DRISKO-CROCKER-FOSTER

Some of the "Coasters" of Maine and New Hampshire

Frances Sterling Drisko

HERITAGE BOOKS
2008

HERITAGE BOOKS
AN IMPRINT OF HERITAGE BOOKS, INC.

Books, CDs, and more—Worldwide

For our listing of thousands of titles see our website
at
www.HeritageBooks.com

Published 2008 by
HERITAGE BOOKS, INC.
Publishing Division
100 Railroad Ave. #104
Westminster, Maryland 21157

International Standard Book Numbers
Paperbound: 978-0-7884-1751-1
Clothbound: 978-0-7884-7338-8

DEDICATION

This book is dedicated to
the memory of my husband

GEORGE DOLBEY DRISKO

16 Nov 1917 – 14 Jan 1994

His love, encouragement and support lives on.

ACKNOWLEDGEMENTS

I wish to thank PICTON PRESS of Rockport, Maine
for their permission to use some of the information
on the DRISKO line
from their book entitled
EARLY PLEASANT RIVER FAMILIES
Of Washington County, Maine
By Darryl B. LAMSON and Leonard F. TIBBETTS
Published 1997

In addition, I wish to thank
Marvin HALL, husband of Mary Ella-10 DRISKO
for his research notes, and family photographs

Clarence Holmes-10 DRISKO, deceased
for his help over many years

Shapleigh Morris-11 DRISKO – son of Clarence Holmes-10 DRISKO

Marian FOSTER-11 Fraser - Bahia, Brazil

Marion SCHOPPEE for her help on the FOSTER line

Betty ANDREWS Storey and
Judith Anne WHITE
for their help on the CROCKER line

There are many, many more to whom I am indebted .

THANK YOU ALL !!!

The records of the DRISKO, CROCKER and FOSTER
families in this book are not complete. And while
no genealogy is 100% accurate, this researcher
has made every effort to verify all of the
information included herein.

TABLE OF CONTENTS

INDEX OF ILLUSTRATIONS

INTRODUCTORY

This book is mainly a genealogy – the recorded history of the descent of three interrelated families, both the male and female lines, who appear at an early time in our country's history.

However, it is also an anthology of some of those people and the memorable events with which they were associated.

Our ancestors were true adventurers. They possessed an indomitable spirit. They went to an unknown land and carved out settlements in the wilderness. Often they worked too hard and died too young. They had large families but lost many of their children to disease and accidents.

In " getting to know them " through my research, I have learned to appreciate their *VISION* of a better life for themselves and their offspring - - - - their *FORTITUDE* in dealing with wilderness settings, and of battling the elements and the enemies; their *COURAGE* to face adversity; their *HEROISM* in defending their homes and settlements; their *PATRIOTISM* in fighting for the freedom to live and die in a country where they could pursue their dreams and ambitions. They truly had a *FREE SPIRIT*.

They were " ordinary " people who accomplished " extraordinary " feats. These are the people who were our ancestors.

Frances STERLING Drisko

FAMILY BACKGROUND

The names of DRISKO, CROCKER and FOSTER appear in Maine and New Hampshire at a very early time in the history of our country. They can be found in almost every town along the coast of Maine, including Machias, Machiasport, Jonesboro, Jonesport, Columbia Falls, Addison, St. George, Bristol, Milport, Steuben, and Cutler to list a few. They are also found among the records of Exeter, Dover, Portsmouth and Newmarket, NH., as well as New Brunswick and Nova Scotia, Canada.

Many of them had occupations as sea captains. Others were shipbuilders, ships' carpenters, seamen, and lighthouse keepers. They made their living from the sea and some of them died there. They were some of the " coasters " of Maine and New Hampshire.

A " coaster ", a vessel and its crew, often carried cargo and/or passengers from port to port along the coast. One such " coaster " was Captain Paul CROCKER. In 1804, as master and part owner of the Schooner *RESOLUTION*, he reportedly sailed the first packet boat from Machias to Boston.

After that, packet boats would travel a regular route along the coast carrying not only passengers and freight, but also mail. The packet comes from the French " paquebot ".

Those who were not sailors often worked in occupations that were closely related. They ran the sawmills that produced the lumber which provided material for boat building in Maine, and was also sent down the coast to provide material for others to build vessels and houses. There were also the very important farmers and merchants who supplied the food and other necessary goods.

These " DOWN-EASTERS " - - the men and their families who settled the wilderness - - were a hardy and adventurous breed. They ultimately endured wars with the French and English; the French and the Indians; and the constant battle with the weather and the sea. Many lost their lives – others survived to become stronger in their resolve to make a better life.

There are as many stories as there are individuals. This book will try to give the reader an overview of some of the people, both men and women, who lived through those times, and who became a part of the history of this country.

Some of these families trace their origins back to the *MAYFLOWER* and England. Others go back to the prominent immigrants such as Tristam COFFIN; the Rev. Joseph HULL; John ALDEN and Priscilla MULLINS; Thomas LOMBARD/LUMBARD who came on the *MARY and JOHN*; the INGERSOLL Family; Reginald/Renold-1 FOSTER, and the PARKERS of Barnstable, MA., etc.

There are many stories of the bravery of the pioneer men and women; including one woman, Margaret STEVENSON Scott, who was hanged as a witch at Salem in 1692.

Some Historical Background on Maine and New Hampshire

Many historians believe that the Vikings may have explored the coast of Maine long before the French and English. They point to such signs of civilization, as the Picture Rocks at Machiasport and the Stone Dam at Norse Pond, Cutler – which indicate that there may have been settlers on the coast as early as the 11th century. It is also believed that other explorers visited the area numerous times between 1598-1605, and that there could have been a permanent settlement as early as 1623.

Louise DICKINSON Rich in her book " The Coast of Maine ", page 63, states " The first ship built in Maine – or in the New World, was the *VIRGINIA* of the Popham Colony in 1607. She was about 30 tons, not a very large vessel. She made voyages up and own the coast collecting furs and delivering salted cod and sassafras root. For about 20 years she was on the tobacco run between Virginia and England; and was finally wrecked off the coast of Ireland. She established a good tradition for seaworthiness and usefulness which Maine ships have always maintained. "

In 1622, two members of the Plymouth Colony of England; Sir Fernando GORGES and Captain John MASON, were granted all of the land between the Kennebec and Merrimac Rivers. Later they divided it. MASON took the area which is now New Hampshire and GORGES the part which is now Maine.

George W. DRISKO in his " History of Machias ", published 1909, stated that   " Machias had a local habitation and a name as early as 1633, only 13 years after the landing of the Pilgrims at Plymouth."

The area was settled by men, and their families, who had searched up and down the coast for a site which could provide them with food and a means of making a livelihood. Shipbuilding and lumbering went hand in hand. Large quantities of wood were needed for building vessels.

By the late 1600's, there were numerous settlements along the coast. The entire area known as Yorkshire County ca 1715/16 - 1760; was then divided into three counties; Lincoln, Cumberland and York.

According to Lemuel NORTON, in his autobiography (1862) " A large percentage of Maine men, and a considerable number of attached women, and even children had traveled, and traveled far."

" Before the Revolutionary War, shipbuilding and shipping had become modest industries in the province. After the Revolution they expanded phenomenally. Around any little Maine harbor could be found men who knew Madras or Marseilles, London or Liverpool, the Yellow Sea, the Tasman Sea, the Gulf of Guinea, or the Bay of Biscay; and could vouch for it with souvenirs, scars and anecdotes acquired there. These were the instructors who brought awareness and cosmopolitan enlightenment to Maine."

Many shipyards dotted the coast in such towns as Addison, Bath, Belfast, Boothbay, Cutler, Eastport, Pembroke, Searsport, and Warren. Although Maine was settled at an early time – it was not one of the original 13 states. Maine was the 23rd state to join the Union. New Hampshire, on the other hand, was one of the original 13 colonies to become a state.

An Englishman, by the name of Martin PRING, landed at the mouth of the Piscatagua in 1603. He was followed by the French explorer Samuel de CHAMPLAIN in 1605 – and Captain John SMITH in 1614.

New Hampshire was settled at Rye (Little Harbor) in 1623; and became part of the Massachusetts Colony in 1641. Many of the original settlers came from Massachusetts and Connecticut. Portsmouth, New Hampshire was settled in 1623 also, and is noted for its shipbuilding and sea related professions.

KEY TO ABBREVIATIONS

bapt	=	baptized
bro	=	brother
bro/o	=	brother of
ca	=	circa/ about
Capt.	=	Captain
d.	=	died
dau	=	daughter
dau/o	=	daughter of
div	=	divorced
Esq.	=	Esquire
Gen.	=	Genealogical
g s	=	gravestone
Hist.	=	History/Historical
int	=	intentions (of marriage)
mag	=	magazine
marr	=	marriage
NB	=	New Brunswick
NS	=	Nova Scotia
p.	=	page
pub	=	published
ref.	=	reference
sis	=	sister
sis/o	=	sister of
son/o	=	son of
States	=	standard two-letter abbreviations
TR	=	Town records
unmarr	=	unmarried
vol	=	volume

DRISCO-DRISKO-DRISKOW-DRISCOW-DRISCOE

The First American Generation

Early records of Maine and New Hampshire have been helpful in establishing certain facts regarding this surname. It is difficult to prove with absolute certainty that the following individual is the immigrant. However, most records indicate, and most researchers believe, that he was the earliest settler of the area.

TEAGUE/TIMOTHY-1 DRISCO +, who appeared in Exeter, New Hampshire as early as 1664; received a grant of land there in 1682. That parcel of land was sold to a Jeremiah CONNER/CONNOR in 1705 by a John DRISCO.

The name of John DRISCO appears on the roll of Captain Nicholas GILMAN'S Scouting Party, 23-25 June 1710; and on the roll of the same company in August 1710.

A JEREMIAH DRISCO resided at Dover, NH and married a Sarah PITMAN before 1682. A CORNELIUS DRISCO, residing at Newmarket, NH, married a Mary CROMMET before 1714, and had sons James and Jeremiah. Cornelius + may have been the son of Jeremiah.

Note: Dover, NH (later part of Strafford County); Exeter and Newmarket (part of Rockingham County) and Wells, Maine (York County) are all in close proximity.

It seems very possible that John and Jeremiah DRISCO were the sons of Teague/Timothy DRISCO.

JOHN DRISCO/DRISKO ++, who had 2 daughters and a son (born between 1683-1688); died at Wells, Maine in 1697. His son John, may have been the John DRISCO who sold the property at Exeter, NH to Jeremiah CONNER/CONNOR in 1705. He married Mary GATCHELL/GETCHELL there before 1709.

++ It may also be more than a coincidence that his daughter Mercy married a Timothy CONNER/ CONNOR, thought to be the son of Jeremiah CONNER/CONNOR; possibly the man who bought land from the aforementioned John DRISCO.

+ According to " Early Pleasant River Families " (1997) by LAMSON and TIBBETTS – " Teague was a nickname often given to Irish immigrants or sailors. "

The given names of John and Jeremiah appear often in the DRISCO/DRISKO line. (The difference between the CO/KO endings to the name (in most cases) is probably due to the fact that people tended to spell names phonetically.

1. TEAGUE/TIMOTHY-1 DRISCO, born ca 1630-40's, possibly England or Ireland, may have been the immigrant and the first of his name to appear in New Hampshire.

Information regarding his wife is not known, possibly a Sarah _____, but he does appear in Exeter, New Hampshire records as early as 1664. His 20 acre land grant was dated 1682. The land was sold by a John DRISCO in 1705 to a Jeremiah CONNER/CONNOR. His wife may have married second to a Benjamin JONES in 1696.

Possible children of Teague/Timothy-1 DRISCO and Sarah ? :
   surname DRISCO

+ 2. JOHN   born 1655-60's probably NH
                      married Sarah EMERSON before 1683
                      died 1697 Wells, Maine (killed by Indians)

His children all married individuals from Exeter or Dover, NH;
and his daughter resided there

+ 3. JEREMIAH   born 1655-60 probably NH
                      married Sarah PITMAN before 1682 at Oyster River (Dover, NH)
                      (she dau/o William PITMAN and _____)

  4. Sarah   born ca 1670's
                      married Nathaniel/ Nathan TAYLOR ++ June 1700
                      witnessed by Sarah WADLEIGH and Margaret TAYLOR
                      (he born 5 Feb 1674; died ca 1703)

References: 1732 NH Census; 1776 NH Census; Dover, NH Vital records 1686-1850 Volume 1; Early Marriages of Strafford, NH, History of Durham, NH

Dictionary of Maine and NH: pages 207/08: DRISCO

" Timothy, alias Teague, appeared in 1673 pledging his 8 acres as security for the child laid to him by Moses GILMAN'S servant Mary PARKER. In 1674 he sold to Philip CARTEE. Taxed 1680-84. "

++ Nathan/Nathaniel TAYLOR was the son of William TAYLOR and Ann-2 WYETH/WYTHE/WISE. Ann was the daughter of Humphrey-1 WYETH +++ and Susannah PAKEMAN, and was born ca 1630; baptized possibly on 18 Oct 1632, and died after 1714 at Exeter, NH. She married 2nd to George PEARSON, and 3rd to Richard CARLE.

+++ Humphrey-1 WYETH/WYTHE was the son of Benjamin-A (Humphrey-B) WYTHE and Emma JANNINGS and was born ca 1591 Suffolk, England.; died ca 1635 at Ipswich, MA. Susanna PAKEMAN was born before 1597 at Nacton, Suffolk, England, and died after 1638 at Ipswich, MA.

The Second American Generation

2. JOHN-2 DRISCO/DRISKO/DRISCOW, most likely the son of Teague/Timothy-1 DRISCO, born ca 1660, was the first of the name to settle in eastern Maine. He appears in the records of Maine (MA) in the late 1600's. It is believed that he settled at Blackpoint (probably Scarboro) near Portland, Maine (then MA) sometime before 1683.

Tradition says that he married an EMERSON, probably a Sarah EMERSON (possibly born 1667, Eng.) and that he was killed by Indians on 16 July 1697 at Wells Township, Maine. Sarah EMERSON was possibly the daughter or sister of Joseph EMERSON.

According to the " Genealogical Dictionary of Maine and NH " page 208, it lists John COOPER of Berwick as the administrator of his estate, dated 10 August 1697. It also states that " his farm was sold to Zachariah GOODALE in 1716 by his daughters." Other data in that reference mentions a John DRISCE in regard to a Wells inquest, John McKENNAY coroner's jury on 15 April 1697.

The WENTWORTH Genealogy, page 252, mentions the marriage of Sara DRISCO to Sylvanus NOCK; stating that her " father is said to have been killed by Indians. She and her sister were named for their mother and aunt, two EMERSONS who came from England. "

Children of John-2 DRISCO/DRISKO and Sarah EMERSON:
   surname DRISCO/DRISKO

+ 5. SARAH   born 4 May 1683 York County, Maine
married Sylvanus NOCK/KNOX/KNOCK/NOCKS 13 Dec 1706 Dover, NH
died ca _____ , NH

+ 6. JOHN   born 28 Dec 1686 Wells, Maine
married Mary GATCHELL/GETCHELL before 1709, NH
(she born 12 Apr 1687 Exeter, NH; died _____)
(she dau/o Samuel GETCHELL/ Elizabeth JONES)

   7. Mercy/Mary   born 20/25 June 1688 Wells, York Co., Maine
married Timothy CONNER/CONNOR ca 1716
(poss son/o Jeremy/Jeremiah CONNER/CONNOR)

3. JEREMIAH-2 DRISCO/DRISKO, brother of above, was born ca 166_, probably at Exeter, NH. He married Sarah-2 PITMAN before 1682 at Oyster River (Dover), Strafford County, NH. She was the daughter of William-1 PITMAN + and Barbara EVANS, and was born ca 166_; died _____. Jeremiah-2 DRISCO died _____.

Child of Jeremiah-2 DRISCO and Sarah PITMAN:
   surname DRISCO

+ 8, CORNELIUS   born ca 168_/169_ probably Dover, NH
married Mary CROMMET before 1714
(she dau/o Philip CROMMET/ Margaret _____) of Lee, Strafford Co., NH
died 1740

unknown as to other siblings

+ WILLIAM-1 PITMAN, a blacksmith, was born ca 1632, as shown by a deposition. He married first, in Boston, MA to a Barbara EVANS on 29 Sept 1653.

It is believed that he married second to an Ann ROBERTS, daughter of William ROBERTS. She was repeatedly mentioned as his wife between 1661 and 1682. On 12 May 1657, he was living on a portion of William ROBERTS' land, and took deed to it in 1664. His will shows that he died in 1682.

Children of William PITMAN and Barbara EVANS:
    surname PITMAN

i. Abigail   born ca 1654-55
                      1m. Stephen-2 WILLEY before 1671
                      (he born ca 1649; died ____)
                      (he son/o Thomas-1 WILLEY + / _____)
                      2m. Edward deFLECHEUR 6 Oct 1710

ii. Mary   born 15 Nov 1657; baptized 8 Dec 1693 Canada ++
                      married Stephen OTIS 16 Apr 1674

        ++ She was taken captive by Indians, taken to Canada, and baptized there

iii. Ezekiel   born 1658; married Elizabeth _____

iv. SARAH   born ca ____; married JEREMIAH-2 DRISCO

Children of William-1 PITMAN and Ann ROBERTS:
    Surname PITMAN

v. Francis   born 1662; married Elizabeth ____ Tibbetts
                      (she widow of Nathaniel TIBBETTS)

vi. John   born 1663; executor of his fathers' will

vii. Nathaniel   born ____; married Deliverance Derry ca 1697
                      (she widow of John DERRY)

viii. Elizabeth   born ____; married Stephen JENKINS

ix. Joseph   born 1669; married Elizabeth _____

x. Ann   born 1672; married John SIAS 1698

xi. Zacharias   born 16__

xii. Hannah   born 16__

xiii. Judith   born 16__; married John HAM 8 Jan 1715

+ Thomas-1 WILLEY, born England; arrived at Oyster River (Dover) , NH before 1645.

The Third American Generation

5. SARA(H)-3 DRISKO/DRISCO/DRISCOE, daughter of John-2 DRISCO/DRISKO and Sarah EMERSON, was born 4 May 1683 at Blackpoint (Scarboro), near Portland/Wells, Maine.

She married on 13 December 1706 a Sylvanus-3 NOCK/KNOX/KNOCK/NOCKS, the Rev. John PIKE officiating. He was the youngest son of Sylvanus-2 NOCK, Sr. (Thomas-1) + and his first wife Elizabeth-3 EMERY (James-2; Anthony-1); and was born 1679 at Wells, York, ME; died ca 1750. (WENT-WORTH Genealogy – page 252)

After their marriage, they resided at Dover, Strafford County, NH. In 1716 they sold their interest in John DRISCO'S estate to Zachariah GOODALE. In 1725 Sylvanus NOCK sold 5 ½ acres of land at Birch Point. In 1730 he was located at Somersworth, Strafford County, NH., when he and two of his brothers (not James) and two sisters gave a deed to John HANSON.

An adm. dated 12 Nov 1750 names S. DRISCO Nock, there being 9 shares for eight children. Ebenezer was listed as his " oldest surviving son "; so it is possible that his son Samuel pre-deceased Sylvanus-3 NOCK.

Children of Sarah-3 DRISCO/DRISKO and Sylvanus-3 NOCK:
  Surname NOCK/KNOX

+ 9. SAMUEL(L)	born 20 Sept 1707 Dover, NH
	married Abigail-3 RICKER
	(she dau/o Maturin-2 RICKER ++ (Geo-1) and Hannah-2 HUNTRESS ++
	(she born 14 Aug 1713, Dover,NH; died 1752)
	died possibly ca 1745
+10. EBENEZER	born 16 May 1710 Dover, NH; 1m. Elizabeth-3 RICKER ca 1736
	(she dau/o John-2 RICKER (Geo-1) and Hannah-2 GARLAND (Jabez-1)
	(she born 15 June 1715; dp before 1760)
	2m. Mary RANDALL Ricker by 1760
	(she wid/o George-3 RICKER ; he born ca 1716/17; died ____)
	(he son/o Maturin-2 RICKER and Hannah-2 HUNTRESS ++)
11. Henry	born 23 Aug 1714 Dover, NH; died before 1750
+12. ESTHER	born 21 Nov 1717 Dover, NH; married Eliphalet CROMWELL
	(he son/o Samuel CROMWELL and Rachel _____)
	(he born 12 Nov 1716 Dover; died ____)
13. Drisco +++	born 21 March 1719 Dover, NH
	dsp 1752 (adm. to brother Ebenezer)
14. Sarah	born 11 July 1721 Dover, NH; died ca 1802
	1m. Ezekiel WENTWORTH (he baptized 5 July 1717 Dover, NH)
	2m. David LYFORD (he born ca 1717 Dover, NH)
15. MERCY	born 11 Oct 1723 Dover, NH
	married Nathaniel-3 RICKER ca 1747
	(he son/o John-2 RICKER and Hannah-2 GARLAND)
	(he born 5 Apr 1724 Somersworth, NH; died 22 Nov 1782 Annapolis, NS)
16. Sylvanus	born ca 1725; res Berwick, ME.; had children 1763-68
17. Rebecca	born ca 1727; married Benjamin VARNEY
	(he son/o Benjamin VARNEY and Martha TIBBETTS)
	(he born ca 1721 Dover, NH; died 21 June 1779 killed by a falling tree)

++ Note: Hannah-2 HUNTRESS, dau/o George-1 HUNTRESS and Mary NUTE, was born ca 1692.
Maturin-2 RICKER was born ca 1686/87.

+ Sylvanus-2 NOCK/KNOCK/KNOX, born ca 1657), was the son of Thomas-1 NOCK and Rebecca-2 TIBBETTS (Henry-1). His first wife Elizabeth-3 EMERY, was the daughter of James-2 EMERY (Anthony-1/Frances _____). Elizabeth –3 EMERY was born ca 1657; married 20 April 1677; and died 6 June 1704 of a " sore throat and other chronical distempers ". Sylvanus-2 was married second to Esther /Hester PHILBROOK Heard (widow) on 12 Nov 1705 Dover, NH.

+++ A Drisco NOCK and Margaret LORD, both of Berwick, were married 15 Sept 1774. He possibly the grandson or namesake of the Drisco NOCK (above). This individual may also be the same person mentioned (# 404) in the Marriage Index of Maine 1743-1891; and (# 145) on the **Revolutionary War** Pension Lists 1792-1841 (CD 145)

References: Dover, NH Births and Marriages, 1693-1838; Genealogical Dictionary of Maine and NH; Genealogy of John and Anthony EMERY (1890).

6. JOHN-3 DRISKO/DRISCO/DRISCOW, brother of above, was born 28 Dec 1686 at Wells, Maine. He married at Salisbury (MA) , a Mary-3 GATCHELL/GETCHELL + . She was the daughter of Samuel-2 GETCHELL and Elizabeth JONES of Exeter, NH. Mary-3 was born 12 April 1687 and was baptized , as an adult, on 18 August 1734 (wife of John) at the 1st Congregational Church of Scarboro, Maine.

John-3 DRISKO and his wife were living in Salisbury (MA/ME) in 1719, when they were deeded land near GETCHELL ROCK in Salisbury; but were in New Meadows, near Brunswick, Maine in 1737. They were both still living in 1750.

Many records, including the Scarboro Church records, spell the name DRISCOW. All members of this family were baptized there, and joined the 1st Church of Scarborough (Maine Historical and Genealogical Recorder). They are also listed in the WENTWORTH Genealogy, published 18__; the Early Settlers of Brunswick, Maine; the Old Norfolk County Court records, and the Salisbury, MA VR; page 74).

Children of John-3 DRISKO/DRISCO and Mary-3 GETCHELL:
    surname DRISKO/DRISCO

18. Sarah	born 21 Jan 1710 Salisbury
	married John SHARP 20 May 1729 1st Congregational Church of Scarboro
	(he born 1706, Salisbury, Essex, MA)
+ 19. JOSEPH	born 21 Dec 1712 Salisbury; baptized 1 Sept 1734 Scarboro
	1m. Elizabeth-3 MITCHELL int pub 21 July 1736
	(she dau/o William-2 MITCHELL of Kittery)
	2m. Mary-5 SMALL int pub 4 May 1746 Portland, ME
	3m. Olive LARRABEE 21/22 Nov 1760
	(she dau/o Thomas LARRABEE and Abigail PITMAN)
	(she born ____; baptized 12 June 1743; died ____)
	died possibly 1790
+ 20. ELIZABETH	born 28 Feb 1714 Salisbury; married Isaac McKENNEY
	on 1 April 1731 at the 1st Congregational Church of Scarboro
	(he served in the **French and Indian War**)
21. Moses	born 19 Aug 1716 Salisbury; baptized 9 May 1736 1st Cong Ch Scarboro
	had land at New Meadows in 1739
22. Judith	born 27 Nov 1718 Salisbury; baptized 18 Aug 1734 Scarboro
23. Joanna	born 31 Oct 1722 Salisbury; baptized 18 Aug 1734 Scarboro
	married Samuel-4 GETCHELL/GATCHELL int pub 24 March 1740 at
	Brunswick, Maine

References: Maine Historical and Genealogical Recorder; WENTWORTH Genealogy; Early Settlers of Brunswick, Maine; Scarboro Church records; Old Norfolk County records; Salisbury, MA VR page 74; Families of Old Salisbury and Amesbury, published 1897; LIBBY Family in America.

++ Ancestry of Mary-3 GETCHELL/GATCHELL

SAMUEL-1 GETCHELL/GATCHELL (Sr.) was probably born in Wales, and came to Salem, MA in 1636 with his brother John. (John resided at Marblehead, MA.)

He was in Salem, MA in 1638 and moved to Hampton, New Hampshire ca 1644 where he owned lots 393a and 393b. He sold his Hampton dwelling on 17 May 1648 to a William GODFREY of Hampton and removed to Salisbury, MA according to SAVAGES' Genealogical Dictionary of New England, published ____.

Samuel-1 GETCHELL/GATCHELL was a " planter "; a " commoner "; and was taxed 1650 and 1652. He received land in 1654 and after. In a deed dated Sept 1658, it stated " after the new mill begins to saw, the next Spring – ".

Samuel-1 GETCHELL married Dorcas _?_ in 1648. She was born ____; died 12 Jan 1684/85 at Salisbury, MA. Samuel-1 had a will dated 2 April 1684; probated 6 Oct 1697.

They had three children: 1. Susanna, born ____, married Joseph NORTON 10 March 1662 at Salisbury; and died there 19 Aug 1724. She was mentioned in her fathers' will – in which he deeded her property .
 2. Priscilla, born 26 Feb 1648/49 at Salisbury; married Solomon RAINSFORD/ RANSFORD ca 1670 and resided in Boston. She was mentioned as the widow Priscilla in 1718 when she was deeded land at Getchell's Rock.   3. SAMUEL-2 GETCHELL/GATCHELL, born 8 Feb 1657/58 at Salisbury; married Elizabeth-2 JONES, daughter of Robert-1 JONES and Joanna OSGOOD on 27 Nov 1679. (Elizabeth-2 JONES was born 24 Dec 1662; died 24 May 1735.)

On 23 Sept 1676, Samuel-2 GETCHELL was credited with pay for serving in Captain Jonathan POOLES' Company, which was stationed at Hatfield, MA during the winter of 1676/77 (MA Archives – Volume 68/69; Soldiers of **King Philips War** by George BODGE, Page 260.)

He was occupied as a shipwright – apprenticed to Thomas MUDGETT – in 1678. Samuel-2 died 7 July 1710 at Salisbury.

SAMUEL-2 GETCHELL/GATCHELL and Elizabeth Jones had 13 children: 1. Hannah, born 1680/81, married Isaac COLBY 1701. 2. Moses, born 1682, married Judith ____. He was a soldier at Salisbury in 1703, and resided there until 1719 when he removed to North Yarmouth; residing there until 1734. He was a selectman at Harpswell in 1740.   3. Eleanor, born 1683; died young   4. Eleanor (2) born 1684, married Benoni CILLEY; and died 1737. 5. Dorcas, born 1685; married Ebenezer-3 AYRES. 6. MARY-3 ++, a twin, married JOHN-3 DRISKO/DRISCO (above).   7. Samuel, born 1687, twin of Mary, married Elizabeth NASON in 1714; and resided at Berwick. 8. Joseph , born ____, married first to Eunice-5 HATCH, and second or third to Mary JOY Gray (widow). 9. Nathaniel born ____, married Susanna LADD; resided at Haverhill, MA; later moving to Wells, Maine. 10. Elizabeth , born ____, married Joseph QUIMBY/QUINBY. 11. Joanna, born 1695; married Noah ROGERS. 12. John, born ca 1697, resided Scarboro; was known as an Indian fighter. 13. Robert, born 1702, married Ruth-3 JONES.

8. CORNELIUS-3 DRISCO, son of Jeremiah-2 DRISCO (Teague/Timothy-1) and Sarah-2 PITMAN, was born ca 1680's or 90's, probably at Exeter/Dover, New Hampshire.

He married Mary-2 CROMMETT before 1714. She was the daughter of Philip-1 CROMMETT/CROMET/ CRUMMETT + and Margaret ____.

Children of Cornelius-3 DRISCO and Mary-2 CROMMETT:
    surname DRISCO   (order of birth uncertain)
  24. Keziah   born ____; baptized 1718 (under age in 1732); married Theodore WILLEY

Children of Cornelius-3 DRISCO, continued:
   surname DRISCO

| 25. Mary | born ____; baptized 1718; 1m. __?__ SAWYER before 1740 |
| | 2m. Salathiel-3 DENBOW ++ ca 1741 |

            Possible child: Elijah DENBOW, born 12 Mar 1741 Dover, NH
                    he married Sarah EMERSON Wiley/Willey; she wid/o Samuel
                    (Reference: Second Boat Nov 1983)

+ 26. JAMES   born ____; adult in 1737; married Mary (poss MASON *) ca 1740

Ref: Genealogical Dictionary of ME and NH: page 208 – Sarah Mason, widow of Joseph MASON ++ of Durham, NH, deeded a
house and 30 acres to daughter Mary Drisco – widow. ++ Joseph-3 MASON, son of John-2 MASON (Robert-1) and Elizabeth
WARDE, was born ca 1693; died before 1763.

| 27. Jeremiah | born ____; baptized 2 Jan 1722/23 |
| 28. Robert | born ____; baptized 15 Feb 1726/27; died young |

+ Ancestry of Mary-2 CROMMETT

+ PHILIP-1 CROMMETT/ CROMET/CRUMMETT purchased land of a Hugh DUNN at Sandy Bank,
above Hook Island Falls, in Lee, Strafford County, New Hampshire. He was licensed to keep a ferry at
Lampril River in 1671. In 1673 he received a grant of six acres adjoining his land. He, and his wife
Margaret, deeded one-half of their property to their son John on 7 June 1710. The other half was deeded to
Cornelius-3 DRISCO, their son-in-law, on 12 March 1714/15.

Children of Philip-1 CROMMETT and Margaret ____:
   surname CROMMETT

i. John	born ____; 1m. Elizabeth THOMAS; 2m. Mary _____
ii. Jeremiah	born ____; killed by Indians 1712
iii. Sarah	born ____; married Thomas FOOTMAN 18 Dec 1691
iv. MARY	born ____ ; married CORNELIUS-3 DRISCO

History of Durham, NH by STACKPOLE and THOMPSON (1913) page 107 states " The following
appear on the roll of a scouting party under the command of Captain James DAVIS in 1712: ----- including
a Timothy CONNER and a Cornelius DRISCO. "

Same reference : Page 123. 20 May 1755 John DRISCO Re: a convention at Exeter, NH to raise three
regiments. It states that Durham, NH contributed nearly a full company under the command of Captain
Winborn ADAMS – including John DRISKO, age 21, husbandman of Durham.
Page 125. Another roll shows that John DRISCO was made a Corporal.

Page 130. Durham 1779 – A committee was appointed to consider the inflated prices and depreciation of
paper money. They agreed to establish prices for certain commodities and that any changes would only be
made in agreement with Portsmouth and neighboring towns. (Signers included James DRISCO).
Page 174. 11 Nov 1715 – name on a petition regarding the choice of a minister. Signed by inhabitants of
Oyster River, Township of Dover, NH (lists Cornelius DRISCO)
Page 178. 6 April 1716 - an Oyster River petition – includes Cornalus DRISCO as one of the signers.

++ Salathiel-1 DENBOW, born ca 1642 – settled at Oyster River (Durham, NH) by 1666. It is believed
that his descendants, who use the name of DINSMORE/DENBOW, later settled at Harrington, Washington
County, Maine. He married a daughter of William ROBERTS, and died before 1714. He had three sons .
1. Salathiel-2, born ____; who married first _____ GRAVES; and second to Rachel PEAVEY. 2.
Richard-2, born ____; who married Mary BUNKER; and 3. Peter-2 , born ____.

Salathiel-3 DENBOW/DENMORE/DINSMORE, and his wife Mary-4 DRISCO Sawyer sold to Ebenezer
SMITH on 21 July 1741 - " 1/5th part of lands in Newmarket and Durham that " belonged to our father,
Cornelius DRISCO, late of Newmarket, deceased."

The Fourth American Generation

9. SAMUEL(L)-4 NOCK/KNOX, son of Sarah-3 DRISCO (John-2) and Sylvanus-3 NOCK/KNOX (Sylvanus-2; Thomas-1) , was born 20 Sept 1707 at Dover, New Hampshire. He married Abigail RICKER, daughter of Maturin RICKER and Hannah HUNT. Abigail was born 18 Aug 1713; died 1752. Samuel-4 NOCK/KNOX died ca 1745 at Somersworth, NH.

Children of Samuel-4 NOCK/KNOX and Abigail RICKER:
　　surname NOCK/KNOX

29. Henry	born ____; a cordwainer
30. Samuel	born ____
+ 31. SOBRIETY	born 14 June 1740; married Moses-3 RICKER
	(he son/o Ephraim-2 RICKER and 2nd wife Sarah WENTWORTH
	(he born 3 Jan 1739; died 26 Oct 1801; served in **Revolutionary War**)
32. Jedediah	born ____; went to Portsmouth, NH; enlisted in **Revolutionary War**
+ 33. DOROTHY	born ca 1747 Dover, NH; married Lemuel-3 RICKER 31 Dec 1771
	(he bro/o Moses-3 RICKER , above)
	(he born 18 Oct 1747, Somersworth, NH; died ____)
	died 26 Nov 1831 (aged 84)
34. Hannah	born ____; married Benjamin CANNEY 19 Sept 1776
	(he son/o Love CANNEY and ____?) Berwick, Maine

10. EBENEZER-4 NOCK/KNOX, brother of above, was born 16 May 1710 at Dover, NH. He married first to Elizabeth-3 RICKER ca 1736. She was the daughter of John-2 RICKER and Hannah GARLAND, and was born 15 June 1715; died before 1756. Ebenezer-4 married second to Mary- 3 RANDALL Ricker before 1760. Mary was the daughter of Samuel-2 RANDALL (Richard-1) and his first wife Elizabeth MAYFIELD. She was the widow of George-3 RICKER. She was born ca 17__; baptized 7 April 1728. They resided Somersworth, NH and purchased the interest in his fathers' estate.

Children of Ebenezer-4 NOCK/KNOX and Elizabeth RICKER:
　　surname NOCK/KNOX

35. Lydia	born 9/19 Mar 1737
	married Willoughby-4 GOODWIN ca 1757 Somersworth, NH
	(he son of John-3 GOODWIN (William-2; Daniel-1)
36. Esther	born ca 1741/42
37. Judith	born ca 1743/44
+ 38. EBENEZER	born 29 July 1746; married Elizabeth GARLAND
39. Thomas	born ca 1748/49; married Sarah SCATES 26 Apr 1772 Berwick
	(she dau/o John SCATES and ____ of Berwick (BVR)

Children of Ebenezer-4 NOCK/KNOX and Mary RANDALL Ricker:
　　surname NOCK/KNOX

+ 40. SYLVANUS	born ca 1760; married Mary PAPOON		
41. Rebecca	born 3 Dec 1762	42. Reuben	born 1 Jan 1767

12. ESTHER-4 NOCK/KNOX, sister of above, was born 21 Nov 1717 at Dover, NH. She married Eliphalet CROMWELL. He was the son of Samuel CROMWELL and Rachel ____; and was born 12 Nov 1716 at Dover, NH; died ____. Esther-4 NOCK/KNOX died ____.

Children of Esther-4 NOCK/KNOX and Eliphalet CROMWELL:
　　Surname CROMWELL

+ 43. LUCY	born 27 Jan 1744 Somersworth, NH; died 3 Jan 1817
	married Daniel-3 RICKER 1762
	(he son/o John-2 RICKER and Hannah-2 GARLAND) (he born ____; died 3 May 1823)

15. MERCY-4 NOCK/KNOX, sister of above, was born 11 Oct 1723 at Dover, NH. She married Nathaniel-3 RICKER ca 1747. He was the son of John-2 RICKER and Hannah-2 GARLAND; and was born 15 Apr 1724; died 22 Nov 1782, Annapolis, Nova Scotia. They resided Somersworth, NH and Newcastle, Maine; moving to Argyle, Nova Scotia around 1766. Nathaniel RICKER obtained a grant of timberland there. Argyle became a prosperous community, engaging mainly in the shipbuilding and seafaring trades. Mercy-4 NOCK/KNOX died _____.

Children of Mercy-4 NOCK/KNOX and Nathaniel RICKER:
   surname RICKER

+ 44. LYDIA	born 24 Sept 1747 Somersworth, NH
	married Jedediah GOODWIN 9 May 1770
45. Benjamin	born 6 May 1755; died unmarried; lost at sea
+ 46. CAPTAIN	born 13 Nov 1757 Somersworth, NH
NATHANIEL, JR.	1m. Anna ROBERTS ca 1781 Argyle, NS; (she born _____; died 1 May 1800)
	2m. Eleanor CURTIS Dalton (she born ca 1757; died 8 May 1817)
+ 47. CAPTAIN PAUL	born 11 Oct 1765 Somersworth, NH
	married Catherine KENTON 30 Dec 1807, NS (later moved to Eastport, ME)
48. Sarah	born _____, NS; died unmarried Argyle, NS

19. JOSEPH-4 DRISKO/DRISCO/DRISCOW, son of John-3 DRISKO (John-2) and Mary-3 GETCH-ELL/GATCHELL, was born 21 Dec 1712 at Salisbury, MA. He was baptized as an adult on 1 Sept 1734 at Scarboro, Maine.

He married first an Elizabeth-3 MITCHELL ++, daughter of William-2 MITCHELL ++ and Elizabeth-2 TENNEY. They had one son. Elizabeth was still living January 1745, and was mentioned in her fathers' will dated at that time. Joseph-4 DRISKO married second a Mary-5 SMALL +++, possibly born 26 June 1724; died before 1760. Intentions were published 4 May 1746 at Portland, Maine.

His third marriage was to Olive LARRABEE on 12/21 Nov 1760 according to the 2nd Congregational Church of Scarboro, Maine records. She was the daughter of Thomas LARRABEE and Abigail PITMAN, and was born _____; baptized 12 June 1743. There was no issue from that marriage. Joseph-4 DRISKO died prior to 1790.

Child of Joseph-4 DRISKO and Elizabeth-3 MITCHELL:
   surname DRISKO/DRISCO

+ 49. JOHN (2nd)	born 1742 Scarboro; baptized 9 Jan 1743 1st Congregational Church Scarboro
	married Mary Johnson CHANDLER int pub 5 Jan 1765 North Yarmouth, ME
	(she dau/o Judah CHANDLER and Martha SEABURY) (she born 25 Oct 1745; died _____)
	died 1830 Addison, Maine (served in the **Revolutionary War**)

Children of Joseph-4 DRISKO and Mary-5 SMALL:
   Surname DRISKO/DRISCO

+ 50. ELIZABETH/	born ca 1747 (according to date on gravestone); died 1835
BETSEY	baptized 16 March 1757 1st Congregational Church Scarboro
	married Joseph TABBUTT, Jr
+ 51. JOSEPH	born 9 June 1748 Addison, ME; died ca 1802/03 (**Revolutionary War**)
	married ca 1770 Rebecca-6 INGERSOLL
	(she dau/o William-5 INGERSOLL and Sarah PARKER)
+ 52. SAMUEL	born _____; baptized 13 Aug 1749 1st Congregational Church Scarboro
GATCHELL	married Mercy CHANDLER (1/2 sister of Mary Johnson CHANDLER)
	(she dau/o Judah-4 CHANDLER and Rebecca SEABURY)(she born 4 Apr 1754; died 8 Mar 1847)
	died ca 1837 Addison, Maine (served in the **Revolutionary War**)

Note: They resided Jonesboro, Maine until 1779/80; then moved to Columbia, Maine

NOTE: A list of inhabitants of Pleasant River taken 17 April 1778 lists the following :
Joseph DRISKO ----- family of 3   Joseph DRISKO, Jr. ------ family of 5
Joseph TIBBETTS, Jr. --- family of 4

All of the DRISKO brothers, Joseph; John, 2nd ; and Samuel , came to Pleasant River with their father before 1770, as shown by their signatures on the Petition to Governor HUTCHINSON of MA, asking for the appointment of a Justice of the Peace for Pleasant River. They were among the first settlers of Pleasant River, and all served in the Militia during the Revolutionary War.

The 1790 Census shows John and Joseph, Jr. residing in Township # 6, west of Machias; later called Addison Ridge. Samuel was residing in Township # 13, later (1796) it was incorporated as Columbia, ME
References: Boston Transcript, 17 July 1812 # 2675; children of Samuel; Maine Historical
and Genealogical Recorder, Volume 9, pages 88 and 89.

++ Ancestry of Elizabeth-3 MITCHELL
WILLIAM-2 MITCHELL, born ca ____, Kittery, Maine; married first an Honor _____?; and resided Isle of Shoals. He married second Elizabeth TENNEY of Kittery before 1715. She was the daughter of John TENNEY and _____?. William-2 MITCHELL died 18 April 1724, killed by Indians.

Children of William-2 MITCHELL and Honor _?_were : 1. Israel who married Mary BERRY 24 Dec 1729. 2. Christopher who married Deborah MILLER, intentions published 5 Apr 1734, and 3. John.
Children of William-2 MITCHELL and Elizabeth TENNEY were : 4/5. Job and William, twins born 24 Apr 1720 6. Mary, born 20 Sept 1722 at Scarboro, married Joseph GETCHELL 17 July 1750 at Scarborough. 7. Relief, born 31 Dec 1724. 8. ELIZABETH-3 born probably 1725/26, married Joseph-4 DRISKO (above). She died before 1746.

References: The MITCHELLS of Kittery, Maine; Maine Historical and Genealogical Recorder, Volume 3, page 1401; Old Kittery and Her Families, STACKPOLE, page 610; Edward SMALL Genealogy Volume 3 pages 1398-1401 and page 1726.

+++ Ancestry of Mary-5 SMALL
EDWARD-1 SMALL, the immigrant, was born ca 16__ in England; and came to America ca 1632/34. He was a magistrate in Kittery, Maine. His wife Elizabeth ____, remained in England; and died there ca 1665. FRANCIS-2 SMALL, son of Edward-1, was born in St. Mary's Parish Biddeford, County Devon, England ca 1625. He married Elizabeth LEIGHTON. She was the daughter of ___ LEIGHTON and ____; and was born ca 1634; died ____. Francis-2 died about 1714 at Truro, MA.

SAMUEL-3 SMALL, born ca 1666, probably at Dover, NH; married Elizabeth HEARD in 1694 at the Parish of Unity, Brunswick, Maine. She was the daughter of James HEARD and Shua CONLEY; and was born ca 1670; died ____. (still living 1737) She married second to James CHADBOURNE.

JOSEPH-4 SMALL, was born 3 Dec 1702 at Kittery, Maine. He married Mary LIBBY on 12 April 1722. She was the daughter of David LIBBY and Eleanor ____; and was born ____; died ____. Joseph-4 SMALL settled in Portland, Maine where he purchased large amounts of property. Children of Joseph-4 SMALL and Mary LIBBY: (all born Kittery) surname SMALL 1. Joseph born 6 Jan 1723. 2. MARY-5 born 26 June 1724. 3. David born 18 June 1726. 4. Isaac born 28 Feb 1727; died Feb 1731. 5. Elizabeth born 18 Mar 1729/30. 6. Daniel born 17 Nov 1731. 7. Eleanor born 28 Aug 1733.

" Soldiers, Sailors and Patriots of the Revolutionary War " Maine - page 216 shows :
DRISKO, John   Captain   MIL
                resided Machias; born Scarborough 1742; died Addison 1830
                married Mary _____   M-1; p 42   MOCA

DRISKO, John   Captain SMITHS' Company   Is
DRISCO, John, Jr.   on UNITY   M-1; p 48
DRISCO, Joseph, Jr.   resided Pleasant River   Is

" Soldiers and Sailors of the Revolutionary War " Massachusetts (COS – DRY   Volume 4; page 979)

DRISKO, JOSEPH (also given as Joseph, Jr.) Pleasant River. Private, Captain Francis SHAW Jr., (Seacoast Company) ; enlisted 9 Sept 1775; discharged 31 Dec 1775; service 4 months and 1 day; Company stationed at Goldsborough, No. 4 Narragaugus and Pleasant River; also Captain John HALLS' Detachment drafted from Militia ; enlisted 24 June 1777; discharged 30 June 1777; service 6 days at Machias; also Captain John HALLS' Detachment drafted from Militia; enlisted 14 Aug 1777; discharged

19 Aug 1777; service 5 days at Machias; also Captain John HALLS' Detachment drafted from Militia; by order of Colonel Benjamin FOSTER; enlisted 15 Sept 1777; discharged 28 Sept 1777; service 14 days at Machias, roll dated Pleasant River.

DRISKO, SAMUEL GATCHELL (brother of Joseph) was listed in the DAR Patriot Index (a publication of all members since 1921) Copyright 1967. He was listed as a Private from MA. It states that he was born 13 Aug 1749, and that he married Mercy CHANDLER, daughter of Judah CHANDLER (he born 13 Aug 1730, Duxbury, MA) and Rebecca SEABURY. Mercy CHANDLER was born 4 April 1754; died 8 March 1847. Samuel Gatchell DRISKO died ca 1837 Addison, Maine. He served several times during the Revolutionary War as follows: Private in Lieut. Joel WHITNEYS' Company; from 16 July 1777 to 7 Oct 1777 at Machias; also 16 Dec 1777 to 7 Jan 1778 at Chaloner's River; and in Captain John HALLS' Company 7 Aug 1779 to 7 Sept 1779 on an expedition to Majorbagaduce (Castine) by order of General LOVELL.

DRISKO, JOHN, 2nd - mentioned in the " History of Machias " by George W. DRISKO, page 169, as " Captain of the Company, who had come to the aid of Machias from Chandler's River now Jonesboro, and Pleasant River." The battle he referred to was the patriots victory on the 12th of July 1775, when they conquered the British ship *MARGARETTA*.

THE FIRST SEA BATTLE OF THE REVOLUTION   12 July 1775

Machias, Maine was originally settled by an " association " of 16 persons during the winter of 1763 for the purpose of building a double sawmill. By 1774 there were some 80 families residing there, plus another 100 single men. It was around this time it became apparent that a split between the colonies and England was inevitable. Although they were quite far removed from Boston, they received news from time to time. They knew of the conflict, between the British and the colonists at Lexington and Concord, which took place on 19 April 1775.

A vessel out of Machias, departing from Boston after this time, was followed by the British vessel *MARGARETTA*; an armed schooner carrying a crew of about 40 men. According to George W. DRISKO, in his book The History of Machias: " the object of the visit of the *MARGARETTA* is said to have been threefold: 1st to see that Captain JONES from Machias, performed his agreement to return to Boston with a load of lumber; 2nd to ' protect' him from trouble with the inhabitants if any should arise; and 3rd to carry to Boston the stores of an armed vessel which had been cast away in the vicinity of Machias a short time before."

The townspeople at Machias, after hearing about the battles, decided that they had endured enough from the British – and were determined that no more of their lumber would be used by the British to build ships or provide shelter for their soldiers.

Having made their decision, the townspeople " in spite of all the adverse circumstances, this little band of patriots became more resolute." As a symbol of their determination, they raised a " Liberty Pole " in front of the Town Hall and made a solemn vow to resist the " Mother country" , and if necessary, sacrifice property and life in defense of their rights and independence.

Arriving at Machias, the *MARGARETTA* anchored off-shore to observe the activities of the townspeople. After a period of time the Captain of the *MARGARETTA*, a Mr. MOOR/MOORE, came ashore in a small boat. He told the people that they would have to remove the pole or that " it will be my painful duty to fire on the town."

The townspeople, stalling for time, told the Captain that they would have to discuss the matter and needed until Monday (it was then Friday) to give him their decision. The real reason was that they needed that time to send to Chandler's River, Pleasant River and other remote settlements for help in their defense of the town.

They extended an invitation to Captain MOOR/MOORE to join them for their Sunday morning church service. They hoped that help would reach Machias by that time and that they might be able to capture the Captain while he attended church – making it much easier for them to take over the *MARGARETTA*.

The plan failed after Mr. MOOR/MOORE, during the sermon, looked out an open window and observed men approaching from the river. Fearing the worst, he made a hasty retreat by jumping out of that window. Reaching his rowboat before anyone could take action to detain him, he rowed quickly back to the *MARGARETTA*. As soon as he was aboard the crew opened fire on the town.

The men of Machias held a meeting, under the leadership of Colonel Benjamin FOSTER. There were about 60 men present, including those from Pleasant River, Jonesboro and Moosebec Reach.

They elected John DRISKO, 2nd + to be the Captain or leader of the Company from Pleasant River.

The plan of action they formulated at that meeting would become " the first known assemblage of colonists in the Province of Maine, (to act) in open hostility to the further dictation of George III and the first directly on the property of Great Britain. "

It was decided that they would use a sloop and a schooner in their pursuit of the *MARGARETTA*. Their plan was to go along side of the British warship, board it, and capture it that way. The schooner, the *FALMOUTH PACKET*, ran onto the rocks and was damaged . The sloop *UNITY* continued on alone. The crew of the *UNITY* had named a Jeremiah O'BRIEN as their Captain. Also aboard the vessel were his five brothers and three brother-in-laws.

After getting close to the *MARGARETTA*, Captain MOOR/MOORE declared " he would fire if the colonists came any closer." The men on the *UNITY* were not to be deterred and, after some strategic problems, the two vessels came together – each firing on the other.

A sharp conflict took place involving muskets at short range. Soon Captain MOOR/MOORE was felled by a shot from one of the men on the *UNITY*. The crew of colonists boarded the *MARGARETTA* – taking command with no further fight. Captain MOOR/MOORE had been mortally wounded, dying the next day. His crew was taken back to Machias, and remained there for some time – as prisoners of war.

The attack on the *MARGARETTA* took place (12 July 1775) more than a year before the Declaration of Independence – and only a few days after the Battle of Bunker Hill.

DRISKOS' book states " Taking all the circumstances of the occasion into view, especially the remote position of Machias from any place where assistance could be obtained, the capture of the *MARGARETTA* must be considered as one of the most bold, energetic and extraordinary occurrences of the times."

The sloop *UNITY* was fashioned into a man-o-war and fitted with guns from the *MARGARETTA*. Its name was changed to the *MACHIAS LIBERTY*; and under the command of Jeremiah O'BRIEN cruised the Bay of Fundy searching for another British vessel, the *DILIGENCE*. They were unable to locate it, but after returning to Machias, they maintained a constant vigil to prevent any further attacks from the British.

Within a few days of their return, the *DILIGENCE* (an 80-ton armed schooner – with 4 four-pound carriage guns) and her tender the *TATAMAGOUCH* appeared in Machias Bay. Captain KNIGHT, the commander of the *DILIGENCE*, went ashore with two of his crew " to make enquiries " about the *MARGARETTA*. They were captured by Captain Stephen SMITH and his men, and taken to Machias where he was informed that he and his crew would be held as prisoners.

Later, a high ranking British officer, Sir George COLLIER was reported to have said – " The damn'd rebels at Machias were a harder set than those of Bunker Hill."

20. ELIZABETH-4 DRISKO/DRISCO/DRISCOW, sister of above, daughter of John-3 DRISKO (John-2) and Mary-3 GETCHELL/GATCHELL, was born 28 Feb 1714 at Salisbury, MA. She married Isaac-3 McKENNEY ++ on 1 April 1731 at the First Church of Scarboro, Maine. Isaac was the son of Robert-2 McKENNEY (John-1) and the widow Rebecca _____ Sparks; and was born 171_; died ____.

++ Isaac " McKANE " (McKENNEY) served as a Private in Captain Thomas PERKINS' Company, enlisting 29 June 1747. This was on scouting duty " to the eastward ." He was also in the Train Band of Scarborough in 1757, under Captain Daniel FOGG; and served in Captain John SMALLS' Company from 14 April – 7 Nov 1760, a period of 34 weeks.

Children of Elizabeth-4 DRISKO/DRISCO and Isaac-3 McKENNEY:
    surname McKENNEY   (order of birth uncertain) (all born Scarboro, Maine)
   53. Jacob   born ca 1732; baptized 5 May 1742; married Temperance _____?
        Note: Resided Greene, Maine. His widow and 4 children : Jacob,Jr; Stephen, and 2 daughters moved to Danville, Maine
+ 54. MOSES   born ca 1734; baptized 5 May 1742; died poss 1806
          1m. Eunice-4 LARRABEE 20 Oct 1762
      (she dau/o John-3 LARRABEE and Mary-5 INGERSOLL) (she born 24 Nov 1741 Scarboro)
          2m. Lucy PLUMMER
   55. Hannah   born ca 1738; baptized 5 May 1742; married Stephen-4 LARRABEE 16 Oct 1760
         (he born 3 Nov 1738; died ____) (bro/o Eunice-4 above)
+ 56. DOROTHY   born ca 1740; baptized 5 May 1742; married Luke-4 LIBBY 1760
         (he son/o John-3 LIBBY and Sarah LIBBY) (he born 15 Aug 1738)
+ 57. ISAAC   born ca 1744; baptized 28 Oct 1744; married Hannah JORDAN 14 Jan 1767
         (he of Scarboro; moved to Danville, Maine)
   58. Priscilla Getchell born _____; baptized 22 March 1746
         married Robert JORDAN ca 1768 Scarboro, Maine
   59. Lydia   born ca 1747; died ca ____
+ 60. LT. WILLIAM   born 11 Feb 1750; baptized 11 May 1750 (served in the **Revolutionary War**)
         married Miriam JORDAN 13 Nov 1783
   61. Joseph   born ca 1754; died ____ (poss at Greene, Maine)

References: First Congregational Church Records, Scarboro, Maine; ++ Southgate's History of Scarborough, Maine 1853; MA Archives : Volume 95; page 407; LIBBY Genealogy; Edward SMALL Genealogy Volume 1; page 501; +++ Maine Historical and Genealogical Recorder, Page 103.

++ Ancestry of Isaac-3 McKENNEY

JOHN-1 McKENNEY, an Irishman and a planter, appeared in a deed of Joshua SCOTTOW at Blackpoint, dated 1 Aug 1668. He may have been single at that time; and his marriage date and wife's name is unknown.

On 12 Jan 1673, John-1 McKENNEY purchased from Robert JORDAN, a tract of land on the Nonsuch River, near Chissemores Hill. This was at Blue Point. He was " on duty " at the fort at Blackpoint/ Scarborough in 1677-78. In 1690 there was a general retreat from that place; and any records of Scarborough were lost. It is not certain where John-1 McKENNEY took his family at that time.

His son, ROBERT-2 McKENNEY, who was born ca 1675, married in 1692, the widow Rebecca _____ Sparks at Portsmouth, NH; and died 23 Sept 1725, aged about 50 years. He is probably the ancestor of most, if not all, of that name in Maine. He resided at the second settlement of Scarborough.

Robert-2 McKENNEY, and his wife, had the following children : 1. John born ___, res. Scarborough; Robert born ____; 3. ISAAC-3 ++ born ____; married Elizabeth-4 DRISKO/DRISCO and resided Scarborough; 4. Henry born ____, resided Cape Elizabeth; 5. Rebecca born ___; married Daniel BURNHAM of Scarboro; 6. Hannah born ____, married William GROVER, res Damariscotta.

26. JAMES-4 DRISCO/ JEREMIAH-4 DRISCO, son of Cornelius-3 DRISCO (Jeremiah-2; Teague/ Timothy-1) and Mary CROMMETT, was born ca 17__ probably at Portsmouth, Rockingham County, NH. He married possibly a Mary MASON. She possibly the daughter of a Joseph MASON and his wife Sarah. They resided Durham, NH. In 1771 Sarah MASON left 30 acres to her daughter Mary DISCO (Drisco).

Child of James/Jeremiah-4 DRISCO:
    surname DRISCO
+ 62. CAPTAIN   born ca 1750 NH ; baptized 15 June 1778 (as an adult) ;   died ca 1812
       JAMES, SR.   1m. Elizabeth WALDEN 12 Aug 1773 (South Church records Portsmouth, NH)
                   2m. Jane _?_; (she born 1765; died 20 Jan 1845 (age 80) Portsmouth, NH

Note: There was possibly another son : Nathaniel DRISCO, who appeared on the 1790 Census, Portsmouth,NH.

THE DRISCO HOUSE AT STRAWBERY BANKE

The house, on Puddle Dock Lane, now part of the Strawbery Banke Museum ++, was built about 1795 by its original owner Captain John SHAPLEY/SHAPLEIGH. He may have used it as a shop in its early years, as during its restoration double front doors were discovered.

John SHAPLEY/SHAPLEIGH was given the title of mariner on the property deeds. However, newspaper advertisements (1790's) suggest that he was also a merchant, selling such items as flour, raisins and lime. Records show that he had a license to sell liquors. An announcement of his " coasting business " was made in April 1800.

Captain James-5 DRISCO, Sr. purchased the John SHAPLEY/SHAPLEIGH House at Strawbery Banke, Portsmouth, NH in 1800. He sold it to James, Jr. the same year. The DRISCOS' were both mariners, and advertisements were often placed in the Oracle of the Day concerning the selling or chartering of ships.

Both James, Sr. and James, Jr. bought other property in the early 1800's and ran a shop down by the wharf they owned. In 1807 James, Jr. died and James, Sr. settled his estate before his own death in 1812. The 1812 inventory of real estate mentions several dwelling houses, a wharf, and a store on Horse Lane.

DRISCO HOUSE at Strawbery Banke, Portsmouth, NH

References: Strawbery Banke Museum, Portsmouth, NH, article by Eileen O'BRIEN, Intern (Jan 1983); Customs Records, Portsmouth, NH Volume III, pages 87-88; St. John's Church records; Portsmouth Record Book Volume 2 ; Rambles About Portsmouth by Charles BREWSTER; North Church records; South Church records; NEH&GR Volume 29,20,62,136,225.

++ STRAWBERY BANKE, is a 10-acre complex of historic buildings in Portsmouth, NH. The 18th Century DRISCO HOUSE is the first building that visitors see upon entering the grounds.

Although it is not the oldest house there, the DRISCO HOUSE has the longest record for having been lived in continuously. Starting in 1795, the house was occupied until the last family moved out in 1957.

By the late 1800's, the once prosperous area was populated by poor European immigrants who called themselves Puddledockers.

In the 1950's , a small group of citizens, after convincing state legislators to include restoration in the urban renewal plan, were successful in getting Strawbery Banke declared a historic site. It opened to the public in 1965, and by 1998 seven of the houses had been completed. The DRISCO HOUSE project began in 1986.

Copied from a gravestone in Maine

Within this grave I lie,
Back to back, my wife and I.
And when the last trump the air shall fill,
If she gets up, I'll just lie still.

Fifth American Generation

31. SOBRIETY-5 NOCK/KNOX, daughter of Samuel-4 NOCK/KNOX (Sarah-3 DRISKO/DRISCO; John-2) and Abigail RICKER, was born 14 June 1740.

She married Moses-3 RICKER ca 1763. He was the son of Ephraim-2 RICKER (George-1) and his second wife Sarah WENTWORTH. He was born 3 Jan 1739; died 26 Oct 1801. Sobriety NOCK/.KNOX died at Lebanon, Maine on 28 Nov 1829, aged 90.

Moses-3 RICKER was a soldier in the **Revolutionary War.** He served in a Company at Pierce's Island 5 Nov 1775. He also served at Crown Point.

Moses RICKER first appeared in Rev. Isaac HASEYS' diary, 3 Feb 1775. Mr. HASEY wrote a deed from Moses GOODWIN to Moses RICKER, 26 Nov 1776. On 14 April 1791, Mr. HASEY wrote in his diary " Moses RICKER raised his house frame " (this was probably a log house). On 27 Oct 1801, Mr. HASEY preached at the funeral of Moses RICKER.

Children of Sobriety-5 NOCK/KNOX and Moses RICKER:
    surname RICKER

63. Henry	born 5 July 1764
64. Abigail	born 3 Oct 1767
+ 65. ELIJAH	born 1 Dec 1769; married Hannah COPPS int pub 10 Nov 1805
	(she dau/o Deacon Samuel COPPS and Hannah HAYES)
	(she born 2 May 1779; died 27 Jan 1861)
66. Hannah	born 8 Oct 1771; died 27 Oct 1842
+ 67. MOSES, JR.	born 1773 Lebanon, ME; married Sally HANSON 28 Dec 1804 Berwick, ME
+ 68. MERCY	born 21 Aug 1777; died 25 Dec 1831 Lebanon, Maine
	married Captain Daniel GRANT 19 Dec 1804
69. Sarah	born 2 March 1780; died 30 Dec 1853
	married Captain Daniel GRANT Dec 1834 (he widower of her sister Mercy)
70. Rebecca	born 13 Jan 1783; died 28 Oct 1879 unmarried EOL

33. DOROTHY-5 NOCK/KNOX, sister of above, was born ca 1747 at Dover, NH. She married Lemuel-3 RICKER on 31 Dec 1771 at Dover. He was the son of Ephraim-2 RICKER and Sarah WENTWORTH. He was the brother of Moses-3, above. Lemuel-3 RICKER was born 17__; died ca 1822 at Milton, NH. Dorothy-5 NOCK/KNOX died 26 Nov 1831, aged 84 years.

Children of Dorothy-5 NOCK/KNOX and Lemuel-3 RICKER:
    surname RICKER   (all born Dover, NH)

+ 71. JEDEDIAH	born 2 March 1773; married Sally WENTWORTH
+ 72. JOANNA	born 11 Aug 1776; married John ROBINSON 31 Dec 1800
73. Ezekiel	born 22 March 1778; died before 1815
74. Dorcas/Dolly	born ca 1780; died 9 June 1860 unmarried EOL
+ 75. SAMUEL	born ca 1784, Maine; married Polly FOSS 17 Oct 1813
+ 76. HANNAH	born ca 1786; married Joseph KNOX 2 Sept 1807
	(he son/o William KNOX and Sarah ALLEY) (he born ca 1790; died 1851 Berwick, ME)
77. Abra	born ____; married Israel DANIELS 26 July 1806 Milton, NH
	(he from Madbury, NH)
78. Sarah Wentworth	born ____

38. EBENEZER-5 NOCK/KNOX, son of Ebenezer-4 NOCK/KNOX (Sarah-3 DRISKO/DRISCO; John-2) and Elizabeth RICKER, was born 29 July 1746. He married Elizabeth GARLAND on 15 Nov 1770. They resided at Somersworth, NH.

Children of Ebenezer-5 NOCK/KNOX and Elizabeth GARLAND:
    surname NOCK/KNOX
79. Elizabeth	born 6 Oct 1771
80. Isaacher	born 3 June 1773; married Mary _?_; (she 2m. Amos SHACKFORD)
	died 1812 ; resided Waterborough, York Co., ME)
81. Henry	born 17 Dec 1775

40. SYLVANUS-5 NOCK/KNOX, ½ brother of above, was the son of Ebenezer-4 NOCK/KNOX and
Mary RANDALL Ricker, and was born ____. He married Mary PAPPOON on ____. She was the daughter
of ____ PAPPOON and ____; and was born ____; died ____. They resided Somersworth, NH.

Children of Sylvanus-5 NOCK/KNOX and Mary PAPPOON:
    surname NOCK/KNOX
82. Thomas	born 28 Jan 1763; died 2 Aug 1771, drowned in the Salmon Falls River		
83. Sarah	born 16 Feb 1766	84. Sylvanus	born 21 March 1768

43. LUCY-5 CROMWELL, daughter of Esther-4 NOCK/KNOX (Sarah-3 DRISKO/DRISCO; John-2)
and Eliphalet CROMWELL, was born 27 Jan 1744 Dover, NH. She married Daniel-3 RICKER ca 1762.
The son of John-2 RICKER and Hannah-2 GARLAND; he was born ____; died 3 May 1823 at Somersworth, NH. Lucy-5 CROMWELL died 3 Jan 1817.

Children of Lucy-5 CROMWELL and Daniel-3 RICKER:
    surname RICKER
85. Esther	born 3 Feb 1763; married Jonathan PINKHAM
86. Ruth	born 28 Mar 1765; married John RICKER
+ 87. JOHN	born 28 Dec 1767; married Elizabeth PINKHAM
88. Caleb	born 15 Jan 1770; married Dorcas HORN
	(she dau/o William HORN and Mary HEARD)
Child: Benjamin Purrington-7 RICKER born 7 Apr 1794; married Elizabeth BICKFORD 24 Aug 1813	
+ 89. ELIAS	born 2 June 1772; married Mary Morrill WITHERELL
	(she dau/o John WITHERELL and Mary ?) (she born 4 July 1782; died 20 June 1856)
90. Hannah	born 18 Oct 1774; married James BISHOP
91. Jeremiah	born 27 Sept 1775; died before 1800
92. Asa (twin)	born 2 April 1777
+ 93. DANIEL (twin)	born 2 April 1777; married Elizabeth EMERY 1 April 1804
	(she dau/o Rev Simon EMERY and Molly HODGDON) (she born 1785; died Feb 1855)
+ 94. ELIPHALET	born 30 June 1779; married Mercy HANSON 22 June 1804 Milton, NH
	(she born 9 Mar 1786; died 26 Mar 1877)
	died 9 March 1850 Wells, Maine
+ 95. PAUL	born 24 Sept 1781; married Elizabeth HAYES 14 Mar 1811; died 1 Jan 1864
	(she dau/o Joseph HAYES and Abigail _?_) (she born 20 Apr 1790; died 5 June 1872)
96. Lucy	born 11 Nov 1784; married Silas DAVIS
97. Eliza	born 11 Mar 1787; married William WITHERELL
98. Rebecca	born 3 May 1789; married Benjamin HAYES 1809

44. LYDIA-5 RICKER, daughter of Mercy-4 NOCK/KNOX (Sarah-3 DRISKO/DRISCO; John-2) and
Nathaniel RICKER, was born 24 Sept 1747 at Somersworth, NH. She married Jedediah GOODWIN on 9
May 1770. The son of Noah GOODWIN and Abigail ____; he was born ____ at Argyle, Nova Scotia; died
____. He was a sailor and farmer. Lydia-5 RICKER died ____.

Children of Lydia-5 RICKER and Jedediah GOODWIN:
    surname GOODWIN
99. Henry	born 18 Jan 1782; married Azuba FROST
100. son (no name)	born ca 17__; died after becoming lost in the woods

46. CAPTAIN NATHANIEL-5 RICKER, JR., brother of above, was born 13 Nov 1757 at Somersworth, NH. He married first at Argyle, Nova Scotia ca 1781 to Anna ROBERTS. She was born ____; died 1 May 1800, Argyle. His 2nd wife was Eleanor CURTIS Dalton. She was born 1757; died at Argyle 8 May 1817.

Captain Nathaniel RICKER was the master of a sailing vessel for many years; mainly carrying lumber. He owned other vessels that were built at Argyle, NS, and was sailing one such vessel with his brother-in-law Jedediah GOODWIN during the Revolutionary War, when they were captured by an American privateer. They were able to re-take their vessel after their captors " partook " of the spirits on board and passed out.

In the diary of Simeon PERKINS, an entry dated 24 Mar 1782 states " Nathaniel RICKER stops briefly at the mouth of Liverpool Harbour enroute to Halifax in his shallop." A shallop was a small half-decked sailing vessel.

Children of Captain Nathaniel-5 RICKER, Jr. and Anna ROBERTS:
   surname RICKER

+ 101. CAPTAIN EBENEZER	born 24 June 1782; 1m. Lucy FROST 15 Jan 1804 Argyle, NS (she dau/o Andrew FROST and Sarah REDDING) (she born 10 Nov 1784; died 10 Feb 1849) 2m. Ruth LARKIN 27 Oct 1852 (she born ____; died 17 Dec 1891) died 20 Mar 1867 Argyle, NS
102. Nathaniel. III	born 28 Dec 1786; died 1812 England, unmarried EOL
+ 103. ELIZABETH	born 1 May 1790; married Solomon MANGRUM 13 Feb 1821 Argyle
+ 104. CAPTAIN BENJAMIN	born 1 Sept 1792; married Sarah FROST 22 Dec 1817 (she born 1794; died 28 Dec 1841) (sister of Lucy, above) died 10 April 1843 Eastport, Maine

   105. Sylvanus ** born 11 Feb 1796   106. William ** born 9 Apr 1798 107. Paul ** born 24 Apr 1800

** The three brothers, all sailors, died ca 1822 in the West Indies along with other members of the ships' crew, after having been given medicine aboard ship. It was suspected that the medicine had been poisoned. Their bodies were never returned to their family and it created a superstition in shipping circles in Nova Scotia thereafter. It was believed that it brought bad luck, and death, to have three brothers sailing on the same vessel.

47. CAPTAIN PAUL-5 RICKER, brother of above, was born 11 Oct 1765 at Somersworth, NH. He married Catherine KENTON on 30 Dec 1807 at Argyle, Nova Scotia. They later moved to Eastport, ME.

Children of Captain Paul-5 RICKER and Catherine KENTON:
   surname RICKER

108. Captain Nathaniel	born 26 Oct 1808; married Anna-7 RICKER 6 Sept 1832 Argyle, NS (she born 28 Nov 1804; died 2 Dec 1856) (she # 270) died 20 Mar 1838; lost at sea in the West Indies
	One child: Sarah Ellen-7 RICKER born July 1833; died July 1836
+ 109. CAPTAIN ROBERT	born 26 April 1811; married Sarah –7 RICKER 8 Feb 1837 Argyle, NS (she dau/o Ebenezer-6 RICKER and Lucy FROST) (she born 10 Sept 1815; died 8 Dec 1873) died 1 Aug 1888 Knowlesville, New Brunswick
+ 110. MARY/MERCY	born 5 June 1813; died 10 May 1868 married David CROWELL 24 Jan 1832 Argyle, NS (he born 8 Feb 1808; died 11 Feb 1886)
+ 111. MARGARET	born 1 Jan 1815; married Joseph JOHNSTON 21 Dec 1835; died 15 May 1890
+ 112. JOHN KNOX	born 12 June 1818; married M ____ M. RICHARDSON 14 Apr 1849 (she born 23 Aug 1826, NC; died 20 Mar 1886 TX) died 14 April 1894 Corsicana, TX
+ 113. DANIEL	born 19 Jan 1821; died 19 Jan 1881 married Lucy Ann-7 RICKER 12 Sept 1847 (she born 26 Mar 1827) (# 287)

49. JOHN-5 DRISKO/DRISCO, 2nd , son of Joseph-4 DRISKO/DRISCO (John-3; 2) and Elizabeth-3 MITCHELL, was born ca 1742 at Scarborough; baptized there 9 Jan 1743 at the First Congregational Church.

He married Mary Johnson-5 CHANDLER ++, daughter of Judah-4 CHANDLER (Joseph-3;2; Edmond-1) and Martha SEABURY of North Yarmouth, Maine. Mary was born 25 Oct 1745; baptized 27 Oct 1745; died after 1830. Their marriage intentions were published 5/15 Jan 1765 (North Yarmouth VR 1:589).

He was the John DRISCO/DRISKO who tradition and Militia records state " was elected Captain of the Pleasant River men " – when they went to the aid of the people of Machias, assisting them in the capture of the British vessel MARGARETTA. John-5 DRISKO, 2nd died Nov 1830 at Addison, Maine – aged 88 years. His obituary was in the *Eastport Sentinel* on 1 Dec 1830.

Children of John-5 DRISKO/DRISCO and Mary-5 CHANDLER:
    surname DRISKO

+ 114. JERUSHA	born 2 June 1765; died 28 Sept 1815 (gs)
	married Joseph WILSON, Jr. 16 Nov 1786 Machias
	(he born 4 Sept 1762 Falmouth; died 25 May 1823 Columbia, ME.)
	(he son/o Joseph WILSON and Mary SWETT)
+ 115. REBECCA	born Oct 1766/67; died 1864
	married David-5 CHANDLER 5 July 1787 North Yarmouth
	(he son/o Jonathan-4 CHANDLER and Rachel MITCHELL)
	(he born 30 June 1752 No. Yarmouth; died ____)
	(resided Great Chebeague Island (now Portland)
+ 116. LORRAINE	born ca 1769/70 ; married Moses-7 PLUMMER, 3rd ca 1790
" Luraney "	(he son/o Moses-6 PLUMMER and Lucy PERKINS; born 1768; died 1846)
	died 20 March 1802 (gs)
117. Moses	born ca 1771; died ca 1789 aged 18 EOL
+ 118. JUDAH	born 4 Nov 1772; died 22 Nov 1849
JOHNSON	married Lucy-7 PLUMMER 10 Jan 1797 ME (she sister/o Moses-7 , above)
	(she born 13 Apr 1777, Washington Co., ME; died 1858)
+ 119. ABIGAIL	born 5 Nov 1775 Addison, ME; died 15 Apr 1837
	married William H-6 BUCKNAM 17 Jan 1796
	(he son/o John-5 BUCKNAM and Mary A. WILSON) (he born 8 Sept 1773; died 1 Jan 1829)
120. Edmund	born ca 1777; died young
+ 121. RELIEF	born 28 June 1780 Addison Ridge; died 15 Feb 1875 Machias, ME
	married Samuel SMITH, int pub 21 March 1804
	(he son/o Moses SMITH, Jr. of North Yarmouth) (he born 2 Dec 1774, MA; died after 1850)
	resided Durham, NH; Nova Scotia and Maine

References: History of Machias by George W. DRISKO 1895; Clarence DRISKO,
Columbia Falls, ME, deceased; Edward SMALL Genealogy.

++ Ancestry of Mary Johnson-5 CHANDLER
MARY JOHNSON-5 CHANDLER, born 25 Oct 1745, was the only child of Judah-4 CHANDLER and his first wife Martha SEABURY. His second wife was Rebecca SEABURY, sister of Martha, by whom he had 8 more children including Mercy-5 CHANDLER who married Samuel Gatchell-5 DRISKO.

JUDAH-4 CHANDLER, was born 13 Aug 1720 at Duxbury, MA. He was the son of JOSEPH-3 CHANDLER (Joseph-2; Edmund-1) and Martha HUNT. According to an ancient deposition in the records of the First Church of North Yarmouth (ME) , Judah CHANDLER was about nine years old (ca 1729) when he went to North Yarmouth with his father.

Early in life he followed the sea. In 1746 and 1753 – he was listed as a " coaster ". Also, in 1746 he received 1/6th of a tract of land on Chebeague, in common with his brother Edmund. It was probably a portion of his fathers' estate.

In 1757 he served as a Private in Captain Solomon MITCHELLS' Train Band. About 1766 he moved to Royalsborough (Durham) near a small pond which flowed into Chandler's River. He built a sawmill on the river soon after he arrived and carried on the business of lumbering. In 1777 he purchased, with others, a tract of land upon which was built another mill. The first mill was located at the head of the falls; its successor was called the " Old Stone Mill ". He was chosen surveyor of lumber. He lived in Durham until his death in 1802, at the age of 82.

50. ELIZABETH/BETSEY-5 DRISKO, half-sister of above, daughter of Joseph-4 DRISKO and Mary-5 SMALL, was born ca 1747 (according to the date on her g s) She was baptized 16 March 1757 in the First Congregational Church of Scarborough, Maine.

She married Joseph-2 TABBUT/TABBUTT, Jr. ++ son of Joseph-1 TABBUT/TABBUTT/TEBBUT, Sr, and possibly Elizabeth SHEPARD/SHEPERD. He was born ca 1748, possibly England; died 1833 at Columbia, Maine. They were married circa 1775 at Pleasant River, Washington County, Maine. They resided at Moose Neck, Pleasant River and Epping. Elizabeth/Betsey-5 DRISKO died 1835.

Children of Elizabeth-5 DRISKO and Joseph TABBUT/TABBUTT, Jr.:
    surname TABBUT/TABBUTT   (all born Columbia, Maine)
+ 122. SUSANNA   born 6 Dec 1776; married David-4 JOY 2 Oct 1796 (as his 2nd wife)
            (he son/o Samuel-3 JOY and Abigail TRACY ; born ca 1771; died bef 1820)
+ 123. THOMAS   *   born 25 April 1778/79; married Catherine CROWLEY 1801/02 ME
            (she born 1784 Cape Elizabeth, ME; died after 1860)
            (she dau/o Jeremiah CROWLEY and Elizabeth JORDAN)
            died before 1 April 1823 Columbia, Maine
  124. Benjamin   born 26 March 1781; married Betsey-5 COLE
        (she dau/o Ebenezer-4 COLE and Elizabeth HALL) (she born ca 1774; died 185_)
            died before 1805 (drowned)
+ 125. JOHN COFFIN   born 2 May 1785; married Betsey-5 COLE TABBUTT Aug 1805
            (she widow of his brother Benjamin # 124)
+ 126. MOSES   born 1 June 1788; married Mary CROWLEY 1812
     (she dau/o John CROWLEY and _?_) (she born 1793; died 1872 Cherryfield, ME)
            died 1868 Columbia Falls, Maine
  127. Olive Drisko   born 13 July 1791; married Samuel-6 TRACY 10 May 1815
            (he born 11 Apr 1794; died 19 Aug 1873)
      (he son /o Rev Christopher-5 TRACY (Jonathan-4; Christopher-3; Jonathan-2; Thomas-1)
            and Anna GETCHELL (John GETCHELL, Jr.)
  128. Abraham   born 13 Feb 1793; died before 1805 (drowned with brother Benjamin)
+ 129. WILLIAM   born 14 May 1798; died 30 July 1886
            married Anne-2 WRIGHT int pub 12 Dec 1819
      (she dau/o John WRIGHT and Katherine IRISH) (she born ca 1799; died 28 March 1884)
  130. Rufus   **   born ca 1801 ; married Phoebe-2 WRIGHT ca 1825; died 20 May 1883
            (she born ca 1802; died 1886) no issue EOL

* Catherine CROWLEY, a first cousin of Mary CROWLEY, married 2nd to John WORCESTER. It is believed that they had a daughter (name unknown). This unnamed daughter may have been the individual who, with Otis-6 TABBUT(T) (Moses-5) , may have been the unmarried parents of Abijah Worcester TABBUTT, born March 1842; died Aug 1918 Columbia Falls, Maine.

** Rufus-6 TABBUTT and his wife had no children of their own, but they adopted and raised Abijah Worcester TABBUTT. Abijah TABBUTT married Aurilla FLOYD on 3 July 1867. He invented the Blueberry Rake, which is still being made at the original location. He is buried in the TABBUT(T) Cemetery near his home. His children were MARY ELLA (1868-1899) who married WILLIAM PITT-9 DRISKO (# 2016); Katie S. (1871-1960) who married Bert ALLEN; Melvin (1874-1882); and Carrie S. (1884-19__) who married Ernest PALMER.   Reference: Maine Historical and Genealogical Recorder Volume 9, pages 88 / 89.

++ Ancestry of Joseph-2 TABBUT(T)/TEBBUT/ TIBBETTS, Jr.
Tradition says that JOSEPH TABBUT/TABBUTT, Sr., born ca 1722, was from Wales; and came to America from London, England ca 1755. He settled at Old Falmouth, Maine. He later resided at Pleasant River and South Addison where he died 25 Sept 1804. On that date his widow Elizabeth (born ca 1726) relinquished her rights to administer the estate of her " late " husband. Joseph TAB-BUT, Sr. had 6 sons and 6 daughters. Of the 4 of his sons, whose names are not known, 3 are said to have drowned. Others were JOSEPH, JR. (above) and William who married first to Elizabeth MacDONALD, and secondly to Rachel KNIGHT. His daughters were Mary/Polly who marr Thomas MANSFIELD; Jemima who marr Eliphalet REYNOLDS; and Elizabeth who married John DAY.

51. JOSEPH-5 DRISKO/DRISCO, brother of above, son of Joseph-4; John-3;2) and Mary SMALL, was born 9 June 1748 at Addison, Washington County, Maine.

He married, ca 1768, Rebecca-6 INGERSOLL, daughter of William-5 INGERSOLL ++ and Sarah PARKER. Rebecca was born 1 Jan 1748; baptized 19 June 1748 at the First Church of North Yarmouth, Maine; died ____ (still living 1835). Joseph-5 DRISKO died about 1802.

Children of Joseph-5 DRISKO and Rebecca- 6 INGERSOLL:
  Surname DRISKO

+ 131. MARY	born ca 1769; married Rev Benjamin-5 DOWNS 16 July 1791 Addison
	(he born 1767; died 10 Nov 1840)
	(he son/o Ebenezer-4 DOWNS and Jane WALTON)
+ 132. CAPTAIN JOHN	born ca 1772; 1m. Phebe PARKER of Steuben, Maine
	2m. Emma KNOWLES Steele Kelly
	(she born ca 1776; died 1854 (aged 88 gs))
133. Olive	born ca 1776; died ____ unmarried EOL
+ 134. HANNAH	born 1778/79; married Daniel-2 McKENZIE int pub 22 Aug 1797
	(he born 1772; died 17 Aug 1870)
	(he son/o Owen-1 McKENZIE and Elizabeth DYER)
	died 184_ Columbia, Maine
+ 135. JOSEPH	born ca 1781; married Eunice PARKER Hill
	(she born 12 Nov 1774; died 19 Jan 1853)
	(she dau/o Elisha-4 PARKER and Eunice JORDAN)
	(she widow of Miles HILL (int pub 10 May 1796)
	died ca 1851 Addison, Maine
136. Lucy	born ca 1783; died 11 Jan 1858
+ 137. JOSIAH	born 6 Sept 1787; married Theodocia CROWLEY 1810; died 2 June 1860
	(she born ca 1790; died 11 Nov 1857 Addison)
	(she dau/o Jeremiah CROWLEY and Elizabeth JORDAN)
138. Rebecca	born ca 1788; died ___ unmarried EOL
+ 139. JEREMIAH	born ca 1790; married Ann FRANKLAND; died 12 Dec 1870
	(she born 22 Nov 1798, NB; died 1878) (**War of 1812**)

Reference: 1850 Census Jonesport, Maine; Maine Families Volume 2, page 65

++ Ancestry of Rebecca-6 INGERSOLL

RICHARD-1 INGERSOLL, born in Bedfordshire, England, came to Salem (MA) in 1629. He married Ann/Agnes LANGLEY on 20 Oct 1616 in England. Richard-1 died ____; his will being proved 2 Jan 1644/45. Ann born ____, England; died 30 July1677. Their children were: Alice; John (died young); LT. GEORGE-2 ; John (2); Joanna/Joan; Sarah; Bathsheba; and Nathaniel.

LT. GEORGE-2 INGERSOLL, born ____; baptized 2 July 1618 England; married circa 1642 to Elizabeth GEORGE. He owned land in Wenham (MA), then removed to Gloucester; and later to Casco Bay. His children were: 1. A son killed by Indians at Falmouth in 1675; 2. George; 3. John; 4. JOSEPH-3 born 4 Oct 1646; 5. Elizabeth (died young); 6. Elizabeth ; 7. Samuel born 1654, d. young; 8. Samuel born 1657.

JOSEPH-3 INGERSOLL, born 1646, married Sarah COE . Her parents were Matthew COE and Elizabeth WAKELY, who were massacred by Indians at Falmouth 5 Sept 1675. Joseph INGERSOLLS' children were: 1. Martha born 1670; 2. John baptized 1676; 3. Stephen born 1674; 4. BENJAMIN-4 born ca 1687; 5. Joseph who married Mary BREWER; and 6. Hannah who married John CLEMENTS.

BENJAMIN-4 INGERSOLL, born ca 1687, first married Mary-4 HUNT, int pub 16 Nov 1711. Mary was the daughter of William-3 HUNT (Samuel-2; William-1) and his wife Sarah-3 NEWMAN (John-2;1). His second wife was Sarah-3 IRESON Parker, daughter of Benjamin-2 IRESON (Edward-1) and Mary-3 LEACH (Richard-2; Lawrence-1); and the widow of Captain James-3 PARKER (James-2; 1).

Children of Benjamin-4 INGERSOLL and Mary HUNT were: 1. Mary born 1713; 2. Benjamin born 1715; 3. WILLIAM-5 born 8 Sept 1717; 4. Martha born 1719; 5. Nathaniel born 1722; 6. Joseph born 1725; 7. Sarah born 1728 , married James-4 PARKER; 8. Hannah born 1730, married Henry TOLMAN; 9. Daniel born 1737, died young; and 10. Possibly another child who died young.

WILLIAM-5 INGERSOLL, born 8 Sept 1717 in Gloucester, MA; married Sarah-4 PARKER 22 Sept 1737. She was the daughter of James-3 PARKER and Sarah –3 IRESON, and was born 14 Oct 1720. Their children were: 1. Sarah born 1738; 2. Lucy born 1742; 3. Mary born 1744; 4. ++ REBECCA-6 born 1 Jan 1748 who married Joseph-4 DRISKO (above); 5. Abigail born 1751; 6. William,Jr. born 1754; 7. Benjamin who married Sarah COLSON.

References: Descendants of Richard INGERSOLL, Salem, MA, pages 2/ 3; The HAMMATT Papers; Town Records of Gloucester, Portland and No. Yarmouth; BABSONS' History of Gloucester; WILLIS' History of Portland; NEH&GR 14: 155; 1850 Census.

52. SAMUEL GATCHELL-5 DRISKO, brother of above, son of Joseph-4 DRISKO (John-3;2) and his second wife Mary SMALL, was born 10 Aug 1749; baptized 13 Aug 1749 at Scarborough, Maine.

He married Mercy-5 CHANDLER at Plantation # 22 (Jonesboro), Maine on 4 July 1773. Mercy was the daughter of Judah-4 CHANDLER (Joseph-3; 2; Edmond-1) and his second wife Rebecca-5 SEABURY ++. Mercy was born 4 April 1754, Chebeague Island, Maine; died 3 May 1810. She and two of her sons, Jonathan and Edward, were buried the same day. She was the sister of Mary-5 Johnson CHANDLER who married John-5 DRISKO.

They resided Pleasant River before 1770; later living in Jonesboro until 1779/80; then removing to Columbia, Maine. Samuel Gatchell-5 DRISKO died at Columbia, Maine on _ Jan 1835.

++ Rebecca-5 SEABURY, born 24 Sept 1723, Bridgewater, MA; died after 1766. She was the daughter of Barnabus-4 SEABURY (Samuel-3; 2; John-1) and Mary JOHNSON. They had 11 children.

Children of Samuel G-5 DRISKO and Mercy-5 CHANDLER:
    Surname DRISKO

+ 140. JONATHAN   born 30 Sept 1774 Jonesboro, ME; died 4 May 1810 Columbia, ME
                        married Sarah Dyer McKENZIE int pub 22 Oct 1796 Columbia Falls, ME
                        (she born ca 1777/78; died 2 Mar 1864 (aged 86 gs)
                        (she dau/o Owen McKENZIE and Elizabeth DYER)

        Note: Sarah McKENZIE married second to Silas-5 TENNEY 10 Sept 1814 Columbia, ME. He was the son/o
             George-4 TENNEY and Deborah-5 INGERSOLL; and was born 1774; died 1833) They had one son :
             Warren-6 TENNEY, born 18__. She married third to John CONNERS/O'CONNOR 4 March 1835.

+ 141. MARY/POLLY   born 26 Oct 1776 Jonesboro, ME; died 8 Mar 1847
                        married Captain Holmes-5 NASH int pub 26 Sept 1796 Columbia, Maine
                        (he son/o Joseph-4 NASH and Elizabeth WASS of Addison Point, ME)
  142. Alethea/Ella   born 11 Feb 1780 Jonesboro, Maine
                        died 10 Feb 1850 Addison   unmarried   EOL
  143. EDMUND   born 24 April 1784 Columbia, Maine; died 4 May 1810 " from a fever "
                        married Elizabeth/Betsey-6 CATES (she born 1790; died ca 1820)
                        (she dau/o Edward-5 CATES and Elizabeth ___?)
                        (she 2m. Isaac HANSCOM 25 Nov 1813 at Machias, ME.)
+ 144. JERUSHA   born 6 Sept 1786 Columbia, ME;   died 27 April 1848 Addison, ME
      (twin)   married Deacon David CORTHELL Dec 1807
                        (he born 1782, MA; died 29 Oct 1868)
+ 145. REBECCA   born 6 Sept 1786 Columbia, ME; married Elisha COFFIN ca 1808
      (twin)   (he born ca 1785; died Aug 1871 (aged 86 gs)
+ 146. SAMUEL   born July 1791 Columbia, Maine
      GATCHELL, Jr. married Mary D. PHINNEY int pub Sept 1814
                        (she born 1796, Machias; died June 1874)
                        (she dau/o Nathaniel PHINNEY, Jr. and Susan MESERVE)
                        died 28 Dec 1865 Columbia, ME; buried Church Hill Cemetery, Addison, ME

References: Boston Transcript #2675 (17 July 1912); Clarence DRISKO Transcript, page 24; Machias Union newspaper 29 Dec 1865; Genealogy of Edward SMALL (CHANDLER Family), page 1079-82; Dr. Leonard F. TIBBETTS.

54. MOSES-5 McKENNEY, son of Elizabeth-4 DRISKO (John-3;2) and Isaac-3 McKENNEY, was born ca 173_ at Scarborough, Maine. He married first, ca 1762, to Eunice-4 LARRABEE ++. She was the daughter of John-3 LARRABEE and Mary-5 INGERSOLL; and was born 24 Nov 1741 at Scarborough, Maine; died ____. His second wife was Lucy PLUMMER on _____. She was the daughter of ____ PLUMMER and _____; and was born ____; died ____. Moses-5 McKENNEY died ca 1806.

Children of Moses-5 McKENNEY and Eunice-4 LARRABEE:
   Surname McKENNEY

+147. DOROTHY	born ca 1763; married DOMINICUS-6 LIBBY 4 Jan/Jun 1790 (# 158)	
	(he son/o Luke-5 LIBBY and Dorothy-5 McKENNEY)	
+ 148. MARY	born ca 1765; married Philip LIBBY	
	died 27 July 1854 (aged 89)	
+ 149. HANNAH	born ____; married William-6 LIBBY 20 Jan 1797 (# 163)	
	(he born 1 Jan 1772; died 1 Apr 1847) (bro/o Dominicus-6, above)	
	died 22 March 1866	
+ 150. BETSEY	born ____; married Dennis LIBBY	
151. Eunice	born ____; married Ebenezer CASELY 4 Nov 1802 Scarboro, ME	
+ 152. MOSES	born ____; married Salome LIBBY 11 June 1799; died 24 Mar 1828	
	(she born 15 Oct 1778; died 1 July 1843)	
153. Lydia	born ____; died at age 74, unmarried EOL	
154. Sally	born ____; married James THURSTON of Danville, Maine	
155. Aaron	born ____	156. Isaac born ____

++ Ancestry of Eunice-4 LARRABEE

Traditions says that WILLIAM-1 LARRABEE was a Frenchman. His birth date is not known, but he married Elizabeth FELT Nov 1655 at Malden, MA. She was the daughter of George FELT and Elizabeth WILKINSON. George FELT was one of the most prominent early settlers of North Yarmouth, ME. William-1 LARRABEE and Elizabeth FELT had 7 children: 1. Stephen; 2. William born 1658, resided Wells, ME; 3. THOMAS-2; 4. John; 5. Isaac born 1664; 6. Benjamin born 1666, married Deborah INGERSOLL; and 7. Samuel.

THOMAS-2 LARRABEE, born ____, married Elizabeth __?, and settled in Scarborough. He later fled , from the Indians, to Kittery in 1690. He returned to Scarborough at the second settlement, and was killed by Indians, along with his son Anthony on 19 April 1723. Thomas-2 LARRABEE was the father of seven children: 1. Thomas who married an Abigail PITMAN ca 1715; 2. Eleanor who married Christopher MITCHELL Dec 1715; 3. Anthony, killed with his father; 4. Benjamin born ca 1700, married Sarah JOHNSON; 5. JOHN-3 who married Mary-5 INGERSOLL; 6. Hannah who married Benjamin RICHARDS; and 7. Jane.

JOHN-3 LARRABEE, born ____; lived and died at Scarborough, ME. He and his wife Mary-5 INGERSOLL had 10 children including EUNICE-4, born 24 Nov 1741; married Moses-6 McKENNEY (above). (Stephen-4 b. 1738, marr Hannah-6 McKENNEY.)

56. DOROTHY-5 McKENNEY, sister of above, was born ca 17__ at Scarborough, Maine. She married Luke-4 LIBBY on 21 Aug 1760 at Scarborough. He was the son of John-3 LIBBY and Sarah LIBBY, and was born 15 Aug 1738 at Scarborough, ME. Luke-4 LIBBY received part of his homestead farm from his fathers' will. He sold it in 1771 to Colonel Benjamin LARRABEE, and bought part of the PROUT estate on which he lived until his death. In 1789, his widow and children sold the property to Reuben FOGG, Jr., and removed to Danville, Maine (now Auburn). Dorothy-5 McKENNEY died there ca 1836.

Children of Dorothy-5 McKENNEY and Luke-4 LIBBY:
   Surname LIBBY

+ 157. REUBEN	born ca 1761; married Elizabeth BURNHAM 6 Feb 1782
+ 158. DOMINICUS	born 13 June 1763 ; bapt Scarborough; died 5 Jan 1836
	married DOROTHY-6 McKENNEY 4 June 1790 (# 147)
159. Eunice	born ca 1765; died 10 Apr 1850 Scarborough; unmarried EOL
+ 160. LUKE	born ca 1767; married Betsey MITCHELL
+ 161. ISAAC	born ca 1768; married Dorothy MESERVE
162. Hannah	born ca 1770; married John VOSMUS of Durham ca Feb 1787
	Ch: John-7 VOSMUS born 11 July 1787; marr Abigail LANE; died 18 Jan 1808 Danville, ME

Children of Dorothy-5 McKENNEY, continued:
  Surname LIBBY
+ 163. WILLIAM   born 1 Jan 1772; married HANNAH-6 McKENNEY 20 Jan 1797 (# 149)
+ 164. HUMPHREY   born ca 1774; married Keziah MESERVE 3 Jan 1799 (served in **War of 1812**)

++ Ancestry of Luke-4 LIBBY

JOHN-1 LIBBY, born in England 1602; died 1682. He came to America around 1630. John-1 LIBBY was (according to the History of Scarborough) " for many years one of the towns' principal planters." He had 12 children ; probably all born in this country. He was employed by a Mr. TRELAWNY in the fishing industry around Richmond's Island from 1635-39. He had two wives – his second wife was the mother of David-2.

DAVID-2 LIBBY, was born ca 1657 at Scarborough. He removed to Portsmouth, NH 1690. He married Eleanor ____. He was a well-to-do farmer who settled (1699) on a piece of property which fronted on the Piscataqua River; since known as LIBBY HILL near Kittery (now Eliot) . His will, dated 6 May 1725, was proven Dec 1736. He was buried on his own farm.

JOHN-3 LIBBY, born 1697 at Portsmouth; married Sarah LIBBY on 14 Nov 1724. She was the daughter of Mathew LIBBY and Elizabeth BROWN. John-3 LIBBY received land in Scarborough from his father. The deed was dated March 1719. Three of his sons, Mathew-4; Nathaniel-4; and Luke-4; settled on parts of his homestead . His other children, Elisha and Allison, received lands in the interior of the town.

John-3 LIBBY had an extra finger on each of his hands, below the little finger. To distinguish him from the many other John LIBBYS in Scarborough at that time, he was called " Five-fingered John LIBBY. " (Others were known as Blue John; Black John; Captain John and Little John).

57. ISAAC-5 McKENNEY, brother of above, was born ca 1744; baptized 28 Oct 1744 at the First Congregational Church of Scarborough, ME. He married Hannah-5 JORDAN on 14 Jan 1767 at Falmouth, Cumberland County, Maine. She was the daughter of Jeremiah-4 JORDAN (Jedediah-3;2; Rev Robert-1) and Keziah HANSCOMB +; and was born ca 1748; died 26 May 1829 at Danville, Androscoggin Co., ME

Children of Isaac-5 McKENNEY and Hannah-5 JORDAN:
  Surname McKENNEY
  165. Moses   born ____; married Mary LARRABEE
  169. Miriam   born (poss) 25 Aug 1769; married John COBB; died 1 Aug 1817 Bath, ME.
  166. Luke   born ____
+ 167. WILLIAM   born ____; married Mary JORDAN 1 June 1785; died before 1798
        (she dau/o James JORDAN/ Elizabeth JORDAN; born ca 1762; died 11 May 1838 Danville, ME)
+ 168. ABRAHAM   born ____; married Mary JORDAN McKenney 1Dec 1798 Durham, ME
        (she wid/o his brother William (above)

+ Keziah HANSCOMB, the daughter of Moses HANSCOMB (Thomas) and Hannah RACKLIFF (William) ; was born ca 1726. Jeremiah-4 JORDAN was born ca 1721; baptized Spurwink, Maine.

60. LIEUTENANT WILLIAM-5 McKENNEY, brother of above, was born 11 Feb 1750; baptized 11 May 1750 Scarborough, ME. He married Miriam-5 JORDAN, sister of Hannah-5 (above) on 13 Nov 1783. Miriam was born ca 1753; died 12 June 1841. She is buried Jordan School Road Cemetery, Auburn, ME. Lt. William-5 McKENNEY, who commanded a company in the **Revolutionary War,** died 27 Jan 1833 at Auburn, Maine and is buried there beside his wife.

Children of Lt. William-5 McKENNEY and Miriam-5 JORDAN:
  Surname McKENNEY

170. Mary Dyer	born _____	174. Jedediah	born _____
171. Phineas	born _____	175. Aaron	born _____
172. Phebe	born _____	176. Hannah	born ca 1797; died after 1876
173. Keziah Haniford	born _____		

62. CAPTAIN JAMES-5 DRISCO, Sr., son of James/Jeremiah-4 DRISCO (Cornelius-3; Jeremiah-2; Teague/Timothy-1) and _____?, was born ca 1750, probably at Portsmouth, NH. He was baptized, as an adult, at the South Church, Portsmouth on 15 June 1778. He married Elizabeth WALDEN on 12 Aug 1773

at Portsmouth. She was the daughter of _____ WALDEN and _____; and was born _____; died _____.
Captain James-5 DRISCO died 1812.

He was the individual who purchased a house on Puddle Dock Lane, Strawbery Banke, from John
SHAPLEY/SHAPLEIGH +++, a mariner/merchant and the original owner. The house, built in 1795, was
purchased by James DRISCO in 1800. He sold it to his son, James, Jr. the same year.

Both James DRISCO, Sr. and James DRISCO, Jr. – were sea captains. The DRISCO family traded with
the West Indies from 1793-1809. Their best year was 1805, during which they imported 4,872 gallons of
molasses; 120,072 pounds of sugar; 2,623 gallons of rum; 11,782 gallons of brandy and 10,774 pounds
of soap from the West Indies.   They also imported various articles from Marseilles, France. In 1807 they
imported 270,000 pounds of sugar from the West Indies.

They were the sole owners or part owners of a number of vessels. See the DRISKO/DRISCO Captains
and Vessel information on pages 217 - 228.

+++ Captain John SHAPLEY/SHAPLEIGH, son of Henry SHAPLEY, Sr. and Elesbeth _____; was born 8 Feb 1759 at Gosport
Township, Rockingham County, NH; married Katherine/ Catherine HUNTRESS 8 Sept 1777. They had three known children :
1. Sally who married William RUGG Sept 1795; and Catherine/Katherine who married William DAMERILL; and 3. A son (name
unknown).

Children of James-5 DRISCO, Sr. and Elizabeth WALDEN:
   Surname DRISCO

177. Izet/Izette	born ca 1774/75; married Abraham SHAW 24 Aug 1797 Portsmouth
+ 178. CAPTAIN JAMES	born ca 1776; married Margarette/Margaretta MENDUM 15 May 1798
JR.	(she born ca 1778; died 13 Mar 1853 (aged 75)
	died 16 June 1807 ; at sea (aged 31)
179. ELIZABETH/	born 1778; baptized 15 June 1778
BETSEY	married Captain William TREFETHEN, JR 18 Dec 1799 at Portsmouth, NH
180. Sarah Huntress	born 22 Mar 1780; baptized 7 May 1780
181. John	born ca 1782; baptized 19 Jan 1783
182. Jeremiah	born ca 1784; baptized 30 Jan 1785
183. Katey	born ca 1786; baptized 7 Nov 1786
184. Nancy	born 26 Sept 1790; baptized 3 Oct 1790
185. Charlotte	born ca 1791/92; baptized 19 Feb 1792
186. Mary D.	born ca 1793/94; died young " of fitts"

References: Birth, Baptism and Funeral records of Portsmouth, NH Churches; Portsmouth Genealogies; records of the South Church,
Portsmouth; NE VR from the Exeter Newsletter (1831-65); NH Gazette records (1765-1800); Strawbery Banke Museum; LDS IGI.

The Sixth American Generation

65. ELIJAH-6 RICKER, son of Sobriety-5 NOCK/KNOX (Samuel-4; Sarah-3 DRISKO; John-2) and Moses RICKER, was born 1 Dec 1769.

He married Hannah COPPS, intentions published at Lebanon, Maine on 10 Nov 1805. Hannah, the daughter of Deacon Samuel COPPS and his wife Hannah HAYES, was born 2 May 1779; baptized 28 Sept 1780; died 27 Jan 1861 at Lebanon., aged 81 years 9 months.

Elijah-6 and Hannah resided on a farm on the River Road , Lebanon. The farm was originally owned by Wilson RICKER. On the 1850 Census of Lebanon, Maine they were listed as follows: Elijah , aged 80; Hannah aged 70; their children : Sobriety aged 44; Hannah 38; and Lewis D. RICKER aged 30. Elijah-6 RICKER died at Lebanon on 26 March 1851; aged 81 years 8 months and 25 days.

Children of Elijah-6 RICKER and Hannah COPPS:
    Surname RICKER   (all children born Lebanon, Maine)
 187. Sobriety   born 19 Sept 1806; died 17 Mar 1877 unmarried   EOL
+ 188. SAMUEL COPPS born 18 Mar 1808; married Annis P. BRIGGS ca 1833
                            (she dau/o Rufus BRIGGS and Elizabeth ___?)
                            (she born ____; died 2 Jan 1883 Cambridge, MA)
                            died 30 July 1880 Corning, NY
+ 189. ZIMRI   born 29 Oct 1809; died 11 June 1880
                            married Caroline D. PARKS 26 Apr 1836 Pittsfield, ME
                            (she born 8 June 1811; died 18 Mar 1897 Boston)
+ 190. ELIJAH, JR.   born 10 June 1810/11; married Mary CLEMENTS 4 July 1838
                            (she dau/o Eben CLEMENTS and Margaret LORD)
                            (she born 9 Sept 1820; died 29 Apr 1900)
                            died 6 Jan 1880 Detroit, Maine
 191. Hannah   born 29 Nov 1812; died 8 Jan 1872 unmarried   EOL
+ 192. GEORGE   born 6 Aug 1814; married Hannah LEARY 1852 Mobile, Alabama
+ 193. MOSES   born 19 June 1816; married Hannah KENT   Wakefield, NH
 194. Lorana   born 16 Oct 1818; died 27 Apr 1820
+ 195. LEWIS DOWNS   born 3 Aug 1820; died 17 Sept 1884 Rochester, NH
                            married Eliza Jane HARTFORD 23 May 1851 Lebanon
                            (she dau/o Lorenzo HARTFORD and Elsie SHOREY)
                            (she born 12 Sept 1830; died 7 Nov 1916)
 196. dau   born _____; died 22 Apr 1823

66. MOSES-6 RICKER, Jr. brother of above, was born ca 1773 at Lebanon, Maine. He married Mary/ Sally HANSON on 28 Dec 1804 at the Second Parish of Berwick, Maine. They were married by the Rev Joseph HILLIARD. The TR list that intentions were published 17 Nov 1804. Sally/Mary was the daughter of ____ HANSON and _____; and was born ____; died Apr 1833. Moses-6 RICKER, Jr. died 31 Oct 1850 at Lebanon, Maine.

Children of Moses-6 RICKER and Sally/Mary HANSON:
    Surname RICKER   (all born Lebanon, Maine)

+ 197. WILLIAM   born 29 Mar 1807; married Martha D. ELLIS before 1823
                            died 1869
 198. Maria   born 8 Jan 1809
 199. Dorcas   born Feb 1815; died Sept 1857 unmarried   EOL
 200. Charles   born 1817; died 1850 unmarried   EOL
+ 201. ELI R.   born 1819; 1m. Maria JACOBS int pub 8 Oct 1837
                            2m. Dorcas JACOBS 6 July 1839 Sanford, Maine

68. MERCY-6 RICKER, sister of above, was born 21 Aug 1777 at Lebanon, Maine. She married Captain Daniel-6 GRANT there on 19 Dec 1804. He was the son of Samuel-5 GRANT (William-4; 3; 2; Peter-1) and ____; and was born possibly 10 Mar 1777; died 10 May 1867. Mercy-6 RICKER died 25 Sept 1831. Captain GRANT married her younger sister Sarah-6 RICKER on 14 Dec 1834. She was born 2 Mar 1780; died 30 Dec 1853. Captain GRANT married third to Rebekah ____ ?. She was born ca 1773, Maine.

Children of Mercy-6 RICKER and Captain Daniel GRANT:

Surname GRANT	(all born Lebanon, Maine)
+ 202. DANIEL	born 22 Aug 1804; married Susan FOSS 13 Dec 1827 (she born 5 June 1806)
203. Polly	born 25 Dec 1807; died Nov 1815
204. Moses Ricker	born 24 Aug 1810; died young
205. Samuel	born 28 Jan 1813; married Esther HANSON; died ca 1843
+ 206. DEPENDANCE	born 10 Dec 1813 gs ; died 12 Nov 1863 (49 yr 11 mos and 2 das) married Mercy HARTFORD (she 2m. Jeremiah SHOREY)
207. Moses Ricker (2)	born 2 Nov 1816; died 23 Feb 1858/59 married Esther BLAISDELL 4 June 1843 (she born 1819; died 20 Nov 1854) ch: Lucy-8 GRANT born 15 May 1845 and Martha-8 GRANT born ca 1852

Reference: Lebanon, Maine VR

71. JEDEDIAH-6 RICKER, son of Dorothy-5 NOCK/KNOX (Samuel-4; Sarah-3 DRISKO; John-2) and Lemuel RICKER, was born 2 Mar 1773 at Dover, NH. He married Sarah/Sally LORD on 19 Feb 1803 at Rochester, NH. She was the daughter of William W. LORD and Mary GARLAND of Milton, NH.

Children of Jedediah-6 RICKER and Sally LORD:

Surname RICKER	
208. James Allen	born 1804; married Eleanor CHAMBERLAIN
+ 209. EZEKIEL	born 9 May 1807; married Joanna W. ROBERTS 20 Nov 1831 (she dau/o George ROBERTS and Mary ROBERTS) (she born 5 Nov 1811; died 29 Apr 1894) died 22 Mar 1857 Somersworth, NH

72. JOANNA-6 RICKER, sister of above, was born 11 Aug 1776 at Dover, NH. She married John ROBINSON on 31 Dec 1800. He was the son of _____ ROBINSON of Farmington, NH.

Children of Joanna-6 RICKER and John ROBINSON:

Surname ROBINSON			
210. Nancy	born 23 May 1801	212. Jane	born 26 Jan 1807
211. Dorothy	born 18 Oct 1802	213. Lemuel	born 21 Nov 1808

75. SAMUEL-6 RICKER, brother of above, was born ca 1784 at Dover, NH. He married Polly FOSS on 17 Oct 1813 at Milton, NH. She was the daughter of ___ FOSS; and was born ca 1787; died 1856 at Milton, NH.

Children of Samuel-6 RICKER and Polly FOSS;

Surname RICKER	
214. Asenath	born 1815; married Thomas A. WARREN
	One child : Thomas A-8 WARREN, Jr. born ____ ; married Hannah DOWNS
215. Hiram	born 1817; married Caroline MESERVE 1839
+ 216. LEONARD	born 12 June 1819; 1m. Lydia M. EDGERLY 12 Apr 1838 2m. Mary Jane WITHAM; 3m. Joanna M. GRANT
+ 217. LOUISA ANN	born 6 Nov 1822; married Luther Dearborn TREFREN 25 Aug 1845 (he born 8 Aug 1817; died 19 Nov 1907 Oregon) died 13 Nov 1910 Ashland, Oregon

Children of Samuel-6 RICKER, continued:

Surname RICKER

218. Wentworth R. * born ca 1825; 1m. Maria B. DOWNS 2 July 1848
(she dau/o James DOWNS and Judith WENTWORTH)
(she born 31 Jan 1832; died 5 Aug 1851)
2m. Lucy E. STEBBINS 12 June 1854
died 26 Mar 1900 San Francisco, CA
Child: Alpheus Smith-8 RICKER born 7 Nov 1849; died 7 Aug 1852
* Wentworth R. RICKER also had a son and dau by his 2nd wife – names and dates unknown

76. HANNAH-6 RICKER, sister of above, was born ca 1786 at Dover, NH. She married Joseph KNOX on 2 Sept 1807. He was the son of William KNOX and Sarah ALLEY; and was born ca 1790 at Berwick, ME; died 16 Nov 1842. Hannah-6 RICKER died 15 Apr 1862.

Children of Hannah-6 RICKER and Joseph KNOX:

Surname KNOX

219. Ephraim	born 18__; 1m. Eliza WINGATE; 2m. Jane DIXON	
220. Augustus	born 18__; married Eliza PRAY of Berwick, Maine	
221. Jefferson	born 18__; 1m. Sally CLEMENTS; 2m. L. HASTINGS	
222. Jacob	born 18__; 1m. Abigail HAYES; 2m. Elizabeth TIBBETTS	
223. Dorothy	born 18__; married Mark MILLETT of Milton, NH	
224. Elizabeth	born 18__; married Moses RANDALL of Berwick	
225. Almira	born 18__; died unmarried EOL	
226. Haven/Hazen	born 18__; died at age 16 EOL	

87. JOHN-6 RICKER, son of Lucy-5 CROWELL (Esther-4 NOCK/KNOX; Sarah-3 DRISKO/DRISCO; John-2) and Daniel RICKER, was born 28 Dec 1767. He married Elizabeth PINKHAM on 16 Nov 1791 at Milton, NH. She was the daughter of _?_ PINKHAM of Rochester, Maine.

Children of John-6 RICKER and Elizabeth PINKHAM:

Surname RICKER

+ 227. LUCY   born 179_; married James BRAGDON 17 Nov 1813 Milton, NH
228. Hannah   born 179_; died ____ unmarried   EOL
229. Zilpha   born 18__; married Ivory BRAGDON 5 Mar 1820 Milton, NH
    2 children: 1. George W-8 BRAGDON born 12 July 1827; married ____ TARBOR
                      2. dau-8 BRAGDON born ____; married ____ RIPLEY
+ 230. ESTHER   born 18 Feb 1809; married Luther GILE 27 May 1830 Rochester, NH
                 (he son/o David GILE and Mary WOOD) (he born 9 Apr 1807)
231. Lois   born ____; married Moses EASTMAN 8 June 1830 (he of Croyden, NH)
232. Jason   born 1816; married Susan W. ____?
                 One child : John T-8 RICKER born ca 1841
233. Blanche   born 18__; married Alvah BERRY of Stratford, NH
                 2 children: Levi-8 BERRY and Addie-8 BERRY – resided Dover, NH

89. ELIAS-6 RICKER, brother of above, was born 2 June 1772. He married Mary Morrill WITHERELL ca 1800 at Lebanon, Maine. She was the daughter of John WITHERELL and Mary ___?; and was born 4 July 1782; died 20 June 1856. Elias-6 RICKER died at Wells, Maine on 11 Apr 1850.

Children of Elias-6 RICKER and Mary WITHERELL:

Surname RICKER

+ 234. SABRINA   born 16 May 1802; married Daniel LARRABEE
                 (he son/o John LARRABEE and Susan LARRABEE)
+ 235. EZRA KIMBALL born 29 Sept 1805; died 1 March 1840 Wells, Maine
                 married Mary March MARR 23 June 1831 (she born 25 Aug 1804)

Children of Elias-6 RICKER, continued:
   Surname RICKER
+ 236. DANIEL   born 27 Feb 1808; married Caroline HIGGINS 4 July 1836
      CROMWELL   (she dau/o Nathaniel HIGGINS of Avon, Maine)
                   (she born 4 July 1814; died 13 Nov 1888, MA.)
                   died 10 Jan 1869 Avon, Maine
  237. Elizabeth Witherell born 22 Mar 1820; died 17 Oct 1876
                   married Reuben GRIGGS 19 May 1844 Dedham, MA.
                   One child : Augustus R-8 GRIGGS born 16 Feb 1845
  238. Lucy Jane   born _____

93. DANIEL-6 RICKER, brother of above, was born 2 April 1777. He married Elizabeth EMERY on 1 April 1804 at Berwick, Maine. She was the daughter of the Rev Simon EMERY and Molly HODGDON; and was born 1785; died Feb 1855 at Fryeburg, Maine. Daniel-6 RICKER died ____.

Children of Daniel-6 RICKER and Elizabeth EMERY:
   Surname RICKER   (all born Monroe, Maine)
+ 239. ISAIAH   born 14 July 1804; married Charlotte BOWEN
  240. George Washington   born 4 Mar 1806
+ 241. SIMEON EMERY born 28 Sept 1808; married Mary Ann HODGKINS
  242. William   born 27 Jan 1811; married Isabell E. LAMBERT 6 July 1839
         One child: Helen Sabena-8 RICKER born 24 Dec 1840; married Edmund BACHELDER
+ 243. BENJAMIN D.   born 15 Sept 1813; married Sophronia BRANCH
+ 244. DANIEL (twin)   born 15 Sept 1813; 1m. _____ (no issue); 2m. Elizabeth METCALFE
  245.Ephraim Lord   born 10 Sept 1816
  246. Stephen Hodgdon born 25 Oct 1818; married Melinda __?__
  247. John   born 2 Nov 1820; married Marianna FISH
  248. Elizabeth   born 1 Nov 1823
+ 249. ROBERT   born 22 Apr 1828; 1m. Mary H. WEED (she born ____; died 29 Nov 1875)
                  2m. Anna ANDERSON Pemberton 11 May 1904

94. ELIPHALET-6 RICKER, brother of above, was born 30 June 1779. He married Mercy HANSON on 22 June 1804 at Milton, NH. She was the daughter of ____ HANSON, and was born 9 March 1786; died 26 March 1877 at Vassalboro, Maine. Eliphalet-6 RICKER died 9 March 1850 at Wells, Maine.

Children of Eliphalet-6 RICKER and Mercy HANSON:
   Surname RICKER
  250. Asenath   born 4 Nov 1804 Somersworth, NH; died 7 May 1894
+ 251. SYRENA B.   born 2 Oct 1807 Somersworth; married Oliver JEPSON 25 Nov 1829
  252. Meshack (m)   born 7 Feb 1810; married Wealthy ____? ca 1831
                died ____; lost at sea
                One child: Horace S-8 RICKER born ca May 1833
  253. Eli   born 20 May 1812 Dover, NH; married Paulina ___? ca 1833
                One child: George B-8 RICKER born ca 1839
+ 254. SOPHRONIA   born 9 Jan 1815; married Hugh GETCHELL
  255. Daniel   born 10 Nov 1817; married Sarah JARVIS; died 20 Nov 1881
                One child: Daniel E-8 RICKER born 6 May 1838
+ 256. JOHN HANSON   born 9 May 1820 Vassalboro, ME
                married Ellen CONY McDavid 12 Dec 1854
  257. Hannah M.   born 3 Nov 1822
  258. Abigail H.   born 21 Oct 1825
  259. George S.   born 29 May 1828; married Elvira HALL 6 Oct 1847 Gardiner, ME.
  260. Charles B.   born 21 July 1833
  261. Rebecca   born ____

95. PAUL-6 RICKER, brother of above, was born 24 Sept 1781. He married Elizabeth HAYES on 14 Mar 1811 at Rochester, NH. She was the daughter of Joseph HAYES and Abigail ____?; and was born 20 Apr 1790, Rochester, NH; died 5 June 1872. Paul-6 RICKER died1 Jan 1864.

Children of Paul-6 RICKER and Elizabeth HAYES:
Surname RICKER
  262. Susan   born 14 Mar 1812; died 2 Mar 1814
  263. Nathaniel Hayes   born 6 Mar 1815; married Mary B. WYATT
                Three children: Mark H-8; Franklin H-8; and Isabella F-8 RICKER
  264. Elizabeth A.   born 2 Mar 1819; married Stephen BERRY 7 July 1839
                  One child: Henry-8 BERRY
+ 265. LUCY JANE   born 13 Oct 1821; married George D. PIKE 14 Dec 1843
+ 266. DANIEL J.   born 9 Mar 1824; married Mary Ann HUTCHINS 19 Jan 1846
+ 267. GEORGE DEXTER   born 31 Oct 1826; married Maria Mehitable MASON 11 Nov 1851
  268. Andrew J.   born 24 Jan 1831; died 16 Feb 1835
  269. Charles A.   born 10 Sept 1833; died 4 June 1863 Boston, MA

101. CAPTAIN EBENEZER-6 RICKER, son of Captain Nathaniel-5 RICKER, Jr. (Mercy-4 NOCK/KNOX; Sarah-3 DRISKO/DRISCO; John-2) and Anna ROBERTS, was born 24 June 1782, probably at Argyle, Nova Scotia.

He was the master of the first square-rigged ship sailing from Yarmouth, Nova Scotia. He owned an interest in several other vessels. After suffering losses during the **War of 1812**, he retired and became a farmer and shipbuilder.

He married first to Lucy FROST on 15 Jan 1804. She was the daughter of Andrew FROST and Sarah REDDING; and was born 10 Nov 1784; died 10 Feb 1849.   His second wife was Ruth LARKIN. They were married on 27 Oct 1852 at Argyle, Nova Scotia. Ruth was born ca 1800; died 17 Dec 1891. Captain Ebenezer-6 RICKER died 20 March 1867.

Children of Captain Ebenezer-6 RICKER and Lucy FROST:
Surname RICKER
  270. Anna   born 28 Nov 1804; married Capt. Nathaniel-6 RICKER 6 Sept 1832 (# 108)
+ 271. ELEANOR   born 10 Oct 1806; married Robert SIMMS 8 June 1827
+ 272. ANDREW   born 13 Aug 1809; married Elizabeth L. B. SIMMS 2 June 1846
  273. Ebenezer, Jr.   born 23 Sept 1811; lost at sea 17 Apr 1829
  274. George Whitfield born 23 May 1813; lost at sea Sept 1842
+ 275. SARAH   born 10 Sept 1815; married CAPT. ROBERT-6 RICKER 8 Feb 1837 (# 109)
+ 276. ELIZABETH   born 28 Mar 1819; married Jeremiah FROST
+ 277. EUNICE   born 7 Mar 1821; married Daniel SARGENT 22 June 1843
+ 278. WILLIAM   born 7 July 1824; married Martha L. FROST Feb 1852 Argyle, NS
+ 279. MARTHA   born 15 Dec 1827; married Freeman HURLBERT 1 Nov 1857
  280. Lucy Jane   born 20 Nov 1831; married Archibald WATSON 11 June 1854

103. ELIZABETH-6 RICKER, sister of above, was born 1 May 1790. She married Solomon MANGRUM on 13 Feb 1821 at Argyle, Nova Scotia. He was a lumberman and farmer.

Child of Elizabeth-6 RICKER and Solomon MANGRUM:
Surname MANGRUM
+ 281. WILLIAM   born 22 Nov 1821 Plymouth, NS; married Sarah H. JONES 20 June 1848
                (she born 25 Mar 1828; died 25 Oct 1877)
                died 9 Apr 1891 Carlisle, New Brunswick

104. CAPTAIN BENJAMIN-6 RICKER, brother of above, was born 1 Sept 1792. He married Sarah

FROST on 22 Dec 1817. She was the daughter of Andrew FROST and Sarah REDDING; and was born ca 1794; died 28 Dec 1841 at Eastport, Maine. (She was the sister of Lucy (above) who married Captain Ebenezer-6 RICKER (# 101). Captain Benjamin-6 RICKER died 10 Apr 1843 at Eastport.

Children of Captain Benjamin-6 RICKER and Sarah FROST:
Surname RICKER	(all children born Argyle, NS; except # 290)
282. Maria	born 1 Oct 1818; died 17 Feb 1819
+ 283. BENJAMIN, JR.	born 9 Oct 1819; married Hannah W. BROOKS 17 Nov 1842
+ 284. MARIA (2)	born 5 Aug 1821; married Uriah CROWELL Jan 1837
+ 285. LYDIA	born 15 June 1823; married Captain Andrew SMITH 25 May 1844
286. Olive	born 14 June 1824; married George BELL 15 Sept 1842
+ 287. LUCY ANN	born 26 Mar 1827; married DANIEL-6 RICKER 12 Sept 1847 (# 113)
+ 288. PAUL	born 25 Dec 1828; married LYDIA ANN-8 SIMMS 20 Aug 1854 (# 745)
+ 289. SYLVANUS	born 20 Oct 1830; married Sarah FROST 14 Mar 1855
290. Jeremiah	born 22 Mar 1834, Eastport, ME; died there 14 Mar 1837

109. CAPTAIN ROBERT-6 RICKER, son of Captain Paul-5 RICKER (Mercy-4 NOCK/KNOX; Sarah-3 DRISKO/DRISCO; John-2) and Catherine KENTON, was born 26 April 1811. He married Sarah-7 RICKER (# 275) on 8 Feb 1837 at Argyle, N S. She was the daughter of Captain Ebenezer-6 RICKER and Lucy FROST; and was born 10 Sept 1815; died 8 Dec 1873 at Knowlesville, New Brunswick.

Captain Robert-6 RICKER was a mariner from early boyhood. He became the master of a sailing vessel which sailed to the West Indies and other foreign ports. He died 1 Aug 1888 at Knowlesville, NB.

Children of Captain Robert-6 RICKER and Sarah-7 RICKER:
Surname RICKER	(all born Argyle, Nova Scotia)
+ 291. OPHELIA	born 17 Dec 1838;
	married Captain Benjamin WHITEHOUSE 1861
292. Byron	born ca 1840; died 1843 EOL
+ 293. EVELENA	born 12 Feb 1843; married Captain Reuben GOODWIN 26 July 1860
294. Byron (2)	born 21 Aug 1845; married Isabella MILLS 3 Feb 1872, NB
	One child: James Wilmot-8 RICKER born 10 Nov 1872
295. Whitfield	born 5 Feb 1847; died May 1872 (drowned)
296. Doran	born ca 1851; died 25 Oct 1872
297. James	born ca 1853; died 1856

110. MARY/MERCY-6 RICKER, sister of above, was born 5 June 1813, NS. She married David CRO-WELL on 24 Jan 1832 at Argyle, NS. He was born 8 Feb 1808; died 11 Feb 1886. She died 10 May 1868.

Children of Mary/Mercy-6 RICKER and David CROWELL:
Surname CROWELL	(all born Argyle, Nova Scotia)
298. Mercy	born 4 Oct 1832; married Thomas DENCH
299. Jane	born 25 Nov 1834; married Charles CARTER
300. John Paul	born 15 Apr 1837; married Lois A. EARLE 8 Jan 1862
301. Elizabeth	born 6 Apr 1839; married William GOODWIN (4 children)
302. Nathaniel	born 25 Jan 1843; married Eleanor EARLE 12 Sept 1869 Riverdale, NS
303. Marietta	born 26 May 1847; married ____ WRIGHT, NH; died before 1907

111. MARGARET-6 RICKER, sister of above, was born 1 Jan 1815. She married John JOHNSTON of Plymouth, Nova Scotia on 21 Dec 1835. He was the son of _?_ JOHNSTON; and was born ____.

Child of Margaret-6 RICKER and John JOHNSTON:
Surname JOHNSTON	
+ 304. JOTHAM	born 7 Aug 1845 Plymouth , NS; married Lydia LARKIN 6 Feb 1867

112. JOHN KNOX-6 RICKER, brother of above, was born 12 June 1818. He married M___M. RICHARDSON on 14 April 1849 at Louisville, Mississippi. She was born 23 Aug 1826 at Asheville, North Carolina; died 20 Mar 1886 at Corsicana, Texas. John Knox-6 RICKER was a sailor in his youth, and later became a carpenter. He died 14 Apr 1894 at Corsicana, Texas.

Children on John Knox-6 RICKER and M.M. RICHARDSON:
Surname RICKER

305. Robert H.	born 14 Feb 1850, Louisville; married Mary M. JOHNSON 20 July 1900 (she born 21 June 1846 Norway; died ____)
306. Frances Elizabeth	born 16 July 1852 , Louisville; married Julius A. DUBOISE 15 Dec 1889
307. John D.	born 15 Aug 1855 Jackson, MS; married Bernie M. BENTON 17 Aug 1879
	Two children: James William-8 born 16 May 1880; and John-8, Jr. born 1 Nov 1883
+ 308. MATTIE A.	born 8 May 1857 Hazelhurst, MS; marr. Edward C. ROTHROCK 18 Oct 1885
+ 309. WILLIAM AUGUSTUS	born 5 Aug 1859 Hazelhurst, MS married Elmira V. HALL 14 Oct 1888
310. Mary E.	born 20 Mar 1861; married William ROTHROCK 15 Aug 1885
+ 311. CHARLES PAUL	born 18 Jan 1863; married Louella E. DOUGLASS 21 Nov 1887
+ 312. LILLY	born 26 Jan 1865; married A. B. DOUGLASS 14 Apr 1886
313. George M.	born 18 Jan 1867; died 1907 unmarried EOL

113. DANIEL-6 RICKER, brother of above, was born 19 Jan 1821. He married Lucy Ann-7 RICKER (# 287) on 12 Sept 1847 at Argyle, Nova Scotia. She was the daughter of Captain Benjamin-6 RICKER and Anna ROBERTS; and was born 26 Mar 1827; died ____. Daniel-6 RICKER was a sailor for many years, and later worked at shipbuilding and farming. He died 19 Jan 1881 at Argyle, NS. Lucy Ann-7 RICKER married second to Andrew RANDALL.

Children of Daniel-6 RICKER and Lucy Ann-7 RICKER:
Surname RICKER

314. Charles Henry	born 23 July 1848; died 4 May 1849
315. Lucinda Lincoln	born 26 Apr 1850; died 22 Mar 1865
+ 316. CHARLES HENRY	born 16 Feb 1853; married Eliza J. TRUSDEN/TWISDEN 23 July 1882 (she born 28 Mar 1858; died 28 Aug 1941) died 2 May 1913 Ipswich, MA.
317. Annie Maria	born 25 May 1855; died 16 Feb 1874
318. Amanda Tillson	born 12 May 1857; died 20 Apr 1859
319. Catherine	born 1 Dec 1858; died 16 Nov 1874
320. Amanda	born 13 May 1861; died 23 Nov 1877
321. Horatio	born 1 June 1866; died 10 Apr 1868
322. Lucinda	born 29 Sept 1867; died 20 Feb 1939 1m. Joseph R. GOODWIN 19 Jan 1907; 2m. Joseph FITZGERALD
323. Edward Sullivan	born 21 May 1871; died 21 July 1872

114. JERUSHA-6 DRISKO, daughter of John-5 DRISKO (Joseph-4; John-3;2) and Mary Johnson CHANDLER, was born 2 June 1765. She married Joseph-5 WILSON, Jr. on 16 Nov 1786 at Machias, Maine. He was the son of Joseph-4 WILSON and Mary-5 SWETT; and was born 4 Sept 1762 at Falmouth, Maine; died ca 1823. Jerusha-6 DRISKO died 8 Sept 1815 at Columbia, Maine.

Children of Jerusha-6 DRISKO and Joseph WILSON, Jr.;
Surname WILSON   (all born Columbia Falls, Maine)

+ 324. JOSEPH WARREN	born 11 Aug 1787; died 10 Dec 1854 Illinois married Elizabeth Chandler PINEO 22 Nov 1817 (she dau/o David PINEO and Priscilla HILL) (she born 24 Jan 1798; died 25 May 1827)
325. Olive	born 23 Dec 1788; died 13 June 1815

Children of Jerusha-6 DRISKO, continued:
  Surname WILSON

+ 326. JOHN DRISKO	born 30 Oct 1790; died ca 1846
	married Hannah COFFIN 12 Dec 1816 Columbia, ME
	(she dau/o Deacon Elisha COFFIN and Ruth-5 CATES)
	(she born 10 May 1797; died 21 May 1849)
+ 327. NATHANIEL	born 27 Feb 1792; died ca 1857
	married Sarah SMITH 1 Nov 1818 Machias, ME. (divorced)
	(she dau/o Samuel SMITH and Sarah KELLEY)
	(she born 11 Jan 1798; died 14 Jan 1883 CA)
	(she 2m. Otis-7 RICKER (# 333)
+ 328. GOWEN	born 26 Mar 1793; married Eliza Ann WESTON 22 Dec 1821
	(she dau/o Timothy WESTON and Ann GOOCH)
	(she born 6 Nov 1803; died 5 May 1880)
	died 18 Dec 1863 MN
329. Relief	born 23 Sept 1794; died 27 June 1883
	married Samuel-6 GARDNER, as his 3rd wife
	(he son/o Ebenezer-5 GARDNER and Damaris MERRILL)
	(he born 13 July 1781; died 1853) resided East Machias, ME.

Note: Samuel GARDNER had 12 children: His 1st wife was Abigail BERRY, by whom he had Atkins born ca 1808; Mary born ca 1809/10; Nathan born ca 1811 ; Caroline born ca 1812; Lucius born 1814; Jonathan born ca 1817; Daniel F. born 1819; Leonard born ca 1821; Rebecca born ca 1823; and Ellen born ca 1829. Harriet; and Samuel, Jr. may have been by 2nd wife. No children from 3rd marriage.

+ 330. STILLMAN A.	born 30 Apr 1796; married Mary Jane MOORE 28 Feb 1838
	(she born Sept 1810; died 30 Mar 1887)
	died 23 Aug 1870 Brewer, Maine
+ 331. JOEL	born 27 June 1797; married Eunice __?__; died ca 1847
332. Mary/Molly	born 15 Jan 1799; married William W. NILES 22 Apr 1830 E. Machias. ME.
333. Otis	born 3 July 1800; 1m. Lucinda CILLEY 7 May 1835
	2m. Sarah SMITH Wilson 24 May 1842
+ 334. ASA	born 7 June 1802; died 14 June 1880 Ohio
	married Rebecca Newell JOY 17 Aug 1730
	(she dau/o Benjamin JOY and Abigail GREEN)
	(she born 3 Oct 1805; died 22 Aug 1883)
+ 335. PUTNAM	born 3 Feb 1804; married Eliza FITTS
	(she born ____; died 22 July 1886)
	died 1 Apr 1883 Brewer, Maine
336. Seward Bucknam	born 5 Dec 1805; married Mary Rachel WESTON 8 Mar 1847
	(she born 1817; died 16 June 1897 CA)
	died 10 April 1866 WA
	One child: Frederick WILSON born ____; died 1897 CA
337. Merrill	born 8 Sept 1807; died 29 Sept 1808
338. William Bucknam	born 8 July 1810; died 9 Nov 1832 unmarried EOL

115. REBECCA-6 DRISKO, sister of above, was born Oct 1766. She married David-5 CHANDLER ++ on 5 July 1787 at North Yarmouth, Maine. David was the son of Jonathan-4 CHANDLER and Rachel MITCHELL; and was born 30 June 1752 North Yarmouth; died ____. They resided Great Chebeague. Rebecca-6 died ____.

Children of Rebecca-6 DRISKO and David-5 CHANDLER:
  Surname CHANDLER   (all children born/ baptized at Great Chebeague)

339. Lucy	born 24 March 1789	342. John	born 26 Feb 1794
340. Jacob	born 24 Sept 1790	343. Rebecca	born ca 1795; bapt 24 Sep 1795
341. Rhoda	born ca 1792/93; bapt 18 Sep 1793	344. David	born ca 1797; bapt 23 Aug 1797

++ Ancestry of David-5 CHANDLER

EDMUND-1 CHANDLER, born ca 1580's England, the immigrant, was in Duxbury, MA. by 1633; possibly with the Pilgrims at Leyden. He died at age 80 - ca 2 May 1662.

JOSEPH-2 CHANDLER was born prior to 1641 at Duxbury, MA. and married Mercy ___?. JOSEPH-3 CHANDLER was born ca 1678/79 at Duxbury. He married Martha HUNT, daughter of Samuel HUNT and Mary ____? on 12 Feb 1700/01 at Duxbury. They were the parents of 9 children: 1. Philip born 21 July 1702, married Rebecca PHILLIPS 16 Dec 1725; 2. Mary born 3 Aug 1704, married Jonas MASON ca 1731; 3. Joshua born 1 July 1706, married Mary WASTE/WEST 27 Nov 1728; 4. Zachariah born 26 July 1708, married Zerviah HOLMES 21 Oct 1736; 5. Edmund born 9 Apr 1710; 6. Ebenezer born 8 Sept 1712; 7. Sarah; 8. Martha ; and 9. JONATHAN-4 born 18 Feb 1717/18 in Duxbury. He married Rachel MITCHELL on 19 Jan 1749.

JONATHAN-4 CHANDLER was a " coaster ", later a " yeoman ". He purchased, in 1746, 650 acres of land on the westerly side of the island of Great Chebeague; and two of his sons, DAVID-5 and Rufus-5 remained there. Jonathan-4 CHANDLER, and his brothers, held the rank of Private in the 1st Company of Militia, commanded by Captain Solomon MITCHELL. (Roll dated 18 May 1757). Jonathan-4 CHANDLER and his wife were received into the 1st Church of Yarmouth. His death is recorded in their church records as 20 July 1786. It also lists his wife's death as 1 Jan 1814 (age 83). Rachel-5 was the daughter of Jacob-4 MITCHELL and his second wife Rachel CUSHING. Children of Jonathan-4 CHANDLER and Rachel MITCHELL were: 1. Tabitha born 18 Sept 1750; died 11 Aug 1756; 2. ++ DAVID –5 (above) 3. Timothy born 20 Oct 1754; 4. Jacob born 19 June 1757; 5. Rachel born 20 May 1761, married Daniel WAITE; 6. Lucy born 12 Oct 1763, married Benjamin WAITE; and 7. Rufus born March 1766.

116. LORRAINE-6 (Luraney) DRISKO, sister of above, was born ca 1769/70. She married Moses-7 PLUMMER, 3rd ca 1790. He was the son of Moses-6 PLUMMER and Lucy PERKINS, and was born ca 1768 at Addison, Maine; died there 5 Sept 1846. Lorraine-6 died 20 Nov 1802 (gs). Moses-7 PLUMMER married second to Hannah WESTON; and third to Susanna JONES Goodwin. He has seven more children.

Children of Lorraine-6 DRISKO and Moses-7 PLUMMER, 3rd:
    Surname PLUMMER

+345. JEREMIAH	born April 1791; married Elizabeth/Betsey-6 WASS before 1819 (she dau/o Wilmot-5 WASS and his 2nd wife Rebecca JORDAN) (she born 8 Sept 1791; died 11 June 1869) died 4 Jan 1850 Addison, Maine
+ 346. MOSES, 4th	born ca 1793; died ca 28 May 1849 + married Abigail/Naby-7 WASS ca 1815

    (she dau/o Christopher-6 WASS and Mary DYER)(she born 23 July 1794; died 31 May 1844)
    + He died aboard the vessel ***BELGRADE*** on a trip to CA with a group of ' 49ers. He was discovered dead in his bunk.

+ 347. BETSEY G.	born 16 Nov 1797; married Captain Holmes Nash-7 WASS

        (he son/o Wilmot-6 WASS and Wealthy DYER) (he born Jan 1791; died 25 Sept 1863)
            died 1 Jan 1879 Harrington, Maine

+ 348. JOHN	born 12 Dec 1799; married Sarah/Sally-7 WASS

        (she dau/o James-6 WASS and Anna DYER) (she born Feb 1800; died 11 May 1857)
            died 23 Feb 1882 Addison, Maine

+ 349. AMOS BUCKNAM born 17 July 1802; married Phebe Coffin-7 WASS int pub 3 Jan 1825
        (she dau/o Joseph-6 WASS and Susan A. COFFIN) (she born ca 1807; died 1847)
            died 20 Feb 1877 Machiasport, Maine

118. JUDAH JOHNSON-6 DRISKO, brother of above, was born 4 Nov 1772 at Chandler's River (now Jonesboro), Maine. He married Lucy Ann-7 PLUMMER on 10 Jan 1797. She was the daughter of Moses-6 PLUMMER (Moses-5) and Lucy PERKINS; and was born 13 April 1777 at Addison, Maine; died 1858. Judah-6 DRISKO died 22 Nov 1849. He served in the **War of 1812**.

Children of Judah Johnson-6 DRISKO and Lucy Ann-7 PLUMMER:
    Surname DRISKO

350. John Perkins	born 20 Oct 1797; died 16 May 1808 EOL
+ 351. WILLIAM JOHNSON	born 15 Aug 1799 Harrington, ME; died 1 Feb 1841 Addison, Maine married Mary B. FRANKLAND 14 Dec 1824 (she dau/o Captain William FRANKLAND and Ann ROSS) (she born 11 Nov 1802, NB; died 9 Oct 1884)

Children of Judah Johnson-6 DRISKO, continued

Surname DRISKO

+ 352. CALEB   born 17 Aug 1801; married Hannah B. COLE 18 Jan 1827
          HASKELL   (she dau/o David COLE and " Nabby " COLBETH)
                            (she born 24 Dec 1806; died 22 Mar 1878)
                            died 10 June 1875
+ 353. LORRAINE   born 27 Jan 1803; married Levi-8 SMALL 6 Feb 1823;
          PLUMMER   (he son/o Daniel-7 SMALL and Phebe COFFIN)
       " Luraney "   died 6 Feb 1830
   354. Moses   born 1 Oct 1804; died 1 Sept 1807   EOL
+ 355. FRANCES   born 7 May 1806; 1m. THOMAS FLETCHER-7 BUCKNAM 11 Apr 1838
                            (he son/o William H. BUCKNAM and Abigail-6 DRISKO (# 119)
                            (he born 15 Feb 1808; died 26 Apr 1846)
                            2m. Colonel James –5 CURTIS 6 Oct 1856 (his 3rd wife)
+ 356. JOHN JEREMIAH born 29 Feb 1808 Addison;   died 8 Nov 1887
          PLUMMER   1m. Lucy Fellows PLUMMER 17 July 1841
                            (she born ca 1807; died 19 Sept 1846) *
                            2m. Permelia Lyon-7 WASS 1 Jan 1849
             (she dau/o Levi WASS and Emma KNOWLES) (she born 3 Oct 1827; died 1871)
                    Reference: * Wayne L. PLUMMER, Moorehead, MN; LDS-IGI
   357. Mariam Perkins   born 19 Nov 1809; died 7 Oct 1884
                            married William Vinal BOWEN 22 Oct 1834
                            (he born May 1803; died 13 Apr 1877) (he was a trader)
              Note: They had no children of their own, but adopted Louisa Everett-7 DRISKO (# 946);
                  daughter of William Johnson-6 DRISKO (# 351). They changed her name to BOWEN.
   358. son   born ca 1812; died after 1840
   359. Betsey Plummer   born 15 May 1814; married John P. ALLEN 14 Feb 1843
                            (he born 10 Feb 1807 Brookline, MA; died 20 Mar 1892)
                            (he son/o Thomas ALLEN and Rachel HERRICK)
                            died Dec 1890/ Jan 1891
   360. Elmira   born 20 Jan 1817; died 26 May 1840   EOL
+ 361. PHILO LEWIS   born 19 Apr 1822; married Caroline Campbell-7 WASS 15 Nov 1864
                            (she born 23 Aug 1836; died 22 July 1921)
                            (she dau/o Levi-6 WASS and Emma KNOWLES)
                            died 3 Oct 1899 ; a ships' caulker
   362. Francis Marion   born 1825; died 184_   EOL

119. ABIGAIL-6 DRISKO, sister of above, was born 5 Nov 1775 at Addison, Washington County, Maine. She married William Henry-6 BUCKNAM on 17 Jan 1796. He was the son of John-5 BUCKNAM (William-4; Samuel-3; Joseph-2; William-1) and Mary A. WILSON; and was born 8 Sept 1773 at Columbia Falls, ME. He died there 1 Jan 1829. Abigail-6 DRISKO died 15 April 1837 at Columbia Falls.

Children of Abigail-6 DRISKO and William-6 BUCKNAM:

Surname BUCKNAM   (all children born Columbia Falls, Maine)

   363. Leonice C.   born 21 Oct 1796; died 1877 GA; unmarried   EOL
+ 364. JOHN   born 31 July 1798; died 24 Nov 1859 Columbia Falls, Maine
                  married Sarah LITTLE 20 Oct 1836 (she born 2 Aug 1812; died 14 June 1861)
   365. Anna Buxton   born 19 Oct 1800; married Lewis Smith-6 SANBORN 19 Feb 1827
                            (he son/o William-5 SANBORN and Priscilla MAYHEW)
                            (he born 24 Aug 1805; died Sept 1887)
                            died 6 Feb 1847 Machiasport, Maine
          Child: Miranda Otis-8 SANBORN born 28 Sept 1829; married Judah J-8 DRISKO # 942
   366. Joseph Warren   born 5 May 1803; died 17 July 1850 unmarried   EOL
+ 367. MARY ANNE   born 19 Aug 1805; married John H. LEE 26 Oct 1830 Boston, MA.

Children of Abigail-6 DRISKO, continued:
   Surname BUCKNAM

+ 368. THOMAS   born 15 Feb 1808 ; married FRANCES-7 DRISKO 11 Apr 1838 (#355)
      FLETCHER   (she dau/o Judah-6 DRISKO (#118) and Lucy PLUMMER)
                   died 26 Apr 1846 Columbia Falls, Maine
  369. WILLIAM H.,JR. born 6 May 1810; married Lucretia Farnham TUCKER 29 Mar 1836
                  (she dau/o Zebediah TUCKER and Lydia WARD; born 20 Aug 1812; died 1870)
                  died 26 June 1882 Columbia Falls, Maine
+ 370. CAROLINE   born 5 Dec 1813; married Frederick Augustus RUGGLES 1847; died 1894
      STONE   (he son/o Thomas RUGGLES and Ruth CLAPP; he born 8 Jan 1801; died 1890)
  371. Sophia Ruggles   born 18 July 1819; married Dr. Christopher Payson SKELTON 20 Oct 1842
                  (he born 23 Jan 1820; died 23 May 1889; he was a Physician in Brooklyn, NY)

121. RELIEF-6 DRISKO, sister of above, was born 28 June 1780 at Addison Ridge, Maine. She married Samuel SMITH , int pub 21 March 1804. He was the son of Moses SMITH, Jr. of North Yarmouth, Maine; and was born 2 Dec 1774 at Athol, MA.; died after 1850. They resided Durham, NH; Nova Scotia and Maine. Relief-6 DRISKO died 15 Feb 1875 at Machias, Washington County, Maine.

Child of Relief-6 DRISKO and Samuel SMITH:
   Surname SMITH

+ 372. MARY   born June 1806 Dunbarton, NH.; died 30 Jan 1875
     CHANDLER   married George E-6 TENNEY , int pub 30 Mar 1828 Columbia, Maine

122. SUSANNA-6 TABBUT/TABBUTT, daughter of Elizabeth-5 DRISKO (Joseph-4; John-3; 2) and Joseph TABBUT, Jr., was born 6 Dec 1776 at Columbia, Maine. She married David-4 JOY on 2 Oct 1796 (as his 2nd wife). He was the son of Samuel-3 JOY (Benjamin-2; Thomas-1) and Abigail-5 TRACY ** (Jonathan-4; Christopher-3; Jonathan-2; Thomas-1), and was born ca 1771; died before 1820.
        Note: He had a son Beriah Smith-5 JOY by his first wife.

** Abigail-5 TRACY, dau/ of Jonathan-4 TRACY and Abigail RIGGS, was born 3 June 1754; and died Aug 1834 at Steuben, ME

Children of Susanna-6 TABBUT and David-4 JOY:
   Surname JOY

373. David, Jr.	born ca 1797 Milbridge, ME	375. son	born ca 18__
	died ca 1871	376. son	born ca 18__
374. dau	born ca 180_		

123. THOMAS-6 TABBUT/TABBUTT, son of Elizabeth-5 DRISKO (Joseph-4; John-3;2) and Joseph TABBUT, Jr., was born 25 April 1778/79 at Columbia, ME. He married Catherine CROWLEY ca 1801. She was the daughter of Jeremiah CROWLEY and Elizabeth JORDAN; and was born ca 1784 at Cape Elizabeth, ME; died ca 1860's at Columbia, ME. Thomas-6 TABBUT/TABBUTT died there ca Feb 1823. .

Children of Thomas-6 TABBUT/TABBUTT and Catherine CROWLEY:
   Surname TABBUT/TABBUTT   (all born Columbia, Maine)

+ 377. DAVID   born Jan 1802; died 18 Aug 1853 Addison, Maine
                married Mary/Polly TUCKER int pub 5 June 1824
                (she dau/o Samuel TUCKER and Esther LEIGHTON)
                (she born 25 July 1804; died 1876)
+ 378. JAMES   born ca 1804 ; married Catherine R. MESERVE 10 Jan 1830
                (she born ca 1809 Cherryfield, ME; died 6 Sept 1892)
                died 28 Mar 1866 Columbia Falls, Maine
  379. Joseph   born ca 1805; married Minerva ____; died 10 Oct 1833; no issue EOL
  380. Richard   born ca 1806; died July 1831 – lost at sea
          married Mary Gowell-7 MERRITT Parker 7 Dec 1827   (she 1m. Ezra Jordan PARKER)

Children of Thomas-6 TABBUT/TABBUTT, continued:
   Surname TABBUT

381. Elizabeth/Eliza	born ca 1808; 1m. William Pitt ROBINSON 6 Jan 1833
	(he born ca 1802; died 9 Jan 1840)
382. Abigail	born ca 1810; married Richard Mansfield ALLEN ca 1840
	died 1864 no issue EOL
383. Elmira	born ca 1812; died young
384. Olive Tracy	born 5 Oct 1814; married Alexander Stockbridge LITCHFIELD
	(he son/o Festus LITCHFIELD and Penelope STOCKBRIDGE)
	(he born 4/5 June 1812 Cohasset, Norfolk, MA ; died 11 Feb 1884)
	died 13 Feb 1897 Boston, MA.
+ 385. JERUSHA	born Sept 1815; married Captain Silas Hillman LOOK ca 1837
WILSON	(he son/o Daniel LOOK and Lois HILLMAN)
(twin)	(he born 14 Oct 1810; died 17 May 1889)
	died 11 May 1895 Jonesport, Maine
386. Hannah A.	born Sept 1815; married James B. ALLEN ca 1848
(twin)	(he son/o Obadiah ALLEN and Mary MANSFIELD)
	died after 1860 no issue EOL
+ 387. THOMAS, JR.	born 11 May 1817; died 24 Apr 1896
	married Thankful Knowles-5 McCASLIN Nov 1840
	(she dau/o Alexander-4 McCASLIN and Abigail KNOWLES)
	(she born 31 Oct 1820; died 20 Dec 1888)
+ 388. JEREMIAH	born ca 1819; died 187_ Columbia Falls, Maine.
	married CATHERINE W-7 TIBBETTS (# 410) int pub 12 Nov 1839
	(she dau/o William-6 TABBUT/TIBBETTS (#129) and Anne WRIGHT
	(she born ca Apr 1822; died 1899)
+ 389. HIRAM	born ca 1820; married Jerusha D. CROWLEY 7 Sept 1845
	(she dau/o Jeremiah CROWLEY and Mehitable DAVIS)
	(she born 8 Nov 1821; died 27 Mar 1892)
	died 29 Mar 1850 ; aboard the vessel *BELGRADE*, from yellow fever
+ 390. LUTHER	born 17 Aug 1822; married Cordelia W. WORCESTER Norton 20 June 1849
INGERSOLL	(she dau/o Leonard WORCESTER and Love M. CORTHELL)
	(she born 16 Aug 1824; died 8 Aug 1915)
	died 15 Oct 1881 Addison, Maine

125. JOHN COFFIN-6 TABBUT/TABBUTT, brother of above, was born 2 May 1785. He married first to Betsey-5 COLE, intentions published 24 Aug 1805 at Columbia, Maine. She was the daughter of Ebenezer COLE and Elizabeth HALL; and was born ca 1774; died 185_ . She was the mother of all of his children. He married second to Elizabeth ROBINSON Cole; the widow of John COLE (brother of Bestey) . Elizabeth was born ca 1798; died 1 Jan 1881. John-6 TABBUT/TABBUTT died 15 Dec 1866 Harrington, ME.

Children of John Coffin-6 TABBUT/TABBUTT and Betsey COLE:
   Surname TABBUT/TIBBETTS   (all born Columbia Falls, Maine)

+ 391. HENRY H.	born ca 1806; died 186_ Columbia Falls, Maine
	1m. Elizabeth/Betsey MAGEE 13 Sept 1838
	(she dau/o John MAGEE and Lucinda LOOK) (she born 1816 ; died 23 Dec 1844)
	2m. Mary Ann DORR 1845 (she born 1823; died 1870)
	(shé dau/o Benjamin DORR and Nellie MAGEE)
392. Ebenezer	born ca 1808; married Mary Gowell-7 MERRITT Parker Tabbut
	intentions pub 30 Nov 1831 Columbia, ME.; (see # 380 – her 3m.)
	died 26 Feb 1873 farmer
+ 393. JOSEPH	born ca 1809; died 13 June 1894 Columbia, Maine
	married Margaret WORCESTER int pub 24 Aug 1830
	(she dau/o John WORCESTER and Mary FERNALD) (she born 1806; died after 1880)

Children of John Coffin-6 TABBUT/TABBUTT, continued:
   Surname TABBUT/TABBUTT
  394. son   born ca 1810/11; died young
+ 395. ALVAH   born ca 1812; married Susanna Freeman DORR int pub 22 Feb 1838
       (she dau/o Benjamin DORR and Nellie MAGEE) (she born 1821; died 187_)
  396. dau   born after 1820; died young

126. MOSES-6 TABBUT/TABBUTT, brother of above, was born 1 June 1788. He married Mary/Polly CROWLEY, intentions published 19 Sept 1812 at Columbia, Maine. She was the daughter of John CROWLEY and Catherine AYERS; and was born ca 1791/92 at Cape Elizabeth, Maine; died 13 Feb 1872 at Cherryfield, ME. Moses-6 TABBUT/TABBUTT, a farmer, died 30 July 1866 at Columbia Falls, Maine.

Children of Moses-6 TABBUT/TABBUTT and Mary CROWLEY:
   Surname TABBUT/TABBUTT
+ 397. OTIS SMITH   born 18 Mar 1813; married Ellen A. COFFIN 28 Jan 1855
                    (she dau/o Deacon David COFFIN and Hannah NASH)
                    (she born ca 1833; died 1899)
                    died 27 June 1879 Columbia Falls, Maine
  398. John Crowley   born 24 Aug 1815 (gs); married Lucy C. WASS 25 May 1841 Columbia
                    (she dau/o Levi WASS and Emma KNOWLES)
                    (she born 19 June 1821; died 30 Dec 1914)
                    died 7 May 1843; drowned in the Machias River
           One child: Ernevesta Abra-8 TABBUT born 27 June 1872; died ___ unmarried
+ 399. SAMUEL   born 3 June 1816; married Harriet J. SMITH 13 Nov 1848
     HILLMAN   (she dau/o Ebenezer SMITH and Deborah FARNSWORTH)
                    (she born 19 Dec 1827; died 27 June 1897)
                    died Oct 1906 (lumberman and farmer)
+ 400. CAROLINE W.   born 23 Apr 1818; married Hillman-7 ALLEN ca 1841; died 1896
                    (he son/o Isaac-6 ALLEN and Judith NASH)
                    (he born 29 Sept 1824; died 6 June 1891)
+ 401. SUSAN JOY   born 14 Oct 1819; married Russell-8 SMITH ca 1844; died 1886
                    (he brother of Harriet (above) , she wife of # 399)
                    (he born 20 Jan 1817; died 1889)
  402. Benjamin Franklin born 9 April 1821; died 11 Aug 1851 (sailor)
  403. Frances Wass   born 6 June 1823; married Ambrose H. STURGIS 16 Sept 1847
          (he son/o James STURGIS and Hannah FAUGHT) (he born ca 1809; died 3 Aug 1879)
+ 404. LOUISA M.   born 17 Sept 1825; married Isaac C. WORCESTER ca 1844
                    (he son/o John WORCESTER and Mary FERNALD)
                    (he born 1817; died 5 Oct 1891)
                    died 11 April 1889
+ 405. AMOS   born 21 Oct 1827; married Juliette Etta ALLEN 10 Sept 1848
     WORCESTER   (she dau/o Abraham ALLEN and Mary WORCESTER)
                    (she born 10 July 1831; died 3 Mar 1914)
                    died 23 July 1900 Addison, Maine
+ 406. MARY ANN   born 17 Nov 1829; married John PUFFER, Jr. ca 1853; died 30 Nov 1860
                    (he son/o John PUFFER and Catherine STANWOOD)
                    (he born 29 July 1824; died ca 1910)
+ 407. ANDREW   born 25 Aug 1832; married Victoria ALLEN 14 Sept 1854
     JACKSON   (she dau/o John ALLEN and Mary Nash LOW)
                    (she born Apr 1838; died 1902)
                    died 19 June 1904 , a blacksmith and farmer
  408. Gilbert LaFayette born 14 Jan 1834; died 2 Oct 1904 lumberman and farmer   EOL
                    married Anna LOW Look 8 Apr 1870
       (she dau/o Enoch LOW, Jr. and Mary INGERSOLL) (she born May 1842; died 1905)

129. WILLIAM-6 TABBUT/TABBUTT, brother of above, was born 14 May 1798. He married Anne-2 WRIGHT, intentions published 12 Dec 1819 at Columbia, Maine. She was the daughter of John WRIGHT and Katherine IRISH; and was born ca 1799; died 28 March 1884. William-6 TABBUT/TABBUTT, a farmer at Columbia Falls, died 30 July 1866.

Children of William-6 TABBUT/TABBUTT and Anne-2 WRIGHT:
   Surname TABBUT/TABBUTT   (all born Columbia Falls, Maine)

409. Nancy	born ca 1820; married Daniel Sawyer CUMMINGS; died 18 June 1896
	(he son/o Samuel CUMMINGS and Elizabeth WHITE)
	(he born 5 Sept 1820; died 26 Apr 1893)
+ 410. CATHERINE W.	born April 1822; died 1899
	married JEREMIAH-7 TABBUT/TABBUTT ca 1839
	(he son/o Thomas-6 TABBUT and Catherine CROWLEY)
	(he born 1819; died 187_) (# 388) a cousin
411. Phebe T.	born ca 1824; married Samuel SARGENT; died 1842
+ 412. MARY E. H.	born ca 1827; died 1862
	married Samuel Cummings WORCESTER ca 1846
	(he son/o Clement Fernald WORCESTER and Tamson Willey CUMMINGS)
	(he born 11 Mar 1824; died 1911)
+ 413. ENOCH	born 3 May 1829; died 16 Dec 1914 Columbia, Maine
LINCOLN	married Eliza Ann TUCKER Wass 25 Nov 1852
	(she dau/o Justus TUCKER and Sarah LEIGHTON) (she born 25 Oct 1828; died 1906)
+ 414. BETSEY SOPHIA	born 16 Dec 1832; married Francis Cummings WORCESTER 1850
	(he born 1 Feb 1826; died 27 Feb 1906)
	died 19 Dec 1897
415. son	born 1835; died young

131. MARY-6 DRISKO, daughter of Joseph-5 DRISKO (Joseph-4; John-3;2) and Rebecca INGERSOLL; was born ca 1769 at Jonesboro, Maine. She married the Rev. Benjamin DOWNS of Steuben, Maine on 16 July 1791 at Addison, Maine. Benjamin was the son of Ebenezer DOWNS and Jane WALTON; and was born ca 1767; died 10 Nov 1840.

 Mary-6 was residing at Frankfort, ME. in 1840 when she and her husband gave Joseph –6 DRISKO (her brother) a quit claim deed to her interest in their mothers' dower (Rebecca INGERSOLL Drisko). Mary-6 DRISKO died 15 Oct 1848. They are buried in the COFFIN Cemetery at Frankfort, ME.

Children of Mary-6 DRISKO and Rev Benjamin DOWNS:
   Surname DOWNS   (1st four children born Steuben, ME; last child at Frankfort, ME)

416. Olive	born 5 Sept 1791	419. Judith	born 9 Mar 1805
417. Ephraim	born 11 Oct 1793	+ 420. BENJAMIN (Jr,)	born 1812
418. Rebecca	born 4 May 1795		

132. CAPTAIN JOHN-6 DRISKO, brother of above, was born ca 1772 at Addison, Maine. He married first to Phebe-5 PARKER ++ of Steuben, Maine. She was the daughter of Elisha-4 PARKER, Jr. and Eunice Jordan who came to Narragaugus Valley from Cumberland County sometime between 1766-79. Phebe PARKER was born 31 Dec 1776, married John-6 DRISKO on 22 Nov 1799, and died before 1821.

Captain John-6 DRISKO married second to Mrs. Emma/Amy KNOWLES Steele Kelley. They were married before 6 Jan 1821. They were married by a Thomas LAMSON, as reported in the local paper on that date. There was no issue from that marriage . Emma/Amy died Oct 1854 at age 88 (gs). According to Washington County, Maine Probate Records, she was married first to Reuben STEELE (1763-1803) and secondly to Thomas KELLEY (1740- 1812/13).

Children of Captain John-6 DRISKO and Phebe PARKER:
   Surname DRISKO

421. Sarah/Sally	born ca 1800 Addison; married Christopher-6 CHANDLER ca 1838-40
	(as his 2nd wife) (he born 18 Oct 1794; died 1882)
	(he son/o Edmund-5 CHANDLER and Hannah BLAISDELL)
	(he 3m. Mary C___ Smith; intentions published 26 Apr 1844 Portland, ME)
	died poss before 1842
+ 422. JOHN (4th)	born ca 1801 Addison; married Lucy Worcester LEIGHTON
	(she born 1801 Columbia; died 1880 Winona, MI)
	(she 2m. John S. BURNS)
	died 21 Nov 1834 (drowned in the Indian River)
+ 423. OLIVETTE/	born ca 1803/04 Addison; 1m. Joseph Prince ROGERS int pub 7/11 Jan 1825
OLIVE	(he born Apr 1789; died 7 Jan 1846 (g s)
	(he son/o Prince ROGERS and Lydia CARR)
	2m. Robert Barton LEIGHTON int pub 9 Aug 1846 Addison
	died before 1870 Addison, Maine
+ 424. MAYHEW C.	born ca 1805-07; married Clarissa WORCESTER; died 1885
	(she dau/o Joseph WORCESTER and Abigail NASH)
	(she born 28 Apr 1811; died 25 Jul 1893)
+ 425. PHEBE PARKER	born Sept 1806; married Nahum Hill LEIGHTON int pub 6 Feb 1828 Addison
	(he son/o Thomas Parritt LEIGHTON and Miriam WORCESTER)
	(he born ca 1803 Crowley's Island; died 13 Mar 1867)
	(he 2m. Mrs. Abigail TUCKER Coffin Crowley)
	died 29 June 1849 (g s) Addison, Maine
+ 426. REBECCA	born 31 Dec 1808; married Andrew Elliot BATSON int pub 20 July 1834
	(he son/o Stephen BATSON and Mary A. ELLIOT)
	(he born 20 Mar 1812; died 1892)
	died 23 Jan 1891 (age 82 g s) Addison, Maine
+ 427. CAPTAIN	born 16 Aug 1810 Addison; 1m. Mary S-7 KILTON in pub 15 Mar 1833
GEORGE	(she dau/o John-6 KILTON and Sarah SAWYER)
WASHINGTON	2m. Margaret-8 FOSTER Gardner 19 Sept 1855 at Machias, ME.
	(she born ca 1819 Machiasport; died 1909 New York)
	died 30 Nov 1878 Syracuse,NY; buried there in Oakwood Cemetery
+ 428. JASON CLAPP	born Feb 1813; 1m. Lucy WORCESTER int pub 15 June 1839
	(she born 1820; died before 1846)
	2m. Mary Ann FARNSWORTH int pub 4 Sept 1846
	(she born ca 1829; died 7 Aug 1904)
	died 29 Oct 1904 carpenter
429. Louraine/Lourania	born ca 1815/16; never married EOL
(male) S.	occupation: house carpenter and seaman at South Addison, Maine
+ 430. JAMES PARKER	born ca 1817; married Rhodell Amanda ARCHER 16 Mar 1843 Addison, Maine
	(she born ca 1820 Cherryfield, ME; died ____)
	(she dau/o Thomas ARCHER and Hannah TUPPER)

++ Ancestry of Phebe-5 PARKER

ROBERT-1 PARKER, the immigrant, first appeared in the Barnstable, MA. Records in 1655 (Volume 1; page 21) – when his holdings were described as being 6 parcels – totaling 60 acres.

He married first ca 1656-57 to Sarah JAMES. She born ca 16__; died June 1664 after the birth of her fourth child. He married 2nd to Patience-2 COBB in Aug 1667. She was the daughter of Henry-1 COBB and Patience-2 HURST. They had 8 children , including BENJAMIN-2 PARKER, who was born 15 Mar 1674 at Barnstable. He married Rebecca/Rebekar-2 LUMBERT/ LUMBARD on 8 Dec 1698. She was the dau/o Thomas-1 LUMBARD/LOMBARD who came to America on the *MARY AND JOHN.*

BENJAMIN-2 PARKER and Rebecca LUMBARD had 10 children: Ebenezer; Hannah; Jacob; ELISHA-3, born Sept 1704; Joseph; Thankful; Hannah (2); Benjamin; Sarah and Rebecca PARKER. ELISHA-3 PARKER , married first to Prudence-4 ATWOOD on 23

Dec 1725 at Truro, MA. She was the daughter of Machiel-3 ATWOOD and Prudence HARDING; and was born 4 July 1709 at Truro. ELISHA-3 PARKER and Prudence ATWOOD had ELISHA-4 PARKER, Jr. , who was born ____; baptized 17 May 1730; married first to Thankful MARCHANT 30 Oct 1760; and second to Eunice JORDAN 15 Nov 1764.

ELISHA-4 PARKER, Jr. and Eunice JORDAN had 9 children: Prudence; Abigail; William; Sarah; EUNICE-5; born 12 Nov 1774, married Joseph –6 DRISKO; James; Elisha III; and Jordan PARKER.

134. HANNAH-6 DRISKO, sister of above, was born ca 1774. She married Daniel McKENZIE , intentions published 22 Aug 1797. Daniel was the son of Owen McKENZIE and Elizabeth DYER, and was born 8 Apr 1772; died 17 Aug 1870 at Columbia, Maine. Hannah-6 DRISKO died ca 184_ at Columbia.

Children of Hannah-6 DRISKO and Daniel McKENZIE:
    Surname McKENZIE   (children all born Columbia, Maine)

+ 431. AMBROSE DYER born 25 Feb 1798; married Sophia TINGLEY ca 1826 New Brunswick
                      (she born 4 July 1802; died 29 Apr 1856)
                      died 28 July 1856

+ 432. JOEL   born ca 1800; married Helena LARRABEE 25 Mar 1824 Machias, ME.
                      (she dau/o Abner LARRABEE and Jane FOSTER)
                      (she born 1803; died after 1850)
                      died 1 May 1852   hanged himself

+ 433. MATILDA   born ca 1802; married Barnard "Barney" McGLAUGHLIN int pub 1 June 1823
                      (he born 1800 Ireland; died after 1870 Maine)
                      died after 1870

+ 434. MARY DYER   born ca 1804; married John MAILEY ca 1823; died 1886
                      (he born ca 1800 Ireland; died 14 Feb 1868)

  435. Lucy Drisko   born ca 1806; married Daniel GRAHAM int pub 24 June 1829

+ 436. DANIEL   born ca 1808/08 ; 1m. Miriam HANNA int pub 2 June 1829 Columbia, ME
                      (she dau/o John HANNA and Jane CAMPBELL)
                      2m. Susan AYERS Conners 7 Nov 1841 (she born ca 1810; died 1 June 1879)

  437. dau   born after 1810; died young

+ 438. JOSEPH DRISKO born ca 1816; married MARIAH STEELE-7 DRISKO 30 Sept 1841
                      (she dau/o Josiah-6 DRISKO and Theodocia CROWLEY)
                      (she born ca 1822; died 1867) (# 454)
                      died 24 Aug 1863 Columbia, Maine

+ 439. DELILAH D.   born ca 1822; 1m. Owen McKENZIE, Jr. 13 Nov 1841
     " Delia "   (he son/o Owen McKENZIE and Persis COLSON)
                      (he born 1821; died 16 Oct 1862 VA of injuries suffered in the **Civil War**)
                      2m. Ephraim HOOPER 5 Sept 1868

135. JOSEPH-6 DRISKO, brother of above, son of Joseph-5 DRISKO (Joseph-4; John-3;2) and Rebecca INGERSOLL, was born ca 1781. He married Eunice-5 PARKER Hill, daughter of Elisha PARKER, Jr. and Eunice JORDAN (sister of Phebe-5 PARKER who married # 132). Eunice-5 PARKER was born 12 Nov 1774; died 19 Jan 1853 at Addison, Maine. Joseph-6 DRISKO, a farmer, died 1851 at Addison.

Children of Joseph-6 DRISKO and Eunice PARKER (Hill) :
    Surname DRISKO

+ 440. ELIZA N./   born ca 1804/05 Addison; married Ebenezer SAWYER int pub 4 Oct 1827
     ELIZABETH N.   (he son/o Nehemiah SAWYER and Rebecca-6 SAWYER)
                      (he born 2 July 1806 Jonesport, ME; died 30 Apr 1878)
                      died 15 Feb 1889 Jonesport, Maine

+ 441. FEAH PARKER born 1807; married Aaron-7 COFFIN, intentions published 10 July 1828
                      (he son/o Matthew-6 COFFIN and Lydia WHITNEY)

  442. Rebecca B.   born ca 1808/09; married Captain John KELLEY (sea captain at Addison)
                      (he born 26 May 1807; died 30 June 1856)

Children of Joseph-6 DRISKO, continued;
  Surname DRISKO

+ 443. EUNICE PARKER born ca 1811 Addison, ME.; married Captain Oliver SAWYER ca 183_
                    (he brother of Ebenezer who married # 440, above)
                    (he born 16 Dec 1809; died 25 Sept 1881)
+ 444. JEREMIAH   born 5 Apr 1812 Addison; died 9 Dec 1893
                    1m. Nancy Shaw PARKER int pub 5 Jan 1836
                    2m. Mary L-7 INGERSOLL
                    (she dau/o Samuel-6 INGERSOLL (Wm-5;4) and Lydia H. LOOK)
                    (she born ca 1818/19; died 2 Oct 1881 (aged 62 yrs; gs)
                    3m. Mrs. Abigail TENNEY Tenney
  445. Jordan   born ca 1814/15; died young
  446. Asenath   born 1817; married William P. INGERSOLL
                    (he born 18 Oct 1809 Centerville, ME; died 23 June 1894 Harrington, ME)
                    (he brother of Mary l. INGERSOLL, above)
                    died 1 Nov 1891; resided Centerville, Maine
       Note: She had no children of her own, but raised Mabelle Asenath-9 DRISKO (# 2328);

137. JOSIAH-6 DRISKO, brother of above, was born ca 1786 at Columbia, Maine. He married Theodocia-3 CROWLEY ca 1810. She was the daughter of Jeremiah-2 CROWLEY and Elizabeth JORDAN; and was born ca 1792, Cape Elizabeth, Maine; died 11 Nov 1857 at Addison, Maine (age 66 gs). Josiah-6 DRISKO resided Addison and died there 2 June 1860/61.

Children of Josiah-6 DRISKO and Theodocia CROWLEY:
  Surname DRISKO
  447. Pamelia   born 1810; died young
+ 448. ZIMRI TABBUT   born 18 Sept 1811, Addison; died 7 Mar 1841 – age 30
                         married Roxalana Hall-7 NORTON 18 Feb 1832
                         (she dau/o Jeremiah B-6 NORTON and Hannah SAWYER)
                         (she born 19 Sept 1811; died 1 Aug 1887)(she 2m. Joseph ALLEY)
+ 449. JEREMIAH   born ca 1812/13; 1m. Jane HUNTLEY ca 1834/35; died 1848
                         2m. Mary J. ALLEN in pub 21 Oct 1844
+ 450. CAPTAIN   born 15 Apr 1815 (gs); married Hannah ALLEN int pub 13 Nov 1836
    EDMUND CURTIS   (she born 16 Dec 1815; died 18 Nov 1902)
                         died 11 Apr 1893
+ 451. BETSEY   born 16 June 1817; married Joseph Patten DORR 1836; died 7 May 1894
  452. Hiram C.   born ca 1818; died ca 1837   EOL
+ 453. THOMAS   born ca 1820/21; 1m. Ellen CROWLEY (she born 1826; died 15 Oct 1882)
      CROWLEY   2m. Mrs. Violetta Morton " Lettie " TIBBETTS Leighton 5 Dec 1883
+ 454. MARIAH STEELE born ca 1822; 1m. Joseph Drisko-7 McKENZIE 1841 (# 438)
                         (he son/o Daniel McKENZIE and Hannah-6 DRISKO (# 134)
                         2m. Antoine LEVENE 14 May 1867 (he born 1820 Canada)
  455. Christiana   born ca 1824; died young
+ 456. CAPTAIN   born Mar 1826; 1m. Mary Ann CROWLEY(she born 1830; died 19 June 1849)
    JOEL WILSON   2m. Sarah W. CROWLEY 2 Nov 1854
                         (she born Sept 1835; died 30 Nov 1908, age 73)
  457. Susan F.   born 31 May 1828; died 9 July 1886 Jonesport, Maine
                         married Ennis ROGERS after 1850 (his 2nd wife)
                         (he son/o Joseph Prince ROGERS and Catherine ENNIS Bryant)
                         (he born 12 Mar 1820 Jonesport, ME; died 28 Apr 1901)
+ 458. NANCY ANN   born Feb 1830; died May 1866
                         married Benjamin Franklin-9 CARVER ca 1850
                         (he son/o Benjamin J-8 CARVER and Mary MANSFIELD)
                         (he born 28 June 1824 Portland, ME; died 10 Nov 1904)

Children of Josiah-6 DRISKO, continued:
    Surname DRISKO
    459. Josiah, Jr.   born ca 1832; died 5 May 1854   EOL
    460. Theodocia   born ca 1834; died young

139. JEREMIAH-6 DRISKO, brother of above, was born ca 1790 at Addison, Washington County, Maine. He served in Captain Holmes NASH's Company of MA Volunteers in the **War of 1812.** His widows' pension papers were # 27859. He married Ann-2 FRANKLAND, daughter of Captain William-1 FRANK-LAND and Ann ROSS; and was born 22 Nov 1798 at St. Andrews, New Brunswick; died 19 July 1878. Jeremiah-6 DRISKO died 12 Dec 1870 at Addison, Maine.

Children of Jeremiah-6 DRISKO and Ann FRANKLAND:
    Surname DRISKO   (children born at Addison, Maine)
    461. dau   born ca 1817; died after 1840
  + 462. ANN   born 28 Oct 1819; 1m. Captain John H. BARTON 24 Nov 1839
        FRANKLAND   (he son/o John BARTON and Mary ELLSWORTH)
                           (he born 19 Oct 1812; died 11 Dec 1843)
                           2m. Green B. STEVENS of Boston, MA on 26 Sept 1847
  + 463. BENJAMIN   born 8 Apr 1821; married NANCY WASS-8 PLUMMER Sept 1845 (# 926)
        FRANKLAND/   (she dau/o John-7 PLUMMER (# 348) and Sarah WASS)
        FRANKLIN   (she born 1823; died 1882)
                           died 7 Sept 1893; buried Church Hill Cemetery, Addison, ME
  + 464. ORAMANDER   born 9 July 1822; 1m. Catherine W. WASS 14 July 1853
        HOWARD   (she born 7 May 1833; died 6 Apr 1900)
                           2m. Mrs. Cecelia LONG Knowles (wid/o Augustus)
                           died 24 Feb 1918 Boston, MA; buried Jamaica Plain, MA
    465. William   born ca 1824; died young
  + 466. CAPTAIN   born born 7 Nov 1826; 1m. Frances A-8 PLUMMER 11 Nov 1849 (# 929)
        PERRIN C.   (she sister of Nancy-8 , above)   (she born ca 1829; died 1860)
                    2m. Eldora Florence HAMILTON (she dau/o Salathiel HAMILTON and Lydia RICH)
                           (she born Nov 1856; died 12 Oct 1928)
                           died 6 May 1910 Provincetown, MA
  + 467. ALONZO S.   born ca 1829; married Elvena A. WASS; died ca 1893
                           (she born ca 1832; died 1851; she dau/o Chipman WASS and Mary CURTIS)
  + 468. MARGARET   born 1831; married Charles L. UNION (he born 1832, MA)
  + 469. EMMA   born 13 Nov 1839; died 23 July 1931 Seattle, WA
        BIGELOW   married Captain John Billings HINCKLEY 1855
                           (he son/o Aaron HINCKLEY and Mary IRONS) (he born ca 1832; died 1900)

140. JONATHAN-6 DRISKO, son of Samuel Gatchell-5 DRISKO (Joseph-4; John-3;2) and Mercy CHANDLER, was born 30 Sept 1774 at Pleasant River (ME). He married Sarah/Sally Dyer McKENZIE , intentions published 22 Oct 1796 at Columbia, ME. She was the daughter of Owen McKENZIE and Elizabeth DYER, and was born ca 1777/78 at Columbia Falls, Maine; died 2 Mar 1864.

Jonathan was elected to Town Office in April 1797; drawn Petit Juror 4 Sept 1797, and elected yearly as Surveyor of Lumber from 1801-08. A mason, Jonathan-6 died May 1810. His widow, married 2nd to Silas TENNEY on 10 Sept 1814, and 3rd to John CONNERS/O'CONNOR on 4 Mar 1835. She died 2 Mar 1864

Children of Jonathan-6 DRISKO and Sarah McKENZIE:
    Surname DRISKO
  + 470. CHANDLER   born 5 May 1799 Columbia, ME; marr Ruth Ruggles WHITNEY + 5 June 1823
        ROBBINS   (she dau/o Joseph-7 WHITNEY and Mary LIBBY)
                           (she born 11 Apr 1805; died 25 Sept 1888; she 2m. Thomas Greenleaf WATTS
                           died 3 June 1845 Jonesboro, Maine

Children of Jonathan-6 DRISKO, continued:
    Surname DRISKO
471. Amasa   born ca 1801
+ 472. ABIGAIL B.   born ca 1803;   died 1828-30
                                married Dennis TRACY 18 Apr 1824 (int pub 3 Aug 1823)
                                (he married 2nd Hannah PEABODY Rowley ca 1831)
+ 473. SARAH JANE   born ca 1807; married Robert SWEENEY ca 1830; died ca 1842
   474. Lucy   born ca 1809; died 1839

                        + Ancestry of Ruth Ruggles-8 WHITNEY
JOHN-1 WHITNEY (THOMAS-A; ROBERT-B) was born in England ca 1589-92, and married Elinor __?__. She was born
1599; died 11 May 1659 at Watertown, MA. John-1 died there 1 June 1673.

JOHN-2 WHITNEY was born 1621, probably in England. He married Ruth REYNOLDS (daughter of Robert who came in
WINTHROP's Fleet 1630). BENJAMIN-3 WHITNEY, born 6 June 1643; married Jane __?__. They had NATHANIEL-4
WHITNEY who was born 14 April 1680 at York, Maine. He married Sarah FORD, daughter of John FORD and Susanna __?__
of Braveboat Harbor, Kittery, Maine. He died at Gorham, Maine.

NAHAM-5 WHITNEY was born 10 Jan 1706/07 at York, Maine. He married Lydia YOUNG on 11 Dec 1730. She was the
daughter of Mathew YOUNG. Their son CAPTAIN NATHAN-6 WHITNEY, was born ca 1745. He married Patience __?__ ca 1771.
He was prominent in Columbia town affairs.

JOSEPH-7 WHITNEY, was born 1782. He married first, on 5 June 1802/03 at Jonesboro, ME; to Mary LIBBY, daughter of
Reuben LIBBY and Rebecca WESTON **, who was born 28 Jan 1783 Jonesborough, Maine; died Oct 1822. Joseph-7 married second
to her sister, Rebecca LIBBY. Joseph-7 died Sept 1860. Ruth Ruggles-8 WHITNEY was the daughter of Joseph-7 and his first wife.

** Rebecca WESTON, daughter of Josiah WESTON and Phebe PARKER (probably of Parker's Island), was born at Falmouth. She
was but a young girl of 15 when she and her sister-in-law, Hannah WATTS Weston (16), carried pewter and powder through the
woods to Machias, Maine (some 16 miles) in an attempt to help provide ammunition for the defenses there. The men of Jonesboro
had met at the home of the WESTON'S before marching to Machias.

141. MARY/POLLY -6 DRISKO, sister of above, was born 26 Oct 1776 at Jonesboro, Maine. She married
Captain Holmes-5 NASH, intentions published 26 Sept 1796, at Columbia, Maine. He was the son of
Joseph-4 ++ NASH and Elizabeth WASS; and was born 9 Aug 1774 at Addison Point; died 20 Oct 1838.
Mary-6 DRISKO died 8 Mar 1847.

Children of Mary-6 DRISKO and Captain Holmes-5 NASH:
    Surname NASH
+ 475. APHATHA/   born 17 July 1797; married Wilmot Wass-5 WILSON 1823; died 1858
       APHPHATHA/   (he son/o Nathaniel-4 WILSON and Mary/Polly WASS)
       APPHIA   (he born 26 Oct 1797 Columbia Falls, ME; died 8 Mar 1884 Somerville, MA)
+476. REBECCA   born 12 Nov 1799;   died 1880
      ALLEN   married Daniel Sawyer-6 WASS Oct 1819 Addison, ME.
               (he son/o Wilmot-5 WASS and Rebecca JORDAN)(he born 22 May 1798; died 7 Aug 1873, IA)
+ 477. ANN S.   born 28 Nov 1801; married David-2 DAVIS Dec 1827; died 1887
               (he son/o Samuel-1 DAVIS and Susannah NASH) (he born Sept 1801; died 1872)
+ 478. GEORGE W.   born 28 May 1804; married Jane PATTEN 16 Apr/28 Aug 1829
               (she dau/o John PATTEN and Pamelia-6 LEIGHTON) (she born 27 Apr 1809 Cherryfield, ME)
                              died 30 July 1854 Boston, MA.
+ 479. JERUSHA   born 26 Nov 1806; married Samuel Robert SUMNER 11 June 1831
       DRISKO   (he son/o John SUMNER and Elizabeth MOORE)
                              (he born 12 Dec 1802, MA; died 1879/80)
                              died 8 Oct 1883 Somerville, MA.
+ 480. MARY E.   born 29 Apr 1809;   died 7 Sept 1901 Addison, Maine
                              married John Lowell ALLINE 22 Feb 1828
               (he son/o Benjamin ALLINE and Lydia PATTEN) (he born 21 July 1803; died 5 Jan 1873)
+ 481. JOSEPH   born 15 May 1812; married Almira BATES , int pub 6 Oct 1834
                              (she born 5 Dec 1816, MA; died 15 Apr 1887) he died 27 June 1893 Addison

Children of Mary-6 DRISKO, continued:
    Surname NASH
482. Holmes, Jr.   born 17 Sept 1814; married Sophia C-6 NASH 10 Nov 1836
              (she dau/o Nathaniel-5 NASH and Sophia COFFIN) (granddau/o Captain John-4 COFFIN)
              died 12 Mar 1886 Atlanta, GA (had 1 child who died young)
483. Miriam   born 2 Jan 1819 Winchester, MA; married George HATHAWAY May 1839
              (he son/o Ebenezer HATHAWAY and Betsey TISDALE)
              (he born 29 May 1805, NH; died 15 July 1882, MA)
              died 15 July 1882 Somerville, MA. (had 3 children, all died young)

                              ++ Ancestry of Captain Holmes-5 NASH
FRANCIS-1 NASH, the immigrant, was at Braintree, MA as early as 1675, and died there 13 Aug 1713. He and, his 2nd wife, Mary
PURCHAS Niles were the parents of JOHN-2 NASH, who was born ca 1698 at Braintree. John-2 married Mary TURBEFIELD on
28 June 1721. She was the daughter of James TURBEFIELD and Mercy CAMPBELL, and was born 16 Sept 1700 at Braintree; died
6 June 1761. John-2 NASH died 7 July 1745.

JOSEPH-3 NASH, son of John-2, was baptized 12 Nov 1727 at Braintree, MA. He married Susannah SHAW, the daughter of Joseph
SHAW and Mary BLANCHARD of Weymouth, MA. She was born 3 Mar 1726; died ca 1790, Maine.

JOSEPH-4 NASH was born 14 July 1750 at Braintree, MA. He died 15 April 1839 at Addison, Maine. His estate was entered for
probate on 3 June 1840. His wife was Elizabeth/Betsey WASS. She was the daughter of Wilmot WASS and Rebecca ALLEN and
was born 13 Sept 1757 at West Tisbury, Martha's Vineyard, MA; and died 23 Sept 1844 at Addison, Maine.
                       References: Marian Fraser, Bahia, Brazil; John B. DRISKO, Easton, PA; Maine Historical Magazine

143. EDMUND-6 DRISKO, brother of above, was born 24 April 1784 at Columbia, Maine. He married
Elizabeth/ Betsey-6 CATES, daughter of Edward-5 CATES (Samuel-4; Edward-3;2; James-1 CATE)
and Elizabeth __?__. She was born ca 1790; died 1820. Edmund-6 died 4 May 1810 " from fever " at
Columbia, Maine. On 13 June his widow was appointed administratrix of his estate. She married second
to Isaac HANSCOM on 25 Nov 1813 at Machias, Maine.

Child of Edmund-6 DRISKO and Betsey-3 CATES:
    Surname DRISKO
+ 484. MERCY   born ca 1809/10; died ca 1844/46
                             married George Handy-6 LONGFELLOW 14 Sept 1834
                             (he son/o Isaac-5 LONGFELLOW ++ and Polly-6 BOYNTON ++)
                             (he 2m. Nancy MERRITT of Addison)

++ ISAAC-5 LONGFELLOW, was the son of JONATHAN-4 LONGFELLOW (NATHAN-3; WILLIAM-2;) and Mercy
 CLARK . Jonathan-4 LONGFELLOW , Esq. came to Machias, Maine in 1776 and built a house that afterwards was kept
as a tavern by his son David-5. Jonathan-4 was the first Justice of the Peace in Maine, east of the Penobscot River. He married
POLLY-6 BOYNTON, the daughter of Amos-5 BOYNTON (DAVID-4; JOSHUA-3; 2; WILLIAM-1) and Polly LIBBY. (Amos
was born 2 Feb 1745. In 1766 he moved from Byfield , MA to Machias, ME. Children of Isaac-5 LONGFELLOW and Polly-6
BOYNTON were: Eri who married Jane STUART (8 ch); Mary who married George BURNHAM (8 ch); Hannah who married
Gridley THAXTER; Addie who died young; GEORGE HANDY (above); Cynthia who 1m. Caleb CROCKER; 2m. Harrison
Gould CROCKER (see CROCKER section # 66 and # 209) ; Margaret B. who 1m. Isaac P. HAM, 2m. Coffin SMITH;
Samuel who married Mary PENNELL (2 ch); and Gates LONGFELLOW.

144. JERUSHA-6 DRISKO, sister of above, was born 6 Sept 1786. She married Deacon David
CORTHELL on __ Dec 1807 at Columbia, Maine. He was a house carpenter, and was the son of Levi
CORTHELL and Deborah CURTIS. David CORTHELL was born ca 1782 at Hingham, MA; died 29 Oct
1868 at Harrington, ME. Jerusha-6 DRISKO died 27 Apr 1848 at Addison, Maine.

Children of Jerusha-6 DRISKO and David CORTHELL:
    Surname CORTHELL   (children all born Addison, Maine)
485. Roxanna   born 1808; married Benjamin MITCHELL
                             (he son/o Thomas MITCHELL and Elizabeth STROUT; he born 1804)
                             died 4 Sept 1836 Harrington, ME (possibly died in childbirth)
                             One child: Roscoe G-8 MITCHELL born __ 1836

Children of Jerusha-6 DRISKO, continued:
  Surname CORTHELL

+ 486. LOUISA   born Feb 1811; married William P. ALLINE Nov 1833; died 4 Dec 1893
                         (he son/o Benjamin ALLINE and Lydia PATTEN)
                         (he born 5 May 1805; died 21 Feb 1887)
  487. Celia D.   born ca 1814; married Henry ALLINE (bro/o William (above)
                         (he born 16 July 1809; died 9 May 1895) tanner/shoemaker
                         died 20 Jan 1899   no issue   EOL
  488. Mary   born 17 Oct 1815; 1m. George DINSMORE 3 Jan 1841; died after 1900
                         2m. Charles R. NASH ca 1851
                         One child: Gilbert M-8 DINSMORE born ca 1843
  489. Julia Ann   born 3 June 1820; married Daniel Webster DINSMORE 25 Dec 1844
                         (he son/o John DINSMORE and Sarah FICKETT)
                         (he born Mar 1819; died 19 Oct 1888) shipbuilder
  490. Cyrene M.   born ca 1822; died 14 Nov 1866
  491. Deborah   born ca 1824; died after 1840
  492. William Johnson   born 10 July 1827; died 1 Nov 1908 Calais, Maine
             married Mary BUCK 16 Dec 1857 (2ch; 1 d y) (she born 1830; died 19 Mar 1910)

145. REBECCA-6 DRISKO, twin sister of above, was born 6 Sept 1786 at Addison, Washington County, Maine. She married Elisha-6 COFFIN ++ on 12 May 1808 at Harrington, Maine. He was the son of Matthew-5 COFFIN and Jane WASS, and was born 1 Jan 1785 at Columbia, Washington County, Maine; died 14 Aug 1871 at Harrington. Rebecca-6 DRISKO died 5 Feb 1851 at Harrington. Elisha-6 COFFIN married second to Lovina FRYE Kent on 20 Dec 1854. He was a farmer at Addison and Harrington.

Children of REBECCA-6 DRISKO and Elisha-6 COFFIN:
  Surname COFFIN   (all born Harrington, ME)

+ 493. JAMES   born 27 Feb 1809; 1m. Catherine DYER   (she born 1810; died 185_)
       CAMPBELL   2m. CORDELIA-8 COFFIN McKenzie 3 Dec 1854 (# 1240)
                        (she dau/o Aaron-7 COFFIN and Feah-6 DRISKO (# 441)
+ 494. FRANCES   born 4 April 1811; married Reuben D-7 COFFIN 24 May 1835
                        (he son/o Richard-6 COFFIN and Hannah WHITTEN)
                        (he born 14 Mar 1812; died 15 Nov 1885)
+ 495. AMOS   born 31 Dec 1813; married Irene MITCHELL 10 Nov 1835
       BUCKNAM   (she dau/o Thomas MITCHELL and Elizabeth STROUT)
                        (she born 27 June 1816; died 27 May 1910)
                        died 11 May 1893 Harrington, Maine
  496. Levi   born 29 Dec 1816; died young
  497. Benjamin Campbell born 16 Sept 1819; married Clarissa-6 NASH 25 Dec 1854
                        (she dau/o John-5 NASH and Amy/Emma FICKETT)
                        (she born 1834/5; died 22 Mar 1920)
                        died 2 May 1906 Boston, MA   no issue   EOL
+ 498. URIAH NASH   born 26 Aug 1823; died 14 June 1893 Harrington, Maine
                        1m. Catherine C. COLSON 18 Nov 1847 Cherryfield, ME
                        (she born 1829; died 20 Feb 1854)
                        2m. Harriet CLEAVES 21 Nov 1855
                        (she dau/o Charles CLEAVES and ? LORD)
                        (she born 19 Mar 1838; died 29 Dec 1924)
+ 499. MERCY JANE   born 27 Mar 1826; married John W-7 COFFIN 1845 (cousin)
                        (he born 30 July 1818; died 2 Oct 1889)
                        died ca 1870's
  500. Almira P.   born 12 Aug 1830; married George PLUMMER 4 Apr 1850 (he born 1825)

++ Ancestry of Elisha-6 COFFIN

PETER-A COFFIN, born ca 1588 Brixton Parish, England , son of NICHOLAS-B COFFIN annd Joan __?__, married about 1608 to Joan KEMBER. She was born ca 1590, Brixton; died 30 May 1661 at Boston, Suffolk County, MA. Peter-A COFFIN died ca Mar 1628 at Brixton, England.

TRISTAM-1 COFFIN, the immigrant, was born ca 1609 at Brixton, Devon, England. He married Dionis STEVENS (born ca 1609) about 1630 at Brixton Parish. Dionis was the daughter of Robert STEVENS (1563-___)(John). Tristam-1 COFFIN died 2 Oct 1681 at Nantucket, MA. His wife died there 6 Nov 1684.

JOHN-2 COFFIN was born 13 Oct 1647 at Haverhill, MA. He married Deborah AUSTIN ca 1668 at Nantucket. Deborah was the daughter of Joseph AUSTIN and Sarah STARBUCK, and was born ca 1649; died 4 Feb 1724. John-2 COFFIN died 5 Sept 1711 at Edgartown, Dukes County, MA.   TRISTAM-3 COFFIN was born ca 1685 at Edgartown, MA. He married Mary BUNKER (born ca 1692 at Nantucket).

RICHARD-4 COFFIN, born 20 Oct 1729 at Edgartown, MA; married Mary/Molly COOKE ca 17__. She was the daughter of _?_ COOKE and was born 18 July 1732 Edgartown; died ____, Addison, ME. MATTHEW-5 COFFIN was born ca 1756 at Edgartown, Dukes, MA. He married Jane WASS, daughter of Wilmot WASS and Rebecca ALLEN on 19 Jan 1780 at Machias, ME. Jane was born 18 Aug 1761 at Tisbury, Dukes, MA; and died 28 Dec 1853 at Columbia, Maine.

Reference: David COFFIN, Bethesda, MD; Coffin Family Newsletter

146. SAMUEL GATCHELL-6 DRISKO (Jr.) , brother of above, was born ca July 1791. He married Mary D. PHINNEY of Machias on 17 Sept 1814; Stephen JONES, Esq. officiated. Mary was the daughter of Nathaniel PHINNEY and Thankful TUPPER, and was born ca 1796; died 18__ .

Samuel Gatchell-6 DRISKO, Jr. operated a shipyard on the Branch Stream at Columbia, Maine. He built the *SAMUEL TRAIN* and the *WAVE* – and possibly other vessels. His business was carried on by his sons George B. and Charles A. DRISKO. Samuel Gatchell-6 DRISKO, Jr. died 28 Dec 1865 at Columbia, Maine. He is buried in Church Hill Cemetery, Addison.

Children of Samuel G-6 DRISKO and Mary PHINNEY:
Surname DRISKO	(all born Columbia, Maine)
+ 501. JERUSHA CORTHELL	born ca 1820; married William Bradford LE BARRON 19 Sept 1839 (he born Aug 1814; died 7 Oct 1886) died after 1904; removed to Oneida, IL before 1850
+ 502. MARY REBECCA	born ca 1823; married Simeon Coffin-6 NASH 19 Sept 1847 (he son o/ Nathaniel-5 NASH ++ and Sophia COFFIN); res. Boston, MA
+ 503. CAPTAIN GEORGE B.	born 5 Mar 1825; married Frances Augusta PLUMMER 3 Aug 1854 (she dau/o Captain Bryce T-8 PLUMMER and Sylvina-7 WASS) (she born 1 Apr 1825; died 28 May 1896) died 10 Sept 1894 ; sea captain and shipbuilder
504. Walter Harris	born ca 1829; died 10 Nov 1855 NY; unmarried; ships' carpenter
505. William F.	born Feb 1832; died 18 Oct 1848 EOL
+ 506. CHARLES A.	born 18 Apr 1835 ; married Theodocia-8 DRISKO 24 Nov 1859 (she dau/o Zimri T-7 DRISKO (# 448) and Roxalana NORTON) (she born Dec 1840; died 18 Sept 1885) # 1261 died 6 Feb 1894; farmer, shipbuilder; lighthouse keeper

++ Nathaniel-5 NASH (Isaiah-4; Joseph-3; John-2) of Addison Ridge. Representative 1834, 1838; married Sophia COFFIN, daughter of Capt. John COFFIN 1817. Sophia was born 29 Sept 1799; died 12 Dec 1888.

147. DOROTHY-6 McKENNEY, daughter of Moses-5 McKENNEY (Elizabeth-4 DRISKO; John-3; 2) and Eunice LARRABEE, was born 14 June 1762. She married DOMINICUS-5 LIBBY (# 158) on 4 Jan 1790. He was the son of Luke-4 LIBBY and Dorothy-5 McKENNEY; and was born 13 June 1763; died 5 Jan 1836. Dorothy-6 McKENNEY died 24 Feb 1817.

Children of Dorothy-6 McKENNEY and Dominicus-6 LIBBY:
Surname LIBBY	
507. Jane	born 12 Oct 1790; died 23 Mar 1874 Danville, Maine

Children of Dorothy-6 McKENNEY, continued:
Surname LIBBY

+ 508. MOSES	born 5 Mar 1792; married Mary Ann LARRABEE 24 Jan 1819	
	(she dau/o Stephen LARRABEE and Priscilla MARTIN)	
	died 28 June 1837 Danville, Maine	
509. Hannah	born 11 Aug 1794; died 9 June 1844	
510. Luke	born 24 Jan 1796; died 23 Jan 1813	
511. Polly	born 14 Oct 1797; married _?_ 5 Mar 1818 Limington, ME; died 25 June 1835	
512. Dominicus	born 24 June 1799; died 14 July 1836	
513. Dorothy	born 20 June 1801; married Jonathan LIBBY; died 9 Sept 1876	
514. William	born 7 Mar 1803; married Mary Ann LIBBY 26 Nov 1847; died 12 Apr 1850	
515. Rufus (twin)	born 10 Aug 1805; died 9 Dec 1846	
+ 516. EUNICE (twin)	born 10 Aug 1805 Pegypscot, ME; died 1 Dec 1876	
	married William McKenney JORDAN 21 Oct 1840 Danville, Maine	

(he son/o James Peables JORDAN and Dorcas McKENNEY)(he born 15 May 1815; died 18 Sept 1872)

148. MARY-6 McKENNEY, sister of above, was born ca 1765 at Scarborough, Maine. She married Philip-4 LIBBY, a farmer, ca 17__. He was the son of Thomas-3 LIBBY and Mary LARRABEE; and was born 16 May 1762 at Scarborough; died 26 Feb 1810. He death resulted when " Philip LIBBY fell from his horse and broke his neck; was found dead in the road." Mary-6 McKENNEY died 27 July 1854, aged 89.

Children of Mary-6 McKENNEY and Philip-4 LIBBY:
Surname LIBBY

517. Eunice	born 5 Jan 1789; died 12 June 1876 unmarried
+ 518. GEORGE	born 18 Apr 1792; 1m. Sally FOSS; 2m. Eliza CARTER
+ 519. MARY	born 20 Oct 1794; married Daniel LIBBY; died 7 June 1874
	(he born 21 Mar 1788; died 8 Dec 1857)
+ 520. MOSES	born 30 Nov 1796; married Fannie SEAVEY
521. Betsey	born 28 Apr 1799; married Eli EDGECOMB 1 Dec 1824
522. Lucy	born 17 Nov 1803; died 28 Aug 1876 unmarried
+ 523. PHILIP	born 19 July 1806; married Catherine HARMON 23 June 1830; died 17 Oct 1870
	(she dau/o Peletiah HARMON and Sally ELWELL ; born ____; died 14 June 1869)

149. HANNAH-6 McKENNEY – see WILLIAM-6 LIBBY (# 163)

150. BETSEY-6 McKENNEY, sister of above, was born ca 17__. She married Dennis-6 LIBBY on 9 Oct 1793 at Scarborough, Maine. He was the son of Ichabod LIBBY and Mary FICKETT; and was born 1771 Scarborough; died 21 Mar 1826 of measles. Bestey-6 McKENNEY died 2 days later, 23 Mar 1826, also the result of measles.

Children of Bestey-6 McKENNEY and Dennis-6 LIBBY:
Surname LIBBY

524. Abner	born 1794; died Sept 1815 unmarried
525. Hanson	born 1796; married Polly MARTIN
526. Eunice	born 1797; died June 1833 unmarried
527. Mary	born June 1799; died Sept 1870 unmarried
528. Lydia	born 1801; married Samuel ROBERTS
529. Caleb	born 10 May 1803; married Lydia BRIGGS
	Child: Dennis Alvra-8 LIBBY born 12 Dec 1828 Danville, Androscoggin Co., ME
530. Dennis	born 16 Apr 1805; married Sarah H. WARREN
+ 531. MOSES	born 8 Aug 1807; married MARGARET M-7 LIBBY 26 Oct 1837 (# 551)
532. Hannah	born 1809; married Jacob S. RICHARDSON 3 Sept 1857
+ 533. SUSAN (twin)	born Feb 1811; married Dennis-7 LIBBY 16 Dec 1838
534. Betsey (twin)	born Feb 1811; married Joseph LANG of Portland

152. MOSES-6 McKENNEY, brother of above, was born ca 17__. He married Salome LIBBY on 11 June 1799 at Scarborough, ME. She was the daughter of Deacon Joshua LIBBY (Andrew; Matthew) and Hannah LARRABEE, was born 15 Oct 1778 Scarboro, ME; died 1 July 1843. Moses-6 McKENNEY died 24 Mar 1828.

Children of Moses-6 McKENNEY and Salome LIBBY:
    Surname McKENNEY
  535. Mahala   born 1803; died Nov 1825   unmarried
  536. Hannah   born 13 Jan 1805; married John CHAPMAN
  537. John   born 20 Feb 1809; married Satira SKILLINGS
  538. William   born 27 Apr 1811; married Delia WARD
+ 539. JOSHUA   born Dec 1813; married Elinor BUGBEE

157. REUBEN-6 LIBBY, son of Dorothy-5 McKENNEY (Elizabeth-4 DRISKO; John-3 ;2) and Luke-4 LIBBY (John; David; John) was born ca 1761 at Scarborough, Maine. He married Elizabeth BURNHAM on 6 Feb 1782 at Scarborough. She was the daughter of ____ BURNHAM and was born 17__; died ____. Reuben-6 LIBBY died before 1789, and his widow removed to Danville, Maine; residing at one time with her brother-in-law Humphrey LIBBY.

Children of Reuben-6 LIBBY and Elizabeth BURNHAM:
    Surname LIBBY   540. Silas   born 17 __; married Mary BOYD; res. KY.   541. Rhoda   born 17__

158. DOMINICUS-6 LIBBY   see DOROTHY-6 McKENNEY (# 147)
160. LUKE-6 LIBBY, brother of above, was born ca 1767 at Scarborough, Maine. He married Betsey MITCHELL ca 17__. She was the daughter of Jonathan MITCHELL and __?_ LOVETT, and was born ca 17__, Cape Elizabeth, Maine; died 15 June 1856. Luke-5 LIBBY died 13 Oct 1800 at Auburn, Maine. His widow 2m. Thomas MURRAY.

Children of Luke-6 LIBBY and Betsey MITCHELL:
    Surname LIBBY
+ 542. JONATHAN   born 29 Feb 1798 Danville, ME; a sailor and fisherman
                       1m. Mary JORDAN (she dau/o William JORDAN of Lisbon, Maine)
                       2m. Dorothy LIBBY
  543. Dorothy   born Feb 1800; married William JORDAN

161. ISAAC-6 LIBBY, brother of above, was born ca 1768 at Scarborough, Maine. He married Dorothy-5 MESERVE on 10 Nov 1793. She was the daughter of William-4 MESERVE (John-3; Clement-2;1) and Margery DEARING; and was born 7 Mar 1773; died 29 Aug 1825 Danville (now Auburn), Maine. Isaac-6 LIBBY died 14 May 1822.

Children of Isaac-6 LIBBY and Dorothy-5 MESERVE:
    Surname LIBBY
+ 544. WILLIAM   born 20 Jan 1795; married Nancy JORDAN
  545. Jonah/Jonas   born 17 Nov 1797; married Hepsibeth HANSCOM 19 Feb 1828 Danville
                       (she dau/o Moses HANSCOM and Mary/Polly McGRAW)
  546. Margaret   born ____; died at age 3
  547. Luke   born 8 Jan 1801; married Mary LARRABEE
  548. Isaac   born 12 Nov 1801; married Abigail S. HANSCOM
  549. Hannah   born 12 Feb 1805; married Charles Peables JORDAN 16 Dec 1824/28
                       (he born 26 Mar 1795 Pejepscot, ME)
     (ch: Isaac-8 JORDAN born ___; died Jan 1865 in the **Civil War** at Andersonville, GA Prison (POW)
  550. Dorothy   born 2 Feb 1807; married Charles PEOPLES 14 Apr 1829; died 21 Jan 1879
+ 551. MARGARET M.   born 28 Mar 1809; died 4 Nov 1863
                       married MOSES-7 LIBBY 26 Oct 1837 (# 531) (he born 8 Aug 1807)

Children of Isaac-6 LIBBY, continued:
  Surname LIBBY
  552. Ann   born 7 May 1811; married William LIBBY 26 Nov 1847
                        (he son/o DOMINICUS-5 LIBBY and Dorothy McKENNEY)
                        (he born 7 Mar 1803; died 12 Apr 1850) EOL
  553. John   born 23 Aug 1813; died 23 Nov 1836

163. WILLIAM-6 LIBBY, brother of above, was born 1 Jan 1772 at Scarborough, Maine. He married
HANNAH-6 McKENNEY (# 149) on 20 Jan 1797. She was the daughter of Moses-4 McKENNEY and
Eunice LARRABEE, and was born ___; died 22 Mar 1866 at Danville. William-6 LIBBY died 1 Apr 1847.

Children of William-6 LIBBY and Hannah-6 McKENNEY:
  Surname LIBBY
  554. Esther   born 7 May 1798; died 19 Oct 1869
  555. Lucy   born 1802; died 22 Mar 1819
  556. Sarah   born 1805; died 8 Feb 1833
  557. Dorothy   born 1808; died 21 July 1835
  558. Gardner   born 1811; died 22 Mar 1836
  559. Philip   born Mar 1816; married Bestey Ann GOSS; died 11 Jan 1846
                        (she dau/o Samuel GOSS of Danville, ME.) (she 2m. Isaac LIBBY)
                        Child: Lucy-8 LIBBY born ____; died at age 19   EOL

164. HUMPHREY-6 LIBBY, brother of above, was born 17__ at Scarborough, Maine. He married
Keziah-5 MESERVE on 3 Jan 1799. She was the daughter of William-4 MESERVE (John-3; Clement-2;1
and Margery DEARING, and was born 17 Nov 1776. According to " LIBBY Family in America ", p. 84 :
" He was a farmer in Danville until the **War of 1812.** He died of fever at ' Saggett's Harbor ' (should be
Sackett's Harbor, Lake Ontario, NY). His widow lived to an old age and died with her daughter Jane. "

Children of Humphrey-6 LIBBY and Keziah MESERVE:
  Surname LIBBY
  560. Emily   born ____; married Israel JONES   (he son/o _?_ JONES and Hannah LIBBY)
  561. Jane   born ____; married Sewall BLANCHARD of Cumberland, Maine
  562. Margaret   born ____; married Levi PRINCE of Pittsfield
  563. Mary   born 7 Mar 1807; married Isaiah KNIGHT of Colebrook, NH
  564. Martha   born ____; married Enoch HOWES of Boston
  565. Hannah   born ____; married John JONES (as his 2nd wife)
                        (he brother of Israel Jones, above)
  566. Keziah   born ____; married Stebben ANDROS of Oswego, New York

167. WILLIAM-6 MC KENNEY, son of Isaac-5 MC KENNEY (Elizabeth-4 DRISKO; John-3; 2) and
Hannah-5 JORDAN, was born ca 17__. He married Mary-7 JORDAN on 1 June 1785 at Pegypscot, ME.
She was the daughter of James-6 JORDAN (Robert-5; John-4; Robert-3; Edward-2; Thomas-1) and
Elizabeth JORDAN, and was born ca 1762; died 11 May 1838. He died 1798, and she married his brother
Abraham-6 MC KENNEY.

Children of William-6 MC KENNEY and Mary-7 JORDAN:
  Surname MC KENNEY
  567. Elizabeth   born 5 Sept 1785
  568. Jonathan   born 5 July 1787; married Sarah JORDAN 17 Nov 1811
  569. Ann   born 3 Aug 1789
  570. William   born 9 Feb 1793   571. Andrew   born 9 June 1798

168. ABRAHAM-6 MC KENNEY, brother of above, was born ca 17__. He married Mary-7 JORDAN on
1 Dec 1798. She was the widow of his brother William (above).

Child of Abraham-6 MC KENNEY and Mary JORDAN:
  Surname MC KENNEY
  572. Abraham   born 12 July 1801

178. CAPTAIN JAMES-6 DRISCO. JR., son of Captain James-5 DRISCO, Sr. (James/Jeremiah-4; Cornelius-3; Jeremiah-2; Timothy-1) and Elizabeth WALDEN, was born ca 1776 probably at Portsmouth, NH. He married Margarette/Margaretta MENDUM on 15 Mat 1798 at Portsmouth. She was the daughter of ___ MENDUM and __?__; and was born ca 1778; died 13 Mar 1853, age 75. Captain James-6 DRISCO, Jr. died 16 June 1807, lost at sea, age 31. They are buried at Harmony Grove Cemetery, Portsmouth NH.

Children of James-6 DRISCO,Jr. and Margarette MENDUM:
  Surname DRISCO
  573. Mary D/E   born ca 1800/01 New Hampshire; married John AMES 30 Nov 1820
         Note: A Mary Elizabeth DRISCO was baptized as an adult , on 23 Oct 1836 at Portsmouth, Rockingham County, NH.
+ 574. CAPTAIN   born ca 1804; 1m. Maria A. TUCKER 12 June 1832
       JOSHUA   (she born ca 1798; died 7 Sept 1834, age 36)
                          2m. Jane B. ___?__ after 1834 (she born ca 1803; died 21 Feb 1877, aged 74)
                          died 30 May 1857, age 53; buried Harmony Grove Cemetery, Portsmouth, NH

179. ELIZABETH/BETSEY-6 DRISCO, sister of above, was born ca 1778; baptized 15 June 1778. She married Captain William TREFETHEN, Jr. on 18 Dec 1799 at Portsmouth, NH. He was the son of William TREFETHEN (Captain Abraham; Henry; Henry) and Lucretia JONES, and was born ca 1768; died 29 Aug 1830 (drowned at Portsmouth, age 62) . Elizabeth-6 DRISCO died at Portsmouth 12 Nov 1850/51.

Captain William TREFETHEN had a considerable estate when he died. Listed were: a mansion house and other buildings on Pleasant St, Portsmouth; a house, land and wharf on Liberty Street; as well as a 1/16 share of DRISCO's Wharf; a 1/5 share in the house and land of Samuel TREFETHEN (a brother); and ¼ of land held in common with his wife.

He was known to have had a ½ interest in the Schooner *LORENZO* (1823-30), and 1/3 interest in the Schooner *JOHN GILMAN* (1825-30). He was also the master of the Schooner *INDUSTRY* (ca 1793); and the Schooner *PINK* (ca 1820).

Children of Elizabeth-6 DRISCO and Captain William TREFETHEN:
  Surname TREFETHEN
  575. Elizabeth Maria   born ca 1803; married Daniel HAM ca 8 May 1831; died 22 Feb 1887
  576. James Drisco   born ca 1806; died Oct 1817   EOL
+ 577. WILLIAM   born ca 1809/10; married Elsa-6 HALEY ; d p 9 Sept 1852 Dover, NH
  578. Lucretia Jones   born 4 May 1813; died 29 Mar 1892 , buried Portsmouth, NH
                          married Archibald Andrew PETERSON ** 14/16 Dec 1837 Portsmouth, NH
                          (he son o/ Adrian/Andrew PETERSON and Frances _?_)
                          (he born 18 Jan 1814 Portsmouth, NH; died 12 Oct 1874 NYC)

      **   Note: In 1834 Archibald PETERSON was a Navy Yard employee in Portsmouth.
                He and his wife removed to New York City ca 1838. He became the proprietor of
                the WALTON HOUSE HOTEL there, located on Franklin Square.

The Seventh American Generation

188. SAMUEL COPPS-7 RICKER, son of Elijah-6 RICKER (Sobriety-5 NOCK/KNOX; Samuel-4; Sarah-3 DRISKO; John-2) and Hannah COPPS, was born 18 Mar 1808 at Lebanon, Maine. He married Annis P. BRIGGS ca 1833. She was the daughter of Rufus BRIGGS and Elizabeth __?__; and was born ca 1812 Detroit, Somerset, ME; died 2 Jan 1883 at Cambridge, MA. Samuel-7 RICKER died 30 July 1880 at Corning, New York.

Children of Samuel Copps-7 RICKER and Annis BRIGGS:
Surname RICKER (all born Detroit, Somerset County, Maine)
579. Charles Augustus born 29 Sept 1834; married Eliza A. SAWYER 15 Dec 1867 IL
  2 children: Ora N-9 RICKER born ca 1868, d y ; Ella L-9 RICKER born 1869, d y
580. Loretta born 9 June 1836; died 16 May 1862
581. Vesta A. born 26 Mar 1842; married Edwin A. MacALLISTER 23 Nov 1863
  1 child: Edward B. MacALLISTER born 31 Dec 1864; married Emma POTTLE
582. Eri S. born 21 June 1844
583. Elizabeth A. born 4 Mar 1850; married George W. NEWMAN 27 Sept 1870
584. Henry R. born 24 Mar 1854; died young

189. ZIMRI-7 RICKER, brother of above, was born 29 Oct 1809 at Lebanon, Maine. He married Caroline D. PARKS on 26 April 1836 at Pittsfield, Maine. She was born 8 June 1811; died 18 Mar 1897 at Boston, MA. Zimri-7 RICKER died 11 July 1880.

Children of Zimri-7 RICKER and Caroline PARKS:
Surname RICKER
585. Oliver Parks born 18 Jan 1837 Pittsfield, Somerset, ME.
  1m. Mary E. WEBSTER; 2m. Emeline TOLMAN Eastman
586. Darius L. born 25 Dec 1838; died 30 June 1862 unmarried EOL
  (killed in the **Civil War** at New Market Crossroads, VA ; served Co. D, 34th Infantry Reg. PA)
587. Elijah A. born 8 July 1841; married Ida M. ROSS 25 Dec 1874
  1 child: Alice B-9 RICKER born 3 Apr 1876; married Philip GREIN; res. CA.
588. Benjamin Franklin born 30 Nov 1844; married Mary Emma NASON 7 Mar 1883
  1 child: Arthur M-9 RICKER born 28 Dec 1883; died unmarried
589. Isabella C. born 27 Aug 1847; married William LOUDON ca 1886, CA
  died 8 Jan 1903 San Francisco, CA (1 child: Mary-9 LOUDON)
590. Theodosia Viola born 26 June 1851; 1m. Ira McCAUSLAND 11 Oct 1873
  2m. Edwin H. GAY 23 Dec 1884
  1 child: Carrie M-9 GAY born 18 Dec 1885; married Clifford SLOCUM
591. Christopher Eugene born 18 Dec 1855; married Ann MILLER 1885, MA
  Twin daughters: Bertha Lillian-9 and _?_-9 RICKER born 15 Oct 1886; d y

190. ELIJAH-7 RICKER, Jr. , brother of above, was born 10 June 1810/11 at Lebanon, ME. He married Mary CLEMENTS on 4 July 1838. She was the dau/of Eben CLEMENTS and Margaret LORD, and was born 9 Sept 1820; died 29 Apr 1900. Elijah-7 RICKER, Jr. died 6 Jan 1880 at Detroit, Somerset Co., ME.

Children of Elijah-7 RICKER, Jr. and Mary CLEMENTS:
Surname RICKER (all born Detroit, Somerset Co., Maine)
592. Hannah Clementine born 14 Feb 1841; married Graham F. FORD
  3 children: George-9, Joseph-9 and Mary-9 FORD
593. Mary Emma born 2 Jan 1846; died 7 Oct 1922 unmarried EOL
594. Edgar born 21 June 1848; died 18 June 1878 unmarried EOL
+ 595. ALFRED LESLIE born 19 Jan 1855; 1m. Mary Eleanor WILLARD 3 Sept 1879
  2m. Leila Ada WORCESTER 27 July 1903
596. Ina Rosalina born 27 Dec 1856; died 5 Sept 1932 unmarried EOL

Children of Elijah-7 RICKER, Jr., continued:
    Surname RICKER
    597. Idella Augusta   born 6 Feb 1859; died 19 May 1948 Melrose, MA unmarried EOL
+ 598. WILBUR ELIJAH born 12 Sept 1861; married Lillian Beatrice GAY 24 Feb 1870

192. GEORGE-7 RICKER, brother of above, was born 6 Aug 1814 at Lebanon, Maine. He married
Hannah LEARY ca 1852 at Mobile, Alabama.

Children of George-7 RICKER and Hannah LEARY:
    Surname RICKER
    599. William Henry   born 22 July 1853   600. Elijah D.   born 15 Jan 1856 Mobile, AL

193. MOSES-7 RICKER, brother of above, was born 19 June 1816 at Lebanon, Maine. He married
Hannah KENT ca ___ at Wakefield, New Hampshire. She was born 23 Apr 1828; died 12 Nov 1885.
Moses-7 RICKER died 3 Apr 1887.

Children of Moses-7 RICKER and Hannah KENT:
    Surname RICKER
    601. Fanny   born ca 1844; still living 1916 Roxbury, MA
    602. William   born ca 1847; married Elmira-8 RICKER 23 Apr 1874, NH (# 617)
            (she dau/o Eli R-7 RICKER (# 201) and 2w. Dorcas JACOBS) (she born 1854; died ____)
                died before 1883, no issue   EOL

195. LEWIS DOWNS-7 RICKER, brother of above, was born 3 Aug 1820 at Lebanon, Maine. He married
Eliza Jane HARTFORD on 23 May 1851 at Lebanon. She was the daughter of ____ HARTFORD and _?_,
and was born ____; died ____. Lewis-7 RICKER died 17 Sept 1884.

Children of Lewis Downs-7 RICKER and Eliza Jane HARTFORD:
    Surname RICKER
    603. Sarah J.   born 6 Aug 1851; died 6 Apr 1857   EOL
    604. Wilson   born 6 Mar 1853; died 7 Feb 1936 , NH
                            possibly married Cora B. PLACE 30 Mar 1883 NH
    605. Lorana   born 26 June 1855; married Frederick R. BUTLER 4 Dec 1882, NH

197. WILLIAM-7 RICKER, son of Moses-6 RICKER, Jr. (Sobriety-5 NOCK/KNOX; Samuel-4; Sarah-3
DRISKO; John-2) and Sally HANSON, was born 29 Mar 1807 at Lebanon, Maine. He married Martha D.
ELLIS at Rochester, NH. They resided at Milton, NH. He was a farmer, and died ca June 1869.

Children of William-7 RICKER and Martha ELLIS:
    Surname RICKER
+ 606. ISAAC   born 1831; 1m. Rosetta TYLER 17 Sept 1853, Maine (divorced)
                          2m. Ellen J. HOLMES 18 Mar 1861, NH (she from Dover, NH)
+ 607. WILLIAM   born 1833; married Harriet M. ELLIS 27 Jan 1858, MA
                          (she dau/o Isaac ELLIS and Charlotte HARTFORD)
+ 608. MARTHA ANN   born 7 Jan 1837; married Christopher HUSSEY 26 July 1857 at Sanford, ME.
                          died 1Oct 1905 Alfred, Maine
    609. Sarah E.   born 1839; married David S. WILLEY int pub May 1858
+ 610. LEWIS   born 15 Apr 1843; died 2 May 1923 Rochester, NH
                          married Mary J. LITTLEFIELD 25 Jan 1867 Somersworth, NH (div 1905)
    611. Phoebe F.   born 1846; married Daniel ELLIS 1 Nov 1869 Dover, NH

201. ELI R-7 RICKER, brother of above, was born ca 1819 at Lebanon, ME. He married 1st to Maria
JACOBS, int pub 8 Oct 1837. She died before 1839, and he married 2nd to Dorcas JACOBS on 6 July
1839 at Sanford, ME. She was the dau/ of George JACOBS, and was born 18 Apr 1819; died 28 Oct 1905.

Children of Eli R-7 RICKER and Dorcas JACOBS:
Surname RICKER

612. Mary Abby	born 1840; 1m. Seth SYLVESTER 8 Nov 1859	
	2m. Simon BENNETT 12 June 1864; 3m. Horace TAYLOR	
613. Emma Caroline	born 1842; married Jackson COLBATH 26 May 1861	
614. George H.	born 1844	
615. Susan	born 1846	
616. Moses H.	born 31 Aug 1850; died 12 Oct 1920 Sanford, Maine	
	married Lillian A. PATCH 20 Feb 1882 (she born ____; died 7 Feb 1944, NH)	
+ 617. ELMIRA	born 1854; 1m. William-8 RICKER 23 Apr 1874 (# 602)	
	2m. Thomas BLAISDELL 13 Mar 1883	
618. Miriam	born 1859; 1m. __?__; 2m. __?__ CLARK; 3m. Frank KRUG, Jr. 5 Oct 1921	

202. DANIEL-7 GRANT, son of Mercy-6 RICKER (Sobriety-5 NOCK/KNOX; Samuel-4; Sarah-3 DRISKO; John-2) and Captain Daniel GRANT, was born 22 Aug 1806 at Lebanon, Maine. He married Susan FOSS on 13 Dec 1827. She was the daughter of _?_ FOSS, and was born 5 June 1806; died ____. Daniel-7 GRANT died ____.

Children of Daniel-7 GRANT and Susan FOSS:
Surname GRANT   (all children born Lebanon, Maine)

619. Susan Elizabeth	born 19 Nov 1828; married ___ BEAN ca 1846-48
Ch: surname BEAN	George born ca 1848
+ 620. LEWIS	born 19 Dec 1829; 1m. Augusta Ann ROLLINS 10 Dec 1848 NY
	(she born 18__ Saco, ME; died bef 1860)
	2m. Mary Jane SANBORN (she born ca 1839 NH; died before 1870)
621. Lois	born 10 Feb 1831; married John W. SPAULDING of Biddeford, ME
+ 622. SOLOMON	born 22 Sept 1832; married Almira R. MANSON 13 June 1853
+ 623. MERCY/MARIA	born 10 July 1834; married Charles Freeman HAYES 20 Aug 1854
+ 624. JOHN	born 1 Apr 1836; died 24 Jan 1910 Berwick, York, ME
625 Delia Ann	born 15 Jan 1841; poss died young
+ 626. DANIEL	born 7 Mar 1843; married Frances A. STERRETT 6 Aug 1869
627. Martha (twin)	born 4 Apr 1845; poss died young
628. Mary (twin)	born 4 Apr 1845; poss died young
+ 629. CAROLINE A.	born 22 May 1848; married William BENNETT 24 July 1867

206. DEPENDANCE-7 GRANT, brother of above, was born 10 Dec 1813 at Lebanon, ME. He married Mercy-5 HARTFORD on 13 Nov 1835 at Lebanon, ME. She was the daughter of Eliakim-4 HARTFORD (Solomon-3; Stephen-2; Nicholas-1) and Charity PERKINS, and was born 29 May 1819 at Crawford Notch, NH; died ____. Dependance –7 GRANT died 12 Nov 1863 (49-11-2 g s) at Lebanon, Maine. His widow married second Jeremiah SHOREY.

Children of Dependance-7 GRANT and Mercy HARTFORD:
Surname GRANT

630. Lucy	born ca 1836, Maine.
631. Martha Maria	born ca 1842, ME; married Charles F. ELLIS 26 May 1868 Rochester, NH

209. EZEKIEL-7 RICKER, son of Jedediah-6 RICKER (Dorothy-5 NOCK/KNOX; Samuel-4; Sarah-3 DRISKO; John-2) and Sarah/Sally LORD, was born 9 May 1807. He married Joanna W. ROBERTS on 20 Nov 1831. She was the daughter of George ROBERTS and Mary ROBERTS, and was born 5 Nov 1811; died 29 Apr 1894. Ezekiel-7 RICKER died 22 Mar 1857 at Somersworth, NH.

Children of Ezekiel-7 RICKER and Joanna ROBERTS:
Surname RICKER

632. Lydia E.	born 24 Aug 1832; died 27 Mar 1913

Children of Ezekiel-7 RICKER, continued:

    Surname RICKER

+ 633. JULIA A.   born 26 Jan 1834 Biddeford, ME; married William LIBBY 5 Feb 1855
  634. Harriet W. (twin) born 16 Nov 1835; died 8 Mar 1884 unmarried   EOL
  635. Martha S. (twin) born 16 Nov 1835 Somersworth, NH; married Robert N. MORRILL
                           died 17 Jan 1907
                           Three children: Harriet, Annie and Elnora (born 1869) MORRILL
  636. George B.   born 11 July 1838 Somerswoth, NH; died 21 Dec 1933
                           1m. Abigail MORRILL 29 Dec 1858 (she born ____ ; died Sept 1885)
                           2m. Adeline FORD Emmons 22 Dec 1886
                One child: George E-9 RICKER born 22 June 1872
  637. Mary W.   born 28 Mar 1840; married George JAMERIN 1865
  638. Ellen S.   born 16 Dec 1841; married Edwin A. GOODWIN
                One child: Irving W-9 GOODWIN born ca 1863; married Margaret J. McKANE 1894
+ 639. WILLIAM LORD   born 24 July 1843 Somersworth, NH; married Sarah A. FRENCH 16 Apr 1867
                           (she born 22 Mar 1844, NH; died 27 Nov 1918, MA)
                           died 5 Jan 1929 Worcester, MA.
+ 640. NATHANIEL   born 22 Mar 1846 Biddeford, ME; married Cinda Ella GRANT 10 Mar 1868
       CLEMENT M.   (she born ____ ; died 5 July 1940, MA)
           (twin)   died 25 June 1914 Haverhill, MA
  641. James A. (twin)   born 22 Mar 1836 ; died 15 May 1864 , killed in the **Civil War**
  642. Fannie A.   born 30 Sept 1850

216. LEONARD-7 RICKER, son of Samuel-6 RICKER (Dorothy-5 NOCK/KNOX; Samuel-4; Sarah-3 DRISKO; John-2) and Polly FOSS, was born 12 June 1819 at Milton, NH. He married first to Lydia M. EDGERLY on 12 Apr 1838. His second wife was Mary Jane WITHAM, who died ca 1866. He married third to Joanna M. GRANT.

Children of Leonard-7 RICKER and Lydia M. EDGERLY:

    Surname RICKER   (all born Milton, NH)
  643. Herbert O.   born 10 Feb 1844; married Sarah A. BOLO 26 Aug 1873
  644. Julia E.   born 7 Feb 1845; died 29 Jan 1891
  645. Arabella C.   born 1847; married Asa WYATT 17 Oct 1874
                           One child: Emma-9 WYATT born 1876; married Herbert S. GLIDDEN
  646. David S.   born 1849; married Georgianna MERRILL 17 Apr 1880

Child of Leonard-7 RICKER and Mary Jane WITHAM:

    Surname RICKER
  647. Imogene   born 2 Aug 1866 at Dover, NH.

Children of Leonard-7 RICKER and Joanna GRANT:

    Surname RICKER
  648. Jennie   born 1867; married Oscar F. HALL 14 Jan 1886
  649. Charles   born 10 Mar 1869; died young
  650. Ida May   born 3 Feb 1872; died 22 Sept 1872
  651. Charles Lewis   born 28 July 1877; 1m. Sarah CARTER 6 Apr 1904 Haverhill, MA.
                           (she born ____ ; died 25 Jan 1910); 2m. Ruth MARSHALL
        2 children: Charles L-9 RICKER, Jr. born 29 Mar 1904 and Gladys M-9 RICKER born July 1905

217. LOUISA ANN-7 RICKER, sister of above, was born 6 Nov 1822 at Milton, NH. She married Luther Dearborn TREFREN on 25 Aug 1845. He was born 8 Aug 1817 at Alton, NH; and died 19 Nov 1907 at Ashland, Oregon. Louisa-7 RICKER died there 13 Nov 1910.

Children of Louisa-7 RICKER and Luther TREFREN:

    Surname TREFREN
  652. Mary Walker born 5 June 1836 Milton, NH   653. Olive Josephine born 8 Dec 1848; died Jan 1851

Children of Louisa-7 RICKER, continued:
   Surname TREFREN

654. George Kelley	born 16 Sept 1852; married Mary Frances JONES 1880 NE
	died Aug 1940 Ashland, Oregon
655. Luther Smith	born 6 Nov 1854 Milton, NH; married Julia K. GREEN 21 Oct 1878 NE
	One child: Olive Marie-9 TREFREN born 3 Sept 1904
656. Levi Woodbury	born 11 Nov 1857; died 20 May 1863 , NH

227. LUCY-7 RICKER, daughter of John-6 RICKER (Lucy-5 CROMWELL; Esther-4 NOCK/KNOX; Sarah-3 DRISKO; John-2) and Elizabeth PINKHAM, and was born 179_. She married James BRAGDON on 17 Nov 1813 at Milton, NH.

Children of Lucy-7 RICKER and James BRAGDON:
   Surname BRAGDON

657. Alonzo born ____marr. Ann PALMER	659. William	born ____
658. Betsey P. born ____	660. Hannah Lois born ____; married William ELLIS

230. ESTHER-7 RICKER, sister of above, was born 18 Feb 1809. She married Luther GILE on 27 May 1830 at Rochester, NH. He was the son of David GILE and Mary WOOD, and was born 9 Apr 1807 at Plaistow, NH; died ____. Esther-7 RICKER died ____.

Children of Esther-7 RICKER and Luther GILE:
   Surname GILE   (all born Plaistow, NH)

661. George Winslow	born 11 May 1837	663. Elvira Lorentina	born 30 June 1844
662. David Washington	born 31 Jan 1842		

234. SABRINA-7 RICKER, daughter of Elias-6 RICKER (Lucy-5 CROMWELL; Esther-4 NOCK/KNOX; Sarah-3 DRISKO; John-2) and Mary M. WITHERILL, was born 16 May 1802 at Lebanon, ME. She married Daniel LARRABEE on 31 Jan 1831. He was the son of John LARRABEE and Susan LARRABEE, and was born 1 July 1805; a ships' carpenter. Sabrina-7 at Gardiner, ME on 27 Feb 1882.

Children of Sabrina-7 RICKER and Daniel LARRABEE:
   Surname LARRABEE

664. Satira J.   born 25 Nov 1831; married William S. HANSCOM; died Sept 1905 (4 ch)
665. James M.   born 4 Dec 1833; married Priscilla WOODARD Sept 1855; res Gardiner, ME (9 ch)

235. EZRA KIMBALL-7 RICKER, brother of above, was born 29 Sept 1805. He married Mary March MARR on 23 June 1831. She was the daughter of _?_ MARR, and was born 25 Aug 1804. Ezra-7 died 1 Mar 1840 at Wells, ME. Mary married second Henry-5 RICKER, son of William-4 RICKER (Richard-3; Maturin-2; George-1) and Amy HOBBS.

Children of Ezra-7 RICKER and Mary M. MARR:
   Surname RICKER

666. Sophia Jane	born 25 June 1832	668. Andrew Jackson born 26 Sept 1836
667. Rebecca Alexandra	born 5 June 1834; died 8 Dec 1843	

236. DANIEL CROMWELL-7 RICKER, brother of above, was born 27 Feb 1808. He married Caroline HIGGINS on 4 July 1836. She was the daughter of Nathaniel HIGGINS and __?__ of Avon, ME. and was born 4 July 1814; died 13 Nov 1888 at Lynn, MA. Daniel-7 RICKER, a farmer, died 10 Jan 1869 at Avon. .

Children of Daniel-7 RICKER and Caroline HIGGINS:
   Surname RICKER

669. Sarepta	born 23 Oct 1839; married Robert HAYES 3 Nov 1863
	2 children: Alva Ricker-9 HAYES and Wentworth Larrabee-9 HAYES

Children of Daniel-7 RICKER, continued:
  Surname RICKER
  670. Delphina Lucy   born 20 June 1841; married James E. Frederick BALLARD 1871
+ 671. NATHANIEL H.   born 25 Apr 1843; married Josephine ROMAINE 22 June 1865
  672. Mary Witherill   born 15 Mar 1845; died 6 June 1876
  673. Sarah Mitchell   born 27 June 1847; married Stephen Jabez DOW 16 Nov 1868
                          3 children: David Elwin-9 DOW; Stephen Ricker-9 DOW and Daisy-9 DOW
  674. Caroline   born 18 Apr 1850; married Joseph O.P. MEYERS 1 Jan 1873
                          1 child: Edwin-9 MEYERS
+ 675. DANIEL L.   born 21 June 1852; married Elizabeth Agnes O'CONNOR 12 Feb 1885
+ 676. JENNIE SABRINA born 4 Apr 1855; married Benjamin Emery PRATT 28 Nov 1873 Avon
+ 677. XARISSA   born 9 May 1857; married Raymond C. ROSS 6 Sept 1875, Maine

239. ISAIAH-7 RICKER, son of Daniel-6 RICKER (Lucy-5 CROMWELL; Esther-4 NOCK/KNOX; Sarah-3 DRISKO; John-2) and Elizabeth EMERY, was born 14 July 1804 at Monroe, Maine. He married Charlotte BOWEN ca 18__. She was the daughter of Nathan BOWEN and Polly HOLMES, and was born 20 Nov 1808; died 25 Nov 1892 at Berwick, ME. Isaiah-7 died 13 Sept 1858 and is buried Monroe, Maine.

Children of Isaiah-7 RICKER and Charlotte BOWEN:
  Surname RICKER
  678. Mary A.   born 16 Feb 1826; died 3 Feb 1859 unmarried   EOL
  679. Elizabeth   born 27 May 1827; died ____ unmarried   EOL
  680. Charlotte   born 25 Dec 1828; married Captain William G. SNOW 28 June 1857
                         (he of Bucksport, Maine) no issue   EOL
  681. Margaret C.   born 20 May 1831; died ____ Lowell, MA.
  682. Lorenzo D.   born 25 Apr 1833; died 2 Feb 1865 , killed in the **Civil War**
  683. Affia Anney   born 22 May 1835; married Edwin M. HAM 11 June 1857 Monroe, Maine
                         (he 2m. her sister Adelaide (# 687 below)
                         2 children: Ida F-9 HAM and Florence Edith-9 HAM
  684. Levi B.   born 17 Feb 1837; died 3 Feb 1859 unmarried   EOL
  685. Lovina B.   born 7 Sept 1839; married Otis J. GETCHELL
                         3 children: Winnie-9, d y; Flora V-9; and Blanche-9 GETCHELL
  686. Freeman Dennis   born 21 Sept 1841
  687. Adelaide R.   born 1 Nov 1843; married Edwin M. HAM (as his 2nd wife)
  688. Francis B.   born 1848   689. Sarah J. born 15 Oct 1850; died 24 Oct 1865

241. REV. SIMEON EMERY-7 RICKER , brother of above, was born 28 Sept 1808. He married Mary Ann HODGKINS of Ellsworth, Maine ca 18__. He was a Baptist minister

Children of Rev Simeon-7 RICKER and Mary Ann HODGKINS:
  Surname RICKER
  690. Trafton G.   born 31 Dec 1833 Waldo, ME; 1m. Elizabeth Jane STURTEVANT
                          (she born ____; died 1871) 2m. Mrs. Catherine ___ Johnson 23 Dec 1872
                          (removed to Wright County, MN)
          References: History of the Upper Mississippi Valley by Edward NEILL, pub 1881; and History of Wright Co., MN 1915.
  691. Mary Ann   born 1836; 1m. Albion McLARES; 2m. George COOMBS
                         3 children: Vernon-9, Fred-9 and Oscar-9 COOMBS; all died before 1914
  692. Hannah Elizabeth born 1839
  693. Merritt Caldwell born 1841
+ 694. JENNIE PHOEBE born 14 Aug 1844; 1m. Joseph H. GRANT; 2m. John D. WELCH;
                         3m. Captain Stephen RICKER; and 4m. Jacob STRANGE
  695. Willard Samuel   born ____
  696. Fannie E.   born ____
  697. Shepard Marshall born ____; resided Elk River, MN

243.   BENJAMIN D-7 RICKER, brother of above, was born 15 Sept 1813. He married Sophronia BRANCH ca 18___. She was born at Waterville, ME. ca 18_. He served in the **Civil War** and died 18 Sept 1887 at Chelsea, MA.

Children of Benjamin-7 RICKER and Sophronia BRANCH:
      Surname RICKER
+ 698. ALONZO E.   born 25 Nov 1835 Monroe, ME; died 17 Apr 1902 Oakfield, Maine
                          1m. Annie FOSTER; 2m. Louisa BROWN Johnson 1894
   699. Milton H.   born 17 June 1839; married Emily F. NORTON
                          died 23 Apr 1919 Old Orchard, Maine
                          1 child: John M-9 RICKER born June 1882; died 22 May 1892
   700. Charles   born 2 Oct 1841 Glenburn, ME; married Harriet N. PLUMMER 3 Sept 1865
   701. William G.   born 1 Oct 1843 Bangor, ME; died 4 Feb 1914 Togus, Maine
                          1m. Matilda N. SHOREY 17 June 1866; 2m. Lucy HOSLEN Hunt 15 July 1908
   702. Melissa   born 2 Mar 1846 Glenburn, Maine
   703. Georgia Anna   born 29 Jan 1849; married Joseph JONES
+ 704. ORREN   born 10 Apr 1850; 1m. Annie LAMBERT (divorced)
                          2m. Flora M. GOWEN 13 Sept 1883 (she born ____; died 25 Feb 1938)
                          died 23 Apr 1933 Chelsea, MA.

244.   DANIEL-7 RICKER, Jr., brother of above, was born 15 Sept 1813. He married first to __?__. She died at Bangor, Maine on 18 Jan 1836. His second marriage was to Elizabeth METCALFE before 1850. She was born 3 Apr 1824; died 23 Mar 1888. Daniel-7 died 9 Oct 1895 at Avon, Maine.

Children of Daniel-7 RICKER, Jr. and Elizabeth METCALFE:
      Surname RICKER
+ 705. AUGUSTA   born ca 1850 Frankfort, ME; married Charles A. DOWNING 25 Jan 1875
                          died 29 Aug 1886 (childbirth)
   706. Annette E.   born 18 May 1852 Freeman, ME; married Charles M. FOSS; died 5 Apr 1914
                          1 child: Charles G-9 FOSS born 1888; married Clarissa ELLSWORTH
   707. Martha   born 1855; died young

249.   ROBERT-7 RICKER, brother of above, was born 22 Apr 1828. His first wife was Mary H. WEED. She was born ca 18__; died 29 Nov 1875. His second wife was Anna ANDERSON of Pemberton, Maine. They were married 11 May 1904. Robert-7 RICKER, a tanner, died ca ____.

Children of Robert-7 RICKER and Mary H. WEED:
      Surname RICKER
   708. Georgianna   born 1849 Glenburn, ME; died before 1860
   709. Philena   born 1851; 1m. Charles OVERHOLT 1866; 2m. Roscoe GRAVES
   710. George W.   born 1853
   711. Mary E.   born 10 Aug 1856 Dexter, ME; married William H. GROVER
                          died 26 Feb 1913 Bangor, Maine
                          1 child: Edwin Albert-9 GROVER born ____ Glenburn, ME
                                             (changed his name to BROWN Oct 1869)
   712. Byron P.   born 1858; died 15 Nov 1895 Bangor, Maine
   713. Charles W.   born 1863 Monroe, ME; 1m. Olivia E. PHILLIPS 30 May 1892
                          2m. Catherine DELAY Dana 13 Apr 1915
                          1 child: Harry Phillips-9 RICKER born 25 Mar 1892; died 26 Mar 1892

251.   SYRENA B-7 RICKER, daughter of Eliphalet-6 RICKER (Lucy-5 CROMWELL; Esther-4 NOCK/KNOX; Sarah-3 DRISKO; John-2) and Mercy HANSON, was born 2 Oct 1807. She married Oliver JEPSON on 25 Nov 1829. He was born ca 18__; died 1 May 1856. She married second to Gilbert ALDRICH on 25 Aug 1858 at China, Maine. She died 18 July 1886.

Children of Syrena-7 RICKER and Oliver JEPSON:
    Surname JEPSON
    714. Elizabeth B.   born 22 Aug 1830; married Samuel EVANS; died 19 Mar 1893   EOL
    715. Eli   born 25 July 1832; (1 ch: Herbert-9 JEPSON born 21 Apr 1859; died 29 Nov 1898)
                    1m. Clara C. RUNNELS (she died 13 Sept 1872); 2m. Martha C. VARNEY
    716. Mary F.   born 26 July 1834; died 15 Oct 1859 unmarried   EOL
    717. Lucy Ann   born 2 Sept 1839; married Joseph C. COOMBS (2 children)
    718. Flavilla   born 9 Oct 1841; married George E. ROBERTS
    719. Lois Maria   born 4 Feb 1844; married Lindley JONES; died 4 Jan 1917

254. SOPHRONIA-7 RICKER, sister of above, was born 9 Jan 1815. She married Hugh GETCHELL, Jr. ca 1832. He was the son of Captain Hugh GETCHELL and Mary RIDEOUT, and was born 24 May 1809; died 29 July 1885 at Litchfield, Maine. Sophronia died there 26 Apr 1876.

Children of Sophronia-7 RICKER and Hugh GETCHELL, Jr.:
    Surname GETCHELL
    720. Lydia Arvilla   born 30 Mar 1833; married A. P. HALL; died Mar 1896 Spokane, WA
    721. LaVendee Augusta born 7 Jan 1835; married Edward E. ROBBINS; died 20 Nov 1912 Bath, ME.
    722. Mary Melvina   born 2 Apr 1837; 1m. Simeon HIGGINS; 2m. Hathaway FICKETT
                    died 18 Feb 1917 Litchfield, Maine
    723. Dora Cecelia   born 6 Feb 1840; married John GILL; died Sept 1885, SD
    724. Albert Dane   born 26 May 1843; married Julia SAVAGE 28 Mar 1868

256. JOHN HANSON-7 RICKER, brother of above, was born 9 May 1820 at Vassalboro, ME. He married Ellen CONY McDavid on 12 Dec 1854 at Augusta, ME. She was the daughter of Samuel CONY, and was born 14 Mar 1829; died 17 May 1898 at Waterville, ME. John H-7 RICKER died 3 Feb 1894 at Augusta.

Children of John-7 RICKER and Ellen CONY (McDavid):
    Surname RICKER
    725. Julia S.   born 7 Apr 1857; married Charles A. BROWN 17 Mar 1874
                    died 4 Oct 1912 Augusta, ME (2 ch: Grace E-9 and Mary L-9 BROWN)
    726. Charles Wesley   born 5 Sept 1859; married Elizabeth D. ACHORN 11 Sept 1878
                    (she dau/o Herman ACHORN and Mercina J. LERMON)
                    died 7 May 1931   (Child : Leonard F-9 RICKER born 20 Mar 1879)
    727. George E.   born 12 July 1861; died 25 June 1921 Bangor, Maine
                    married Margaret WHITTINGHAM (she born 23 Oct 1862; died _____)
           2 children: George E-9 (born 1886) and Ralph E-9 RICKER (born 3 July 1887)
    728. Mary C.   born ca 1864; died ca 1871
    729. Sarah W.   born 1 Jan 1866; married Charles D. PLUMMER 27 July 1887
                    (he born 21 Dec 1844 Richmond, Maine)
           1 child: Remington Gaubert-9 PLUMMER born 22 Mar 1888
    730. Joseph G.   born 23 Feb 1870; 1m. Edith FENNIMORE Johnson 26 Apr 1897
           2m. Theresa L. ELLIS 25 Feb 1908; 3m. Irene DURGIN Stevens 26 June 1925
           1 child: Alice Irene-9 RICKER born 20 Nov 1908

265. LUCY JANE-7 RICKER, daughter of Paul-6 RICKER (Lucy-5 CROMWELL; Esther-4 NOCK/ KNOX ; Sarah-3 DRISKO; John-2) and Elizabeth HAYES, was born 13 Oct 1821. She married George D. PIKE on 14 Dec 1843 at Chelsea, MA. She died 18 Nov 1887 at Rochester, NH.

Children of Lucy-7 RICKER and George PIKE:
    Surname PIKE
    731. Flora born ___; married Arthur RICHARDSON   734. Charles E. born 25 Feb 1845;
    732. Lizzie born ___; married Charles HOYT   died 27 Jan 1909
    733. Mary Abbie   born 1850; married George A. BLACKMAN; died 26 June 1917 Portland, ME

266. DANIEL J-7 RICKER, brother of above, was born 9 Mar 1824. He married Mary Ann HUTCHINS ca 18__. She was born 19 Jan 1826; died 27 Sept 1896 at Chelsea, MA. He died there 21 Jan 1891.

Children of Daniel J-7 RICKER and Mary Ann HUTCHINS:

Surname RICKER	(all born Chelsea, MA)
735. Julia	born 2 Mar 1845; died 9 Feb 1851
736. George	born May 1847; died 14 Feb 1851
737. Susan C.	born 9 May 1850; died 23 Feb 1851
738. Charles W.	born 7 Apr 1852; 1m. Caroline G. RYDER, MA.; died 3 Jan 1918
	(she born ____; died 5 Mar 1912 Chelsea, MA); 2m. Anna W. CORBETT
	2 children: Frank F-9 (born Nov 1873) and Gertrude-9 RICKER born 1882; d y
739. Ella M.	born 18 Aug 1854
+ 740. WALTER P.	born 12 Oct 1863; married Mary Arvie HASKELL 29 Oct 18__ MA
	died 15 June 1925 Everett, MA.

267. GEORGE DEXTER-7 RICKER, brother of above, was born 31 Oct 1826. He married Maria Mehitable MASON on 11 Nov 1851 at Boston, MA. She was born ca 18__; died 19 Mar 1885. He was a druggist and died 10 Dec 1881 at Boston, MA.

Children of George D-7 RICKER and Maria MASON:

Surname RICKER	
741. George Fabian	born 1856; married Marie F. HENLEY 1884
742. Isabel Harkins	born 1859; died 25 Oct 1910 Newton Highlands, MA.
	married John GLOVER, Jr. 12 Sept 1878 (he born ca 18__; died 12 June 1922)
	3 ch: Abbie-9 GLOVER, Mildred-9 GLOVER and John-9 GLOVER

271. ELEANOR-7 RICKER, daughter of Captain Ebenezer-6 RICKER (Nathaniel-5; Mercy-4 NOCK/ KNOX; Sarah-3 DRISKO; John-2) and Lucy FROST, was born 10 Oct 1806, probably at Argyle, Nova Scotia. She married Robert SIMMS, Jr. of Plymouth, Nova Scotia on 8 June 1827 at Argyle. He was the son of Robert SIMMS and Mary RAPP, and was born 12 Apr 1792; died 20 Mar 1868. He was a shipbuilder and farmer. Eleanor-7 RICKER died 9 July 1865 at Plymouth, NS.

Children of Eleanor-7 RICKER and Robert SIMMS, Jr.:

Surname SIMMS	(all born Plymouth, Nova Scotia)
743. Ebenezer	born 11 Mar 1828; married Wealthy J. CROCKER 1854; died 1898
744. George W.	born 11 July 1829; married Martha ENSLOW 1856
+ 745. LYDIA ANN	born 12 Mar 1831; married PAUL-7 RICKER 20 Aug 1854 (# 288)
746. Jeremiah F.	born 2 Mar 1833; married Emily H. JOHNSON 1860
747. Ruth Ellen	born 22 Nov 1835; married James H. Van BUREN 1856
748. Maria	born 5 Jan 1837; married Weymouth HURLBERT 1863
749. Webster	born 11 Oct 1839; married Ellen J. SPINNEY 1863
750. Sophronia	born 31 Aug 1840; married Nehemiah CROCKER 1864
751. Nathaniel	born 24 Aug 1842; married Sarah A. HARDING 1867
752. Lucy	born 8 Oct 1844; married David Mc KAY
753. Catherine Kenton	born 19 May 1848; married John WHITEHOUSE 1870

272. ANDREW-7 RICKER, brother of above, was born 13 Aug 1809 at Argyle, Nova Scotia. He married there on 2 June 1846 to Elizabeth l. B. SIMMS. She was the daughter of Robert SIMMS and Lucy BARROWS, and was born 29 June 1819; died 29 June 1914. Andrew-7 RICKER, a shipbuilder and farmer, died at Argyle on 3 May 1892.

Children of Andrew-7 RICKER and Elizabeth SIMMS:

Surname RICKER	(all born Argyle, Nova Scotia)
+ 754. ELEANORA J.	born 17 Aug 1847; marr Elihu WHITEHOUSE 6 Oct 1867

Children of Andrew-7 RICKER, continued:
   Surname RICKER
   755. George Jackson   born 17 Aug 1849; died 25 Oct 1854
+ 756. ABNER JACKSON born 23 Apr 1858; married Fannie Sargent DOANE 6 Jan 1887
   757. James H.   born 12 Dec 1860; married Grace COOK 20 Aug 1891

275. SARAH-7 RICKER - see CAPTAIN ROBERT-6 RICKER (# 109)
276. ELIZABETH-7 RICKER, sister of above, was born 28 Mae 1819 at Argyle, NS. She married Jeremiah FROST there on 30 Jan 1846. He was the son of Jeremiah FROST and Eunice SPINNEY, and was born 28 July 1820; died 17 Oct 1877 at Knowlesville, NB. Elizabeth-7 RICKER died there Mar 1892.

Children of Elizabeth-7 RICKER and Jeremiah FROST:
   Surname FROST   (all born Argyle, Nova Scotia)
   758. Lois   born 17 Oct 1846; married William KENNEY 13 Nov 1868; died 10 Oct 1874
              1 ch: Elizabeth-9 KENNEY born 25 Sept 1871; married Abijah RANKIN 20 Nov 1899
   759. Lydia   born 24 June 1848; married David SWEENEY 24 Dec 1883 NB
              3 ch: Ida-9 born 1884; Albina-9 born 1886; and Norman-9 SWEENEY born 26 July 1888
   760. Parazanda   born 4 Aug 1850; 1m. Norman KENNEY 13 Dec 1874 NS
              2m. Maurice ROBBINS 6 May 1879 (no issue)
              died Oct 1912 Argyle, NS
   761. Elizabeth   born 10 July 1852; died 12 Dec 1852
   762. James G.   born 25 Nov 1853; married Zephora/Zipporah-8 MANGRUM 17 Mar 1878
              died 28 Mar 1906 NB   (she # 783)
   763. Calvin   born 10 Aug 1864; married Estella KENNEY (she dau/o James M. KENNEY)

277. EUNICE-7 RICKER, sister of above, was born 7 Mar 1821. She married Daniel SARGENT on 22 June 1843 at Argyle, Nova Scotia. He was the son of William SARGENT and Maria WORTHEN, and was born 5 June 1812; died 27 Feb 1900. He was a farmer and shipbuilder. Eunice-7 RICKER died 13 Nov 1889 at Argyle, NS.

Children of Eunice-7 RICKER and Daniel SARGENT:
   Surname SARGENT   (all born Argyle, NS)
   764. Andrew   born July 1846; married Alvah FORBES; died 17 May 1894 Glenwood, NS
             2 ch: Adelbert-9 (born 1875) and Albert-9 SARGENT (born 1877; died 1896)
   765. Martha   born Sept 1847; married W. W. FROST 11 Feb 1875 Argyle, NS
             died 29 Nov 1882 Argyle, NS
             3 ch: Theora-9 (born 1876); Lillian S-9 (born 1878) and Bessie-9 FROST (born 1881)
   766. Augusta   born 28 July 1851; married Benjamin CROWELL 11 Mar 1875 (# 797)
             (he son/o Uriah CROWELL and Maria RICKER)
             (he born 18 June 1843, NS; died _____)
   767. Wilson   born 11 Jan 1855; married ___?___
           3 ch : Rockhart B-9, born 1886; Percy E-9, born 1888; Herbert M-9 SARGENT, born 1890
   768. Robert M.   born 24 Apr 1858   769. Lavinia   born 29 Feb 1860

278. WILLIAM-7 RICKER, brother of above, was born 7 July 1824. He married first to Martha L. FROST ca Feb 1852 at Argyle, Nova Scotia. She was the daughter of Theodore K. FROST, and was born 15 Aug 1829; died 16 Feb 1867. His second marriage was to Susan RAYMOND on 28 Nov 1872. She was the daughter of Job RAYMOND and Phebe HATFIELD; and was born 13 Nov 1820; died _____ . William-7 RICKER, a sailor and shipbuilder, died 26 June 1896.

Children of William-7 RICKER and Martha FROST:
   Surname RICKER   (all born Argyle, NS)
+ 770. FLORENCE   born 21 Nov 1852; married Joseph R. GOODWIN 31 Dec 1875
      ASHTON   died 4 June 1902 Kemptville, NS

Children of William-7 RICKER, continued:
  Surname RICKER
+ 771. MATURIN MORSE   born 7 June 1855; married Alfaretta ROBERTS 1877 Argyle, NS
  772. Theodore Seth H.   born 4 Feb 1857; died 17 Nov 1892; unmarried   EOL
  773. Sarah Lennie   born 1 Jan 1861; died ____; unmarried   EOL

279. MARTHA-7 RICKER, sister of above, was born 15 Dec 1827. She married Freeman HURLBERT on 1 Nov 1857 at Kemptville, Nova Scotia. He was born 20 Mar 1826; died Dec 1893. Martha-7 RICKER died 30 Apr 1914 at Riverside, CA.

Children of Martha-7 RICKER and Freeman HURLBERT:
  Surname HURLBERT
  774. Frederick   born Oct 1858
  775. Etta   born 22 Dec 1860; married Frederick BRAGG Oct 1890   EOL
  776. Lelia   born 1866; married John S. FRANTZ 31 Aug 1906 CA.
  777. Lucinda   born 1868; married John DAWSON 3 July 1892
  778. Eva   born 1874; died 1892

281.   WILLIAM-7 MANGRUM, son of Elizabeth-6 RICKER (Nathaniel-5; Mercy-4 NOCK/KNOX; Sarah-3 DRISKO; John-2) and Solomon MANGRUM, was born 22 Nov 1821 at Plymouth, Nova Scotia. He married Sarah H. JONES on 20 June 1848 at Shelburne, NS. She was born 25 Mar 18828; died 25 Oct 1877 at Mainstream, New Brunswick. He died 9 Apr 1891 at Carlisle, New Brunswick.

Children of William-7 MANGRUM and Sarah JONES:
  Surname MANGRUM
  779. Elizabeth S.   born 7 Apr 1849 Kemptville, NS; married James GASCOYNE May 1869
        died 4 July 1880 Brighton, NS
  780. Susannah   born 13 Apr 1851 Kemptville; died 3 Nov 1878 Blaine, Maine
        married Albert SHAW Sept 1875 Bridgewater, Maine
  781. John Whitefield   born 4 Feb 1853 Kemptville; married Aramantha SHAW 2 Jan 1880, ME.
  782. Thomas William   born 3 Dec 1854 Kemptville; married Harriet CAMPBELL 27 July 1875
  783. Zipporah/Zephora   born Jan 1858 Argyle, NS; married James-7 FROST (# 762) Mainstream, NB
  784. Lucy A.   born 30 Jan 1860 Argyle; married Samuel ORSER Nov 1874
  785. Caroline   born 17 Mar 1861 Argyle; married Thomas McKENNA Hyde Park, MA.
  786. Phillip M.   born 4 Oct 1863 Mainstream, NB; died 4 Nov 1872   EOL
  787. Sarah J.   born 7 Apr 1864 Mainstream; married J. H. WHEATON Woodstock, NB
  788. Augusta   born 14 May 1866 Mainstream; married C. H. LUCE Hyde Park, MA.

283. **BENJAMIN-7 RICKER**, son of Benjamin-6 RICKER (Nathaniel-5; Mercy-4 NOCK/KNOX; Sarah-3 DRISKO; John-2) and Sarah FROST, was born 9 Oct 1819 at Eastport, Maine. He married Hannah W. BROOKS on 17 Nov 1842 at Eastport. She was born ca 1827; died 15 Oct 1883 at Eastport. Benjamin-7 RICKER was the Chief of Police there, and died 1 May 1879.

Children of Benjamin-7 RICKER and Hannah BROOKS:
  Surname RICKER
  789. Benjamin B.   born 4 Mar 1844; marr Susie S. PERKINS 4 Apr 1871; died 4 Sept 1885 Estpt
  790. Albert W.   born 24 Jan 1849; died 20 Jan 1850
  791. Eliphalet F.   born 25 Apr 1850; died 30 June 1887
        married Elizabeth A. HUNT McCafferty 4 May 1876
        (she dau/o Louis HUNT; she born 18__; died 7 Nov 1902)
  792. Beresford   born 27 Jan 1852; died 3 Feb 1853
  793. George W.   born 16 Oct 1854; died 23 Nov 1855
  794. Andrew F.   born ca 18__; died 6 July 1860
  795. Charles W.   born 13 Aug 1860; died 9 July 1865

Children of Benjamin-7 RICKER, continued:
   Surname RICKER
+ 796. CARRIE A.   born 17 Oct 1865; 1m. Alonzo H. FOUNTAIN 6 Apr 1881
                          (he born ca ____; died 23 June 1881); 2m. Benjamin V. BRADSHAW

284. MARIA-7 RICKER, sister of above, was born 5 Aug 1821. She married Sea Captain Uriah
CROWELL ca Jan 1837. He was the son of Daniel CROWELL and Experience ATWOOD, and was
born 4 Oct 1817; died 28 Sept 1898. Maria-7 RICKER died 22 Dec 1905.

Children of Maria-7 RICKER and Captain Uriah CROWELL:
   Surname CROWELL
   797. Benjamin L.   born 18 June 1843; married Augusta M-8 SARGENT 11 Mar 1875 (# 766)
                          (she dau/o Daniel SARGENT and Eunice-7 RICKER (# 277)
   798. Sarah Ellen   born 16 Sept 1845; married Emery FROST Feb 1866; died 10 Nov 1884
   799. Elizabeth   born 6 Dec 1847; married J. A. RAYNARD 10 Mar 1881
   800. Asa K.   born 13 May 1850; married Eliza HALSTEAD 16 Mar 1877
   801. George S.   born 22 Apr 1852; married Emily C. VICKERY 20 Sept 1892
   802. Rebecca   born 8 July 1855; married John HAYES 26 Dec 1874 Argyle, NS.
   803. Mary   born 13 Oct 1857; married James F. ROBERTS 1 Oct 1878
   804. Lois T.   born 23 Jan 1859; married William CROWELL 19 Jan 1881
                          died 5 Sept 1896 Argyle, NS.
   805. Phebe T.   born 13 Aug 1861; married Joseph M. PORTER 15 June 1883
              died 15 May 1893 (poss. from childbirth) 1 ch: Blanche-9 PORTER born 29 Apr 1893

285. LYDIA-7 RICKER, sister of above, was born 15 June 1823. She married Captain Andrew SMITH, of
Barrington, NS on 25 May 1844. He was the son of Aram SMITH and Abigail KENNEY, and was born 21
Mar 1819; died 1865. She went to sea with her husband, and her children were born there. She died 28
Aug 1866 at St. John's, New Brunswick.

Children of Lydia-7 RICKER and Captain Andrew SMITH:
   Surname SMITH
+ 806. MELINDA   born 29 May 1845; married Levi HOPKINS 12 Nov 1867
   807. Susan   born Feb 1847; died 1860 Rio de Janeiro
+ 808. ADELIA   born Sept 1849; married William Watson FROST 9 Sept 1887

287. LUCY ANN-7 RICKER - see DANIEL-6 RICKER (# 113)
288. PAUL-7 RICKER, brother of above, was born 25 Dec 1828. He married LYDIA ANN-8 SIMMS
(# 745) on 20 Aug 1854 at Argyle, NS. She was the daughter of Eleanor-7 RICKER (# 271) and Robert
SIMMS , and was born 12 Mar 1831; died 16 June 1893 Argyle, NS. Paul-7 died there on 12 June 1900.

Children of Paul-7 RICKER and Lydia Ann-8 SIMMS:
   Surname RICKER   (all born Argyle, NS)
   809. Odessa   born 28 May 1855; married Albert W. FROST 1 Jan 1878
   810. Frederick B.   born 4 Sept 1858; died 2 Apr 1859   EOL
   811. Frank   born 18 Feb 1860; died ____ unmarried EOL
   812. Stanley B.   born 25 July 1861; married Jeanette CROSBY 1 Jan 1888 NS
   813. Bowman Noyes   born 23 Feb 1864; married Daisy Alberta CHAPMAN 20 Nov 1900
                         One child: Murray Franklin-9 RICKER born 19 Sept 1901
   814. Sophronia   born 4 Aug 1866; married John W. RAYNARD 19 Dec 1901
                         died 20 May 1917 Raynardton, NS.

289. SYLVANUS-7 RICKER, brother of above, was born 20 Oct 1830. He married Sarah FROST on 14
Mar 1855 at Argyle, NS. She was the daughter of Jeremiah FROST and Eunice SPINNEY, and was born 1
Jan 1830; died 6 Jan 1886. Sylvanus-7 RICKER died 31 Mar 1906 at Glenwood, NS.

Children of Sylvanus-7 RICKER and Sarah FROST:
    Surname RICKER
   815. James D.   born 21 Jan 1857; died 20 Apr 1857
+ 816. ADA B.   born 28 Aug 1858; married Lemuel CROWELL 12 Dec 1885
   817. James Dexter   born 7 June 1861; died 3 July 1868
   818. Benjamin Lewis born 24 Jan 1863; died 16 Feb 1869
   819. Sarah   born 16 Nov 1864; died 3 Jan 1866
   820. Forrester   born 29 Aug 1866; married Mary A. CROSBY 2 Jan 1907
                One child: Amelia Adeline-9 RICKER born 17 Jan 1908
+ 821. GILES   born 23 Nov 1869; married Ella Maude GULLIVER 30 June 1897
   822. Jessie Curtis   born 26 Aug 1872; married Walter BARTLETT Sept 1903

291. OPHELIA-7 RICKER, daughter of Robert-6 RICKER (Paul-5; Mercy-4 NOCK/KNOX; Sarah-3 DRISKO; John-2) and Sarah-7 RICKER, was born 17 Dec 1838 at Argyle, NS. She married Captain Benjamin J. WHITEHOUSE ca 1861. He was born 15 Oct 1838. Ophelia-7 RICKER 2m. James FROST.

Children of Ophelia-7 RICKER and Benjamin WHITEHOUSE:
    Surname WHITEHOUSE
   823. Edna   born 17 Dec 1861; married Delancy ROBERTS; resided Neponset, MA.
   824. Doran   born 25 Nov 1863; died ___ , drowned at sea
   825. Robert S.   born 18 Sept 1868; died 5 May 1886 , drowned in the Argyle River

293. EVELENA-7 RICKER, sister of above, was born 12 Feb 1843. She married Captain Reuben GOODWIN on 26 July 1860 at Beverly, MA.

Children of Evelena-7 RICKER and Captain Reuben GOODWIN:
    Surname GOODWIN
   826. Clara E.   born 23 Sept 1861; married Leonard ROBERTS 6 Jan 1883; res. Block Is., NY
   827. Byron M.   born 10 Aug 1864; died 18 Aug 1865
   828. Mansfield   born 17 Sept 1866; died 6 July 1867
   829. Augusta B.   born 24 Sept 1871; married Emerson ROBERTS 16 Apr 1890
   830. Lindsey B.   born 30 July 1877; married Cornelia HINES 13 Feb 1901

304. JOTHAM-7 JOHNSTON, son of Margaret-6 RICKER (Paul-5; Mercy-4 NOCK/KNOX; Sarah-3 DRISKO; John-2) and John JOHNSTON, was born 7 Aug 1845 at Plymouth, Nova Scotia. He married Lydia LARKIN on 6 Feb 1867.

Children of Jotham-7 JOHNSTON and Lydia LARKIN:
    Surname JOHNSTON (all born Plymouth, NS)

| 831. Margaret J. | born 25 Apr 1869 | 833. Mary L. | born 27 Apr 1876 |
| 832. Ruth l. | born 21 Mar 1871 | 834. Lelia R. | born 15 Dec 1877; died 13 Apr 1906 |

308. MATTIE A-7 RICKER, daughter of John Knox-6 RICKER (Paul-5; Mercy-4 NOCK/KNOX; Sarah-3 DRISKO; John-2) and M. M. RICHARDSON , was born 8 May 1857 at Hazelhurst, Mississippi. She married Edward C. ROTHROCK on 18 Oct 1885 at Athens, Texas. He was born 25 July 1861 at Brookhaven, Mississippi; died 7 Dec 1889 at Anderson County, TX. Mattie-7 RICKER died 18 June 1906, TX.

Children of Mattie-7 RICKER and Edward ROTHROCK:
    Surname ROTHROCK
   835. George   born 23 July 1886 Corsicana, TX.
   836. Edward (Jr. ?) born Aug 1888 Dallas, TX; died Sept 1888 Corsicana, TX.
   837. Beatrice   born 30 Aug 1889

309. WILLIAM AUGUSTUS-7 RICKER, brother of above, was born 18 Jan 1863 at Hazelhurst, MISS.

He married Elmira V. HALL on 14 Oct 1888 at Corsicana, TX. She was born 7 Sept 1872 at Oglesby, TX.

Children of William-7 RICKER and Elmira HALL:
    Surname RICKER
    838. Rupert Paul   born 19 Dec 1889 Corsicana   840. Mabel Allen   born 1 June 1894
    839. Lee   born 10 June 1892; died 11 June 1892

311. CHARLES PAUL-7 RICKER, brother of above, was born 18 Jan 1863 at Hazelhurst, Mississippi. He married Louella E. DOUGLASS on 21 Nov 1887 at Corsicana, TX. She was born 6 Mar 1870; died ___. Charles Paul-7 RICKER died 1 Nov 1897 Corsicana, TX.

Children of Charles P-7 RICKER and Louella DOUGLASS:
    Surname RICKER
    841. Myrtle Louise   born 20 Aug 1888; married Walter GLASS at Fort Worth, TX
                              One child: Althea Louise-9 GLASS born 4 July 1905
    842. Aleen   born 18 Dec 1891   843. Robert   born 20 Mar 1894

312. LILLY-7 RICKER, sister of above, was born 26 Jan 1865 at Hazelhurst, Mississippi. She married A. B. DOUGLASS on 14 Apr 1886 at Corsicana, TX. He was born 14 Apr 1845, MS; died ____.

Children of Lilly-7 RICKER and A. B. DOUGLASS;
    Surname DOUGLASS
    844. Joseph   born 28 Mar 1887   848. Fred H.   born 31 Aug 1900
    845. Annie   born 6 July 1889   died 6 Nov 1900
         married _?_ CLENDON June 1906   849. Roland E.   born 13 Sept 1901
    846. Newton E.   born 9 Jan 1892   850. Louise A.   born 22 Apr 1903
    847. Edward S.   born 11 Dec 1896; died 6 Nov 1906

316. CHARLES HENRY-7 RICKER, son of Daniel-6 RICKER (Paul-5; Mercy-4 NOCK/KNOX; Sarah-3 DRISKO; John-2) and Lucy Ann-7 RICKER, was born 16 Feb 1853 at Argyle, Nova Scotia. He married Eliza J. TRUSDEN/TWISDEN on 23 July 1882 at Ipswich, MA. She was born 28 Mar 1858; died 28 Aug 1941 at Wareham, MA. Charles H-7 RICKER, a baker, died 2 May 1913 at Ipswich, MA.

Children of Charles H-7 RICKER and Eliza TRUSDEN/TWISDEN:
    Surname RICKER   (all born Ipswich, MA.)
    851. Charles F.   born 18 Feb 1883; died 24 Aug 1883
    852. Charles Chester   born 4 Nov 1885; married Martha Etta THAYER Dodge 28 Apr 1907
                             died 2 Oct 1908 Ipswich, MA.
                             One child: Arthur Milton-9 RICKER born 22 July 1908
  + 853. ARTHUR S.   born 24 Aug 1888; married Nora M. PERRY 2 Apr 1910 Ipswich
                             (she dau/o Joseph PERRY and Mary ARSENAULT)
                             (she born 1890 Prince Edward Is.; died ____)
    854. Grace M.   born 8 May 1894; married John G. MANSFIELD 28 Feb 1910
                             (he son/o John MANSFIELD and Helen GRANT) (he born 1892)

324. JOSEPH WARREN-7 WILSON, son of Jerusha-6 DRISKO (John-5; Joseph-4; John-3;2) and Joseph-5 WILSON, Jr., was born 11 Aug 1787 at Columbia Falls, Maine. He married Elizabeth Chandler PINEO on 22 Nov 1817 at Machias, ME. She was the daughter of David PINEO and Priscilla HILL, and was born 24 Jan 1798; died 25 May 1827 at Campobello, New Brunswick. Joseph-7 WILSON died 10 Dec 1854 at St. Charles, Illinois.

Children of Joseph Warren-7 WILSON and Elizabeth PINEO:
    Surname WILSON   (all born Columbia, Maine)
    855. Coffin G.   born 24 Nov 1818; died young

Children of Joseph Warren-7 WILSON, continued:
  Surname WILSON
  856. John Lyman   born 24 Feb 1820; died 3 Jan 1910 St. Cloud, MN
                    1m. Cordelia MORGAN; 2m. Mrs. Harriet N. RICHMOND Corbett 13 Nov 1855 (4 ch)
  857. Joseph Patten   born 16 Mar 1822; married Mary CORBETT; died 18 Feb 1900 MN.
+ 858. BUSHROD   born 18 July 1824; married Priscilla Ousley YANTIS Oct 1856
      WASHINGTON   died 4 Mar 1900 Oregon

326. JOHN DRISKO-7 WILSON, brother of above, was born 30 Oct 1790 at Columbia Falls, Maine
He married Hannah Coffin on 12 Dec 1816 at Columbia. She was the daughter of Deacon Elisha COFFIN
and Ruth-5 CATES (Samuel-4; Edward-3;2; James-1 CATE), and was born 10 May 1797; died 21 May
1849. John D-7 WILSON, a shipbuilder at Brewer, Maine , died ca 1846.

Children of John Drisko-7 WILSON and Hannah COFFIN:
  Surname WILSON   (all born Brewer, Maine)
  859. Ambrose   born 5 Jan 1818; died 6 Mar 1871 unmarried EOL
  860. Cordelia   born 18 Apr 1819; died 27 July 1822   EOL
  861. Louisa   born 10 Nov 1820; died 10 July 1822   EOL
  862. Winfield S.   born 12 Nov 1822; married Nancy J. HATCH 4 June 1864 Bangor, ME.
  863. Cordelia R.   born 7 July 1825; died 12 Mar 1834   EOL
  864. James R.   born 25 Feb 1829; died ca 185_ unmarried   EOL
  865. George P. (twin) born 28 June 1831; died 17 Mar 1833   EOL
  866. Robert P. (twin) born 28 June 1831; died 7 Jan 1833   EOL
  867. Julia A.   born 10 May 1835; died 12 Mar 1836   EOL
  868. Hannah F.   born 28 Jan 1837

327. NATHANIEL-7 WILSON, brother of above, was born 27 Feb 1792 at Columbia Falls, Maine. He
married Sarah/Sally SMITH on 1 Nov 1818 at Machias, Maine. She was the daughter of Samuel SMITH
and Sarah KELLEY, and was born 11 Jan 1798; died 14 Jan 1883 at San Francisco, CA. Nathaniel-7
WILSON died 12 Sept 1857 at East Machias, Maine.

Children of Nathaniel-7 WILSON and Sarah/Sally SMITH:
  Surname WILSON   (all but the last child, born at Machias, Maine)
  869. Eliza Jane   born 29 Oct 1819; married Rev Edward VERY 2 Sept 1839; died CA.
  870. Frederick A.   born 3 Nov 1822; died ca 1878 CA
  871. Henry Clay   born 2 June 1825; married Susan KELLAR; died 7 Mar 1864 CA.
                    (she born 13 Apr 1833; died _____)
  872. George Osborne   born 12 June 1827; died 14 Jan 1879 , poss CA.
                    married Mary Amelia SANDERSON (CA.)
                    (she dau/o George SANDERSON and Elizabeth KIMBALL)
                    (she born 1 May 1837, NY; died 3 July 1888)
  873. Mary Lucretia   born 7 Jan 1830; died 12 Jan 1833
  874. Nathaniel Irving   born 7 Jan 1832 East Machias; died 10 Mar 1885 CA.
                    1m. Mary Caroline HALL 25 Oct 1858; 2m. Malvina Chase PELTON

328. GOWEN-7 WILSON, brother of above, was born 26 Mar 1793 at Columbia Falls, Maine. He married
Eliza Ann WESTON on 22 Dec 1821 at East Machias, Maine. She was the daughter of Timothy WESTON
and Ann GOOCH, and was born 6 Nov 1803; died 5 May 1880. Gowen-7 WILSON died 18 Dec 1863 at
St. Augusta, MN.

Children of Gowen-7 WILSON and Eliza WESTON:
  Surname WILSON   (all children born East Machias, Maine)
  875. Horatio Nelson   born 12 Mar 1823; married Mary SOUTHARD ca 1848
                    died 16 Feb 1852 East Machias

Children of Gowen-7 WILSON, continued:
Surname WILSON

876. Charles Warren	born 18 June 1825; married Elizabeth Stewart McNUTT 16 Jan 1851 died 21 June 1873 MN.	
877. Gilbert Longfellow	born 13 July 1827; died 18 Jan 1857	
878. Lorenzo Dow	born 18 Oct 1829; died 1851 unmarried EOL	
879. Gowen W.	born 16 Feb 1832; died ____ unmarried	
880. Timothy Weston	born 27 May 1834; died ____ unmarried	
881. Joseph F.	born 8 June 1836; married Lucy McNUTT Stimson 21 July 1870; died MN.	
882. Benjamin F.	born 4 Dec 1838; died young	
883. Eliza Ann	born 17 May 1841; died young	
884. James Martin	born 13 Aug 1842; married Ida D. WARREN 25 Dec 1871	
885. Francis H.	born 17 Sept 1844; died ____ unmarried	
886. Emily Florence	born 10 Mar 1847; married Henry G. RISING 1872	
887. Andrew B.	born 3 Nov 1849; died ____ unmarried	

330. STILLMAN A-7 WILSON, brother of above, was born 30 Apr 1796 at Columbia Falls, Maine. He married Mary Jane MOORE on 28 Feb 1838 at Portland, Maine. She was born ca Sept 1810; died 30 Mar 1887. Stillman-7 WILSON died 23 Aug 1870 at Brewer, Maine.   Note: Stillman-7 WILSON is listed in " Benton County, Oregon Pioneers ", also the California Pioneers Society (15 June 1849).

Children of Stillman-7 WILSON and Mary Jane MOORE:
Surname WILSON

888. George Stillman	born 26 Jan 1839; died 5 Apr 1840
889. William Henry	born 4 Apr 1841; married Hannah M. BLAKE; died 20 Jan 1876
890. Stillman A. , Jr.	born 27 Dec 1842; married Delphis HOLYOKE at Brewer, ME died 1 Nov 1911 Brewer
891. John Dwight	born 5 Aug 1846

331. JOEL-7 WILSON, brother of above, was born 27 June 1797 at Columbia Falls, Maine. He married Eunice __?__ ca 18__.

Children of Joel-7 WILSON and Eunice __?__:
Surname WILSON

892. Mary W.	born 20 Aug 1840; dy	895. Elizabeth Augusta	born 2 Jan 1846 IL
893. Francis Edgar	born 19 May 1842; dy	896. Mary Chandler	born 24 Dec 1847 ME.
894. Ellen Louisa	born 16 Aug 1843		

334. ASA-7 WILSON, brother of above, was born 7 June 1802 at Columbia Falls, Maine. He married Rebecca Newell-8 JOY ++ on 17 Aug 1830 at Ellsworth, ME. She was the dau/of Benjamin –7 JOY and Abigail GREEN, and was born 3 Oct 1805; died 22 Aug 1883. Asa-7 WILSON died 14 June 1880, OH.

Children of Asa-7 WILSON and Rebecca JOY:
Surname WILSON

897. William W.	born 14 Aug 1832	900. Asa Putnam	born 7 Aug 1842
898. Mary Relief	born 23 Apr 1836; d y	901. Henrietta	born ca 1845
899. Benjamin Joy	born 1 Jan 1840		

Ancestry of Rebecca Newell-8 JOY

THOMAS-1 JOY, the immigrant, son of Thomas-A JOY and Frances PAULETT, was born ca 1611 Norfolk, England. He emigrated to America before 1637 when he married Joan GALLOP at Boston, Suffolk, MA. She was the daughter of John GALLOP and Christobel BRUSHETT, and was born 20 Sep 1618 at Bridgeport,Dorsetshire, England. They were the parents of JOSEPH-2 JOY, born 1 Feb 1645 at Boston, MA. He married Mary PRINCE on 29 Aug 1667 at Hingham, MA. She was the daughter of John PRINCE and Margaret SKILLINGS, and was born 29 July 1649 at Hingham, died 23 June 1726 at Scituate, MA. Joseph-2 JOY died 31 May 1697 at Hingham.

JOSEPH-3 JOY, born 30 July 1668 at Hingham, MA; married Elizabeth ANDREWS 22 May 1690 at Hingham. She was the daughter of Thomas ANDREWS and Ruth _?_; and was born 22 Sep 1665 at Hingham; died 10 Sep 1743 at Hingham, MA. Joseph-3 JOY died there on 29 April 1716.

DAVID-4 JOY, son of Joseph-3; was born 28 Feb 1693 at Hingham, MA. He married Ruth FORD on 13 Oct 1738 at Pembroke, Plymouth, MA. She was born 7 Sept 1698 at Pembroke; died July 1772 at Killingly, Windham, CT. David-4 JOY died 13 Apr 1739 at Rehoboth, Bristol, MA.

Their son, BENJAMIN-5 JOY, was born 20 May 1719 at Rehoboth, MA. He married Sarah Sawyer CUMMINGS on 10 June 1740 at Rehoboth. She was the daughter of Josiah CUMMINGS and Mary FRIZZELL, and was born 11 Mar 1722; died 26 Sept 1803 at Plainfield, Sullivan, NH. Benjamin-5 JOY died there 11 Mar 1810.

BENJAMIN-6 JOY (Jr.) was born 9 Dec 1748 at Killingly, Windham, CT. He married Rebecca SMITH on 1 Aug 1765 at Ellsworth, Hancock, ME. She was the daughter of John SMITH and Rebecca DAY, and was born 25 Jan 1749 at Saco, York, ME; died 5 Oct 1830. BENJAMIN-7 JOY, born 24 Dec 1768, married Abigail GREEN on 23 Aug 1795 at Reading, Middlesex, MA. She was the dau/of John GREEN & Abigail GEARY, and was born 8 June 1772 at Reading, ME. Their daughter was Rebecca Newell-8 JOY.

335. PUTNAM-7 WILSON, brother of above, was born 3 Feb 1804 at Columbia Falls, Maine. He married Eliza FITTS ca 18__. She was the daughter of _?_ FITTS and was born ___; died 22 July 1886 at Brewer, ME. Putnam-7 WILSON died there 1 Apr 1883.   Note: Putnam-7 WILSON listed in " Benton County, Oregon Pioneers "

Children of Putnam-7 WILSON and Eliza FITTS:
  Surname WILSON

902. Eliza Adelaide	born 1 Mar 1841	904. Jerusha Drisko	born ca 1847; died unmarried
903. Josephine A.	born 14 June 1844	905. Marshall Putnam	born 24 Feb 1850; d y

345. JEREMIAH-7 PLUMMER, son of Lorraine-6 DRISKO (John-5; Joseph-4; John-3;2) and Moses-7 PLUMMER, was born ca Apr 1791 at Addison, Maine. He married Elizabeth/Betsey-6 WASS before 1819. She was the daughter of Wilmot-5 WASS and his second wife Rebecca JORDAN, and was born 8 Sept 1791; died 11 June 1869. Jeremiah-7 PLUMMER died 4 Jan 1850 at Addison..

Children of Jeremiah-7 PLUMMER and Betsey-6 WASS:
  Surname PLUMMER

+ 906. ELIZABETH ANN born ca 1819; married Jacob Adams DAVIS 1839
       (he son/o Samuel DAVIS and Susanna NASH) (he born ca 1810; died 6 Jan 1872)
  907. dau   born ca 1820; died young
  908. Stillman Wass   born 31 Dec 1821; died 1843 unmarried   EOL
+ 909. CAPTAIN   born May 1824; married Jane H. WARD July 1852
       WILLIAM   (she dau/o William WARD) (she born Aug 1828; died 30 Dec 1910)
       WILMOT   died 24 July 1902 Addison   sea captain
  910. Miriam Perkins   born ca 1826; married Aaron Tucker SMALL 26 Dec 1847
                          (he born 9 May 1825; died 1890)
  911. Rebecca Wass   born Sept 1828; married Isaiah Nash MERRITT; died 22 Apr 1907   EOL
  912. Marion Handy   born ca 1831; died 1853 (age 22) unmarried

346. MOSES-7 PLUMMER, 4th, brother of above, was born ca 1793 at Addison, Maine. He married Abigail/Nabby-7 WASS ca 1815. She was the daughter of Christopher-6 WASS and Mary DYER, and was born 23 July 1794 at Addison; died there 31 May 1844. Moses-7 PLUMMER died 28 May 1850 aboard the vessel BELGRADE. He was a ships' steward and was discovered dead in his bunk.

Children of Moses-7 PLUMMER and Abigail WASS:
  Surname PLUMMER

  913. Lorraine   born ca 1818; married David WASS ca 1832; died ca 1894
                          (he son/o John Adams WASS and Anna DYER)
  914. Christopher Wass born ca 1825; married Lydia ALLEN, int pub 11 Dec 1843
  915. Mary Jane   born ca 1828; died 1835
                Note: There were reportedly three more children who died in infancy

347. BETSEY G-7 PLUMMER, sister of above, was born 16 Nov 1797 at Addison, Maine. She married Captain Holmes Nash-7 WASS ca 18__. He was the son of Wilmot-6 WASS and Wealthea DYER, and was born Jan 1791; died 25 Sept 1863 at Harrington, Maine. Betsey-7 PLUMMER died there 1 Jan 1879.

Children of Betsey-7 PLUMMER and Holmes Nash-7 WASS:
  Surname WASS
916. son   born ca 18__; died young
917. Rebecca   born 20 July 1818;   died 25 Oct 1883; married John T.-8 PLUMMER ca 1837
          (he son/o Jeremiah-7 PLUMMER and Frances FELLOWS) (he born July 1812; died 1880)
918. Julia Ann   born ca 1819; 1m. Uriah WASS ca 1839; 2m. Reuben F. WASS ca 186_
          (he 1m. Martha Ann GILMAN on 26 Nov 1835 at Kennebec, Maine)
919. Emeline C.(triplet) born 22 Sept 1821; married Frederick WHITE ca 1863; died 1917
920. Orva   (triplet) born 22 Sept 1821; died young
921. Almira W. (triplet) born 22 Sept 1821; died young
922. Lorraine   born ca 1823; died young
923. Elizabeth B.   born 8 Oct 1825 Addison; marr Christopher CURTIS, Jr ca 1845; died ca 1891
924. Almira W. (2)   born June 1828 Harrington, ME; married Henry HAMILTON 1 Oct 1848
                                  died 31 Aug 1920 Marlboro, MA.
+ 925. CHARLES S.   born Feb 1833 Addison; 1m. Louisa A. RAMSDELL 18 Jan 1855
                                  2m. Elizabeth A. SMITH 24 Feb 1881

348. JOHN-7 PLUMMER, brother of above, was born 12 Dec 1799 at Addison, Maine. He married Sarah/Sally WASS ca 18__. She was the daughter of James-6 WASS and Anna DYER, and was born ca Feb 1800; died 11 May 1857. John-7 PLUMMER, a farmer, died 23 Feb 1882 at Addison, Maine.

Children of John-7 PLUMMER and Sally WASS:
  Surname PLUMMER
+ 926. NANCY WASS   born ca 1823 Harrington, ME
                      married BENJAMIN FRANKLIN-7 DRISKO ca 1845 (# 463)
                      (he son/o Jeremiah-6 DRISKO (# 139) and Ann FRANKLAND)
                      (he born 8 Apr 1821; died 7 Sept 1893)
927. dau   born ca 1825; died young
928. Lucy   born 2 Feb 1827; marr David Coffin CURTIS 10 Nov 1847; died 19 Oct 1903
+ 929. FRANCES A.   born ca 1829; married Captain PERRIN C-7 DRISKO ca 1849 (# 466)
                      (brother of above; he born ca 1826)
930. James W.   born ca 1831; married Elizabeth-8 LEIGHTON int pub 29 Sept 1855
                    (she dau/o Aaron-7 LEIGHTON and Bethia WAKEFIELD) (she born ca 1834)
931. Rinaldin W.   born ca 1834; married Clara M-8 LEIGHTON 27 Sept 1862
                      (she sister of above, she born ca 1835; died _____)
932. Henry L.   born ca 1840; died _____ unmarried

349. AMOS BUCKNAM-7 PLUMMER, brother of above, was born 17 July 1802 at Addison, Maine. He married Phebe Coffin-7 WASS, intentions published 3 Jan 1825 at Harrington, ME. She was the daughter of Joseph-6 WASS and Susan A. COFFIN, and was born ca 1807; died ca 1847. Amos B-7 PLUMMER, a ships' carpenter, died 20 Feb 1877 at Machiasport, Maine.

Children of Amos Bucknam-7 PLUMMER and Susan COFFIN:
  Surname PLUMMER
933. George W.   born ca 1826; married Matilda A. __?__ (had 3 children; all died young)
934. Harriet E.   born ca 1831; married __?__ BICKNER
935. Joseph Wass   born ca 1833; died ca 1898
936. Lucy Perkins   born ca 1833/34; married Elisha Green-8 COFFIN (# 1402)
+ 937. CAPTAIN AMOS   born ca 1836; married Elizabeth M-8 COFFIN 3 July 1856 (# 1403)
       BUCKNAM, JR. (she born ca 1838; died 12 Mar 1883)

Children of Amos Bucknam-7 PLUMMER, continued:

Surname PLUMMER

+ 938. CAPTAIN   born 10 Apr 1837 Harrington, ME;   died 26 June 1926 Addison, Maine
     VORANUS   1m. Susan Coffin WASS Apr 1858; 2m. Mary Elizabeth NASH 20 July 1872
     COFFIN   3m. Ada F. CROWLEY Merritt Ingersoll 13 June 1914
+ 939. HARLAND E.   born ca 1840; married Judith A. TOBEY 14 May 1860; died 1879
                    Note: Reportedly, there were 3 more children who died young

351. WILLIAM JOHNSON-7 DRISKO, son of Judah-6 DRISKO (John-5; Joseph-4; John-3;2) and Lucy PLUMMER, was born 15 Aug 1799 at Harrington, Washington County, Maine. He married Mary Barker-2 FRANKLAND on 14 Dec 1824. She was the daughter of Captain William-1 FRANKLAND and Ann ROSS, and was born 11 Nov 1802 at Grand Manaan, New Brunswick; died 9 Oct 1884 at Machiasport, Maine. William-7 DRISKO died 1 Feb 1841 at Addison, Maine.

Children of William Johnson-7 DRISKO and Mary FRANKLAND:

  DRISKO

 940. William Frankland born 11 Oct 1825; died 10 Nov 1826
+ 941. LUCY ANN   born 7 Feb 1828 Harrington, ME
            married Luther Ingersoll SAWYER 15 Mar 1849; (he born 11 June 1823; died 29 May 1898)
 942. JUDAH   born 3 July 1830 Addison, ME; 1m. Miranda Otis SANBORN 1 Jan 1855
    JOHNSON (2nd) (she dau/o Lewis SANBORN and Anna B. BUCKNAM # 365)
            (she born 28 Sept 1829; died 12 Mar 1884 Machiasport, ME)
            2m. Sophia Wilson ALLEN Strout (she born 13 May 1840; died 19 Jan 1924)
            died 1 Mar 1912 Harrington, Maine
 943. Alice Frankland born 12 Oct 1832; died 12 Feb 1866 unmarried
 944. Elmira J. (Myra) born 18 Jan 1835; (adopted by Baker SAWYER of Steuben)
            married Captain Temple Cook-7 COFFIN 26 Oct 1881 (as his 2nd wife)*
            (he son/o William Thorndike-6 COFFIN ** and Hannah PLUMMER)
            (he born 3 Feb 1828; died 4 Mar 1900 at the Sailors Snug Harbor, NY)
            died 21 June 1926 Addison, Maine
         Note: * Temple-7 COFFIN was married first to Margaret S. HALL (1826- 1880)
    ** William Thorndike-6 COFFIN, born 1797, son/o Temple-5 COFFIN (1772-1856) and Ann THORNDIKE
(1776- 1860); Richard-4 COFFIN (1729-____) and Mary COOKE; Tristam-3; John-2; Tristam-1 COFFIN.

 945. Amanda/Margaret born 3 Mar 1837; died young
 946. Louisa E.   born 18 Sept/Oct 1839; died 9 Oct 1909 (age 69) unmarried
        (adopted by her aunt Mariam-7 DRISKO Bowen (# 357); used the name BOWEN)

352. CALEB HASKELL-7 DRISKO, brother of above, (called Haskell) was born 7/17 Aug 1801. He was named after Dr. Caleb HASKELL, a resident physician at Columbia, Maine 1797-1801 or later. Dr. HASKELL was born at Harvard, MA 31 May 1762, and after practicing a few years at Columbia, ME. he returned to MA.   Caleb Haskell-7 DRISKO married Hannah COLE on 18 Jan 1827 at Addison. She was the daughter of David COLE and " Nabby " COLBETH of Harrington, and was born 24 Dec 1806; died 22 Mar 1878 at Addison. Caleb H-7 DRISKO, a ships' carpenter, died 10 June 1875.

Children of Caleb Haskell-7 DRISKO and Hannah COLE:

  Surname DRISKO   (children all born at Addison, Maine)
 947. Sophia   stillborn 1826
+ 948. SOPHIA S.   born 15 Mar 1827; married Benjamin A. SHUTE 12 Sept 1852 Addison
            (he from Boston, MA.)
 949. Almira   born 25 Dec 1829; died Jan 1830
 950. Miriam F.   born 20 July 1831; died 21 Sept 1832
+ 951. FRANCIS   born 31 Aug 1833; married Alice Everlina WASS 14 Dec 1861 Addison
    MARION (she dau/o Enos WASS and Lydia COLE)(she born Apr 1843; died 19 Oct 1875 gs)
           died 21 Feb 1901   ships' carpenter

Children of Caleb Haskell-7 DRISKO, continued:
    Surname DRISKO
+ 952. ABIGAIL SLADE   born 13 Oct 1835 ; died 21 June 1886 Steuben, ME
      " Abby "   married John Bucknam-8 LEIGHTON 19 Oct 1856
    (he son/o Handy-7 LEIGHTON and Rebecca WASS) (he born 4 Apr 1832; died 20 May 1900, ME)
  953. Mariam   born Sept 1837 ; died before 1850
+ 954. FANNY M./   born 31 Aug 1838; 1m. Captain John Wass DYER 5 Dec 1856
    FRANCES MARIA (he son/o Captain William Vinal DYER and Eliza WASS)
                  (he born ca 1835; died 1856) resided Biddeford, Maine
                  2m. Benjamin Ludden CRANE after 1870
  955. John Perkins   born 23 July 1839; died 21 July 1866 at Panama (sailor)
  956. Alcander Thomas born 20 July 1841; died ____ carpenter
  957. twins   born 2 July 1843; d y   958. Horatio   born 25 Aug 1844 (sailor)
        Some information on the above family from an article in Yankee Magazine (12 Sept 1964)
          entitled " Picture Behind a Picture " by Lowell A. NORRIS.

353. LORRAINE PLUMMER-7 DRISKO, sister of above, was born 27 Jan 1803 at Jonesboro, Maine. She married Levi-8 SMALL on 6 Feb 1823. He was the son of Daniel-7 SMALL and Phebe COFFIN of Harrington, Maine and was born ca 1793; died 4 July 1835 at Addison, ME. Levi-8 SMALL was a ship owner. (He married second to Alice Bentley FRANKLAND, intentions published 28 July 1833 at Addison). Lorraine-7 DRISKO died 6 Feb 1830.

Children of Lorraine-7 DRISKO and Levi-8 SMALL:
    Surname SMALL
  959. Lucy Ann   born ca 1825; married Henry-6 NASH 21 Nov 1847; died 31 Oct 1889
    (he son/o William-5 NASH and Mary COFFIN) (he born 13 June 1819; died 21 Nov 1906; EOL)
  960. Adoniram <u>Judson</u> born ca 1826 ; married Elizabeth BROWN 27 Jan 1856 Addison
                  (she born ca 1834, NB; died Feb 1869)
  961. Emeline   born ca 1828; died June 1844

355. FRANCES-7 DRISKO, sister of above, was born 7 May 1806. She married THOMAS FLETCHER-7 BUCKNAM (# 368) on 11 Apr 1838. He was the son of Abigail-6 DRISKO (# 119) and William H-6 BUCKNAM , and was born 15 Feb 1808; died 26 Apr 1846 at Columbia Falls, ME. Frances-7 married 2nd to Colonel James-5 CURTIS on 6 Oct 1856 at Columbia (his 3rd wife). Frances-7 died 21 July 1893.

Children of Frances-7 DRISKO and THOMAS FLETCHER-7 BUCKNAM:
    Surname BUCKNAM
  962. Eliza Frances   born 20 May 1839 Columbia Falls, ME; died 8 July 1915
                  married Captain Robert Perkins-8 PLUMMER 18 Mar 1888
    he son/o Moses-7 PLUMMER and Hannah-5 WESTON; he born 11 Sept 1816; died 18 May 1891; EOL
  963. William Sanborn born 20 Dec 1840; died 14 Nov 1841
  964. Martha Washington born 24 Aug 1842; died 6 Apr 1843
  965. Caroline   born 4 Sept 1843; died 7 May 1844
  966. Frances   born 29 Apr 1845; died 10 Nov 1845

356. JOHN JEREMIAH-7 DRISKO, brother of above, was born 29 Feb 1808 at Addison, Maine. (He was called John J. and Jeremiah). He married first to Lucy Fellows PLUMMER on 17 July 1841. She was the daughter of Jeremiah PLUMMER and Frances FELLOWS, and was born ca 1807 at Addison; died 19 Sept 1846 (age 39 gs). His 2nd wife was Permelia Lyon-7 WASS of Columbia, ME. They were married on 1 Jan 1849 at Addison. She was the daughter of Levi WASS and Emma KNOWLES, and was born 3 Oct 1827; died 1871.

They appeared on the 1850 and 1860 Census as residing at Addison. According to the deeds, they were residents of Machiasport, ME. In 1864 when " Pamelia " sold the house lot in Addison to Francis Marion

DRISKO (a nephew). Jeremiah-7 DRISKO purchased land at Machiasport at about the same time. Although he did not appear on the 1870 Census, he was still living there in 1880; and on 29 May 1886 conveyed land to his daughter Mary Olivia Cates; the land purchased from Adkins S. CATES – plus another strip of land conveyed to him by Susan C. Cates et al (Reg. Book 174; page 428) John Jeremiah-7 DRISKO died 8 Nov 1887.

Children of John Jeremiah Plummer-7 DRISKO and Pamelia/Permelia WASS:
    Surname DRISKO

967. Mary Olivia	born 2 Jan 1850, Addison; married Captain Joseph Willard CATES 6 July 1867 (he born 21 May 1840; died 1 Sept 1914)(sea captain at Machiasport, ME) died May 1941 Addison, Maine
+ 968. LEVI WASS	born ca 1851 Addison, 1m. Emma L. PALMER (she dau/o Charles PALMER of Machias)
(used DRISCO)	(she born 20 July 1849; died 7 Jan 1877 South Bend, IN) 2m. Sarah Jane KAISER 19 Nov 1879 Chicago, IL died 9 Nov 1885 Chicago, IL
969. Lucy Emma	born 1 Jan 1856; 1m. Edward Augustus P. HUSON 1 Jan 1876 (div by 1880) 2m. Charles PADGETT Chicago, IL
970. George B.	born 6 July 1859; died 10 Sept 1860
+ 971. BURT/BERT WILLIAM	born 27 May 1868 Machiasport, ME: married Ada DILL of Gardiner, ME. died 2 June 1948 Gardiner, ME.

361. PHILO LEWIS-7 DRISKO, brother of above, was born 19 Apr 1822. He was named after Philo LEWIS, a local dignitary. He married Caroline Campbell-7 WASS of Columbia, Maine on 15 Nov 1854. She was the daughter of Levi-6 WASS and Emma KNOWLES; and was born 23 Aug 1836; died 1921. Philo Lewis-7 DRISKO, a ships' caulker who worked in Leander KNOWLES shipyard, died 3 Oct 1899.

Children of Philo-7 DRISKO and Caroline WASS:
Surname DRISKO	(all children born Addison, Maine)
972. Mary Louise	born 29 Sept 1856; died 25 May 1875 unmarried
973. Frances Bucknam	born 23 June 1862; died 1 Mar 1934 Addison married Harvey L. RAMSDELL 26 Nov 1913 Calais, Maine
+ 974. WILLIAM JOHNSON, 2nd	born 8 Sept 1866; married Martha Sherman BUCKNAM 27 June 1901 (she dau/o Captain Benjamin Franklin BUCKNAM * and Sarah WASS) (she born 8 Nov 1875; died 4 Feb 1965 (SSDI)

  * Captain Benjamin F. BUCKNAM was the master of the : *J W DRISKO*; *CALLAO*; and *ANNIE L MORSE/ANNIE L MOWE* and the Bark *ZELINDA* (of which he was the first master).

364. JOHN-7 BUCKNAM, son of Abigail-6 DRISKO (John-5; Joseph-4; John-3;2) and William H. BUCKNAM, was born 31 July 1798 at Columbia Falls, Maine. He married Sarah LITTLE there on 20 Oct 1836. She was born at Edmunds on 2 Aug 1812; died at Columbia Falls 14 June 1861. John-7 BUCKNAM, a farmer, died 24 Nov 1859.

Children of John-7 BUCKNAM and Sarah LITTLE:
Surname BUCKNAM	(children born at Columbia Falls, Maine)
975. Robert William	born 2 Aug 1837; 1m. Nancy H. STILES 2 Dec 1862 (she born ca 1839; died 25 Dec 1863) 2m. Mary Ann-8 LEIGHTON 24 Feb 1866 (she born 1845; died __ MO) died 6 July 1878 Columbia, Maine
976. George Little	born 15 June 1840; died 16 Apr 1888 Whiting, Maine married Ellen B. CRANE 2 Sept 1866 (she born 30 July 1844; died 5 Nov 1924)
977. Captain Frederick A. R.	born 30 Apr 1842; died 30 May/Nov 1867 (a sea captain from Columbia Falls, ME; he was lost at sea on the Schooner *FANNY and MAY*)
978. Louisa Gertrude	born 17 Apr 1845; died 28 June 1863 unmarried EOL

367. MARY ANNE-7 BUCKNAM, daughter of Abigail-6 DRISKO (John-5; Joseph-4; John-3; 2) and William-6 BUCKNAM (John-5; William-4; Samuel-3; Joseph-2; William-1) was born 19 August 1805 . She married John H. LEE on 26 Sept 1830 at Boston, Suffolk, MA. He was the son of _____ LEE, and was born ca 18__. They moved to California in Aug 1849. Mary Anne-7 BUCKNAM died 24 Nov 1875 at Washington, CA.

Children of Mary Anne-7 BUCKNAM and John H. LEE:
>   Surname LEE

979. John Howard C.	born 18 Aug 1831 Boston, MA; died 22 May 1869 Sacramento, CA
980. Anna Marie	born ca 1833; 1m. David JONES; 2m. Harrison IVEY 25 May 1868
981. William Henry	born ca 1834 Rochester, NY; died 17 Nov 1879 Sacramento, CA
Harrison	1m. Emma S. GRAFF ca 1858; 2m. Martha A. GARFIELD 29 Dec 1860
+ 982. WILLARD	born 10 July 1837 Lowell, MA; died 12 Dec 1902 Sacramento, CA
MALCOLM	married Emma Ann BOGART 28 Nov 1860 Benicia, CA
983. Amanda Melvina	born ca 1838 Mexico, IN; married Len HARRIS

368. THOMAS FLETCHER-7 BUCKNAM - see FRANCES-7 DRISKO (# 355)

369. WILLIAM H-7 BUCKNAM, Jr. , brother of above, was born 6 May 1810 at Columbia Falls, Maine. He married Lucretia Farnham-7 TUCKER on 29 Mar 1836. She was the daughter of Zebediah-6 TUCKER and Lydia WARD, and was born 20 Aug 1812; died 1870. William-7 BUCKNAM, Jr., a blacksmith and farmer, died 26 June 1882 at Columbia Falls, Maine.

Children of William-7 BUCKNAM, Jr. and Lucretia TUCKER:
>   Surname BUCKNAM

984. Abigail Lydia	born 10 Apr 1837 Columbia Falls, ME; died 25 Sept 1864
	married Albion T. KINGSLEY 12 Sept 1857; (he born 1837; died _____)
985. Eleazer Ring	born 27 Aug 1838 Columbia; married Maggie MUNDLE 14 Mar 1883
	(she born 26 Mar 1856, NB; died 1924)
986. William F.	born 30 Oct 1841; died 25 Apr 1844
987. Anna S.	born 1849, MA.; died 19__ unmarried EOL

370. CAROLINE STONE-7 BUCKNAM, sister of above, was born 5 Dec 1813 at Columbia Falls, Maine. She married Frederick Augustus-7 RUGGLES on 11 Oct 1847 at Columbia, Maine. He was the son of Thomas-6 RUGGLES and Ruth CLAPP, and was born 8 Jan 1801; died 27 Dec 1890 at Columbia Falls. Caroline Stone-7 BUCKNAM died 4 Apr 1894.

Children of Caroline Stone-7 BUCKNAM and Frederick-7 RUGGLES:
>   Surname RUGGLES

988. Emily Bucknam	born 10 Oct 1850 Columbia Falls, died Aug 1887 unmarried EOL
989. Maria Elizabeth	born 20 Apr 1852; died 1920 (a portrait artist)

Note: Another child is said to have died in infancy

372. MARY CHANDLER-7 SMITH, daughter of Relief-6 DRISKO (John-5; Joseph-4; John-3;2) and Samuel SMITH, was born ca June 1806 at Dunbarton, New Hampshire. She married George E-6 TENNEY, intentions published 30 Mar 1828 at Columbia, Maine. He was the son of David-5 TENNEY and Mercy STEVENS, and was born Feb 1799; died 15 Aug 1885 at Machias. Mary C-7 SMITH died there on 30 Jan 1875.

Children of Mary C-7 SMITH and George-6 TENNEY:
>   Surname TENNEY

990. son	born ca 1829; died young
991. Mary Jane	born ca Jan 1831; married Jacob PENNIMAN ca 1848 / 49
	(he son/o William F. PENNIMAN and Olive-4 CROCKER , # 254 CROCKER)
	died 3 Feb 1875 Machias, Maine

Children of Mary C-7 SMITH, continued:
Surname TENNEY
+ 992. BENJAMIN F. born July 1834; died 3 Mar 1875 Machias, Maine
married Sabrina A-7 GARDNER 20 Dec 1858; (she dau/o John-6 GARDNER and Susan BERRY)

377. DAVID-7 TABBUT/TIBBETTS, son of Thomas-6 TABBUT/TIBBETTS (Elizabeth-5 DRISKO; Joseph-4; John-3;2) and Catherine CROWLEY, was born Jan 1802. He married Mary/Polly TUCKER, intentions published 5 June 1824. She was the daughter of Samuel TUCKER and Esther LEIGHTON, and was born 25 July 1804 at Columbia, Maine; died 13 May 1876 at Oconto, Wisconsin. David-7 TABBUT/ TIBBETTS, a ships' carpenter at Addison Point, died 18 Aug 1853.

Children of David-7 TABBUT/TIBBETTS and Mary TUCKER:
Surname TABBUT/TIBBETTS
993. Catherine W. born 17 May 1825; married Richard-7 COFFIN, Jr. 6 Dec 1846
(he born 24 Oct 1822; died 27 Mar 1885)
died 1860 Addison, Maine no issue EOL
+ 994. JULIA ANN born ca 1828; 1m. Joseph H. PAIGE ca 1845; 2m. Levi LINDSEY; res. WI
995. James Richard born ca 1830; married Mary Elizabeth __?__ (5 sons and 3 dau)
996. Joseph born ca 1834; married Philena C. __?__ (had children)
997. Mary/May born ca 1836
+ 998. HILLMAN LOOK born ca 1838; 1m. Alida Elizabeth FOLSOM of WI.
(she dau/o Cyrus G. FOLSOM and Miranda HANSCOM)(she born ca 1849; died 1883)
2m. Adaline WHITE 1887
999. David C. born ca 1841; died ____, WI
1000. Arthur B. born ca 1843; married Mary Lucretia THOMPSON 18 June 1865
(she dau/o Gideon THOMPSON and Hannah-7 LEIGHTON)
1001. Lucy born ca 1845; died Feb 1860

378. JAMES-7 TABBUT/TIBBETTS, brother of above, was born ca 1804 at Columbia, Maine. He married Catherine R. MESERVE on 10 Jan 1830 at Columbia. She was the daughter of ____ MESERVE and was born ca 1809 at Cherryfield; died 6 Sept 1892 at Columbia Falls, Maine. James-7 TABBUT/TIBBETTS, a farmer, died there 28 March 1866.

Children of James-7 TABBUT/TIBBETTS and Catherine MESERVE:
Surname TABBUT/TIBBETTS (children born Columbia Falls, Maine)
+ 1002. EMELINE born 2 Oct 1830; married Aaron Worcester-7 ALLEN ca 1848
BRADFORD died 1861
+ 1003. ELIZABETH born 3 Apr 1832; married ERI HATHAWAY-8 DRISKO 9 Jan 1851
ROBINSON died ca 1872
+ 1004. FRANCES born 4 Mar 1834; married ERI HATHAWAY—8 DRISKO 1873
(he was married first to her sister, above, he # 1327)
died ca 1926
1005. James Augustus born ca 1838; married Elizabeth B. COLE 9 Nov 1862 Columbia, ME.
(she dau/o John COLE and Elizabeth ROBINSON)
+ 1006. HELENA born 22 Jan 1841; married John B-7 GRANT ca 1856; died ca 1920
AUGUSTA (he son/o Edward-6 GRANT and Elsie DORR)
1007. Rebecca born 8 Oct 1843; 1m. Alpheus B. DORR ca 1859
2m. Hollis/Horace TENNEY ca 1867
1008. Harriet Amanda born 9 June 1846; married Edwin R. NORTON 10 July 1880
(he son/o James NORTON and Mary DENNISON)
died 3 Sept 1931
1009. Sarah Drisko born 17 Feb 1850; 1m. Ephraim-8 GRANT, 2nd on 20 July 1893
2m. Valentine ABBOTT 1 Jan 1910
died 25 Sept 1940 Cherryfield, Maine

385. JERUSHA WILSON-7 TABBUT/TIBBETTS, sister of above, was born Sept 1815 at Columbia, Maine. She married Captain Silas-7 Hillman LOOK ca 1837. He was the son of Daniel-6 LOOK and Lois HILLMAN; and was born 14 Oct 1810; died 17 May 1889. Jerusha-7 TABBUT/TIBBETTS died 11 May 1895 at Jonesport, Maine.

Children of Jerusha Wilson-7 TABBUT/TIBBETTS and Silas-7 LOOK:
  Surname LOOK
+ 1010. WILLARD G.   born ca 1838; married Electa Ann-6 PINEO 23 Nov 1861
                        (she dau/o William-5 PINEO and Abitha DUNBAR)
                        died 3 Apr 1868   result of a shooting accident
  1011. Mary Emily   born ca 1840; married William Warren SMITH; died ca 1867
                        (he son/o Stephen E. SMITH and Deborah WHITE) (he born ca 1846; died 187_)
  1012. Julia A.   born Jan 1847; married Charles Albert WOODARD 186_; died 9 Apr 1892
                        (he son/o Charles M. WOODARD and Sylvia WALKER; he born 4 July 1848)
  1013. Horatio Nelson born ca 1849; d. 1860   1015. James W.   born Mar 1855; died ca 1936
  1014. George H.   born ca 1851: d. 1870   1016. Israel Peasley born 1859/60; d y

387. THOMAS-7 TABBUT/TIBBETTS, Jr., brother of above, was born 11 May 1817 at Columbia, Maine. He married Thankful Knowles-5 McCASLIN, intentions published 24 Nov 1840. She was the daughter of Alexander-4 McCASLIN and Abigail KNOWLES; and was born 31 Oct 1820; died 20 Dec 1888. Thomas-7 TABBUT/TIBBETTS died 24 Apr 1896.

Children of Thomas-7 TABBUT/TIBBETTS, Jr. and Thankful-5 McCASLIN:
  Surname TABBUT/TIBBETTS   (children born Columbia, Maine)
+1017. HANNAH   born 27 Oct 1842; married Nathaniel-7 WHITE 1 Dec 1860
       MARIA   (he son/o Ichabod-6 WHITE and Pamelia NASH)
+1018. ABIGAIL   born 5 May 1844; married William Howard-8 WORCESTER 29 Mar 1866
       McCASLIN   (he son/o William-7 WORCESTER and Frances INGERSOLL)
  1019. Lavona C.   born June 1846; died 29 Mar 1861
  1020. Alexander T. born Dec 1848; died young
  1021. Philena N.   born ca 1853; married Irving BARTLETT after 1870
  1022. Susie Emma   born May 1859; married Albert B-9 LEIGHTON ca 1881
        (twin)   (he son/o Jason C-8 LEIGHTON and Jane WORCESTER)
  1023. John (twin) born May 1859; died ____

388. JEREMIAH-7 TABBUT/TIBBETTS, brother of above, was born ca 1819 at Columbia Falls, Maine. He married his cousin, CATHERINE W-7 TIBBETTS (# 410), intentions published 12 Nov 1839 at Columbia. She was the daughter of William-6 TABBUT/TIBBETTS and Anne WRIGHT, and was born ca Apr 1822; died ca 1899. Jeremiah-7 TABBUT/TIBBETTS, a **Civil War** veteran, died 187_ at Columbia Falls, Maine.

Children of Jeremiah-7 TABBUT/TIBBETTS and Catherine W. TIBBETTS:
  Surname TABBUT/TIBBETTS
  1024. Zimri Drisko   born ca 1841; married Phidelia-9 WORCESTER 23 Nov 1863
                        (she dau/o James-8 WORCESTER and Elsie GRANT)
                        died 25 Aug 1886   **Civil War** veteran
  1025. Rufus Drisko   born ca 1844; died 23 Mar 1863 from yellow fever; unmarried EOL
  1026. Phebe A.   born ca 1847; 1m. George W. BOWLEY 2 Oct 1866; 2m. ____ HERRICK
  1027. Antoinette Sophia born 24 Jan 1851; died 1933
           married John Dillingham-9 HATHAWAY 1871 (he son/o Paul-8 HATHAWAY and Nancy WILSON)
                 One child: John-10 HATHAWAY born 18 Apr 1873 Columbia Falls, Maine
  1028. Amanda E.   born ca 1854; died 1899 unmarried   EOL
+1029. ZEPHANIAH ALLEN born Feb 1856; married Grace CURRIER 13 Feb 1902; died 24 May 1930
  1030. Isyander T.   born ca 1858; died ____; resided South America

389. HIRAM-7 TABBUT/TIBBETTS, brother of above, was born ca 1820 at Columbia, Maine. He married Jerusha D-4 CROWLEY there on 7 Sept 1845. She was the daughter of Jeremiah-3 CROWLEY and Mehitable DAVIS, and was born 8 Nov 1821; died 27 Mar 1892 at Lewiston, ME. Hiram-7 died 29 Mar 1850, aboard the vessel *BELGRADE*, from yellow fever. The vessel was en route from Rio de Janeiro to California.

Children of Hiram-7 TABBUT/TIBBETTS and Jersuha-4 CROWLEY:
  Surname TABBUT/TIBBETTS
  1031. George S.   born 1846; died 26 July 1864
  1032. Augusta A.   born 1848; married Ephraim-8 GRANT,2nd 4 Sept 1864
                           (he son/o Calvin-7 GRANT and Roxanna WORCESTER)
                (he born May 1843; died 28 Feb 1909) (he 2m. Sarah-7 Drisko TIBBETTS (# 1009)

390. LUTHER INGERSOLL-7 TABBUT/TIBBETTS, brother of above, was born 17 Aug 1822 at Columbia, Maine. He married Cordelia Wilson WORCESTER Norton on 20 June 1849 at Columbia. She was the daughter of Leonard WORCESTER and Love CORTHELL, and was born 16 Aug 1824; died 8 Aug 1915. Luther-7 died 15 Oct 1881 at Addison, Maine.

Children of Luther Ingersoll-7 TABBUT/TIBBETTS and Cordelia WORCESTER:
  Surname TABBUT/TIBBETTS   (children born Addison, Maine)
  1033. Elmira Josephine   born 7 Apr 1850; married Loring Alfred CATES 11 Feb 1871
                           (he son/o Nathaniel CATES and Nancy __?__)
                           (he born 6 Feb 1847; died 4 Jan 1914; lost at sea aboard *USS OKLAHOMA*
  1034. Leonard Alphonso   born 18 Apr 1853; married Mercy Ellen McDONALD 2 Oct 1880
                           died 26 Feb 1903 Addison, Maine
  1035. Edvyanna B.   born 18 Jan 1855; married George W. LEWIS; died 11 Jan 1929
+1036. VIOLETTA   born 20 June 1858; 1m. Oscar Enoch-9 LEIGHTON ca 1877
       MORTON   2m. THOMAS CROWLEY-7 DRISKO 5 Dec 1877 (# 453)
       " Lettie "   (he son/o Josiah-6 DRISKO (# 137) and Theodocia CROWLEY)
  1037. Leslie Artell   born 8 Aug 1860; died 26 July 1933, a seaman
                           1m. Alice Jane McCARTY 14 Nov 1880 (divorced)
                           2m. Elizabeth LEIGHTON Dauphine 1905; 3m. Fannie KELLEY White 1922
  1038. Burton Luther   born 30 Dec 1863; married Cora Ella AUSTIN 2 Jan 1892
                           died 4 Sept 1907 Jonesport, Maine
  1039. Lena Rivers   born 1 Feb 1867; married Edgar Moses DERNIER July 1891
                           died 25 July 1952 Detroit, Michigan

391. HENRY H-7 TABBUT/TIBBETTS, son of John Coffin-6 TABBUT/TIBBETTS (Elizabeth-5 DRISKO; Joseph-4; John-3;2) and Betsey COLE, was born ca 1806. He married first to Elizabeth/Betsey MAGEE on 13 Sept 1838 at Columbia, ME. She was the daughter of John MAGEE and Lucinda LOOK, and was born ca 1816; died 23 Dec 1844. He married his second wife was Mary Ann DORR ca 1845. She was the daughter of Benjamin DORR and Nellie MAGEE, and was born ca 1823; died ca 1870. Henry-7 TABBUT/TIBBETTS died ca 186_ at Columbia Falls, Maine.

Children of Henry-7 TABBUT/TIBBETTS and Betsey MAGEE:
  Surname TABBUT/TIBBETTS
  1040. Minerva   born ca 1839; died young
+1041. LUCINDA V.   born Oct 1842; died ca 1914
                           married Asa Tucker-8 WORCESTER 31 Aug 1862
                           (he son/o Clement Fernald-7 WORCESTER and Tamson CUMMINGS)
+1042. ELIZABETH   born 1 July 1844 Columbia, ME; married George A-2 YOUNG 3 July 1869
       MAGEE   (he son/o John-1 YOUNG and Mary Ann WORCESTER)
  1043. Darius A.   born Apr 1847; died after 1900   unmarried
  1044. Isaiah M.   born 16 Aug 1849; married Martha A. LUNT; died 29 Mar 1921

Children of Henry-7 TABBUT/TIBBETTS, continued:
   Surname TABBUT/TIBBETTS
1045. Lowell Washington born May 1851; died 18 Mar 1938 unmarried   EOL
1046. Sarah E.   born 1853; married Charles W. DORR
1047. Enos D.   born 8 May 1856; married Maria Maude TRACY 30 Oct 1892; died ca 1942
1048. Alpheus   born ca 1859; married Ida M. WORCESTER 3 June 1891; died 1892

393. JOSEPH-7 TABBUT/TIBBETTS, brother of above, was born ca 1809 at Columbia Falls, Maine. He married Margaret WORCESTER, intentions published 24 Aug 1830 at Columbia. She was the daughter of John WORCESTER and Mary FERNALD, and was born ca 1806; died ____. Joseph-7 died 13 June 1894 at Columbia, Maine.

Children of Joseph-7 TABBUT/TIBBETTS and Margaret WORCESTER:
   Surname TABBUT/TIBBETTS
1049. Jerome B.   born Dec 1831; married Ellen P. FARDY int pub 11 Apr 1856; died 4 Oct 1914
1050. George Stillman   born 1833; died ____
1051. Jotham M.   born 30 Nov 1837; married Mary Ann SNOW 17 Mar 1857
                         died 1 Mar 1921 Chelsea, MA
1052. John Worcester   born ca 1846; married Phebe Tucker WORCESTER ca 1870; died Easton,NH

395. ALVAH-7 TABBUT/TIBBETTS, brother of above, was born ca 1812 at Columbia Falls, Maine. He married Susanna Freeman DORR, intentions published 22 Feb 1838. She was the daughter of Benjamin DORR and Nellie MAGEE, and sister of Betsey who married Henry-7 TABBUT/TIBBETTS, above. She was born ca 1821; died 187_. Alvah-7 TABBUT/TIBBETTS died ca 1898 at Harrington, Maine.

Children of Alvah-7 TABBUT/TIBBETTS and Susanna DORR:
   Surname TABBUT/TIBBETTS   (children born Columbia Falls, Maine)
1053. Ambrose Snow   born ca 1842; died 21 Aug 1898   committed suicide
                        1m. Sophronia REED Tucker ca 1863; 2m. Margaret A. FOSS Dec 1892
1054. William J.   born Nov 1843; died 22 Feb 1912 Addison, Maine
                        married Eliza Ann WOOD 2 June 1871(she born Jul 1847; died 17 June 1926)
1055. Elizabeth   born Oct 1856; married George Washington ROCKWELL ca 1877; died 1908

397. OTIS SMITH-7 TABBUT/TIBBETTS, son of Moses-6 TABBUT/TIBBETTS (Elizabeth/Betsey-5 DRISKO; Joseph-4; John-3;2) and Mary CROWLEY, was born 18 Mar 1813 at Columbia Falls, Maine. He married Ellen Amanda-7 COFFIN on 28 Jan 1855 at Addison. She was the daughter of Deacon David-6 COFFIN and Hannah NASH; and was born ca 1833; died 1899. Otis-7 TABBUT/TIBBETTS, a lumberman, died 27 June 1879 at Columbia Falls, Maine.

Children of Otis-7 TABBUT/TIBBETTS and Ellen-7 COFFIN:
   Surname TABBUT/TIBBETTS
1056. John Crowley   born 20 June 1855; married Harriet M. DUNPHY June 1876
                        died 15 Aug 1936 Seattle, WA
1057. David Lorenzo   born 7 Feb 1859; died 12 Mar 1928 unmarried
1058. Fred B.   born Oct 1860; married Mary Elizabeth LAWRENCE 15 Oct 1898; died 1923
1059. Annie C.   born 13 Mar 1863; married Wilbur-7 PETERSON 24 Dec 1889; died ca 1944
1060. Bion Bradbury   born 11 Jan 1865 Addison; married Frances Evelyn MORRIS 13 Jan 1900
                        died 28 June 1945
1061. Ida M.   born ca 1867; married Frank B. MILLER 19 June 1892; died 1921

399. SAMUEL HILLMAN-7 TABBUT/TIBBETTS, brother of above, was born 3 June 1816 at Columbia Falls, Maine. He married Harriet J. SMITH on 13 Nov 1848. She was the daughter of Ebenezer SMITH and Deborah FARNSWORTH, and was born 19 Dec 1827; died 27 June 1897. Samuel-7, a farmer and lumberman, died Oct 1906.

Children of Samuel H-7 TABBUT/TIBBETTS and Harriet SMITH:
  Surname TABBUT/TIBBETTS
  1062. Lydia D.   born May 1850; died 22 Jan 1925
                           married Benjamin Leighton-6 PINEO 3 Sept 1870
                           (he born 14 Aug 1848; died 22 Sept 1888, the result of an accidental shooting)
  1063. Theresa N.   born 4 Feb 1852; married Walter H-9 ROCKWELL 1875; died 1914
  1064. Franklin Pierce   born May 1854; married Clara B-9 GRANT 28 June 1912; died 1925
  1065. Milton Hillman   born ca 1857;   died 21 Oct 1890 Columbia Falls
                           married Cora A-7 DORR 24 Dec 1880 Columbia Falls, ME.
                           (she dau/o Thomas T. DORR (Jonathan) and Olive LORD; born 1861 CF)

400. CAROLINE W-7 TABBUT/TIBBETTS, sister of above, was born 23 Apr 1818 at Columbia Falls, Maine. She married Hillman-7 ALLEN ca 1841. He was the son of Isaac-6 ALLEN and Judith NASH, and was born 29 Sept 1824; died 6 June 1891. Caroline W-7 TABBUT/TIBBETTS died ca 1896.

Children of Caroline-7 TABBUT/TIBBETTS and Hillman-7 ALLEN:
  Surname ALLEN   (children born at Columbia, Maine)
  1066. Isaac Nash   born Oct 1842; married Mary Ann CONLEY 29 June 1862; died 13 Aug 1863
  1067. Frances D.   born 1844; married Uriah Nash-9 INGERSOLL 1865; died 1886
  1068. Horace F.   born 29 Apr 1846; married Emma-8 BRIDGHAM 29 Aug 1868; d. 1 Apr 1901
  1069. Benjamin Franklin born 20 Jan 1849; died 8 Mar 1918 Columbia Falls, Maine
         1m. Mary Frances-2 MAILEY 5 Oct 1872; 2m. Abbie Sophia-7 FARNSWORTH 17 Mar 1883
  1070. Anna A.   born 11 July 1852; marr Rev Milton F-8 BRIDGHAM 3 July 1878; died 7 Sept 1923
  1071. Judith A.   born Sept 1855; died 15 Aug 1860
  1072. Gilbert E.   born July 1857; died 15 Dec 1881
  1073. Mary O.   born July 1859; married Eugene W-8 GRAY ca 1879; died 1923

401. SUSAN JOY-7 TABBUT/TIBBETTS, sister of above, was born 14 Oct 1819 at Columbia Falls, Maine. She married Russell-8 SMITH ca 1844. He was the son of Ebenezer-7 SMITH and Deborah FARNSWORTH, and was born 20 Jan 1817; died 1889. Susan-7 died 1886.

Children of Susan-7 TABBUT/TIBBETTS and Russell-8 SMITH:
  Surname SMITH   (children born Columbia, Maine)
  1074. Bartlett Campbell born Feb 1845; died 18 Mar 1908
                           married Electa Brown-10 INGERSOLL 7 Nov 1868
  1075. John R.   born 30 June 1847; died 2 Oct 1914
     1m. Abbie J-7 DORR int pub 25 Nov 1876; 2m. Almeda Tucker-9 WORCESTER int pub 26 Nov 1886
  1076. Orland Eri   born 1849; married Augusta V-9 SMALL int pub 15 Apr 1872
                           died ____ (abandoned his family, went West)
  1077. Mary Louisa   born 1852; died 1927
  1078. Andrew J.   born 1853; died ____ unmarried
  1079. Adelaide L.   born May 1855; married George M-8 COFFIN 1872; died 1917
  1080. Edgar Emerson   born Feb 1857; married Sophia Helen-3 BARNEY 21 Dec 1878; died 1925 ME.

404. LOUISA M-7 TABBUT/TIBBETTS , sister of above, was born 17 Sept 1825 at Columbia Falls, Maine. She married Isaac Case-7 WORCESTER, intentions published 15 June 1844 at Columbia. He was the son of John-6 WORCESTER and Mary FERNALD, and was born ca 1817; died 5 Oct 1891 at Columbia Falls. Louisa-7 died there 11 Apr 1889.

Children of Louisa-7 TABBUT/TIBBETTS and Isaac WORCESTER:
  Surname WORCESTER   (children born Columbia Falls, Maine)
+ 1081. CECELIA A.   born 26 May 1846; died 21 Oct 1885 Columbia Falls, Maine
                           married Captain Ira G. THOMPSON 31 Aug 1867
                           (he son/o John THOMPSON and Miriam V. NORTON) (he born Aug 1835)

Children of Louisa-7 TABBUT/TIBBETTS, continued:
  Surname WORCESTER
+ 1082. MARY ANN   born ca 1847; married Herrick-6 NASH 1 Sept 1866
                   (he son of John-5 NASH and Sylvania SMITH) (he born 1841; died 188_)
  1083. Julia Tabbut   born Jan 1851; married Philander-7 WHITE 17 June 1875 (as his 2nd wife)
                (he son /o Ichabod-6 WHITE and Pamelia-6 NASH) (he born Dec 1843; died 1916)
                One child: Frank H WHITE born Mar 1877; married Jennie-9 COFFIN
  1084. Arnold William   born 1857; died Oct 1878
                (lost at sea, off Cape Cod, aboard the Schooner *EVELYN*)
  1085. Susan Edith   born 12 Aug 1861; died 11 Feb 1887
                married John Billings-8 WASS 2 Jan 1886
        (he son/o Nathaniel-7 WASS and Clarinda NASH) (he born 23 Feb 1856; died 1925)
        1 child: Susan Edith-9 WASS born 30 Dec 1886; married Eathiel-9 LEIGHTON ca 1907
  1086. Lillian Belle   born 1 Sept 1866; married Charles-6 PINEO 10 Nov 1888; died 3 Aug 1908
                (he born 3 Jan 1861; died 17 Dec 1935)

405. AMOS WORCESTER-7 TABBUT/TIBBETTS, brother of above, was born 21 Oct 1827 at Columbia Falls, Maine. He married Juliette Etta-7 ALLEN on 10 Sept 1848 at Columbia. She was the daughter of Abraham-6 ALLEN and Mary WORCESTER, and was born 10 July 1831; died 3 Mar 1914. Amos-7 TABBUT/TIBBETTS, a farmer and lumberman, died 23 July 1900 at Addison, Maine.

Children of Amos-7 TABBUT/TIBBETTS and Juliette ALLEN:
  Surname TABBUT/TIBBETTS
  1087. Edmund Drisko   born June 1849 Columbia, ME; died 2 July 1907 Addison, Maine
                married Melvina-3 BARNEY 25 Oct 1870
                (she born Mar 1852; died 20 Sept 1939)
  1088. Benjamin Franklin born 5 Feb 1851 Columbia Falls, ME;
                married Sarah A. FIELD 29 Oct 1875; died 1 June 1924 Bremerton, WA
      (she dau/o David FIELD and Caroline ?) (she born 1 June 1858; died 18 July 1935, WA)
  1089. Amos Everett   born Feb 1855 Centerville, ME; died 8 Feb 1924 Addison, ME.
                married Effie-5 CROWLEY 28 Nov 1881
  1090. Idella E.   born Jan 1860; died young
  1091. Rosa E.   born 29 Nov 1861 Centerville, ME; died 21 Apr 1898
                married Frank-7 THOMPSON 4 Nov 1882

406. MARY ANN-7 TABBUT/TIBBETTS, sister of above, was born 17 Nov 1829 at Columbia Falls, Maine. She married John-8 PUFFER, Jr. on 8 Nov 1853 at Columbia, Maine. He was the son of John-7 PUFFER and Catherine R. STANWOOD; and was born 29 July 1824 at Frankfort, Maine; died 1910. Mary Ann-7 TABBUT/TIBBETTS died 30 Nov 1860, eight days after giving birth to a set of twins.

Children of Mary Ann-7 TABBUT/TIBBETTS and John PUFFER, Jr.:
  Surname PUFFER   (children born Columbia, Maine)
  1092. Ida Emeline   born 1 Nov 1854; married James-8 BRIDGHAM 2 Dec 1876
                (he son/o Joseph-7 BRIDGHAM and Deborah WHITTEMORE)
                (he born 4 Mar 1854; died 1921)
  1093. Priscilla Charlotte born 28 Feb 1858; married John V. NEWBURY ca 1890
                died 1920   school teacher
  1094. George H. (twin) born 22 Nov 1860; died 24 Nov 1860
  1095. Charles   (twin)born 22 Nov 1860; died 5 Dec 1860

407. ANDREW JACKSON-7 TABBUT/TIBBETTS, brother of above, was born 25 Aug 1832 at Columbia Falls, Maine. He married Victoria A. ALLEN on 14 Sept 1854 at Columbia. She was the daughter of John T. ALLEN and Mary Nash LOW; and was born Apr 1838; died 1902. Andrew-7 TABBUT/TIBBETTS, a blacksmith, died 19 June 1904.

Children of Andrew-7 TABBUT/TIBBETTS and Victoria ALLEN:
   Surname TABBUT/TIBBETTS
1096. Charles Herbert   born 27 Dec 1858; married Frances WASS 4 Feb 1882
                       (she born 20 Apr 1859; died 12 Dec 1949)
1097. William Bartlett   born May 1867; died ____ unmarried

410. CATHERINE W-7 TABBUT/TIBBETTS   see JEREMIAH-7 TIBBETTS (# 388)
412. MARY E. H-7 TABBUT/TIBBETTS, daughter of William-6 TABBUT/TIBBETTS (Elizabeth-5 DRISKO; Joseph-4; John-3;2) and Anne WRIGHT, was born ca 1827 at Columbia Falls, Maine. She married Samuel Cummings-8 WORCESTER on 21 June 1846 at Columbia. He was the son of Clement Fernald-7 WORCESTER and Tamson Willey CUMMINGS; and was born 11 Mar 1824; died 1911. Mary E H-7 TABBUT/TIBBETTS died 11 Mar 1862 at Centerville, Maine.

Children of Mary-7 TABBUT/TIBBETTS and Samuel WORCESTER:
   Surname WORCESTER
1098. Francis L.   born June 1847; died 13 Oct 1860
1099. Phebe Tucker   born Apr 1850; married John Worcester-5 TIBBETTS 1870; died 1926
1100. Lory S.   born 8 June 1852; died ca 1898, CA.   multiple sclerosis
                       married Julia-9 WORCESTER 16 Nov 1872 (she born 1858; died 1945)
1101. Electa Ann   born 24 Apr 1854; married William P. JORDAN; died 1940
1102. Ignatius S.   born ca 1857; married Rose BERGER of WA.; died ____, a lumberman

413. ENOCH LINCOLN-7 TABBUT/TIBBETTS, brother of above, was born 3 May 1829 at Columbia Falls, Maine. He married Eliza Ann TUCKER on 25 Nov 1852. She was the daughter of Justus S. TUCKER and Sarah LEIGHTON, and was born 25 Oct 1828; died 1906. Enoch L-7 TABBUT/TIBBETTS died 16 Dec 1914 at Columbia, Maine.

Children of Enoch L-7 TABBUT/TIBBETTS and Eliza Ann TUCKER:
   Surname TABBUT/TIBBETTS   (children born Columbia, Maine)
1103. George Levi   born 1855; 1m. Mary A-8 COFFIN 23 Mar 1878
                       2m. Sarah J. WHITTEN ca 1899
1104. Francis Marion born 7 Feb 1860; married Anna Belle COTTON 31 July 1886
                       (she born 26 June 1867; died 30 Sept 1944 MA.)
                       died 7 May 1903 Boston, MA
1105. Mary Elizabeth   born 1862; died ca 1885 unmarried

414. BETSEY SOPHIA-7 TABBUT/TIBBETTS, sister of above, was born ca Jan 1832 at Columbia Falls, Maine. She married Francis Cummings-8 WORCESTER (brother of Samuel, above). He was born 1 Feb 1826; died 27 Feb 1906. Betsey-7 died 19 Dec 1897.

Children of Betsey-7 TABBUT/TIBBETTS and Francis C-8 WORCESTER:
   Surname WORCESTER
1106. Leonice L.   born Jan 1851;   died ca 1916
                       1m. Jefferson TUCKER ca 1871; 2m. Vandeluer LOW 1887
1107. George E.   born 26 Aug 1852; died 28 Apr 1856
1108. Mary Ann   born Dec 1856; died 20 July 1859
1109. Caroline Sophia born Mar 1859; married Milton C. REED 8 Apr 1876
          (he son/o Stephen REED and Ann THORNTON) (he born Mar 1854; died 9 Sept 1928)
1110. Anne Betsey   born 11 Jan 1863; 1m. Lassell-6 CORTHELL ca 1880
                       2m. Leander F. WHITE (he son/o William WHITE and Susan JOHNSON)
                       died 9 Feb 1946 North Reading, MA
1111. George F.   born 1865; married Lillie M. YOUNG 11 Oct 1890
1112. Wilbur M.   born Sept 1867; married Susanna Davis-9 BEAL 2 July 1888; died 1941
                       (she born May 1870; died 1950)

Children of Betsey-7 TABBUT/TIBBETTS, continued:
  Surname WORCESTER
  1113. child   born ca 1871; died young
  1114. Forrester R.   born ca 1874; married Minnie L. BRACY 3 July 1894; died ca 1922
                             (she born 22 July 1876; died 1950)
  1115. Adrianna P.   born 26 Apr 1876; 1m. Joel A. WHITE 21 Apr 1894
                             2m. Charles L. FOREN 30 June 1914

420. BENJAMIN-7 DOWNS, Jr. , son of Mary-6 DRISKO (Joseph-5; 4; John-3;2) and the Rev Benjamin DOWNS, was born ca 1812 at Frankfort, Maine. He married first to _?_. She was born ____; died ____. His second wife was Betsey __?__. She was born ca 1831; died ___.

Children of Benjamin DOWNS, Jr. and ___?___:
  Surname DOWNS
  1116. Melissa   born ca 1841   1117. Reed (m) born ca 1843   1118. Teresa born ca 1845
  1119. Benjamin W. born ca 1847   1120. Joshua   born 1850

422. JOHN-7 (4th) DRISKO, son of John-6 DRISKO (Joseph-5;4; John-3; 2) and Phebe PARKER, was born ca 1801 at Addison, Maine. He married Lucy Worcester-7 LEIGHTON ca 1820/21. She was the daughter of Thomas Parritt-6 LEIGHTON and Miriam WORCESTER + of Addison, Maine. She was born ca 1801 at Plantation # 12, later Columbia, Maine.; and died July 1880. John-7 DRISKO died 21 Nov 1834, he drowned in the Indian River, Addison. Lucy married second to John S. BURNS (1803- 1866) on 12 Feb 1839. She had 3 more children by her 2nd husband. They were James E.; Charles E.; and Lucy BURNS.

Children of John-7 DRISKO and Lucy-7 LEIGHTON:
  Surname DRISKO
  1121. Lorenzo   born ca 1822; died young
  1122. Abdon R.   born ca 1824; died 5 June 1858 unmarried
 +1123. PHEBE PARKER   born 26 July 1826 Addison, ME; died 29 Nov 1866 Jaffa
                          married Abraham Lincoln NORTON, int pub 15 Dec 1849
        (he son/o Jeremiah Beal NORTON and Hannah SAWYER) (he born 20 Jan 1823; died 29 Aug 1881)
 +1124. PRISCILLA ANN   born 17 Mar 1828 Addison, ME; died 6 Apr 1902, MI
                          1m. Captain Ackley Ezra-7 NORTON, int pub 15 Dec 1849 Addison, Maine
        (he son/o Phineas M-6 NORTON and Frances E-7 BEAL; he born 1828; died 1 Jan 1871 Chelsea, MA)
                          2m. Captain Albert BARTMAN in MI; he born Germany; a sea captain
              + Miriam WORCESTER Leighton was living with Ackley and Priscilla DRISKO Norton in 1850, aged 79
 +1125. GEORGE ALVIN   born 23 Nov 1830 Addison, ME; died 28 July 1905, MI
                          married Elizabeth/Lizzie C. SKINNER 3 Dec 1852
        (she dau/o Justin SKINNER and Rachel CUMMINGS) (she born 1834; died 12 Apr 1920, MI)
  1126. John A.   born 1833/34; 1m. Charlotte L. PARKER 5 Jan 1862
                          (she dau/o James PARKER and Mary FARLEY; she born 1841; died ca 1868) no issue
                          2m. Calcida/ Cassie A. BLUNT no issue
                          (she dau/o Thomas BLUNT and Ann FARLEY; she born 1847, ME; removed to WI)

Note: John A. DRISKO, as reported in the Land Patent reports of the Bureau of Land Management (Eastern States Land Office), purchased land in Wisconsin and Michigan. Document # 1776 shows 160 acres of land purchased at Traverse City, Delta County, Michigan on 15 Sept 1874. Document # 31414 shows 80 acres of land in Menasha, Forest Co, Wisconsin purchased on 30 June 1882. Document # 31415 shows another 200 acres purchased there on the same date. On 6 Apr 1891 he purchased 180 acres of land at Marquette, Iron County, Michigan.

THE ADAMS COLONY

George Jones ADAMS, a former actor , alcoholic, and cast-out Mormon preacher , arrived in Washington County, Maine around the 1st of January 1861. He immediately started preaching, to anyone who would listen, about his self-proclaimed " Church of the Messiah ".

ADAMS had written a covenant ++ for his "church " and he preached that the coming of the Messiah was imminent. He told the people of the area, the Old Testament prophecies needed to be fulfilled, namely that all Jews should return to Palestine. He was looking for converts to go to Palestine with him, to labor for God and prepare for their return. He considered himself to be the " chosen servant of the Lord."

For a year and a half, he spoke to people all over Maine and New Hampshire. Some responded quite enthusiastically. He settled in Lebanon, Maine; and began publishing a small monthly magazine which he named the " *Sword of Truth* " . Each issue of the publication spoke about the imminent return of the Jews.

At Indian River, ME his " Church of the Messiah " began to thrive after two leaders of the community were baptized by him. The two were Abe McKENZIE, a businessman, and Warren WASS, a ships' captain.

Not everyone liked the Rev ADAMS, however, and they were quite vocal about it. One such person, a Timothy DRISKO (by birth a DRISCOLL – by choice a DRISKO) +++, " a God-fearing Methodist, merchant and earnest keeper of the welfare of Indian River " – viewed Mr. ADAMS as the " the devil himself. " Tim DRISKO attempted to reduce ADAMS to a laughing stock; little realizing that there would be another DRISKO, in Machias, who would succeed in exposing Mr. ADAMS prior life.

Morey WASS, also an Indian River resident, agreed with Tim DRISKO that Mr. ADAMS was " a silver-tongued orator who had beguiled the entire community ". His feelings about Mr. ADAMS were so strong that he wrote to Springfield, Missouri (where Mr. ADAMS had been cast out from the Mormon Church) and to several other communities in Vermont and New Jersey; asking them to send information about Mr. ADAMS to the local newspaper – the *MACHIAS UNION.*

Due to the efforts of Mr. WASS; Mr. George W. DRISKO and the *MACHIAS UNION* received more than 50 letters stating that George Jones ADAMS was " an unworthy and extremely wicked man. "

George W. DRISKO had been critical of the Rev. Mr. ADAMS from the outset and had published some derogatory articles. On 5 June 1866, after Morey WASS visited the *MACHIAS UNION* newspaper – Mr. DRISKO began and editorial campaign to discredit Mr. ADAMS and to warn the residents of Addison, Indian River and Jonesport.

Mr. DRISKO stated in his newspaper that " even a smart fellow like Abe McKENZIE had been taken in – Gram Burns and her whole tribe – the Ben ROGERS and the NORTONS were supporting the hare-brained scheme of emigrating to that land which was cursed of God 2000 years ago and had not been ' worth a continental ' since -- -- ."

The Rev Mr. ADAMS became upset by these assertions – and with his Palestine venture at stake, he began to lose his temper, loudly proclaiming his innocence. Everyone had an opinion about Mr. ADAMS. There were those who believed whole-heartedly in him, and those who were solidly opposed. Even after all of the bad publicity, Mr. ADAMS was still able to convince 157 " *Downeast Americans* " to board the *NELLIE CHAPIN* (a 3-masted Bark built at the Leander KNOWLES shipyard, Addison, ME.) on 10 August 1866 for the journey to Palestine. They were to be known as the ADAMS COLONY at Jaffa.

Despite the objections of George W. DRISKO, many members of the DRISKO clan would go with Mr. ADAMS. One of ADAMS most ardent supporters was Lucy LEIGHTON Drisko Burns. She was the widow of John-7 DRISKO (# 422) who had drowned at Indian River at age 33. Mrs. Burns , age 66, recruited more people than any other individual, except Mr. ADAMS himself. Her second husband, John S. BURNS also went with her to Jaffa.

Five of Lucy's children would accompany her; including her oldest daughter Phebe Parker-8 DRISKO Norton (# 1123), along with her husband Abraham Lincoln NORTON and their five children. Phebe would die there. Lucy's two sons by her second husband, Charles and James BURNS, were also members of the Colony. Her daughter Priscilla Ann-8 DRISKO Norton (# 1124), who was the wife of Captain

Ackley Ezra NORTON, took their five children. Lucy's son George Alvin-8 DRISKO (# 1125) and his wife Elizabeth SKINNER Drisko +++ took their daughter Julie. George had helped pre-fabricate living units which were taken with them on board the *NELLIE CHAPIN*.

Other DRISKO family members included Benjamin Kelley-8 ROGERS (# 1128), son of Olivette-7 DRISKO and Joseph Prince ROGERS. He was accompanied by his wife Lucy LEIGHTON Rogers, and their five children. Their youngest child, George-9 ROGERS, age 2, would die there.

Abitha D-8 LEIGHTON (# 1137) daughter of Phoebe-7 DRISKO and Nahum Hill LEIGHTON, was married to Uriah LEIGHTON. Of the 3 children who went with them- 2 died in Palestine. When Abitha refused return to Maine with her husband, he divorced her on the grounds of desertion and married a second time to Anna S. DYER. He was a fisherman. Another 13 LEIGHTON relatives made the journey, making a total of 46 persons related to the DRISKO family, almost 1/3 of the Colony.

As is often the case, things seemed rosier from a distance. It was a rough sea voyage and when they arrived at Jaffa, conditions there were not as Mr. ADAMS had portrayed them. They lived on the beach for months while negotiations continued with the officials of the area. The children died from dysentery and living in extremely unsanitary conditions. Most of the Colony members became disillusioned and returned home to Maine in less than a year. A few remained there and became agents for Thomas Cook, Ltd., a tour agency.

It was an era when a number of small religious sects came into being (Ex: the Shakers, and the Oneida Community) for various reasons. Possibly they were searching for what they perceived would be a " better life."

++ Covenant : An agreement among members of a church to hold to certain points of doctrine, faith, etc.
+++ Timothy DRISKO (nee DRISCOLL - see page 213. Unattached Families , for descendants) was a farmer at Addison, having emigrated from Ireland. His wife was Rachel CUMMINGS Skinner. His two step-daughters, Elizabeth SKINNER, the wife of George Alvin DRISKO, and Nancy SKINNER, the wife of Moses LEIGHTON, became part of the ADAMS Colony in spite of his public opposition to it. According to the *MACHIAS UNION* newspaper, May 1881, Timothy DRISKO " was very ill, living in Indian River " with his daughter, who was the wife of George M. EMERSON – It was reported that her husband died aboard the Brig *MARENA* in Rio de Janeiro, South America on 1 Jan 1881, age 35. "

423. OLIVETTE/OLIVE-7 DRISKO, sister of above, was born ca 1803 at Addison, ME. She married first to Joseph Prince-6 ROGERS (as his 2nd wife), intentions published 11 Jan 1825. He was previously married to Mrs. Catherine ENNIS Bryant . Joseph Prince-6 ROGERS was the son of Prince-5 ROGERS and Lydia CARR of Jonesport, ME, and was born Apr 1789 at Montville, ME; died 7 Jan 1846 at Addison.

Olive-7 DRISKO married second to Robert Barton-7 LEIGHTON (1798-1865) (as his 3rd wife), intentions published 9 Aug 1846 Addison, ME. He was the son of Thomas Parritt-6 LEIGHTON and Miriam WORCESTER. He was married first to Margaret BARFIELD (4 ch); and 2nd to Eliza–7 DYER (7 ch). Olive-7 DRISKO and Robert-7 LEIGHTON had no children. He was a lumberman and fisherman at Addison. Olive-7 DRISKO died before 1870. She and her husband are buried at Hall's Hill Cemetery.

Children of Olivette/Olive-7 DRISKO and Joseph Prince-7 ROGERS:
    Surname ROGERS
+ 1127. REBECCA   born ca 1826
        DRISKO   married Jason Clapp-4 CROWLEY int pub 13 Dec 1848 Addison
+ 1128. BENJAMIN   born 14 June 1829 Jonesport, ME.; died 21 Sept 1879 Jonesport
        KELLEY   married Lucy Drisko-8 LEIGHTON 12 Apr 1851
            (she dau/o Curtis-7 LEIGHTON and Philena EMERSON) (she born 21 Dec 1833; died 8 Jan 1921)
  1129. Rufus D.   born ca 1833
+ 1130. CORDELIA H.   born 14 Sept 1835 Jonesport, ME
                         married James Campbell-4 CROWLEY 8 Mar 1852
  1131. Sarah Jane   born ca 1839/40
  1132. Catherine Esther born ca 1842

424. MAYHEW C-7 DRISKO, brother of above, was born ca 1805 at Addison, Maine. He married Clarissa WORCESTER ca 18__. She was the daughter of Joseph WORCESTER and Abigail NASH of Columbia, Maine; and was born Apr 1811; died 25 July 1893. Mayhew-7 DRISKO, a ships' carpenter at Addison, died ca 1885.

Children of Mayhew-7 DRISKO and Clarissa WORCESTER:
Surname DRISKO
1133. Luthera   born ca 1838; died 1880 unmarried   EOL
1134. Lucy W.   born ca 1842/43; died 1919 at West Roxbury, MA
          married John Hartley ALBEE 2 July 1872 Machias, ME (he born ca 1837; died 18__)
+ 1135. AUGUSTUS W. born 16 Dec 1845; married Clara L. HALL; died 17 Feb 1925 S. Portland, ME
          (she born 1865; died 1 June 1917) (she dau/o Levi HALL and Betsey TABBUT)

425. PHEBE PARKER-7 DRISKO, sister of above, was born Sept 1806 at Addison, Maine. She married Nahum Hill-7 LEIGHTON, intentions published 6 Feb 1828 at Addison. He was the son of Thomas Parritt-6 LEIGHTON, and was born 1803 Columbia, Maine; died 13 Mar 1867 at Addison. Phebe Parker-7 DRISKO died 29 June 1849 at Addison, after the birth of her 13th child. Nahum-7 LEIGHTON married second to Abigail 6 COFFIN Tucker Crowley on 9 Apr 1860.

Children of Phebe Parker-7 DRISKO and Nahum-7 LEIGHTON:
Surname LEIGHTON
1136. Mary Jane   born 17 July/Sept 1828 Addison, ME; died 18 Oct 1889 Columbia, ME
          married James Monroe McCASLIN 2 Aug 1847
     (he son/o Alexander McCASLIN and Abigail KNOWLES ; he born 12 June 1822; died 6 Jan 1907)
+1137. ABITHA D.   born 1830 Addison; married Uriah Wass-8 LEIGHTON 1852
          (he son/o John-7 LEIGHTON and Eunice WRIGHT)
1138. Captain Harris H. born 1 May 1832; married Elvina A-8 LEIGHTON 9 Oct 1852
          (she sister of Uriah-7 LEIGHTON, above ; she born 9 Dec 1834/5; died 8 Sept 1919)
          died 18 Aug 1921 Addison, Maine no issue   EOL
1139. Avery W.   born 3 June 1834; died 10 Dec 1853 Staten Island, NY (smallpox)
+ 1140. CAPTAIN   born 3 Nov 1835 Addison, ME; died 9 Feb 1917 Milbridge, Maine.
   JASON DRISKO   married MARY ELIZABETH-8 DRISKO 20 Oct 1860 (# 1270)
          (she dau/o Edmund C-7 DRISKO and Hannah ALLEN)
          (she born 14 May 1842; died 7 Aug 1868 at sea)
According to records held at the Maine Historical Society, Portland, Maine – Jason Drisko-8 LEIGHTON served in the **1st Regiment of the Maine Artillery** during the **Civil War**, from 1862-65.

There are also " miscellaneous papers of Captain Jason Drisko-8 LEIGHTON of Milbridge, Maine. containing papers of the Bark *I SARGENT*, the Schooner *CRYSTAL PALACE*, and the Brigs *G F BUCKNAM, J W SAWYER* and the *MARY E LEIGHTON*, consisting of ships' papers, captains accounts with owners and crew, and shippers; bills of lading for the *I SARGENT* and *CRYSTAL PALACE*; bills and receipts for the *CRYSTAL PALACE* reflecting the cost of ship repairs, wharfage, pilotage and the like."   MS 68-159 – (2,3,5,9,10)
1141. James Parker   born 1837; died 185 _
+ 1142. SARAH A.   born 17 July 1839 Addison, Maine; died 3 Feb 1900 Milbridge, Maine
          married Ezra S-7 STROUT ca 1860
     (he son/o Lewis-6 STROUT and Lydia SMITH)(he born 2 Feb 1835; died 13 Oct 1905)
+ 1143. REBECCA   born 16 Nov 1840 Addison, Maine; died 1913
   DRISKO   married David Beriah-6 JOY 29 Sept 1857
+ 1144. LUCY W.   born ca 1842; died 17 Mar 1912 Gouldsboro, Maine
          married Charles William-7 TRACY 21 Jan 1865
          (he son/o Eri-6 TRACY and Hannah ASHE) (he born 20 Mar 1833; died 16 Aug 1896)
+ 1145. LAURA DRISKO born 8 Jan 1844; died 20 Jan 1916 Milbridge, Maine
          married John Henry FOSTER 20 Jan 1866; (he born 21 Jan 1841; died 1890 Milbridge)
          (he son/o William Godfrey FOSTER and Catherine CAMPBELL Ray)
1146. Porter   born ca 1845; d y   1147. Nahum, Jr.   born ca 1846; died 190_ EOL

Children of Phebe Parker-7 DRISKO, continued:
    Surname LEIGHTON
+ 1148. PHEBE PARKER born 29 June 1849; married Captain Warren FOSTER 31 May 1873
                    (he born 24 Apr 1846; died 1908 Milbridge)(he brother of John, above)

426. REBECCA-7 DRISKO, sister of above, was born 31 Dec 1808 at Addison, Maine. She married
Andrew Elliot-8 BATSON on 10 Aug 1834 (intentions published 20 July 1834) at Addison. He was the
son of Captain Stephen-7 BATSON (William-6; Stephen-5; John-4;3;2; Stephen-1) and Mary ELLIOT
of Addison, and was born 20 Mar 1812; died 10 Apr 1892 at Addison. He was a farmer at South Addison.
Rebecca-7 DRISKO died 23 Jan 1891 at Addison.

Children of Rebecca-7 DRISKO and Andrew BATSON:
    Surname BATSON   (all children born Addison, Maine)
    1149. Almira H.   born Nov 1836; died 14 May 1892
        (twin)   married George Henry CHANDLER ca 1858 (he born July 1834; died 19 Nov 1860)
                      One child: Mary E. CHANDLER born ca 1860
+ 1150. OLIVETTE M.   born Nov 1836; died 11 Mar 1926
        (twin)   married Benjamin Franklin REYNOLDS, Jr. 1859
    (he son/o Benjamin F- REYNOLDS and Anna CHANDLER; he born Apr 1837; died 18 Dec 1915)
+ 1151. CAPTAIN   born 26 Nov 1838; married Adrianna Abigail CARTER int pub 8 Aug 1871
    ADRIAN ABBOTT   (she born 9 Dec 1853; died 15 Dec 1936)
    1152. Captain   born Dec 1840; 1m. Josephine B. ALLEN; 2m. unknown
        John Drisko   3m. Ruth D. CARTER Drisko 10 Jan 1882
                          (she wid/o Everett-8 DRISKO # 1167, and sister of Adrianna CARTER)
                          died 7 July 1926 Addison, Maine (sea captain and farmer)
    1153. Captain Franklin born 6 Dec 1842; died 5 May 1918 Boston, MA
        Jones   married Mary Ann LOOK intentions published 2 Jan 1867 Harrington, Maine
                          (she born Dec 1846; died 5 Feb 1912)
    1154. Harriet Elvena   born July 1845; married Francis Edgar WASS 1870; died 26 Oct 1930
    1155. Anne Rebecca   born 16 Aug 1848; died June 1922; school teacher
        (Annie R.)   marr. William N-9 INGERSOLL 7 Oct 1871(he b. Dec 1849; d. 28 Feb 1923)
                1 child: Herbert N. INGERSOLL born ca 1872; married Carrie LAKEMAN 16 Nov 1898
    1156. Andrew Arthur   born 20 Aug 1851; died 17 May 1908   (he a seaman and farmer)
                          married Eliza Emma MERRITT 17 July 1881 (she born 21 Feb 1856; died 19 Aug 1936)
Note: Lorrain S. DRISKO (# 429), brother of Rebecca, resided with this family according to the 1860 Federal Census for Addison,
Maine. In 1870 he resided with Everett-8 DRISKO (# 1167), son of Jason Clapp-7 DRISKO (# 428).
                    Reference: Darryl LAMSON, Warrensburg, MO; 1860/70 Census Addison, Maine

427. CAPTAIN GEORGE WASHINGTON-7 DRISKO, brother of above, was born 16 Aug 1810 at
Addison, Washington County, Maine. He married first to Mary S-7 KILTON ++, intentions published 15
May 1833 at Jonesboro, Maine. She was the daughter of John-6 KILTON and Sarah W. SAWYER, and
was born 31 Mar 1814; died after 1850 and before 1855. They resided Addison, Jonesboro and Belfast,
Maine – and removed to Boston, MA ca 1848 when Mary-7 began studying medicine there. She was
preparing to become one of the first woman doctors – but there is no record that she reached that goal.

Captain George W-7 DRISKO, married second to Margaret-8 FOSTER Gardner of Machiasport, MEon
19 Sept 1855 at Machias. She was the daughter of Nathan-7 FOSTER (# 457 FOSTER section) and
Sarah G-4 CROCKER (# 98 CROCKER), and was born ca 1819 at Machiasport, Maine. She was married
1st to George W. GARDNER, a ships' carpenter, on 26 Sept 1841. They had two daughters, Sarah Josephine and Henrietta/Marietta GARDNER. (see FOSTER Section). Margaret-8 FOSTER died 12 Aug
1909 at Syracuse, Onondaga Co., NY. She is buried in the DRISKO plot at Oakwood Cemetery, that city.

Captain George-7 DRISKO was a master mariner, a sea captain at Addison, Belfast, Cutler, Jonesboro and
Jonesport, Maine, as well as Boston, MA. He died 30 Nov 1878 at Syracuse, NY and is buried there.

Children of Captain George W-7 DRISKO and Mary S-7 KILTON:
    Surname DRISKO

1157. Laura	born ca 1834; died 16 Mar 1843 Jonesboro, Maine
+ 1158. MATILDA J.	born ca 1835, Jonesboro; married Asa WESTON of MA.; died before 1911
	(he born 1832 Sandwich, MA; died ____)
+ 1159. VANDELIA	born Jan 1837 Jonesboro; married James C. LEWIS 23 Nov 1859 Boston
(Fannie/Fanny)	(he son of Nicholas LEWIS and Olive C. __?___)
	(he born Jan 1831, ME; died 4/14 Oct 1903)
	died 10 Nov 1880 Somerville, MA; buried Grove Cemetery Belfast, ME cancer
1160. Augustus W.	born 3 Nov 1838 Jonesboro; died 23 May 1844 Rogue Island (Jonesboro)
1161. Hubert	born ca 1840/41 Jonesboro; died ____ (poss before 1854/55)
1162. dau	born and died 1844; gs reads Infant dau of Geo W/ Mary DRISKO
	buried Rogue Island, Shorey's Cove Jonesboro
+ 1163. EVERARD	born 1845/46 Belfast, Waldo County, Maine
IRVING	1m. Emma S-8 WHITNEY ca 1874
	(she dau/o William-7 WHITNEY and Sophronia __?__)
	(she born 185_; died 26 May 1877)
	2m. Flora A. HARPER before 1880

Children of Captain George W-7 DRISKO and Margaret-8 FOSTER:
    Surname DRISKO

+ 1164. GEORGE	born 19 Jul 1856 Machiasport, Maine
AUGUSTUS	married Amelia A. GREEN ca 1880 at East Syracuse, NY
	(she dau/o Henry GREEN, Jr. and Nancy A. FINCK)
	(she born 16 May 1861; died 20 July 1919)
	died 30 Apr 1936, Syracuse, NY; buried Oakwood Cemetery, Syracuse, NY
1165. Laura	born ca 1860, Maine; died at age 3 months

++ Ancestry of Mary-7 KILTON

THOMAS-1 KILTON, the immigrant, was born ca 16__, in ____, Scotland. He married Susannah __?__.
THOMAS-2 KILTON, was born ca 16__, probably at Boston, MA. He married Jane-3 BLAKE on 25 Jan 1685. She was the daughter of Edward-2 BLAKE and Agnes BENT. Thomas-2 KILTON died 18 Oct 17__ at Dorchester. MA.

Their son, JONATHAN-3 KILTON, was born 14 Dec 1691 at Milton, MA. He married first to Mary-3 BIRD on 4/14 Feb 1718. She was the daughter of Thomas-2 BIRD (Thomas-1) and Thankful ATHERTON. Jonathan-3 KILTON died ca Apr 1752.

JONATHAN-4 KILTON, was born 27 May 1730 at Dorchester, MA. He married Margaret LUCAS. She was born 23 Apr 1735; died 14 Dec 1817. Jonathan-4 KILTON died 20 Nov 1804 at Athol, MA.

BENJAMIN-5 KILTON, son of Jonathan-4, was born 3 Dec 1765 at Athol. He married Mary Parris RUSSELL on 26 Oct 1765 at Barre, MA. She was the daughter of William RUSSELL and Katherine BENT; and was born 6 Apr 1763 at Athol; died 21 Apr 1835 at Jonesboro, Maine.

JOHN-6 KILTON, was born 8 Jan 1787 at ___, NH. He married Sarah/Sally W. SAWYER on 16 June 1810 at Jonesboro, Maine. She was born ca 1792; died 23 Jan 1861. John-6 KILTON died 17 Dec 1854 at Jonesboro. He was a Private in the **War of 1812**, and served one year at the Fort in Machias, Maine.

428. JASON CLAPP-7 DRISKO, brother of above, was born Feb 1813 at Addison, Maine. He married first to Lucy-7 WORCESTER, intentions published 15 June 1839; married 27 Oct 1839. She was the daughter of Joseph-6 WORCESTER and Abigail NASH; and was born 1820; died ca 1845/46. His second marriage was to Mary Ann-7 FARNSWORTH, intentions published 4 Sept 1846. She was the daughter of Levi-6 FARNSWORTH and Delia Speare WATTS of Jonesboro, Maine. She was born Dec 1830; died ____ (still living 1900). Jason C-7 DRISKO, a ships' carpenter, was still living 1900.

Children of Jason C-7 DRISKO and Lucy-7 WORCESTER:

Surname DRISKO	(children born Jonesboro, Maine)
1166. Harriet R.	born ca Oct 1840/41; married Daniel Shepard-4 NOYES 5 Nov 1859
(Hattie)	(he son/o Phineas-3 NOYES and Lydia Holmes-3 TABBUTT)

Children of Jason Clapp-7 DRISKO, continued:
   Surname DRISKO
+ 1167. EVERETT W.   born ca 1842; married Ruth D. CARTER 25 June 1865
                     died 20 May 1880   ships' carpenter
Children of Jason C-7 DRISKO and Mary Ann-7 FARNSWORTH:
   Surname DRISKO
1168. Julia C.   born Feb 1848 Jonesboro, ME
                1m. John W. FEENEY 2 Apr 1865 (he born 1843; died 1884)
   1 ch: Ulva Mabel-9 FEENEY born 1869; marr Charles F. CRANDON 18 Apr 1888; died 11 Aug 1889)
          2m. Frederick S. COFFIN 13 Mar 1886 (div);3m. Henry Alvin GARNETT 17 Feb 1906
1169. Child   born ca 1849; died young   EOL
1170. James Hamilton   born 1851/52; died 27 Dec 1867   EOL
1171. Delia M.   born 7 July 1854; died 12 Mar 1895
                married Ansel Jeremiah-8 TUPPER 6 June 1877
(he son /o Decatur B-7 TUPPER and Lois White NORTON; born 17 Apr 1854; died 14 Feb 1908 NH)
             1 child: Hattie M-9 TUPPER born 1892; died 1897
    1172. Lucy F.   born 1858; d y   1173. Child   born after 1860; d y

430. JAMES PARKER-7 DRISKO, brother of above, was born ca 1817 at Addison, Maine. He married
Amanda Whitney-3 ARCHER on 16 Mar 1843 at Addison. She was the daughter of Thomas-2 ARCHER
and Hannah-7 TUPPER of Columbia and Cherryfield, Maine. Amanda-3 was born 20 Apr 1820 at Cherryfield; and died 14 July 1904. James Parker-7 DRISKO, a sailor and farmer, died after 1880.

Children of James P-7 DRISKO and Amanda ARCHER:
   Surname DRISKO
1174. Dana Boynton   born 23 Mar 1843; died 11 Mar 1845
+ 1175. AMANDA   born Jan 1847; died ca 1915 unmarried
     RHODELLA   (had one son – no further information)
1176. Laura J.   born 31 Jan 1852; died 16 Mar 1863
1177. Ellis   born 1856; died ____
1178. Jane W.   born 1859; died 20 Oct 1937
            married John VAN BUSKIRK 30 Apr 1882 (he born ca 1846; died 30 Apr 1931)

431. AMBROSE DYER-7 MC KENZIE, son of Hannah-6 DRISKO (Joseph-5;4; John-3;2) and Daniel
McKENZIE, was born 25 Feb 1798 at Columbia, Maine. He married Sophia TINGLEY ca 1826 at ____,
New Brunswick. She was born 4 July 1802 ____, Kings County, New Brunswick; and died 29 Apr 1856,
New Brunswick. Ambrose-7 died there 28 July 1856.

Children of Ambrose Dyer-7 McKENZIE and Sophia TINGLEY:
   Surname McKENZIE
1179. Pamela	born 25 July 1827	1184. Daniel	born Nov 1833; died 1834
1180. James	born 26 Jan 1829	1185. Ann	born ____
1181. William	born 13 Apr 1830	1186. Ambrose, Jr.	born ____
1182. Mary	born 16 Oct 1831	1187. Charles Frederick born 12 Sept 1844;	
1183. Elizabeth	born Jan 1833; died 1834		died 1885

432. JOEL-7 McKENZIE, brother of above, was born ca 1793 at Columbia, ME. He married Helena-6
LARRABEE on 25 Mar 1824. She was the daughter of Abner-5 LARRABEE and Jane-5 FOSTER; and
was born ca 1802; died ____, ME. Joel-6 McKENZIE died, by hanging himself, on 1 May 1852 at
Columbia, Maine.

Children of Joel-7 McKENZIE and Helena-6 LARRABEE:
   Surname McKENZIE   (children born at Columbia, Maine)
1188. Child   born ca 1825

Children of Joel-7 McKENZIE, continued:
Surname McKENZIE

1189. Betsey	born ca 1827; married Samuel-4 LAWRENCE 7 Sept 1846	
	(he son/o Aaron-3 LAWRENCE and Lucy H-7 LEIGHTON)	
1190. Hannah	born ca 1829	1196. Augusta C. born ca 1841
1191. Leonice	born ca 1831	married John RADLEY Mar 1855
1192. Helen	born ca 1833	1197. Jeremiah born ca 1844
1193. Child	born ca 1835	1198. Delbert born ca 1848; died 1850 (age 2)
1194. Benjamin	born ca 1837	
1195. Almira	born ca 1839; married Joseph SUTCLIFF int pub 3 May 1856	

433. MATILDA-7 McKENZIE, sister of above, was born ca 1802 at Columbia, ME. She married Barnard " Barney " McGLAUGHLIN, intentions published 1 June 1823 at Columbia. He was born ca 1800 in IRE.

Children of Matilda-7 McKENZIE and Barnard McGLAUGHLIN:
Surname McGLAUGHLIN

1199. Daniel	born 24 Mar 1824 Machias, ME; 1m. Delia COLSON 10 Dec 1840	
	(she born ca 182_; died ca 1841)	
	2m. Abigail LOVETT int pub 8 June 1842	
1200. John	born 28 June 1826, Columbia; married Lucy A SMITH int pub 17 Aug 1848	
1201. Mary Ann	born 3 Sept 1830; died 1915	1205. Charles A. born 20 May 1842
1202. Eliza J.	born 11 Mar 1833; died 1839	1206. Isabella born May 1845
1203. Francis M.	born Nov 1835	married George H. ALLEN
	married Juliet WOOD 1856	1207. Edwin born Apr 1851
1204. Barnard, Jr.	born ca 1838	

434. MARY DYER-7 McKENZIE, sister of above, was born ca 1804 at Columbia, Maine. She married John MAILEY; intentions published at Columbia 31 Aug 1823. He was an Irish immigrant, and was born ca 1800 _____, Ireland; died 14 Feb 1868 Columbia, Maine. Mary-7 died 1886.

Children of Mary Dyer-7 McKENZIE and John MAILEY:
Surname MAILEY

1208. Catherine	born ca 1824; married Charles McCARTY; divorced; died 10 May 1890
	Two children: Catherine-9 (born 1842) and Jeremiah-9 McCARTY (born Nov 1843)
1209. John Nelson	born Nov 1829; died 1905

436. DANIEL-7 McKENZIE, brother of above, was born ca 1808/09 at Columbia, Maine. He married first to Miriam HANNA, intentions published 2 June 1829 at Columbia. She was the daughter of John HANNA and Jane CAMPBELL, and was born ca 1807; died 3 Oct 1840. He married second to Susan P. AYERS on 7 Nov 1841. She was born ca 1810; died 1 June 1879.

Children of Daniel-7 McKENZIE and Miriam HANNA:
Surname McKENZIE

1210. Ambrose I.	born ca 1831; died 1852
1211. Alonzo S.	born Apr 1834; died 1844
1212. George E.	born ca 1835; married Frances CALKINS 1861
1213. John Hanna	born ca 1837; 1m. Matilda E. STUART 14 Nov 1858
	2m. Jane CLARK 19 Dec 1863; 3m. Amelia A. CROCKER 13 July 1867
1214. Julia A.	born Oct 1840; 1m. Hiram T. BERRY June 1861
	(he son/o Freeman BERRY and Hannah __?__)
	2m. Ivory TRAFTON 19 Dec 1873

438. JOSEPH DRISKO-7 McKENZIE, brother of above, was born ca 1816 at Columbia, Maine. He married MARIAH STEELE-7 DRISKO (# 454) his cousin, on 30 Sept 1841 at Columbia. She was the

daughter of Josiah-6 DRISKO (# 137) and Theodocia CROWLEY, and was born ca 1822; died 1867.
Joseph D-7 McKENZIE died at Columbia, Maine on 24 Aug 1863.

Children of Joseph-7 McKENZIE and Mariah-7 DRISKO:
    surname McKENZIE   (first 4 children born Columbia, ME; last 4 born Centerville, ME)

1215. Sophia L.	born ca 1842; died 1858	1219. Theodocia O.	born 8 Aug 1851
1216. Arthur D.	born Feb 1844; died 1847	1220. Mary Alice	born 9 Jan 1854
1217. Horace Greeley	born ca 1846; died ____	1221. Millard Fillmore	born 29 Nov 1856
1218. Oscar	born Feb 1849; died young	1222. Ezra Josiah	born 19 June 1858

439. DELILAH D-7 McKENZIE, (Delia) sister of above, was born ca 1822 at Columbia, Maine. She
married first to Owen-3 McKENZIE on 13 Nov 1841 at Columbia. He was the son of Owen-2 McKENZIE
and Persis COLSON, and was born ca 1821 Columbia; died on 16 Oct 1862 at Camp Stetson, VA of
of injuries sustained in the **Civil War.** Delilah-7 married second to Ephraim HOPPER on 5 Sept 1868.

Children of Delilah-7 McKENZIE and Owen-3 McKENZIE:
    surname McKENZIE   (children born at Addison, Maine)
    1223. Christiana   born ca 1844
    1224. William Forrester born 12 Nov 1846 Ellsworth, ME.; died 7 Jan 1885 Addison, ME.
                              married Elizabeth Ann WORCESTER 14 Feb 1865 Columbia Falls, ME.
                              (she born 1843; died Apr 1925, MA)

1225. Adah Emily	born ca 1849	1227. Clara D.	born 13 Feb 1858
1226. Oscar D.	born 16 June 1854	1228. Isabelle	born 18 Feb 1861

440. ELIZA/ELIZABETH N-7 DRISKO, daughter of Joseph-6 DRISKO (Joseph-5;4; John-3;2) and
Eunice PARKER, was born ca 1804/05 at Addison, ME.. She married Ebenezer-7 SAWYER, intentions
published 4 Oct 1827 at Addison. He was the son of Nehemiah-6 SAWYER and Rebecca-6 SAWYER,
and was born 2 July 1806; died 30 Apr 1878. He was a ships' carpenter at Jonesport. Eliza N-7 DRISKO
died 15 Feb 1889 at Jonesport, ME.

Children of Eliza-7 DRISKO and Ebenezer-7 SAWYER:
    Surname SAWYER   (children born at Jonesport, Maine)

+ 1229. STEPHEN E.	born 12 Oct 1828; married Dorcas Elizabeth KELLEY; died 20 Feb 1910
	(she born ca 1838; died ____)
1230. Eunice D.	born 8 Feb 1830; married Henry KELLEY; died 22 Dec 1910
+ 1231. JOSEPH W.	born 5 Dec 1831; married Rebecca E. WATTS 4 Feb 1855; died 9 Dec 1876
1232. Mary Emily	born 15 Mar 1833; married Benjamin Otis BRYANT 23 Apr 1854; died 1923
1233. Eliza Ann	born 10 May 1835; married John SAWYER; died 4 June 1912
1234. Lois Mansfield	born ca 1837; married Samuel James JENKINS 12 Dec 1866; died 11 Aug 1877
1235. Harriet Newell	born ca 1839; married Reuben S. BEAL ca 1859
+ 1236. EBENEZER J.	born 5 July 1840; married Philena Augusta KELLEY; died 1917
+ 1237. GEORGE W.	born ca 1842; married Mary Elizabeth KELLEY; died 1878
1238. Clara Emma	born ca 1844; married Jewett BRYANT 3 Aug 1867; died 7 Oct 1931
1239. William H	born ca 1846/47; married Mary A. SAWYER

441. FEAH PARKER-7 DRISKO, sister of above, was born ca 1808 at Addison, ME. She married Aaron-
7 COFFIN, intentions published 10 July 1828 at Addison. He was the son of Matthew-6 COFFIN +
(Matthew-5; Richard-4; Tristam-3; John-2; Tristam-1) and Lydia WHITNEY, and was born 1806; died
____, CA. Feah Parker-7 DRISKO died 6 Mar 1880 at Lewiston, Maine.

Children of Feah P-7 DRISKO and Aaron-7 COFFIN:
    Surname COFFIN

+ 1240. CORDELIA M.	born ca 1830; 1m. Joseph-3 McKENZIE 26 Feb 1852
	2m. JAMES CAMPBELL-7 COFFIN (as his 2nd wife) 31 Dec 1854 (# 493)

Children of Feah Parker-7 DRISKO, continued:
Surname COFFIN

1241. Martha M.	born ca 1835	1245. William H. born 1844
1242. Frederick S.	born ca 1837	married Lizzie E. BERRY 1 June 1867 Machias
1243. Appheus L.	born ca 1839	1246. George W. born ca 1847; resided CA
1244. Mary F.	born ca 1842; married Seth D. WAKEFIELD 1859	

+ Matthew-6 COFFIN was born ca 1781. A farmer, he resided with his son Aaron in 1850 at Centerville, Maine.

443. EUNICE PARKER-7 DRISKO, sister of above, was born ca 1810 at Addison, Maine. She married Captain Oliver-7 SAWYER ca 1830/31. He was the son of Nehemiah SAWYER and Rebecca-6 SAWYER of Addison, and was born 16 Dec 1809; died 25 Sept 1881. Eunice Parker-7 DRISKO, died Mar 1850 (age 39). Oliver-7 SAWYER, a shipbuilder and sea captain at Jonesport, Maine; married second to Mary M. NORTON ca 1851, and had 7 more children : Mary; Oliver; Wellington; Ellery A.; Orlando T.; William A.; and Lillian B. SAWYER. Resided Jonesport, Maine.

Children of Eunice-7 DRISKO and Captain Oliver-7 SAWYER:
Surname SAWYER

1247. Elizabeth D.	born ca 1832; married Barnabas C. BEALE
1248. Rebecca	born ca 1834; married Jefferson DOBBINS
1249. Frederick A.	born ca 1836; married Melinda Jane FOSS 15 June 1863 (9 ch)

444. JEREMIAH-7 DRISKO, brother of above, was born 5 Apr 1812 at Addison, Washington County, Maine. He married first to Nancy Shaw-6 PARKER of Steuben, Maine (his cousin), intentions published 5 Jan 1836. She was the daughter of William-5 PARKER ++ and Polly GRACE; and was born 21 Sept 1815, Steuben; died ca 1838. He married second Mary L-8 INGERSOLL of Centerville, Maine ca 1839. She was the daughter of Samuel-7 INGERSOLL (William-6; 5; Benjamin-4; Joseph-3; George-2; Richard-1) and Lydia LOOK, and was born 19 July 1819; died 2 Oct 1881, aged 62 years. He married 3rd to Mrs. Abigail TENNEY Tenney on 30 June 1883. Jeremiah-7 DRISKO served as a Representative to the Maine Legislature in 1876 from Centerville, Maine. He died at Centerville 9 Dec 1893.
++ William-5 PARKER the son of Elisha-4 PARKER (Elisha-3; Benjamin-2; Robert-1 of Barnstable, MA) and Eunice JORDAN, was born 7 Apr 1770 Steuben, Maine; married Polly GRACE ca 1795. He was the brother of Eunice-5 PARKER Hill Drisko, the mother of Jeremiah-7 DRISKO, above.

Child of Jeremiah-7 DRISKO and Nancy Shaw-6 PARKER:
Surname DRISKO

1250. Elizabeth Maria	born ca 1837; 1m. Francis Marion AYERS 2 Oct 1858; died ca 1906
	(he born 1835; died 1880, killed on his gold claim CA)
	2m. _____ TENNEY; 3m. John SMITH of Bath, Maine

Children of Jeremiah-7 DRISKO and Mary L-8 INGERSOLL:
Surname DRISKO

+ 1251. AUGUSTUS MELVILLE	born ca 1840; married Leonice G. GRACE 6 Nov 1864 (she dau/o William B. GRACE and Rebecca Lucy STROUT died ca 1869 Saginaw, Michigan
+ 1252. FRANCIS JASPER	born ca 1842; married Nancy LORD 24 June 1865 died 27 Dec 1928 Harrington, Maine
+ 1253. SEWALL MARSTON	born 4 July 1844; married Helen Augusta CALER 4 June 1864 (she dau/o John B. CALER and Nancy FOSTER)(she born 1845; died 1918)
+ 1254. JULIA B.	born July 1853; married Frank R. DYER 1876
1255. Bertha M.	born 14 May 1859; died 23 May 1861 (gs)
+ 1256. BION L.	born 7 July 1863 Centerville, ME; married Ada ALLEN 4 July 1893 (she dau/o John ALLEN and Drucilla ALLEN) (she born 17 Nov 1874; died 15 Feb 1967 San Luis Obispo, CA) died 18 Jan 1936 Northville, South Dakota

448. ZIMRI TABBUT-7 DRISKO, son of Josiah-6 DRISKO (Joseph-5; 4; John-3; 2) and Theodocia

CROWLEY, was born 18 Sept 1811 at Addison, Maine. He married 18 Feb 1832 to Roxalana Hall-7 NORTON. She was the daughter of Jeremiah Beal-6 NORTON and Hannah SAWYER, and was born 19 Sept 1811; died 1 Aug 1887. Zimri Tabbut-7 DRISKO died 7 Mar 1845 (gs). Roxalana-7 married 2nd to Joseph ALLEY, a fisherman and laborer, born ca 1798. She had three more children before 1850 : Jane (born 1844); Amanda (born 1846); and Hannah ALLEY (born 1848).

Children of Zimri-7 DRISKO and Roxalana-7 NORTON:
Surname DRISKO   (children born Jonesport, Maine)
1257. Sylvina Hall   born ca 1833; marr Thomas Francis CUMMINGS 1851; died 21 Aug 1873
          (he son/o Francis CUMMINGS and Mary KELLEY)(he born 25 Mar 1829; died 10 May 1898)
1258. Elmira G.   born 2 Apr 1835; died 29 Sept 1895
                         married Robert M. ALLEY 7 July 1850 Jonesport, ME..
                         (he son/o Joshua ALLEY and Lydia BEAL)
+ 1259. ALEXANDER   born 21 Dec 1836; married Sophia B. FAULKINGHAM
       MILLIKEN   died 15 Dec 1901
+ 1260. JEREMIAH   born 2 Dec 1838; 1m. Mary Sabra ALLEY; 2m. Annie/Anna B/V KELLEY
       NORTON   (she born Nov 1857; died 22 Dec 1936)
                         died 19 Dec 1899 seaman and fisherman
+ 1261. THEODOCIA   born Dec 1840; married CHARLES A-7 DRISKO 1859 (# 506)
                         died 18 Sept 1885

449. JEREMIAH-7 DRISKO, brother of above, was born ca 1812 at Addison, Maine. he married first to Jane-7 HUNTLEY ca 18__. She was the daughter of Daniel-6 HUNTLEY and Rachel-7 GARDNER, and was born ca 1815; died 15 Oct 1843. His second wife was Mary Jane-7 ALLEN. They were married on 21 Oct 1844 at Columbia, Maine. She was the daughter of Abraham-6 ALLEN and Mary/Polly WORCES-TER, and was born ca 1823; died ____, WA. Jeremiah-7 DRISKO died of typhoid fever on 25 May 1848.

Children of Jeremiah-7 DRISKO and Jane-7 HUNTLEY:
Surname DRISKO
+ 1262. CAPTAIN   born Dec 1836/37; married Hannah Norton KELLEY 14 Sept 1859 at Addison
       HIRAM   (she dau/o Aaron KELLEY and Rebecca S. NORTON)
       CROWLEY   (she born 16 Oct 1841; died 1920)
1263. Mary Eliza   born 1838; died 1839 (aged 11 mo.) gs
1264. Arthur Albee.   born ca Oct 1840; died 19 Aug 1841 (aged 10 mo.) gs
+ 1265. CAPTAIN   born 28 July 1843 Jonesport, Maine
       THOMAS   married Francesca T. SAWYER 1866 at Lancaster, St. John, New Brunswick
       ARTHUR   (she dau/o Levi B. SAWYER and Jane Barfield-8 LEIGHTON)
                        (she born 31 May 1847; died 11 Jan 1938)
1266. Charles A.   born ca 1846; died 3 Aug 1882 Seattle, WA
1267. David   born ca 1848; died young

450. CAPTAIN EDMUND CURTIS-7 DRISKO, brother of above, was born 15 Apr 1815 at Addison, Maine. He married Hannah W. ALLEN on Columbia, Maine on 30 Nov 1836 at Addison. She was the daughter of Abraham ALLEN and Mary WORCESTER, and was born 16 Dec 1815; died 27 Nov 1902 at Milbridge, Maine. Captain Edmund-7 DRISKO died 11 Apr 1893 at Jonesport, Maine.

Children of Captain Edmund-7 DRISKO and Hannah ALLEN:
Surname DRISKO
1268. Child   born ca 1837; died young
1269. Henry B.   born 11 July 1838; married Aurilla A. MADDEN 1 Dec 1865 of Cherryfield
                         (she 2m. Stillman WALLACE 3/5 Feb 1872 at Columbia Falls, ME)
                         died 5 Aug 1868 **
+ 1270. MARY   born 14 May 1842 Addison, ME.; died 7 Aug 1868 **
       ELIZABETH   married CAPTAIN JASON D-8 LEIGHTON 20 Oct 1860 (# 1140)

Children of Captain Edmund-7 DRISKO, continued:
Surname DRISKO

+ 1271. ZIMRI TABBUT(T)	born 4 Mar 1845; married Susan C. FIELD 23 Jan 1869/70 (she born 23 Sept 1852; died 8 Feb 1931, WA) died 27 Dec 1925 Medina, WA
+ 1272. IDA FRANCES	born 6 Apr 1849; 1m. Ira S. WALLACE 1 Feb 1868 Milbridge, Maine (he born 12 Jan 1848; died 5 Oct 1883, CA) 2m. Fred A. WALLACE 1 Feb 1888 no issue died Nov 1936 Milbridge, Maine
+ 1273. EDMUND W.	born 4 June 1853/55; married Clara J. GRAY 1880; died 18 Jan 1899 (she born 15 Jan 1855; died 25 Aug 1918)

** Both Henry (# 1269) and his sister Mary Elizabeth (# 1270), died from yellow fever. They were aboard the Brig *RAVEN*, which was enroute from Cienfuegos (a seaport on the southern coast of Cuba) to New York. Henry was listed as a seaman on the 1860 Census. His only son, Henry Jr., was born on 20 Oct 1868; died 27 July 1869 at age 9 mo. 7 da. (gs).

Mary Elizabeth-7, the wife of the vessels' captain, JASON D. LEIGHTON, died two days after her brother. Besides her husband, she was survived by two young daughters, Carrie (# 1830) and Lucretia Small (# 1831) LEIGHTON.

451. BETSEY-7 DRISKO, sister of above, was born 16 June 1817 at Addison, Maine. She married Joseph Patten-6 DORR, intentions published 18 Nov 1836 at Columbia. A ships' carpenter, he was the son of Jonathan-5 DORR and Judith N. WORCESTER; and was born 22 June 1813; died 1896. Bestey-7 DRISKO died 7 May 1894 at Jonesport, Maine.

Children of Betsey-7 DRISKO and Joseph P-6 DORR:

Surname DORR	(children born Indian River, Maine)
+ 1274. JULIA S.	born ca 1838; married Truman Wilson MAGEE 18 Dec 1855 Columbia, ME (he born 16 Apr 1837; died 8 May 1871, CA) died 14 Oct 1901 Stockton, CA
1275. Captain Joseph Patten, Jr.	born July 1841; married Julia Drisko-9 SMITH 10 July 1877 (she dau/o William-8 SMITH and Emma H. WASS) (she born Apr 1860; died July 1939)
1276. William Augustus	born ca 1845; married Sarah E. RANDALL 25 Dec 1873 died 6 Feb 1883 Stockton, CA
1277. Isabella C.	born ca 1848; died 10 Sept 1864
1278. Emma F.	born ca 1852; died 4 June 1873
1279. Mary Ann	born 9 Feb 1854 Addison; died 29 Oct 1892 Addison, Maine married Timothy Driscoll CUMMINGS 4 Dec 1877
1280. Bion B.	born ca 1856
1281. Arthur A.	born 13 Aug 1859; died 31 Oct 1913 married Flora M. KELLEY 27 May 1893 (she born 22 Sept 1874; died 1943)

453. CAPTAIN THOMAS CROWLEY-7 DRISKO, brother of above, was born ca 1820/21 at Columbia, Maine. He married first, ca 1847, to his cousin Barbara Ellen-4 CROWLEY, daughter of Thomas J-3 CROWLEY and Barbara A. THOMPSON McDonald. She was born 28 Aug 1826 at Addison; died 15 Oct 1882. His second wife was Mrs. Violetta Morton-8 (Lettie) TIBBETTS Leighton (# 1036). They were married on 5 Dec 1883. " Lettie " was the daughter of Luther I. TIBBETTS and Cordelia Wilson WORCESTER Norton; and the widow of Oscar Enoch-9 LEIGHTON. She was born 20 Dec 1858; died 21 June 1910 at Boston, MA. Captain Thomas C-7 DRISKO was a sea captain at Addison, Maine 1850-80.

Children of Captain Thomas-7 DRISKO and Ellen CROWLEY:
Surname DRISKO

+ 1282. CAPTAIN ALMON R.	born 6 Mar 1849; died 30 Mar 1913 married Orrie/Aura Anna-5 CROWLEY (she born 3 Feb 1854; died 28 Jan 1920) (she dau/o Mathew C-4 CROWLEY and Elizabeth Ann CROWLEY)

Children of Captain Thomas-7 DRISKO, continued:
    Surname DRISKO

+ 1283. CAPTAIN EDGAR EVERSON	born 25 Aug 1850 Jonesport, ME; died 1920 married Gertrude Emily EMERSON 15 Aug 1874 at Indian River (Jonesport) (she born Sept 1854; died 1945)
1284. George Todd	born 1855; died 15 July 1894 Sullivan, Maine
1285. Orilla V.	born 1857; married John E. SIMPSON 17 Jan 1880 Addison
+ 1286. HARVEY McKENZIE	born 1866; married Jennie Maude PENLEY died after 1934; resided Bridgton, Maine

Children of Thomas-7 DRISKO and Lettie TIBBETTS Leighton:
    Surname DRISKO

1287. Grace D.	born ca 1884; died young EOL
1288. Maude C.	born Mar 1892, MA; married Charles/Clarence BLACKINGTON died before 1930 no issue EOL
1289. Mildred G.	born 30 May 1898; died 15 May 1945 EOL

    Note: Maude and Mildred resided with their uncle, Horatio NORTH at Addison, ME in 1900.

454. MARIAH STEELE-7 DRISKO see JOSEPH-7 DRISKO (# 438)

456. CAPTAIN JOEL WILSON-7 DRISKO, brother of above, was born Mar 1826 at Columbia, Maine. He married first, ca 1848, to his cousin Mary Ann-4 CROWLEY. She was the daughter of Thomas J-3 CROWLEY and Barbara THOMPSON McDonald; and was born ca 1830; died 19 June 1849. No issue. His second wife, Sarah W-4 CROWLEY, was the younger sister of his first wife. She was born Sept 1834; died 30 May 1908 (age 78). Captain Joel W-7 DRISKO died 3 June 1909 at Sailors Snug Harbor, New York. He was a sea captain at Addison from 1860- ____.

Children of Captain Joel-7 DRISKO and Sarah-4 CROWLEY:
    Surname DRISKO

1290. Faustina W.	born ca 1855/56; married John H. WOOSTER 28 Oct 1872 Machiasport, ME
1291. Mary A.	born Feb 1861; married James Frederick DOBBINS 18 Aug 1881
1292. Capt. Orren Willis	born ca 1863; married Melinda E. BICKFORD 27 Jan 1888 Children: Ralph-8 DRISKO born ca 1889; died 1918 **World War 1; and** Faustina born 18__.
+ 1293. CHARLES CHANDLER	born 21 Feb 1865; married Phebe DODGE 16 Jan 1897 Addison, Maine died 18 Mar 1956 Burlingame, CA
1294. Irving L.	born 2 July 1867; died 23 Apr 1871 EOL
1295. Minnie B.	born 30 Aug 1871; married Horatio A. DOBBINS 14 Mar 1891 (he born 9 Nov 1868; died 15 Dec 1910 – lost at sea) died 28 May 1904 (suicide – burned to death) Jonesport, ME.
1296. Maurice W.	born ca 1876

458. NANCY ANN-7 DRISKO, sister of above, was born Feb 1830 at Columbia, Maine. She married Benjamin Franklin-9 CARVER ca 1850. He was the son of Benjamin J-8 CARVER and Mary MANS-FIELD, and was born 28 June 1824 at Portland, ME; died 10 Nov 1904. Nancy Ann-7 DRISKO died May 1866. He married second to Abbie BAGLEY Apr 1868. She was born 21 Dec 1841; died 12 Mar 1923. They had 2 children: Charles F., born Feb 1870; and Ella E., born 19 Dec 1873.

Children of Nancy Ann-7 DRISKO and Benjamin-9 CARVER:
    Surname CARVER

+ 1297. AMELIA F.	born ca 1851; 1m. Daniel James MANSFIELD 10 Aug 1870 (he born 12 May 1848; died ____) 2m. Nathaniel Church DAVIS ca 18__ (he born 21 Apr 1854; died ____)
+ 1298. JUSTINA A.	born 18 Nov 1852; died 25 July 1940 marr Edwin Allen KELLEY 28 July 1872 Columbia, ME (he born Dec 1846)
+ 1299. AUGUSTUS FELLOWS	born Jan 1855; married Annie M. SANBORN 11 Dec 1880; died 23 Mar 1889 (she born 5 Feb 1863; died 19 Mar ____)

Children of Nancy-7 DRISKO, continued:
    Surname CARVER

+ 1300. JUDSON	born 25 July 1857; died 23 July 1950
HOWARD	married Carrie A. WOODMAN 21 July 1879 (born 1862; died 26 Feb 1890)
+ 1301. WILLIAM L.	born Feb 1859; married Martha A. GUPTILL; died 1929
	(she born 19 Aug 1865 Lubec, ME; died Mar 1939)
+ 1302. GEORGE	born 6 Nov 1860; died 19 Mar 1944
BROWN	married Evelyn Willard-9 LOOK (# 1741)
	(she born 21 Nov 1863/8 Jonesboro, ME; died 26 Nov 1927)
1303. Volney B.	born 24 Apr 1865 Jonesport, ME; died 11 Aug ____

462. ANN FRANKLAND-7 DRISKO, daughter of Jeremiah-6 DRISKO (Joseph-5; 4; John-3; 2) and Ann FRANKLAND, was born 28 Oct 1819. She married first to Captain John H-7 BARTON on 24 Nov 1839. He was the son of John BARTON and Mary ELLSWORTH, and was born 19 Oct 1812; died 11 Dec 1843. She married second to Green B. STEVENS of Boston, MA. on 26 Sept 1847.

Children of Ann Frankland-7 DRISKO and Captain John BARTON:
    Surname BARTON

1304. Henry	born 28 May 1840; died 26 July 1840
1305. Henrietta	born 28 May 1840; died 26 July 1840
1306. Hamilton C.	born July 1841; died 21 Oct 1844 (age 3 years)

463. BENJAMIN FRANKLIN-7 DRISKO, brother of above, was born 8 Apr 1821 at Addison, Maine. He married Nancy Wass-8 PLUMMER, intentions published 8 Sept 1845. She was the daughter of John-7 PLUMMER and Sarah-7 WASS, and was born 1823 Harrington, ME; died 1882 (gs). Benjamin Franklin-7 DRISKO, better known as Franklin, was a ships' carpenter. He resided his entire life at Addison where he was a Selectman in 1867-68, and 1872. He died 7 Sept 1893 (gs).

Children of Benjamin Franklin-7 DRISKO and Nancy-8 PLUMMER:

Surname DRISKO	(children born at Addison, Maine)
+ 1307. JULIA E.	born 13 Jan 1846; married Coffin Stephen-8 LEIGHTON 25 Dec 1866
	(he son/o Aaron-7 LEIGHTON and Bethia WAKEFIELD)
	(he born 17 Apr 1845; died 14 Feb 1928)
	died 24 Aug 1915 Arlington, MA.
+ 1308. ELIZA V.	born 13 Oct 1848; died 10 Dec 1897
	married Harrison Nash-8 LOOK 10 Apr 1869
+ 1309. HOWARD	born 13 Dec 1852; died 18 Dec 1928
PERRIN	married Mary A. FUREY 22 May 1883 (she born 6 July 1863)
1310. Benjamin, Jr.	born ____; died in infancy EOL

464. ORAMANDER HOWARD-7 DRISKO, brother of above, was born 9 July 1822 at Addison, ME. He married 1st to Catherine W-8 WASS on 14 July 1853. She was the daughter of N. Jones-7 WASS and Lois LOOK, and was born 7 May 1833; died 6 Apr 1900. He married 2nd to Mrs. Cecelia Ann LONG Knowles, daughter of the Rev Charles C. LONG and Hannah FRIEND, and the widow of Augustus KNOWLES. According to the 1850 Census, he was a ships' carpenter. He moved to Boston at a later date, and was occupied in the contracting and building business with his sons. Oramander-7 died 24 Feb 1918 at Boston. .

Children of Oramander-7 DRISKO and Catherine-8 WASS:
    Surname DRISKO

+ 1311. FRED HOWARD	born 10 Dec 1858, Addison; married Evelyn Alice-9 WASS 14 Dec 1881
	died 7 June 1939 Boston, MA.
+ 1312. ALONZO B.	born 11 Jan 1866, Addison; married Mary PHILBRICK; died 3 June 1958

466. CAPTAIN PERRIN C-7 (Perry) DRISKO, brother of above, was born 7 Nov 1826 at Addison, ME.

He married 1st to FRANCES A-8 PLUMMER (# 929) on 11 Nov 1849. She was the daughter of John-7 PLUMMER(#348) and Sarah-7 WASS, and was born ca 1829. His 2nd wife was Eldora Florence HAMILTON. According to the 1850/60 Censuses (Addison, ME) Perrin-7 was a sea captain. He died 6 May 1910 at Provincetown, MA.

Child of Captain Perrin C-7 DRISKO and Frances A-8 PLUMMER:
    Surname DRISKO
+ 1313. HENRY   born ca 1853/4 Addison; died 1935
       BROOKS   married Florence COLLIER of Melrose, MA 1879 (she born ca 1857; died 1945)
Child of Captain Perrin C-7 DRISKO and Eldora HAMILTON:
    Surname DRISKO
1314. William   born 18__; died 19__ Hyannis, MA.

467. ALONZO S-7 DRISKO, brother of above, was born ca 1829 at Addison, Maine. He married Elvena WASS ca 1852. She was the daughter of Chipman WASS and Mary CURTIS. She was born ca 1832; died ca ____. They had three daughters, all of them dying in their early twenties.

Children of Alonzo-7 DRISKO and Elvena WASS:
    Surname DRISKO   1315. Ella born 18 __   1316. Laura born 18__   1317. Clara born 18__

468. MARGARET-7 DRISKO, sister of above, was born ca 1831 at Addison, Maine. She married Charles L. UNION ca 18__. He was the son of __?__ UNION and was born ca 1832, MA; died ____.

Children of Margaret-7 DRISKO and Charles L. UNION:
    Surname UNION 1318. Frank L. born 18__   1319. Marguerite born 18__   1320. Susie born 18 __

469. EMMA BIGELOW-7 DRISKO, sister of above, was born 13 Nov 1839 at Addison, Maine. She married Captain John Billings HINCKLEY on 18 July 1855. He was the son of Aaron HINCKLEY and Mary IRONS, and was born ca 1832; died 1900. He was a sea captain at Addison, ME in 1870. Emma-7 DRISKO died 23 July 1931 at Seattle, WA.

Children of Emma-7 DRISKO and John HINCKLEY:
    Surname HINCKLEY

1321. Merrill R.	born 20 Dec 1858 Addison, ME; married Amy EATON of Boston, MA
	died 7/9 June 1942 Prairie Grove, South Dakota
1322. Perrin Drisko	born 10 Nov 1861; married Anna Lucretia HINST
1323. Albert Leopold	born 16 Dec 1864; married Dora Alvina HINST; died Nov 1944 Oakland, CA
1324. Maude Evelyn	born 5 Aug 1867; married John Edward McGUIRE 6 July 1891 ID
1325. Mabel	born May 1871 Boston, MA; died 5 Oct 1902 ID unmarried EOL

470. CHANDLER ROBBINS-7 DRISKO, son of Jonathan-6 DRISKO (Samuel Gatchel-5; Joseph-4; John-3;2) and Sarah McKENZIE, was born 5 May 1799 at Columbia Falls, ME. He married Ruth Ruggles-6 WHITNEY ++ on 5 June 1823. She was the daughter of Joseph –5 WHITNEY and Mary C. LIBBY, and was born 11 Apr 1805; died 25 Sept 1888. Chandler Robbins-7 DRISKO died 3 June 1845 at Jonesboro, ME. He is buried in back of Eugene DRISKOS' house in Jonesboro. His widow married 2nd to Thomas G. WATTS.

Children of Chandler Robbins-7 DRISKO and Ruth Ruggles-6 WHITNEY:
    Surname DRISKO
1326. George West   born 10/20 Oct 1824 Jonesboro, ME; died 20 Aug 1910 Machias, ME
          married Esther C-6 NASH 19 Sept 1852
      (she dau/o Jesse L-5 NASH and Sarah NASH) (she born 1824; died 1909) no issue EOL
      Note: He was the editor and part owner of the *MACHIAS UNION* newspaper for many years;
       and was the author of the " Life of Hannah WESTON " and the " History of Machias ".

Children of Chandler Robbins-7 DRISKO, continued:
Surname DRISKO

+ 1327. ERI	born 2 Mar 1827 Jonesboro, ME; died 1878
HATHAWAY	1m. Elizabeth Robinson TABBUT 9 Jan 1851
	(she born 5 Apr 1832; died 18__) (# 1003)
	(she dau/o James-7 TABBUT (# 378) and Catherine MESERVE)
	2m. Fannie Brewster-8 TABBUT 30 June 1873 (# 1004)
	(she born 4 Mar 1840; died ____ (living 1900)
+ 1328. JOSEPH	born 11 Oct 1829 Jonesboro
WHITNEY	married Isabel Frances FARNSWORTH 11 Oct 1853
1329. Sarah E.	born 2 Apr 1832; died 20 Aug 1847 EOL
1330. Martha W.	born 2 Nov 1834; died 20 Mar 1852 EOL
1331. Jonathan H.	born 22 May 1838; died 28 July 1839 EOL
+ 1332. JERUSHA	born 16 July 1840; married Lorenzo BRIDGHAM 12 Mar 1864
CORTHELL	(he son/o of Andrew BRIDGHAM and Ann DOWNS)
	died 8 Nov 1915 (resided 1860 with Thomas WATTS ; Whitneyville, ME
1333. Catherine S.	born 21 June 1842; died 9 Dec 1847 EOL

++ Ancestry of Ruth Ruggles-6 WHITNEY

BENJAMIN-1 WHITNEY, the immigrant, was born 6 June 1643. He married Jane POOR ca ____. She was born ca 1647; died 14 Nov 1690. NATHANIEL-2 WHITNEY was born 14 Apr 1680; married Sarah FORD ca ____; died ca 1768. Sarah was born ca 1685. NATHAN-3 WHITNEY, born 10 Jan 1706/07; married Lydia YOUNG, and had NATHAN-4 born 30 Apr 1742. He married Patience BARNARD/BERNARD (born 1742; died 1840) They were the parents of JOSEPH-5 WHITNEY born 17 Feb 1782, who married Mary C. LIBBY and had Ruth Ruggles-6 WHITNEY, born 3 Apr 1805.

472. ABIGAIL B-7 DRISKO, sister of above, was born ca 1803 at Columbia, ME. She married Dennis TRACY, int pub 3 Aug 1823 (married 18 Apr 1824). He was born ca 1798 in Ireland. Abigail-7 DRISKO died ca 1829-30. Dennis-1 TRACY married 2nd to Hannah PEABODY Rowley on 16 Jan 1831. She was the daughter of Solomon PEABODY and Lydia ALLEY. They had 2 ch: Dennis F. and John L. TRACY

Children of Abigail-7 DRISKO and Dennis-1 TRACY:
Surname TRACY

+ 1334. DEBORAH	born 1824; 1m. William Wass NICHOLS 14 June 1848; s/o Ward NICHOLS
McKENZIE	2m. Jeremiah CUMMINGS 1850; he drowned in 1864 in NY Harbor
	3m. Luther Humphrey CALLAGHAN 1868; 4m. William RAFTER 24 Feb 1875 Machias. ME.
	died ca 1893 Harrington, Maine
+ 1335. AMASA	born 23 Feb 1826 Jonesboro, ME; died 5 Mar 1905 Addison, ME.
DRISKO	1m. Rebecca Drisko-8 SAWYER 28 May 1855; 2m. Susie D. ROBBINS 17 Oct 1893
+ 1336. AMOS L.	born 1828; married Abigail Crowley GRAY int pub 11 July 1852
	(she dau/o William GRAY and Lydia WHITNEY)
	died 31 Jan 1888 Columbia Falls, Maine

473. SARAH JANE-7 DRISKO, sister of above, was born ca 1807. She had two sons (father unknown), and later married Robert SWEENEY, intentions published 22 May 1825 at Columbia, Maine. He was born ca 18__; died ca 1839 at Cherryfield, Maine. Sarah-7 DRISKO died there ca 1842.

Children of Sarah-7 DRISKO and __?__:
Surname DRISKO 1337. Barney C. born ca 1822; laborer   1338. Zebra born 27 Nov 1828
Child of Sarah-7 DRISKO and Robert SWEENEY:
Surname SWEENEY
1339. Charles W.   born 11 May 1831; died 23 May 1906, CA ; was called " Loring "
Note: This son was raised by Daniel Merritt NASH. Resided Columbia, ME. 1860-80 and removed to Santa Cruz, CA ca 1889

475. APHPHATHA/APHATHA/APPHIA-7 NASH, daughter of Mary-6 DRISKO (Samuel Gatchell-5; Joseph-4; John-3; 2) and Holmes-5 NASH, was born 17 July 1797 at Addison, Maine. (Marian Fraser of

Bahia, Brazil, a direct descendant, states that she is certain the spelling should be Aphphatha because her mother wanted to name her after Aphphatha but intended to use only one ph. Aphphatha-7 NASH married Wilmot Wass-5 WILSON, intentions published 10 Feb 1823 at Columbia, Maine. He was the son of Nathaniel-4 WILSON and Mary WASS, and was born 26 Oct 1797 at Columbia Falls, ME; died 8 Mar 1884 at Somerville, MA. Aphphatha-7 NASH died 9 Apr 1858 at Charlestown, MA.

Children of Aphphatha-7 NASH and Wilmot-5 WILSON:

	Surname WILSON	
+ 1340.	MARY ELIZABETH	born 24 Dec 1823 Machias, ME; 1m. Captain Joseph B. LORING 4 Apr 1841 (he born 18__; died 1852 , lost at sea) 2m. Captain Gilman COLSON (he born 16 Mar 1813 Addison, ME; died 17 May 1879) died 15 Oct 1905 Columbia Falls, Maine
+ 1341.	MARIA	born 4 Mar 1826; married Eri Hathaway-8 SMITH 20 Nov 1846 (he son/o Ebenezer-7 SMITH and Deborah FARNSWORTH) (he born 24 May 1825; died 19 June 1903)
1342.	dau	born ca 1828; poss d y 1344. Mary Otis born 6 Sept 1834
1343.	son	born ca 1830; died ___ died 10 June 1840 EOL

476. REBECCA ALLEN-7 NASH, sister of above, was born 12 Nov 1799. She married Daniel Sawyer-6 WASS on ___ Oct 1819 at Addison, Maine. He was the son of Wilmot Wass-5 WASS and Rebecca JORDAN, and was born 22 May 1798; died 7 Aug 1873 at Grundy Center, Iowa. Rebecca Allen-7 NASH died 14 May 1880 at Eldora, Iowa.

Children of Rebecca-7 NASH and Daniel-6 A WASS:

	Surname WASS	(first 5 children born at Addison, Maine)
+ 1345.	RUFUS WADSWORTH	born 17 Aug 1820; married Mary Adams GULLIVER 15 Aug 1846, MA died 7 Aug 1900 South Dakota
1346.	Harriet LeBaron	born 2 Nov 1821; married Thomas G-1 COPP 22 Nov 1842 died 13 Sept 1950 Del Rapids, Iowa
		One daughter: Harriet Agnes-9 COPP born ca 1843; married Daniel MEADER
1347.	George Nash	born 22 Dec 1822; died 15 Aug 1848 at sea
1348.	Anne Rebecca	born 19 Apr 1824; married Charles H. WALKER 1844; died 1904
1349.	dau	born ca 1827; died young EOL
1350.	Mary Jane	born 30 May 1830; died 14 Feb 1845 (gs) EOL
+ 1351.	HOLMES NASH	born 10 Jan 1832; died 4 Apr 1914 Clear Lake, Iowa 1m. Arathusa L. WILSON; 2m. Mary Elizabeth-9 McLAURY Burnison
+ 1352.	NAPOLEON BONAPARTE	born 8 Dec 1834; married Julia __?__ before 1865 died 5 Sept 1902 Los Angeles, CA
1353.	Anna Elizabeth	born 29 Jan 1836; died 8 Mar 1902 Iowa married Morrison B. SARGENT 29 June 1856 Iowa

477. ANN S-7 NASH, sister of above, was born 28 Nov 1801 at Addison, Maine. She married her second cousin, David-2 DAVIS, ca Dec 1827 at Addison. He was the son of Samuel-1 DAVIS and Susanna NASH, and was born ca Sept 1801; died 7 Jan 1872. He was a ships' carpenter. Ann S-7 NASH died 21 Nov 1887 at East Machias, Maine.

Children of Ann-7 NASH and David-2 DAVIS:

	Surname DAVIS	(children born Addison, Maine)
1354.	A. Helen	born ca 1829; died 30 Aug 1866; unmarried
1355.	Captain Galen W.	born ca 1831; died 30 July 1880 Florida (sea captain at Addison 1850-60)
1356.	Ellis Vespatian	born 25 May 1836; died 29 Dec 1916 Jonesport, ME. married Emeline E. MALOON 17 Mar 1861 (she dau/o Benjamin MALOON and Deborah ELLIS) (she born ca 1841)

478. GEORGE W-7 NASH, brother of above, was born 28 May 1804 at Addison, Maine. He married Jane-7 PATTEN on 28 Aug 1829 at Cherryfield, Maine. She was the daughter of John-6 PATTEN and Pamelia-6 LEIGHTON, and was born 27 Apr 1809 at Cherryfield,; died 16 Jan 1889. George W-7 NASH died 30 July 1854 at Boston, MA.

Children of George W-7 NASH and Jane-7 PATTEN:
Surname NASH
1357. Pamelia Ann   born 2 June 1830; died Oct 1835   EOL
1358. Elizabeth C.   born 5 Aug 1832; married Charles L. MELOON 4 Apr 1855 Boston, MA
1359. Gilbert M.   born 29 Aug 1834; married Mary E. MARTIN 12 Dec 1859; died Dec 1864
1360. Mary Emma   born 12 Feb 1837; married George DRAPER of Dedham, MA 21 Feb 1860
1361. Georgianna W.   born 5 Dec 1839; died 12 Feb 1898
                       1m. Lucas BAKER of MA.; 2m. John C. NICHOLS of Somerville, MA
1362. Olivia P. (twin) born 18 July 1844; married George M. BALL of Dedham, MA
1363. Osborn P. (twin) born 18 July 1844; married Annie POWERS of Pawtucket, Rhode Island

479. JERUSHA DRISKO-7 NASH, sister of above, was born 26 Nov 1806 at Addison, Maine. She married Samuel Robert-8 SUMNER on 11 June 1831 at Gouldsboro, Maine. He was the son of John Gabriel-7 SUMNER (John-6; Samuel-5; Clement-4; William-3; 2; 1) and Elizabeth MOORE, and was born 12 Dec 1802 at Boston, MA; died 1879/80. Jerusha D-7 NASH died 18 Oct 1883 at Somerville, MA.

Children of Jerusha Drisko-7 NASH and Samuel-8 SUMNER:
Surname SUMNER   (children born Addison, Maine)
1364. Stafford B.   born 19 Feb 1833   1367. Mary R.   born 21 Apr 1838
                     died May 1851, MA; EOL   1368. John Holmes born 25 Mar 1840
1365. Thaddeus E.   born 9 Sept 1834
1366. William R.   born 8 June 1836; died Dec 1856 unmarr EOL
          REF: Descendants of William SUMNER of Dorchester, MA by William S. APPLETON, Boston 1879.

476. MARY E-7 NASH, sister of above, was born 29 Apr 1809 at Addison, Maine. She married John Lowell-5 ALLINE on 22 Feb 1828 at Addison. He was the son of Benjamin-4 ALLINE and Anna LOWELL, and was born 21 July 1803; died 5 Jan 1872. He was a farmer and master shoemaker, residing at Addison, Maine 1850. Mary-7 NASH died at Addison , Maine on 7 Sept 1901.

Children of Mary-7 NASH and John-5 ALLINE:
Surname ALLINE
+ 1369. HENRY W.   born May 1829; died 5 Sept 1905; a school teacher and surveyor
                      1m. Sarah S. KELLER 13 Jan 1858 Maine
                      (she born 1831 E. Machias, ME; died 18 July 1880 Remsen, Iowa)
                      2m. Maria E. EMMETT ca 1883
1370. Alfred A.   born ca 1831/32; died after 1888; he a ships' caulker
          married Orilla-6 NASH 26 Nov 1854 Addison (she born 11 Dec 1831; died 19 Sept 1856)

1371. Jerome B.   born Aug 1834; died 1902 ; a farmer and a tinsmith
                      married Delia E-6 NASH 8 Oct 1859
          (she dau/o Oliver-5 NASH and Deborah SMITH) (she born 20 Sept 1833; died May 1913)
               One child: Aurilla/Orilla F-9 ALLINE born 1861; died 1944 unmarried

1372. Miriam P/F.   born ca 1837; married Anson Morris-7 CLAPP 9 Jan 1866; died after 1876
1373. Frederick L.   born ca 1839; died 4 Feb 1894 Addison, ME;   unmarried

481. JOSEPH-7 NASH, brother of above, was born 15 May 1812 at Addison, Maine. He married Almira BATES, intentions published 6 Oct 1834 at Addison. She was born 5 Dec 1816 at Kingston, MA; died 15 Apr 1887. Joseph-7 NASH, a farmer, grocer and postmaster at Addison, died 27 June 1893.

Children of Joseph-7 NASH and Almira BATES:
   Surname NASH
   1374. son   born ca 1835/6; died 184_   EOL
   1375. John Hamilton   born ca 1843 Addison; married Eudora M-8 LOOK 9 May 1863
         Bates   (she born 18 Dec 1845; died Dec 1885)
   1376. Milton L.   born 2 Jan 1848; died 2 Dec 1853

484. MERCY-7 DRISKO, daughter of Edmund-6 DRISKO (Samuel Gatchell-5; Joseph-4; John-3; 2) and Elizabeth/ Betsey CATES, was born ca 1809/10 at Columbia, Maine. She married George Handy-6 LONGFELLOW on 14 Sept 1834 at Machiasport, Maine. George-6 LONGFELLOW was the son of Isaac-5 LONGFELLOW and Polly-6 BOYNTON ++ (Amos-4; David-3; Joshua-2; William-1) (History of the BOYNTON Family, page 20) He was born 13 June 1810 at Machias, Maine; died there 22 Apr 1894. Mercy-7 DRISKO died before 1847. George Handy-6 LONGFELLOW married second to Nancy W. MERRITT of Addison on 24 Apr 1847. Nancy was born Jan 1820; died Apr 1903.

Children of Mercy-7 DRISKO and George H-6 LONGFELLOW:
   Surname LONGFELLOW
   1377. Augusta E.   born ca 1835/6 Machias, Washington County, Maine
+ 1378. JOSEPHINE   born ca 1837/8 Machias; married Captain Warren-8 WASS,Esq 15 Aug 1863
        HALL   (he son/o Henry-7 WASS and Susanna BROWN) (he born 11 Feb 1821)
                 died 20 Apr 1918 Somerville, MA
   1379. George A.   born ca 1841
   1380. Isaac Ham   born ca 1843   1381. Edward   born ca 1854/56; died young
       ++ Polly-6 BOYNTON was born 1776, MA; died 5 May 1861 (age 83) Machias, Maine

486. LOUISA-7 CORTHELL, daughter of Jerusha-6 DRISKO (Samuel Gatchell-5; Joseph-4; John-3; 2) and Deacon David CORTHELL, was born Feb 1811 at Addison, Maine. She married William P-5 ALLINE, a house and ships' carpenter, ca Nov 1833. He was the son of Benjamin-4 ALLINE and Lydia PATTEN, and was born 5 May 1805; died 21 Feb 1887. Louisa-7 CORTHELL died 4 Dec 1893.

Children of Louisa-7 CORTHELL and William-5 ALLINE:
   Surname ALLINE
   1382. Henrietta   born ca 1834; married Henry L. BROWN 9 Oct 1853 Milbridge, ME.
           (he son/o James BROWN and Priscilla JORDAN) (he born Apr 1825; died Aug 1901)
   1383. Benjamin W.   born July 1836; died Oct 1838
   1384. Sidney A.   born ca 1840; died 17 Nov 1861 in the **Civil War;** unmarried
+ 1385. ARTHUR H.   born 11 Aug 1847 Harrington, ME; married Alice A. GARNETT
       (she dau/o Bela GARNETT and Mary WILLEY) (she born 19 Feb 1851; died 8 Aug 1909)
       died 23 Apr 1893 multiple sclerosis

493. JAMES CAMPBELL-7 COFFIN, son of Rebecca-6 DRISKO (Samuel Gatchell-5; Joseph-4; John-3; 2) and Elisha-6 COFFIN, was born 27 Feb 1809 at Harrington, Maine. He married first to Catherine DYER, intentions published 27 Oct 1832 at Harrington. She was born ca 1808/09 at Cape Elizabeth, Maine; died 185_ at Harrington. His second marriage was to CORDELIA M-8 COFFIN McKenzie on 31 Dec 1854 (# 1240). She was the daughter of Aaron-7 COFFIN and Feah Parker-7 DRISKO (# 441) and was born ca 1830; died 1891.

Children of James Campbell-7 COFFIN and Catherine DYER:
   Surname COFFIN
   1386. Frances M.   born ca 1833/34
   1387. Rebecca C.   born ca 1835; married Edward E. SWETT 4 Oct 1854
   1388. Mary E.   born ca 1836; married George E. BROWN 25 Nov 1855 Harrington, Maine
   1389. Julia S.   born ca 1840
   1390. Nathan Harris born ca 1843   1391. Henry A.   born ca 1846/47

Children of James Campbell-7 COFFIN and Cordelia M-8 COFFIN:
    Surname COFFIN

1392. Caroline S.	born ca 1859; died young
1393. Captain Charles	born May 1861; died ____ sea captain at Harrington, ME
Everett	married Almeda Frances-7 COLE 29 July 1885 (she born Aug 1858)
1394. Captain Herbert	born ca 1864; married Ada May-7 COLE 1 Feb 1888
W.	(she dau/o Lyman-6 COLE and Christiana COLBERT
	(she born Jan 1868; died 19__; sister of Almeda-7, above)
	died 15 Mar 1930 Hartford, CT
1395. Caroline S. (2)	born Dec 1866
	married George Napoleon-7 COLE int pub 28 Aug 1883 Harrington, ME
	(he born 1860; died 1941) (he son/o George-6 COLE)

494. FRANCES-7 COFFIN, sister of above, was born 4 Apr 1811 at Harrington, Maine. She married Reuben D-7 COFFIN on 24 May 1835 at Addison. He was the son of Richard-6 COFFIN and Hannah WHITTEN, and was born 14 Mar 1812; died 15 Nov 1855 at North Perry, Maine. Frances-7 COFFIN died before 1881. He married second to Mercy Ann-6 NASH Merritt 5 June 1881.

Children of Frances-7 COFFIN and Reuben-7 COFFIN:
    Surname COFFIN

1396. Nancy C.	born ca 1836/37		
1397. George H.	born ca 1838; died 24 Aug 1864 unmarried		
	(died at Petersburg, VA ; killed in the **Civil War**)		
1398. Hannah Augusta	born ca 1840; married Rev John S. PECKHAM (as his 2nd wife)		
	(he born ca 1840; died ca 186_)		
1399. Lorenzo M.	born ca 1843; died 186_ in the **Civil War**; unmarried		
1400. Mary J.	born ca 1845	1401. Ada	born ca 1852

495. AMOS BUCKNAM-7 COFFIN, son of Rebecca-6 DRISKO (Samuel Gatchell-5; Joseph-4; John-3; 2) and Elisha-6 COFFIN, was born 30 Dec 1813 (LDS-IGI) at Washington County, Maine. He married Irene MITCHELL on 10 Nov 1835 at Harrington, Maine. She was the daughter of Thomas J. MITCHELL and Elizabeth A. STROUT, and was born 27 June 1816; died 27 May 1910. Amos-7 COFFIN died 11 May 1893 at Harrington.

Children of Amos-7 COFFIN and Irene MITCHELL:
    Surname COFFIN   (children born Harrington, Maine)

1402. Elisha Green	born ca 1836/37; married Lucy Perkins-8 PLUMMER (# 936)
	(she born 1834; died 189_) (she sister of Amos-8 PLUMMER, below)
1403. Elizabeth M.	born ca 1838; married Captain Amos Bucknam-8 PLUMMER 1856 (# 937)
1404. Captain Samuel	born ca 1843; 1m. Lucretia Rosina MITCHELL Nov 1863
Moody	2m. Sylvia Louise WHITE 24 Nov 1874
	died 5 Apr 1879 Harrington, Maine sea captain at Harrington, ME

+ 1405. EUGENE AMOS	born ca 1853; 1m. Malintha J-9 LOOK 18 May 1872
	(she born 1855; divorced before 1897; died ____)
	2m. Mary Ann FLAGG Kent 22 Jan 1898 (she born Apr 1844, Canada)

498. URIAH NASH-7 COFFIN, brother of above, was born 26 Aug 1823 at Harrington, Maine. He married first to Catherine C-6 COLSON on 18 Nov 1847 at Cherryfield, Maine. She was the daughter of Samuel-5 COLSON and Mariah B. WILLEY, and was born 1829; died 20 Feb 1854. No issue. His second marriage was to Harriet E-5 CLEAVES on 21 Nov 1855. She was the daughter of Charles-4 CLEAVES and __?__ LORD, and was born 19 Mar 1838; died 29 Dec 1924 at Harrington. Uriah-7 COFFIN died 14 June 1893 at Harrington.

Children of Uriah-7 COFFIN and Harriet CLEAVES:
    Surname COFFIN

1406. Captain Charles	born Oct 1856; died 1905; a sea captain at Harrington, Maine
	married Georgia E. COLE 2 Mar 1881(
	(she dau/o Amos COLE and Eliza J. CARTER)(she born Jan 1863; died 1905)
1407. Harriet L.	born Feb 1858; died 1862 EOL
1408. Catherine A.	born 1859; died 1905; 1m. William PREBLE 23 Oct 1877
" Katie "	(he born 1852; died before 1888)
	2m. Ira W-7 NASH ca 1888; 3m. George F. TARBOX 24 Sept 1904
+ 1409. JOHN	born 4 May 1863; died 30 June 1926 Winthrop, MA marine engineer
BARTLETT	married Effie Cora RANDALL 12 Nov 1885 (she born 1862; died 192_)
1410. Voranus L.	born 1865; died 1870 EOL
1411. Ulysses Grant	born 1867; married Katie B. RAMSDELL 1887; died 1905
	(she born 1865; died 1905)
1412. Frances C.	born 1868; married Captain Warren M. WHITE 31 Dec 1885
	(he born 1864; died 1943)
1413. Jennifer M.	born Mar 1872; married Winslow J. RAMSDELL 1888
" Jennie "	(he born 1865; died ____)
+ 1414. URIAH N, JR.	born June 1879; married Annie Louise TALBOT 5 June 1901, MA
	(she born 1882; died 1966)
	died 13 Oct 1946; buried Peabody, MA

499. MERCY JANE-7 COFFIN, sister of above, was born 27 Mar 1826 at Harrington, Maine. She married John W-7 COFFIN, her cousin, intentions published 12 Sept 1845 at Harrington. He was the son of Richard-6 COFFIN and Hannah WHITTEN, and was born 30 July 1818; died 2 Oct 1889. Mercy Jane-7 COFFIN died 18__.

Children of Mercy Jane-7 COFFIN and John W-7 COFFIN:

Surname COFFIN	(1st child born at Harrington, ME; the other 4 at Cherryfield, ME)
1415. Howard M.	born ca 1847; married Harriet W. TUCKER 16 Mar 1871
1416. Elmira Emma	born Sept 1849; 1m. Forrester DAVIS 8 Sept 1867
	2m. Charles Lewis-8 COFFIN 27 Mar 1878
1417. Charles H.	born 5 May 1852 ; died 23 Sept 1900
	married Mary Elizabeth-8 GRAY 18 Dec 1875 (she born 1858; died 1 Apr 1939 Augusta, ME)
1418. Aylmer P.	born ca 1855 1419. Reuben Dyer born 1868

501. JERUSHA CORTHELL-7 DRISKO, daughter of Samuel Gatchell-6 DRISKO (Samuel Gatchell-5; Joseph-4; John-3; 2) and Mary PHINNEY, was born ca 1820 at Columbia, Maine. She married William Bradford LE BARON on 19 Sept 1839 at Addison, Maine. he was the son of William-4 LE BARON (Lemuel-3; Lazarus-2; Francis-1) and Elizabeth LE BARON, and was born 1 Aug 1814; died 7 Oct 1886. Jerusha Corthell-7 DRISKO died after 1904.

Children of Jerusha Corthell-7 DRISKO and William-5 LE BARON:
    Surname LE BARON

1420. Elizabeth born 17 Apr 1841	1421. Mary D. born 26 Apr 1848
died 27 Dec 1902 unmarried	1422. Sarah Ann born 15 Dec 1853

502. MARY REBECCA-7 DRISKO, sister of above, was born ca 1823 at Columbia, Maine. She married Simeon Coffin-6 NASH on 19 Sept 1847 at Addison. He was the son of Nathaniel-5 NASH and Sophia COFFIN (daughter of Captain John COFFIN). Simeon-6 NASH was born ca 1823; died ____. They resided Boston, MA.

Children of Mary Rebecca-7 DRISKO and Simeon-6 NASH:

Surname NASH 1423. Isabella	born 1848	1424. Kitty born 18__

503. CAPTAIN GEORGE B-7 DRISKO, brother of above, was born 5 Mar 1825 at Columbia, Maine. He married Frances Augusta-9 PLUMMER on 3 Aug 1854. She was the daughter of Captain Bryce T-8 PLUMMER ++ and Sylvina A-7 WASS, and was born 1 Apr 1835; died 28 May 1896 in Boston, MA. The funeral and burial was in Addison, ME. Captain George-7 DRISKO was a master shipbuilder and sea captain at Addison (1860 -   ). He died 10 Sept 1894 at Taunton, MA; and is buried in Church Hill Cemetery, Addison, Maine.

Children of Captain George B-7 DRISKO and Frances A-9 PLUMMER:
  Surname DRISKO   1425. Mary E. born 1857/60, teacher   1426. Lewis F.   born 1868

++ Captain Bryce Tinning-8 PLUMMER, born ca 1805, was a sea captain. He married first to Sylvina-7 WASS, int pub 10 Nov 1831. They had 8 children: Maria born ca 1833; FRANCES AUGUSTA (above); Eliza born 1836; Mary O. born 1839; William born ca 1842; Martha born 1844; Lewis born ca 1845 and John born 1848 at Addison, Maine. He married second to Sarah J. KELLEY and had 2 more children.

506. CHARLES A-7 DRISKO, brother of above, was born 17 Apr 1835 at Addison, Maine. He married Theodocia- 8 DRISKO (#1261) on 24 Nov 1859. She was the daughter of Zimri-7 DRISKO and Roxalana NORTON, and was born ca 1840; died 18 Sept 1885. They resided in Columbia, ME. most of their lives, where Charles-7 DRISKO was a ships' carpenter. They were listed on the 1880 Census at Machiasport where he was listed as Keeper of the Libby Island Lighthouse. Charles-7 DRISKO died 6 Feb 1894.

Children of Charles A-7 DRISKO and Theodocia-8 DRISKO:
  Surname DRISKO   (born Columbia, Maine)
  1427. William J.   born ca 1861 (listed as Assistant Lighthouse Keeper on 1880 census)
  1428. Mary J.   born Feb 1863; died 10 Nov 1864   EOL
  1429. Justin M.   born 13 Aug 1866; died 18 Aug 1866   EOL
+ 1430. GERTRUDE B.   born 1870; died 1925
  1431. Millard B.   born 22 Feb 1875; 1m. Ellie E, PICKARD 19 Aug 1896 at Phillips, ME
                        2m. Edna E. GROVER 4 July 1908 (she born 1887; died 1938 Phillips, ME)
                        died 1943; buried Riverside Cemetery, Phillips, Maine
              Note: Millard-8 DRISKO left Columbia, Maine ca 1895 to study engineering in Galesburg, IL
              He was a Civil Engineer employed by a Boston firm in 1925. Had children but they all died young.

508. MOSES-7 LIBBY, son of Dorothy-6 McKENNEY (Moses-5; Elizabeth-4 DRISKO; John-3 2) and Dominicus-5 LIBBY, was born 5 Mar 1792. He married Mary Ann LARRABEE on 24 Jan 1819 at Danville, Maine. She was the daughter of Stephen LARRABEE and Priscilla MARTIN, and was born ca 18__; still living at age 87 (_____). Moses-7 LIBBY, a Methodist, died 28 June 1837.

Children of Moses-7 LIBBY and Mary Ann LARRABEE:
  Surname LIBBY
  1432. John Nelson   born 2 Mar 1820; died unmarr; (he was blind; a farmer and a tradesman)
  1433. Asenath   born 10 July 1823; died Sept 1844 unmarried
  1434. Dorothy Jane   born 19 May 1825; died 13 Mar 1843
  1435. Stephen L.   born 3 Dec 1827; died 9 May 1831
  1436. Dominicus   born 5 Dec 1829; died 3 May 1864; member of 7th **ME. Volunteers, Civil War**
  1437. Lorenzo F.   born 9 July 1831; died 10 July 1831
  1438. Priscilla Martin born 3 June 1832; 1m. Charles HEARN 13 July 1856
                        (he born 18__; died 5 May 1867)
                        2m. Charles W. WALLACE 15 Sept 1870 no issue   EOL
  1439. Mary Ann   born 16 Oct 1836; died 23 Dec 1853

516. EUNICE-7 LIBBY, twin sister of above, was born 10 Aug 1805 at Pegypscot, Androscoggin County, ME. She married William McKenney JORDAN, a farmer, on 21 Oct 1840 at Danville, ME. He was the son of James Peables JORDAN ++ and Dorcas McKENNEY, and was born 15 May 1815 at Cape Elizabeth, Cumberland Co., ME; died 18 Sept 1872 at Danville, ME. Eunice-7 LIBBY died there 1 Dec 1876.

Children of Eunice-7 LIBBY and William JORDAN:
Surname JORDAN	(children born Danville, Maine)
1440. Hannah	born 11 Nov 1841; died 12 Nov 1841
1441. Rufus Libby	born 28 Aug 1843; died 6 Apr 1845
1442. William Albert	born 24 June 1846; married Belinda McKENNEY Oct 1869 Scarboro, ME
	died 6 Nov 1936 Auburn, Maine

++ JAMES PEABLES- JORDAN, son of Lieut. BENJAMIN- JORDAN and Abigail PEABLES, was born 31 Mar 1781 at Cape Elizabeth, Maine; married Dorcas McKENNEY 4 Apr 1803; died ca 1839. Lieut. Benjamin- JORDAN, born ca 1738, was the son of NATHANIEL- JORDAN and Dorothy HILL. Nathaniel- JORDAN, born 1696, was baptized Spurwink, ME and was the son of DOMINICUS- JORDAN and Hannah TRISTAM. Dorothy HILL was the daughter of Ebenezer HILL and Abiel SNELL.

518. GEORGE-7 LIBBY, son of Mary-6 McKENNEY (Moses-5; Elizabeth-4 DRISKO; John-3; 2) and Philip-4 LIBBY, was born 18 Apr 1792 at ___. He married first to Sally FOSS ca 18__. She was the daughter of ____ FOSS, and was born ___; died ___. His second wife was Eliza CARTER.

Children of George-7 LIBBY and Sally FOSS:
Surname LIBBY	
1443. Eunice	born 8 Dec 1819; married Cyrus KING
1444. Moses	born Apr 1822; unmarried
+ 1445. WILLIAM HENRY	born Apr 1825; married Lydia S. TYLER; died 30 Jan 1862
	(she dau/o Abraham TYLER and Eunice SEAVEY)
	(Lydia 2m. George E. JOHNSON 18 Feb 1868)

519. MARY-7 LIBBY, sister of above, was born 20 Oct 1794. She married Daniel- LIBBY ca 18__. He was the son of Elijah LIBBY and Mary DRESSER, and was born 21 Mar 1788; died 8 Dec 1857. She died 7 June 1874.

Children of Mary-7 LIBBY and Daniel LIBBY:
Surname LIBBY	
1446. Philip	born 23 Jan 1817; died 20 June 1877 unmarried
1447. Stephen	born ____; died in infancy
1448. Amos	born 11 Aug 1822; 1m. Elizabeth HAINES 16 Jan 1849
	(she dau/o Asa HAINES and Hannah MILLIKEN)(born 18__; died 1 Mar 1874)
	2m. Mary RICE 24 June 1878 (she dau/o Samuel RICE and Abigail TYLER)
	One child: Emily Jane LIBBY born 28 Jan 1850; married Living G. HILL 1872

520. MOSES-7 LIBBY, brother of above, was born 30 Nov 1796 at ____. He married Fannie SEAVEY ca 1835. She was the daughter of Job SEAVEY and Betsey TYLER, and was born ca ____; died 29 Oct 1872. Moses-7 LIBBY died 29 Jan 1879.

Children of Moses-7 LIBBY and Fannie SEAVEY:
Surname LIBBY	
+ 1449. JOSEPH WHITE	born 27 Jan 1836; married Marie Louise BLOUIN
	(she dau/o Leon BLOUIN and Lizzie _?_ of New Orleans, LA)
1450. Thomas	born 22 Nov 1837; died 14 Sept 1842
1451. Phebe	born 12 June 1841; died Dec 1856
1452. Thomas Seavey	born 20 Oct 1846; married Emma E. MARSTON 5 Nov 1865
	(she dau/o Joseph MARSTON and Susan ELLIS)
	Ch: Thomas Franklin-9 LIBBY born 18 July 1866

523. PHILIP-7 LIBBY, brother of above, was born 19 July 1806. He married Catherine HARMON on 23 June 1830. She was the daughter of Pelatiah HARMON and Sally ELWELL, and was born 18__; died 14 June 1869. Philip-7 LIBBY died 17 Oct 1870.

Children of Philip-7 LIBBY and Catherine HARMON:
    Surname LIBBY
    1453. Roxanna Foss   born 22 Nov 1830 Saco, ME; married Hezekiah DREW Sept 1859
    1454. Mary E.   born 22 Jan 1833; married David WARREN Aug 1863

531. MOSES-7 LIBBY see MARGARET M-7 LIBBY (# 551)
533. SUSAN-7 LIBBY, daughter of Betsey-6 McKENNEY (Moses-5; Elizabeth-4 DRISKO; John-3; 2) and Dennis-6 LIBBY, was born Feb 1811. She was the twin sister of Betsey-7 (# 534). She married a Dennis-7 LIBBY on 16 Dec 1838. He was the son of Alexander-6 LIBBY and Elizabeth-6 LIBBY, and was born 21 Jan 1816 at Pownalborough, Maine. He was a farmer there and died 24 Mar 1860. Susan-7 died 8 May 1875 at Charlestown, MA.

Children of Susan-7 LIBBY and Dennis-7 LIBBY:
    Surname LIBBY
    1455. Almira   born 24 July 1839; died 14 Apr 1841   EOL
    1456. Delia   born 21 Mar 1842
    1457. Appleton   born 17 Aug 1845; died 8 May 186_   EOL
              (he was a member of **Co.H, 32nd Maine Volunteers, Civil War;** died in camp)
+ 1458. ADDIE M.   born 18 Feb 1850; married Estus A. MORRILL of MA 4 May 1869
    1459. Ella E.   born 21 Apr 1854; died 8 July 1854   EOL

539. JOSHUA-7 McKENNEY, son of Moses-6 McKENNEY (Moses-5; Elizabeth-4 DRISKO; John-3; 2) and Salome LIBBY, was born Dec 1813. He married Elinor BUGBEE ca 18__. She was the daughter of _?_ BUGBEE and Abigail LIBBY, and was born 18__; died ____. Joshua-7 McKENNEY died ____, MN.

Children of Joshua-7 McKENNEY and Elinor BUGBEE:
    Surname McKENNEY
    1460. John Henry G.   born 18__; died ____; resided Minnesota
    1461. Moses Benjamin born ca 1841; married Frances Alice LEWIS 15 Oct 1870
        Franklin   (she dau/o Samuel LEWIS and Frances WILDING of Manchester, ENG)
              One child: Frances Lewis-8 McKENNEY born 22 Aug 1876
    1462. Abby Libby   born 184_; resided Minnesota; died ____ unmarried
    1463. Joshua   (twin) born 184_; resided Minnesota; died ____ unmarried
    1464. Mary Ellen (twin) born 184_; married Jerome B. CHAPMAN

542. JONATHAN-7 LIBBY, son of Luke-6 LIBBY (Dorothy-5 McKENNEY; Elizabeth-4 DRISKO; John-3; 2) and Betsey MITCHELL, was born 29 Feb 1798 at Danville, Maine. He married first to Mary JORDAN ca 18__. She was the daughter of William JORDAN of Lisbon, Maine, and was born 18__; died 9 Sept 1850. His second wife was Dorothy-7 LIBBY (#513). She was the daughter of Dominicus-6 LIBBY and Dorothy-6 McKENNEY (# 147), and was born 30 June 1801; died 9 Sept 1876. Jonathan-7 LIBBY, a sailor, fisherman and farmer, died 11 Nov 1866.

Children of Jonathan-7 LIBBY and Mary JORDAN:
    Surname LIBBY
    1465. Elizabeth   born 13 Nov 1825; married Lemuel TURNER
+ 1466. WILLIAM T.   born 8 Aug 1828; married Elizabeth HARRIMAN July 1851
              (she dau/o Charles HARRIMAN and Betsey BURBANK of Chatham, NH)
    1467. Mary J.   born 6 Mar 1833; married John STEVENS
    1468. Louisiana   born 19 Aug 1835; married James WAGG

544. WILLIAM-7 LIBBY, son of Isaac-6 LIBBY (Dorothy-5 McKENNEY; Elizabeth-4 DRISKO; John-3; 2) and Dorothy MESERVE, was born 20 Jan 1795 in Danville (now Auburn) Maine. He married Nancy JORDAN ca 1822. She was the daughter of John JORDAN and Margaret PEABLES, and was born 18__; died 6 May 1843. William-7 LIBBY died 18 Nov 1836 at Danville.

Children of William-7 LIBBY and Nancy JORDAN:
    Surname LIBBY
    1469. Isaac   born 1823; married Susan TARBOX
    1470. Hannah   born 182_; married Joseph JORDAN
    1471. Margaret   born 18__; died ____
    1472. Elizabeth   born 18__; married William CURTIS of Wisconsin

551. MARGARET M-7 LIBBY, sister of above, was born 28 Mar 1809 at Danville, Maine. She married MOSES-7 LIBBY (# 531) on 26 Oct 1837. He was the son of Betsey-6 McKENNEY and Dennis-6 LIBBY, and was born 8 Aug 1807 Danville, ME; died ____. Margaret-7 LIBBY died 4 Nov 1863.

Children of Margaret M-7 LIBBY and Moses-7 LIBBY:
    Surname LIBBY
    1473. Luella   born 2 Sept 1838; died 28 Jan 1850   EOL
    1474. Nellie L.   born 28 Apr 1842; married Stephen B. WORCESTER 31 May 1875
    1475. Moses Leroy   born 20 July 1854; married Emma E. JENNESS 17 May 1879   EOL

574. CAPTAIN JOSHUA-7 DRISCO, son of James-6 DRISCO (Captain James-5; James/Jeremiah-4; Cornelius-3; Jeremiah-2; Teague/Timothy-1) and Margarette MENDUM, was born ca 1804 at Portsmouth, New Hampshire. He married first to Maria A. TUCKER on 12 June 1832 at Portsmouth. She was the daughter of Samuel TUCKER and Margaret __?__, and was born ca 1798; died 7 Sept 1834, age 36. His second wife was Jane B. __?__, whom he married after 1834. She was born ca 1803; died 21 Feb 1877, aged 74. Joshua-7 DRISCO died 30 May 1857 (age 53) and is buried at Harmony Grove Cemetery, Portsmouth, NH.

Child of Joshua-7 DRISCO and Maria TUCKER:
    Surname DRISCO
    1476. Margaret M.   born 183_; married Charles E. COFFIN 3 Jan 1853
Children of Joshua-7 DRISCO and Jane B. __?__:
    Surname DRISCO
    1477. Izette S.   born 184_; married Augustus WALDEN 18 Aug 1862
    1478. James E.   born 2 Nov 1846; died 8 July 1911, age 65
                             buried Harmony Grove Cemetery, Portsmouth, NH

577. WILLIAM-7 TREFETHEN, son of Elizabeth/Betsey-6 DRISCO (Captain James-5; James-4; Cornelius-3; Jeremiah-2; Timothy-1) and Captain William TREFETHEN, was born ca 1809/10 , probably at Portsmouth, NH. He married Elsa-6 HALEY 16 Sept 1834. She was the daughter of Samuel-5 HALEY (Samuel-4; Thomas-3; 2; 1) and was born 22 Apr 1809; died ____.

Children of William-7 TREFETHEN and Elsa HALEY:
    Surname TREFETHEN
    1479. Elizabeth Mary   born 4 July 1835   1480. William Franklin   born 16 Oct 1836

The Eighth American Generation

595. ALFRED LESLIE-8 RICKER, son of Elijah-7 RICKER, Jr. (Elijah-6; Sobriety-5 NOCK/KNOX; Samuel-4; Sarah-3 DRISKO; John-2) and Mary CLEMENTS, was born 19 Jan 1855 at Detroit, Somerset County, Maine. He married first to Mary Eleanor WILLARD on 3 Sept 1879 at Pine Valley, Nevada. She was born 19 Dec 1856, CA; died 26 Oct 1895 at Cottonwood, Arizona.

He married second on 27 July 1903 to Leila Ada WORCESTER at Pittsfield, Maine. She was the daughter of John WORCESTER and Eleanor WHEELER; and was born 11 Nov 1865 at Etna, Maine; died 30 Apr 1930 at Carmel, Maine. Alfred-8 RICKER died 21 Jan 1938 at Kennebunk, Maine.

Children of Alfred-8 RICKER and Mary E. WILLARD:
   Surname RICKER
1480. Maud	born 9 Nov 1880 Palisade, Nevada
1481. Clyde Willard	born 7 July 1882 Detroit, Maine; died ____ unmarried
1482. Mary	born 25 Jan 1884 Detroit, Maine; died ____ unmarried
1483. Edgar Alfred	born 26 Aug 1885, Detroit,ME; married Amelia Angel SOUSA 10 Feb 1907
1484. George Alex	born 19 June 1888 Santa Rosa, CA; died 12 June 1889 San Francisco, CA

Children of Alfred-8 RICKER and Leila WORCESTER:
   Surname RICKER
+ 1485. LESLIE	born 11 Oct 1905 North Reading, MA; died 19 July 1967, Lewiston, ME
ALFRED	married Natalie Ann TRUE 1 June 1930

598. WILBUR ELIJAH-8 RICKER, brother of above, was born 12 Sept 1861 at Detroit, Maine. He married Lillian Beatrice DAY on 24 Feb 1870 at Concord, MA. She was the daughter of Charles E. DAY and Emma PITMAN. Wilbur-8 RICKER died 31 Dec 1930 at Melrose, MA.

Children of Wilbur-8 RICKER and Lillian DAY:
   Surname RICKER
1486. son	born 29 June 1892 Boston, MA
1487. Lillian Adeline	born 12 Jan 1894 Revere, MA; married William Damon PORTER 8 May 1917
1488. Dorothy Dean	born 18 Mar 1899 Boston, MA; marr Francis M. PENDERGAST 27 Oct 1924

606. ISAAC-8 RICKER, son of William-7 RICKER (Moses-6, Jr.; Sobriety-5 NOCK/KNOX; Samuel-4; Sarah-3 DRISKO; John-2) and Martha ELLIS, was born ca 1831. He married first Rosetta TYLER on 17 Sept 1853 at Lebanon, Maine. They were divorced. His second wife was Ellen J. HOLMES of Dover, NH. They were married 18 Mar 1861 at Alton, NH. She was born ca 1825; died 14 Feb 1903 at age 78.

Children of Isaac-8 RICKER and Rosetta TYLER:
   Surname RICKER   (children born Rochester, NH)
1489. Lizzie	born ca 1854; married Willard ELLIS 1 Mar 1872 Haverhill, MA
1490. Martha Rosetta	born 1855; married John L. SAWYER 28 Sept 1878
1491. Clara E.	born 1856; married John P. JONES 1 Sept 1877

       One child: Bertha-10 JONES born 1878; married Arthur DURGIN

607. WILLIAM-8 RICKER, brother of above, was born ca 1833. He married Harriet M. ELLIS on 27 Jan 1858 at Lowell, MA. She was the daughter of Isaac ELLIS and Charlotte HARTFORD, and was born 18__ Lebanon, Maine; died there 9 Dec 1907. William-8 RICKER died 19 Apr 1869 at Lowell, MA.

Children of William-8 RICKER and Harriet ELLIS:
   Surname RICKER
1492. Vesta Emma	born 13 Jan 1860 Great Falls, New Hampshire

       1m. Frank G. GRANT(he born 1855); 2m. Albert E. ELLIS; 3m. Fred S. DREW
       One child: Gladys Maxine-10 DREW born 4 Nov 1894 Lebanon, Maine

608. MARTHA ANN-8 RICKER, sister of above, was born 7 Jan 1837. She married Christopher HUSSEY on 26 July 1857 at Sanford, Maine. She died 1 Oct 1905 at Alfred, Maine.

Children of Martha Ann-8 RICKER and Christopher HUSSEY:

Surname HUSSEY				
1493. Charles	born 18__		1496. Lizzie	born 18__
1494. Mary Jane (twin) born 18__			1497. Herbert	born 18__
1495. Cora (twin) born 18__			1498. Phebe	born 18__
			1499. Martha	born 18__

610. LEWIS-8 RICKER, brother of above, was born 15 Apr 1843. He married Mary J. LITTLEFIELD on 25 Jan 1867 at Somersworth, NH. They were divorced 1905. He died 2 May 1923 at Rochester, NH.

Children of Lewis-8 RICKER and Mary LITTLEFIELD:

Surname RICKER	(children born Rochester, NH)
1500. Lottie	born 1868; married Wesley BEALE
1501. Lewis Daniel	born 25 Dec 1874; married Carrie M. PRICE 1900
1502. Grace M.	born 26 Aug 1878
1503. William A.	born 14 Feb 1880; married Carrie May FURBUSH
	Two children: Wayne-10 RICKER born 17 Apr 1911, and Paul-10 RICKER born 1913

617. ELMIRA-8 RICKER, daughter of Eli R-7 RICKER (Moses-6, Jr.; Sobriety-5 NOCK/KNOX; Samuel-4; Sarah-3 DRISKO; John-2) and Maria JACOBS, was born ca 1854. She married first to William-8 RICKER (# 602) on 23 Apr 1874, NH. No issue. She married second to Thomas BLAISDELL on 13 Mar 1883 at Rochester, NH.

Children of Elmira-8 RICKER and Thomas BLAISDELL:

Surname BLAISDELL	
1504. Ida May	born 18__; married Earl GORDON 1914
1505. Mary Ella	born 18__; married George __?__
1506. Thomas	born 18__; died ____ unmarried
1507. Ada Elizabeth	born 18__; married Edward DAY
1508. Alonzo E.	born 18__; married Lillian HERSOM 1910

620. LEWIS D.-8 GRANT, son of Daniel-7 GRANT (Mercy-6 RICKER; Sobriety-5 NOCK/KNOX; Samuel-4; Sarah-3 DRISKO; John-2) and Susan FOSS, was born 19 Dec 1829 at Lebanon, Maine. He married 1st to Augusta Ann ROLLINS on 10 Dec 1848 in New York. She was the daughter of _?_ ROLLINS, and was born ca 18__ Saco, ME; died before 1860. He married second to Mary Jane SANBORN. She was the daughter of _?_ SANBORN, and was born ca 1839, NH; died before 1870. He removed to Lawrence and Lowell, MA, and died 3 Apr 1898 at Dover, NH; buried Lawrence, MA.

Child of Lewis D-8 GRANT and Mary Jane SANBORN:

Surname GRANT	
1509. Frank	born 13 Dec 1863 Lawrence, Essex, MA; died 3 Nov 1952 Concord, NH married Elizabeth " Lizzie " HOYT/HOITT 14 Aug 1882 Dover, NH (she born 11 Oct 1864 Berwick, ME; died 15 Oct 1956 Dover, NH)

622. SOLOMON-8 GRANT, brother of above, was born 22 Sept 1832 at Lebanon, Maine. He married Almira R. MANSON on 13 June 1853 at South Berwick, ME. She was the daughter of Solomon (?) MANSON, and was born ca 1835 at Kennebunkport, Maine; died East Rochester , NH after 1890. Solomon-8 GRANT died 24 Mar 1890 at Rochester, NH.

Children of Solomon-8 GRANT and Almira MANSON:

Surname GRANT

1510. Francena " Fannie" born ca 1856 Lebanon, ME; marr George LANGDON 1873; died 3 May 1906

Children of Solomon-8 GRANT, continued:
    Surname GRANT
    1511. Emma   born ca 1858   1512. Mary   born ca 1860

623. MERCY/MARIA-8 GRANT, sister of above, was born 10 July 1834 at Lebanon, Maine. She married Charles Freeman HAYES on 20 Aug 1854 at Lebanon, ME. He was the son of George HAYES and Lydia _?_, and was born ca 1831, NH; died ____. They resided Rochester, NH ca 1850. Mercy-8 died there between 1870-1880.

Children of Mercy/Maria-8 GRANT and Charles HAYES:
    Surname HAYES   (all children born at North Rochester, Strafford, NH)

1513. Fannie Augusta	born 2 Apr 1856	1517. Annie Laurie	born 12 Oct 1863
1514. James Buchanan	born 23 Nov 1857	1518. Nettie Maria	born 7 Oct 1865
1515. Arthur Herbert	born 2 Jan 1860	1519. Florence Leona	born 17 Apr 1869
1516. Charles Winfield	born 24 Apr 1861		

624. JOHN-8 GRANT, brother of above, was born 1 Apr 1836 at Lebanon, Maine. He married Lydia A. ESTES on 25 Mar 1858 at Somersworth, NH. She was the daughter of _?_ ESTES, and was born ca 1839 Berwick, ME; died 5 Nov 1865. John-8 GRANT died 24 Jan 1910 at Berwick, York, Maine.

Children of John-8 GRANT and Lydia ESTES:
    Surname GRANT   (all children born Berwick, Maine)
    1520. Frank W.   born ca 1858; died 10 Aug 1865   1523. Flora A.   born ca 186_
    1521. John   born ca 1860   married Frank R. FOLSOM 24 Jan 1888
    1522. Pluma A.   born ca 186_; married John W. DUFNEY 26 Nov 1884

626. DANIEL-8 GRANT, brother of above, was born 7 Mar 1843 at Lebanon, Maine. He married Frances " Fannie " STERRETT on 6 Aug 1869. She was the daughter of _?_ STERRETT, and was born Aug 1845 at Hodgdon, Maine; died 2 Feb 1914. Daniel-8 GRANT died 26 Jan 1914 at Lebanon, Maine.

Children of Daniel-8 GRANT and Frances STERRETT:
    Surname GRANT   (all children born Lebanon, Maine)
    1524. Babe (?)   born ca 1860   1526. Lillian May   born 17 Feb 1872
    1525. Harry Linden born 15 May 1870; died 1941

629. CAROLINE " CARRIE " A-8 GRANT, sister of above, was born 22 May 1848 at Lebanon, Maine. She married William B. BENNETT on 24 July 1867 at Lebanon. He was the son of Job BENNETT and Sarah _?_, and was born ca 1845 at Rockport, MA; died ___.

Children of Caroline-8 GRANT and William BENNETT:
    Surname BENNETT
    1527. Agnes Caroline   born 22 June 1868; married Robert M. LILLEY
    1528. Mildred   born 29 Sept 1871; married William E. PHILLIPS

633. JULIA A-8 RICKER, daughter of Ezekiel-7 RICKER (Jedediah-6; Dorothy-5 NOCK/KNOX; Samuel-4; Sarah-3 DRISKO; John-2) and Joanna ROBERTS, was born 26 Jan 1834 at Biddeford, Maine. She married William LIBBY on 5 Feb 1855 at Somersworth, NH. He was born 26 Oct 1834 at Newington, NH; died ____. Julia-8 RICKER died ____.

Children of Julia-8 RICKER and William LIBBY:
    Surname LIBBY   (first 4 children born at Evansville, Wisconsin)

1529. Frank	born 23 Nov 1855; died 17 May 1856	1532. William Ernest	born 3 July 1865
1530. Maybelle Inez	born 18 Dec 1856	1533. Henry Elmer	born 12 July 1872 VA
1531. Irvin Aston	born 17 July 1860	1534. Emily Gertrude	born 25 May 1875

639. WILLIAM LORD-8 RICKER, brother of above, was born 24 July 1843 at Somersworth, NH. He married Sarah A. FRENCH on 16 Apr 1867 at Somersworth. She was born 22 Mar 1844 at Moultonboro, NH; died 27 Nov 1918 at Worcester, MA. He died there 5 Jan 1929.

Children of William L-8 RICKER and Sarah FRENCH:
    Surname RICKER
    1535. James E.   born 4 Oct 1867 Somersworth, NH; married Bertha H. HERSEY 13 July 1917 MA.
+ 1536. WILLIAM   born 6 Aug 1869 Somersworth, NH
        WOOSTER   married Mrs. Gertrude M. FISHER Tuttle 30 May 1897 MA
    1537. George F.   born 16 Sept 1871; died 31 Dec 1873

1538. Herbert H.	born 28 May 1875; died 20 Feb 1879	1541. Arthur E	born 9 Mar 1880
1539. Frederick E	born 1 Apr 1877; died 25 Feb 1879	1542. Grace	born 23 Dec 1886
1540. Annie J.	born 14 July 1878; died 4 Mar 1879		died 5 Sept 1887

640. NATHANIEL CLEMENT M-8 RICKER, brother of above, was born 22 Mar 1846 at Biddeford, ine. He married Cinda Ella GRANT on 10 Mar 1868 at Somersworth, NH. She was born 18__; died 5 July 1940 at Haverhill, MA. Nathaniel-8 RICKER died 25 June 1914 at Haverhill.

Children of Nathaniel-8 RICKER and Cinda Ella GRANT:
    Surname RICKER

1543. Edgar Sylvester	born 21 Sep 1869	1545. Alice May	born 11 Feb 1881
	died 4 Feb 1940	1546. James Linden	born 10 Mar 1883
1544. Mabel Natalie	born 29 Mar 1871		died 12 Apr 1889

671. NATHANIEL HIGGINS-8 RICKER, son of Daniel-7 RICKER (Elias-6; Lucy-5 CROMWELL; Esther-4 NOCK/KNOX; Sarah-3 DRISKO; John-2) and Caroline HIGGINS, was born 25 Apr 1843 at Avon, Maine. He married Josephine T. ROMAINE on 22 June 1865 at Galveston, Texas. She was born 4 Apr 1844 New York City, NY; died 27 Aug 1906 at Galveston. Nathaniel-8 RICKER was a contracting engineer, and died ca 1912 at Hitchcock, TX.

Children of Nathaniel H-8 RICKER and Josephine ROMAINE:
    Surname RICKER   (children born at Galveston, Texas)
    1547. John Romaine   born 24 May 1870; married Julia Hurd SHAW 8 Jan 1896
             3 ch: Norman Hurd-10 RICKER born 11 Oct 1896; Vivian Cunningham-10 RICKER
                   born 24 Oct 1898; and Julia Hurd-10 RICKER born 14 Aug 1908.
    1548. Nathaniel Higgins born 14 Aug 1871; died Dec 1872
    1549. Carrie Elizabeth   born Nov 1872; died 17 Nov 1872
    1550. Josephine Theresa born 28 Dec 1873; died 14 Nov 1876
    1551. Charles Custer   born 1 Aug 1876; married Sue Mary COOPER 24 Dec 1902
             1 son: Nathaniel Higgins-10 RICKER born 14 Oct 1904 (blind)
    1552. Edwin Estell   born 19 Dec 1878; died 3 Aug 1883
    1553. Hortense Higgins born 27 Oct 1881
    1554. Edwina Estelle   born 31 Dec 1883
    1555. Josephine Romaine born 24 May 1885; died 1 June 1885
    1556. Inez Isabell   born 13 June 1886; married Randolph W. WEST
           2 children: Sally Josephine-10 WEST and Randolph W-10 WEST

675. DANIEL LARRABEE-8 RICKER, brother of above, was born 21 June 1852 at Avon, Maine. He married Elizabeth Agnes O'CONNOR on 12 Feb 1885 at Galveston, Texas. She was born ca 18__; died 18 Feb 1938. Daniel L-8 RICKER died 25 Nov 1936.

Children of Daniel Larrabee-8 RICKER and Elizabeth O'CONNOR:
    Surname RICKER
+ 1557. CAROLINE AGNES born 19 May 1887; married Jesse Crockett WORTHINGTON

Children of Daniel Larrabee-8 RICKER, continued:
Surname RICKER

+ 1558. HAZEL F.	born 3 Oct 1891; 1m. James A. BLOCKER; 2m. Julian MONTANA
1559. Mary Elizabeth	born 1 Mar 1896; married Albert French WESTFALL 14 Mar 1929
+ 1560. NATHALIE H.	born 22 July 1897; married Leo Joseph STILL 1928
+ 1561. DANIEL L.,JR.	born 28 Dec 1898; married Eugenia Elizabeth McENTIRE 31 Aug 1930
1562. James O'Connor	born 8 Jan 1905; married Margaret Norma MATTIMORE
	2 children: Patricia M-10 RICKER born 13 July 1935 and Carol Jean-10 RICKER born 24 Apr 1938; died 20 Oct 1938
1563. Philip Aloysius	born Mar 1913; married Norma Hortense GONZALES 1936

676. JENNIE SABRINA-8 RICKER, sister of above, was born 4 Apr 1855 at Avon, Maine. She married Benjamin Emery PRATT on 28 Nov 1873 at Avon.

Children of Jennie-8 RICKER and Benjamin PRATT:
Surname PRATT

1564. Blanche M.	born 30 Jan 1874 Avon; married Leon J. EMERSON 22 Apr 1893
1565. Myrtle B.	born 5 Dec 1875 Kingsfield, ME; married Edward W. MYERS 24 Dec 1896
1566. Jennie V.	born 24 Feb 1878 Farmington, ME; died 13 June 1886 Phillips, ME.
1567. Harry Emery	born 12 Oct 1879 Farmington; married Blanche P. PRATT 23 Aug 1904

677. XARISSA-8 RICKER, sister of above, was born 9 May 1857 at Avon, Maine. She married Raymond C. ROSS on 6 Sept 1875 at Phillips, Maine.

Children of Xarissa-8 RICKER and Raymond ROSS:
Surname ROSS

1568. Harold	born 18__		1571. Atherton	born 18__
1569. Winifred	born 18__		1572. Verna	born 18__; married Ernest E. MOSES
1570. Delerna	born 18__		1573. Della	born 18__

694. JENNIE PHOEBE-8 RICKER, daughter of the Rev Simeon-7 RICKER (Daniel-6; Lucy-5 CROMWELL; Esther-4 NOCK/KNOX; Sarah-3 DRISKO; John-2) and Mary Ann HODGKINS, was born 14 Aug 1844 at Ripley, Maine. She married first to Joseph Hiram GRANT. He served in the **Civil War** and died 1865 at a hospital in Washington, DC. Her second husband was John D. WELCH.

She married third to Captain Stephen RICKER on 26 Apr 1876 at Portland, Maine. He was a sea captain, and was the son of Joel RICKER and Hulda CHANDLER. He was born 2 Oct 1817; died ____ at Portland, Maine. Her fourth husband was Jacob STRANGE. They resided Duluth, Minnesota.

Child of Jennie-8 RICKER and Joseph GRANT:
Surname GRANT
+ 1574. GENEVA HELEN born 22 Apr 1865; married Alton K. WENTWORTH 30 Nov 1884

Children of Jennie-8 RICKER and John D. WELCH:
Surname WELCH

1575. Willard Everett	born 18__; died in OR	1577. Frank Dermott	born 18__
1576. Albert Elmer	born 18__; died in the **Phillipine War**		

698. ALONZO E-8 RICKER, son of Benjamin-7 RICKER (Daniel-6; Lucy-5 CROMWELL; Esther-4 NOCK/KNOX; Sarah-3 DRISKO; John-2) and Sophronia BRANCH, was born 25 Nov 1835 at Monroe, ME. He married first to Annie FOSTER ca 18__. She was the daughter of ____ FOSTER, and was born ca 18__; died before 1874. He married second to Louisa BROWN Johnson ca 1874 at Oakfield, Maine. She was the daughter of William BROWN and Sarah PORTER, and was born ca 1855; died 16 June 1933 at Brownville, Maine. Alonzo-8 RICKER died 17 Apr 1902 at Oakville, Maine.

Child of Alonzo-8 RICKER and Annie FOSTER:
    Surname RICKER
    1578. Annie   born ca 1868 Oakfield, ME; 1m. ? MERRILL
                             2m. Frederick BROWN 12 May 1896
 Children of Alonzo-8 RICKER and Louisa BROWN:
    Surname RICKER
    1579. Alonzo   born 1874 Oakfield; died 27 Mar 1896
    1580. Arabella   born 1875 Auburn, ME; married Stephen F. McFARLAND 27 Sept 1889
                     2 children: Lester Eugene-10 McFARLAND born 1893; and Charlotte
                                 May-10 McFARLAND born 1895 Lewiston, Maine.
    1581. Mabel   born ca 1876; married James S. IRELAND
                     1 child: Mary V. IRELAND born 21 Aug 1918
    1582. Orren Newton   born 11 Jan 1877; married Mary Davidson GIBSON 1 Aug 1918
                     (she dau/o James GIBSON and Annie WILSON) (she born 18__; died 6 Sept 1960)
                     died 22 June 1975 Howland, Maine
                     3 children: Agnes-10 RICKER born 6 June 1919; James Orren-10 RICKER
                          born 15 July 1921, and Jan Violet-10 RICKER born 17 Feb 1923

704. ORREN-8 RICKER, brother of above, was born 10 Apr 1850 at Glenburn, Maine. He married first to Annie LAMBERT ca 18__. She was the daughter of Lewis LAMBERT and Mary J. ERSKINE, and was born 15 July 1849 at Brewer, Maine, died 6 Oct 1922. They were divorced. His second wife was Flora M. GOWEN. They married on 13 Sept 1883 at Waterville, Maine. She was born ca 18__; died 25 Feb 1938 at Chelsea, MA. He died there on 23 Apr 1933.

Children of Orren-8 RICKER and Annie LAMBERT:
    Surname RICKER
    1583. Kerry   born 25 Jan 1875   1584. Lewis W.   born 18__
Children of Orren-8 RICKER and Flora GOWEN:
    Surname RICKER
    1585. Jennie Estella   born 29 Aug 1885 Farmingdale, ME; 1m. Ernest H. ROBINSON 17 Aug 1912
                           (he son /o Hubert ROBINSON and Mary WILLIAMS)
                           2m. Joseph B. TAYLOR 26 Nov 1919
    1586. Orinda G.   born 29 Sept 1888 Randolph, Maine; died 30 Jan 1891
    1587. Fred Harold   born 17 July 1891; died 8 June 1892
    1588. Ernest Leroy   born 2 Apr 1893 Chelsea, MA; married Grace Leona MAY 19 Apr 1921
    1589. Sophronia   born 25 Feb 1897 Chelsea, MA; married Philip L. GARDINER 28 Aug 1913
                    1 child: Norman Bucher-10 GARDINER born 20 Feb 1917 Randolph, Maine
    1590. Frederick Roland born 22 Mar 1899 Chelsea, MA; 1m. Alice PUSHARD 29 May 1918
                           (she born 1898; died 8 Apr 1928)
                           2m. Helen M. SHEA Barter 1 June 1930; 3m. Eleanor RANKIN Hubbard 1941
    1591. Vera Dorothy   born 1 Aug 1905

705. AUGUSTA-8 RICKER, daughter of Daniel-7 RICKER, Jr. (Daniel-6; Lucy-5 CROMWELL; Esther-4 NOCK/KNOX; Sarah-3 DRISKO; John-2) and Elizabeth METCALFE, was born ca 1850 at Frankfort, Maine. She married Charles A. DOWNING on 25 Jan 1875 at Ripley, Maine. He was the son of __?__ DOWNING and was born ca 18__; died ____. She died 29 Aug 1886, after the birth of her fifth child.

Children of Augusta-8 RICKER and Charles A. DOWNING:
    Surname DOWNING   (children born Ripley, Maine)
    1592. Herbert Plummer born 30 Aug 1879; married Cora MARSH 20 Dec 1905
    1593. Laura Leora   born 30 Apr 1880; married Ernest Charles FARRAR 6 Apr 1906
    1594. Roscoe Metcalfe born 13 June 1882; married Susan Eldredge JONES 4 July 1908
    1595. Florence Gusta   born 6 Oct 1884; married Bart James FOLSOM 2 Nov 1907
    1596. Charles Stillman born 29 Aug 1886; died ____ unmarried

740. WALTER P-8 RICKER, son of Daniel J-7 RICKER (Paul-6; Lucy-5 CROMWELL; Esther-4 NOCK/KNOX; Sarah-3 DRISKO; John-2) and Mary Ann HUTCHINS, was born 12 Oct 1863 at Chelsea, MA. He married Mary Arvie HASKELL on 29 Oct 1884 at Everett, MA. She was the daughter of Byron T. HASKELL and Mary F. MATTHEWS, and was born ca 18__; died 14 July 1921 at Reading , MA. He died 15 June 1925.

Children of Walter-8 RICKER and Mary Arvie HASKELL:
  Surname RICKER   (children born Chelsea, MA)
  1597. Edith Pearl   born 20 Feb 1886; married Earl ANSBERRY 15 Nov 1907
  1598. Lloyd Eugene   born 25 Jan 1888
  1599. George Valentine born 14 Feb 1890, MA ; married Anna __?__; died Oct 1971 Dedham, MA
                    (she born 6 June 1890; died Dec 1979 Dedham, Ma)

745. LYDIA ANN-8 SIMMS   see PAUL-7 RICKER (# 288)
754. ELEANORA J-8 RICKER, daughter of Andrew-7 RICKER (Captain Ebenezer-6; Nathaniel-5; Mercy-4 NOCK/KNOX; Sarah-3 DRISKO; John-2) and Elizabeth SIMMS, was born 17 Aug 1847 at Argyle, Nova Scotia. She married Elihu WHITEHOUSE on 6 Oct 1867 at Argyle. He was born there on 28 Sept 1844; was a fisherman and woodworker; and died ____. Eleanora-8 RICKER died 13 May 1892 at Glenwood, Nova Scotia.

Children of Eleanora-8 RICKER and Elihu WHITEHOUSE:
  Surname WHITEHOUSE
  1600. Ida Belle   born 25 Dec 1869 Glenwood, NS; married Archibald MORRELL 25 Feb 1892
  1601. Arthur Jackson born 29 June 1883 Glenwood; married Emma NICKERSON

756. ABNER JACKSON-8 RICKER, brother of above, was born 23 Apr 1858 at Argyle, Nova Scotia. He married Fannie Sargent DOANE on 6 Jan 1887 at Barrington, NS. She was the daughter of James Hervey DOANE, and was born 12 Mar 1864; died ____. Abner-7 RICKER died 2 Apr 1942 at Glenwood, NS.

Children of Abner Jackson-8 RICKER and Fannie DOANE:
  Surname RICKER   (children born Glenwood, Nova Scotia)
  1602. Charlotte Eleanor born 14 Sept 1889; married Thomas Uhlman KILLAM 9 May 1912
                    One child: Florence-10 KILLAM born 1 May 1916 Fernie, British Colombia
  1603. Helen Sophia   born 24 Oct 1891
  1604. Annie Louise   born 9 Nov 1894; died Sept 1942
  1605. James Allison   born 19 Sept 1896; died 26 Aug 1918 (killed in France in **World War I**)
  1606. Andrew Jackson   born 27 Sept 1898; married Dorothy Jean BAIN 16 July 1920
                    (she dau/o Nathan BAIN and Ina __?__)
  1607. Elizabeth Grace   born 13 Sept 1900

770. FLORENCE ASHTON-8 RICKER, daughter of William-7 RICKER (Captain Ebenezer-6; Nathaniel-5; Mercy-4 NOCK/KNOX; Sarah-3 DRISKO; John-2) and Martha l. FROST, was born 21 Nov 1852 at Argyle, Nova Scotia. She married Joseph R. GOODWIN on 31 Dec 1875 at Argyle, NS He was from Kemptville, NS, where Florence-8 RICKER died 4 June 1902.

Children of FLORENCE ASHTON-8 RICKER and Joseph GOODWIN:
  Surname GOODWIN   (children born Kemptville, NS)
  1608. Letitia H.   born 7 Nov 1876   1610. William   born 21 Aug 1882
  1609. Ezra A.   born 2 Jan 1879   1611. Sarah Emma born 23 May 1887
                    died 20 May 1895   1612. Aubrey   born 15 June 1890

771. MATURIN MORSE-8 RICKER, brother of above, was born 7 June 1855 at Argyle, Nova Scotia. He married Alfaretta ROBERTS ca 1877 at Argyle. She was the daughter of Hiram ROBERTS and Martha NICKERSON, and was born 20 Oct 1859, NS.

Children of Maturin Morse-8 RICKER and Alfaretta ROBERTS:
   Surname RICKER
   1613. Martha N.   born 5 Mar 1878 Argyle, Nova Scotia
   1614. Carrie Jane   born Oct 1879l died 29 July 1941 unmarried
   1615. Alice   born ca 1881 Argyle, NS
 + 1616. WHITFIELD W.   born ca 1883 Gloucester, MA; married Sarah E. CURRAN 4 Feb 1910
   1617. Hiram R.   born 8 Aug 1885 Gloucester; married Mae A. MONAGLE 15 Oct 1913
                          (she dau/o Charles MONAGLE and Mary DOHERTY)
 + 1618. OSBORNE F.   born 12 Nov 1886 Gloucester; married Margaret McNEIL 12 Nov 1910
   1619. Frances A.   born 20 Nov 1890 Malden, MA; married Lowell D. AREY 6 June 1918 MA.
   1620. Richard Theodore born 3 Sept 1892 Malden; married Roxy Evelyn GODDARD 6 Dec 1922

796. CARRIE A-8 RICKER, daughter of Benjamin-7 RICKER, Jr. (Benjamin-6; Nathaniel-5; Mercy-4 NOCK/KNOX; Sarah-3 DRISKO; John-2) and Hannah BROOKS, was born 17 Oct 1865 at Eastport, ME. She married first to Alonzo H. FOUNTAIN on 6 Apr 1881. He was born ca 18__; died 23 June 1881. She married her second husband, Benjamin V. BRADSHAW, before 1888 at LaConner, Skaget Co., WA.

Children of Carrie-8 RICKER and Benjamin BRADSHAW:
   Surname BRADSHAW   (children born Skaget County, WA)
   1621. Edgar R.   born 22 Mar 1888; d. Jan 1974 Mt. Vernon, WA.   1622. Leonard T. born 30 Mar 1891
   1623. Vaughan V born 19 July 1892; d. Dec 1969 Mt. Vernon   1624. Clarence D. born 18 Apr 1894; dy

806. MELINDA-8 SMITH, daughter of Lydia-7 RICKER (Benjamin-6; Nathaniel-5; Mercy-4 NOCK/KNOX; Sarah-3 DRISKO; John-2) and Captain Andrew SMITH, was born 29 May 1845, at sea. She married Levi HOPKINS on 12 Nov 1867. He was the son of __?_ HOPKINS of Bear Point, NS.

Children of Melinda-8 SMITH and Levi HOPKINS:
   Surname HOPKINS
   1625. Andrew Leslie   born Mar 1872   1627. Amelia   born 10 Mar 1882
   1626. Lydia Gertrude   born 13 Nov 1874; died 1881

808. ADELIA-8 SMITH, sister of above, was born Sept 1849, at sea. She married William Watson FROST on 9 Sept 1887.

Children of Adelia-8 SMITH and William FROST:
   Surname FROST   1628. Francis G.   born 29 June 1888   1629. Lucy M.   born 5 May 1893

816. ADA B-8 RICKER, daughter of Sylvanus-7 RICKER (Benjamin-6; Nathaniel-5; Mercy-4 NOCK/KNOX; Sarah-3 DRISKO; John-2) and Sarah FROST, was born 28 Aug 1858 at Argyle, NS. She married Lemuel CROWELL on 12 Dec 1885 at Argyle. He was a ships' carpenter at Gloucester, MA.

Children of Ada B-8 RICKER and Lemuel CROWELL:
   Surname CROWELL
   1630. Sarah Redding   born 21 Nov 1886 Argyle Head, NS
   1631. Angus Clifton   born 3 Mar 1893, MA; died 24 May 1894
   1632. Henry Clifton   born 6 June 1894

821. GILES-8 RICKER, brother of above, was born 23 Nov 1869 at Argyle, Nova Scotia. He married Ella Maude GULLIVER on 30 June 1897 at Hudson, MA. She was born 8 Jan 1872 at Douglaston, New Brunswick; died 7 June 1943 at Hudson, MA. Giles-8 RICKER died there 22 Feb 1940.

Children of Giles-8 RICKER and Ella GULLIVER:
   Surname RICKER
   1633. Everett Giles   born 13 May 1898; died 1946 unmarried

Children of Giles-8 RICKER, continued:
  Surname RICKER
  1634. Mildred Maud   born 29 July 1899 Hudson, MA
                           married Charles Winthrop LEARNED 15 June 1929
    (he son/o Herbert LEARNED and Harriet HOUGHTON) (he born 19 July 1900)
  1635. Florence Ada   born 22 Jan 1901 Hudson, MA
                           married James Campbell COOLIDGE 24 June 1923
    (he son/o Charles COOLIDGE and Margaret CAMPBELL)   (he born 6 Aug 1900)
+ 1636. VIOLA HELEN   born 29 Nov 1902 Marlboro, MA; married Carl Douglas PHIPPS 19 Mar 1933
  1637. Percival James   born 30 Nov 1904; died 1922 unmarried
+ 1638. RUBY EDITH   born 9 Aug 1908 Hudson, MA; married Patrick Joseph MURPHY 19 Feb 1939
  1639. Mary Ella   born 16 Dec 1909 Hudson, MA; married Theron A. LOWDEN 6 July 1935
  1640. Henry Lemuel   born 22 May 1912 Hudson, MA; married Elva Marjorie BURKLE 26 Sept 1943
    (she dau/o Henry BURKLE and Marjorie O'HEARN)(she born 3 Jan 1918, MA)
+ 1641. RICHARD W.   born 12 Sept 1915 Hudson, MA; married Isabelle Burnham KING 21 June 1946
  1642. Mabel Arlene   born 3 Oct 1917, Hudson; married Rundell Rinehart SCHROEDER
                           (he born 18 Jan 1910; died July 1979 Torrance, CA)

853. ARTHUR S-8 RICKER, son of Charles Henry-7 RICKER (Daniel-6; Paul-5; Mercy-4
NOCK/KNOX; Sarah-3 DRISKO; John-2) and Eliza TRUSDEN/TWISDEN, was born 24 Aug 1888 at
Ipswich, MA. He married Nora M. PERRY on 1 Apr 1910 at Ipswich. She was the daughter of Joseph G.
PERRY and Mary ARSENAULT, and was born ca 1890 on Prince Edward Island; died ____ .

Children of Arthur S-8 RICKER and Nora M. PERRY:
  Surname RICKER   (children born Ipswich, MA)
  1643. Yvonne   born 6 Feb 1916 ; married Alfred E. BEAUCHANIN 15 Nov 1937
  1644. Grace Elizabeth born 27 Aug 1917; marr Richard D. KIERNAN 30 Dec 1942; d. Nov 1981 MA
    (he son/o Felix KIERNAN and Florence DELANO) (he born 1916 Wareham, MA)
  1645. Stanley Grant   born 1 July 1919; married Loretta J. ST. GERMAINE 15 Nov 1941
    (she dau/o Joseph ST. GERMAINE and Marie BAKER)
  1646. Mary Ethel   born 10 Aug 1922; married James S. BORHO 12 July 1947
    (he son/o Alexander BORHO and Juliana HEMSTEDT) (he born 1924 North Dakota)

858. BUSHROD WASHINGTON-8 WILSON, son of Joseph Warren-7 WILSON (Jerusha-6 DRISKO;
John-5; Joseph-4; John-3;2) and Elizabeth PINEO, was born 18 July 1824 at Columbia Falls, Washington
County, Maine. He married Priscilla Ousley YANTIS 19 Oct 1856 at Linn, Oregon. She was the daughter
of James Madison YANTIS and Sarah Ann HAMILTON; and was born 4 Jan 1838 at Saline County, MO;
died 9 Dec 1911 at New York, NY. Bushrod W-8 WILSON died 4 Mar 1900 at Corvallis, Benton Co., OR.

Children of Bushrod W-8 WILSON and Priscilla YANTIS:
  Surname WILSON
  1647. LaFayette   born 26 Oct 1857, Oregon; died ca 1899
                           married Inez ST. CLAIR 6 Oct 1886 Corvallis, OR
    (she dau/o Wayman ST. CLAIR and Mahala Jane JOHNSON) (she born May 1866 OR)
                1 ch: Bertha-10 WILSON born 5 Mar 1891; died Oct 1960 Oak Park, IL)
                           married Joseph A. GANONG
  1648. John Hamilton   born ca 1858 Saline Co., MO; d y
  1649. Eliza Belle   born 25 Apr 1859 Saline Co., MO
                           married J. Bernard WALKER 23 Mar 1887
  1650. Minnie Augusta   born ca 1860 Saline Co., MO; d y
  1651. James Offin   born 14 Mar 1861 Saline Co., MO; died 31 Aug 1904
                           married Lulu SMITH 1 Oct 1891
  1652. Clara Helen   born ca 1861 Saline Co., MO; d y
  1653. Joseph Hamilton   born 1 Aug 1863; died 2 May 1919; married Effa May HANDY 8 Aug 1894

Children of Bushrod W-8 WILSON, continued:
   Surname WILSON
   1654. Robert Justice   born 02 June 1866 Saline Co., MO
   1655. Otis Lincoln   born 7 June 1870 Saline Co., MO
                          married Amelia Romeyn WILLIAMS 25 Jan 1893
   1656. Thomas Edwin   born 18 June 1872, Saline Co., MO; died 1921
                          married Margaret KING Collings 4 Aug 1898
   1657. Minnie Augusta   born 18 Mar 1877 Benton Co., OR
   1658. Cara Helen Mary born 17 Feb 1879 Benton Co., OR; died 9 Nov 1932 Boise, ID
                          married William Hale WICKS 16 Nov 1904 Benton, OR   (2 ch)
                          (he son/o Francis WICKS and Alice M ?)
                          (he born 30 Nov 1880 Macon Co, IL; died 2 Nov 1959 Boise, ID)
                          Reference: Benton County, Oregon Pioneers and LDS- IGI records

906. ELIZABETH ANN-8 PLUMMER, daughter of Jeremiah-7 PLUMMER (Lorraine-6 DRISKO; John-5; Joseph-4; John-3; 2) and Elizabeth-6 WASS, was born ca 1819 at Addison, Maine. She married Jacob Adams-2 DAVIS on 27 Oct 1839. He was the son of Samuel-1 DAVIS and Susanna NASH, and was born ca 1810; died 6 Jan 1872 at Addison. Elizabeth/Eliza-7 PLUMMER died ____.

Children of Elizabeth-8 PLUMMER and Jacob-2 DAVIS:
   Surname DAVIS   (children born Addison, Maine)
   1659. Algernon A.   born ca 1841; died 2 May 1871 Augusta, Maine
   1660. Stillman P.   born Oct 1843; died young
   1661. George Adams   born 18 Feb 1852; died ____   seaman
   1662. Irving Handy   born 13 Jan 1854; marr Sarah Carolyn HOYT 16 Oct 1883 at Bar Harbor, ME
                          (she born 1 Oct 1862; died 9 Apr 1935)

909. CAPTAIN WILLIAM WILMOT-8 PLUMMER, brother of above, was born May 1824 at Addison, Maine. He married Jane H. WARD on __ July 1852 at Cherryfield, Maine. She was the daughter of William WARD, and was born Aug 1828; died 30 Dec 1910 at Addison. William W-8 PLUMMER, a sea captain and farmer, died 24 July 1902 at Addison.

Children of Captain William W-8 PLUMMER and Jane WARD:
   Surname PLUMMER   (children born Addison, Maine)
   1663. Theresa W.   born Oct 1853; died 7 Apr 1863
   1664. Marion Handy   born Jan 1858; died 6 Apr 1871
   1665. William N.   born June 1864; died 1937; a blacksmith
            married Ida B-7 COLSON 26 Oct 1889 (she born June 1865; died 5 July 1935)
   1666. Albert Dyer   born 1 Oct 1868; died 20 Aug 1916; a house painter
            married Mary C-9 KNOWLES 27 June 1894 (she born 21 Jan 1869; died 5 Nov 1955 CA)

925. CHARLES S-8 WASS, son of Betsey G-7 PLUMMER (Lorraine-6 DRISKO; John-5; Joseph-4; John-3; 2) and Captain Holmes NASH-7 WASS, was born Feb 1833 at Addison, Maine. he married first to Louisa A-8 RAMSDELL on 18 Jan 1855 at Addison. She was the daughter of Jesse-7 RAMSDELL and Eunice Look-6 HILLMAN, and was born 1833 at Harrington, ME; died 1880. He married his second wife, Elizabeth/Lizzie SMITH, on 24 Feb 1881. She was the daughter of ____ SMITH, and was born Feb 1837.

Children of Charles S-8 WASS and Louisa RAMSDELL:
   Surname WASS
   1667. Holmes S.   born 1856; died young
   1668. John Plummer   born 16 Aug 1862 Addison, ME
                          married Lulu C-9 LEIGHTON Austin 21 July 1885
   (she dau/o Luther P-8 LEIGHTON and Caroline S. KELLEY)(she born 18 Apr 1866; died 1957)
   1669. Betsey   born ca 1866

Children of Charles S-8 WASS, continued:
     Surname WASS
     1670. Gilbert Holmes   born ca 1868; died ____ ; Leominster, MA,   a grocer
                                  married Lillian Maude-7 DICKINSON 3 Aug 1889
(she dau/o Talbot S-6 DICKINSON and Susan HAYLAND)(she born 13 Apr 1869; died Oct 1938 MA)

926. NANCY WASS-8 PLUMMER   see BENJAMIN FRANKLIN-7 DRISKO (# 463)
929. FRANCES A-8 PLUMMER   see CAPTAIN PERRIN-7 DRISKO (# 466)
937. CAPTAIN AMOS BUCKNAM-8 PLUMMER, JR., son of Amos Bucknam –7 PLUMMER
(Lorraine-6 DRISKO; John-5; Joseph-4; John-3; 2) and Susan COFFIN, was born ca 1836, probably at
Harrington, Maine. He married Elizabeth/Lizzie-8 COFFIN there on 3 July 1856. She was the daughter of
Amos Bucknam-7 COFFIN and Irene MITCHELL, and was born ca 1838; died 12 Mar 1883 at Harrington.
Captain Amos-8 PLUMMER, sea captain at Machiasport, died there 1890.

Children of Captain Amos-8 PLUMMER, Jr. and Elizabeth-8 COFFIN:
     Surname PLUMMER
     1671. Milton E.   born ca 1858; died ____ ; a sailor at Harrington, ME.
                                  married Mary Elizabeth-7 NASH (she born ca 1858)
                                  (she dau/o Wilmot W-6 NASH and Mary-7 DINSMORE)
     1672. Lavina C.   born ca 1863; married Lincoln HENDERSON 30 May 1881, MA.
     1673. Lucy   born ca 1871

938. CAPTAIN VORANUS COFFIN-8 PLUMMER, brother of above, was born 10 Apr 1837 at
Harrington, ME. He married 1st to his cousin, Susan Coffin-8 WASS, ca Apr 1858 at Harrington. She was
the daughter of Wilmot G-7 WASS and Frances PLUMMER, and was born 7 Aug 1840 at Addison; died
1870. He married 2nd at Addison on 20 July 1872 to Mary Elizabeth/Lizzie-6 NASH. She was the daughter
of William N-5 NASH and Jane Coffin SMALL, and was born 11 Nov 1836; died 13 Aug 1911. Captain
Voranus-8 PLUMMER died 26 June 1926 at Addison. He was a sea captain, lumberman and shipbuilder.

Children of Captain Voranus-8 PLUMMER and Susan C-8 WASS:
     Surname PLUMMER
     1674. Gertrude A.   born 8 Dec 1864; died 15 Jan 1954 Addison, Maine
                                  married Melvin Longfellow CLEAVES 6 Aug 1881
(he son/o Benjamin F. CLEAVES and Angeline LONGFELLOW) (he born Aug 1859; died Jan 1940)
     1675. Harland E.   born 23 Oct 1867; died 11 Apr 1907 Addison
                                  married Sarah B-8 CHANDLER 25 Oct 1890
(she dau/o Nathaniel-7 CHANDLER & Elizabeth A-8 TUPPER; she born 24 Jul 1871; died 27 Apr 1934)
     1676. Walter W.   born Aug 1870; died ____ ; a Lighthouse Keeper at Addison
                                  married Rhoda M-9 WHITE 19 Apr 1890 (she born Mar 1868; died 25 Feb 1910)

939. HARLAND E-8 PLUMMER, brother of above, was born ca 1840 at Harrington, ME. He married
Judith A. TOBEY on 14 May 1860 at Machias, Washington Co., ME. She was the daughter of Charles
TOBEY and Lydia GARDNER of Machiasport, and was born there Sept 1838; died 1914. Harland-8
PLUMMER died 1879.

Children of Harland-8 PLUMMER and Judith TOBEY:
     Surname PLUMMER
     1677. Asenath M.   born Apr 1861; died 1950; married Willard D-8 COFFIN 1882
             (he son of John-7 COFFIN and Mary E. ALLEN)(he born Apr 1855; died 26 Dec 1913)
     1678. Geneva A.   born Sept 1870; died 1919 unmarried

941. LUCY ANN-8 DRISKO, daughter of William Johnson-7 DRISKO (Judah-6; John-5; Joseph-4;
John-3; 2) and Mary FRANKLAND, was born 7 Feb 1828 at Harrington, ME. She married Luther Inger-
soll-8 SAWYER on 15 Mar 1849 at Addison. He was the son of Joseph-7 SAWYER and Wealthy DYER,

and was born 11 June 1823; died 29 May 1898. Lucy Ann-8 DRISKO died 12 Dec 1906 at Jonesport, ME..

Children of Lucy Ann-8 DRISKO and Luther I-8 SAWYER:
    Surname SAWYER   (children born Addison, Maine)
    1679. William Johnson born 21 Oct1850
                           married Almeda Longfellow-9 INGERSOLL 15 Apr 1874 at Columbia, ME.
                           (she dau/o Fonze Green Hill-8 INGERSOLL and Lucy C. WORCESTER)
                           (she born 18 Nov 1854; died 1906)
    1680. Walter Preston   born 14 May 1854; died 15 Aug 1922 Machias, Maine
                           married Annie Serena-9 TUPPER 28 June 1879
                           (she dau/o William L-8 TUPPER and Elizabeth F-7 KILTON)

942. JUDAH JOHNSON-8 DRISKO, brother of above, was born 3 July 1830 at Addison, Maine. He married first on 1 Jan 1855 to Miranda O-7 SANBORN ++. She was the daughter of Lewis-6 SANBORN and Anne B. BUCKNAM, and was born 28 Sept 1829 at Machiasport, Maine; and died there 12 Mar 1884. He married second to Mrs. Sophia Wilson-8 ALLEN Strout on 15 June 1896. They resided at Harrington, Maine in 1905. Sophia was the daughter of Samuel-7 ALLEN and Jane B. COFFIN, and was born May 1840; died 19 Jan 1924. She was the widow of Captain Francis-7 STROUT. All of his children were from the first marriage. Captain Temple C-8 ALLEN, Sophias' brother, resided with them in 1900. Judah-8 DRISKO, a ships' caulker, died at Harrington 1 Mar 1912.

Children of Judah Johnson-8 DRISKO and Miranda SANBORN:
    Surname DRISKO
    1681. Annie/Anne   born 12 Apr 1855; married Seth W. LINCOLN 12 Nov 1874
          Buxton   (he son/o Captain William Seth LINCOLN and Hannah PHINNEY)
                        (he born 24 Feb 1843, Machiasport, ME; his father was a sea captain)
                        died 1 Jan 1942; resided Worcester, MA
  + 1682. WALDO   born 22 June 1857 Addison, ME.; died 1929 Bartlesville, Oklahoma
          BENTLEY   married Jennie Gertrude BURNHAM 11 Nov 1879
                        (she born 8 June 1861; died after 1924)
  + 1683. MARY   born 5 Feb 1861 Addison, ME.; died 10 Feb 1931 Worcester, MA
          FRANKLAND   married Rev Francis Arthur SANBORN 24 Dec 1884
                        (he son/o Cyrus SANBORN and Susan GARDNER)
                        (he born 19 Dec 1860; died 26 July 1933)
    1684. Mabel E.   born 1866; died 3 June 1901 Colorado Springs, Colorado

++ Ancestry of Miranda O-7 SANBORN

JOHN-1 SANBORNE, born 1620, the son of WILLIAM (A) SANBORNE of Brimpton, Berks, England and Anna BACHILER, is said to have come to America with his maternal grandfather, the Rev Stephen BACHILER, ca 1632. He was known as Lieutenant John SANBORNE, and he was married twice. His first wife was Mary TUCK , daughter of Robert TUCK. She was born ca 16__; died 30 Dec 1668, shortly after the birth of her ninth child. His second wife was Margaret PAGE Moulton, daughter of Robert PAGE; and widow of William MOULTON. They had one child.

JOHN-2 SANBORNE, was born ca 1649 at Hampton, New Hampshire. He married Judith-2 COFFIN, daughter of Tristam-1 COFFIN of Newbury, MA. She was born 4 Dec 1653; died 17 May 1724. John-2 SANBORNE died 23 Sept 1727. They were the parents of 10 children: Judith; Mary; Sarah; Deborah; John; Tristam; ENOCH-3; Lydia; Peter and Abner.

ENOCH-3 SANBORN(E) was born ca 1685 at Hampton, NH. In 1707 he went with Captain CHESLEYS' expedition to Port Royal. He married first to Elizabeth DENNETT of Portsmouth, NH in 1709. His second marriage, on 1 Apr 1736, was to Mehitabel BLAKE Godfrey; daughter of John BLAKE and widow of Jonathan GODFREY.

ENOCH-4 SANBORN, son of Enoch-3 and his first wife, was born ca 17__; baptized 28 June 1724. He was an Ensign in the British Army at the capture of Cape Breton. He resided most of his life in Hampton Falls; later moving to Machias, Maine. He married four times – first to Mary MORRILL on 3 Dec 1747. She died in 1752 and he married second to Sarah GREEN Sanborn on 27 Nov 1752. His third wife was Phebe SANBORN, and his fourth was the widow Hannah Day, whom he married in 1772.

WILLIAM-5 SANBORN, born 8 Oct 1773, was the son of Enoch-4 and his 4th wife Hannah Day. Captain William-5 SANBORN lived and died at Machias, Maine. He married first to Mary-3 CROCKER (# 18 CROCKER section) on 21 Feb 1796. She was the daughter of John-2 CROCKER (# 4) and Jane FREEMAN Berry of Bristol and Machias. She was born ca 1774; died 5 Apr 1797 in childbirth. His second wife was Priscilla MAYHEW. She was born ca 1773; died 1846. They were married on 4 Nov 1798. LEWIS-6 SANBORN was born 24 Aug 1805 at Machias, Maine.. He married Anna B. BUCKNAM on 27 Feb 1827. She was born 19 Oct 1800; died 6 Feb 1847. They were the parents of William; MIRANDA O-7; Anna J; and Eugene B. SANBORN. Reference: The American SANBORNS; published ____ .

948. SOPHIA S-8 DRISKO, daughter of Caleb Haskell-7 DRISKO (Judah-6; John-5; Joseph-4; John-3; 2) and Hannah COLE, was born 15 Mar 1827 at Addison, Maine. She married Benjamin A. SHUTE on 12 Sept 1852 at Addison. He was from Boston, MA.

Child of Sophia S-8 DRISKO and Benjamin SHUTE:
Surname SHUTE
+ 1685. MARTHA H.   born ca 187_; 1m. __?__ WHITE; 2m. FRED M-9 DRISKO ca 1900
    " Mattie "   (he son/o Francis Marion-8 DRISKO (# 951) and Alice E.WASS)

951. FRANCIS MARION-8 DRISKO, brother of above, was born 31 Aug 1833 at Addison, Maine. He married Alice Everlena WASS on 14 Dec 1861 at Addison, by Hiram TABBUTT, Esq. . She was the daughter of Enos WASS and Lydia COLE; and was born Apr 1843; died Oct 1875 (gs). Francis Marion-8 DRISKO died 21 Feb 1901 at Addison.

Children of Francis Marion-8 DRISKO and Alice E. WASS:
Surname DRISKO
1686. Walter Wass   born 1863; married Flora KNOWLES
1687. Sophia S.   born 8 May 1867; married __?__ SPENCER; died 5 July 1951 Springvale, ME.
+ 1688. FRED M.   born 18 May 1870 Harrington, ME.; died 24 Aug 1934
    married Mrs. MARTHA H. (Mattie) SHUTE White (# 1685) ca 1900
1689. John T.   born 1875; died 7 Jan 1899 (age 24) gs , So. Addison, Maine

952. ABIGAIL SLADE-8 (Abby) DRISKO, sister of above, was born 13 Oct 1835 at Addison, ME. She married John Bucknam-8 Godfrey LEIGHTON on 17 Oct 1856 at Addison. He was the son of Handy-7 LEIGHTON and Rebecca WASS, and was born 4 Apr 1832 at Steuben, ME.; died there 20 May 1900. Abby-8 DRISKO died 21 June 1886. John-8 LEIGHTON married 2nd to Hattie E. RAY on 2 Oct 1887.

Children of Abigail-8 DRISKO and John-8 LEIGHTON:
Surname LEIGHTON   (children born at Steuben, Maine)
1690. Frances A./Fannie born 21 Oct 1858; married Charles SMITH 16 Mar 1881 Cherryfield, ME.
1691. Hattie H.   born ca 1868; resided West Sullivan, Maine
1692. Maud   born 10 July 1873; died 6 June 1875   EOL

954. FRANCES/FANNY MARIA-8 DRISKO, sister of above, was born 31 Aug 1838 at Addison, Maine. She married first to Captain John Wass DYER on 5 Dec 1856. He was the son of Captain Vinal DYER and Eliza WASS of Addison, and was born ca 1835; divorced before 1860. According to the 1860 and 1870 Censuses, Frances-8 was residing with her parents (no children listed). She married second, after 1870, to Benjamin Ludden CRANE of Boston, MA.

Child of Frances-8 DRISKO and Benjamin Ludden CRANE:
Surname CRANE
1693. Alice   born ca 1876; married Samuel CURTIS; died 4 July 1930 (age 54)

968. LEVI WASS-8 DRISCO (used CO instead of KO), son of John Jeremiah-7 DRISKO (Judah-6; John-5; Joseph-4; John-3; 2) and Pamelia WASS, was born ca 1851 at Addison, Maine. He married first to Emma L. PALMER ca 18__ . She was the daughter of Charles PALMER of Machias, Maine, and was born 20 July 1849; died 7 Jan 1877, South Bend, IN; one week after the birth of her son Palmer L-9 DRISCO. Levi-8 DRISCO married second to Sarah Jane KAISER on 19 Nov 1879 at Chicago, Illinois. She was born ca 18__; died after 1935. At the time of his death, 9 Nov 1885, Levi-8 DRISCO was employed by the Lakeshore and Michigan Central Railroad, as yard master at Chicago.

Child of Levi-8 DRISCO and Emma PALMER:
Surname DRISCO
+ 1694. PALMER L.   born 1 Jan 1877 So. Bend, IN; married Myrtle ALLEN 20 June 1899 So. Bend
   (COLE)   (she born 29 Apr 1879 White Pigeon, MI; died 14 Oct 1960)
                          (she dau/o Wilbur ALLEN and Cynthia E. WARREN)
                          died 3 Feb 1966 South Bend, St. Joseph Co., Indiana
Note: Shortly before his marriage, Palmer L. DRISCO changed his name to COLE. It was the surname of the family who raised him (Martin and Eliza COLE). After his mothers' death, when he was about a week old, his father went to Chicago leaving him behind.

Children of Levi-8 DRISCO and Sarah Jane KAISER:
Surname DRISCO
+ 1695. LEE WASS   born 28 Aug 1880 Chicago, IL; married Helen V. RAY of Brooklyn, NY
                          (1935 – he was a retired Naval officer)
+1696. CADDIE PRESENT born 2 Dec 1884, Chicago; married Ben O. BROWN

971. BURT/BERT WILLIAM-8 DRISKO, brother of above, was born 27 May 1868 at Machiasport, Washington Co., ME. His mother, Pamelia WASS, died when he was very young. He married Ada Isabel DILL of Gardiner, Maine on 24 Sept 1892. She was born ca 1873; died 1956. Bert told his sons, that on his 10th birthday (27 May 1878) he was in Havana Harbor with his brother-in-law Captain Joseph Willard CATES. He owned his own trucking firm, and resided at Gardiner, ME. until his death on 2 June 1948.

Children of Bert-8 DRISKO and Ada Isabel DILL:
Surname DRISKO   (children born Gardiner, Maine)
1697. Mildred Olivia   born 189_; died young
+ 1698. LEVI BERT   born 30 June 1893; died 25 Dec 1967 Gardiner, ME.
               married Addie L. HAMILTON 18 May 1918 (she born 1892; died 20 Feb 1968)
+ 1699. EARL   born 21 Apr 1900; married Sarah B. GOODWIN 25 Nov 1918
   WINFIELD   (she born 6 Mar 1898; died Apr 1969 Gardiner, Maine)
                        died 29 Aug 1967
1700. Linwood Alton   born 22 June 1908; died 29/30 July 1982 Gardiner, Maine
                        married Angie E. LYONS 12 Mar 1907 (no issue)
                        (she born 27 Aug 1909, ME; died Sept 1994 Gardiner, Maine)

974. WILLIAM JOHNSON-8 DRISKO (2nd), son of Philo Lewis-7 DRISKO (Judah-6; John-5; Joseph-4; John-3; 2) and Caroline WASS, was born 6 Sept 1866 at Addison, Maine. He was a graduate of MIT, Class of 1895; and at the time of his retirement was Associate Professor of Physics at MIT. During his teaching years, he operated the homestead farm at Addison Ridge; known as the DRISKO FARM.
He married his cousin, Martha-8 Sherman BUCKNAM of Columbia Falls, Maine, on 27 June 1901. She was the daughter of Benjamin Franklin-7 BUCKNAM and Sharon WASS, and was born 8 Nov 1875; died 4 Feb 1965. William Johnson-8 DRISKO died 4 Aug 1943 at Bangor, Maine.

Children of William Johnson-8 DRISKO and Martha-8 BUCKNAM:
Surname DRISKO
1701. Benjamin   born 9 Oct 1902 Malden, MA; died 10 May 1987 Camden. ME.
   Bucknam   1m. Rose THOMPSON Oct 1930 (divorced)
               2m. Doris E. CROCKETT Feb 1937 (div); 3m. Mrs. Sarah CUNNINGHAM Mann 197_
1702. John Bucknam   born 1 May 1906, Winchester, MA; married Eunice D. BROWN 17 Sept 1932
1703. Caroline   born 16 Apr 1909; 1m. O. Pitman KELLER; 2m. Rex ROBERTS (he born IA)
                      resided Groton, MA

982. WILLARD MALCOLM-8 LEE, son of Mary Anne-7 BUCKNAM (Abigail-6 DRISKO; John-5;

Joseph-4; John-3;2) and John H. LEE, was born 10 July 1837 at Lowell, MA. He married Emma Ann BOGART/ BOGERT on 28 Nov 1860 at Benicia, CA. (her birth and death dates are unknown) Willard-8 LEE died 12 Dec 1902 Sacramento, CA.

Children of Willard Malcolm-8 LEE and Emma BOGART/ BOGERT:
Surname LEE

1704. Homer Willard	born 24 Sept 1861; died 15 Sept 1926
	married Rita M. L. CARRINGTON 17 Oct 1885 Sacramento, CA
1705. Roseanna	born 22 Feb 1863; died 31 July 1864
1706. Eliza May	born 21 Aug 1866; marr Arthur E. GARDNER 17 Oct 1885; died 6 Aug 1944
+ 1707. KING HIRAM	born 7 June 1870 Broderick, CA; died 5 Mar 1948 Sacramento, CA
	married Lillian Mae KING 13 July 1899
1708. Judson Bogart	born 29 Aug 1872; married Etta GORE 30 Apr 1892; died 18 Jan 1947
1709. Arthur Malcolm	born 11 Aug 1875 Yolo, CA; died 31 Jan 1895 Broderick, CA
1710. Reuben Benjamin	born 1 Dec 1877; married Nancy MORSE; died 4 Apr 1934
1711. William Henry	born 18 Apr 1880; married Agnes SULLIVAN; died 24 May 1947

992. BENJAMIN F-8 TENNEY, son of Mary Chandler-7 SMITH (Relief-6 DRISKO; John-5; Joseph-4; John-3; 2) and George-6 TENNEY, was born ca July 1834. He married Sabrina A-7 GARDNER on 20 Dec 1858 at Machias, Washington County, Maine. She was the daughter of John-6 GARDNER and Susan BERRY, and was born ca 1832; died 2 May 1906. Benjamin-8 TENNEY died 3 Mar 1875 at Machias. Sabrina-7 GARDNER married second to Winslow BATES, Esq. on 8 Nov 1875.

Children of Benjamin F-8 TENNEY and Sabrina-7 GARDNER:
Surname TENNEY

| 1712. Francis Atwood | born ca 186_; dy | 1714. Mary Eva | born ca 1867 |
| 1713. George Irving | born ca 1863; dy | | married Joseph S. BUCKNAM |

994. JULIA ANN-8 TIBBETTS, daughter of David-7 TIBBETTS (Thomas-6; Elizabeth-5 DRISKO; Joseph-4; John-3; 2) and Mary TUCKER, was born ca 1828. She married Joseph H. PAIGE, intentions published 24 Apr 1845 at Addison, Maine. He was born ca 1824, MA; died 186_, WI. Her second husband was Levi LINDSEY. They resided Wisconsin, where she died ca 1890.

Children of Julia Ann-8 TIBBETTS and Joseph PAIGE:
Surname PAIGE

| 1715. John Frank | born ca 1845 | 1717. Nellie | born 185_; 1m. Ned PAIGE (cousin) |
| 1716. Charles Foster | born ca 1849 | | 2m. __?__ MATTHEWS |

998. HILLMAN LOOK-8 TIBBETTS, brother of above, was born ca 1838. He married first to Alida Elizabeth FOLSOM of Oconto, Wisconsin. She was the daughter of Cyrus G. FOLSOM ++ and Miranda HANSCOM of East Machias, Maine, and was born ca 1849; died 1883. Hillman-8 married second to Adaline WHITE. He died ca ____, WA.

++ Cyrus Gooch FOLSOM was the son of John Dearborn FOLSOM and Hannah GOOCH, and was born 4 Oct 1801 at East Machias, ME. He married Miranda HANSCOM June 1836 at East Machias.

Children of Hillman Look-8 TIBBETTS and Alida FOLSOM:
Surname TIBBETTS

1718. Ermina	born ____	1722. Harry Leslie	born ____
1719. Frederick	born ____	1723. Amy Doris	born ____
1720. David Clifford	born ____	1724. Julia Bernice	born ____
1721. Foster	born ____; died young		

1002. EMELINE BRADFORD-8 TABBUT/TIBBETTS, daughter of James-7 TABBUT/TIBBETTS

(Thomas-6; Elizabeth-5 DRISKO; Joseph-4; John-3; 2) and Catherine MESERVE, was born 2 Oct 1830 at Columbia Falls, Maine. She married Aaron Worcester-7 ALLEN on 17 Jan 1848 at Columbia. He was the son of Abraham-6 ALLEN and Mary W-7 WORCESTER, and was born ca 1820 at Columbia, ME; died there 22 July 1881. Emeline B-8 TABBUT/ TIBBETTS died 27 Mar 1861.

Children of Emeline-8 TABBUT/TIBBETTS and Aaron W-7 ALLEN:
   Surname ALLEN
   1725. Joseph Crandon   born Jan 1849; married Direxa Jane HARRINGTON 25 Apr 1874
           (she dau/o Joseph HARRINGTON and Octavia HARTFORD) (she born Aug 1856; died 1939)
   1726. Mary Emeline   born July 1854; married Stillman Guptill YOUNG 1 June 1873
         (he son/o Freeman G.YOUNG and Sarah HAMILTON)(he born 23 June 1852; died 12 Oct 1878)
                             (he lost at sea aboard the Schooner *EVELYN*)
   1727. Melvena Chandler born 20 Dec 1856; married Clement Uriah-8 WORCESTER 1874
                             (he born 5 Apr 1851; died 1925)
     2 ch: Willbury Waldo-10 born 27 Sept 1875, ME; & Lucius R-10 WORCESTER born 12 Feb 1880 , NH
   1728. Aaron W., Jr.   born ca 1860

1003. ELIZABETH ROBINSON-8 TABBUT/TIBBETTS   see ERI HATHAWAY-8 DRISKO (# 1327)
1004. FRANCES BREWSTER-8 TABBUT/TIBBETTS see (# 1327)
1006. HELENA AUGUSTA-8 TABBUT/TIBBETTS, sister of above, was born 22 Jan 1841 at Columbia Falls, Maine. She married John Billings-7 GRANT on 10 Apr 1856 at Columbia. He was the son of Edward-6 GRANT and Elsie DORR, and was born 17 July 1836; died 10 Dec 1912. Helen-8 died 1920.

Children of Helena Augusta-8 TABBUT/TIBBETTS and John-7 GRANT:
   Surname GRANT   (children born Columbia Falls, Maine)
   1729. Rufus Meserve   born Nov 1857; married Lucy E-8 NORTON 3 Nov 1881; died 1931
   1730. Laura Estelle   born 27 June 1860; died 1 June 1921 Harrington, Maine
                         married Captain Gilbert H-9 LEIGHTON 28 Jan 1888
         (he son/o Sewell-8 LEIGHTON and Sophronia OAKES) (he born Sept 1856; died 19 Apr 1939)
   1731. John B., Jr.   born 20 Nov 1861; married Mabel Eldora TIBBETTS 17 Sept 1886
                         (she born 27 Apr 1870; died _____)
   1732. William G.   born May 1864; died 1942
                         married Minerva COLE 14 Feb 1893 (she born Oct 1868; died 2 Apr 1957)
   1733. Gilbert Leslie born 6 Dec 1867; married Clara Belle HARTFORD 15 Apr 1893
                         (she born 24 Dec 1873; died 26 May 1955)
   1734. Clayton   born Mar 1870; married Florence A-6 TIBBETTS 19 Apr 1893
                         (she born Sept 1874; died 1936)
   1735. Forester P.   born 7 May 1872; married Lettie E. HARTFORD 24 May 1893
                         (she born Dec 1875; died _____)
   1736. Lorey Worcester born 17 Sept 1874; married Charlotte W-6 TIBBETTS 27 Oct 1900
                         (she born 27 Mar 1882; died 27 Mar 1947)
                         died 12 Jan 1969 Bangor, Maine
   1737. Edward   born 8 Apt 1876; died 26 Mar 1941   unmarried

1010. WILLARD G-8 LOOK, son of Jerusha Wilson-7 TABBUT/ TIBBETTS (Thomas-6 TABBUT/ TIBBETTS; Elizabeth-5 DRISKO; Joseph-4; John-3; 2) and Silas-7 LOOK, was born ca 1838. He married Electa Ann-6 PINEO on 23 Nov 1861 at Jonesboro, Maine. She was the daughter of William O-5 PINEO and Abitha DUNBAR, and was born May 1838; died 16 Oct 1892 at Jonesport, Maine. Willard-8 LOOK died 3 Apr 1868 at Jonesboro; as the result of a shooting accident.

Children of Willard-8 LOOK and Electa Ann-6 PINEO:
   Surname LOOK   (children born Jonesboro, Maine)
   1738. Captain Oscar born 27 Nov 1862; died 8 Apr 1940 Jonesport, Maine   sea captain
         William   1m. Mary Ann SAWYER 26 Jan 1889;   2m. Frances Eleanor JOY ca 1917

Children of Willard-8 LOOK, continued;
  Surname LOOK
  1739. Electa Ann   born Jan 1864; died July 1865
  1740. Captain Bert   born 7 May 1866; married Minnie REED 21 Dec 1889 Boothbay, ME.
      Sidney   (she born Feb 1865; died 7 Mar 1946)
                         died 5 Aug 1937 Jonesport, Maine   sea captain
+ 1741. EVELYN   born 21 Nov 1868; died 26 Nov 1927
      WILLARD   married George Brown-8 CARVER 11 Nov 1885 (# 1302)
                         (he son/o Benjamin F-7 CARVER, Jr. and Nancy Ann-7 DRISKO (# 458)
                         (he born 6 Nov 1860; died 19 Mar 1944)

1017. HANNAH MARIA-8 TABBUT/TIBBETTS, daughter of Thomas-7 TABBUT/TIBBETTS
(Thomas-6; Elizabeth-5 DRISKO; Joseph-4; John-3; 2), and Thankful McCASLIN, was born 27 Oct 1842
at Columbia, Maine. She married Nathaniel-7 WHITE there on 1 Dec 1860. He was the son of Ichabod-6
WHITE and Pamelia NASH, and was born 12 June 1839 at Columbia; died ____.

Children of Hannah-8 TABBUT/TIBBETTS and Nathaniel WHITE:
  Surname WHITE
  1742. Hattie   born 5 Apr 1866; died 2 Jan 1872
  1743. Milton Bridgham born 2 Apr 1868 Columbia, ME; married Cora SMART 6 May 1891, MA.
                        (she born 12 Apr 1868; died ____)

1018.. ABIGAIL McCASLIN-8 TABBUT, sister of above, was born 5 May 1844 at Columbia, Maine.
She married William Howard-8 WORCESTER on 29 Mar 1866 at Columbia. He was the son of William
Bingham-7 WORCESTER and Frances Campbell INGERSOLL, and was born 9 June 1845; died 22 Mar
1924. Abigail-8 died 12 Apr 1918.

Children of Abigail-8 TABBUT and William H. WORCESTER:
  Surname WORCESTER   (children born Columbia, Maine)
  1744. Iva Bernice   born 17 Sept 1867; died 10 Oct 1871   EOL
  1745. Ina Gertrude   born 6 Feb 1879; died 1956
                         1m. Albert F. ALLEN ca 1906; 2m. George R. SMITH 30 June 1939
  1746. Ralph Bertram   born 18 Sept 1871; died 14 Mar 1872
  1747. Nathan Shaw   born 1 Mar 1873; died 15 Apr 1873
  1748. Bertha Edna   born 5 Mar 1875; died 8 Sept 1889
  1749. Irving Bartlett born 20 Aug 1878; died Sept 1966
                         1m. Susie N. CLARK 26 Oct 1894; 2m. Ida WILLIAMS
  1750. Thomas Howard   born 25 Nov 1884; died 12 Dec 1939
                         married Effie H. ALLEN 30 May 1914 (she born Oct 1888; died 1931)

1029. ZEPANIAH ALLEN-8 TIBBETTS, son of Jeremiah-7 TABBUT/TIBBETTS (Thomas-6; Eliza-
beth-5 DRISKO; Joseph-4; John-3;2) and Catherine W. TIBBETTS, was born Feb 1856. He married
Grace G. CURRIER ca 18__. She was the daughter of Hugh L. CURRIER and Harriet CONANT, and
was born ca 1876 at __. MA; died ca 1960 at Bangor, Maine. Zephaniah-8 TIBBETTS died 24 May 1930
at Harrington, Maine

Children of Zephaniah-8 TIBBETTS and Grace CURRIER:
  Surname TIBBETTS
+ 1751. EDNA   born ca 1903; married Maurice G. BLACK; died 17 Jan 1981
  1752. George Otis   born 29 Nov 1904; married Beatrice L. NICHOLS; died 6 Aug 1997
+ 1753. GRACE   born 24 June 1907; died 11 Mar 1992
      KATHLEEN   married Harris H. VAGUE 29 Jan 1938 Bangor, ME;
                       (he born ca 1888; died 19 Dec 1980 Bangor, ME)
+ 1754. ALLEN ZEPHANIAH born 18 Mar 1909; married Mary Jane GRANT; died 20 Aug 1993

Children of Zephaniah-8 TIBBETTS, continued:
   Surname TIBBETTS

1755. Louis G.	born 12 Feb 1912; died 19 Apr 1996 Bangor, ME		
	married Marguerite M. GRANT		
1756. Pheobe	born ca 1912; married ____ O'PALENICK		
1757. Leslie	born ca 1914	1759. Phillip	born ca 19__
1758. Maynard	born ca 19__; died 1966	1760. Blanche	born ca 19__

1036. VIOLETTA MORTON-8 TIBBETTS see THOMAS CROWLEY-7 DRISKO (# 453)

1041. LUCINDA V-8 TABBUTT, daughter of Henry H-7 TABBUT (John Coffin-6; Elizabeth-5 DRISKO; Joseph-4; John-3; 2) and Betsey MAGEE, was born Oct 1842. She married Asa Tucker-8 WORCESTER, as his 2nd wife, on 31 Aug 1862. He was the son of Clement Fernald-7 WORCESTER and Tamson CUMMINGS, and was born 8 Sept 1830; died 7 June 1923 at Columbia Falls, Maine. Lucinda V-8 died 1914.   Note: Asa-8 WORCESTER had 5 children from his first marriage .

Children of Lucinda V-8 TABBUT and Asa-8 WORCESTER;
   Surname WORCESTER   (children born Columbia Falls, Maine)
   1761. Everett Vanleason born 22 Mar 1863; died 18 May 1925
                married Lenora E-9 NORTON 13 July 1904 (she born 4 Aug 1882; died 16 Apr 1968)
   1762. Harriet Farrell   born 8 May 1866; died 27 June 1946
                1m. George C-8 COFFIN ca 1892; 2m. Henry L-9 WILLEY 21 Apr 1906
   1763. Minnie E.   born 19 May 1868; died 2 Aug 1924
                1m. Amherst HARTFORD 9 Oct 1885; 2m. Franklin D. HARTFORD 31 Dec 1894
   1764. Della P.   born 8 June 1870; marr Charles C-9 WORCESTER ca 1888; died 1951
   1765. Amy C.   born 17 Dec 1872; married John BRYANT 7 June 1892; died 1 Apr 1965
   1766. Philander A.   born 23 May 1875; died 8 Sept 1942; married Lenora-6 TIBBETTS 14 Apr 1900
   1767. Laura Isabell   born 11 July 1877; died 1951
                married Daniel Webster HARTFORD 5 Dec 1896 (he born 1875; died 1964)
   1768. Sadie   born 16 Nov 1879; married George TRUSSELL 1 Aug 1903; died 28 Apr 1947
   1769. Louise B.   born 16 Apr 1883; married James TENAN 15 Mar 1902; died 6 Dec 1942
 + 1770. QUEEN B.   born 16 July 1887; married JOSEPH WILLARD-10 DRISKO 30 Oct 1907
                (he son/o George Camelo-9 DRISKO (# 2002) and Sarah MAGEE)
                died 18 Mar 1984 Addison, Washington County, Maine

1042. ELIZABETH MAGEE-8 TABBUT, sister of above, was born 1 July 1844. She married George A-2 YOUNG on 3 July 1869 at Columbia, Maine. he was the son of John-1 YOUNG and Mary Ann WORCESTER, and was born ca Oct 1849; died 1921. Elizabeth M-8 TABBUTT died 1 Nov 1924.

Children of Elizabeth-8 TABBUT and George-2 YOUNG:
   Surname YOUNG
   1771. child   born and died 1870
   1772. Flora T.   born 14 Jan 1872 Columbia, ME; married Leander F-8 GRANT ca 1891; died 1903
   1773. John Herbert   born 17 May 1874; died 19 Dec 1954;
                married Elizabeth M-4 DONOVAN 12 May 1902
   1774. Colon M.   born Jan 1876; married Blanche N. CORLISS 1 Feb 1909
   1775. Mary A.   born Apr 1879; died 4 July 1911   unmarried
   1776. George N.   born Mar 1881; died 1922
                1m. Flora E-10 SMITH 5 Aug 1905; 2m. Louise E-10 WASS 22 June 1909
   1777. Agnes E.   born May 1883; married Charles H. MATTHEWS 2 Oct 1901
   1778. unnamed child   born ____; died young

1081. CECELIA A-8 WORCESTER, daughter of Louisa M-7 TABBUT/TIBBETTS (Moses-6; Elizabeth-5 DRISKO; Joseph-4; John-3; 2) and Isaac Case-7 WORCESTER, was born 26 May 1846 at

Columbia Falls, Maine. She married Captain Ira G. THOMPSON on 31 Aug 1867 at Columbia Falls. He was the son of John THOMPSON and Miriam Vincent-6 NORTON, and was born Aug 1835; died 19__. Cecelia-8 WORCESTER died 21 Oct 1885 at Columbia Falls.

Children of Cecelia-8 WORCESTER and Ira G. THOMPSON:
   Surname THOMPSON   (children born Columbia Falls, Maine)

1779. Mary Ellen	born 1 Dec 1871; married Ellington Ellery-9 LEIGHTON 1903; died 1942
1780. Junietta L.	born ca 1873; died 19__ unmarried
1781. John Ira	born June 1878; married Emma_Lila-7 CALER 3 July 1899
1782. Ina	born May 1880; married Irvin S. FELT, resided MA.

1082. MARY ANN-8 WORCESTER, sister of above, was born ca 1847 at Columbia Falls, Maine. She married Herrick-6 NASH on 1 Sept 1866 at Columbia Falls. He was the son of John-5 NASH and Sylvania SMITH, and was born ca 1841; died 18__. Mary Ann-8 died ___.

Children of Mary Ann-8 WORCESTER and Herrick-6 NASH:
   Surname NASH

| 1783. Gilbert M. | born ca 1868 | 1785. Charles M. born 1873 |
| 1784. Emily M. | born 1870 | 1786. Fannie A. born 1875 |

1123. PHEBE PARKER-8 DRISKO, daughter of John-7 DRISKO (Captain John-6; Joseph-5; 4; John-3; 2) and Phebe PARKER, was born 26 July 1827 at Addison, Maine. She married Abraham Lincoln-7 NORTON, intentions published 15 Dec 1849. He was the son of Jeremiah Beal-6 NORTON (Elihu-5) and Hannah SAWYER, and was born 20 Jan 1823; died 29 Aug 1881. Phebe Parker-8 DRISKO died 29 Nov 1866 at Jaffa, Palestine. Abraham-7 NORTON married second to Henrietta Bernice LORD Cole on 1 Mar 1873 at Addison.

Children of Phebe P-8 DRISKO and Abraham Lincoln-7 NORTON:
   Surname NORTON   (children born Addison, Maine)

1787. George Edgar	born 30 Oct 1851; died 27 Oct 1874 St. Martin Island, MI
1788. Lucy Ada	born 15 June 1853; died 1 Nov 1919 unmarried
1789. John Lincoln	born 31 Mar 1855; married Carrie Bernice COLE 19 Dec 1881 (his step-sister)
	(she dau/o Coffin COLE and Henrietta B. LORD)
1790. Rebecca Ann	born 6 July 1858; married Charles H. MANSFIELD, int pub 25 Mar 1882
1791. Daniel John	born 6 Apr 1860; married Helen G. COFFEY ca 1885
1792. William S.	born 22 July 1862; died Jan 1864

1124. PRISCILLA ANN-8 DRISKO, sister of above, was born 17 Mar 1828 at Addison, Maine. She married first to Captain Ackley Ezra-7 NORTON ca 1847. He was the son of Phineas-6 NORTON and Frances Ella-7 BEAL, and was born ca 1828; died 1 Jan 1871 at Chelsea, MA. Captain NORTON was the master of the Schooner *ELVIRA CONANT* which was built 1863 at Addison Ridge by Leander KNOWLES. Priscilla-8 DRISKO married second to Captain Albert BARTMAN ca ____ at ____, Michigan. He was born ca 18__ in ____, Germany.

Children of Priscilla-8 DRISKO and Captain Ackley-7 NORTON:
   Surname NORTON   (children born Addison, Maine)

1793. Alice Bentley	born 26 Dec 1848; married John COFFEY 24 Sept 1872, MI
1794. Esther Church	born 13 Apr 1852; married Asa E. CAMP Oct 1874, MI
1795. Everett Eugene	born ca 1858; died 1912 MN; unmarried
+ 1796. LOVEATUS	born ca 1861; died ca 1932 Manistique, Michigan
PLUMMER	married Mildred Christiana-9 LEIGHTON 1891
	(she dau/o Langdon-8 LEIGHTON and Matilda- 2 DRISCOLL/DRISKO)
	(she born ca 1870; died 1924 Manistique, MI)
1797. Lewella	born ca 1863; married Charles TROWNSELL; died 1930

1125. GEORGE ALVIN-8 DRISKO, brother of above, was born 23 Nov 1830 at Addison, Maine. He married Elizabeth/ Lizzie C. SKINNER ++ on 3 Dec 1852. She was the daughter of Justin SKINNER and Rachel CUMMINGS, and was born 15 Dec 1834; died 12 Apr 1920 at Escanaba, MI. George-8 DRISKO, called Alvin, went with the Palestine Emigration Society (the ADAMS Colony) to Palestine in 1866.

After returning to the US, he moved to the Upper Peninsula of Michigan in 1868, and was engaged in fishing there until 1879. He discovered a shoal in Lake Michigan ca 1880 (later named DRISCO Shoal), which was then marked with a government buoy. He died at Misery Bay, MI on 28 July 1905. He and his wife are buried at Lakeview Cemetery, where his gravestone reads Captain George A. DRISKO. (On 15 Sept 1874 , at the Land Office in Traverse City, Delta County, Michigan (Document # 1775 of the Land Patent Report ; Bureau of Land Management – Eastern States) he acquired 155.6 acres of homestead land. NOTE: This land was described in the Federal Township and Range System – which used a survey system of meridians, baselines, townships and ranges. It was public-domain land and was generally obtained by Federal Land Grants – either purchased or homesteaded.)

Children of George Alvin-8 DRISKO and Elizabeth SKINNER:
  Surname DRISKO
+ 1798. JULIA   born 3 Feb 1855 Addison, ME; married Norman A. EDDY 3 Sept 1873, MI.
       ELILLIAS   (he born 1848 Coburg, Canada; died Nov 1917 Montana)
                      died 20 Apr 1920 Misery Bay, Michigan
    1799. Rachel L. born 1858; d y   1800. George B. born 1859; d y   1801. Lurenna born ca 1869, MI; d y

1127. REBECCA DRISKO-8 ROGERS, daughter of Olivette/Olive-7 DRISKO (Captain John-6; Joseph-5; 4; John-3; 2) and Joseph Prince ROGERS, was born ca 1826 at Jonesport, Maine. She married Jason Clapp-4 CROWLEY, intentions published 13 Dec 1848 at Addison. He was the son of James-3 CROWLEY and Abigail-6 COFFIN Tucker, and was born June 1826; died 10 Feb 1907 at Addison. Rebecca Drisko-8 ROGERS died there 3 Feb 1899.

Children of Rebecca Drisko-8 ROGERS and Jason Clapp-4 CROWLEY:
  Surname CROWLEY   (children born Addison, Maine)
  1802. Ellen D.   born 1 Oct 1850; married George H-9 WASS ca 1872; died 1942
  1803. Mary Ann   born 30 Oct 1852
                       1m. Jeremiah Norton-5 FAULKINGHAM , int pub 24 Aug 1868 Addison
                       2m. Charles W-8 HALL 1888
  1804. Olivette   born 18 July 1854; married Adelbert L-8 NORTON ca 1872; died 1924
  1805. Joseph Avery   born 11 Sept 1855 (blind); died 26 June 1926 unmarried
  1806. Burlon Worth   born 9 Oct 1857; died 2 Apr 1923 Addison, Maine
                       married Orriana Warren CHURCH Dorr 22 June 1878 Jonesport, ME
                       (she born 10 Mar 1858; died 23 Sept 1934)
  1807. Irving Jason   born 23 Dec 1859; died 6 Sept 1948
                       married Theressa S-9 DRISKO 21 Jan 1882 (# 1915)
                       (she dau/o Alexander-8 DRISKO (#1259) and Sophia FAULKINGHAM)
                       (she born 16 July 1863; died 9 July 1941)
  1808. Elvena Rebecca born 18 Dec 1861; married Charles W-8 HALL ca 1879; died 1880
  1809. Susan   born ca 1864; d y   1810. Carrie Estelle   born ca 1866; died ca 1881

1128. BENJAMIN KELLEY-8 ROGERS, brother of above, was born 14 June 1829 at Jonesport, Maine. He married Lucy-8 Drisko LEIGHTON on 12 Apr 1851. She was the daughter of Curtis-7 LEIGHTON and Philena EMERSON, and was born 21 Dec 1833; died 8 Jan 1921 at Jonesport, ME. Benjamin-8 ROGERS and Lucy-8 LEIGHTON were among the group who emigrated to Palestine in 1866. He died 21 Sept 1879 at Jonesport, Maine.

Children of Benjamin Kelley-8 ROGERS and Lucy-8 LEIGHTON:
  Surname ROGERS
  1811. Eleanora P.   born 13 Oct 1851 Addison, ME; married Warren Ennis CROWLEY 29 Jan 1870
       " Nora "   (he son/o Matthew C. CROWLEY and Elizabeth Ann CROWLEY)
                       (he born 1846; died ____ at sea)
                       died 15 Feb 1915 Jonesport, Maine

Children of Benjamin Kelly-8 ROGERS, continued:
   Surname ROGERS
   1812. Theresa L.   born 8 July 1854, Addison; married Abram Billings KELLEY 21 June 1873
         (he son/o Aaron KELLEY and Rebecca S. NORTON) (he born 12 Oct 1836; died 24 Jan 1909)
   1813. Bradford   born ca 1858; died before 1900
   1814. Arthur R.   born 15 Nov 1860 Jonesport, ME; married Amanda C. DAVIS 27 June 1885
         (she dau/o David DAVIS and Eliza WHITE) (she born June 1863; died 1949)
   1815. George   born ca 1863; died 8 Oct 1866 Jaffa, Palestine
+ 1816. ALTON V.   born 9 June 1867 Jaffa, Palestine
         1m. JULIA A-9 SAWYER 24 Sept 1890 Jonesport, ME (# 1897)
         2m. Sara T. AUSTIN (she dau/o Junius AUSTIN and Elizabeth THOMPSON)
         died 31 July 1957 Ellsworth, ME (ship builder at Jonesport)
   1817. Clifton M.   born 15 June 1870 Jonesport, ME; married Geneva May FRENCH
      (she dau/o Lorenzo FRENCH and Adrianna JOHNSON)(she born 17 Oct 1873; died 11 June 1935)
         died 25 Mar 1947 Bangor, Maine   a bookkeeper

1130. CORDELIA H-8 ROGERS, sister of above, was born 14 Sept 1835 at Jonesport, Maine. She married James Campbell-4 CROWLEY on 8 Mar 1852 at Addison. He was the son of James-3 CROWLEY and Abigail–6 COFFIN Tucker, and was born 11 Oct 1831; died 16 May 1922 at the Sailors Snug Harbor, NY. Cordelia-8 ROGERS died 4 Dec 1890.

Children of Cordelia-8 ROGERS and James C-4 CROWLEY:
   Surname CROWLEY   (children born at Addison, Maine)
   1818. Abbie F.   born 6 Dec 1853; died 14 Sept 1855
   1819. Adelbert Enos   born 9 Mar 1856; died 8 Oct 1892 Indian River
         married Charlotte A-5 CROWLEY 20 Sept 1877; (she born 18 Aug 1858; died 18 July 1953)
   1820. Colin Campbell   born 2 July 1858; died 26 Jan 1869
   1821. Flora M.   born 2 July 1861; died 14 Feb 1880
         married Orrin W-5 CROWLEY 27 Aug 1878 (he born 1856, ME; died 14 Oct 1940, NY)

1135. AUGUSTUS W-8 DRISKO, son of Mayhew-7 DRISKO (Captain John-6; Joseph-5; 4; John-3; 2) and Clarissa WORCESTER, was born 16 Dec 1845 at Addison, Maine. He married Clara L. HALL 26 Dec 1893. She was the daughter of Levi HALL and Betsey TABBUTT of Farmingdale, ME; and was born ca 1865; died 1 June 1917. Augustus-8 DRISKO died 17 Feb 1925 at South Portland, Maine.

Children of Augustus-8 DRISKO and Clara HALL:
   Surname DRISKO
   1822. Henry A.   born 1895; died 1917
   1823. Chester C.   born after 1900; died 28 Dec 1961; resided South Portland, ME
         married Ruth J. DEMPSTER 10 Oct 1928 (she born ?; died 18 Jan 1967)
   1824. Bessie H.   born 19__; married Martin E. McINTYRE 9 Feb 1921 So. Portland, ME

1137. ABITHA D-8 LEIGHTON, daughter of Phebe Parker-7 DRISKO (Captain John-6; Joseph-5; 4; John-3; 2) and Nahum Hill-7 LEIGHTON, was born ca 1830 at Addison, ME. She married Uriah Wass-8 LEIGHTON on 19 Aug 1852. He was the son of John-7 LEIGHTON and Eunice WRIGHT, and was born 10 Aug 1830 at Addison, died there 11 Aug 1910. Abitha D-8 LEIGHTON died at Jaffa on 6 Dec 1885.

Abitha and Uriah LEIGHTON went with the Palestine Emigration Society to Jaffa, Palestine where two of their daughters died as a result of unsanitary conditions. When Abitha refused to go back to the States with her husband, he divorced her on the grounds of desertion. He married second to Anna S. DYER on 9 May 1874 at Addison, Maine. He was a fisherman at Indian River.

Children of Abitha-8 LEIGHTON and Uriah-8 LEIGHTON:
   Surname LEIGHTON
   1825. Idella W.   born 1854 Addison; died 1867 Jaffa, Palestine

Children of Abitha-8 LEIGHTON, continued:
  Surname LEIGHTON
  1826. James Avery   born 2 Oct 1856; died 6 May 1858 Addison, Maine
+ 1827. RALPH I.   born 18 Aug 1859; married Mary Jane CLARK
                           (she dau/o George CLARK and Ellen WENTWORTH)
  1828. Flora L.   born 1865 Addison; died Nov 1866 Jaffa, Palestine

1140. CAPTAIN JASON DRISKO-8 LEIGHTON, brother of above, was born 3 Nov 1835 at Addison, Maine. He married MARY ELIZABETH-8 DRISKO (# 1270) on 20 Oct 1860 at Jonesport, Maine. She was the daughter of Edmund C-7 DRISKO (# 450) and Hannah W. ALLEN, and was born 14 May 1842 at Addison, ME; died 7 Aug 1868 of yellow fever, while on board the Brig *RAVEN*. Her husband, Capt. Jason LEIGHTON, was the master of the vessel. It was enroute from Cuba to New York.

Captain Jason D-8 LEIGHTON was a **Civil War** veteran; having served with the **1ˢᵗ Regiment of the Maine Artillery.** He married second to Helen Georgia RICH on 13 Oct 1880 at Milbridge, Maine. She was the daughter of William RICH and Sybil S. LEIGHTON, and was born 22 Jan 1852 Milbridge, died 30 Oct 1935. Captain Jason-8 LEIGHTON died 9 Feb 1917 at Milbridge, Maine.

Children of Captain Jason-8 LEIGHTON and Mary ELIZABETH-8 DRISKO:
  Surname LEIGHTON
  1829. Avery D.   born 10 May 1861, New York City; died 18 July 1861
+ 1830. CARRIE C.   born 30 Sept 1862 Addison, ME; married Orrin P. SWANTON 29 May 1887
          (he son of Joseph B. SWANTON and Katherine TUCKER) (he born 9 May 1863; died 1926)
+ 1831. LUCRETIA   born 11 Oct 1864 Milbridge, ME; died 24 Jan 1950 Milbridge
        SMALL   married Abraham Lincoln-8 WALLACE 25 Mar 1886
   (he son/o Samuel C. WALLACE and Harriet Almira SANBORN) (he born Apr 1865; died Jan 1939)

1142. SARAH A-8 LEIGHTON, sister of above, was born 17 July 1839 at Addison, Maine. She married Ezra S-7 STROUT ca 1860 at Milbridge, Maine. he was the son of Lewis-6 STROUT (Joseph-5; 4; 3; 2; Christopher-1) and Lydia SMITH, and was born 2 Feb 1835 at Milbridge; died there 13 Oct 1905. Sarah-8 LEIGHTON died 3 Feb 1900 at Milbridge. They are buried in Evergreen Cemetery.

Children of Sarah-8 LEIGHTON and Ezra STROUT:
  Surname STROUT   (children born Milbridge, Maine)
+ 1832. CORA M.   born 29 May 1861; died 7 Feb 1896 Milbridge
        LEIGHTON   married Captain Lewis B. PINKHAM 6 Feb 1879 Milbridge
          (he son/o David PINKHAM and Louise STROUT) (he born 5 Aug 1858; died 11 Sept 1923)
  1833. Laura J.   born 23 Feb 1863 Milbridge; died there 25 Apr 1906
                           1m. Napoleon-8 LEIGHTON 16 July 1882 Milbridge, ME;
                           2m. Nathan Everett-9 LEIGHTON 29 Aug 1896 Harrington, ME
                           (he born 31 May 1858 Milbridge, ME; died there 28 June 1941)
+ 1834. ARVILLA M.   born 5 Sept 1864; died 25 Dec 1892
                           married Herbert O. STROUT 25 Dec 1880 (he born 19 May 1859)
  1835. Martha Rowena   born 13 Mar 1866; died 8 May 1933 Addison, ME
                           married Darius Dickey-9 JOY (# 1841) 12 May 1887
                           (he born 14 Apr 1864; died 12 Mar 1943)
  1836. Avery   born 5 Mar 1868; died Aug 1868 (5 months old)
  1837. Lena/Linnie   born 5 Mar 1869; died 31 Oct 1924/34
                           married Lewis Fred NEAL/ NEIL 8 Aug 1886; he from Waltham, MA
+ 1838. CAPTAIN   born 9 Nov 1870 Milbridge, ME ; died 28 Feb 1935 Newport, ME
        GEORGE V.   1m. Florence STROUT 1891; div ; 2m. Mary EAKINS 16 Oct 1915
  1839. William E   born 23 May 1876; died 21 Mar 1892

1143. REBECCA DRISKO-8 LEIGHTON, sister of above, was born 16 Nov 1840 at Addison, Maine. She married David Beriah JOY on 29 Sept 1857 at Milbridge, ME. He was the son of Beriah Smith JOY and Phebe COX, and was born 11 Aug 1837 at Addison; died there 15 Oct 1912. Rebecca Drisko-8 LEIGHTON died 11 Jan 1913 at North Haven, Maine.

Children of Rebecca Drisko-8 LEIGHTON and David Beriah JOY:

Surname JOY	(children born Addison, Maine)
1840. Phebe L.	born 29 Jan 1862; died 12 Aug 1877 Columbia, Maine
1841. Darius Dickey	born 14 Apr 1864; died 12 Mar 1943 Addison, ME.
	married Martha Rowena-8 STROUT 12 Mar 1887 (# 1835)
1842. Viola L.	born 28 Mar 1866; died 11 Oct 1883
1843. David E.	born 20 Nov 1867; married Mary E. BURNS 1 Jan 1894

    (she dau/o John W. BURNS and Julia FLAHERTY) (she born 15 Apr 1871; died 11 Apr 1946)
    died 29 Nov 1959 Arlington, MA (aged 92 yr; 9 days)

1844. Margaret B.	born Apr 1871; married William E-9 WASS 28 Oct 1893 Machias, ME.

    (he son/o Edwin R-8 WASS and Elizabeth BURNS) (he born Oct 1852; died 7 June 1930)
    died 3 Jan 1925 Machias, Washington County, Maine

1845. Harris Webster	born 4 Aug 1876; married Flora M. BEAL; died 27 Oct 1955 Jonesboro, ME

    (she dau/o Darius Dickey BEAL/ Sabrina SAWYER)(she born 30 June 1880; died 8 Dec 1961)

1846. Susan E.	born 9 Feb 1878; married Emery WOOSTER (he born 1884; died 1968)

    died Mar 1981 at 103 years of age

1144. LUCY W-8 LEIGHTON, sister of above, was born ca 1842 at Addison, ME. She married Charles William TRACY on 20 Jan 1865 at Jonesport, ME. He was the son of Eri TRACY and Hannah ASHE, and was born 12 Mar 1833 at Gouldsboro, ME.; died there 16 Aug 1896. Lucy W-8 LEIGHTON died at Gouldsboro 17 Mar 1912.

Children of Lucy-8 LEIGHTON and Charles TRACY:

Surname TRACY	(children born Gouldsboro, Maine)
1847. Asenath E.	born 1 Jan 1866; died 1 Nov 1866
1848. Jason L.	born 6 Aug 1868; died ____ unmarried
1849. Ella B.	born 19 Feb 1870; died ____; resided CA.
1850. John Handy	born 22 May 1872; married Alice Belle BUNKER 14 Oct 1896
	(she dau/o Uriah BUNKER and Hannah CLEAVES) (she born 2 July 1878; died 1976)
	died 17 Oct 1954 Bucksport, Maine
1851. Hattie J.	born 7 Nov 1874; married John D. TRACY; died 2 Sept 1954
1852. Carrie E.	born 10 Sept 1877; 1m. George RICE; 2m. Fred SMITH

1145. LAURA DRISKO-8 LEIGHTON, sister of above, was born 8 Jan 1844 at Addison, Maine. She married John Henry FOSTER on 20 Jan 1866 at Milbridge, Maine. He was the son of Captain William Godfrey FOSTER (a sea captain) and Catherine CAMPBELL Ray, and was born 21 Jan 1841 at Milbridge; died there 1890. Laura Drisko-8 LEIGHTON died 20 Jan 1916 at Milbridge.

Children of Laura Drisko-8 LEIGHTON and John Henry FOSTER:

Surname FOSTER	
1853. Katie Campbell	born 23 Nov 1866, Milbridge; died 3 Apr 1880
1854. Hannah F.	born 8 Mar 1872, Columbia, ME; married __?__ KEENAN
1855. Raymond Leighton	born 16 June 1886 Milbridge, Maine

1148. PHEBE PARKER-8 LEIGHTON, sister of above, was born 29 June 1849 at Addison, Maine. She married Captain Warren FOSTER on 31 May 1873 at Columbia, ME. He was the son of William Godfrey FOSTER and Catherine CAMPBELL Ray, and brother of John Henry FOSTER, above. Captain Warren Foster was born 24 Apr 1846 Milbridge, Maine; died there 1908. Phebe P-8 LEIGHTON died 2 Feb 1923.

Children of Phebe Parker-8 LEIGHTON and Captain Warren FOSTER:
    Surname FOSTER
    1856. Mary   born 1 May 1874 Columbia,ME; died 21 Dec 1958 Milbridge, ME
                            married Elias Burt GRIFFIN (he son/o John W. GRIFFIN and Ida BRACEY)
    1857. Margaret Dyer   born 8 May 1880 Columbia Falls, ME; died 21 Oct 1950 unmarried

1150. OLIVETTE M-8 BATSON, daughter of Rebecca-7 DRISKO (Captain John-6; Joseph-5; 4; John-3; 2) and Andrew Elliot BATSON, was born Nov 1836 at Addison, Maine. She married Benjamin Franklin REYNOLDS, Jr. ca 1859. He was the son of Benjamin Franklin REYNOLDS and Anna CHANDLER, and was born Apr 1837; died 18 Dec 1915. Olivette-8 BATSON died 11 Mar 1926 at Addison, Maine.

Children of Olivette-8 BATSON and Benjamin REYNOLDS, Jr.:
    Surname REYNOLDS   (children born South Addison, Maine)
    1858. Child   born 186_; died young
    1859. Annie R.   born July 1865; married Levi L-8 HALL 1887; died 1917
    1860. Howard L.   born Aug 1868; marr Blanche Jane DYER 11 Jan 1896; died 3 Feb 1957, MA.
                            (she dau/o Horace-9 DYER and Clara E. STINSON)
    1861. Warren Willis   born 9 Oct 1871; died 19 Apr 1956
            married Carrie M. CARTER 27 Apr 1895 (she dau/o William CARTER and Millicent __?__)

1151. CAPTAIN ADRIAN ABBOTT-8 BATSON, brother of above, was born 26 Nov 1838 at Addison, ME. He married Adrianna Abigail " Ada " CARTER, intentions published 8 Aug 1871. She was the daughter of Job CARTER and Mary Jane FRIEND of W. Levant and Addison, and was born 9 Dec 1853; died 15 Dec 1936. Captain Adrian-8 BATSON died 2 Apr 1917. He was a sea captain at South Addison, ME.

Children of Captain Adrian-8 BATSON and Adrianna CARTER:
    Surname BATSON   (children born Addison, Maine)
+ 1862. COLIN ANDREW born 22 Oct 1872; died 11 Jan 1953
                            married Sarah Alden BEAL 12 Mar 1910
    1863. Berlin P.   born Apr 1883; married Catherine Morse TABBUTT
                            (she dau/o Edward H. TABBUTT/ Jane Erin Emmett McNAMARA)
                            (she born 27 Nov 1889; died June 1983)
                            died ca 1923 (machinist at East Boston, MA)
    1864. Alice G.   born Oct 1891   1865. Ruth A.   born Jan 1898

1158. MATILDA-8 DRISKO, daughter of Captain George Washington-7 DRISKO (Captain John-6; Joseph-5; 4; John- 3; 2) and Mary S-7 KILTON, was born ca 1835 at Jonesboro, ME. She married Asa WESTON ca 1853. He was the son of _?_ WESTON and was born ca 1832 at Sandwich, Barnstable Co., MA; died ____. He was listed on the 1860 and 1870 Censuses (Boston, MA) as an Engineer; residing in the 12th Ward. Matilda-8 DRISKO died before 1911.

Children of Matilda-8 DRISKO and Asa WESTON:
    Surname WESTON
    1866. George   born ca 1854 Boston, MA
    1867. Laura P.   born ca 1855/56 Boston; married Frank Harvey ROBBINS
                            (he son/o John ROBBINS and Susan A. __?__) (he born 10 Jan 1849 Woburn, MA)
                            One child: Cora May ROBBINS born 19 Dec 1871 Woburn, MA
    1868. Mary L.   born Nov 1859 Boston, MA
    1869. Warren Herbert   born 1863, Boston, MA; res. 11 Clifton Pl., Roxbury, MA 1911
    References: Census; Notes on the Kilton Family, Jonesboro, ME.; Woburn (MA) Records 1640-1873, published 1890, page 227.

1159. VANDELIA/ FANNY/ FANNIE-8 DRISKO, sister of above, was born Jan 1837 at Jonesboro, Washington County, Maine. She married James C. LEWIS + on 23 Nov 1859 at Boston, Suffolk County, MA. He was the son of Nicholas S. LEWIS and Olive C. _?_ of Belfast, Waldo County, Maine; and was born there 25 Jan 1831 (gs) ; died there 14 Oct 1903 (gs). Vandelia/Fannie-8 DRISKO died 10 Nov 1880 (43yr 11 mo) in Somerville, MA of cancer. Vandelia-8, her husband and their oldest child are all buried at Grove Cemetery, Belfast, Maine.

Children of Vandelia-8 DRISKO and James C. LEWIS:
Surname LEWIS
1870. Herschel W.   born ca Aug 1860, ME; died 18 May 1874 Belfast, ME.
1871. Donald   born 1862, Belfast (was blind) 1911 res. Knox Station, Waldo, ME.
1872. Sanford S.   born 26 Sept 1865 Belfast; 1911 res. 50 Holyoke St., Somerville, MA
+ 1873. HERSCHEL   born ca 1874, MA; married Nettie E. __?__ ca 1899
      WILDER ++   (she born 1874, Maine; died ____)

+ Obituary – 22 Oct 1903 BELFAST (ME) REPUBLICAN JOURNAL
" James C. LEWIS died very suddenly of heart disease at his home in Somerville, MA., Oct 14th, at the age of 72 yr, 8 mo and 19 da. He was a native of Belfast, and a brother of the late Sanford S. and George W. LEWIS. He was a boat builder by trade, and it was his boat shop, where the Maine Central Freight Depot now stands, that the great fire of 12 Oct 1865 originated. He married Fannie DRISCO of Belfast and after her death remarried. His second wife, who survives him, lived in MA. At one time he owned and occupied the farm in Northport (ME) now owned by Edward C. WOODBURY, but has lived in MA. for many years. He leaves three sons who live in MA, and two sisters, Mrs. Rebecca Files of Thorndike and Mrs. Wales I. Miller of Belfast. The interment was in Grove Cemetery in Belfast."

++ LEWISIANA, Vol. XV, page 212, states " 1896 Herschel Wilder LEWIS , AB – Harvard University "; Vol. XVII, page 162 lists the latest report from the US Commissioner of Education – High School Principals 1907 – includes Herschel W. LEWIS – Littleton, MA. 1910 Federal Census, New Ipswich, Hillsborough County, NH lists his occupation as a teacher at a Private Academy.
References: Notes on the Kilton Family of Jonesboro, Maine; 1910 Census Ipswich, NH; 1850 MA Census

1163. EVERARD IRVING-8 DRISKO, brother of above, was born ca 1846 at Belfast, Waldo County, Maine. In 1870, he was single, and resided in Boston, MA with his sister Matilda-8 DRISKO Weston. His occupation was listed as that of Engineer. He was married first to Emma S-8 WHITNEY +++ of Woburn, MA. ca 1874. She was the daughter of William-7 WHITNEY and Sophronia __?__, and was born 185_; died 26 May 1877. She was buried " near her father ", possibly at Woburn / Granville, MA. Everard-8 married second to Flora Abioner HARPER before 1880 at Belfast, Maine. She possibly the daughter of William H. HARPER and Harriet ?; and was born 8 June 1853, MA; died 1 June 1947 (age 93) at Los Angeles, CA. They resided (1911/20) at Deer Park, Spokane County, Washington.

NOTE: Everard-8 DRISKO, stated that he was a " clerk ", and a resident of CA (1863) when he enlisted as a Private in the **Civil War** at MA on 23 Apr 1863, and served with the **Massachusetts 2nd Cavalry Regiment (F Co)**. He was promoted to Full Bugler , and was mustered out of the service at Fairfax Court House, VA on 20 July 1865.

Child of Everard-8 DRISKO and Emma S-8 WHITNEY:
Surname DRISKO
1874. Ethel Whitney   born ca 1875/76

Children of Everard-8 DRISKO and Flora A. HARPER:
1875. Russell   born 14 July 1880 Boston, MA; died 14 Feb 1909 Boston
                       married Anna KENDALL ca 1901 (she born 18__, Boston, MA; died ca 19__)
1876. Winslow   born ca 1884 MA; resided w. parents in 1920 at Deer Park, WA.

+++ Ancestry of Emma S-8 WHITNEY

JOHN-1 WHITNEY (Thomas-A; Robert-B) was born 1589 in England, and settled at Watertown, MA June 1635. He married, in England, an Elinor _?_ . She was born 1599; died 11 May 1659 at Watertown. He married 2nd to Judith CLEMENT on 29 Sept 1659. He died 1 June 1673 at Watertown. JOHN-1 WHITNEY had 10 children by his first wife. JOSHUA-2 WHITNEY was born 5 July 1635 at Watertown, MA. He married first to Lydia __?__; 2nd to Mary __?__ (she died 1671) and 3rd to Abigail TARBELL. WILLIAM-3 WHITNEY was the son of Joshua-2 and his 3rd wife, and was born 28 Feb 1678. He married Lydia PERHAM on 1 Mar 1700 at Chelmsford, MA. She was born ___; died 24 Aug 1716. He married 2nd to Margaret MYRICK at Newton, MA on 25 Apr 1717. She was born 1683; died ____.

DEACON JOHN-4 WHITNEY, born ca 1718 at Groton, MA , married Elizabeth __?__. She was born 1719; died 14 May 1790. John-4 died 13 Nov 1793 at Canaan, CT. They had ELIJAH-5 WHITNEY, born 17__; married Chloe BECKLEY on 24 Sept 1772. They were the parents of WILLIAM-6 WHITNEY, born 22 Feb 1774 at Hartford, CT; married Prudence BROWN at Norwich, VT in 1807. Prudence was born 14 Nov 1790; died 20 Oct 1856 at Boston. William-6 WHITNEY died 14 Nov 1859. They had 10 children. WILLIAM-7 WHITNEY was born 6 June 1819 at Norwich, VT. He married Sophronia __?__; resided Woburn, MA and died at Union Grove, IL. On 29 Oct 1865. He was the father of Emma-8 WHITNEY.

1164. GEORGE AUGUSTUS-8 DRISKO, half-brother of above, son of Captain George Washington-7 DRISKO (Captain John-6; Joseph-5; 4; John-3; 2) and his second wife Margaret-8 FOSTER Gardner, was born 19 July 1856 at Machiasport, Washington County, Maine.

He married in 1880 to Amelia A-7 GREEN ++ at East Syracuse, Onondaga County, NY, the Rev Isaac SWIFT, pastor of the Presbyterian Church of East Syracuse, officiating. Amelia , called " Minnie " was the daughter of Henry GREEN, Jr. and Nancy A-6 FINCK, and was born 16 May 1861 at Poughkeepsie, Dutchess County, New York; died 20 July 1919 at Syracuse, Onondaga County, NY.

George A-8 DRISKO was employed by the Remington Rand Corp. in Syracuse for 40 years. He was a stationary engineer; retiring from that company in 1930. He was a member of the Brotherhood of Stationary Engineers, Union # 6708. He died 30 Apr 1936 in Syracuse, NY and is buried at Oakwood Cemetery, with his wife, in that city.

Children of George Augustus-8 DRISKO and Amelia-7 GREEN:
  Surname DRISKO
+ 1877. EVA FRANCES born 19 Sept 1881 Syracuse, NY
                    married Orson Fowler BUTTS 21 June 1917 (as his 2nd wife)
                    died 30 Apr 1942 East Syracuse, NY; buried Warners Cemetery, Onon. Co., NY
  1878. Nancy   born 9 March 1884; died the same day
+ 1879. HENRY   born 29 May 1891 Lyons, Wayne County, NY
      WILLIAM   married Leah Belle DOLBEY 1 Sept 1914 at Oneida, Madison County, NY
    (H. William) (she dau/o William Henry DOLBEY and Nellie FANNING)
       " Bill "   (she born 31 Aug 1890 Frankfort, NY; died May 1969 Carthage, NY)
                    died 6 Apr 1953 Syracuse, NY (peritonitis from a ruptured appendix)

George Augustus-8 DRISKO (1856 – 1936)

++ Ancestry of Amelia A-7 GREEN

ANDREAS-1 FINCK, the immigrant, came to America in 1709 with the second large group of Palatines. His age at that time was recorded as 34. He was accompanied by his wife (believed to be a Maria GERLACH) and one son, Christian-2 FINCK, 9 years old. CHRISTIAN-2 FINCK, born ca 1700 in Germany; married Catherine EAKER/ACKER, and died ca 1744. He was one of the original patentees of the Stone Arabia (NY) Patent.

They had ANDREAS-3 FINCK, born 2 Sept 1731, NY. He married Catherine Elizabeth LOUCKS/LAUX on 14 Dec 1742. Their son MAJOR ANDREW-4 FINCK, born 1 Feb 1751, served with distinction in the **Revolutionary War.** He married Maria MARKELL/ MERCKEL, and died 2 Feb 1820.   Major Andrew-4 FINCK and Maria had 4 children including CHRISTIAN ANDREW-5 FINCK, born 24 Aug 1789 at Stone Arabia, NY. He married first to Nancy EAKER/ACKER on 7 Nov 1813. She was born ca 17__; died ca 1823/24. He married 2nd to Margaretha FINCK on 10 July 1825. She was born ca 1795.   ANDREW-5 FINCK and his first wife had 5 children including NANCY-6 FINCK who was born 20 Mar 1823 Montgomery County, NY.; died 18__. She married Henry GREEN, Jr. They were the parents of AMELIA-7 GREEN (above).

1167. EVERETT W-8 DRISKO, son of Jason Clapp-7 DRISKO (Captain John-6; Joseph-5; 4; John-3; 2) and Lucy WORCESTER, was born ca 1842. He married Ruth D. CARTER on 25 June 1865. She was the daughter of Job CARTER and Mary Jane FRIEND, and was born Mar 1844; died 3 July 1926, Addison, Maine. Everett-8 DRISKO was a member of **Company H, First Maine Heavy Artillery** in the **Civil War.** He died 20 May 1880. His widow married second to John Drisko-8 BATSON (# 1152).

Children of Everett-8 DRISKO and Ruth D. CARTER:
    Surname DRISKO
1880. Hattie   born 29 June 1868 Jonesboro, ME; died 23 Sept 1892
                married Frank Aymar SAWYER 3 Jan 1891 (he born 12 Feb 1871; died 29 Sept 1932)
+ 1881. ARTHUR   born 7 June 1870 Jonesboro; died 10 Feb 1956 Addison, ME.
                married Lucy Faustina PLUMMER 4 Dec 1892
        (she dau/o Loveatus PLUMMER and Georgia LOOK) (she born 2 May 1871; died 26 Jan 1954)
    1882. Josephine Lucy   born 20 Jan 1872; died 4 May 1892

1175. AMANDA RHODELLA-8 DRISKO, daughter of James Parker-7 DRISKO (Captain John-6; Joseph-5; 4; John-3; 2) and Amanda Whitney-3 ARCHER, was born Jan 1847, ME. She was never married, but had one son by William Hawley-8 EMERSON. He was the son of Dr. John-7 EMERSON and Louisa JACKSON, and was born Sept 1831; died unmarried 20 Aug 1906. Amanda-8 DRISKO resided Jonesport and Westbrook, Maine; and died 24 Aug 1915.

Child of Amanda Rhodella-8 DRISKO (and William H. EMERSON):
    Surname DRISKO
1883. Perlin Winslow born 6 Dec 1876 Addison, ME; 1m. Inez BICKFORD 21 June 1894; div bef 1900
    " Perley "   (she dau/o Justus W. BICKFORD and Alfaretta CHURCH)
            2m. Agnes Elizabeth TRACY 30 Oct 1901 (she born 7 Dec 1882; died 25 March 1967)
            died 17 Apr 1952 Westbrook, ME; buried Woodlawn Cemetery (hotel worker)

1229. STEPHEN E-8 SAWYER, son of Eliza N-7 DRISKO (Joseph-6; 5; 4; John-3; 2) and Ebenezer SAWYER, was born Feb 1828/29 at Jonesport, Washington County, Maine. He married Dorcas Elizabeth KELLEY ca 18__. She was the daughter of _____ KELLEY, and was born ca 1838; died ____.

Children of Stephen-8 SAWYER and Dorcas KELLEY:
    Surname SAWYER   (children born Jonesport, Maine)

1884. Lowell A.	born ca 1858; d y	1889. Lizzie E.	born ca 1872
1885. Ella May	born ca 1859; d y		married William DUPEE
1886. George W.	born Mar 1863/65	1890. Frank B.	born July 1873
married Mary E. FLAHERTY 21 May 1891		marr Henrietta FAULKINGHAM 11 Nov 1893	
1887. Anna May	born ca 1868; d y	1891. Nellie R.	born ca 1875; d y
1888. Eben J.	born 1870; d y	1892. Lowell (2)	born ca 1879; d y

1231. JOSEPH W-8 SAWYER, brother of above, was born 5 Dec 1831 at Jonesport, ME. He married Rebecca E. WATTS on 4 Feb 1855. She was the daughter of Stephen Jones WATTS and Elizabeth Brown SAWYER, and was born 15 Aug 1834; died 13 Apr 1905. She was the granddaughter of Samuel WATTS, Jr. and Mary / Polly NOYES. Joseph-8 SAWYER died 9 Dec 1876 Jonesport, Maine.

Children of Joseph-8 SAWYER and Rebecca WATTS:
    Surname SAWYER   (children born Jonesport, Maine)
    1893. Lester   born 21 Oct 1858; died 9 Dec 1876   1895. Cora L.   born ca 1870
    1894. Eugene M. born 17 Apr 1862; died 5 June 1900

1236. EBEN J-8 SAWYER, brother of above, was born July 1840 at Jonesport, Maine. he married Philena Augusta KELLEY ca 18__. She was the daughter of __?__ KELLEY, and was born July 1849, Maine.

Children of Eben-8 SAWYER and Philena KELLEY:
    Surname SAWYER
    1896. Stephen   born Feb 1872; married Laura LAKEMAN 8 Aug 1903 Jonesport, ME
  + 1897. JULIA A.   born June 1875; married ALTON V-9 ROGERS 24 Sept 1890 (# 1816)
                            (he son/o Benjamin-8 ROGERS (# 1128) and Lucy LEIGHTON)
                            (he born 9 June 1867 Jaffa, Palestine; died 31 July 1957)
                            (he a shipbuilder at Jonesport, Maine)
    1898. Eliza   born ca 18__; died at age 2

1237. GEORGE W-8 SAWYER, brother of above, was born ca 1842 at Jonesport, Maine. he married Mary Elizabeth KELLEY ca 18__. She was the daughter of __?__ KELLEY, and was born Aug 1841.

Children of George W-8 SAWYER and Mary Elizabeth KELLEY:
    Surname SAWYER
    1899. Edith May   born 16 June 1878, Milbridge, ME
                            married Melvin S. MITCHELL of Harrington, ME 6 Dec 1899

1240. CORDELIA M-8 COFFIN, daughter of Feah Parker-7 DRISKO (Joseph-6; 5; 4; John-3; 2) and Aaron-7 COFFIN, was born ca 1830, Maine. She married first to Joseph-3 McKENZIE on 26 Feb 1852 at Columbia, Maine. he was the son of Owen-2 McKENZIE and Persis COLSON, and was born Feb 1810; died 22 Oct 1852. She married second to JAMES CAMPBELL-7 COFFIN (# 493) on 31 Dec 1854. Children of second marriage listed under # 493.

Child of Cordelia-8 COFFIN and Joseph-3 McKENZIE:
    Surname McKENZIE
    1900. Agnes   born Oct 1852; married John R. RANDALL , int pub 1 June 1878 Harrington, ME
                   (he son/o Stillman RANDALL and Catherine DICKSON)(he born ca 1848)

1251. AUGUSTUS MELVILLE-8 DRISKO, son of Jeremiah-7 DRISKO (Joseph-6; 5; 4; John-3; 2) and his 2nd wife Mary INGERSOLL, was born ca 1840 at Centerville, ME. He married on 6 Nov 1864 at Harrington, ME. to Leonice Gertrude GRACE of Harrington, ME. She was the daughter of William B. GRACE and Rebecca Lucy STROUT, and was born 26 Aug 1846; died 19__, SD They moved to Saginaw, Michigan in 1867; where he died in 1869. She married second to __?__ PERRY.

Children of Augustus Melville-8 DRISKO and Leonice Gertrude GRACE:
    Surname DRISKO
  + 1901. ALICE MAUDE born 12 Feb 1866, ME; married William PINKERTON of South Dakota
  + 1902. WILLIAM   born ca 1869 Saginaw, MI; married Minnie WILSON of Mansfield, So. Dakota
         HERBERT   (she dau/o ANSON WILSON and Sarah MOULTON)
                       died 26 Jan 1936 Aberdeen, South Dakota
         Note: William Herbert-9 DRISKO, Sr., was a wholesale hardware dealer in Aberdeen, SD

1252. FRANCIS JASPER-8 " JAP " DRISKO, brother of above, was born 8 Sept 1842 at Centerville, ME. He married Nancy Abby-8 LORD on 24 June 1866. She was the daughter of James-7 LORD and Betsey FOGG, and was born May 1845; died 1913. They resided at Harrington, ME. Clarence DRISKO of Columbia Falls, ME. had the benefit of some of his genealogical research, which was done prior to 1924. At that time " Jap " was in his 82nd year and was " confined to his bed ". He died 27 Dec 1928 at Harrington. His work, along with that of Clarence-10 DRISKO and many others, have helped preserve the history of the DRISKO family.

Children of Francis Jasper-8 DRISKO and Nancy LORD:
Surname DRISKO

1903. Ernest H.	born ca 1867/68; died before 1880; EOL
1904. Bertha G.	born 1869; died ____; unmarried; resided New Jersey 1924 EOL
1905. JOSEPHINE	born 5 May 1872; married James William CARTY 5 Mar 1892
KNOWLES	(he born 20 Nov 1851, NS; died 5 Sept 1941)
	died 16 Feb 1944 Rockville Center, NY
1906. Isabel	born 6 June 1879; died Mar 1956 Mexico City, unmarried

1253. SEWALL MARSTON-8 DRISKO, brother of above, was born ca 1844 at Centerville, Maine. He married Helen Augusta-6 CALER on 4 June 1864 at Machias, Washington County, Maine. She was the daughter of John Barton-5 CALER and Nancy Lord-2 FOSTER, and was born 22 July 1845; died 1918. Sewall-8 DRISKO died 1912 at Harrington, Maine.

Children of Sewall-8 DRISKO and Helen-6 CALER:
Surname DRISKO

1907. Ralph Leslie	born ca 1868; married Ruth Pearl CUMMINGS; resided NH
	One child: Paul Leslie-10 DRISKO born 21 Feb 1916; died young
1908. Mildred Estelle	born 4 Mar 1874; married William ROWLEE/ROWELL, Jr. 21 Oct 1895
" Millie "	(he born ____; died 5 Sept 1931) (he of Lancaster, NH)
+ 1909. MELVILLE	born 8 Aug 1875; married Nettie W. MAHONEY 23 Dec 1899
AUGUSTUS	(she dau/o William MAHONEY and Rose HOWE of Machias, ME)
	(she born 27 Oct 1877; died 23 Dec 1961)
1910. Mary H.	born Mar 1881; died June 1932 unmarried

1254. JULIA B-8 DRISKO, sister of above, was born ca 1861 possibly at Centerville, Maine. She married Frank R-8 DYER, intentions published 6 Nov 1876 Addison, ME. He was the son of Silas Briggs-7 DYER and Julia A. INGERSOLL, and was born June 1857; died 192_ at Corea (Gouldsboro) Maine.

Children of Julia-8 DRISKO and Frank-8 DYER:
Surname DYER   1911. Calla M. born ca 1879; married Winslow YOUNG 19 June 1899; died ca 1949
(he son/o Nathaniel YOUNG) (he born ca 1874; died 1939)

1256. BION L-8 DRISKO, brother of above, was born 7 July 1863 at Centerville, Maine. He married Ada ALLEN on 4 July 1893. She was the daughter of John ALLEN and Drucilla ALLEN, and was born 17 Nov 1874; died 15 Feb 1967 at San Luis Obispo, CA. Bion L-8 DRISKO died 18 Jan 1936 at Northville, SD
NOTE: On 18 July 1907, Bion L. DRISKO acquired 160 acres of homestead land in South Dakota according to information from the Bureau of Land Management (Land Patent Report for Montana, ND and SD) Document # 7369.

Children of Bion L-8 DRISKO and Ada ALLEN:
Surname DRISKO

1912. Alice M.	born 19 Jan 1896 Centerville, ME; married Grover S. ROBERTS 25 Dec 1922
	(he born 13 Dec 1896; died May 1976) (He from Ipswich, So. Dakota)
	died Mar 1982 SD (celebrated their 50th wedding anniversary 1972)
1913. Ethel May	born 19 Feb 1901, SD; married Ernest JOHNSON of Northville, SD;
	died 16 Oct 1987 San Luis Obispo, CA

1259. ALEXANDER MILLIKEN-8 DRISKO, son of Zimri-7 DRISKO (Josiah-6; Joseph-5; 4; John-3; 2) and Roxalana-7 NORTON, was born 21 Dec 1836 at Jonesport, Maine. He married Sophia B-4 FAULK-INGHAM ca 1859. She was the daughter of John P-3 FAULKINGHAM and Elizabeth HORN, and was born 19 Sept 1833, Nova Scotia,; died 20 Dec 1927, Jonesport. Alexander-8 DRISKO was an Assistant Lighthouse Keeper according to the 1860 Census, Jonesport, Maine. He died there 15 Dec 1901.

Children of Alexander M-8 DRISKO and Sophia-4 FAULKINGHAM:
Surname DRISKO
1914. Melissa D.   born 10 Nov 1861; married Danforth Orlando FRENCH, int pub 7 Aug 1883
                  (he son/o Albert FRENCH and Margaret LANG) (he born Mar 1862; died 6 Jan 1922)
1915. Theressa S.   born 16 July 1863 Addison, ME; died there 9 July 1941
     (12 ch)   married Irving Jason-9 CROWLEY 21 Jan 1882 Harrington,. ME   (# 1807)
                  (he son/o Jason C-8 CROWLEY and Rebecca Drisko-8 ROGERS (# 1127)
                  (he born 23 Dec 1859; died 6 Sept 1948)
1916. Alice D.   born May 1868; married Samuel S. NEWBERRY 5 June 1894; died 1953
                  (he born Mar 1845; died Mar 1900) EOL

1260. JEREMIAH NORTON-8 DRISKO, brother of above, was born 2 Dec 1838 at Jonesport, ME. He married 1st to Mary Sabra-7 ALLEY. She was the daughter of John-6 ALLEY and Elizabeth-7 BEAL, and was born 1841 at Beals, ME.; died 9 Dec 1876. His 2nd wife was Annie Victoria KELLEY. She was the adopted daughter of J. HALL, and was born Nov 1857; died 22 Dec 1936. Jeremiah-8 DRISKO, a fisherman and seaman, died 1900.

Children of Jeremiah-8 DRISKO and Mary Sabra-7 ALLEY:
Surname DRISKO
1917. Zimri Tabbut   born Nov 1859; died young
1918. Abigail L.   born 1862; marr Capt Horace Marston DUNBAR 12 Sept 1881; died 11 June 1886
                  (he son/o William Marston DUNBAR and Mary S. WOODARD)
                  (he born 9 Feb 1853, NH; died 11 Sept 1923)
1919. Mary E.   born 1866; died June 1875
1920. Eliza Evelyn born 19 Feb 1871; died 28 Dec 1938 Beals
                  married Jeremiah Beal-8 ALLEY 7 May 1888
         (he son/o Reuben-7 ALLEY and Sarah ROBINSON)(he born 1 Jan 1871; died 19 Sept 1946)
1921. Susan A.   born 2 Sept 1875; married Augustus Oramander-9 BEAL 20 Dec 1890
                  (he son/o Barnabas Coffin-8 BEAL and Elizabeth Drisko SAWYER)
1922. Leroy A.   born 2 Oct 1879; married Sarah C. ALLEY 26 May 1904; died 2 Jan 1960
1923. Sadie Ellen   born 5 Mar 1885; married George Franklin-9 BEAL 11 June 1900
1924. Flora L.   born 21 Mar 1892; married Edward L-10 BEAL 2 July 1913; died 4 Apr 1971
1925. Ellis Wass   born 19 Aug 1895; marr Christiana B. ALLEY 19 May 1915; died 17 Nov 1964
                                 (she born ca 1896; died 22 Aug 1964 Beals)

1261. THEODOCIA-8 DRISKO   see CHARLES A-7 DRISKO (# 506)

1262. CAPTAIN HIRAM CROWLEY-8 DRISKO, son of Jeremiah-7 DRISKO (Josiah-6; Joseph-5; 4; John-3; 2) and Jane HUNTLEY, was born Dec 1836/37 at Jonesport, Maine. He married Hannah Norton-5 KELLEY on 14 Sept 1859. She was the daughter of Aaron-4 KELLEY and Rebecca Sawyer NORTON, and was born 16 Oct 1841; died 1920. Hiram-8 DRISKO, a sea captain at Jonesport 1860-1910, died 1920.

Children of Hiram-8 DRISKO and Hannah-5 KELLEY:
Surname DRISKO
1926. Georgia Anne   born 14 June 1860 Jonesport, ME; died there 22 June 1941
                  married George T. JENKINS 30 June 1877 Addison, Maine
(he son/o Samuel J. JENKINS and Margaret THORNTON)(he born 2 Oct 1857, NB; died 28 Aug 1915)
+ 1927. LAURA JANE   born 24 Oct 1871 Jonesport; died 23 Sept 1958   Reference: LDS- IGI Maine
                  married Rubin Edgar WILSON 31 Jan 1891 Jonesport
         (he son /o William WILSON and Laura WESCOTT)(he born 13 Oct 1871; died 1 July 1950)

1265. CAPTAIN THOMAS ARTHUR-8 DRISKO, brother of above, was born 28 July 1843 at Jonesport/ Indian River, Maine. He married Francesca T. SAWYER ca 1866 at Lancaster, New Brunswick. She was the daughter of Levi Bagley SAWYER (a sailor at Jonesport, ME) and Jane Barfield-8 LEIGHTON ; and was born 31 May 1847; died 11 Jan 1938. Thomas-8 DRISKO, a master mariner (1870-1900), died 1904. He resided Jonesport, Maine 1880.

Children of Captain Thomas Arthur-8 DRISKO and Francesca SAWYER:
Surname DRISKO

1928. Captain Ralph Burton	born 12 Apr 1867 Jonesport; married Winifred PARKIN 11 Sept 1889 Jonesport (she dau/o John L. PARKIN and Clarissa LEIGHTON) died 6 Oct 1948 Sailors Snug Harbor, New York

Child: (1928a) Ralph Burton-10 DRISKO, Jr. born 189_; died 11 Mar 1924.
He was swept overboard the Steamship *LILLIAN LUCKENBACK* on passage from New York to San Francisco.

1929. Mabel D.	born ca 1870/71; 1m. Rev Everett L. WALBRIDGE 2 July 1891 2m. ___?__ RUSH/RUST; resided MA. 1938
1930. Grace D.	born Oct 1872/73 Jonesport; married Edgar A-9 WORCESTER 1 Oct 1901 (he son/o Joseph W-8 WORCESTER and Eva ALLEN) (he born 30 Oct 1877; died 11 Feb 1968)
1931. Jane Barfield	born 1875; married Dr. John P. BYRON 21 July 1896 Jonesport

1270. MARY ELIZABETH-8 DRISKO   see CAPTAIN JASON D-8 LEIGHTON (# 1140)

1271. ZIMRI TABBUT-8 DRISKO, brother of above, son of Captain Edmund Curtis-7 DRISKO (Josiah-6; Joseph-5; 4; John-3; 2) and Hannah ALLEN, was born 4 Mar 1845 at Milbridge, Maine. He married Susan C. FIELD on 23 Jan 1869 at Milbridge. She was the daughter of David FIELD and Caroline GRANT, and was born 23 Sept 1852; died 8 Feb 1931, WA. They resided at Milbridge until about 1890, then moved to the Pacific Coast. Zimri-8 DRISKO died 27 Dec 1925 at Medina, WA.

Children of Zimri-8 DRISKO and Susan FIELD:
Surname DRISKO

1932. Henry B. 3rd	born 1 June 1871 Milbridge; died 30 Mar 1949 Seattle, WA 1m. Jessie M. SEAMON 16 Nov 1895; 2m. Bertha L. McCASLIN 10 Oct 1924
+ 1933. WILLIAM F.	born 3 Sept 1872 Milbridge,ME; died Dec 1935 married Jennie BISHER 4 Sept 1901 (she born 22 Aug 1874; died Nov 1965)
+ 1934. GUY C.	born 29 Jan 1881 Addison, ME; 1m. Mary JONES Smith 4 Nov 1908 2m. Anna GOODWIN; 3m. ____?___
+ 1935. ELTON B.	born 5 Mar 1886 Addison; 1m. Mabel HESTON 3 Nov 1908 (she born 188_; died 18 Oct 1940)
	2m. Della M. ELLIS Galligan 18 Dec 1942 (she born 23 Dec 1898; died July 1975 Seattle, WA.)

1272. IDA FRANCES-8 DRISKO, sister of above, was born 6 Apr 1849 at Milbridge, Maine. She married first to Ira S-7 WALLACE on 1 Feb 1868 at Milbridge. He was the son of Moses-6 WALLACE and Catherine SAWYER, and was born 12 Jan 1848; died 5 Oct 1883 at Modesto, CA. She married second to Fred A-7 WALLACE (brother of Ira) on 1 Feb 1888.

Children of Ida F-8 DRISKO and Ira-7 WALLACE:
Surname WALLACE

1936. Minnie C.	born 15 Mar 1869
1937. Newell H.	born 5 Oct 1873; married Clara M. LEIGHTON 13 Nov 1897
1938. Belle D.	born 10 May 187_, CA; died 7 Oct 1887

1273. EDMUND W-8 DRISKO, brother of above, was born 4 June 1855 at Milbridge, Maine. He married Clara J-8 GRAY, intentions published 6 Apr 1880. She was the daughter of Jeremiah-7 GRAY and Mercy-6 NASH, and was born 15 Jan 1855; died 25 Aug 1918. Edmund-8 DRISKO died 18 Jan 1899, ME.

Children of Edmund-8 DRISKO and Clara GRAY:
　　Surname DRISKO
　　1939. Eulalia F.　　　　born 9 Feb 1884 Jonesport, ME; died 1934 Gorham, Maine
　　　　　　　　　　　married Charles H-9 WASS 24 Nov 1906
　　　　　　(he son/o Judson-8 WASS and Mary-8 WASS) (he born 9 Sept 1886; died 1909)

1274. JULIA S-8 DORR, daughter of Betsey-7 DRISKO (Josiah-6; Joseph-5; 4; John-3; 2) and Joseph Patten DORR, was born ca 1838 at Indian River, Maine. She married Truman Wilson MAGEE on 18 Dec 1855 at Columbia, Maine. He was the son of ____ MAGEE, and was born 16 Apr 1837; died 8 May 1871, CA. Julia-8 DORR died 14 Oct 1901 at Stockton, CA.

Children of Julia-8 DORR and Truman W. MAGEE:
　　Surname MAGEE

1940. Franklin B.	born 18__	1944. Gertrude	born 18__
1941. Nancy Ella	born 18__	1945. Rebecca	born 18__
1942. Julia	born 18__		
1943. John	born 18__; poss marr Beatrice H. DORR 2 Sept 1903 Columbia Falls, ME		

1282. CAPTAIN AL(A)MON R-8 DRISKO, son of Thomas-7 DRISKO (Josiah-6; Joseph-5; 4; John-3; 2) and Ellen CROWLEY, was born 6 Mar 1848. He married Orrie A/ Aura Anna-5 CROWLEY ca 1873. She was the daughter of Matthew C-4 CROWLEY and Betsey CROWLEY, and was born 3 Feb 1854; died 28 Jan 1920 at Jonesport, Maine. Al(a)mon –8 DRISKO, a sea captain and grocer, died 30 Mar 1913.

Children of Captain Al(a)mon-8 DRISKO and Orrie CROWLEY:
　　Surname DRISKO　　　　　(children born Addison, Maine)
+ 1946. LEON ROWELL born Aug 1874/76; died Dec 1934 Belfast, Maine
　　married Caroline Goldsmith RUMERY 26 June 1900 (she born 1875; died 8 Dec 1953 Evanston, IL)
　　1947. Milton C.　　　born 8 Oct 1877; married Minnie ___?___
　　　　　　　　　died 28 Apr 1935 Los Angeles, CA ; was a school teacher and author; ME / MA.
　　1948 Ellen E.　　　　born Feb 1885

1283. CAPTAIN EDGAR EVERSON-8 DRISKO, brother of above, was born Sept 1850 at Jonesport, Maine. He married Gertrude Emily-8 EMERSON on 15 Aug 1874 at Indian River / Jonesport, Maine. She was the daughter of Aaron Wass-7 EMERSON and Salome J-7 WASS, born Sept 1854; died 1945. Edgar E-8 DRISKO died 5 Jan 1920 at Jonesport, Maine.

Children of Edgar Everson-8 DRISKO and Gertrude-8 EMERSON:
　　Surname DRISKO
+ 1949. MERTON　　　born 5 July 1880 Addison, ME; died 9 Aug 1961 Addison
　　EMERSON　　marr Addie S. EMERSON 22 Apr 1908 Addison (born 9 Apr 1890; died 31 Aug 1957)
　　1950. Irene H. born 20 May 1882; married John A. CHASE Readfield, ME 10 Mar 1904; died May 1974

1286. HARVEY " Harry " McKENZIE-8 DRISKO, brother of above, was born ca 1866 at Jonesport, ME. He married Jennie Maud PENLEY. She was born ca 1874; died 8 Nov 1965. They resided Bridgton, ME

Children of Harvey (Harry)-8 DRISKO and Jennie Maud PENLEY:
　　Surname DRISKO
　　1951. George Thomas　born 11 Feb 1908,ME; died 25 June 1975 Bridgton, ME
　　　　　　　　　married Avis B. LAMONT of E. Hiram, ME on 31 Oct 1931
　　　　　　　　　(she born 5 Nov 1910, ME; died 22 Mar 1993 Bridgton, Cumberland, ME)
　　　　　son: George T-10 DRISKO, Jr. born 193_; married Daphine K. McALLISTER 14 June 1957
　　1952. Evelyn Salome　born 28 Sept 1914; died Oct 1984 Bridgton, ME
　　　　　　　　　married Albert R. SMITH, Jr. on 28 Nov 1935 (he born 16 July 1912; died 29 Jul 1988)
　　1953. Arthur Almon　born (poss) 16 July 1917 ME; died 17 Aug 1992 Harrison, York, ME

1293. CHARLES CHANDLER-8 DRISKO, son of Captain Joel W-7 DRISKO (Josiah-6; Joseph-5; 4; John-3; 2) and Sarah W. CROWLEY, was born 21 Feb 1865 at Machias, ME. He married Phebe DODGE on 16 Jan 1897 at Addison, ME. She was the daughter of Thomas Ellison O. DODGE and Melinda M. DAY, and was born 18 July 1876 at Augusta, ME; died 24 July 1963 at San Mateo, CA. Resided at Machias, ME; removed to CA ca 1923. Charles-8 DRISKO died 18 Mar 1956 at Burlingame, CA.

Children of Charles C-8 DRISKO and Phebe DODGE:
   Surname DRISKO
+ 1954. THOMAS   born 10 July 1897; married Alice J. DOW 19 Sept 1918
      ELLISON   died 30 Oct 1987 Santa Rosa, Sonoma County, CA
+ 1955. FLORENCE A/E. born Nov 1898; married William E. CLARK 16 Aug 1919; living 1989
  1956. Ralph C.   born 5 Jan 1901; died June 1973 Cranford, NJ;   EOL
  1957. Madeline R.   born ca 1905; married __?__; One ch: surname unknown: Phoebe-10
  1958. Kathleen M.   born 1 Oct 1908; married ____?__
        2 ch: (surname unknown) Laverne-10 born 19__; and John-10 born 19___; died before 1989
  1959. Marvin   born 13 Apr 1910; died 19 Mar 1942   no issue   EOL
  1960. Vivian   born ca 1912; married ?_; 1 Ch: Ralph-10 (surname unknown)_

1297. AMELIA F-8 CARVER, daughter of Nancy A-7 DRISKO (Josiah-6; Joseph-5; 4; John-3;2) and Benjamin F-9 CARVER, was born ca 1851. She married 1st to Daniel James MANSFIELD on 10 Aug 1870. He was born 12 May 1848. She married 2nd to Nathaniel Church DAVIS; he was born 21 Apr 1854.

Children of Amelia F-8 CARVER and Nathaniel DAVIS:
   Surname DAVIS 1961. Myron R. born 18__   1962. Frederick L. born 18__   1963. Frank M. born 18__

1298. JUSTINA A-8 CARVER, sister of above, was born 18 Nov 1852. She married Edwin Allen KELLEY on 28 July 1872 at Columbia, ME. He was born Dec 1846. Justina A-8 died 25 July 1940.

Children of Justina-8 CARVER and Edwin Allen KELLEY:
   Surname KELLEY
+ 1964. GERTRUDE N. born Mar 1877; married Mark C. ALLEN 21 July 1900 Woodstock, ME
+ 1965. EDWIN A., JR. born Aug 1882; married Ethel Rosamond BEAL 16 Mar 1904 Jonesport, ME
                (she born 19 May 1888; died 28 Oct 1956)

1299. AUGUSTUS FELLOWS-8 CARVER, brother of above, was born Jan 1855. He married Annie M. SANBORN on 111 Dec 1880. She was born 5 Feb 1863; died 19 Mar ___. Augustus-8 died 23 Mar 1889.

Children of Augustus Fellows-8 CARVER and Annie SANBORN:
   Surname CARVER
+ 1966. BURTON   born Sept 1881; married Nettie Wallace BICKFORD 10 Jan 1903
      EUGENE   (she born 27 May 1885; died Apr 1965)
+ 1967. FRANK LEON born 13 Feb 1886 Jonesport, ME; married Mildred Arletta HALL 17 Mar 1914
              (she born 12 Feb 1891 Jonesport, ME; died ____)

1300. JUDSON HOWARD-8 CARVER, brother of above, was born 25 July 1857. He married first to Carrie A. WOODMAN on 21 July 1879. She was born 1862; died 26 Feb 1890. He married 2nd to Lena Rose FAULKINGHAM on 4 July 1894. She was born Aug 1873. Judson-8 CARVER died 23 July 1950.

Children of Judson-8 CARVER and Carrie WOODMAN:
   Surname CARVER
+ 1968. BERNARD F./ born 5 Apr 1880/81 Jonesport, ME; died Mar 1971 Westbrook, ME.
  FRANK BERNARD married Georgia Ann TRACY (# 2387) 9 Oct 1901 Jonesport, ME
              (she born 27 Aug 1880 Columbia Falls, ME; died ____)
  1969. Irving L.   born June 1884

Children of Judson-8 CARVER and Lena Rose FAULKINGHAM:
   Surname CARVER
   1970. Gertrude N.   born 22 Dec 1895; died Oct 1963 Maine
     married Charles G. STEVENS 10 Apr 1917 Jonesport, ME (he born 24 Oct 1894; died Dec 1974 ME)
+ 1971. JUDSON H., JR. born 16 Jan 1902; married Doris L. KELLEY; died 19 May 1986
   1972. Carrie A.   born 19 May 1906; married Oscar G. HAYWOOD 13 May 1933 Jonesport
     One child: Richard –10 HAYWOOD born 19__

1301. WILLIAM L-8 CARVER, brother of above, was born Feb 1859. He married Martha A. GUPTILL ca ____. She was born 19 Aug 1865 at Lubec, Maine; died March 1939. William-8 died 1929.

Children of William-8 CARVER and Martha GUPTILL:
   Surname CARVER
   1973. Evelyn A.   born 13 Sept 1887 Jonesport, ME:
             married Clinton M. CROWLEY of Addison on 21 July 1907
             (he born Aug 1883 Addison, ME; died 19 Apr ____)
   1974. Leroy L.   born July 1889; died before 1939
             married Bertha L. GARNETT 18 Mar 1916 Jonesport, ME
+1975. BYRON B.   born Mar 1891; married Rhoda V. SAWYER 23 May 1914 Jonesport, ME
             (she born 13 Apr 1892 Jonesport, ME; died 29 Oct 1986)
+ 1976. GLEN LEWIS   born Jan 1896; married Frances E. CARVER; died 29 Dec 1959

1302. GEORGE BROWN-8 CARVER, brother of above, was born 6 Nov 1860. He married Evelyn Willard-9 LOOK (# 1741) on11 Nov 1885. She was the daughter of Willard-8 LOOK and Electa Ann-6 PINEO, and was born 21 Nov 1863/8 Jonesboro, ME; died 26 Nov 1927. George-8 died 19 Mar 1944.

Children of George-8 CARVER and Evelyn LOOK:
   Surname CARVER
+ 1977. GUY HERRICK born 27 Apr 1886 Jonesport, ME
             married Susie Olive BEAL 1 Aug 1906 Jonesport, Maine
+ 1978. WILLARD   born 14 Oct 1887 Jonesport, ME
     LOOK   married Ethel Alta CROWLEY 30 Aug 1911 Jonesport, Amine
             (she born 25 Sept 1889 Addison, ME;)
   1979. Minnie E.   born 8 Sept 1897; died July 1974 Yarmouth, Maine
             married Archie F. KNAPP 1 Jan 1916 Jonesport, ME

1307. JULIA E-8 DRISKO, daughter of Benjamin Franklin-7 DRISKO (Jeremiah-6; Joseph-5; 4; John-3; 2) and Nancy PLUMMER, was born 13 Jan 1846 at Addison, ME. She married Coffin Stephen-8 LEIGHTON on 25 Dec 1866. He was the son of Aaron-7 LEIGHTON and Bethia WAKEFIELD, and was born 17 Apr 1845; died 14 Feb 1928 at Arlington, MA. They are buried in Church Hill Cemetery, Addison, ME. Coffin S-8 LEIGHTON served in the **Civil War – Company G, 11th Maine Infantry Regt.** from 29 Oct 1861 - 18 Nov 1864. He was wounded in his left leg and right hand. In 1900 he resided at Cambridge, MA.

Children of Julia E-8 DRISKO and Coffin S-8 LEIGHTON:
   Surname LEIGHTON   (children born Addison, Maine)
   1980. Gertrude May   born 5 Jan 1868; died 13 Sept 1883 Addison
   1981. Walstein H.   born June 1870; married Gertrude F. PETERSON 14 Oct 1897
             (she born 1870 Cambridgeport, MA; died ____)
             (she dau/o Pelham B. PETERSON and Amelia CROWLEY)
     One child: Gladys P-10 LEIGHTON born 11 Aug 1899 Columbia Falls, ME.
   1982. Blanche B.   born July 1872; married Leverett DUNBAR (he born Jan 1873, ME)
     One child: Marion-10 DUNBAR born Apr 1895 Cambridge, MA
   1983. Winifred Scott born 6 Feb 1874; died 24 Mar 1900
   1984. Harland P.   born Aug 1877   1985. Bernard F.   born Mar 1881

1308. ELIZA V-8 DRISKO, sister of above, was born 13 Oct 1848 at Addison, Maine. She married Harrison N-8 LOOK on 10 Apr 1869. He was the son of Robert Miller-7 LOOK and Cordelia HEATH, and was born 14 Feb 1839; died 10 Dec 1906. Eliza-8 DRISKO died 10 Dec 1897.

Children of Eliza-8 DRISKO and Harrison LOOK:
 Surname LOOK
 1986. Irving N.   born 12 Jan 1872; married Sadie __?__ ca 1902; died 13 Dec 1926

1309. HOWARD PERRIN-8 DRISKO, brother of above, was born 13 Dec 1852 at Addison, Maine. He married Mary Agnes-2 FUREY on 22 May 1883 at East Boston, MA. She was the daughter of James-1 FUREY and Catherine HUGHES, and was born 6 July 1863, Ireland; died 12 Feb 1934 Boston, MA. Howard-8 DRISKO died 18 Dec 1928 at Quincy, MA.

Children of Howard-8 DRISKO and Mary Agnes FUREY:
 Surname DRISKO
 1987. Agnes N.   born 13 Apr 1884; married Frederick N. CUTTER; died ca 1971
                       (he born 21 Apr 1876; died 18 July 1932
 1988. Seldon F.   born 22 Apr 1886; married Ardell LA PURL (she born 6 Jan 1889 Woburn, MA)
 1989. Raymond H.   born 4 May 1895 Boston, MA; married Mary A. NOLAN
                       died 23 Dec 1921 Dorchester, MA

1311. FRED HOWARD-8 DRISKO, son of Oramander Howard-7 DRISKO (Jeremiah-6; Joseph-5; 4; John-3; 2) and Catherine WASS, was born 10 Dec 1858 at Addison, Maine. He married Eva / Evelyn Alice-9 WASS on 14 Dec 1881. She was the daughter of Joseph W-8 WASS and Susan C-8 LOOK, and was born 9 Oct 1860; died 1947. They resided at Boston, MA. Fred-8 DRISKO died 7 June 1939, MA.

Children of Fred H-8 DRISKO and Eva / Evelyn-9 WASS:
 Surname DRISKO
 1990. Bertrand Irving   born 20 Feb 1885 Boston, MA; grad. Yale University 1906; died 8 Jan 1911
 1991. Arthur Howard   born 8 June 1888; graduated Yale University 1910; died 6 Aug 1977
                       married Mary ELLIOT   no issue   EOL
 1992. Alice S.   born 15 Feb 1891; died 19 Sept 1948   unmarried   EOL
 1993. Katherine W.   born 15 Aug 1893; married Paul N. SWAFFIELD; died 16 Feb 1944

1312. ALONZO B-8 DRISKO (called " Lon " or " Nibs "), brother of above, was born 11 Jan 1866 at Addison, Maine. He married Mary Littlefield PHILBRICK ca 18__. She was the daughter of ____ PHILBRICK, and was born 27 Mar 1868; died 20 June 1953. Alonzo-8 DRISKO died 3 June 1958, MA.

Children of Alonzo-8 DRISKO and Mary PHILBRICK:
 Surname DRISKO
+ 1994. HAROLD   born 20 Jan 1895 Boston, MA; graduated Yale University 1916
    PHILBRICK   married Ruth THOMPSON 6 June 1923; died 7 Dec 1981 Newton, MA.
                     (she born 28 Feb 1898, MA; died June 1987 Hollis, NH)
+ 1995. HELEN   born 11 May 1897; married Otto P. MANN; died June 1984
                     (he born 8 June 1895; died Jan 1984)

1313. HENRY BROOKS-8 DRISKO, son of Captain Perrin-7 DRISKO (Jeremiah-6; Joseph-5; 4 ; John-3; 2) and Frances PLUMMER, was born ca 1853/54 at Addison, Maine. He married Florence COLLIER of Melrose, MA ca 1879. She was the daughter of ____ COLLIER, and was born 1857, MA; died ca 1945. Henry-8 DRISKO died 1935.

Children of Henry B-8 DRISKO and Florence COLLIER:
 Surname DRISKO
 1996. Edna   born 1880; died young Addison, Maine

Children of Henry B-8 DRISKO, continued:
    Surname DRISKO

+ 1997. GRACE PLUMMER	born 1882/83 Boston, MA; married Fred BUCKNAM of Machias, Maine (he son/o Eugene M. BUCKNAM and Paulina KIETH) (he born 20 Sept 1875; died 10 Sept 1918, MA)
1998. Gerald Perrin	born 1885 Chelsea, MA; died 1912
1999. Vera	born 15 Nov 1889 Boston, MA; died May 1973 Natick, MA.
2000. Ethel	born 14 Sept 1900; married George RAU; died May 1983 (he born 20 Aug 1901; died Nov 1958, MA)

Reference: Holbrook Collection, Volume 342, page 54 and Volume 360, page 260

1327. ERI HATHAWAY-8 DRISKO, son of Chandler Robbins-7 DRISKO (Jonathan-6; Samuel G-5; Joseph-4; John-3; 2) and Ruth Ruggles WHITNEY, was born 2/8 Mar 1827 at Jonesboro, Maine. He married first to Elizabeth Robinson-5 TABBUTT on 9 Jan 1851. She was the daughter of James-7 TABBUT and Catherine MESERVE, and was born 5 Apr 1832; died before 1873.

He married second to Fannie BREWSTER–5 TABBUT, younger sister of Elizabeth , intentions published 30 June 1873. Fannie was born 4 Mar 1834; died 3 Nov 1926. Eri H-8 DRISKO died 5 Jan 1878 at Columbia Falls, Maine.

Children of Eri Hathaway-8 DRISKO and Elizabeth-8 TABBUT:
    Surname DRISKO   (children born Columbia, Maine)

+ 2001. REV RAYMOND CHANDLER	born 22 Aug 1852; married LAURA ISABEL-9 DRISKO 17 July 1878 (she dau/o Joseph W-8 DRISKO (# 1328) and Isabel FARNSWORTH) (she born 26 Oct 1860 ; died Apr 1953, Florida) died 19 June 1937 Pomona, Florida
+ 2002. GEORGE CAMELO	born 15 Apr 1854; married Sarah MAGEE; died 26 Oct 1944 (she dau/o John MAGEE and Esther DORR) (she born 24 Apr 1859; died 6 Jan 1955)
2003. Irene Frances	born 13 Sept 1857; married Charles WHITE, int pub 16 June 1875 (he from Jonesport, Maine)
+ 2004. EDWIN IRWIN	born 6 Dec 1859; married Hattie A. DONAVAN 17 June 1880 (she born 16 Apr 1860; died 4 Mar 1937) died 14 Nov 1928
2005. Rosa L.	born Feb 1863; married William Flagg WHITE, Jr. 19 Aug 1881 (he son/o William F. WHITE, Sr. and Susan L. JOHNSON Jonesport, ME) **

** William Flagg WHITE, Sr. was born ca 1824 at Machiasport, ME. He married Susan L. JOHNSON ca 1848 at Machias, ME. She was the daughter of Joseph Brookins JOHNSON and Nancy WESCOTT, and the granddaughter of Stephen Otis JOHNSON and Patience BRYANT.

+ 2006. RUTH E.	born June 1870; 1m. Charles F. ATWATER 11 July 1891 2m. Michael W. MURPHY 4 Oct 1916
2007. Katie	born 1868; died 1885 age 17 EOL
2008. Grace E.	born ca 1873/74; married Ernest McCLENITHAN 2 Oct 1906; no issue EOL
+ 2009. ERI HASKELL	born 25 Sept 1877; died 1 Feb 1971 Columbia Falls, Maine. married Susie Ethel ALLEN 29 Oct 1904 (she born 27 Apr 1886; died 9 Mar 1976)

1328. JOSEPH WHITNEY-8 DRISKO, brother of above, was born 11 Oct 1829 at Jonesboro, Maine. He married Isabel Frances-6 FARNSWORTH ++ on 11 Oct 1853. She was the daughter of Cyrus-5 FARNS-WORTH and Mary Thompson WATTS, and was born 6 Dec 1836; died 14 Sept 1911 Jonesboro, Maine. Joseph Whitney-8 DRISKO resided at Jonesboro, ME his entire life, and was a farmer and lumberman. He took an active part in town affairs – serving one term in the State Legislature as a representative, 1877. Joseph W-8 DRISKO died Sept 1913.

Joseph Whitney-8 DRISKO (1829-1913)   *Isabel F-6 FARNSWORTH (1836-1911)*

Children of Joseph Whitney-8 DRISKO and Isabel Frances FARNSWORTH:
  Surname DRISKO

+ 2010. EUGENE   born 24 Dec 1853, Jonesboro, ME; died 14 Mar 1943 Jonesboro
   CYRUS or   1m. Asenath Ingersoll BARTON 2 Sep 1875
   Cyrus Eugene   (she born 21 June 1852; died 10 July 1876)
                      2m. Arathusa B. SMITH 12 Oct 1884
           (she dau/o Asa K. SMITH and Hannah PENNELL)(she born Jan 1861; died 1923)
+ 2011. CORA EDITH   born 14 Aug 1855; died 1939
                      married Eri Wellington-8 LOOK 21 June 1874
           (he son/o Henry-7 LOOK and Roxanna KILTON) (he born 21 Jan 1856)
+ 2012. LAURA ISABEL born 26 Oct 1859/60; died 1953/54
                      married RAYMOND C-9 DRISKO 17 July 1878 (# 1991)
+ 2013. ESTHER RUTH   born 5 Apr 1862/63; died 1959
                      married Noyes Watts-8 FISH 7 Aug 1880 Jonesboro, ME.
           (he son/o Ansel-7 FISH and Mary Jane WATTS) (he born Sept 1853; died 1936)
+ 2014. LIZZIE MADGE born 22 Oct 1866; died 10 July 1964
   (twin)   married George W Gates-8 FISH 28 June 1884
+ 2015. LUCY MAUD   born 22 Oct 1866; died 4 Oct 1931
   (twin)   married Frank Herbert HUGHES 3 Oct 1883
+ 2016. WILLIAM PITT born 1 Dec 1869 Harrington, ME; died 7 Aug 1901 Centerville, Maine
   FESSENDEN   1m. Mary Ella TABBUTT 27 July 1892
           (she dau/o Abijah TABBUT and Aurilla FLOYD) (she born 28 Apr 1868; died 19 July 1899)
                      2m. Rosa May/Mae BAGLEY 7 June 1900
+ 2017. ALICE MAY   born 19 Jan 1872 Jonesboro, ME; married Arthur Franklin LINDSEY
+ 2018. JOSEPHINE   born 15 Feb 1874 Jonesboro, Maine
   FRANCES   married Frank Marshall ALLEN 19 Apr 1901 (he born 18__; died 1956)
   (twin)   died 1965, buried Ruggles Cemetery, Columbia Falls, Maine
  2019. Shapleigh   born 15 Feb 1874; married Myra Louella NOYES 3 May 1903
   Chandler   (she born 24 Feb 1876; died July 1952)
   (twin)   died Mar 1938   EOL
+ 2020. JAMES   born 24 Mar 1879 Jonesboro, ME.; died 15 July 1966 Jonesport, ME
   WALKER   married Annie Lydia NOYES 28 Nov 1900
                      (she dau/o George NOYES and Clara BRIDGHAM)

MATTHIAS-1 FARNSWORTH, the immigrant, was born ca 1612 at Lancashire, England. He was a resident of Lynn, MA. in 1657; and moved to Groton around 1660 where he was a selectman. During the Indian raid on Groton, 17 Mar 1676, he and his family escaped to Concord. They returned about two years later. His first wife is unknown. His second wife was probably Mary FARR; daughter of George FARR, a shipbuilder. Mary was born 16__; died 1717. Matthias-1 FARNSWORTH died 21 Jan 1689.

BENJAMIN-2 FARNSWORTH was born 1667 at Groton. He married Mary PRESCOTT ca 1695. She was the daughter of Jonas PRESCOTT and Mary LAKER, and was born 3 Feb 1674 Lancaster; died 28 Oct 1735. Benjamin-2 died 15 Aug 1733.
JONAS-3 FARNSWORTH was born 4 Oct 1713 at Groton.. He married ca 1739 to Thankful WARD. She was the daughter of Obadiah WARD and Joanna MIXER, and was born 15 Feb 1712 Sudbury; died 1 May 1799.

ISAAC-4 FARNSWORTH was born 9 Aug 1750 at Worcester, and married Abigail HILL ca 1769 at Scarboro, Maine. She was the daughter of Joseph HILL (Valentine HILL) and was born 1752; died 1829 at Jonesboro, Maine. His second wife was Martha BARTH of Granville, Nova Scotia. Issac-4 FARNSWORTH, went to Nova Scotia with the Expedition of his uncle Amos. After his marriage at Scarboro, he returned to Annapolis, NS for a few years, where he built and warranted a large dike. Only weeks before his guarantee was to expire, the dike broke and placed him in financial ruin. He removed to Maine, and was one of the early settlers of Jonesboro, where he aided the revolting Colonists.

CYRUS-5 FARNSWORTH, father of Isabel-6 FARNSWORTH, was born 7 Jan 1795 at Jonesboro. His first wife was Mary SCHOPPEE Palty, born 1799; died 1829 at age 30. His 2nd wife was Mary Thompson WATTS. She was the daughter of David WATTS and Abigail NOYES, born 19 Mar 1807 Jonesboro; died there 13 Feb 1899. Cyrus-5 died 14 Aug 1874 Jonesboro, ME.

1332. JERUSHA CORTHELL-8 DRISKO, sister of above, was born 16 July 1840 at Jonesboro, Maine. She married Lorenzo-7 BRIDGHAM on 12 Mar 1864. He was the son of Andrew M-6 BRIDGHAM ++ and Ann DOWNES of Whitneyville. He was born 1836; died ____. Jerusha-8 DRISKO died 8 Nov 1915.

Children of Jerusha-8 DRISKO and Lorenzo BRIDGHAM:
    Surname BRIDGHAM
    2021. Willie   born 18__   2022. Murray   born 18__   2023. George   born 18__
    +2024. WILSON born 18__; married Abbie M. FLYNN 28 Oct 1893 Whitneyville, ME
    2025. May   born 18__   2026. Dana   born 18_

+ + Andrew M. BRIDGHAM was one of four brothers residing in Washington Co., ME in 1840. He had come in the 1830's and kept a tavern at Marion. Three of the BRIDGHAM brothers, including Andrew, married three DOWNES sisters – all daughters of Eben DOWNES who settled at Steuben, ME, coming from Oxford County at an early time. Alden BRIDGHAM married Margaret DOWNES; Alvin married Jane DOWNES; Andrew married Ann DOWNES, and Levi BRIDGHAM married Lucinda KILTON.

1334. DEBORAH MC KENZIE-8 TRACY, daughter of Abigail-7 DRISKO (Jonathan-6; Samuel Gatchell-5; Joseph-4; John-3;2) and Dennis-1 TRACY, was born ca 1824. Her first marriage was to William Wass NICHOLS on 14 June 1848 at Addison, Washington Co., ME. He was the son of Ward NICHOLS; and was born 18__; died 1850. She married 2nd to Jeremiah Norton CUMMINGS ca 1850. He was the son of Samuel CUMMINGS and Elizabeth WHITE, born 31 Jul 1825. She married 3rd to Luther Humphrey CALLAGHAN in 1868; and 4th to William RAFTER on 24 Feb 1875 at Machias, ME.

Child of Deborah-8 TRACY and William NICHOLS:
    Surname NICHOLS   2027. William W.   born ca 1849
Children of Deborah-8 TRACY and Jeremiah CUMMINGS:
    Surname CUMMINGS
    2028. Sarah J. born 1853   2029. Sybil D.   born 1855   2030. John   born 1860

1335. AMASA DRISKO-8 TRACY, brother of above, was born 23 Feb 1826 at Jonesboro, Maine. He married first to Rebecca Drisko-8 SAWYER on 28 May 1855 at Addison. She was the daughter of Joseph-7 SAWYER and his 2nd wife Mary W. YEATON, and was born 15 Jan 1834 at Addison, died 1892. He married second to Susie D. ROBBINS on 17 Oct 1892. She was born May 1844; died after 1900. Amasa Drisko-8 TRACY died 5 Mar 1905 at Addison.

Children of Amasa-8 TRACY and Rebecca D-8 SAWYER:
    Surname TRACY   (children born at Addison, Maine)
+ 2031. ELZENA G.   born ca 1857; marr Ferdinand M. MERRITT 12 May 1881; died 1944

Children of Amasa-8 TRACY, continued:
>   Surname TRACY
>   2032. Edward W.   born 18 Aug 1862; died 24 Mar 1920;   unmarried
>   2033. John F.   born 4 May 1872; died 24 Apr 1946 Addison, ME
>   married Estella May LAMSON 7 Sept 1926 Addison, ME (she born 16 May 1871; died 24 Apr 1946)

1336. AMOS L-8 TRACY, brother of above, was born ca 1828 at Columbia Falls, Maine. He married Abigail Crowley-6 GRAY, intentions published 11 July 1852 at Addison, Maine. She was the daughter of William-5 GRAY and Hannah-6 WHITNEY, and was born 5 Jan 1833 at Machiasport, Washington County, Maine; died 1902. Amos L-8 TRACY died 31 Jan 1888 at Columbia Falls.

Children of Amos L-8 TRACY and Abigail-6 GRAY.
>   Surname TRACY
> + 2034. BELINDA J.   born Sept 1853; married Moses-8 WORCESTER 12 July 1883 (as his 2nd wife)
>   died ca 1900 Columbia Falls, Maine
> + 2035. AMASA DRISKO   born 16 Apr 1855 Columbia, ME; married Mary Caroline STEVAR ca 1879
> + 2036. MARY E.   born ca 1858; married George H. BOWLES 28 Dec 1889; died ca 1900
> + 2037. AMOS W.   born Mar 1861; married Corris A. NORTON 21 Jan 1893
>   died June 1910 Jonesport, Maine
> + 2038. JOHN   born 3 Nov 1863 Columbia Falls, ME; married Flora R. I. BUTLER 6 July 1886
>   FRANKLIN   (she born 29 Dec 1868, MN; died 22 Sep 1958 Calais, ME)
>   died 26 Jan 1917 Calais, Washington Co., Maine
> + 2039. ASA MERRILL   born 4 Apr 1865 Columbia Falls; married Sarah J-10 WORCESTER 1 Jan 1893
>   died 5 Aug 1926 Columbia Falls, Maine
> + 2040. ELIZA ANN   born May 1869; married Ransom Nash BUTLER 19 Aug 1891 (bro/o Flora)
>   2041. Charles G.   born ca 1871 Bucks Harbor, ME; died ca 1889 (age 18)
> + 2042. WM. HENRY   born 28 Mar 1873; married Delilah-10 WORCESTER 7 May 1907
>   2043. Elizabeth E.   born 12 May 1874; married John H. CONNERS 17 Oct 1894; died 16 Jan 1898
>   2044. Grace E.   born 14 Sept 1878; married John H. CONNERS 22 Jan 1900

1340. MARY ELIZABETH-8 WILSON, daughter of Aphphatha-7 NASH (Mary-6 DRISKO; Samuel G-5; Joseph-4; John-3; 2) and Wilmot WILSON, was born 24 Dec 1823 at Machias, ME. She married 1st to Captain Joseph LORING on 4 Apr 1841 at Addison, ME. He was born ?; died ca 1852, lost at sea. They had one son, Joseph-9 LORING, Jr. (# 2045), born ca 1848, ME; died 1852, NY. Her 2nd marriage was to Captain Gilman COLSON. He was the son of Mary-5 COLSON (William-4) and was born 16 Mar 1813 at Addison, ME; died 17 May 1879 at Somerville, MA. Mary E-8 WILSON died 15 Oct 1905 at Columbia Falls, Maine.

Child of Mary E-8 WILSON and Captain Gilman COLSON:
>   Surname COLSON
> + 2046. GILMAN (Jr.)   born Apr 1858, ME; married Emma __?__ ca 1885/86
> + 2047. MARY   born 11 Aug 1865 Lexington, MA; died 9 Dec 1951
>   AUGUSTA   married Edward Bissell CURTIS 31 Dec 1885 Somerville, MA
>   (he born 20 Feb 1853 Machias, ME; died 14 Apr 1927 Machias)

1341. MARIA-8 WILSON, sister of above, was born 4 Mar 1826 at Machias, Maine. She married Eri Hathaway-8 SMITH on 20 Nov 1846 at Columbia, ME. He was the son of Ebenezer-7 SMITH and Deborah FARNSWORTH, and was born 24 May 1825 at Columbia; died there 19 June 1903. Maria-8 WILSON died 8 June 1876.

Children of Maria-8 WILSON and Eri Hathaway-8 SMITH:
>   Surname SMITH   + 2048. WINFIELD SCOTT born 20 Sept 1848 Columbia, Maine
>   married Matilda Alvenia-5 JORDAN 6 Sept/Dec 1873
>   (she dau/o Ebenezer-4 JORDAN and Harriet R. YOUNG) (she born Dec 1852; died 29 Jan 1909)

Children of Maria-8 WILSON, continued:
  Surname SMITH   (children born Columbia, Maine)
  2049. Anna   born Mar 1850; married Julius E. WHITE; died ca 1926
  2050. Winslow M.   born 1852; 1m. Evelyn S. WHITE 24 July 1872; 2m. Jennie __?__
  2051. Philena B.   born Dec 1856; married John W. CHANDLER ca 1877

1345. RUFUS WADSWORTH-8 WASS, son of Rebecca Allen-7 NASH (Mary-6 DRISKO; Samuel Gatchell-5; Joseph-4; John-3; 2) and Daniel Sawyer-6 WASS, was born 17 Aug 1820 at Addison, ME. He married Mary Adams GULLIVER on 15 Aug 1846 at Boston, MA. She was the daughter of _____ GULLIVER, and was born 5 Mar 1831, MA.; died 21 Oct 1890 at Grundy Center, Iowa. Rufus-8 WASS died 7 Aug 1900 at Beresford, South Dakota.

Children of Rufus-8 WASS and Mary A. GULLIVER:
  Surname WASS
+ 2052. GEORGE FRANCIS born 23 Jan 1849; MA; married Emma C. WEGESTEIN 7 Mar 1882, IA
  2053. Louise Hinckley   born 3 Dec 1850 Addison, ME; married John R. CARLETON 15 May 1877, IA
  2054. Idolette D.   born 7 Feb 1852; married Harlow W. HIGHLEY
+ 2055. JOHN NICHOLS born 6 Mar 1854 Addison; married Harriet _?_ Garwood 26 July 1892, SD
  2056. Daniel S.   born Apr 1855; died young
  2057. Lester L.   born 7 Mar 1858, Iowa; died Dec 1864 Iowa
+ 2058. VICTOR CURTIS born 14 Oct 1864 Hudson, IA; married May STEVENS; died 19 Jun 1948,MN.

1351. HOLMES NASH-8 WASS, brother of above, was born 10 Jan 1832 at Addison, Maine. He married first to Arathusa Louise-7 WILSON on 15 Nov 1853 at Machias, Washington County, Maine. She was the daughter of David Gardner-6 WILSON and Lydia-6 LONGFELLOW, and was born ca Nov 1833; died of pneumonia on 10 Dec 1864 at Eldora, Iowa. His second wife was Mary Elizabeth McLAURY Burnison of Iowa. She was a widow, and had one daughter from a previous marriage.

Children of Holmes-8 WASS and Arathusa-7 WILSON:
  Surname WASS
  2059. Louisa H.   born 28 Nov 1854 Machias, ME; died 1920
                          married John G. ROBERTSON 4 Jan 1876, IA
  2060. Lydia J.   born 1856/57, Iowa; married C. H. FAY
  2061. Helen L.   born 24 May 1859 Belle Plaine, Iowa; married George G. WALKER (a cousin)
        (he son/o Charles H. WALKER and Rebecca-7 WASS) (he born 1849 Addison, ME; died ____)
  2062. Edward   born ca 1861, Iowa; died 1864
Child of Holmes-8 WASS and Mary Elizabeth McLAURY :
  Surname WASS
  2063. Arathusa Leone   born 6 Sept 1870, IA; married James B. PEDELTY 19 Oct 1893; died 1958 IA

1352. NAPOLEON BONAPARTE-8 WASS, brother of above, was born 8 Dec 1834 at Addison, ME. He married Julia _?_ before 1865. She was born ca 1847; died 14 Apr 1871. Napoleon-8 WASS died 5 Sept 1902 at Los Angeles, CA.

Children of Napoleon-8 WASS and Julia __?__:
  Surname WASS
  2064. Harriet   born ca 1865; married __?__ HUSE   2066. dau born ca 1868; marr ? MacCLAY
  2065. George   born ca 1866; died ____ unmarried   2067. Nellie born 2 Mar 1870; dy

1369. HENRY W-8 ALLINE, son of Mary-7 NASH (Mary-6 DRISKO; Samuel Gatchell-5; Joseph-4; John-3; 2) and John Lowell-5 ALLINE, was born ca 1828 at Steuben, Maine. He married first to Sarah S. KELLER on 13 Jan 1858. She was the daughter of John KELLER and Susan ?, and was born ca 1831 at East Machias, Maine; died 18 July 1880 at Remsen, Iowa. He married second to Maria E. EMMETT ca 1883. She was born Oct 1839, Canada; died 19__. Henry-8 ALLINE died 25 Sept 1905.

Children of Henry-8 ALLINE and Sarah S. KELLER:
    Surname ALLINE
+ 2068. EMMA KELLER born ca 1859; died after 1905 IA/CO
                      married John Hezekiah WINCHELL ca 1883
  2069. Mary Frances   born ca 1860 East Machias; married Andrew C. MORGAN; died 11 Apr 1933
  2070. Josiah Keller   born ca 1862; died after 1905
  2071. Anna Lowell   born ca 1864; married Wilton BROWN; died 15 Dec 1934 Ottumwa, Iowa
  2072. Charles F.   born 1865; died after 1905

1378. JOSEPHINE HALL-8 LONGFELLOW, daughter of Mercy-7 DRISKO (Edmund-6; Samuel Gatchell-5; Joseph-4; John-3; 2) and George Handy-6 LONGFELLOW, was born ca 1837/38 at Machias, Maine. She married Captain Warren-8 WASS, as his 2nd wife, on 15 Aug 1863 at Addison, Maine. He was the son of Henry-7 WASS and Susanna BROWN, and was born 11 Feb 1821; died ____. He was a sea captain at Addison, Maine, and was the master of the *NELLIE CHAPIN* which took the Adams Colony to Jaffa, Palestine. Josephine Hall-8 LONGFELLOW died 20 Apr 1918 at Somerville, MA.

Children of Josephine-8 LONGFELLOW and Captain Warren WASS:
    Surname WASS
  2073. Handy   born 18__; married Sarah PRATT
  2074. James   born 18__;
  2075. Cora   born 18__; married Edwin Haschal ANSELL ca 1890; resided MA.
    (he son/o William H. ANSELL/ Hannah WESTON)(he born 24 Apr 1861 Sherbrooke, QE, Canada)
  2076. Alice   born 18__; married William CLOUTMAN

1385. ARTHUR H-8 ALLINE, son of Louisa-7 CORTHELL (Jerusha-6 DRISKO; Samuel Gatchell-5; Joseph-4; John-3; 2) and William P-5 ALLINE, was born 11 Aug 1847 at Harrington, Maine. He married Alice A. GARNETT before 1869. She was the daughter of Bela GARNETT and Mary WILLEY, and was born 19 Feb 1851; died 8 Aug 1909. Arthur-8 ALLINE died 23 Apr 1893 at Harrington, Maine.

Children of Arthur-8 ALLINE and Alice GARNETT:
    Surname ALLINE   (children born Harrington, Maine)
  2077. Sidney   born Apr 1869; died ____ a sailor
  2078. Lizzie E.   born 24 Sept 1880; died 16 Oct 1909 Columbia, ME.
                    married Eugene KELLEY 22 July 1899 Harrington, Maine

1405. CAPTAIN EUGENE AMOS-8 COFFIN, son of Amos-7 COFFIN (Rebecca-6 DRISKO; Samuel Gatchell-5; Joseph-4; John-3; 2) and Irene MITCHELL, was born July 1853 at Harrington, Maine. he married Malintha J-9 LOOK on 18 May 1872 at Harrington. She was the daughter of Levi T-8 LOOK and Delia WHITE, and was born Apr 1855; died ____. They were divorced before 1897. He married second to Mary Ann FLAGG Kent on 22 Jan 1898. Eugene Amos-8 COFFIN died 19__.

Children of Captain Eugene Amos-8 COFFIN and Malintha-9 LOOK:
    Surname COFFIN
  2079. Myra W.   born 1873; married Charles Eben WHITE 2 Mar 1892 Harrington, ME
  2080. Eugene   born 1875
+ 2081. HARLAND   born 29 Nov 1876; died Apr 1966 Steuben, Maine
                    married Emma WARD (she born 1883; died ____)
  2082. Amos   born 1877; married Della M. WARD 14 Jan 1893 Harrington, ME (she born 1879)

1409. JOHN BARTLETT-8 COFFIN, son of Uriah Nash-7 COFFIN (Rebecca-6 DRISKO; Samuel Gatchell-5; Joseph-4; John-3; 2) and Catherine COLSON, was born ca 1863 at Harrington, Maine. He married Effie Cora RANDALL on 12 Nov 1885 at Portland, Maine. She was the daughter of Abner RANDALL and Margaret-6 NASH, and was born ca 1862 Harrington, ME; died 1926. John Bartlett-8 COFFIN died 30 June 1926 at Winthrop, MA.

Child of John B-8 COFFIN and Effie Cora RANDALL:
    Surname COFFIN
2083. Hazel born 1890; married Marshall Thomas ATWOOD; died 1970 (he born 1888; died 1968)

1414. URIAH NASH-8 COFFIN, JR., brother of above, was born June 1879 at Harrington, Maine. He married Annie Louise PILLSBURY Talbot on 5 June 1901 at Boston, MA. She was the daughter of _?_ PILLSBURY and ? RICHARDS, and was born 15 Nov 1882, Portland, ME; died 30 June 1966. She was adopted by her aunt Carrie RICHARDS Talbot, and used that name. Uriah-8 died 13 Oct 1946, MA.

Children of Uriah Nash-8 COFFIN, Jr. and Annie Louise TALBOT:
    Surname COFFIN
2084. Beryl Elspeth   born 12 May 1903; died 31 Dec 1987 Melrose, MA
        married Warner Whitman WAYNE (he born 8 Oct 1893; died Aug 1966 Melrose, MA)
2085. Carrie Eva   born 1906; married James E. DUCROW
        (he born 17 Dec 1905; died Apr 1969 Melrose, MA)

1430. GERTRUDE B-8 DRISKO, daughter of Charles A-7 DRISKO (Samuel Gatchell-6; 5; Joseph-4; John-3; 2) and Theodocia-8 DRISKO (Zimri-7; Josiah-6; Joseph-5;4; John-3; 2), and was born ca 1870. She never married, but had one son who went by the name DRISKO. She died ca 1925.

Child of Gertrude B-8 DRISKO and __?__ :
    Surname DRISKO
2086. Harry M.   born Dec 1888; died before 1925 (Note: Harry was raised by Hollis J. LEIGHTON)
    married Edith I. FOLSOM ca 19__ ; (she dau/o William FOLSOM and Eunice PARNELL)
      (she born 26 Nov 1892, MA; died I Jan 1951)(she 2m. Wentworth LEIGHTON)

1445. WILLIAM HENRY-8 LIBBY, son of George-7 LIBBY (Mary-6 McKENNEY; Moses-5; Elizabeth-4 DRISKO; John-3;2) and Sally FOSS, was born Apr 1825. He married Lydia S. TYLER. She was the daughter of Abraham TYLER and Eunice SEAVEY, and was born ___. William Henry-8 LIBBY died 30 Jan 1862. Lydia married 2nd to George E. JOHNSON 18 Feb 1868.

Children of William Henry-8 LIBBY and Lydia TYLER:
    Surname LIBBY
2087. George   born 18 June 1849; died 3 Nov 1851
2088. Sarah Ann   born 29 July 1850; died 25 Oct 1851
2089. Georgianna   born 29 Mar 1852; married Albert ROBINSON
2090. Sally   born 19 Nov 1854; married Robert GRAFFAM 12 Mar 1873
2091. Eunice Buzzell   born 16 Mar 1861

1449. JOSEPH WHITE-8 LIBBY, son of Moses-7 LIBBY (Mary-6 McKENNEY; Moses-5; Elizabeth-4 DRISKO; John-3; 2) and Fannie SEAVEY, was born 27 Jan 1836. He married Marie Louise BLOUIN ca 18__. She was the daughter of Leon BLOUIN and Lizzie _?_ of New Orleans, LA.

Children of Joseph White-8 LIBBY and Mary Louise BLOUIN:
    Surname LIBBY   2092. Fanny Edith   born 4 Sept 1878

1458. ADDIE M-8 LIBBY, daughter of Susan-7 LIBBY (Betsey-6 McKENNEY; Moses-5; Elizabeth-4 DRISKO; John-3; 2) and Dennis LIBBY, was born 18 Feb 1850. She married Estus/Estes A. MORRILL on 4 May 1869, ME. He was the son of _?_ MORRILL of Charlestown, MA; and was born ca 1845.

Children of Addie-8 LIBBY and Estus MORRILL:
    Surname MORRILL
2093. Maude L. born 7 Oct 1870; died 1872 2095. Ethel M. born 8 Sept 1875, Charlestown
2094. Vernon H. born 4 Jan 1873   2096. Charles Sumner born 28 May 1880; died Nov 1963

1466. WILLIAM T-8 LIBBY, son of Jonathan-7 LIBBY (Luke-6; Dorothy-5 McKENNEY; Elizabeth-4 DRISKO; John-3; 2) and Mary JORDAN, was born 8 Aug 1828 at Danville, Maine. He married Elizabeth HARRIMAN ca July 1851. She was the daughter of Charles HARRIMAN ++ and Betsey W. BURBANK, and was born ca 183_ at Chatham, NH; died ____. William T-8 LIBBY died ____.

William T-8 LIBBY went to Boston, MA. when he was about 22 years of age. He worked as a clerk/salesman in several dry goods stores. He returned to Auburn, Maine in 1868.

Children of William T-8 LIBBY and Elizabeth HARRIMAN:
    Surname LIBBY
    2097. Eva   born 21 Aug 1860 Boston, Suffolk Co., MA
    2098. Gertrude A.   born 19 Oct 1864 Boston , MA
    2099. Justin F.   born 4 Nov 1867 Boston, MA

++ Charles-5 HARRIMAN, was the son of Amos-4 HARRIMAN (Joshua-3; Matthew-2) and Nancy ?, and was born 5 July 1789 at Chatham, New Hampshire. He married Betsey W. BURBANK 21 July 1815 at Conway, NH. She was born 24 July 1795 at Boscawen Township, NH

Model of a two-masted Schooner
Made by George Dolbey-10 DRISKO

Part of National Ocean Service Map # 13326
Showing DRISKO ISLAND and LITTLE DRISKO ISLAND (lower left of map)
Off the coast of Maine - in the Western Bay - West of GREAT WASS ISLAND

The Ninth American Generation

1485. LESLIE ALFRED-9 RICKER, son of Alfred Leslie-8 RICKER (Elijah-7; 6; Sobriety-5 NOCK; Samuel-4; Sarah-3 DRISKO; John-2) and Mary E. WILLARD, was born 11 Oct 1905 at Reading, MA. He married Natalie Ann TRUE on 1 June 1930 at Winslow, Maine. She was the daughter of Samuel TRUE and Caroline Elizabeth MOORE, and was born 28 July 1907 at Clinton, Maine; died 8 Jan 1986 at Pine Bluff, North Carolina. Leslie-9 RICKER died 19 July 1967 at Lewiston, Maine.

Children of Leslie-9 RICKER and Natalie TRUE:
   Surname RICKER
   2100. John Merrill   born 2 Mar 1931 Carmel, Maine
   2101. Norman Edward   born 31 July 1933 Waterville, ME; married Carole F. COOPER 3 June 1956
   2102. James Malcolm   born 12 Mar 1935; died 9 Apr 1935
   2103. Merle Ellen   born 6 Dec 1936; died next day
   2104. Maetta Rose   born 31 Jan 1941 No. Vassalboro, ME.; marr Ronald H. SAWYER 1 Oct 1960
   2105. Timothy Lee   born 7 Apr 1948 Northbridge, MA.

1536. WILLIAM WOOSTER-9 RICKER, son of William Lord-8 RICKER (Ezekiel-7; Jedediah-6; Dorothy-5 NOCK; Samuel-4; Sarah-3 DRISKO; John-2) and Sarah FRENCH, was born 6 Aug 1869 at Somersworth, NH. He married Mrs. Gertrude M. FISHER Tuttle on 30 May 1897 at Gardner, MA. She was the daughter of Charles FISHER and Harriet ATWOOD, and was born 18__; died 1 May 1945 at Worcester, MA. William W-9 RICKER died there 12 Nov 1949.

Children of William W-9 RICKER and Gertrude FISHER:
   Surname RICKER   (children born Worcester, MA)
   2106. Frederick William born 1 Feb 1899; married Jessie FORTUNE; died May 1979, MA
       (she dau/o Angus FORTUNE and Margaret MacINNES; born 5 Aug 1898 Glace Bay, N S)
            One child: Jessica Marcia RICKER born 31 May/July 1933 Worcester, MA
   2107. Dorothy G.   born 23 Sept 1901
   2108. Ruth Lillian   born 7 June 1907; died Jan 1974, MA
                            married Willis Whittemore CURRY 8 Mar 1929
       (he son/o John K. CURRY and Bertha SAUNDERS ; born 4 Oct 1905; died Oct 1982, MA)

1557. CAROLINE AGNES-9 RICKER, daughter of Daniel Larrabee-8 RICKER (Daniel-7; Elias-6; Lucy-5 CROMWELL; Esther-4 NOCK; Sarah-3 DRISKO; John-2) and Elizabeth O'CONNOR, was born 19 May 1887 at Willow Point, Texas. She married Jesse Crockett WORTHINGTON on 30 Dec 1912 at Willow Point. He was the son of Nicholas Crockett WORTHINGTON and Sarah Jane WHITLOCK, and was born 28 May 1883, TX; died July 1957.

Children of Caroline Agnes-9 RICKER and Jesse WORTHINGTON:
   Surname WORTHINGTON   (children born Oklahoma City, Oklahoma)
   2109. Jessie Bernice   born 28 Aug 1916; married Arthur William PINDAR 22 Feb 1941
   2110. Olga Helen   born 22 Jan 1918; married George C. HUPP 27 June 1942
   2111. Merle Frances   born 8 Mar 1924; married Donald Roy LARKIN 24 Aug 1944
   2112. Dorothy Agnes   born 22 Dec 1925

1558. HAZEL FRANCES-9 RICKER, sister of above, was born 3 Oct 1891 at Willow Point, Texas. She married first to James A. BLOCKER ca 1907. Her second marriage was to Julian MONTANA before 1909, and her 3rd marriage was to Ira J. KINNEY.

Child of Hazel F-9 RICKER and James BLOCKER:
   Surname BLOCKER
   2113. James A. (Jr.)   born 17 June 1908 Fort Worth, TX; died June 1973, CA.
                            married Bessie Lee RAPPORT

Children of Hazel F-9 RICKER and Julian MONTANA:
    Surname MONTANA
    2114. Julian J., Jr.   born 26 Sept 1909 Fort Worth, TX; died 19 May 1996, CA.
                     married Ruth VAN EPPO 26 Aug 1929 (she born 4 Nov 1909; died 30 May 1996)
    2115. Amelia E.   born 28 Mar 1912 Oklahoma City, OK; died May 1974, CA
                     married A. James LOPEZ 10 June 1933
    2116. Cecil F.   born 22 Oct 1913 Oklahoma City, OK
    2117. Vincent R.   born 17 Nov 1915 Oklahoma City; married Cicely KELLEY 30 Dec 1947
    2118. Maurice G.   born 25 May 1918 Oklahoma City, OK; died Apr 1970, CA.
                     married Helen ROBBY 6 Aug 1938

1560. NATHALIE HELEN-9 RICKER, sister of above, was born 22 July 1897 at Willow Point, Texas. She married Leo Joseph STILL ca 1928. He was the son of Mathias STILL and Frances PRING, and was born 16 Feb 1897 at Atchison, KS., died Feb 1963, CA. She died 24 Nov 1996 San Diego, CA.

Children of Nathalie-9 RICKER and Leo J. STILL:
    Surname STILL   2119. Leo Joseph, Jr. born 17 Apr 1929 San Diego, CA
    2120. Frances Helen   born 15 Feb 1930 Pasadena, CA   2121. Raymond A. born 2 July 1933 Atchison

1561. DANIEL L-9 RICKER, brother of above, was born 28 Dec 1898 at Willow Point, Texas. He married Eugenia Elizabeth McENTIRE on 31 Aug 1930 at Bridgeport, Texas. She was the daughter of A. M. McENTIRE and Mollie PRESCOTT; born 6 Dec 1900; died Aug 1975, TX. He died Feb 1973, TX

Children of Daniel L-9 RICKER and Eugenia McENTIRE:
    Surname RICKER
    2122. Anna Marie   born 17 Oct 1933 Bridgeport, TX   2124. Larry Gene   born 14 Nov 1937
    2123. April Agnes   born 9 Dec 1935 Bridgeport, TX

1574. GENEVA HELEN-9 GRANT, daughter of Jennie Phoebe-8 RICKER (Simon-7; Daniel-6; Lucy-5 CROMWELL; Esther-4 NOCK; Sarah-3 DRISKO; John-2) and Joseph GRANT, was born 22 Apr 1865. She married Alton K. WENTWORTH on 30 Nov 1884 at Ripley, Maine. He was the son of William WENTWORTH, and was born 18__; died 19__. They resided at Albion, Maine in 1914.

Children of Geneva Helen-9 GRANT and Alton WENTWORTH:
    Surname WENTWORTH   (children born Albion, Maine)
    2125. John K.   born 23 Oct 1886; d. Dec 1977, ME   2127. Helen G.   born 18 Oct 1890
    2126. Hilda E.   born 19 Jan 1888; d. Nov 1969, MA 2128. Sydney D.   born 29 Dec 1897
                     marr Weston L. AMES 29 June 1913 Albion, Maine

1616. WHITFIELD W-9 RICKER, son of Maturin Morse-8 RICKER (William-7; Captain Ebenezer-6; Nathaniel-5; Mercy-4 NOCK; Sarah-3 DRISKO; John-2) and Alfaretta ROBERTS, was born ca 1883 at Gloucester, MA. He married Sarah E. CURRAN on 4 Feb 1910 at Malden, MA. She was the daughter of Robert CURRAN and Bridget McKANE, and was born 18__; died 31 July 1927 at Malden, MA. Whitfield-9 RICKER, a shipper, died 26 July 1946 at Malden, MA.

Children of Whitfield-9 RICKER and Sarah CURRAN:
    Surname RICKER   (children born Malden, MA)
    2129. Whitfield W., Jr. born 4 July 1910   2131. son   born 4 Feb 1912
                     died Aug 1910   2132. Alice Gertrude born 23 May 1914
    2130. Frances Mary   born 4 July 1910   2133. Robert Maturin born 5 Nov 1915

1618. OSBORNE F-9 RICKER, brother of above, was born 12 Nov 1886 at Gloucester, MA. He married Margaret Mc NEIL on 12 Nov 1910 at Malden, MA. She was the daughter of Neil Mc NEIL and Sarah IRVING, and was born ca 1891 at Sydney, NS; died 19__. Osborne-9 died 3 Aug 1949 at Melrose, MA.

Children of Osborne-9 RICKER and Margaret Mc NEIL:
    Surname RICKER   (children born at Melrose, MA)
    2134. Osborne F.,Jr.   born 19 Nov 1911   2137. Lawrence Herbert   born 5 May 1917
    2135. Bernard Theodore born 29 Jan 1913; d. Feb 1968   died 14 Apr 1996, NH
    2136. Edward Robert   born 19 Aug 1915; d. Oct 1980   2138. Unnamed twins born/died 26 Mar 1923

1636. VIOLA HELEN-9 RICKER, daughter of Giles-8 RICKER (Benjamin-7; 6; Nathaniel-5; Mercy-4 NOCK; Sarah-3 DRISKO; John-2) and Ella GULLIVER, was born 29 Nov 1902 at Marlboro, MA. She married Carl Douglas PHIPPS on 19 Mar 1933 at Hudson, MA. He was the son of John H. PHIPPS and Florence G. HILL; and was born 14 May 1900; died 1916 Nov 1999. Viola-9 RICKER died 15 Sept 1990.

Children of Viola-9 RICKER and Carl PHIPPS:
    Surname PHIPPS
    2139. Janet Ellen   born 7 Jan 1939   2141. Douglas Henry   born 22 Jan 1943
    2140. Nancy Ella   born 3 June 1941

1638. RUBY EDITH-9 RICKER, sister of above, was born 9 Aug 1908 at Hudson, MA. She married Patrick Joseph MURPHY on 19 Feb 1939 at Hudson, MA. He was the son of Dennis MURPHY and Bridget HARRINGTON, and was born 7 Aug 1890; died 8 May 1968. He was a police officer in Cambridge, MA. Ruby Edith-9 died 28 July 1995 Cambridge, MA.

Children of Ruby Edith-9 RICKER and Patrick MURPHY:
    Surname MURPHY
    2142. George Richard   born 15 Jan 1942   2144. Patricia Eileen   born 16 Dec 1949
    2143. David James   born 17 Jan 1945

1641. RICHARD WALTER-9 RICKER, brother of above, was born 12 Sept 1915 at Hudson, MA. He married Isabelle Burnham KING on 21 June 1946 at Brunswick, Maine. She was the daughter of Arthur W. KING and Marian E. PUSHARD, and was born 17 June 1921.

Children of Richard-9 RICKER and Isabelle KING:
    Surname RICKER
    2145. Karen Ella   born 23 Mar 1949   2146. Richard W., Jr.   born 13 Sept 1951

1682. WALDO BENTLEY-9 DRISKO, son of Judah Johnson-8 DRISKO,2nd (William Johnson-7; Judah-6; John-5; Joseph-4; John-3; 2) and Miranda SANBORN, was born 22 June 1857 at Addison, Maine. He married Jennie Gertrude BURNHAM on 11 Nov 1879 at Worcester, MA. She was the daughter of __?__ BURNHAM and was born 8 June 1861 at Worcester; died 19__. Waldo-9 DRISKO died 19__.

Children of Waldo Bentley-9 DRISKO and Jennie BURNHAM:
    Surname DRISKO
    + 2147. THEODORE   born 7 Apr 1880 Worcester, MA; married Bertha HOWES
            BENTLEY   (she born 9 Mar 1883, IL; died May 1975 Havana, Mason County, IL)
    + 2148. EUGENE   born 13 June 1882 Worcester; 1m. Pearl BROUGHTEN (she from Abilene, KS
            SANBORN   2m. Betty SMITH (she from Topeka, KS)
    2149. Judah Johnson   born 14 Oct 1884 Abilene, KS; married Molly McCLURE of Topeka, KS
                             died Oct 1964 Tulsa, OK   EOL
    2150. Mae Burnham   born 12 Mar 1889 Abilene, KS; married Hollis J. JONES (he of Topeka, KS)
    + 2151. PHILIP   born 5 Feb 1891 Abilene; married Blanche HENDERSON
            JOSLYN   **   (she born 1 Sept 1904, Independence, MO; died Sept 1981 Odessa, TX)
    2152. Waldo Edwin **   born 2 Feb 1893 Abilene; died ___ unmarried   EOL
    2153. Marion Louise   born 24 July 1897 Abilene; married Harris James ELDER of Bartlesville, OK
    + 2154. CHARLES   born 8 Nov 1900 Abilene; married Lela Esper SEARS
            LYMAN   died Aug 1987 Bartlesville, Washington County, Oklahoma

** # 2151 and 2152 are mentioned in " The Oklahoma Spirit of '17 " , a biographical volume, compiled by W E WELCH, J S ALDRIDGE, and L V ALDRIDGE , pub 1920. It lists the Oklahoma soldiers of **WW I.** Philip J. DRISKO, was a sailor; his brother served in the Army as a Private. They were both from Bartlesville, Washington County, Oklahoma.

1683. MARY FRANKLAND-9 DRISKO, daughter of Judah Johnson-8 DRISKO (William Johnson-7; Judah-6; John-5; Joseph-4; John-3; 2) and Miranda SANBORN, was born 5 Feb 1861 at Machiasport, Washington County, Maine. She married the Rev Francis Arthur SANBORN on 24 Dec 1884. He was the son of Cyrus P. SANBORN and Helen Jane SANBORN, and was born 19 Dec 1860; died 26 July 1933. Francis Arthur SANBORN was a minister at Turner, Maine and at Wilton and Gloucester, MA. After retiring he removed to Worcester, MA. Mary Frankland-9 DRISKO died 10 Feb 1931 at Topsfield, MA.

Child of Mary Frankland-9 DRISKO and Rev Francis Arthur SANBORN:
    Surname SANBORN
+ 2155. HELEN   born 31 Dec 1888 Machiasport, ME
              FRANKLAND married Eleazer CARVER II 15 June 1911 Salem, NH
(he son/o Eleazer CARVER I and Marcella A. TIBBETTS; born 8 Dec 1885 Milo, ME; died 6 Dec 1966)

1685. MARTHA H-9 SHUTE   see   FRED M-9 DRISKO (below) # 1688
1688. FRED M-9 DRISKO, son of Francis Marion-8 DRISKO (Caleb Haskell-7; Judah-6; John-5; Joseph-4; John-3; 2) and Alice WASS, was born 18 May 1870 at Harrington, Maine. He married his cousin, Mrs. MARTHA H-9 (Mattie) SHUTE White (# 1685 above) ca 1900. She was the daughter of Benjamin A. SHUTE and Sophia S-8 DRISKO (Caleb H-7; Judah-6; John-5; Joseph-4; John-3; 2) and was born 187_; died 19__. She was married first to __?__ WHITE and had a son, Stanwood WHITE ++, who was adopted by Fred-9 DRISKO.   Fred-9 DRISKO died 24 Aug 1934.

Child of Fred-9 DRISKO and Martha-9 SHUTE (White):
    Surname DRISKO
2156. Paul Humphrey   born 3 Aug 1901; married Mildred E. NOBLE of Ft. Kent, ME. On 5 Aug 1929
                         died Mar 1977 South Yarmouth, MA (res Norwalk, CT.)
              One child: Paul Humphrey-11 DRISKO, Jr. born 4 Mar 1932; died 27 Dec 1999, MA)
    ++ Stanwood WHITE Drisko was born 9 Aug 1890; married Gladys HAMMOND; died 29 Dec 1924

1694.   PALMER L.-9 DRISCO Cole, son of Levi Wass-8 DRISCO (John Jeremiah-7; Judah-6; John-5; Joseph-4; John-3; 2) and Emma PALMER, was born 1 Jan 1877 at South Bend, Indiana. His mother died 6 days after his birth (7 Jan 1877) from complications of childbirth. As a baby he was cared for by, Martin COLE and his wife Eliza, friends of the DRISCO family. Soon after the death of his mother, Palmers' father, Levi-8 DRISCO, went to Chicago, Illinois, leaving his infant son with the COLE family. Levi-8 married second ca 1879, and had more children, but never sent for Palmer.

Shortly before his marriage, Palmer-9 DRISCO had his name legally changed to COLE – honoring the couple who raised him. Palmer-9 DRISCO Cole married Myrtle ALLEN on 20 June 1899 at South Bend, Indiana. She was the daughter of Wilbur R. ALLEN and Cynthia E. WARREN, and was born 29 Apr 1879 at White Pigeon, Michigan; died 14 Oct 1960 at South Bend, IN. Palmer-9 died Feb 1966 at South Bend.

Children of Palmer-9 DRISCO Cole and Myrtle ALLEN:
    Surname COLE
2157. Allen   born ca 1901; died 1902   EOL
+ 2158. BRADFORD   born 11 July 1906 South Bend, IN; died Nov 1981 South Bend
    DRISCO   married Arlene ESCH 26 Oct 1929
              (she dau/o Edward ESCH and Edith IRELAND; she born 31 Oct 1907; died 8 Apr 1998)
2159. Cynthia Jane   born 2 Aug 1909; married James C. GILLIS; died Oct 1978 So. Bend
                       (he born 29 Jan 1908; died Feb 1979 South Bend, IN)
2160. Palmer D., Jr.   born 25 May 1913; married Avis Joan HALL

1695. LEVI WASS-9 DRISCO, half brother of above, son of Levi-8 DRISCO and his 2nd wife Sarah J. KAISER, was born 28 Aug 1880 at Chicago, Illinois. He married Helen V. RAY of Brooklyn, New York. She was the daughter of __?__ RAY, and was born 18__; died 19__. Levi Wass-9 DRISCO was a retired Naval officer in 1935, and died ca 19__.

Children of Levi Wass-9 DRISCO and Helen V. RAY:
    Surname DRISCO
2161. Lee James   born 10 Feb 1919, NY; died Mar 1977 Rocky Point, Suffolk County, NY
2162. Mary Carolyn   born ca 19__

1696. CADDIE PRESENT-9 DRISCO, sister of above, was born 2 Dec 1884 at Chicago, Illinois. She married Ben O. BROWN ca 19__. He was the son of __?__ BROWN and was born ca 18__; died ____. Caddie Present-9 DRISCO died 19__.

Child of Caddie Present-9 DRISCO and Ben BROWN:
    Surname BROWN
2163. Jane   born 19__; married Norman LARSEN 1 Aug 1934

1698. LEVI BERT-9 DRISKO, son of Burt William-8 DRISKO (John Jeremiah-7; Judah-6; John-5; Joseph-4; John-3; 2) and Ada DILL, was born 30 June 1893 at Gardiner, Maine. He married Addie L. HAMILTON on 18 May 1912. She was the daughter of ____ HAMILTON and was born ca 189_; died 20 Feb 1970. They resided Gardiner, Maine, where Levi Bert-9 died on 25 Dec 1967.

Children of Levi Bert-9 DRISKO and Addie HAMILTON:
    Surname DRISKO   (children all born Gardiner, Maine)
+ 2164. OLIVER   born 22 Aug 1915; married Maybelle F. BAKER 20 Apr 1935
      CARROLL   (she born 23 Mar 1914; died 28 Oct 1989 Bath, ME)
      REED   died 12 Oct 1992 Bath, Maine
+ 2165. HARRY LEE   born 16 Sept 1918, ME; married Beulah M. BAKER 9 July 1938
                died 31 July 1995 Gardiner, Maine
+ 2166. GEORGIANNA born ca 19__; 1m. Roy G. GREEN 13 Mar 1954 ; 2m. __?__

1699. EARL WINFIELD-9 DRISKO, brother of above, was born 21 Apr 1900 at Gardiner, Maine. He married Sarah B. GOODWIN on 25 Nov 1918. She was the daughter of __?__ GOODWIN, and was born 6 Mar 1898; died Apr 1969 at Gardiner, Maine. Earl W-9 DRISKO died 29 Aug 1967.

Children of Earl W-9 DRISKO and Sarah GOODWIN:
    Surname DRISKO
2167. Bert W.   born 9 Feb 1922, ME; married Dorothy THORNE; died 14 Jan 1986
2168. Kenneth Earl   born 17 June 1926, ME; died 17 May 1991, CA.
2169. Thelma Isabel   born 15 July 1927; married Edward Frank BOUDWAY; died Sept 1998 FL
2170. Ruth Esther   born 19__; 1m. Harry STONIER, Jr. 15 June 1951 ; 2m. Ronald GERARD

1707. KING HIRAM-9 LEE, son of Willard Malcolm-8 LEE (Mary Anne-7 BUCKNAM; Abigail-6 DRISKO; John-5; Joseph-4; John-3; 2) and Emma BOGART/BOGERT, was born 7 June 1870 at Broderick, CA. He married Lilian Mae KING on 13 July 1899. King Hiram-9 LEE died 5 Mar 1948 at Sacramento, CA.

Children of King Hiram-9 LEE and Lilliam Mae KING:
    Surname LEE
2171. Rollin King   born 20 Feb 1901; died Dec 1967
2172. Flora   born ca 1903/04
+ 2173. CLINTON   born 26 Nov 1906 Sacramento, CA; died 20 Jan 1986 Bodega Bay, CA
      HIRAM   married Rhonda Alice ALDRICH

1741. EVELYN WILLARD-9 LOOK   see GEORGE BROWN-8 CARVER (# 1302)

1751. EDNA-9 TIBBETTS, daughter of Zephaniah-8 TIBBETTS (Jeremiah-7; Thomas-6: Elizabeth-5 DRISKO; Joseph-4; John-3;2) and Grace CURRIER, was born Feb 1856 at Columbia Falls, Maine. She married Maurice G. BLACK on 22 May 1920. He was born ca 1888; died 11 Oct 1978. Edna-9 TIBBETS died 17 Jan 1981 at Bangor, Maine.

Children of Edna-9 TIBBETTS and Maurice BLACK:
   Surname BLACK
   2174. Maurice G., Jr.   born ca 1921; died 8 July 1995
+ 2175. LLOYD EVAN   born 23 Mar 1924; died 23 Jan 2000
                        married Vivian E. KNOWLTON 21 Dec 1943

1753. GRACE KATHLEEN-9 TIBBETTS, sister of above, was born 24 June 1907 at Columbia Falls, Maine. She married Harris H. VAGUE on 29 Jan 1938 at Bangor, ME. He was born ca 1888; died 19 Dec 1980 at Bangor. Grace-9 TIBBETTS died 11 Mar 1992 at Bangor, and is buried at Maple Grove Cemetery .

Children of Grace K-9 TIBBETTS and Harris VAGUE:
   Surname VAGUE
   2176. Marilyn   born ca 19__; married James DeBERRY
   2177. Glenice/Glennice born ca 19__; married Merwin E. WELCH 1 Aug 1958

1754. ALLEN ZEPHANIAH-9 TIBBETTS, brother of above, was born 18 Mar 1909 at Columbia Falls, Maine. He married Mary Jane GRANT on _ Sept 1931 at Cherryfield, ME. She was the daughter of James Alden GRANT and Linnie Elizabeth WAKEFIELD; and was born 18 Feb 1913; died 7 July 1979 at Bangor, Maine. Allen Z-9 TIBBETTS died 20 Aug 1993 at Bangor, Maine.

Children of Allen Zephaniah-9 TIBBETTS and Mary Jane GRANT:
   Surname TIBBETTS
+ 2178. PHILLIP MONROE born 32 Mar 1932; died 21 June 1973 Orrington, ME
                        married Charlotte Emily KATEN 27 May 1951 Orrington
+ 2179. DENNIS A.   born ca 193_; married Sandra E. WILBUR 1 June 1960

1770. QUEEN B-9 WORCESTER   see JOSEPH WILLARD-10 DRISKO (# 2312)

1796. LOVEATUS PLUMMER-9 NORTON, son of Priscilla-9 DRISKO (John-7; Captain John-6; Joseph-5; 4; John-3; 2) and Captain Ackley Ezra NORTON, was born ca 1861 at Addison, ME. He married Mildred Christiana-9 LEIGHTON ca 1891, MI. She was the daughter of Langdon-8 LEIGHTON and Matilda-2 DRISCOLL/ DRISKO (Timothy-1) ++, and was born ca 1870; died 1924 Manistique, MI. Loveatus-9 NORTON died there ca 1932.   ++ (See unattached DRISKO families # 10, pages 213-14)

Children of Loveatus-9 NORTON and Mildred C-9 LEIGHTON:
   Surname NORTON

2180. Alton A.	born ____	2182. Alice	born ____
2181. Perry	born ____	2183. Ethel	born ____

1798. JULIA ELILLAS-9 DRISKO, daughter of George Alvin-8 DRISKO (John-7, Jr.; Captain John-6; Joseph-5; 4; John-3; 2) and Elizabeth C. SKINNER, was born 3 Feb 1855 at Addison, Maine. She married Norman Alexander EDDY on 3 Sept 1873, MI. He was the son of Ashael EDDY and Mary Ann DRINK-WATER, and was born 19 Aug 1848,Coburg, Ontario, Canada; died Nov 1917. Julia-9 died 20 Apr 1911.

Children of Julia-9 DRISKO and Norman EDDY:
   Surname EDDY   (1st 3 born St. Martin's Is., MI; others born Escanaba, Delta Co., MI)

2184. Mary Elizabeth	born 17 Oct 1874	2187. Lurenna Mildred born 6 July 1881
2185. Alvin Wellington	born 15 Feb 1877; d. 23 May 1951	(e). Clarence Norman born 22 Mar 1886
2186. Christina Bell	born 7 Feb 1879; d. 22 Mar 1936	(f). Emeline Varco born 1 Mar 1898

1816. ALTON V-9 ROGERS, son of Benjamin Kelley-8 ROGERS (Olive-7 DRISKO; Captain John-6; Joseph-5; 4; John-3; 2) and Lucy-8 LEIGHTON, was born 9 June 1867 at Jaffa, Palestine. He married 1st to JULIA A-9 SAWYER (# 1897) on 24 Sept 1890. She was the daughter of Eben J-8 SAWYER and Philena KELLEY, and was born June 1875. They divorced, and he married 2nd to Sara T-9 AUSTIN on 15 Nov 1902. She was the dau/o Junius Noble-8 AUSTIN and Elizabeth THOMPSON, and was born 20 Apr 1880; died 17 Aug 1944. Alton-9, a ship builder at Jonesport, ME, died 31 July 1957 at Ellsworth, ME.

Children of Alton V-9 ROGERS and Julia-9 SAWYER:
  Surname ROGERS
  2188. Harris B.   born 31 May 1893; died Feb 1973 Ellsworth, Maine
                           married Elsie E. MORRISON 18 Nov 1916 Ellsworth, ME
                           (she born 13 Oct 1896; died June 1978, CA)
  2189. Roland E.   born 4 Feb 1897; died Jan 1990
                           married Evelyn CHURCH 19 Jan 1918 Bar Harbor, Maine
  2190. Charles M.   born May 1900; married Nellie M. CLARK (of Appleton ,ME) on 14 Feb 1930

1827. RALPH I-9 LEIGHTON, son of Abitha D-8 LEIGHTON (Phoebe-7 DRISKO; Captain John-6; Joseph-5; 4; John-3; 2) and Uriah Wass-8 LEIGHTON, was born 18 Aug 1859 at Addison, Maine. He married Mary Jane CLARK on 26 Jan 1888 at Jaffa, Palestine. She was the daughter of George W. CLARK and Ellen WENTWORTH, and was born 6 Apr 1859 at Rochester, NH; died 18 Oct 1934 at Jerusalem.

Children of Ralph I-9 LEIGHTON and Mary Jane CLARK:
  Surname LEIGHTON   (children born Jerusalem)
  2191. Oscar I.   born 2 Mar 1889; died 15 May 1890
+ 2192. ALBERT WENTWORTH born 11 Aug 1890; died 8 July 1954

1830. CARRIE C-9 LEIGHTON, daughter of Mary Elizabeth-8 DRISKO (Edmund C-7; Josiah-6; Joseph-5; 4; John-3; 2) and CAPTAIN JASON D-8 LEIGHTON (# 1140) (Phebe Parker-7 DRISKO; Captain John-6; Joseph-5; 4 ; John-3; 2) was born 30 Sept 1862 at Addison, ME. She married Orrin P. SWANTON on 29 May 1887 at Milbridge, Maine. He was the son of Joseph Bernard SWANTON and Katherine D. TUCKER, and was born 9 May 1863 Cherryfield, Maine; died 22 Oct 1926 Milbridge, Maine. Carrie C-9 LEIGHTON died there 26 Aug 1955.

Children of Carrie-9 LEIGHTON and Orrin SWANTON:
  Surname SWANTON   (children born at Milbridge, Maine)
  2193. Joseph B.   born 29 Apr 1889; died July 1971 Old Orchard Beach, Maine
                           married Clara WHEELOCK 5 Nov 1913 Portland, ME.
  2194. Carl   born 10 Mar 1894; married Mildred WHITE; died 26 Oct 1966 Bath, ME
                           (she born 2 Aug 1897; died Mar 1981 Bath, Maine)
  2195. Iona T.   born 20 May 1899; died Jan 1984 Milbridge, Maine
                           married Darien H. McGRAW 12 May 1927
          (he son/o Henry McGRAW and Caroline GAVIN)(he born 2 Oct 1902; died 23 Dec 1989)

1831. LUCRETIA SMALL-9 LEIGHTON, sister of above, was born 11 Oct 1864 at Milbridge, Maine. She married Abraham Lincoln " Linc " WALLACE on 25 Mar 1886 at Milbridge. He was the son of Samuel Clark WALLACE and Harriet Almira SANBORN, and was born 23 Apr 1865; died 8 Jan 1939 Milbridge. He was a barber, and was the Milbridge Postmaster. Lucretia-9 LEIGHTON died 24 Jan 1850. They are buried at Evergreen Cemetery, Milbridge, Maine.

Children of Lucretia-9 LEIGHTON and Abraham " Linc " WALLACE:
  Surname WALLACE   (children born Milbridge, Maine)
  2196. Mary Eliza   born 13 Aug 1887; died 25 Mar 1953 Canton, MA
                          married Vernon Kelley BRACKETT 31 Dec 1910
       (he son/o Benjamin BRACKETT and Clara FICKETT)(he born 27 June 1885; died Aug 1969 , ME)

Children of Lucretia-9 LEIGHTON, continued:
Surname WALLACE
2197. Jason Drisko   born 17 July 1889; died 2 Dec 1973 Dayton, Ohio
    married Effie-11 LEIGHTON 2 Sept 1911
    (she dau/o Everett U-9 LEIGHTON and Minnie " Ada " WILLEY
    (she born 11 Dec 1890; died Mar 1986 Dayton, OH)
      One child: Betty Renee'-11 born 17 July 1918, CT; died Apr 1985, OH
    married James CONNELLY (she was an Army nurse in **World War 2**; served in India)
2198. Harriet Almira   born 11 Mar 1892; died 17 Mar 195_ EOL
    married Chester DORR 25 Dec 1917 (he born 3 Jul 1894; died Sept 1977 Cherryfield, ME
2199. Helen Georgia   born 25 Oct 1896; died 26 Feb 1989 Camden, Maine
    married Harry E. FREEMAN 14 Mar 1940 (he born 28 May 1889; died 16 Feb 1977)
      One son: Harry –11 FREEMAN (Jr. ?) born ca 19__

1832. CORA M. LEIGHTON-9 STROUT, daughter of Sarah A-8 LEIGHTON (Phebe Parker-7 DRISKO; Captain John-6; Joseph-5; 4; John-3;2;) and Ezra S-7 STROUT, was born 29 May 1861 at Milbridge, ME. She married Captain Lewis B. PINKHAM on 6 Feb 1879 at Milbridge. He was the son of David PINK-HAM and Louise STROUT, and was born 5 Aug 1858; died 11 Sept 1923. Cora M. L-9 STROUT died 7 Feb 1896 at Milbridge.

Children of Cora M L-9 STROUT and Captain Lewis PINKHAM:
Surname PINKHAM

2200. David L.	born ca 1880; died 1900	2202. Elmer E.	born ca 1903
2201. Alta H.	born ca 1884; died 1944		died ca 1944

1834. ARVILLA M-9 STROUT, sister of above, was born 5 Sept 1864 at Milbridge, Maine. She married Herbert O. STROUT, a mariner, on 21 Dec 1882 at Harrington, ME. He was the son of Otis STROUT and Eliza JOY, and was born May 1859 Milbridge, ME; died ____. Arvilla-9 STROUT died 25 Dec 1892.

Children of Arvilla-9 STROUT and Herbert STROUT:
Surname STROUT
2203. Raymond E. born Nov 1884 2204. Winslow H. born June 1890; marr Grace M. JORDAN (2 ch)

1838. CAPTAIN GEORGE V-9 STROUT, brother of above, was born 9 Nov 1870 at Milbridge, ME. He married 1st to Florence A. STROUT ca 1891. She was the dau/o Almon STROUT and Julia TENNEY, and was born Dec 1873; died 1936. They divorced. He married 2nd to Mary EAKINS on 16 Oct 1915.

Children of Captain George-9 STROUT and Florence STROUT:
Surname STROUT   (children born Milbridge, Maine)
2205. Almon C.   born 1 Mar 1896; died 16 May 1896
2206. Basil Harry   born 21 June 1898; married Florence M. HALL; died June 1963

1862. COLIN ANDREW-9 BATSON, son of Captain Adrian Abbott-8 BATSON (Rebecca-7 DRISKO; Captain John-6; Joseph-5;4; John-3;2) and Adrianna " Ada " CARTER, was born 22 Oct 1872 at Addison, Maine. He married Sarah Alden BEAL on 12 Mar 1910. She was the daughter of Franklin BEAL and Harriet TIRRELL, and was born 18__; died Nov 1945. Colin-9 BATSON died 11 Jan 1953.

Child of Colin-9 BATSON and Sarah BEAL:
Surname BATSON
+ 2207. ROBERT   born 12 June 1919; married Helen Marion COOTS; died before 1968
    ANDREW   (she dau/o Harold Roscoe COOTS and Marion Grace WOODSON)
        (she born 13 Oct 1921) (she 2m. Athill Hillston MORAN 25 Mar 1968)

1873. HERSCHEL WILDER-9 LEWIS, son of Vandelia/Fannie-8 DRISKO (Captain George W-7;

Captain John-6; Joseph-5; 4; John-3; 2) and James C. LEWIS, was born ca 1874 at Boston / Somersworth, MA. He was a graduate of Harvard University, class of 1896, where he earned a Bachelor of Arts degree. He was an educator, and served as a school principal (1907) in Littleton, MA. He later resided at Ipswich, Hillsborough County, NH (1910). He married Nettie __?__ ca 1899. She was born ca 1874, Maine.

Children of Herschel-9 LEWIS and Nettie __?__:
    Surname LEWIS
    2208. Richard J.   born 5 Apr 1901, MA.; died Jan 1985 Keene, NH
    2209. Howard A.   born 3 June 1904, MA.; died June 1981 Newport, NH

1877. EVA FRANCES-9 DRISKO, daughter of George Augustus-8 DRISKO (Captain George Washington-7; Captain John-6; Joseph-5; 4; John-3; 2) and Amelia A. " Minnie " GREEN, was born 19 Sept 1881 at Syracuse, Onondaga County, New York.

She married Orson Fowler BUTTS, as his 2nd wife, on 21 June 1917 at East Syracuse, New York. Orson BUTTS, the son of Francis BUTTS , was born 1 Feb 1878; died 2 Oct 1942. His first wife was Carrie M. BENN, by whom he had 4 children. (1. Laura who married J. D. GREEN; 2. Edith who married Horace SCHRAY; 3. Orson BUTTS, Jr.; and 4. a daughter who died in infancy.) Eva Frances-9 DRISKO died 30 Apr 1942 at Syracuse, NY. She and her husband are buried in Warners Cemetery, Onondaga County, NY.

Children of Eva-9 DRISKO and Orson F. BUTTS:
    Surname BUTTS   (children born Syracuse, Onondaga Co., NY)
+ 2210. JANE ANNA   born 18 Mar 1918; married William J. O'DONNELL 2 Nov 1940
                          (he son/o George O'DONNELL and Catherine DILLON; he born 2 Oct 1915)
    2211. Betty Lucille   born 29 July 1919; married Albert " Hap " GRABOSKE 17 May 1941
                          died Aug 1978 East Syracuse, NY; no issue EOL (2 adopted children)
    2212. Robert Charles born 27 Mar 1922; died 2 Dec 1922; buried Warners Cemetery
+ 2213. DONALD   born 28 Sept 1925; married Eleanor June CARD 18 Nov 1950
        FREDERICK   (she dau/o Hadwin CARD and Norma _?_)(she born 10 June 1930)

Eva Frances-9 DRISKO (1881-1942)   *Henry William-9 DRISKO (1891-1953)*

1879. HENRY WILLIAM-9 " Bill " DRISKO, brother of above, was born 29 May 1891 at Lyons, Wayne County, New York. He married Leah Belle-4 DOLBEY ++ on 1 Sept 1914 at Oneida, Madison County.

NY. She was the daughter of William Henry DOLBEY, Jr. and Nellie FANNING, and was born 31 Aug 1890 at Frankfort, Herkimer County, NY; died 17 May 1969 at Carthage, Jefferson County, NY. For most of his adult life, Henry William " Bill " DRISKO worked as a baker. At the time of his death, 6 April 1953, he was the owner of the HOME BAKERY in North Syracuse, NY. He died after an illness of four days, as a result of peritonitis caused by a ruptured appendix. He and his wife are buried in Oakwood Cemetery, Syracuse, Onondaga County, New York.

Children of Henry William-9 " Bill " DRISKO and Leah Belle-4 DOLBEY:
    Surname DRISKO   (children born Syracuse, Onondaga County, NY)
+ 2214. ELLEN   born 23 July 1915; married John Henry ECKELAMN, MD 1 May 1937
        AMELIA   (he son/o John ECKELMAN and Marie _____)
+ 2215. GEORGE   born 16 Nov 1917; died 14 Jan 1994 North Syracuse, NY
        DOLBEY   married Frances Jean STERLING 31 Jan 1947 Syracuse, NY
        " Jack "   (she dau /o Charles Lee STERLING and Hazel F. DOTY)(she born 3 June 1927)

++ Ancestry of Leah Belle-4 DOLBEY

STEPHEN WESLEY-1 DOLBEY, possibly born between 1790-1800 at _____, CT; married Abbie-Ann (Anna) LYON 17 Nov 1821 at Oxford, New Haven County, CT. She was the daughter of Hezekiah LYON and Sarah HENDRIX, and was born 9 Oct 1803 at Fairfield, CT; died 18 Feb 1877 at Cleveland, Oswego County, NY. Stephen-1 DOLBEY died between 1847-50, CT.

WILLIAM HENRY-2 DOLBEY, SR. was born 11 Sept 1833, CT; married Ellen Amelia-4 CROFUTT on 27 Nov 1858 at Stratford, CT. She was the daughter of Samuel-3 CROFUT/CROFUTT (Samuel-2; 1) and Sarah Jane-7 CULVER (Stephen-6; Amos-5; Stephen-4; Joshua-3; 2; Edward-1), and was born 1 Sept 1837,CT; died ca 1926 at Oneida, Madison County, NY. She and her first husband are buried in the Cleveland (NY) Cemetery. William-2 DOLBEY moved to Oswego County, NY. shortly after his marriage, and was engaged in the lumbering business. He owned property in the Scriba Patent there, and died at the age of 37, on 4 May 1872. His widow married second to Dr. Kinsman BROGA on 7 Sept 1879.

WILLIAM HENRY-3 DOLBEY, JR, the youngest son of William Henry-2, Sr. was born 15 Apr 1870 at Dakins Bay, Oswego County, NY. He married first to Nellie FANNING on 25 Dec 1888. She was the daughter of Irish immigrants Patrick FANNING and Bridget __?__. She was born 8 Aug 1871; died 15 Oct 1930 at Syracuse, NY. They divorced ca 1898, and he married second to Anna R. PATTEN in 1912. William H-3 DOLBEY, Jr. died at Auburn, Cayuga County, NY on 5 July 1944. LEAH BELLE-4 DOLBEY was the twin daughter of William H-3 DOLBEY, Jr. and Nellie FANNING. The other twin, Lena Belle-4 DOLBEY, was stillborn.

1881. ARTHUR WILLIAM-9 DRISKO, son of Everett-8 DRISKO (Jason Clapp-7; Captain John-6; Joseph-5; 4; John-3; 2) and Ruth CARTER, was born 7 June 1870 at Jonesboro, ME. He married Lucy Faustina PLUMMER on 4 Dec 1892 at Jonesboro, ME. She was the daughter of Loveatus PLUMMER and Georgia LOOK, and was born 2 May 1871, died 26 Jan 1954. Arthur-9 DRISKO died 10 Feb 1956 at Addison, Maine.

Children of Arthur-9 DRISKO and Lucy F. PLUMMER:
    Surname DRISKO
+ 2216. FELLOWS E.   born 1 July 1898, Maine; married Flora L. CROWLEY 21 June 1924
                          (she born 8 Apr 1904, ME; died 14 July 1977 Addison)
                          died 23 Nov 1987 Addison, Maine (age 89)
  2217. Iona D.   born Aug 1899; died 16 Aug 1938 Melrose, MA.
                          married Austin L. SMITH of Milford, ME 31 Aug 1924

1897. JULIA A-9 SAWYER see ALTON V-9 ROGERS (# 1816)
1901. ALICE M-9 DRISKO, daughter of Augustus Melville-8 DRISKO (Jeremiah-7; Joseph-6; 5; 4; John-3; 2) and Leonice Gertrude GRACE, was born 12 Feb 1866 at _____, Maine. She married William Alexander PINKERTON of South Dakota. He was born 18__; died 19__. Alice M-9 died 19__.

Children of Alice-9 DRISKO and William PINKERTON:
    Surname PINKERTON   (3 other children of this marriage died young)
    2218. William Grace (twin) born 30 May 1896; died May 1977 Aberdeen, SD
    2219. Harry A.   (twin) born 30 May 1896; died Mar 1982 Aberdeen, SD
        The twins enlisted in **World War 1** on 9 Apr 1917; returned 1919.

1902. WILLIAM HERBERT-9 DRISKO, brother of above, was born ca 1869 at Saginaw, Michigan. He married Minnie WILSON of Mansfield, South Dakota before 1903. She was the daughter of Anson WILSON and Sarah MOULTON, and was born 18__; died 19__. William Herbert-9 DRISKO was a retired wholesale dealer (1926) residing in Aberdeen, South Dakota. He died there on 26 Jan 1936. (His son, Melville-10 DRISKO, stated Wm.-9 died of a heart attack while on a train enroute to Aberdeen from Minneapolis, MN.

Children of William Herbert-9 DRISKO and Minnie WILSON:
Surname DRISKO

2220. Marian	born ca 1903	
2221. Fern	born 3 Sept 1904; died 11 Nov 1992 St. Paul, MN	
	married Marshall Allan FROST 30 June 1928 (he born 1902 MN; died 1972 GA)	
	2 children: Marilyn-11 and Marshall-11 FROST, II (both died young)	
2222. Gladys	born ca 1906/07; died at age 2 EOL	
2223. Alice M.	born 16 Apr 1907; died 1 Jan 1997 Sioux Falls, SD	
	married Donald GAMBREL (he born 23 June 1906 SD; died 26 Mar 1990, SD)	
2224. William H., Jr.	born 3 Aug 1909; died May 1966 Minnesota	
+ 2225. MELVILLE ANSON, SR.	born 7 Feb 1911; married Margaret Marie RENNIX 14 July 1935	
	(she dau/o George RENNIX and Ellen HANSON)	
	(she born 5 Nov 1911; died 24 May 1997 Chesterfield, VA)	
	died 3 Feb 1990 Aberdeen, Brown Co, SD; buried Riverside Cemetery	

1905. JOSEPHINE KNOWLES-9 DRISKO, daughter of Francis Jasper-8 DRISKO (Jeremiah-7; Joseph-6; 5; 4; John-3; 2) and Nancy LORD, was born 5 May 1872. She married James CARTY on 5 Mar 1892. He was the son of ____ CARTY, and was born 18__; died 19__. Josephine-9 DRISKO died 16 Feb 1944.

Children of Josephine-9 DRISKO and James CARTY:
Surname CARTY

2226. Ruth	born 16 June 1893; married Fred D. TRACY; died 1 Dec 1989 Bridgeport, CT
2227. James Francis	born 31 Aug 1895
2228. Elmer Lord	born 6 Feb 1902
2229. Lester Ames	born 15 Nov 1906

1909. MELVILLE AUGUSTUS-9 DRISKO, son of Sewall M-8 DRISKO (Jeremiah-7; Joseph-6; 5; 4; John-3; 2) and Helen CALER, was born 8 Aug 1875 at Harrington, Maine. He married Nettie Mae MAHONEY on 23 Dec 1899. She was the daughter of William MAHONEY and Rose HOWE, and was born 27 Oct 1877; died 23 Dec1961at Orono, Maine. Melville-9 DRISKO had a blacksmith shop and later a garage at Harrington, Maine. He died 9/10 Jan 1958 at Bangor, Maine.

Children of Melville-9 DRISKO and Nettie Mae MAHONEY:
Surname DRISKO

+ 2230. SEWALL M.	born 12 Mar 1901; married Anna McGREGOR 3 Sept 1927
	died 17 Oct 1971 at Milford, Worcester, MA.
2231. Helen A.	born 25 May 1903; died 6 Feb 1994 Bloomington, IL
	married Cecil J. CUTTS 4 Sept 1926 (he born 6 Feb 1902; died Sept 1976 Bangor, ME)
+ 2232. ROSE	born ca 19__; married Maxwell KELLEY of Jonesport, ME 28 June 1930
	(he born 7 Sept 1909; died 4 Nov 1991)
2233. Ralph L.	born 12 Jan 1908, Maine; married Marjorie I. CUTTS 10 June 1939
	died June 1973 Buffalo, NY; buried at Boothbay Harbor, Maine

1927. LAURA JANE-9 DRISKO, daughter of Hiram-8 DRISKO (Jeremiah-7; Josiah-6; Joseph-5; 4; John-3; 2) and Hannah KELLEY, was born 24 Oct 1871 at Jonesport, Maine. She married Reuben/Rubin Edgar-3 WILSON there on 31 Jan 1891. He was the son of William E-2 WILSON (Wm-1) and Laura WESCOTT, and was born 13 Oct 1871; died 1 July 1950. Laura-9 DRISKO died 23 Sept 1958.

Children of Laura Jane-9 DRISKO and Reuben/Rubin-3 WILSON:
    Surname WILSON   (all children born Jonesport, Maine)
    2234. Myron Loyce   born 26 Aug 1891; married Bernice HIGGINS 17 Sept 1911; died 29 Jul 1956
        (she dau/o Silas T. HIGGINS and Phoebe Mabel KELLEY)
        (she born 19 June 1891 Jonesport, ME; died 7 Mar 1981 Machias, ME)
            (3 children incl. Leon A-11 WILSON born 14 June 1921; died 30 Dec 1922)
    2235. Frank Eugene   born Nov 1892; died 6 Apr 1921
    2236. Percy Howard   born 26 Aug 1895; married Julia MORANG 6 Apr 1921; died 19 July 1932
        (she born ca 1897 Jonesport, Maine; died _____)

1933. WILLIAM F-9 DRISKO, son of Zimri-8 DRISKO (Edmund-7; Josiah-6; Joseph-5; 4; John-3; 2) and Susan FIELD, was born 3 Sept 1872 at Milbridge, Maine. He married Jennie BISHER on 4 Sept 1901. She was the daughter of _?_ BISHER, and was born 18__; died 19__. William-9 DRISKO died Dec 1935.

Children of William-9 DRISKO and Jennie BISHER:
    Surname DRISKO
    2237. William H. (twin) born 9 Oct 1902; died 13 Dec 1989 Seattle, Kings County, WA.
    2238. Harry (twin)   born 9 Oct 1902   2239. Evelyn Winifred born 21 Aug 1904
        died May 1983 New Castle, Indiana   2240. Helen J.   born 8 Jan 1907

1934. GUY C-9 DRISKO, brother of above, was born 29 Jan 1881 at Indian River, Maine. He married first to Mary JONES Smith on 4 Nov 1908. His second wife was Anna GOODWIN.

Child of Guy-9 DRISKO and Mary JONES Smith:
    Surname DRISKO
    2241. Clarence C.   born 10 Sept 1909; married Cleo TORREY; died 9 Aug 1992 Seattle, WA
        One child: Daniel Clarence-11 DRISKO born 19 July 1939
  Child of Guy-9 DRISKO and Anna GOODWIN:
    Surname DRISKO
+ 2242. DOROTHY   born 4 Nov 1918; died Jan 1987 Bremerton, Kitsap, WA
        1m. Robert LOWRY; 2m. Fred PEABODY July 1946

1935. ELTON B-9 DRISKO, brother of above, was born 5 Mar 1886 at Addison, ME. He married first to Mabel HESTON on 3 Nov 1908. She was the daughter of _ ?_ HESTON, and was born 1888; died 18 Oct 1940. His 2nd marriage was to Mrs. Della M. Galligan on 18 Dec 1942. She was born 23 Dec 1898; died July 1975, Seattle, King Co., WA.

Children of Elton-9 DRISKO and Mabel HESTON:
    Surname DRISKO
    2243. Margaret L.   born 21 June 1910; married Chan O. BURROWS 1 Oct 1946 (divorced)
    2244. Elton B., Jr.   born Sept 1912; died 10 Oct 1943

1946. LEON ROWELL-9 DRISKO, son of Alamon R-8 DRISKO (Thomas-7; Josiah-6; Joseph-5; 4; John-3; 2) and Orrie CROWLEY, was born 5 Mar 1886 at Addison, Maine. He married Caroline G. RUMERY on 26 June 1900. She was the daughter of Newell RUMERY and Olive J. HINCKLEY, and was born 14 Aug 1875; died 9 Dec 1953 at Evanston, Illinois. Leon-9 DRISKO died Dec 1934 at Belfast, ME.

Children of Leon-9 DRISKO and Caroline RUMERY:
    Surname DRISKO
    2245. Marian   born ca 19__   2247. Jeanette   born ca _____
    2246. Lena R.   born 19__; marr John R. NORTH, Jr. 25 June 1938 (he from Palmer, MA)

1949. MERTON EMERSON-9 DRISKO, son of Edgar Everson-8 DRISKO (Thomas-7; Josiah-6; Joseph-5;4; John-3; 2) and Gertrude EMERSON, was born 5 July 1880 at Addison, Maine. He married Addie

Sophia-9 EMERSON on 22 Apr 1908. She was the daughter of Christopher P-8 EMERSON and Cora A-6 TIBBETTS, and was born 9 Apr 1890; died 1957. Merton E-9 DRISKO died 9 Aug 1961 at Addison, ME.

Children of Merton-9 DRISKO and Addie S. EMERSON:
   Surname DRISKO
2248. Donald E.   born 14 Dec 1908, ME; died 28 Dec 1985 Bangor, Penobscot County, ME.
      Child: Edgar E-11 DRISKO   born 19__; poss marr Josephine H. CHURCH 14 Dec 1953
2249. Gertrude   born 19__
2250. Ella M.   born 25 Aug 1911; died 15 May 1997 Harbor, Hancock, ME
           married Roger S. CUNNINGHAM 25 Dec 1937
2251. Cora H.   born 13 June 1913; married Reginald F. GRAY 13 Mar 1937; died Mar 1984
           (he born 13 Nov 1914; died 19 June 1992 Hancock, ME)
2252. Agnes   born 23 Aug 1915 Addison, ME; died 1925   EOL
2253. Julia V.   born 19__; married Gordon M. CROWLEY 10 Oct 1938
2254. John Merton   born 12 Aug 1922 Jonesport, ME; died 19__ Togus, ME (auto accident)

1954. THOMAS ELLISON-9 DRISKO, son of Charles C-8 DRISKO (Joel W-7; Josiah-6; Joseph-5; 4; John-3; 2) and Phebe DODGE, was born 10 July 1897 at Machias, Washington County, Maine. He married Alice J. DOW on 19 Sept 1918. Thomas E-9 DRISKO died 30 Oct 1987 at Santa Rosa, CA.

Children of Thomas Ellison-9 DRISKO and Alice J. DOW:
   Surname DRISKO
2255. Thomas E., Jr. born 29 Oct 1919; d. 5 Mar 1987   2257. Richard Warren + born 26 Nov 1925
2256. Robert Donald born 20 July 1923; d. 7 Apr 1987 CA. 2258. Ruth Alice   born 12 Dec 1926
+ Richard W-10 DRISKO, PhD, in 1987, was a senior chemist at the Naval Civil Engineering Laboratory, Port Hueneme, CA. He was an international expert in protection coatings, and was named Engineer of the Year in 1986 by the Western Region of the National Association of Corrosion Engineers.

1955. FLORENCE-9 DRISKO, sister of above, was born Nov 1898 at Machias, Maine. She married William E. CLARK of East Machias, ME on 6 Aug 1919. She was living (1989) at 2140 Santa Cruz Avenue, Apt B-207, Menlo Park, CA.   Reference: Dr. Richard W-9 DRISKO (# 2257) above

Children of Florence-9 DRISKO and William CLARK:
   Surname CLARK
2259. William E. born 19__   2260. Ruth born 19__ 2261. Barbara born 19__   2262. Robert born 19__

1964. GERTRUDE M/N-9 KELLEY, daughter of Justina-8 CARVER (Nancy Ann-7 DRISKO; Josiah-6; Joseph-5;4; John-3;2) and Edwin Allen KELLEY, was born March 1877. She married Mark C. ALLEN on 21 July 1900 (both residing at Woodstock, Maine) MVR.

Children of Gertrude-9 KELLEY and Mark C. ALLEN:
   Surname ALLEN 2263. Mason born 18 Feb 1902; d.Oct 1975 Portland, ME 2264. Parker born ca __

1965. EDWIN A-9 KELLEY, JR., brother of above, was born 6 Aug 1882. He married Ethel Rosamond BEAL on 16 March 1904 at Jonesport, ME. She was born 19 May 1888; died 28 Oct 1956. Edwin-9 died Dec 1968 at South Freeport, Maine.

Children of Edwin-9 KELLEY, Jr. and Ethel BEAL:
   Surname KELLEY   (all children born at Jonesport, Maine)
2265. Millard A   born 1 Dec 1905; died May 1978 Jonesport, Maine
           married Velma A. BEAL 26 March 1928 at Jonesport
2266. Leemont R.   born 19 March 1907; married Beatrice C. BEAL 15 June 1928 Jonesport
2267. Allen   born June 1913
2268. Margaret   born 14 May 1916; died 18 Jan 2000 Zephyrhills, FL
           married John R. FAULKINGHAM 10 June 1933 Jonesport

1966. BURTON EUGENE-9 CARVER, son of Augustus Fellows-8 CARVER (Nancy Ann-7 DRISKO; Josiah-6; Joseph-5;4; John-3;2) and Annie M. SANBORN, was born Sept 1881. He married Nettie Wallace BICKFORD on 10 Jan 1903. She was born May 1884; died ____.

Children of Burton E-9 CARVER and Annie SANBORN:
   Surname CARVER

2269. Madeline	born 12 Sept 1905; died 18 June 1993	2271. Genevieve (twin)	
2270. Elmer (twin) born 27 March 1908; died 17 July 1976		born 27 Mar 1908	

1967. FRANK LEON-9 CARVER, brother of above, was born 13 Feb 1886 at Jonesport, ME. He married Mildred Arletta HALL 17 Mar 1914 at Jonesport, ME. She was born 12 Feb 1891 at Jonesport, ME.

Children of Frank Leon-9 CARVER and Mildred HALL:
   Surname CARVER

2272. Arletta Annie	born 26 May 1914; married Carroll F. CROWLEY 1 June 1939 Jonesport, ME
2273. Helen Arlena	born 25 Feb 1922

1968. BERNARD FRANK-9 CARVER, son of Judson Howard-8 CARVER (Nancy-7 DRISKO; Josiah-6; Joseph-5;4; John-3;2) and Carrie A. WOODMAN, was born 5 Apr 1880/81 at Jonesport, ME. He married Georgia Ann TRACY ca ____. She was born 27 Aug 1880 Columbia Falls, ME; died ____. Bernard-9 CARVER died March 1971 at Westbrook, Maine.

Children of Bernard F-9 CARVER and Georgia TRACY:
   Surname CARVER

2274. Cecil Frank	born 12 Feb 1902 Jonesport, ME; died 4 Dec 1991
	married Rena PHANEUF 18 Aug 1928 (she born 24 Nov 1905; died Oct 1985 Westbrook)
2275. Volney Becker	born 10 Aug 1903 Jonesport; marr Emily M. GREEN 6 Dec 1922 Westbrook
2276. Perley Winslow	born 9 May 1906/07 Westbrook, ME; died 29 Mar 1975 Westbrook, ME
	married Mildred May HOPKINS 31 Mar 1928 Westbrook, ME
	(she born 16 Oct 1907; died 27 May 1991 Westbrook, ME)
2277. Irving Llewellyn	born 21 Sep 1909; died May 1984 Gaston, CT
	married Pearl HALL 13 June 1935 Westbrook
2278. Donald Woodman	born 21 Aug 1910 Westbrook; died 28 June 1997 Portland, ME
	married Angelina MARTELL 7 May 1932 Portland, ME
2279. Frank Bernard, Jr.	born 29 Mar 1913 Westbrook; died May 1986 Sebago Lake, Cumberland, ME
	married Helen Marie BICKFORD 26 Apr 1944 Westbrook
	(she born 16 Jan 1911; died May 1987 Sebago Lake, ME)
2280. Howard Amasa	born 29 May 1920 Westbrook, Maine
	married Ruth Carolyn DAVIS 30 Aug 1941 Westbrook

1971. JUDSON HOWARD-9 CARVER, JR., half-brother of above, son of Judson-8 CARVER and his second wife Lena R. FAULKINGHAM, was born 16 Jan 1902. He married Doris L. KELLEY 11 Feb 1922 at Jonesport, Maine. Judson-9 CARVER died 19 May 1986 at Jonesport, ME.

Children of Judson-9 CARVER, Jr. and Doris KELLEY:
   Surname CARVER

2281. Merton L.	born 192_; married Dorothy G. AREY/CARVER 19 May 1949 Portland, ME		
2282. John	born ca 192_		
2283. Charles	born 29 Apr 1930; died 29 Dec 1972	2284. Judson H. III	born ca 1935

1975. BYRON B-9 CARVER, son of William-8 CARVER (Nancy-7 DRISKO; Josiah-6; Joseph-5;4; John-3;2;) and Martha GUPTILL, was born 26 Mar 1891. He married Rhoda V. SAWYER 23 May 1914 at Jonesport, ME. She was born 13 Apr 1892 at Jonesport, ME; died 29 Oct 1986 at Cape Elizabeth, ME. Byron-9 CARVER died Oct 1966 at Westbrook, Maine.

Children of Byron-9 CARVER and Rhoda V. SAWYER :
   Surname CARVER
  2285. Virginia Mae   born 6 Oct 1914; died 23 June 1984
  2286. Velma Lee   born 14 Nov 1917; died 4 Apr 1939 at Rutland
  2287. Pauline Vaughan born 1 Feb 1922; married Breen O. MORANG of Portland, ME on 28 Sept 1940
                      (he born 9 July 1917; died Dec 1980 Portland, ME)

1976. GLEN LEWIS-9 CARVER, brother of above, was born Jan 1896. He married Frances E. CARVER
ca 19___.   She was born ___ at Jonesport, Maine. Glen-9 CARVER died 29 Dec 1959.

Children of Glen-9 CARVER and Frances CARVER:
   Surname CARVER
  2288. Dale   born 19__   2289. Constance   born 25 Jan 1934; died 17 Nov 1986

1977. GUY HERRICK-9 CARVER, son of George-8 CARVER (Nancy Ann-7 DRISKO; Josiah-6;
Joseph-5;4; John-3;2) and Evelyn LOOK, was born 27 Apr 1886 at Jonesport, Maine. He married Susie
Olive BEAL 1 Aug 1906 at Jonesport, Maine . She was born 14 Jan 1889 at Beals Island, ME. Guy H-9
CARVER died May 1968 at Beals, Washington Co., Maine.

Children of Guy-9 CARVER and Susie Olive BEAL:
   Surname CARVER
  2290. Sylvia Evelyn   born 4 Feb 1905/06
  2291. Oscar Look   born 31 Mar 1909; died 13 June 1974 Beals, Maine
                      married Mary L. COFFIN 30 Mar 1931 (he of Beals, Maine)
  2292. Mina B.   born 25 Oct 1919, Beals, ME; married Melrose L. KENT 23 Feb 1946
                      (he born 7 Apr 1913; died Feb 1966)
  2293. Guy Herrick, Jr. born 8 May 1926

1978. WILLARD LOOK-9 CARVER, brother of above, was born 14 Oct 1887 at Jonesport, Maine. He
married Ethel Alta CROWLEY 30 Aug 1911 at Jonesport, ME. She was born 25 Sept 1889 at Addison, ME
Willard L-9 CARVER died Jan 1968 at Jonesport.

Children of Willard-9 CARVER and Ethel CROWLEY:
   Surname CARVER
  2294. Evelyn Alberta   born 29 Jan 1912; died 19 Jan 1945
      married Percy W. BRYANT 15 Nov 1930 Jonesport, ME (he born 7 May 1907; died 25 May 1995)
  2295. Dorothy Electra   born 21 Sep 1914; died 25 July 1991
      married Gordon J. PLUMMER of Harrington 20 Oct 1937 (he born 11 Apr 1913; died 4 Aug 1990)
  2296. Ann Miller   born 19 Mar 1922; married Loren H. LAKEMAN 12 Dec 1939 Jonesport, ME
  2297. Minnie Grace   born 1 Mar 1924; married Clifford JOHNSON of Machias 29 Oct 1941
  2298. Willard L., Jr   born 2 Nov 1927
  2299. Byron Fred   born 23 May 1932; married Freda I. BRUCH of Geneva, NY on 10 Apr 1954

1994. HAROLD PHILBRICK-9 DRISKO, son of Alonzo-8 DRISKO (Oramander-7; Jeremiah-6; Joseph-
5; 4; John-3; 2) and Mary PHILBRICK, was born 20 Jan 1895 at Boston, MA. He was a graduate of
Yale University, class of 1916. He married Ruth THOMPSON of Fall River, MA on 6 June 1923. She was
the daughter of Dr. Richard THOMPSON and Annie Minerva SMITH, and was born 28 Feb 1898; died
June 1987 at Hollis, NH. Harold-9 DRISKO died 7 Dec 1981 at Wellesley, MA.

Children of Harold P-9 DRISKO and Ruth THOMPSON:
   Surname DRISKO
  2300. Ruth   born 19__; married John (Jack) A. ROGERS (divorced) poss 2 children
+ 2301. RICHARD   born 25 Nov 1928, NJ; 1m. Elizabeth GRAY of Rahway, NJ
       BURTON   2m. Katherine GRAY Pearson (sister of his first wife)

1995. HELEN-9 DRISKO, sister of above, was born 11 May 1897 at Boston, MA. She married Otto P. MANN ca 19__. He was the son of ___ MANN, and was born 8 June 1895; died Jan 1984 at Beverly, NJ.

Children of Helen-9 DRISKO and Otto MANN:
   Surname MANN
   2302. Philip   born 19__   2303. Harold   born 19 __

1997. GRACE PLUMMER-9 DRISKO, daughter of Henry Brooks-8 DRISKO (Captain Perrin-7; Jeremiah-6; Joseph-5;-4; John-3; 2) and Florence COLLIER , was born ca 1882/83 at Boston, MA. She married Fred BUCKNAM of Machias, Maine ca 19__. He was the son of Eugene M. BUCKNAM and Paulina KIETH, and was born 18__; died 1918. Grace-9 DRISKO died 1950.

Children of Grace Plummer-9 DRISKO and Fred BUCKNAM:
   Surname BUCKNAM   Reference: Holbrook Collection Volume 342, page 54
   2304. Austin   born 16 Apr 1910, MA; died 12 Dec 1998 , VA
   2305. Earl   born 19__   2306. Francis born 24 June 1913, MA; died Mar 1978

2001. REV. RAYMOND CHANDLER-9 DRISKO, son of Eri Hathaway-8 DRISKO (Chandler Robbins-7; Jonathan-6; Samuel Gatchell-5; Joseph-4; John-3; 2) and Elizabeth TABBUTT/TIBBETTS, was born 22 Aug 1852 Columbia, ME. He married his cousin LAURA ISABEL-9 DRISKO on 17 July 1878. She was the daughter of Joseph Whitney-8 DRISKO (Chandler Robbins-7; etc.) and Isabel FARNSWORTH, and was born 26 Oct 1860; died 1953. Rev. Raymond-9 DRISKO died 19 June 1937.

Child of Raymond-9 DRISKO and Laura Isabel-9 DRISKO:
   Surname DRISKO   2307. Margaret   born 16 June 1890; died 21 Feb 1908   EOL

2002. GEORGE CAMELO-9 " CAM " DRISKO, brother of above, was born 15 Apr 1854 at Columbia, Maine. He married Sarah MAGEE on 30 June 1874 at Columbia Falls, Maine. She was the daughter of John MAGEE and Esther DORR, and was born 24 Apr 1859; died 6 Jan 1955 (age 95). George Camelo-9 DRISKO , a lumberman, died 26 Oct 1944.

Children of George Camelo-9 DRISKO and Sarah MAGEE:
   Surname DRISKO
   2308. Elizabeth   born Oct 1875; died 9 Mar 1900   unmarried EOL
 + 2309. HARRY E.   born 11 Feb 1878; married Lillian WORCESTER
          (she dau/o Algernon WORCESTER and Nancy TRACY) (she born 20 Feb 1876; died 1960 gs)
                 died 8 Aug 1976 Addison, Maine
   2310. Mae/Mamie S.   born 2 Mar 1880; died June 1972 , CA
               1m. John A. FITZHENRY 14 May 1898 (div); 2m. Henri PRESCOTT no issue   EOL
   2311. Inez   born 11 Nov 1882; 1m. Ellis CLARK; 2m. William KIMBALL
 + 2312. JOSEPH   born 28 Oct 1885; died 22 Dec 1976
       WILLARD   married Queen B-9 WORCESTER 20 Oct 1907 (# 1770)
                 (she dau/o Asa T. WORCESTER and Lucinda TABBUTT (# 1041)
   2313. Hugh R.   born 13 May 1892; died 15 Nov 1915
             He died from burns received while a passenger on a train. Ayers Junction, Washington Co., ME.
                 The boiler head of the engine blew out and the steam burned him fatally.
   2314. Mildred Etta   born 22 Feb 1894; married Clyde LEGACY 15 Nov 1915; died 9 May 1991
                 (he born 22 Nov 1892; died Dec 1965 Princeton, ME)
       (1 ch: Clydene F-11 LEGACY who marr Kenneth R. SAVAGE 21 July 1938; resided Princeton, ME)
 + 2315. GEORGE C. JR   born 15 Apr 1898; died 5 Nov 1978 Addison, Maine
                 1m. Christine SMITH 10 Sept 1921(divorced)
                 2m. Wilma/Hilena BUBAR 25 Dec 1925 (she born ___; died 5 May 1994)

2004. EDWIN IRWIN-9 DRISKO, brother of above, was born 6 Dec 1859 at Columbia, Maine. He married Hattie Ann DONAVAN on 17 June 1880 at Columbia Falls. She was the daughter of Elizabeth DONAVAN and _?_, and was born 16 Apr 1860; died 4 Mar 1937. Edwin I-9 DRISKO died 14 Nov 1928.

Children of Edwin Irwin-9 DRISKO and Hattie DONAVAN:
Surname DRISKO   (children born Columbia Falls, Maine)
+ 2316. CHARLES C.   born 6 May 1881; married Bessie Rena-9 LEIGHTON 21 Sept 1910
                         (she born 31 Dec 1887, ME; died 23 Jan 1990 – age 102 years)
                         died 22 Nov 1968 Columbia, Maine , a farmer
2317. Hannah M.   born Apr 1885; married William A. CLEAVES 2 May 1910 (2 ch)
2318. Hattie E.   born 27 Dec 1887; died 2 Nov 1990, CA ; unmarried (age 102 years)
2319. Effie M.   born 12 Jan 1893; died Mar 1987
                         1m. Roy H. HATHAWAY 29 Mar 1910; 2m. Howard LONGFELLOW
                         (1 ch: Russell –11 HATHAWAY ; he born 15 Dec 1910; died Mar 1969)

2006. RUTH E-9 DRISKO, sister of above, was born June 1870 at Columbia Falls, ME. She married first to Charles ATWATER on 11 July 1891 at Steuben, ME. He was the son of William R. ATWATER and Priscilla LEIGHTON, was born 27 Jan 1858; died 1908. She marr 2nd to Michael MURPHY on 4 Oct 1916

Children of Ruth-9 DRISKO and Charles ATWATER:
Surname ATWATER
2320. Frances P.   born 18__; married James H. NEALY 30 Oct 1923 (both res. Bangor, ME)
2321. Carl   born 18__   2324. Marie   born ____
2322. Lila   born ____   married Kenneth C. WILSON 20 Aug 1921
2323. Pauline   born ____   2325. Charles, Jr.   born ____

2009. ERI HASKELL-9 DRISKO, half-brother of above, son of Eri Hathaway-8 DRISKO and his 2nd wife, Fannie Brewster-5 TABBUT, was born 25 Sept 1877 at Columbia Falls, ME. He married Susie Ethel ALLEN on 29 Oct 1904 at Machias, ME. She was the daughter of Benjamin ALLEN and Abbie FARNS-WORTH, and was born 27 Apr 1886 at Columbia Falls; died 9 Mar 1976 at Machias. Eri-9 DRISKO died 1 Feb 1971 at Machias, Maine.

Children of Eri Haskell-9 DRISKO and Susie ALLEN:
Surname DRISKO
2326. Lawrence M.   born 19__; married Phyllis M ROCKWELL of Portland, ME on 16 June 1934
2327. Dr. Elliot H.   born 1917; married Elizabeth WINSHIP
                         (she born 21 Apr 1915; died 18 Apr 1994 Yonkers, NY)

2010. EUGENE CYRUS-9 DRISKO, son of Joseph Whitney-8 DRISKO (Chandler-7; Jonathan-6; Samuel G-5; Joseph-4; John-3; 2) and Isabel Frances FARNSWORTH, was born 24 Dec 1853 at Jonesboro, ME. He married first to Asenath Ingersoll-8 BARTON on 2 Sept 1875. She was the daughter of Lewis-7 BARTON and Eliza Asenath CALER, and was born 21 June 1852; died 10 July 1876, shortly after the birth of her only child. He married 2nd to Arethusa/Arrie B. SMITH on 12 Oct 1884. She was the daughter of Asa K. SMITH and Hannah PENNELL, and was born Jan 1861; died 1923. Eugene Cyrus-9 died 1943.

Child of Eugene Cyrus-9 DRISKO and Asenath-8 BARTON:
Surname DRISKO
2328. Mabelle Asenath   born 21 June 1876 Centerville, ME; died 1965 TX
                married David McNAUGHTON (he born 1874 ME; died 5 Jul 15 May 1850 Miami FL)
                      (he son/o George McNAUGHTON and Sarah J. McDERMOTT)
         1 son: Lewis Winslow-11 McNAUGHTON born 23 Apr 1902; died 25 Feb 1969 TX.
             Note: Mabelle-10 was raised by Asenath-7 DRISKO # 446
Children of Eugene Cyrus-9 DRISKO and Arethusa SMITH:
Surname DRISKO
2329. Mina E. born 20 Oct 1889; marr Maurice C. WILSON 3 Feb 1916   2330. Joseph   born 18__; dy

2011. CORA EDITH-9 DRISKO, sister of above, was born 14 Aug 1855 at Jonesboro, Maine. She married Eri Wellington-8 LOOK on 21 June 1874. He was the son of Henry Sawyer-7 LOOK and Roxanna H. KILTON, and was born 21 Jan 1856; died after 1945. Cora Edith-9 died 13 Dec 1939.

Child of Cora Edith-9 DRISKO and __?__:
    Surname DRISKO
    2331. Walter Breckenridge born 19 Oct 1874; died 13 Sept 1943
            Note: An entry in the diary of Joseph W-8 DRISKO, father of Cora-9, made on 9 May 1875, stated
            that " this child was deserted by mother ". Raised by his grandparents, he used the name DRISKO.
Children of Cora Edith-9 DRISKO and Eri Wellington-8 LOOK:
    Surname LOOK
    2332. Rosswell Lawrence   born 5 Oct 1876
    2333. Mabel F.   born July 1879; died ____; unmarried
    2334. Cecile Vinton   born 9 Jan 1883; married __?__ DURGIN
    2335. Laura Raymond   born 14 Dec 1886; died 1 Apr 1981 Medway, MA
                              married Edward L. STRICKLAND of Franklin, MA.

2012. LAURA ISABEL-9 DRISKO see REV RAYMOND C-9 DRISKO (# 2001)
2013. ESTHER RUTH-9 DRISKO, sister of above, was born 5 Apr 1862 at Jonesboro, Maine. She married Noyes Watts FISH on 7 Aug 1880. He was the son of Ansel H. FISH and Mary Jane WATTS, and was born Sept 1853; died 1936. Esther Ruth-9 DRISKO died 1959.

Children of Esther Ruth-9 DRISKO and Noyes Watts FISH:
    Surname FISH
    2336. Esther D.   born 1883; married David Leon SINFORD 9 Dec 1914; died 1958
    2337. Bertha M.   born 1884; married Edward O'BRIEN 5 Apr 1903; died 1980
    2338. Fred H.   born 1887; married Susie WHITNEY; died 1978
    2339. Nellie W.   born 1895; married Noble Willis SNOWDEAL 16 July 1916; died 5 Jan 1980
    2340. Marjorie B.   born 18__; Albert E. WHITNEY 17 June 1917 (he from Jonesboro, ME)

2014. LIZZIE MADGE-9 DRISKO, sister of above, was born 22 Oct 1866 at Jonesboro, Maine. She was the twin of Lucy Maud-9 DRISKO. She married George Gates-8 FISH on 28 June 1884. He was the son of Ansel Henry-7 FISH and Mary Jane WATTS, and the brother of Noyes Watts FISH, above. George Gates-8 FISH was born 22 Aug 1858; died ____. Lizzie Madge-9 DRISKO died 10 July 1964.

Children of Lizzie Madge-9 DRISKO and George Gates-8 FISH:
    Surname FISH   (order of birth uncertain)
    2341. Lucy M.   born 18__; married Lawrence M. TRACY 21 Aug 1919 (he # 2411)
    2342. Georgia L.   born 18__; married Willie N. MORRIS 15 Aug 1915 (he of Jonesboro, ME)
    2343. Beth   born 18__   2344. Cecile   born ca 18__

2015. LUCY MAUD-9 DRISKO, twin sister of above, was born 22 Oct 1866 at Jonesboro, Maine. She married Frank Herbert HUGHES on 3 Oct 1883 at Machias, Maine. He was the son of _____ HUGHES, and was born Oct 1861; died ____. Lucy Maud-9 DRISKO died 4 Oct 1931.

Children of Lucy Maud-9 DRISKO and Frank HUGHES:
    Surname HUGHES   2347. Leigh Drisko born Jan 1890, RI.; res. Ohio
    2345. Wayne   born 18__   enlisted **WW 1** on 21 Sept 1917 at Auxbridge, MA
    2346. Willie born 18__; d y   2348. Isabel   born 18__

2016. WILLIAM PITT FESSENDEN-9 DRISKO, brother of above, was born 1 Dec 1869 at Harrington, ME. He married first to Mary Ella-7 (Mamie) TABBUTT on 27 July 1892 at Harrington. She was the daughter of Abijah Worcester TABBUTT and Aurilla FLOYD, and was born 28 Apr 1869 at Columbia Falls, ME; died 19 July 1899 at Centerville, ME, 1 week after the birth of twin daughters. He married his second wife, May/Mae BAGLEY, on 7 June 1900. (She married twice more). William Pitt-9 died 7 Aug 1901 (age 31) at Centerville, Maine.

*** William Pitt-9 DRISKO and a Mr. GILMAN jointly owned a granite quarry. After Mr. GILMAN was killed in an explosion at the quarry, the business failed and William Pitt-9 DRISKO went into the lumbering business. He was the namesake of a prominent citizen of Maine, William Pitt FESSENDEN (1806-1869). Mr. FESSENDEN was a US Congressman; a US Senator under Presidents Abraham LINCOLN and Andrew JOHNSON. He was also Secretary of the Treasury under LINCOLN. He was only 16 years old when he graduated from Bowdoin College (ME). His father was Samuel FESSENDEN, & his godfather was Daniel WEBSTER.

Children of William Pitt-9 DRISKO and Mamie TABBUTT:
    Surname DRISKO

+ 2349. CLARENCE HOLMES — born 30 Sept 1893 Jonesboro, ME; died 19 Mar 1991 Columbia, ME
  married Almira/ Myra Mabel MORRIS 15 Sept 1918
  (she dau/o Henry F. MORRIS, Jr. and Ida M. MARTIN)

+ 2350. FRANK EUGENE — born 20 Dec 1894 Jonesboro, ME; 1m. Maude A. STEWART 22 Jan 1915
  (she born 14 Apr 1892; died 13 Jan 1977 Harrington, ME.)
  2m. Julia A. Sewell; (she born 16 Dec 1900; died 21 June 1995 Caribou, ME)
  died 20 Nov 1995 Caribou, Maine; buried Columbia, ME.

2351. Melvin Tabbutt — born 16 Jan 1896 Jonesboro, ME; married Ethel PERKINS 13 Sep 1923 (2 ch)
  (she born 23 Mar 1902, KS; died Mar 1984 San Antonio, TX)
  died 1 Nov 1982 San Antonio, Bexar County, Texas

+ 2352. EDNA — born 17 May 1897; married Chester S. BURTCH; died 1984 CA
  (he born 4 Dec 1893; died Jan 1983 San Luis Obispo, CA)

+ 2353. MAMIE/MARY ELLA (twin) — born 12 July 1899; married Marvin HALL 26 Dec 1930
  died 8 July 1936 Washington, DC

2354. Marion (twin) — born 12 July 1899; married Edward Payson TUCKER 24 Feb 1940
  (he born 13 Apr 1895; died 18 Feb 1993)
  died 25 Mar 1993; buried Columbia Falls, Maine.

William Pitt-9 DRISKO (1869-1901)

Mary Ella-7 TABBUT (1869-1899)

Child of William Pitt-9 DRISKO and May/Mae BAGLEY:
    Surname DRISKO
2355. Ruth — born ca Oct 1900; died 3 Mar 1901   EOL

+ Ancestry of Mary Ella-7 (Mamie) TABBUTT

PHILIP-1 FLOOD/FLOYD, the immigrant, arrived in New Jersey from the Isle of Guernsey. He settled in Newbury, MA ca 1680. He was born ca 16__; died 1705.　His son, HENRY-2 FLOOD/FLOYD, was the father of ANDREW-3 FLOOD/FLOYD of Surry, Hancock Co., ME; who was born ca ____, and married Sarah-5 HOPKINSON. She was the daughter of John-4 HOPKINSON (Caleb-3; 2; Michael-1).

ANDREW-3 FLOOD/FLOYD was the father of the REV JOHN HOPKINSON-4 FLOYD, who was born 23 Apr 1768/70 at Waltham, MA. He was a Methodist lay minister and lumberman. He married Phebe W. SWETT on 14 Apr 1796. She was the daughter of Joseph SWETT and Jemima WORMWOOD, and was born 16 Sept 1777; died 30 Dec 1828.

Their 3rd son, David Swett-5 FLOYD, was born at Surry on 16 Oct 1809, and married Huldah-7 SINCLAIR on 8 May 1834. She was the daughter of Thomas-6 SINCLAIR and Dorothy ALLEN, and was born Oct 1813, ME; died ca 1876. They were the parents of 5 children, including Rolla D-6 FLOYD who married first to Theodocia Drisko-7 ALLEN Chandler, the daughter of Abraham-6 ALLEN and Mary/Polly-7 WORCESTER, and second to Mary Jane CLARK Leighton (widow of Ralph LEIGHTON, # 1827).

AURILLA-6 FLOYD, oldest daughter of David-5, was born 19 Oct 1842 at Surry, ME.; married Abijah Worcester TABBUTT +++ ca 1867, and died ca 1914. Abijah was born 25 Mar 1842; died 3 Aug 1918. Their daughter was Mary Ella-7 TABBUTT (above).

+++ Abijah Worcester TABBUTT, whose ancestry is uncertain, was a farmer at Columbia Falls, Maine. He was affectionately called a " Jack of all trades ".　In 1883 he invented the " Blueberry Rake ".　He had adapted it from the design of rakes used to harvest cranberries. His first rake had eight teeth and a handle attached to the back of a dust-pan like scoop. In a few years the rake had twelve teeth and an improved handle. Before the turn-of-the-century he was producing about 200 rakes a year.

By 1918, after his grandson, Clarence Holmes-10 DRISKO (# 2349) had graduated from college, he was producing rakes with as many as 25 teeth, and was selling them for $.65 apiece. They sold about 2,000 rakes that year.

After Abijah Worcester TABBUTT died (3 Aug 1918), two of his grandsons (Clarence and Frank) inherited the business. They expanded production, but soon after Frank decided to turn the business over to Clarence. Frank wanted to pursue other interests. Clarence-10 DRISKO made all of his rakes during the summer months, and spent his winters teaching and serving as a high school principal in Bangor, Maine until 1954. After that time, the rakes were made during the winter months, still at the shop Clarences' grandfather had built for that purpose. In 1971, Clarence suffered a broken hip and pelvis, and as a result his son-in-law Verrill WORCESTER, Jr., and two other men took over the operation and kept the plant in production.

The " Blueberry Rakes ", changed many times over the years, until they contained as many as 40 to 60 teeth. They sold about 3,000 rakes at $ 22.50 each in 1979. Berry raking isn't all the rakes are used for. Many were purchased by tourists and souvenir hunters. They used the rakes as letter holders, ornaments, and conversation pieces.

Abijah Worcester TABBUT (1842-1918)　　　　　*Aurilla-6 FLOYD (1842-1914)*

2017. ALICE MAY-9 DRISKO, sister of above, was born 19 Jan 1872 at Jonesboro, Maine. She married Arthur Franklin LINDSEY of Harrington, ME on 10 Dec 1893. He was the son of Edward W. LINDSEY and Abbie Jane WESCOTT, and was born 22 May 1866, New Brunswick . Alice May-9 died 6 Sept 1917.

Children of Alice May-9 DRISKO and Arthur LINDSEY:
  Surname LINDSEY
  2356. Hazel V.   born 27 Nov 1895; d. 1 Nov 1988   2358. Walter K.   born 19__
  2357. Darrell Enos born 8 Aug 1899; d. 17 June 1917   marr Erma M. WENTWORTH 15 Dec 1926

2018. JOSEPHINE FRANCES-9 DRISKO, sister of above, was born 15 Feb 1874 (possibly baptized 1 Apr 1874) at Jonesboro, Maine. She married Frank Marshall-9 ALLEN on 19 Apr 1901. He was the son of Benjamin Franklin-8 ALLEN and Mary Frances-2 MAILEY, and was born 19 June 1874; died 1956. Josephine F-9 DRISKO died 1965 at Columbia Falls, Maine, and are buried there in the Ruggles Cemetery.

Children of Josephine Frances-9 DRISKO and Frank Marshall-9 ALLEN:
  Surname ALLEN
  2359. Fred   born 19__; d y   2360. Harold W. born 19__; res Columbia Falls, ME
  2361. J. Drisko   born 19__; resided Rumford, RI
  2362. Joy   born 20 Feb 1907; married _?_ CHEVALIER; died 22 May 1995 , ME.
  2363. Frances M.   born July 1917; died 19 July 1967; resided Tacoma Park, MD
                      married Robert L. McCONNAUGHY 20 July 1936 Washington., DC
                      (he born 13 Aug 1915; died 14 Mar 1993 Alexandria, VA)
  2364. June   born 1921; died 1939
  2365. Shapleigh C. born 19__; married Frances M. BOUDREAU 22 Dec 1946; res. Bangor, ME

2020. JAMES WALKER-9 DRISKO, brother of above, was born 24 Mar 1879 at Jonesboro, Maine. He married Annie Lydia NOYES on 28 Nov 1900. She was the daughter of George NOYES and Clara BRIDGHAM, and was born 15 Feb 1881; died 1947. James-9 DRISKO died 11 July 1966 at Jonesboro.

Children of James-9 DRISKO and Annie NOYES:
  Surname DRISKO
  2366. Felice A.   born 11 Jan 1902; died Sept 1966 Castine, Hancock, Maine
        marr Ralph J. REYNOLDS 30 June 1921 Jonesboro, ME (he born 5 June 1898; died 22 Feb 1990)
  2367. Leander   born 19__
  2368. Thelma L.   born 24 July 1906; ; died 4 Dec 1999 Jonesport, Maine
        marr Richard W. PEASLEY 19 Aug 1930 (he born 28 Aug 1902; died July 1972 Jonesport)
  2369. Donald   born 20 July 1908; died 20 Dec 1994 Jonesboro, Maine

2024. WILSON L-9 BRIDGHAM, son of Jerusha-8 DRISKO (Chandler R-7; Jonathan-6; Samuel G-5; Joseph-4; John-3; 2) and Lorenzo BRIDGHAM. He marr Abbie FLYNN 28 Oct 1893 at Whitneyville, ME

Children of Wilson L-9 BRIDGHAM and Abbie FLYNN:
  Surname BRIDGHAM
  2370. Ruth E.   born ca Dec 1893/94; died Aug 1979
                     married Hazen R. LIBBY on 14 Aug 1915 (he of Calais, Maine)
  2371. Calla   born 28 Aug 1895; died July 1983 Bangor, Maine
                     married Harold J. EMERY 12 Sept 1917 (both of Bangor, ME)
  2372. Claire   born ca 18__; married Merrill A. JONES of Cutler, ME on 24 Dec 1918
                     (he born 3 Mar 1890; died Aug 1976 Portland, Maine)
  2373. Carl   born poss 17 Dec 1900; died May 1970   2374. Blanche   born ca ____

2031. ELZENA G-9 TRACY, daughter of Amasa Drisko-8 TRACY (Abigail-7 DRISKO; Jonathan-6; Samuel G-5; Joseph-4; John-3; 2) and Rebecca D-8 SAWYER, was born ca 1857 at Addison, Maine. She married Ferdinand Milliken-8 MERRITT on 12 May 1881 at Addison, the Rev Mr. HARDEN, officiating..

He was the son of Curtis-7 MERRITT and his 3ʳᵈ wife Sarah W. NICHOLS, and was born 1850; died 1932 at Chadron, Nebraska. Elzena-9 TRACY died there ca 1944. (Note: Machias Union newspaper reported 14 June 1881, that they " started from their home in Addison 23 May (1881) for the Black Hills of Dakota Territory ". He was a millwright.)

Children of Elzena-9 TRACY and Ferdinand-8 MERRITT:
  Surname MERRITT
  2375. Wilbur Tracy   born 29 Jan 1882; died Feb 1969 unmarried
  2376. Evelyn   born 18__; died young
  2377. Harry C.   born 188_; married Georgia HADDON 13 May1908; died Jan 1964
  2378. Fred Harris   born 18__; died 192_ as the result of an automobile accident
  2379. Ferdinand, Jr.   born 1 July 1895; married Elvina Marie DEEN; died Nov 1967
                          (she born 3 June 1904; died June 1985)
  2380. Charles D.   born 19 Dec 1898; married Edna __?__; died Oct 1961; resided St. Louis, MO

2034. BELINDA-9 TRACY, daughter of Amos L-8 TRACY (Abigail B-7 DRISKO; Jonathan-6; Samuel G-5; Joseph-4; John-3; 2) and Dennis TRACY, was born Sept 1853. She married Moses-8 WORCESTER, 3ʳᵈ on 12 July 1883 at Columbia Falls, Maine. (as his 2ⁿᵈ wife) He was the son of Amos-7 WORCESTER and Sarah WARD, and was born Aug 1829; died 4 Feb 1904 at Columbia, Maine. (His first wife was Abigail J. DORR, with whom he had 5 children) He was a **Civil War veteran**, and was a day laborer at CF.

Children of Belinda-9 TRACY and Moses-8 WORCESTER:
  Surname WORCESTER   (children born at Columbia Falls, Maine)
  2381. William Wesley   born 15 Dec 1883; died 10 July 1958 Columbia Falls, Maine
        " Willie "   married Laura C. GRANT 24 Sept 1909; she born 6 Jan 1894; died 3 Aug 1987)
  2382. Moses Jefferson born 18 Jan 1886; died 11 Oct 1918 influenza
                         marr Lettie Lee GRANT Worcester 8 Aug 1914; (she born 31 May 1881; died 14 Dec 1918)
  2383. Mary A.   born Dec 1887; died 2 July 1908
                         married Augustus Winslow/William CARTER 13 May 1905
                         (he born 27 Dec 1880; son/o Ezekiel CARTER and Louise FRYE)
 +2384. MARCIA   born 30 May 1889; died 12 June 1983 Howland, Maine
        EVELYN   married Austin Eugene-8 HARMON 1 Oct 1913
                         (he son/o Austin Turner-7 HARMON and Harriet ARMSTRONG)
                         (he born 21 Apr 1887; died 27 Nov 1934)
  2385. John Palmer   born Feb 1891; died ca 1913 after losing his arm in a shooting accident   EOL
  2386. Elizabeth M.   born Mar 1894; died ca 1910 unmarried   EOL

2035. AMASA DRISKO-9 TRACY, brother of above, was born 16 Apr 1855 at Columbia, Maine. He married Mary Caroline STEVAR ca 1879. She was the daughter of George STEVAR and Martha ??, and was born 28 Sept 1857, VA; died 21 Jan 1936 Westbrook, ME. Amasa-9 was a laborer and a fisherman..

Children of Amasa Drisko-9 TRACY and Mary STEVAR:
  Surname TRACY
 + 2387. GEORGIA ANN born 27 Aug 1880 Columbia Falls, Maine
          married Bernard Frank/Frank Bernard-9 CARVER (# 1968) on 9 Oct 1901 Jonesport, ME
  2388. Agnes Elizabeth   born 7 Dec 1882 Columbia Falls, ME.; died 25 Mar 1967
                          married Perlin Winslow-9 DRISKO 30 Oct 1901 (as his 2ⁿᵈ wife) (# 1883)
        (he son/o Amanda Rhodella-8 DRISKO)(he born 6 Dec 1876; died 17 Apr 1952 Westbrook, ME)
  2389. Fannie E.   born ca 1883/84; married Harry McFARLAND 29 Dec 1909 Westbrook, ME
  2390. Jennie M.   born 30 Sep 1885; died Dec 1971 Gorham, Maine
                          married Omer W. BRIGHTMAN 14 Dec 1905 Jonesport, Maine
  2391. Martin L.   born 9 June 1886; died Jan 1964 ME; married Ella M. BERRY 27 Aug 1910
  2392. Fred D.   born ca 1887; poss married Ruth-10 CARTY (she born 16 June 1893)
  2393. Clara   born 11 Nov 1888; died Dec 1973 Hallowell, Maine
        married George C. BERRY 16 Aug 1913 Westbrook, ME. (he born 30 Oct 1878; died Aug 1962, ME)

2036. MARY E-9 TRACY, sister of above, was born ca 1858. She married George H. BOWLES, son of Stephen BOWLES and Ann _?_, on 28 Dec 1889; and died ca 1900. George was born ca 1855, Maine.

Children of Mary E-9 TRACY and George BOWLES:
Surname BOWLES   2394. Helen   born 18__   2395. John   born 18__

2037. AMOS W-9 TRACY, brother of above, was born March 1861 at Addison, ME. He married Corris A. (Sandy) NORTON 21 July 1893. Amos-9, a laborer in a sardine factory, died June 1910 at Jonesport, ME

Children of Amos-9 TRACY and Corris NORTON:
Surname TRACY
2396. Sylvanus R.   born 27 May 1899; died June 1973 Prospect Harbor, Maine
    married Grace E. BARTLETT 3 Jan 1924 (she born 16 Dec 1906; died Nov 1976 Prospect Harbor
2397. Vernard C.   born 20 Apr; marr Kathleen E. LUNT 28 Feb 1929; died 4 July 1988, MA
          (she poss born 1 Nov 1907; died 20 Nov 1996, RI)

2038. JOHN FRANKLIN-9 TRACY, brother of above, was born 3 Nov 1863 at Columbia Falls, Maine. He married Flora Rosetta Isabel BUTLER on 6 July 1886 at Columbia Falls. She was the daughter of Peter BUTLER and Laura A-6 NASH, and was born 29 Dec 1868 MN; died 22 Sept 1958 Calais, ME. As a youth he worked as a ship's cook and second mate. In 1897 he left the sea to become a farmer. John F-9 TRACY died 26 Jan 1917 at Calais, ME. An account of his death appeared in the Calais Advertiser. It stated that " he was a section foreman on the Maine Central Railroad and was killed while working. " An Arthur CASEY, a farmer, was arraigned before the local judge, and was charged with his murder.

Children of John Franklin-9 TRACY and Flora BUTLER:
Surname TRACY
+ 2398. FLORA   born 4 June 1887 Columbia Falls, ME; died Sept 1974 Kennebunkport, ME
    ROSETTA   married Arthur M. ALLEN 28 May 1907
  2399. Eliza Ann   born 6 Nov 1888 Columbia Falls, ME.; died 4 July 1907
          married Melvin Samuel TENNEY 3 June 19__
          One child: Ruby Ethel-11 TENNEY born 19__
+ 2400. CHARLES   born 20 Apr 1890 Columbia Falls, ME.; died 29 Apr 1964 Vancouver, BC
    GILBERT   married Maggie Craig LEITH 12 Oct 1914 Kenora, Ontario, Canada
          (she dau/o William LEITH and Annie NICHOLL)(she born ca 1893 Ireland)
+ 2401. ELIZABETH   born 9 June 1893 Columbia Falls, ME.; died Dec 1971, NH
    ELLA   married Loring Josiah WILLEY 12 Oct 1912
+ 2402. JOSEPHINE   born 15 Aug 1895 Jonesboro, ME.; died Jan 1988
    FRANKLIN   1m. Alden SEELEY (no issue); 2m. Frank B. KELLY 15 May 1915
          3m. Fred L. CAMERON 11 July 1934
+ 2403. VICTOR   born 12 Apr 1897 Jonesboro, ME; died Oct 1976 Concord, NH
    THURLOW   married Fidelia Jane GREENLAW 4 May 1921 Baileyville, Maine
          (she dau/o Charles GREENLAW and Nettie WILKINS)
+ 2404. AMOS PETER   born 28 Apr 1900 Jonesboro
          married Priscilla BURGESS 7 July 1934 Conway, NH
          (dau/o Edward BURGESS and Rosie BUTLER)
+ 2405. HARRIETTE   born 31 March 1904 Jonesboro
    ESTELLE   married John Russell FITZSIMMONS 24 Aug 1923
+ 2406. ETHEL MAE   born 16 Nov 1906 Woodland, ME; died 26 Aug 1991
          married Carroll W. DUDLEY 1 July 1922
  2407. Annie Laurie   born 2 March 1904/14; died 22 Sept 1915   EOL

2039. ASA MERRILL-9 TRACY, brother of above, was born 4 Apr 1865 at Columbia Falls, Maine. He married Sarah J-10 WORCESTER on 11 Jan 1893 at Columbia Falls. She was the daughter of Leander Knowles-9 WORCESTER and Julia A. DORR French; and was born __; died __. Asa-9 died 5 Aug 1926.

Children of Asa M-9 TRACY and Sarah WORCESTER:
   Surname TRACY
   2408. Merrill   born 21 Feb 1893; marr Elsie NORTON 9 Nov 1912 Jonesport, ME; died 14 Aug 1995
   2409. Alice   born 18__
   2410. Harvey   born 18__; poss marr Ella L. KELLEY/ROBINSON 30 Nov 1919 Jnspt
   2411. Lawrence M.   born 18__; married Lucy M-10 FISH (# 2341) 21 July 1919 Jonesboro
   2412. Everett B.   born 20 July 1900; died Feb 1965 Maine
                            married Susie A. TIBBETTS 27 Dec 1924 (both of Jonesport, ME)
                            (she born 26 Feb 1900; died 28 Dec 1996 Jonesport, ME)
   2413. William   born 22 Oct 1902 Jonesport; died there Apr 1980
   2414. Amos   born 10 June 1909; died July 1966 Maine
                            married Leonice HAYWOOD 16 Sept 1931 Jonesport, Maine
                            (she born 27 July 1914; died 27 Jan 1995, Maine)
   2415 Frank Small   born 1 Aug 1915; died Jan 1980 Jonesport, Maine
   2416. Sara   born 19__   2417. Abbie born 19__; married Carleton H. ROLFE 3 Jan 1931

2040. ELIZA ANN-9 TRACY, sister of above, was born May 1869 at Columbia Falls, Washington Co.,
Maine. She married Ransom Nash BUTLER on 19 Aug 1891. He was the son of Peter BUTLER and Laura
A. NASH, and brother of Flora BUTLER (above). He was born 4 Aug 1866, ME; died May 1905.

Children of Eliza Ann-9 TRACY and Ransom Nash BUTLER:
   Surname BUTLER
   2418. Fred   born ca 1892   2420. Clarence   born ca 1896
   2419. Frank   born ca 1894   2421. Roger   born ca 1898

2042. WILLIAM HENRY-9 TRACY, brother of above, was born 28 March 1873 at Bucks Harbor, Maine.
He married first to Delia L. (Lila) WORCESTER/WORSTER on 7 May 1907. He married second to Lucy
L. WALLACE/Wright/WRIGHT/ Wallace on 25 Nov 1931 at Jonesport, Maine.

Children of William H-9 TRACY and Delia WORSTER:
   Surname TRACY
   2422. Ada M.   born 18 May/Dec 1910; died Oct 1972 Buck Creek, Tippecanoe, IN
                           married Ivan FLAHERTY 17 May 1926 Columbia Falls, ME
   2423. Marion C.   born 18 May/Dec 1910; died June 1985 Milbridge, Maine
                           married Chester W. LOVEJOY 6 March 1929
   2424. Ethel   born ____
   2425. Maud   born ____
   2426. Jessie   born ____; married Maurice W. ALLEY 23 Apr 1939 Columbia Falls, ME
   2427. Frank   born ____; 1m. Helen DINSMORE 16 June 1940 Columbia Falls
                           2m. Madeline E. TIBBETTS 3 Feb 1951 Columbia Falls

2046. GILMAN-9 COLSON, Jr. , son of Mary Elizabeth-8 WILSON (Aphphatha-7 NASH; Mary-6
DRISKO; Samuel Gatchell-5; Joseph-4; John-3; 2) and Captain Gilman COLSON, was born Apr 1858,
ME. He married Emma _?_ ca 1885/86. She was born June 1861, ME. He was a sailor/cook.

Children of Gilman COLSON and Emma __?__:
   Surname COLSON
   2428. Olive   born Nov 1886
   2429. Mary D.   born Sept 1894
                         married Virgil E. MAREAN (of Portland, ME) 17 Sep 1911

2947. MARY AUGUSTA-9 COLSON, sister of above, was born 11 Aug 1865 at Lexington, MA. She
married Edward Bissell CURTIS on 31 Dec 1885 at Somerville, MA. After their marriage they resided in
Boston and Cambridge , MA; spending summers at his home in Machias, ME. Shortly after the birth of

their first or second child they moved to Machias permanently. Edward CURTIS owned timberland; the Machias drugstore; and was President of the Machias Electric Light. Company. He was the son of Abel CURTIS and Mercy LONGFELLOW, and was born 20 Feb 1853 Machias; died 15 Apr 1927 Machias, Maine. He was a wholesale flour salesman and postmaster for Machias. Mary Augusta-9 died 9 Dec 1951 in Machias, and they are buried there in Court Street Cemetery.

Children of Mary Augusta-9 COLSON and Edward Bissell CURTIS:
   Surname CURTIS
+ 2430. EDWARD GILMAN   born 7 Sept 1886; died 21 March 1970 Bronxville, NY
                              married Mary Helen SEELBACH 28 Oct 1920
+ 2431. JOSEPHINE NASH   born 6 Apr 1889 Cambridge, MA; died 3 July 1941 Minneapolis, MN
                              married William Silliman FOSTER
+ 2432. MARY   born 24 July 1892 Machias, ME; died 27 Aug 1984 Orleans, MA
                              1m. Dr. Farrar COBB 1919; 2m. Lawrence A. THAYER 30 June 1953

2048. WINFIELD SCOTT-9 SMITH, son of Maria-8 WILSON (Aphphatha-7 NASH; Mary-6 DRISKO; Samuel Gatchell-5; Joseph-4; John-3; 2) and Eri Hathaway-8 SMITH, was born 20 Sept 1848 at Columbia, Maine. He married Matilda Alvenia-6 JORDAN on 6 Dec 1873. She was the daughter of Ebenezer-5 JORDAN and Harriet R. YOUNG, and was born 6 Dec 1852 at Mariaville, Maine; died 29 Jan 1909. Winfield Scott-9 SMITH was a saddle and harness maker, and died ____.

Children of Winfield-9 SMITH and Matilda-6 JORDAN:
   Surname SMITH
2433. Eben E.   born 10 Mar 1875   2434. Alla (f)   born 6 June 1877
       marr Mary P. McMILLAN 30 Sept 1903 (both of Kingman, ME)

2052. GEORGE FRANCIS-9 WASS, son of Rufus Wadsworth-8 WASS (Rebecca-7 NASH; Mary-6 DRISKO; Samuel Gatchell-5; Joseph-4; John-3; 2) and Mary Adams GULLIVER, was born 23 Jan 1849, MA. He married Emma C. WEGENSTEIN on 7 Mar 1882 at Grundy Center, Iowa. She was the daughter of Henry WEGENSTEIN and was born 31 Dec 1862, NJ; died 9 Dec 1941, KS. George F-9 died 1920.

Children of George-9 WASS and Emma WEGENSTEIN:
   Surname WASS
2435. George   born ca 1883; d y   2438. Lettie   born ca 1888; d y
2436. Louise   born 1884; d y   2439. Mary A.   born ca 1890; died 1915
2437. Ida Maud   born 5 Feb 1886, Iowa   2440. Frances   born 189_; res. MN
       married J. Claude MILLER; died 5 Nov 1942, KS.   married J. E. CHAPMAN

2055. JOHN NICHOLS-9 WASS, brother of above, was born 6 Mar 1854 at Addison, Maine. He married Harriet __?__ Garwood on 26 July 1892 at Beresford, South Dakota. (She had a daughter from a prior marriage). She was born ca 18__; died 11 Apr 1909. He married second, but had no more children.

Children of John Nicholas-9 WASS and Harriet __?_ Garwood:
   Surname WASS   (children born Beresford, SD)
2441. Lloyd M.   born 25 May 1893; married Rose Elizabeth STUESSI June 1916
2442. Wayne   born ca 1899; died 28 Nov 1921 unmarried EOL

2058. VICTOR CURTIS-9 WASS, brother of above, was born 14 Oct 1864 at Hudson, Iowa. He married May STEVENS ca 1892. He died 19 June 1948 at ___, Minnesota.

Children of Victor-9 WASS and May STEVENS:
   Surname WASS
2443. Harold   born 4 Jan 1893; died Aug 1968,MN   2445. Lowell   born 18___
2444. Hazel   born   18__   2446. Rolland born 14 Nov 1906; died Oct 1980

2068. EMMA KELLER-9 ALLINE, daughter of Henry W-8 ALLINE (Mary-7 NASH; Mary-6 DRISKO; Samuel Gatchell-5; Joseph-4; John-3; 2) and Sarah S. KELLER, was born ca 1859. She married John Hezekiah WINCHELL ca 1883. Emma Keller-9 ALLINE died after 1905 IA/CO.

Children of Emma Keller-9 ALLINE and John H. WINCHELL:
   Surname WINCHELL
+ 2447. RUTH LOWELL born 4 Sept 1890 Plymouth Co., IA; died 5 Nov 1950 Tucson, AZ
                 married Frank Moe STEPHENS 6 July 1916 CO.
  (he son/o Peter STEPHENS and Ida MOE; he born 29 Jan 1889 Denver, CO; died 21 Sept 1982 Denver)

   2448. John H. born 29 Aug 1892 LaMars, IA; died Dec 1970 Washington, DC
          1m. Harriet Meredith PARMALEE 3 Aug 1918
          2m. Teresa J. CONNOLLY 17 May 1936

2081. HARLAND-9 COFFIN, son of Eugene-8 COFFIN (Amos-7; Rebecca-6 DRISKO; Samuel Gatchell-5; Joseph-4; John-3; 2) and Malintha LOOK, was born 29 Nov 1876. He married Emma WARD ca 19__. She was born 1883; died 19__. Harlan-9 COFFIN died Apr 1966 Steuben, Maine.

Children of Harland-9 COFFIN and Emma WARD:
   Surname COFFIN
2449. Vera   born 1904; married Ray EVANS 25 May 1935
2450. Harland E.   born 19 Feb 1909; married __?__ before 1929
                 died 28 Feb 1970 Talmadge, Maine
          One child: Richard Eugene-11 COFFIN born 1929
                poss married Iona V. SORENSON of Milbridge, ME
2451. Charlotte   born ca 1910; married __?__ LEIGHTON

The Tenth American Generation

2147. THEODORE BENTLEY-10 DRISKO, son of Waldo Bentley-9 DRISKO (Judah Johnson-8; William Johnson-7; Judah-6; John-5; Joseph-4; John-3; 2) and Jennie BURNHAM, was born 7 Apr 1880 at Worcester, MA. He married Bertha HOWES ** of Illinois. She was born 9 Mar 1883, IL; died May 1978 at Havana, Mason County, Illinois. Theodore-10 DRISKO died _____.

Children of Theodore-10 DRISKO and Bertha HOWES:
Surname DRISKO
2452. Blanche May   born ____   2453. Mabel Eugenia   born _____
          ** Bertha HOWES had a son, Othello Frank __?__, who was adopted by Theodore-10 DRISKO.
                    He married __?__ from Oregon and had no children.

2148. EUGENE SANBORN-10 DRISKO, brother of above, was born 13 June 1882 at Worcester, MA. He married first to Pearl BROUGHTEN ca 19__ at Abilene, KS. His second wife was a Betty SMITH.

Children of Eugene-10 DRISKO and Pearl BROUGHTEN:
Surname DRISKO   2454. Mary Gertrude born 19__   2455. William H.   born 19__; dy
Child of Eugene-10 DRISKO and Betty SMITH:
Surname DRISKO
2456. Robert Eugene   born 20 July 1923, CA; married ? from Long Beach, CA; died Apr 1987

2151. PHILIP JOSLYN-10 DRISKO, brother of above, was born 5 Feb 1898 at Abilene, Kansas. He married Blanche HENDERSON of Independence, MO ca 19__. She was born 1 Sept 1904; died Sept 1981 at Odessa, TX. Philip-10 DRISKO died June 1945. Served in the US Navy in WW 1.

Child of Philip Joslyn-10 DRISKO and Blanche HENDERSON:
Surname DRISKO
2457. Philip Benjamin   born 19__; married Edna Louise KIRK (she from Waco, TX) no issue EOL

2154. CHARLES LYMAN-10 DRISKO, brother of above, was born 8 Nov 1900 at Abilene, Kansas. He married Lela Esper SEARS of Bartlesville, Oklahoma ca 19__. She was born 23 Sept 1901; died 12 March 2000. Charles-10 died Aug 1987 Bartlesville.

Children of Charles Lyman-10 DRISKO and Lela SEARS:
Surname DRISKO
+ 2458. WILLIAM   born 15 Mar 1925 Bartlesville, OK; married Doris DANIEL of Bartlesville
      WALDO   (she born 7 May 1926; died 26 Nov 1991, OK)
+ 2459. CHARLES   born 27 Oct 1928 Bartlesville; married Nancy WALKER
      HERBERT   (she from Lufkin, Texas)
   2460. Richard Reed   born 6 July 1931 Bartlesville; married Ann ROBERTS of Bartlesville
                 One child: Julia Ann-12 DRISKO born 1 Sept 1957 San Antonio, Texas

2155. HELEN FRANKLAND-10 SANBORN, daughter of Mary Frankland-9 DRISKO (Judah Johnson-8; William Johnson-7; Judah-6; John-5; Joseph-4; John-3; 2) and the Rev Francis Arthur SANBORN, was born 31 Dec 1888 at Machiasport, Maine. She married Eleazer CARVER II on 15 June 1911 at Salem, NH. He was the son of Eleazer CARVER I (William; Rev Eleazer) and Marcella Adelaide TIBBETTS, and was born 8 Dec 1885 at Milo, Maine; died 3 Jan 1967 Milo.

Children of Helen F-10 SANBORN and Eleazer CARVER II:
Surname CARVER
+ 2461. ELEAZER III   born 31 Aug 1912 Milo, Maine
                 married Thelma Louise BUSHEY 19 Oct 1936 at Shelby, Ohio
                 (she dau/o Paul BUSHEY and Nellie WILSON) (she born 10 Oct 1912)

Children of Helen F-10 SANBORN, continued:
    Surname CARVER
+ 2462. JOHN   born 7 June 1914; married Dorothy EADE 19 Jan 1946
                               (she dau/o John EADE and Elizabeth __?__)
    2463. Eugene Sanborn   born 15 Sept 1916; married Phyllis D. PEARL 16 June 1942
                               (she dau/o Simon PEARL and Elizabeth SANBORN)
                               (she born 7 May 1920 W. Boxford, MA;   )
    2464. Marcella Frankland born 14 June 1918; died 15 Oct 1933 Milo, Maine
    2465. Francis Speed   born 21 Feb 1921 Milo, ME; died 2 May 2000 Saratoga, NY
                               1m. Ann Marie LA PADULA 18 Sept 1946, NY
          (she dau/o James LA PADULA and Ida EVANGELISTA)(she born July 1927 Brooklyn, NY; div)
                     One child: Robert James-12 CARVER born 24 June 1949 White Sulphur Springs, WV
                               2m. Martha Lois WARD 12 May 1956
                               (she dau/o Erwin WARD and Isabella ?) (she born 17 July 1926 Deposit, NY)
    2466. William   born 14 Oct 1924; died 15 Aug 1978 unmarried; resided Milo, Maine
+ 2467. ALBION   born 29 Apr 1928 Milo, Maine
        MINOT   married Fern Alice NASON 21 Jan 1953 Dover- Foxcraft, Maine
                               (she dau/o Carroll NASON and Carrie CUTHBERTSON)
                               (she born 29 Apr 1934 Milo, ME;   )
+ 2468. JOSEF TODD   born 17 Aug 1930, Milo,Maine
                               married Annegrethe KISLING 8 Feb 1954 Dover-Foxcraft, Maine
                               (she dau/o Christian KISLING and Ane Margarethe POULSEN)
                               (she born 2 Sept 1935 Denmark; divorced)

2158. BRADFORD DRISCO-10 COLE, son of Palmer L-9 DRISCO Cole (Levi Wass-8 DRISCO; John Jeremiah-7 DRISKO; Judah-6; John-5; Joseph-4; John-3; 2) and Myrtle ALLEN, was born 11 July 1906 at South Bend, Indiana. He married Arlene ESCH on 26 Oct 1929. She was the daughter of Edward ESCH and Edith IRELAND; and was born 31 Oct 1907; died 8 Apr 1998. Bradford-10 COLE died Nov 1981, IN.

Children of Bradford Drisco-10 COLE and Arlene ESCH:
    Surname COLE
    2469. Nancy   born 19 Feb 1932 Cleveland, OH; married Ervin WESLOSKI 12 Oct 1957
    2470. Marcia   born 3 July 1935 Cleveland; married Lawrence TOWNE 26 Feb 1959

2164. OLIVER CARROLL REED-10 DRISKO, son of Levi Bert-9 DRISKO (Burt William-8; John Jeremiah-7; Judah-6; John-5; Joseph-4; John-3; 2) and Addie HAMILTON, and was born ca 1915/16 probably at Gardiner, ME. He married Maybelle F. BAKER 20 Apr 1935 at Gardiner, ME. She was the daughter of _?_ BAKER and was born 23 Mar 1914, ME; died 28 Oct 1989 at Bath, Maine. Oliver-10 DRISKO died 12 Oct 1992 (age 77).

Children of Oliver-10 DRISKO and Maybelle/Mabel BAKER:
    Surname DRISKO
    2471. Dawn M.   born 193__; married Austin G. McGEE of Randolph, ME on 8 Mar 1954
    2472. Faith E.   born 19__ ; married Alston R. STUTZ 4 Jan 1958
    2473. Ronald L.   born 19__;   a chemist

2165. HARRY LEE-10 DRISKO, brother of above, was born 16 Sept 1918 at Gardiner, ME. He married Beulah M. BAKER, sister of Maybelle (above) 9 July 1938 at Gardiner. She was born ca 19__; died 19__. Harry-10 DRISKO died 31 July 1995 at Gardiner, Maine.

Children of Harry-10 DRISKO and Beulah BAKER:
    Surname DRISKO
    2474. Richard born 19__; an airline pilot   2475. Robert + born 19__; worked in electronics
        + Possibly the Robert E. DRISKO who married Dale L. BOYNTON 1 Aug 1959, Maine.

2166. GEORGIANNA-10 DRISKO, sister of above, was born ca 19__, probably at Gardiner, Maine. She married first to Roy G. GREEN 13 Mar 1954. She married second to __?__.

Child of Georgianna-10 DRISKO and Roy GREEN:
    Surname GREEN   2476. Sandra   born ca 19__; married ___?__ FLAHERTY

2173. CLINTON HIRAM-10 LEE, son of King Hiram-9 LEE (Willard Malcolm-8; Mary Anne-7 BUCKNAM; Abigail-6 DRISKO; John-5; Joseph-4; John-3; 2) and Lilliam Mae KING, was born 26 Nov 1906 at Sacramento, CA. He married Rhonda Alice ALDRICH ca 19__. She was born 16 Feb 1910; died 15 Sep 1989 Bodega Bay, CA. Clinton H-10 LEE died Jan 1986 at Bodega Bay, Sonoma, CA.

Children of Clinton Hiram-10 LEE and Rhonda ALDRICH:
    Surname LEE
+ 2477. RANCH ALDRICH born ca 19__; 1m. Dolores Anne SCHIELE; 2m. Diane WALKLEY
  2478. Rhonda   born ca 19__; married George HENAS
  2479. Patricia   born ca 19__; married Richard F. JACOBSEN
               2 children : Kris-12 JACOBSEN, and Karen-12 JACOBSEN
  2480. King   born ca 19__

2175. LLOYD EVAN-10 BLACK, son of Edna-9 TIBBETTS (Zephaniah A-8; Jeremiah-7; Thomas-6; Elizabeth-5 DRISKO; Joseph-4; John-3;2) and Maurice G. BLACK, was born 23 March 1924 at Bangor, Maine. He married Vivian E. KNOWLTON on 21 Dec 1943. He died 23 Jan 2000 at Bangor, Maine.

Children of Lloyd Evan-10 BLACK and Vivian KNOWLTON:
    Surname BLACK
  2481. Lois E.   born 19__; married Thomas NEWMAN 1 Aug 1964
              One child: Lawrence NEWMAN born 19__
  2482. Lloyd Evan   born 19__   2483. Geraldine born 19__

2178. PHILLIP MONROE-10 TIBBETTS; son of Allen Zephaniah-9 TIBBETTS (Zephaniah A-8; Jeremiah-7; Thomas-6; Elizabeth-5 DRISKO; Joseph-4; John-3; 2) and Mary Jane GRANT, was born 31 Mar 1932 at Cherryfield, ME. He married Charlotte Emily KATEN on 27 May 1951 at Orrington, ME. She was the daughter of Charles Francis KATEN and Ella Victoria ?, and was born 13 Jan 1932 at Orneville, ME. Phillip-10 TIBBETTS died 21 June 1973, and is buried at Pine Hill Cemetery, Orrington, Maine.

Children of Phillip-10 TIBBETTS and Charlotte KATEN:
    Surname TIBBETTS
+ 2484. KATHERINE ANN born 28 Mar 1952; 1m. Mark SHOTWELL 9 Oct 1976 Waterville, ME; (div)
              2m. Jiminez CORTEZ 17 Aug 1985 Honolulu, Hawaii
  2485. Gail Louise   born 10 Apr 1953 Bangor, ME; married James CRUSE 26 Apr 1996 Denver
+ 2486. LARRY PHILLIP born 5 Sep 1956; 1m Heidi CLUCKEY 25 Dec 1976 Eastport, ME (div)
              2m. Cheryl CASTO 10 Feb 1990 Columbus, OH
+ 2487. BRENDA LEE   born 3 Aug 1958 Ft. Lauderdale, FL
              1m. David Duane DRAWDY 26 Apr 1979 Honolulu, HI. (div)
              2m. Mark Anthony BOYORAK 18 Aug 1984 Hampden, Maine

2179. DENNIS A-10 TIBBETTS, brother of above, was born 19__. He married Sandra Elizabeth WILBUR on 1 June 1960. She was the daughter of Bernard A. WILBUR and Ruby Mae DARLING.

Children of Dennis-10 TIBBETTS and Sandra WILBUR:
    Surname TIBBETTS
  2488. Lori Jean   born
  2489. Karen Lynn   born 19__; married Peter Alan HENDERSON
              One child: Ashlie Nikole-12 HENDERSON born 19__

2192. ALBERT WENTWORTH-10 LEIGHTON, son of Ralph I-9 LEIGHTON (Abitha D-8; Phoebe-7 DRISKO; Captain John-6; Joseph-5; 4; John-3; 2) and Mary Jane CLARK, was born 11 Aug 1890 at Jerusalem, Palestine. He married Clara Norine BRENDEL on 1 July 1913. She was the daughter of __?__ BRENDEL , and was born 20 Mar 1890 at Knob Noster, Missouri; died 5 Dec 1941 at Independence, MO.

Albert W-10 LEIGHTON, in honor of his step-father, adopted the surname of LEIGHTON-FLOYD. He returned to the US in 1912. He and his mother homesteaded land in Montana the next year. He returned to Palestine in 1930, where he built the first cinema in Jerusalem on the original FLOYD property. In 1936, he and his wife returned to Independence, Missouri, where he died on 8 July 1954.

Children of Albert W-10 LEIGHTON-FLOYD and Clara BRENDEL:
   Surname LEIGHTON-FLOYD

+ 2490. HOWARD W.	born 21 Dec 1914 Opheim, Montana
	married Katherine M. BERGERSON 21 Oct 1936
+ 2491. LOIS NORINE	born 28 Aug 1918 Opheim; married James STILWELL 17 Feb 1940
2492. Frances	born 19__; died young
+ 2493. RALPH E.	born 4 Aug 1922 Knob Noster, MO; married Betty Jane GROSS 10 Sept 1943

2207. ROBERT ANDREW-10 BATSON, son of Colin Andrew-9 BATSON (Captain Adrian-8; Rebecca-7 DRISKO; Captain John-6; Joseph-5;4; John-3;2) and Sarah Alden BEAL, was born 12 June 1919. He married Helen Marion COOTS ca ___. She was the daughter of Harold Roscoe COOTS and Marion Grace WOODSON; and was born 13 Oct 1921. Robert-10 BATSON died before 1968.

Children of Robert-10 BATSON and Helen COOTS:
   Surname BATSON

 + 2494. CHERYL ANN born 4 Apr 1947 Brockton, MA.
                married Douglas Wood FREEMAN 29 Mar 1969
  (he son/o Leonard Allen FREEMAN and Dorothy Helen WOOD)(he born 12 Mar 1945 Taunton, MA)
   2495. Colin Andrew   born 8 Aug 1953

2210. JANE ANNA-10 BUTTS, daughter of Eva Frances-9 DRISKO (George Augustus-8; Capt. George Washington-7; Captain John-6; Joseph-5; 4; John-3; 2) and Orson Fowler BUTTS, was born 18 Mar 1918 at Syracuse, Onondaga County, New York. She married William J. O'DONNELL on 2 Nov 1940 at East Syracuse, NY. He was the son of George O'DONNELL and Catherine DILLON, and was born 2 Oct 1915

Children of Jane Anna-10 BUTTS and William J. O'DONNELL:
   Surname O'DONNELL   (children born Syracuse, NY)
  2496. Lawrence James   born 13 Aug 1943; died 13 July 1973 (suicide)
 + 2497. ANNE LUCILLE born 2 Feb 1946 ; married James Willard COUGHENOUR ** 1 July 1967
          (he born 26 Nov 1942; son/o Willard OLLER, Sr. and Antoinette Pearl CHAPIN)
      ** James Willard COUGHENOUR was born Willard OLLER, Jr. His parents divorced and his mother married
      Harry Morton COUGHENOUR. He legally adopted Willard and changed his name to James Willard COUGHENOUR.
      Harry M. COUGHENOUR was born 13 Feb 1911; died 24 Sept 1992 East Syracuse, NY.
 + 2498. JAMES   born 11 Nov 1947; married Diane Lynne CAVANAUGH 14 Feb 1976
     FREDERICK   (she dau/o Walter E. CAVANAUGH and Alice Rose SWEENEY)
 + 2499. DAVID   born 15 Nov 1952; married Cynthia GRIFFIN 9 Aug 1975
     WILLIAM   (she dau/o William Jos. GRIFFIN and Barbara BABINE) div May 1984
 + 2500. RICHARD FRANCIS born 9 Nov 1955; married Nancy HATALA
 + 2501. KAREN MARIE born 19 Feb 1958; married Anthony HICKS 26 Apr 1984
  2502. Margaret Ann   born 16 June 1960; married Robert CORRICE 21 Aug 1982; divorced

2213. DONALD FREDERICK-10 BUTTS, brother of above, was born 28 Sept 1925 at Syracuse, Onondaga County, NY. He married Eleanor June CARD on 18 Nov 1950 at East Syracuse, NY. She was the daughter of Hadwin CARD and Norma __?__, and was born 10 June 1930. Donald-10 worked for the New York Central Railroad, later moving to Honolulu, HI; then returning to the Syracuse, NY area.

Children of Donald F-10 BUTTS and Eleanor CARD:
    Surname BUTTS   (children born Syracuse, NY)
    2503. Donald F., Jr.   born 15 Sept 1951; married Karen SOLBERG 23 Mar 1985
+ 2504. NORMA JUNE   born 9 Sept 1952; 1m. David BARTHOLOMEW (divorced)
                              2m. Terry GOLLINGER 10 Jan 1981
    2505. Robert Arthur   born 13 Jan 1955
+ 2506. THOMAS ORSON born 5 Feb 1958; married JoAnn SHIBLEY 15 June 1980

2214. ELLEN AMELIA-10 DRISKO, daughter of Henry William-9 DRISKO (George Augustus-8; Captain George Washington-7; Captain John-6; Joseph-5; 4; John-3; 2) and Leah Belle DOLBEY, was born at Syracuse, Onondaga County, New York. She married John Henry ECKELMAN, MD on 1 May 1937 at East Syracuse, NY. He was the son of John ECKELMAN and Marie _____, and was born Jan 1916. They were divorced. Ellen-10 DRISKO graduated from the Syracuse City Normal School, a teacher training institution, in 1935. She worked, for a time, in the office of the A. E. NETTLETON Co., a manufacturer of fine shoes for men. Later she taught elementary school for many years in the Carthage (NY) Central School District.

Children of Ellen Amelia-10 DRISKO and John Henry ECKELMAN:
    Surname ECKELMAN
+ 2507. JOHN ALLEN   born 17 Dec 1938 Syracuse, NY
                        married Anne Marie BINGLE 8 Feb 1959 Carthage, NY
                        (she born 7 Aug 1941; dau/o Harry BINGLE and Genevieve WISNER)
+ 2508. BERNARD   born 31 July 1940, Harrisville, Lewis County, NY
        CARL   1m. Sharon Marie SAYER 28 Feb 1959 Carthage, NY
  (she dau/o Colin SAYER and Ruth Ella LENNOX)(she born 27 July 1939; NY; died 25 Nov 1991 OH)
                        2m. Paula Marie HENDRICK 6 June 1992 Hamilton, Ohio
                        (she born 15 May 1957; dau/o Ronald HENDRICK and ____ HOOPER)
+ 2509. WILLIAM   born 4 Dec 1941 Harrisville, NY
        DWIGHT   married Carol Marie KNAPP 28 Apr 1962 Carthage, NY
                        (she born 18 Jan 1942; dau/o Harold A. KNAPP and Cora V. HEWITT)
    2510. Jane Ellen   born 15 Nov 1950, Carthage, Jefferson County, NY

2215. GEORGE DOLBEY-10 " Jack " DRISKO, brother of above, was born 16 Nov 1917 at Syracuse, Onondaga County, NY. He was a graduate of Eastwood High School, Class of 1935. After high school he worked for Gaylord Bros., Inc., a Library Supply manufacturer, and attended University College of Syracuse University evenings, to study Electrical Engineering.

In 1942 he enlisted in the **US Army Air Corps**;and served in the **Signal Corps Unit attached to the 8th Air Force** in England. He returned to the US at the end of the **World War 2**, receiving an honorable discharge at Rome (NY) Air Force Base in the fall of 1945. He returned to Syracuse University full time to finish his studies. In the fall of 1946 he began working at radio station WAGE (later WHEN) as a broadcast engineer, and later program director. In 1954 he returned to Gaylord Bros. Inc where he worked (for another 30 years) as an Industrial Engineer in various capacities, retiring from the Engineering Dept. in Mar 1984 as Manager for Systems Development.

He married Frances Jean STERLING on 31 Jan 1947 at Syracuse, NY, by the Rev Thomas KIRKWOOD, pastor of the 2nd Reformed (Dutch) Church . She was the daughter of Charles Lee STERLING and Hazel Frances DOTY, and was born 3 June 1927 at Syracuse, NY. George Dolbey-10 DRISKO died 14 Jan 1994 at North Syracuse, NY. He is buried in the North Syracuse Cemetery.

Children of George-10 DRISKO and Frances STERLING:
    Surname DRISKO   (children born Syracuse, NY)
    2511. Linda Lee   born 11 June 1951; 1m. Charles John HICKOK 15 May 1976 Aurora, NY (div)
                        2m. John Michael HURLEY 11 June 1994 North Syracuse, NY

Children of George Dolbey-10 DRISKO, continued:
  Surname DRISKO

| 2512. Charles Eric | born 27 July 1953; married Patricia Ann TEMPLE 17 Mar 1979 North Syracuse divorced Sept 1984 no issue   EOL |
| + 2513. DANA STERLING | born 29 July 1958 married Jennifer Lynn REYNOLDS 17 Sept 1983 North Syracuse, NY (she born 23 Apr 1961; dau/o John REYNOLDS and Patricia DAIR) |

2216. FELLOWS E-10 DRISKO, son of Arthur William-9 DRISKO (Everett-8; Jason Clapp-7; Captain John-6; Joseph-5; 4; John-3; 2) and Faustina PLUMMER, was born 1 July 1898, Maine. He married Flora L. CROWLEY 21 June 1924 at Addison, ME. She was the daughter of ___ CROWLEY and was born 8 Apr 1904; died 14 July 1997 at Addison, Maine. Fellows-10 DRISKO died there 23 Nov 1987.

Children of Fellows-10 DRISKO and Flora CROWLEY:
  Surname DRISKO

2514. Donald A.	born 1925; died 2 Dec 1939 EOL
2515. Barbara M.	born 192_; married Neil Irving PLUMMER 28 Oct 1944
2516. Alan F.	born 19__

2225. MELVILLE ANSON-10 " Jack " DRISKO, son of William Herbert-9 DRISKO (Augustus Melville-8; Jeremiah-7; Joseph-6; 5; 4; John-3; 2) and Minnie Irene WILSON, was born 7 Feb 1911 at Aberdeen, SD. He married Margaret Marie RENNIX on 14 July 1934 at Chicago, Illinois. She was the daughter of George Weekly RENNIX and Ellen HANSON, and was born 5 Nov 1911 at Hankinson, North Dakota; died 24 May 1997 at Chesterfield, Virginia. Melville-10 DRISKO, Sr. died 3 Feb 1990 at Aberdeen, South Dakota. Both are buried in Riverdale Cemetery, Aberdeen.

Children of Melville A-10 DRISKO, Sr. and Margaret RENNIX:
  Surname DRISKO

+ 2517. MELVILLE ANSON, JR.	born 26 July 1935 Chicago, Illinois married Alice Jane SAUNDERS 8 June 1958 at Cadet Chapel, West Point, NY
	(she dau/o Walter Ellis SAUNDERS and Mary Jewell SMITH)(she born 10 Mar 1936 Roanoke, VA)
+ 2518. RICHARD WILLIAM	born 5 May 1938 Davenport, IA; 1m. Joyce WALDROP ca 1962 2m. Brenda __?__ ca 1975; 3m. Florence __?__ 1981
+ 2519. MARY MARGARET	born 29 Sept 1944 Troy, New York married Robert L. McCALL, III 2 Sept 1967 Fort Benning, Georgia

2230. SEWALL M-10 DRISKO, son of Melville Augustus-9 DRISKO (Sewall-8; Jeremiah-7; Joseph-6; 5; 4; John-3; 2) and Nettie Mae MAHONEY, was born 12 Mar 1901 probably at Harrington, Maine. He married Anna McGREGOR of So. Gouldsboro, ME. on 3 Sept 1927. She was the daughter of _____ McGREGOR and was born 19__; died 19__.Sewall-10 DRISKO died 17 Oct 1971 at Hopedale, PA.

Children of Sewall-10 DRISKO and Anna McGREGOR:
  Surname DRISKO   2520. Murray   born 19__   2521. Anita   born 19__

2232. ROSE-10 DRISKO, sister of above, was born ca 19__ Harrington, ME. She married Maxwell J. KELLEY of Jonesport, ME on 28 June 1930. He was the son of _?_ KELLEY and was born 7 Sept 1909; died 4 Nov 1991.

Children of Rose-10 DRISKO and Maxwell J. KELLEY:
  Surname KELLEY

2522. Lionel D.	born 25 May 1931; died 26 Jan 2000 married Jean D. COUSINS 27 Oct 1953 (she of E. Blue Hill, ME)
2523. Ralph	born 19__; married Earline M. BEALE 15 June 1958, Maine
2524. Gregory	born 19__

2242. DOROTHY-10 DRISKO, half-sister of above, daughter of Guy-9 DRISKO and his 2nd wife Anna GOODWIN, was born 4 Nov 1918. She married first to Robert LOWRY ca 19__. They divorced; no issue. She married 2nd to Fred PEABODY on July 1946. Dorothy-10 died Jan 1987 at Bremerton, Kitsap, WA.

Children of Dorothy-10 DRISKO and Fred PEABODY:
    Surname PEABODY   2525. Jerry D. born 16 Feb 1947   2526. Ronnie G. born 29 Jan 1949

2301. RICHARD BURTON-10 DRISKO, son of Harold Philbrick-9 DRISKO (Alonzo-8; Oramander-7; Jeremiah-6; Joseph-5; 4 ; John-3; 2) and Ruth THOMPSON, was born 25 Nov 1928, N J. He married first to Elizabeth GRAY of Rahway, NJ ca 195_. She was the dau/o _? GRAY and Alice SWINTON, and was born 4 Apr 1932; died 1 Feb 1977. Res. Hollis, NH. Richard-10 married 2nd to Katherine GRAY Pearson.

Children of Richard B-10 DRISKO and Elizabeth GRAY:
    Surname DRISKO
+ 2527. RICHARD LINDSAY born 6 Nov 1954; married Debbie Artha KNEER (she born 11 Dec 1960)
+ 2528. KATHERINE   born 4 July 1956; married Marc/Mark METIVIER; (he born 27 Dec 1954)
+ 2529. JOHN T. born 14 Apr 1958; married Cynthia A BOOTHBY 20 July 1984; she born 10 Nov 1954

2309. HARRY E-10 DRISKO, son of George Camelo-9 DRISKO (Eri Hathaway-8; Chandler R-7; Jonathan-6; Samuel G-5; Joseph-4; John-3; 2) and Sarah MAGEE, was born 11 Feb 1878 at Columbia, ME. He married Lillian WORCESTER ca 1898/99. She was the daughter of Algernon WORCESTER and Nancy TRACY, and was born 20 Feb 1876; died 1960 (gs). Harry-10 DRISKO died 8 Aug 1975 age 97

Children of Harry E-10 DRISKO and Lillian WORCESTER:
    Surname DRISKO
+ 2530. LLOYD   born 26 Sept 1900 Machias, ME; died 11 June 1995 Addison, ME
        HARRY   1m. Dorothy B. STROUT 16 Dec 1922   (she born 1903; died 1939)
                       2m. Juanita L. ROBINSON 23 July 1941
+ 2531. OTHELLO   born ca 1904; married Kathleen PLUMMER; died 26 Mar 1957 Haverhill, MA
                       (she born 29 July 1903; died 13 Jan 2000 Haverhill, MA)

2312. JOSEPH WILLARD-10 DRISKO, brother of above, was born 28 Oct 1885 at __, Maine. He married QUEEN BESS-9 (Queenie Bess) WORCESTER (# 1770) on 30 Oct 1907. She was the daughter of Asa T-8 WORCESTER and Lucinda-8 TABBUTT (# 1041), and was born 16 July 1887; died 18 Mar 1984. Joseph-10 DRISKO died 22 Dec 1976.

Children of Joseph W-10 DRISKO and Queen B-9 WORCESTER:
    Surname DRISKO
  2532. Frances M.   born 10 Feb 1909, ME; she was a school teacher; died 2 Apr 1998
                       1m. Donald HIGGINS 11 Oct 1929 (3 ch) div; 2m. Harold F. NICKERSON 28 Aug 1940
+ 2533. KEITH (Babe) born 28 June 1912 Tibbettstown, ME.; died 21 Oct 1996 Columbia Falls, ME
        CLARK   married Donna A. RAMSDELL 7 Mar 1941
  2534. Hughene R.   born 23 Nov 1915; married Frederick A. HODGINS 19 Oct 1936 (poss 5 ch)
                       (he born 23 Mar 1913; died 20 Mar 1995 Eddington, Penobscot, ME)
+ 2535. JOSEPH W., Jr. born 16 Jan 1919; married Almeda BEAL 5 June 1940
                       died 10 Jan 1973; widow resided Columbia Falls, Maine 1997

2315. GEORGE CAMELO-10 DRISKO, JR., brother of above, was born 15 Apr 1898 at __, Maine. He married first to Christine SMITH of Lubec, ME on10 Sept 1921. They divorced and he married 2nd to Wilma/ Hilena BUBAR of Danforth, ME on 25 Dec 1925. She poss born 8 Mar 1900, ME; died 5 May 1994 Machias, Washington Co.,ME.   George-10 DRISKO, Jr. died 5 Nov 1978 at Machias, Maine.

Child of George C-10 DRISKO, Jr. and Christine SMITH:
    Surname DRISKO   2536. Frederick   born 192_

Child of George C-10 DRISKO, Jr. and Wilma BUBAR:
    2537. Joan H.   born 192_; married Stanley S. BAILEY 28 Feb 1954; res Cherryfield, ME.
                                     (he born 24 Aug 1926; died Mar 1970)

2316. CHARLES C-10 DRISKO, son of Edwin I-9 DRISKO (Eri Hathaway-8; Chandler-7; Jonathan-6;
Samuel G-5; Joseph-4; John-3; 2) and Hattie DONAVAN, was born 6 May 1881 at Columbia Falls, ME.
He married Bessie Rena-9 (Susie)LEIGHTON on 21 Sept 1910 at Columbia, Maine. She was the daughter
of Fonze Green Hill-8 LEIGHTON ++ and Gennetta Allison WORCESTER, and was born 31 Dec 1887;
died 23 Jan 1990 at Milbridge, Maine (age 102). Charles-9 DRISKO died 22 Nov 1968 at Columbia, ME.

++ Fonze Green Hill-8 LEIGHTON was the son of Daniel-7 LEIGHTON; and was born 18 Sept 1832 at Columbia, Maine;
    died 3 Oct 1899. He married Gennetta Allison WORCESTER on 26 June 1869 at Columbia, Maine. She was the daughter of
                              Moses WORCESTER and Diadama SMITH, and was born 27 Jan 1848.

Child of Charles C-10 DRISKO and Bessie-9 LEIGHTON:
    Surname DRISKO   2538. Gennetta Leighton born 1912; died 1956 unmarried   EOL

2349. CLARENCE HOLMES-10 DRISKO, son of William Pitt-9 DRISKO (Joseph Whitney-8; Chandler
Robbins-7; Jonathan-6; Samuel G-5; Joseph-4; John-3; 2) and Mamie E. TABBUTT, was born 30 Sept
1893 at Jonesboro, Maine.

He married Almira (Myra) Mabel MORRIS on 15 Sept 1918. She was the daughter of Henry F. MORRIS,
Jr. ++ and Ida M. MARTIN, and was born 15 Sept 1897 at Addison, Maine; died 17 Mar 1951 at Bangor,
ME. Clarence H-10 DRISKO, an educator, was a teacher then principal of the Bangor (ME) High School,
retiring in 1954. At the age of 86 he was still involved in the making of " Blueberry Rakes ".

His grandfather, Abijah Worcester TABBUTT, invented the rake in 1883. (see page 170) Clarence-10
DRISKO was an avid family history researcher, having provided information to many people and produced
a 29-page typescript on " The Ancestors and Some of the Descendants of Joseph DRISKO ". (The original
copy is housed at the Bangor (ME) Public Library. Clarence-10 died 9 Mar 1991 (age 97) at Columbia,
ME. He was a remarkable man, who lead a full and productive life.

Children of Clarence Holmes-10 DRISKO and Myra MORRIS:
    Surname DRISKO
+ 2539. WILLIAM   born 17 May 1925 Bangor, Maine
        HENRY   married Carolyn A. WORCESTER 12 Aug 1948
                         (she dau/o Alden WORCESTER and Laura MAWHINNEY)
+ 2540. CHANDLER   born 12 Aug 1927 Jonesport, ME.; died 31 Dec 1977 Cleveland, OH
        ROBBINS   married Ramona C. STROUT 11 July 1953
                         (she dau/o Carroll STROUT and Ida WORCESTER)
+ 2541. MARILYN IDA   born 3 Oct 1930 Bangor, ME
                         married Verrill R. WORCESTER, Jr. 15 Sept 1950
                         (he son /o Verrill WORCESTER, Sr. and Erma WHITE)
+ 2542. SHAPLEIGH   born 10 Aug 1932 Columbia Falls, Maine
        MORRIS   married Barbara L. BARRON 28 Aug 1955 Nashua, Iowa
                         (she dau/o Rev Dr. Ralph J. BARRON and Lucille VOLZ)

++ Henry F. MORRIS, Jr., son of Henry, Sr., was born 11 Apr 1866 at Columbia Falls, Maine, and died 21 May 1933 at Jonesport,
Maine. He married Ida M. MARTIN on 11 Apr 1890 at Columbia Falls. She was the daughter of Joseph MARTIN and Josephine
HAMMOND, and was born 12 Oct 1868 at Columbia Falls, died 2 Jan 1950 at Bangor, Maine.

2350. FRANK EUGENE-10 DRISKO, brother of above, was born 20 Dec 1894 at Jonesboro, ME. He
graduated from Columbia Falls High School, studied at Bates College, and was a graduate of the
University of Maine. He was an educator and school superintendent for many years in the Harrington
(ME) and Mechanic Falls school systems.

He married first to Maude A. STEWART on 22 Jan 1915. She was the daughter of Otis STEWART and Albertina YOUNG, and was born 14 Apr 1892, Gouldsboro, ME; died 13 Jan 1977. His 2nd wife was Julia _?_ Kelley. She was born 16 Dec 1900; died 21 June 1995. He died 20 Nov 1995, just one month short of his 101st birthday. He spent the last part of his life at Caribou, ME. where 3 of his step-children lived. He was survived by his daughters, 4 step-children ++, 25 grandchildren and 22 great grandchildren. He is buried at Mailey Hill Cemetery, Columbia, Maine.

Children of Frank Eugene-10 DRISKO and Maude STEWART:
   Surname DRISKO
   2543. Natalie Tabbutt   born 9 Dec 1921; 1m. Myron L. FICKETT 3 June 1938 Harrington, ME
                            2m.__?__ CUSHMAN; 1996 resided Honolulu, HI
   2544. Norma Maude   born 5 Dec 1925; married Garfield E. HIGGINS 23 Mar 1955 Mechanic Falls
              ++ Marjorie Anderson; Captola Paul; Sheldon KELLEY; and Gail Demura.

2352. EDNA J-10 DRISKO, sister of above, was born 17 May 1897 at Jonesboro, Maine. She married Chester Swan BURTCH ca 19__. He was the son of ___ BURTCH and was born 4 Dec 1893; died 22 Jan 1983 at San Luis Obispo, CA. Edna-10 DRISKO died there 12 Feb 1984.

Children of Edna-10 DRISKO and Chester BURTCH:
   Surname BURTCH
   2545. Allen born 19__; died (age 15)   2546. Allison born 19__: died 1923   2547. Dorothy born 19__

2353. MARY ELLA-10 " Mamie " DRISKO, sister of above, (twin sister of # 2354) was born 12 July 1899 at Centerville, Maine. She married Marvin F. HALL on 26 Dec 1930 at Columbia Falls, Maine. He was the son of Dr. Frank J. HALL and Rowena M. RUSSELL, and was born 26 May 1905 at Dallas, TX; living at Scarsdale, NY 1997.

Marvin HALL was a graduate of the University of Michigan, Class of 1926, and was an Engineer. He worked for many years for the Washington (DC) Gas and Light Company. Mary Ella/Mamie-10 DRISKO was a graduate of Colby College, Maine, and was teaching in Wellesley, MA when she met her future husband. They resided in Washington, DC, where she died 8 July 1936, after the birth of her second child. Marvin HALL married second to Anita McCORD in 1938.

Mary Ella-10 " Mamie " DRISKO (1899 – 1936)

Children of Mary Ella-10 DRISKO and Marvin HALL:
  Surname HALL
+ 2548. MARY PAMELA born 19 Sept 1932 Washington, DC
                    married William E. HUTH 11 Aug 1962 New York City, NY
+ 2549. DAVID DRISKO born 8 July 1936 Washington, DC; married Diana LONG 24 Sept 1960
                    (she born 11 May 1938; dau/o Hugh LONG and Hilda JARMAN)

2384. MARCIA EVELYN-10 WORCESTER, daughter of Belinda-9 TRACY (Amos L-8; Abigail B-7 DRISKO; Jonathan-6; Samuel G-5; Joseph-4; John-3;2) and Moses-8 WORCESTER, 3rd , was born 30 May 1889. She married Austin Eugene-8 HARMON 1 Oct 1913. He was the son of Austin Turner-7 HARMON and Harriet ARMSTRONG; and was born 21 Apr 1887; died 27 Nov 1934. Marcia-10 died 12 June 1983 at Howland, ME.

Children of Marcia-10 WORCESTER and Austin Eugene HARMON:
  Surname HARMON
  2550. Austin Eugene, Jr   born 10 May 1914; died 23 June 1959
                             married Evada L. JEFFERY 5 Jan 1941, ME.
  2551. Christine Elizabeth born 29 Sept 1917; married Melton C. HOMPTON 17 Sept 1936, ME.
  2552. Frederick Leon, Sr. born 15 July 1930 Huntsville, Madison Co. AR

2387. GEORGIA ANN-10 TRACY see # 1968 BERNARD FRANK-9 CARVER

2398. FLORA ROSETTA-10 TRACY, daughter of John Franklin-9 TRACY (Amos L-8; Abigail-7 DRISKO; Jonathan-6; Samuel G-5; Joseph-4; John-3;2) and Flora BUTLER, was born 4 June 1886 at Columbia Falls, Maine. She married Arthur M. ALLEN on 28 May 1907.

Children of Flora –10 TRACY and Arthur ALLEN:
  Surname ALLEN
  2553. Hollis F.   born 8 Aug 1907; died Aug 1985 Gorham, Maine
                       married Roxie M. BASSETT 20 June 1937 Addison, Maine
  2554. Lyman P.   born 6 Nov 1914; died June 1973 Maine
                       married Olia SMITH 22 May 1937 Harrington, Maine
                       (she born 22 Nov 1917; died 16 Apr 1991)
  2555. Myra F.   born 20 Sept 1918; married Kenneth C. GREENLAW 17 Aug 1935 Milbridge

2400. CHARLES GILBERT-10 TRACY, brother of above, was born 20 Apr 1890 at Columbia Falls, ME. He married Maggie Craig LEITH on 12 Oct 1914 at Kenora, Ontario, Canada. She was the daughter of William LEITH and Annie NICHOLL. Charles Gilbert-10 TRACY died 29 Apr 1964 at Vancouver, BC.

Children of Charles-10 TRACY and Maggie LEITH:
  Surname TRACY
  2556. Annie Rachel born 18 July 1915 Minaki, Ontario, Canada; married Sam NEWMAN 1 June 1935
+ 2557. CHARLES G.,JR born 15 Nov 1916 Kamsack, Saskatchewan, Canada
                    1m. Gay WILLIAMS 30 June 1937
                    2m. Rowena Jean SMITH 28 Dec 1946 Whitehorse, Yukon Territory
                    died 8 Mar 1986 Fort St. John, British Columbia, Canada
  2558. Flora   born 3 Feb 1919 Kamsack, Saskatchewan, Canada
     Margaret Isabel married Edward John SIMS 14 June 1947 Winnipeg, Manitoba, Canada
                    Ch: Robert John-12 SIMS born 4 Apr 1949 Winnipeg, Manitoba
+ 2559. JOHN WM.   born 5 June 1921 Kamsack, Saskatchewan, Canada
     FRANKLIN   married Dora Katherine RHEAULT 21 July 1945 Redditt, Ontario, Canada
+ 2560. DOROTHY   born 19 Apr 1923 Kamsack, Saskatchewan, Canada
     MAUDE   1m. Gordon SKINNER _____ at _____, British Columbia, Canada
                    2m. Josiah THARP 20 June 1942 Winnipeg, Manitoba, Canada

Children of Charles-10 TRACY, continued:
Surname TRACY

+ 2561. LEIGH ALLEN   born 14 Jan 1926 Kamsack, Saskatchewan, Canada
    (AMOS)   married Mary WASYLYNCHUK 17 Feb 1951 Edmonton, Alberta, Canada
+ 2562. VICTOR   born 20 July 1928 Winnipeg, Manitoba, Canada
    SAMUEL   married Katherina WESELOWSKI 30 June 1951 Winnipeg
+ 2563. SHARON   born 5 May 1937 Winnipeg, Manitoba
    ROSIE   1m. John SHYMKIW 5 June 1954; 2m. William J. JOHNSTONE 30 Dec 1972
        3m. Ralph PARLIN 8 Sept 1990 Long Beach, CA

2401. ELIZABETH ELLA-10 TRACY, sister of above, was born 9 June 1893 at Columbia Falls, Maine. She married Loring/Loren Josiah WILLEY 12 Oct 1912. She died Dec 1971 at Conway, New Hampshire.

Children of Elizabeth Ella-10 TRACY and Loring/Loren WILLEY:
Surname WILLEY

2564. Loren Franklin   born 26 July 1914; died 12 Aug 1994 Conway, NH
2565. John Frederick   born 19 Jan 1916; died July 1987 Conway, NH

2402. JOSEPHINE FRANKLIN-10 TRACY, sister of above, was born 15 Aug 1895 at Jonesboro, Maine. She married first to Alden SEELEY; and second to Frank B. KELLEY on 15 May 1915. Her third husband was Fred L. CAMERON on 11 July 1934. He was the son of George CAMERON and Addie DIXON. Josephine-10 TRACY died 11 Jan 1988 at Bangor/ Princeton, Maine.

Children of Josephine F-10 TRACY and Frank KELLEY:
Surname KELLEY

2566. Lois <u>Irene</u>   born 18 June 1917; married Keith GREENLAW 13 Jan 1934
        (he born 21 Apr 1913; died 24 July 1997 Princeton, Washington, ME)
2567. Leroy F.   born 12 Oct 1919
2568. Perley M. (Bud)   born 30 July 1921 (a Methodist minister); died Oct 1974 ME.
        married Paula D. STUBBS 15 May 1948 Bangor, Maine

2403. VICTOR THURLOW-10 TRACY, brother of above, was born 12 Apr 1897 at Jonesboro, Washington Co., Maine. He married Fidelia Jane GREENLAW 4 May 1921 at Baileyville, Maine. She was the daughter of Charles GREENLAW and Nettie WILKINS. Victor-10 TRACY died 31 Oct 1976.

Children of Victor-10 TRACY and Fidelia GREENLAW:
Surname TRACY

+ 2569. WINONA   born 7 June 1922 Portland, ME.; 1m. Larry GARVEY
    VICTORIA   2m. Frank E. ALEXANDER 21 Nov 1942
+ 2570. NETTIE   born 5 July 1923 Calais, Maine; 1m. __?_ GORMAN
    ISABEL   2m. Clifford G. HOLDEN 17 Aug 1952
  2571. Randolph G.   born 10 Aug 1925; married ?; 2 ch: Kathleen and Miranda TRACY
+ 2572. GWENDOLYN   11 Oct 1926 Woodland, Maine
    CAROLINE   married Raymond Howard SHAW 17 Feb 1946 South Portland, Maine

  2573. Ethel May   born 20 Sept 1928; married Wilfred SPRING 21 June 1952 Worcester, MA
+ 2574. CONRAD   born 16 Aug 1933 Baileyville, Maine
    THURLOW   1m. Rhonda Margaret THURLOW; 2m. Alice May HAGLER 5 Sep 1954
+ 2575. ALGERNON P.   born 12 Jan 1935; married Alicia M. EMERY
+ 2576. SYLVIA DESMA born 26 Dec 1936; married Fred KEYS
  2577. Nadine Varie   born 8 Oct 1938; married Frederick H. DOUGHTY 18 Aug 1957
        2 children : Carole-12 and Kevin-12 DOUGHTY (no further info)
  2578. Victor Leroy   born 12 May 1940; married __?__
        2 children: Laurie-12 and Sheryl-12 TRACY (no further info)

2404. AMOS PETER-10 TRACY, brother of above, was born 28 Apr 1900 at Jonesboro, Maine. He married Priscilla BURGESS on 7 July 1934 at Conway, NH. She was the daughter of Edward BURGESS and Rosie BUTLER. Amos-10 died March 1987 at Texarkana, Bowie County, TX.

Children of Amos P-10 TRACY and Priscilla BURGESS:
   Surname TRACY
  2579. Rose Flora   born 22 Nov 1935; died 25 Nov 1935
+ 2580. AMOS P. JR   born 3 Nov 1937 Calais, ME; married Bernice V. MC CURDY 1 Dec 1959
+ 2581. MARY E.   born 9 Dec 1938 Woodland, ME; married Denis ROBBINS 7 Dec 1957
  2582. Lawrence Stillman born 26 Nov 1939; died March 1940
  2583. Gloria Loraine   born 30 Nov 1940 Calais; married Romeo D. SOUCY 1 Dec 1961 (2 ch)

2405. HARRIETTE ESTELLE-10 TRACY, sister of above, was born 31 Mar 1904 at Jonesboro, Maine. She married John Russell FITZSIMMONS on 24 Aug 1923. Harriette-10 died July 1976 at Wyckoff, NJ

Children of Harriette-10 TRACY and John FITZSIMMONS:
   Surname FITZSIMMONS
+ 2584. ELIZABETH I.   born 22 Mar 1924; married _____ FITZSIMMONS
  2585. Margaret Jo   born 20 July 1927; married Edward STOUT
  2586. John F.   born 6 Aug 1934; married Betsey J. FOX of Calais, ME 10 Dec 1954
  2587. Lloyd G.   born 30 Aug 1936; married Joyce E. PIKE 23 Feb 1957
  2588. Paul I.   born 11 Aug 1941; died Nov 1975   2589. Merl R.   born 31 May 1943

 2406. ETHEL MAE-10 TRACY, sister of above, was born 16 Nov 1906 at Woodland, Maine. She married Carroll W. DUDLEY ++ on 1 July 1922. Ethel-10 TRACY died 26 Aug 1991, Maine.
++ Carroll DUDLEY, possibly born 5 Feb 1903; died Jan 1974 at Waterville, Kennebec, ME

Children of Ethel-10 TRACY and Carroll DUDLEY:
   Surname DUDLEY
  2590. Agnes L.   born 10 Apr 1929; died 1964; married ? (a New Jersey mail carrier)
  2591. Ada Lois   born 27 Oct 1932; married Raymond C. DUDLEY 17 Aug 1951 W. Lubec, ME
  2592. Frances E.   born 13 Dec 1933; died Apr 1976
                  married Bernard J. GOMM 6 June 1953 (he born 4 Feb 1926; died Feb 1976)
  2593. Donna L.   born 4 Sept 1939; married Charles B. CASTLE 1 May 1962

2430. EDWARD GILMAN-10 CURTIS, son of Mary Augusta-9 COLSON (Mary Elizabeth-8 WILSON; Aphphatha-7 NASH; Mary-6 DRISKO; Samuel G-5; Joseph-4; John-3;2) and Edward Bissell CURTIS, was born 7 Dec 1886 at Machias, ME. He married Mary Helen SEELBACH on 28 Oct 1920. She was the daughter of Louis SEELBACH and Marie DURBECK, and was born 13 Apr 1897 Louisville, KY; died 4 Mar 1997 (six weeks short of her 100th birthday). Edward Gilman-10 CURTIS was a Harvard graduate and a patent attorney. He had an office in the Lincoln Building in New York City. They lived in Bronxville, NY where he died 21 March 1970.

Children of Edward Gilman-10 CURTIS and Mary Helen SEELBACH:
   Surname CURTIS
  2594. Mary Gilman   born 9 Aug 1922; graduate of New York University
     “ Gil “   married John Reynolds BROOKS 5 Mar 1949 at Bronxville, NY
                    (he born 22 Feb 1918 Chicago, IL)
       2 ch: Lila Curtis BROOKS born 11 Dec 1950 Naples, Italy (unmarr)
          John Winthrop BROOKS born 13 Feb 1955 Bronxville, NY (unmarr)
+ 2595. ANNE RAQUET born 21 Oct 1925 NYC; graduate of Vassar College
                 married J. (Jacob) Wayne FREDERICKS
+ 2596. ELEANOR   born 18 Nov 1926 NYC; graduate of Wellesley College, an artist
     COLSON   married Jan Samuel F. van HOOGSTRATEN 4 July 1953 The Netherlands

Children of Edward Gilman-10 CURTIS, continued:
     Surname CURTIS
+ 2597. EDWARD   born 18 Aug 1930 Bronxville, NY; died 15 Mar 1984 (suicide)
     MOREY   married Margaret Gwendolyn KELLER 22 Sept 1962 Bronxville, NY

2431. JOSEPHINE NASH-10 CURTIS, sister of above, was born 6 Apr 1889 at Cambridge, MA. She married William Silliman FOSTER on 22 July 1918 at Machias. ME. He was the son of William Carlos FOSTER and Katherine Frances LANGDON; and was born 15 Oct 1886 Water MILL, LI; died 2 Jan 1926 of pneumonia. He had a PhD in Psychology from Cornell University, and was a Professor of Psychology at the University of Minnesota. Josephine Nash-10 CURTIS, a graduate of Wellesley, with a PhD from Cornell University, died of cancer on 3 July 1941 at Minneapolis, MN. Their ashes are buried in the FOSTER plot at the cemetery in Water MILL, LI

Child of Josephine-10 CURTIS and William FOSTER:
     Surname FOSTER
+ 2598. MARIAN   born 2 July 1922; married Alexander S. FRASER Aug 1953
  2599. Harriet Wilson   24 Apr 1925 Minneapolis, MN; unmarr; PhD in Psychology

2432. MARY-10 CURTIS, sister of above, was born 24 July 1892 at Machias, Maine. She attended Wheaton College and studied nursing. She married first to Dr. Farrar Crane COBB 2 Sept 1919 at Brooklin, MA. (as his 2nd wife) He was the son of Sanford Hoadley COBB and Mary Elizabeth CAPEN, and was born 6 May 1867 Saugerties, NY; died 29 May 1944. She married second to Lawrence Alden THAYER on 30 June 1953 at Osterville, MA. He was born 14 May 1905; died Sept 1955 at Osterville, MA.   Mary-10 CURTIS died 27 Aug 1984 at Orleans, MA.

Child of Mary-10 CURTIS and Dr. Farrar COBB:
     Surname COBB
  2600. Sanford   ++   born 23 March 1926 Boston, MA
                          married Doris Jean STEELE 3 Feb 1951 Albany, NY
                          (she was the dau/o Nester Lane STEELE and Elsie Mae KLUCHER)
                          (she born 27 Apr 1928 Corning, NY)
                  Ch: 1. Stephen Edward-12 COBB born 9 Apr 1952 Albany, NY
                                 1m. Roberta BOILINI; divorced
                                 2 m. Josefina CWIERZ 20 Dec 1983 Las Vegas, NV
                                 (she from Mislenice, Poland) (no issue)
                      2. Thomas Gerard COBB born 9 June 1960 Miami, FL; a chef; unmarried

          ++ Sanford-11 COBB graduated from the Albany Medical School of Union University,
                          and is an anesthetist. He lives in Jacksonville, FL

2447. RUTH LOWELL-10 WINCHELL, daughter of Emma Keller-9 ALLINE (Henry W-8; Mary-7 NASH; Mary-6 DRISKO; Samuel Gatchell-5; Joseph-4; John-3; 2) and John Hezekiah WINCHELL, was born 4 Sep 1890 at Plymouth County, Iowa. She married Frank Moe STEPHENS on 6 July 1916 , CO. He was the son of Peter STEPHENS and Ida MOE, and was born 29 Jan 1889 at Denver, CO; died there on 21 Sep 1982. Ruth L-10 WINCHELL died 5 Nov 1950 at Tucson, AZ.

Children of Ruth Lowell-10 WINCHELL and Frank STEPHENS:
     Surname STEPHENS
  2601. William   born 30 July 1918 Arden, NV; died 12 Feb 1997 Peoria, AZ
                          married ____ JONES 14 Sept 1940 Denver, CO
  2602. Robert Lawrence born ca 19__

The Eleventh American Generation

2458. WILLIAM WALDO-11 DRISKO, son of Charles Lyman-10 DRISKO (Waldo Bentley-9; Judah Johnson-8; William Johnson-7; Judah-6; John-5; Joseph-4; John-3; 2) and Lela Esper SEARS , was born 15 Mar 1925 at Bartlesville, Oklahoma. He married Doris DANIEL of Bartlesville, ca 1945.

Children of William Waldo-11 DRISKO and Doris DANIEL:
  Surname DRISKO
  2603. William Michael   born 25 Mar 1946 Bartlesville, OK
  2604. Thomas Lynn   born 19 Oct 1949 Bartlesville
  2605. Charles Richard   born 10 Oct 1955 Tulsa , Oklahoma

2459. CHARLES HERBERT-11 DRISKO, brother of above, was born 27 Oct 1928 at Bartlesville, Oklahoma. He married Nancy WALKER of Lufkin, Texas ca 19__.

Children of Charles Herbert-11 DRISKO and Nancy WALKER:
  Surname DRISKO
  2606. Diana   born 13 Jan 1956 Victorville, CA
  2607. David Charles born 30 Mar 1958 Victorville, CA
                       marr Robin Eileen Bagby MILLBERN 15 Oct 1988 Lake Murray, OK
                       Child: Jasper Thomas-13 DRISKO born 1989
  2608. Timothy Lee   born 16 Sept 1961 Las Vegas, Nevada

2461. ELEAZER-11 CARVER, III, son of Helen Frankland-10 SANBORN (Mary Frankland-9 DRISKO; Judah Johnson-8; William Johnson-7; Judah-6; John-5; Joseph-4; John-3; 2) and Eleazer CARVER,II, was born 31 Aug 1912 at Milo, Maine. He was a railroad engineer, and married Thelma Louise BUSHEY on 19 Oct 1936 at Shelby, Ohio. She was the daughter of Paul F. BUSHEY and Nellie M. WILSON, and was born 10 Oct 1912. He died 5 Sept 1977 at Dover-Foxcroft, Maine.

Children of Eleazer-11 CARVER, III and Thelma BUSHEY;
  Surname CARVER
  2609. Helen Marie   born 10 Dec 1937 Shelby, OH; died 24 Aug 1938 Belleville, Ohio
  2610. Eleazer IV   born 27 Jan 1939 Milo, Maine
  2611. James Edward   born 8 Nov 1940 Milo, Maine
  2612. Richard Andrew born 25 June 1942 Milo, Maine

2462. JOHN (Jack) –11 CARVER, brother of above, was born 7 June 1914 at Milo, Maine. He married Dorothy EADE on 19 Jan 1946. She was the daughter of John EADE and Elizabeth __?__, and was born 4 Aug 1913, died 29 Sept 1995 at Peabody, Essex, MA. They resided Merrimac, MA.

Children of John-11 CARVER and Dorothy EADE:
  Surname CARVER
  2613. Priscilla Ann born 6 Apr 1949 Jamaica Plain, MA
  2614. John Eade   born 28 Sept 1953 Haverhill, MA

2467. ALBION MINOT-11 CARVER, brother of above, was born 29 Apr 1928 at Milo, Maine. He married Fern Alice NASON on 21 Jan 1953 at Dover-Foxcroft, Maine. She was the daughter of Carroll NASON and Carrie CUTHBERTSON, and was born 29 Apr 1934 at Milo, Maine.

Children of Albion Minot-11 CARVER and Fern NASON:
  Surname CARVER (1st four children born Dover-Foxcroft, ME; last two Plymouth, MA)

2615. Michael Anton	born 14 Mar 1954	2618. Jeffrey Owen	born 22 Aug 1960
2616. Kenneth Mark	born 17 Aug 1955	2619. Lois Ellen	born 3 July 1964
2617 Marcella Donne	born 2 Oct 1958	2620. Lisa Helen	born 23 Feb 1967

2468. JOSEF TODD-11 CARVER, brother of above, was born 17 Aug 1930 at Milo, Maine. He married Annegrethe KISLING on 8 Feb 1954 at Dover-Foxcroft, Maine. She was the daughter of Christian KISLING and Ane Margarethe POULSEN, and was born 2 Sept 1935, Denmark. They were divorced.

Children of Josef Todd-11 CARVER and Annegrethe KISLING:
    Surname CARVER
    2621. Todd Frankland   born 29 Oct 1954 Dow AFB, Bangor, Maine
    2622. Franz Josef   born 14 June 1956 Ladd AFB, Fairbanks, Alaska
    2623. Dane Pierre   born 3 June 1960 Chaumont AFB, ____, France
    2624. Brett Lancelot   born 5 Mar 1961 Kings, Lynn Co., Suffolk, England
    2625. Ladd Kisling   born 11 Nov 1962 Travis AFB, CA

2477. RANCH ALDRICH-11 LEE, son of Clinton Hiram-10 LEE (King Hiram-9; Willard Malcolm-8; Mary Anne-7 BUCKNAM; Abigail-6 DRISKO; John-5; Joseph-4; John-3; 2) and Rhonda ALDRICH, was born ca 19__. He married first to Dolores Anne SCHIELE, and second to Diane WALKLEY.

Children of Ranch Aldrich-11 LEE and ? :
    Surname LEE
    2626. Dona   born ca 19__; 1m. Edwin O'NEAL; 2m. Marty GROSSMAN
        2 ch: Cynthia-13 O'NEAL and Charles-13 O'NEAL
    2627. Linda Elaine   born ca 19__; married David OPALINSKY
        1 ch: Isaac-13 OPALINSKY
    2628. Laura   born ca 19__; 1m. David BLOOM; 2m. David MILLER
        2 ch: Casey-13 MILLER and Morgan Amber-13 MILLER
    2629. Randall   born ca 19__
    2630. Clinton A. (Jr)   born ca 19__; married Christie GARCIA (1 child: Nicole-13 LEE)
    2631. Scott A.   born ca 19__

2484. KATHERINE ANN-11 TIBBETTS, daughter of Phillip Monroe –10 TIBBETTS (Allen Zephaniah-9; Zephaniah Allen-8; Jeremiah-7; Thomas-6; Elizabeth-5 DRISKO; Joseph-4; John-3;2) and Charlotte KATEN, was born 28 Mar 1952, ME. She married first to Mark SHOTWELL on 9 Oct 1976 at Waterville, Maine. They divorced and she married second to Jiminez CORTEZ on 17 Aug 1985 at Honolulu, HI.

Child of Katherine–11 TIBBETTS and Mark SHOTWELL:
    Surname SHOTWELL
    2632. Christine L.   born 27 June 1977; not married to Blaze PIMOCA
        Child: Megan Cortez PIMOCA born 20 Feb 1999 Honolulu, HI
Child of Katherine-11 TIBBETTS and Jiminez CORTEZ:
    Surname CORTEZ   2633. Jiminez (Jr)   born 16 June 1986 Honolulu, HI

2486. LARRY PHILLIP-11 TIBBETTS, brother of above, was born 5 Sep 1956 at Bangor, Maine. He 1st married Hidie/Heidi CLUCKEY on 25 Dec 1976 at Eastport, ME. (She was born 5 Jan 1959, ME) They divorced. He married 2nd to Cheryl CASTO on 10 Feb 1990 at Columbis, OH. She was born 10 Feb 1954.

Children of Larry-11 TIBBETTS and Heidi CLUCKEY:
    Surname TIBBETTS
    2634. Janet Madline   born 27 May 1978 Denver, CO   2635. Stephen Michael   born June 1980
Child of Larry-11 TIBBETTS and Cheryl CASTO:
    Surname TIBBETTS   2636. Samantha Jean   born 14 May 1989 Columbus, OH

2487. BRENDA LEE-11 TIBBETTS, sister of above, was born 3 Aug 1958 at Ft. Lauderdale, FL. She married first to David Duane DRAWDY on 26 Apr 1979 at Honolulu, HI. He was born 2 May 1955 at Seattle, WA. They divorced. She married second to Mark Anthony BOYORAK on 18 Aug 1984 at Hampden, ME. He was the son of John G. BOYORAK and Jean LEVASSEUR, and was born 22 Sep 1960 at Bangor, Maine.

Children of Brenda Lee-11 TIBBETTS and David DRAWDY:
   Surname DRAWDY
  2637. David Brent **   born 24 July 1979, Honolulu, HI; unmarried (** goes by the surname of BOYORAK)
          Child: Nathaniel James WILCOX born 29 Jul 1999 Bangor, Maine
          Mother: Amanda WILCOX (she born 14 June 1977 Bangor, ME)
  2638. Anthony Chase   born 4 Apr 1981 Oshkosh, WI
                  died 6 Apr 1989 Boston, MA; buried Mt. Hope Cemetery, Bangor, Maine
Children of Brenda Lee-11 TIBBETTS and Mark BOYORAK:
   Surname BOYORAK (both children born Bangor, Maine)
  2639. John Matthew   born 18 Feb 1984   2640. Robert Phillip   born 7 Feb 1986

2490. HOWARD W-11 LEIGHTON-FLOYD, son of Albert Wentworth-10 LEIGHTON (Ralph I-9; Abitha D-8; Phoebe-7 DRISKO; Captain John-6; Joseph-5; 4; John-3; 2) and Clara BRENDEL, was born 21 Dec 1914 at Opheim, Montana. He married Katherine M. BERGERSON on 21 Oct 1936. She was the dau/of ?_ BERGERSON and was born 30 Nov 1917 at Kalispell, Montana. Resided at Rogers, AR in 1987

Children of Howard-11 LEIGHTON-FLOYD and Katherine BERGERSON:
   Surname LEIGHTON-FLOYD
  2641. Barbara K.   born 9 June 1937 Independence, MO; married Donald HITT
  2642. Albert   born 2 Feb 1939

2491. LOIS NORINE-11 LEIGHTON-FLOYD, sister of above, was born 28 Aug 1918 at Opheim, MT. She married James Howard STILWELL on 17 Feb 1940. He was born 5/6 July 1917, died June 1989, OR .

Children of Lois-11 LEIGHTON-FLOYD and James STILWELL:
   Surname STILWELL (children born Independence, MO)
  2643. James Edward   born 22 Feb 1947; married Janice ROBBINS 2 Oct 1971
                  (she born 30 Aug 1950) resided Roseville, CA
  2644. Cherie Norine   born 4 July 1948; married Val BATTI 9 June 1968; divorced
  2645. Stephen Leroy born 24 May 1949; married Sharon BROWN 12 Apr 1969(she born 15 Sept 1950)
  2646. Deborah Mae born 4 Sept 1950; married Thomas WOODS 16 Aug 1971 (he born 2 Nov 1950)

2493. RALPH E-11 LEIGHTON-FLOYD, brother of above, was born 4 Aug 1922 at Knob Noster, MO . He married Betty Jane GROSS on 10 Sept 1943. She was born 1 May 1925 at Kansas City, MO.

Children of Ralph-11 LEIGHTON-FLOYD and Betty GROSS:
   Surname LEIGHTON-FLOYD (children born at Independence, MO)
  2647. Charles E.   born 28 Dec 1947
  2648. Diane Louise   born 30 Dec 1949; married D. Larry McCONNELL
  2649. Jane Ellen (twin) born 2 Dec 1951; married Thomas H. SANDGREN
  2650. Julia Anne (twin) born 2 Dec 1951; married Terry N. THACKER

2494. CHERYL ANN-11 BATSON, daughter of Robert-10 BATSON (Colin Andrew-9; Captain Adrian Abbott-8; Rebecca-7 DRISKO; Captain John-6; Joseph-5;4; John-3;2) and Helen COOTS, was born 4 Apr 1947 at Brockton, MA. She married Douglas Wood FREEMAN on 29 Mar 1969. He was the son of Leonard Allen FREEMAN and Dorothy Helen WOOD, and was born 12 Mar 1945 at Taunton, MA.

Children of Cheryl-11 BATSON and Douglas FREEMAN:
   Surname FREEMAN
  2651. Douglas Allen   born 7 Mar 1972 Attleboro, MA
                  married Angela Dawn BRUNSON 8 June 1996 Dallas, TX
  2652. Jason Christopher born 27 Dec 1974 Attleboro, MA
                  married Melissa Marie MILLER 1 Aug 1998 So. Hamilton, MA
                  (she dau/o John Albert MILLER and Darlene Louise KAUTH)

2497. ANNE LUCILLE-11 O'DONNELL, daughter of Jane Anna-10 BUTTS (Eva Frances-9 DRISKO; George Augustus-8; Captain George W-7; Captain John-6; Joseph-5; 4; John-3; 2) and William J. O'DONNELL, was born 2 Feb 1946 at Syracuse, Onondaga County, NY. She married James Willard COUGHENOUR on 1 July 1967 at E. Syracuse, NY. He was the son of Willard OLLER, Sr and Antoinette Pearl CHAPIN; and was born 26 Nov 1942. He was adopted by his step-father, Harry COUGHENOUR.

Children of Anne Lucille-11 O'DONNELL and James Willard COUGHENOUR:
  Surname COUGHENOUR
  2653. Jason James   born 7 Nov 1976; res. with Kellie J. DOANE (she born 26 Aug 1974)
        Ch: surname COUGHENOUR   William Jason   born 16 Feb 2000 Syracuse, NY
  2654. Kevin James   born 4 Oct 1978

2498. JAMES FREDERICK-11 O'DONNELL, brother of above, was born 11 Nov 1947 at Syracuse, Onondaga County, New York. He married Diane Lynn CAVANAUGH on 14 Feb 1976 at Newark, NY. She was the dau/of Walter Edward CAVANAUGH and Alice Rose SWEENEY, and was born 4 July 1949.

Children of James F-11 O'DONNELL and Diane CAVANAUGH:
  Surname O'DONNELL 2655. Sara Beth born 11 Feb 1981   2656. Jessica Lynn born 16 May 1983

2499. DAVID WILLIAM-11 O'DONNELL, brother of above, was born 15 Nov 1952 at Syracuse, Onondaga Co., NY. He married Cynthia GRIFFIN on 9 Aug 1975 at Newburyport, MA. She was the daughter of William Joseph GRIFFIN and Barbara BABINE; and was born 19 Jan 1954. They were divorced May 1984. David-11 O'DONNELL married 2nd to Kathleen Ann FONTAINE on 17 June 1994 at Hopedale, MA. She was the daughter of Wilfred Anthony FONTAINE and Fahy SULLIVAN, born 17 July 1961.

Children of David W-11 O'DONNELL and Cynthia GRIFFIN:
  Surname O'DONNELL (all born at Wakefield, Rhode Island)
  2657. Amy Elizabeth   born 2 Dec 1976, RI   2659. David Griffin born 19 May 1980 RI
  2658. Katelyn   born 23 Sept 1978, RI
Child of David-11 O'DONNELL and Kathleen FONTAINE:
  Surname O'DONNELL   2660. Jacob Daniel   born 31 Jan 1997

2500. RICHARD FRANCIS -11 O'DONNELL, brother of above, was born 7 Nov 1955 at Syracuse, New York. He married Nancy Ann HATALA on 16 June 1979 atVoorheesville, NY. She was the daughter of Joseph Michael HATALA and Beverly June BRAULT, and was born 23 Aug 1960.

Children of Richard-11 O'DONNELL and Nancy Ann HATALA:
  Surname O'DONNELL 2661. Josh William born 16 Aug 1985 2662. Ethan Patrick born 19 June 1990

2501. KAREN MARIE-11 O'DONNELL, sister of above, was born 19 Feb 1958 at Syracuse, New York. She married Anthony Kenneth HICKS on 26 April 1984. He was the son of Kenneth HICKS and Annie Colette FIELDERMAN, and was born 30 May 1957.

Children of Karen-11 O'DONNELL and Anthony HICKS:
  Surname HICKS
  2663. Jennifer Ann   born 14 Sept 1988   2664. Andrew Kenneth born 16 Nov 1992 VA

2504. NORMA JUNE-11 BUTTS, daughter of Donald Frederick-10 BUTTS (Eva Frances-9 DRISKO; George Augustus-8; Captain George W-7; Captain John-6; Joseph-5; 4; John-3; 2) and Eleanor June CARD, was born 9 Sept 1952 at Syracuse, Onondaga County, New York. She married first to David BARTHOLOMEW ca 19__. They divorced. She married 2nd to Terry GOLLINGER on 10 Jan 1981.

Children of Norma-11 BUTTS and David BARTHOLOMEW:
Surname BARTHOLOMEW 2665. Jennifer M. born 13 May 1975   2666. Wendy Ann born 16 Feb 1977

2506. THOMAS ORSON-11 BUTTS, brother of above, was born 5 Feb 1958 at Syracuse, New York. He married JoAnn SHIBLEY on 15 June 1980. She was the daughter of ____ SHIBLEY and was born ____-.

Children of Thomas Orson-11 BUTTS and JoAnn SHIBLEY:
    Surname BUTTS
  2667. Mykel Lyn (f)   born 8 Sept 1983   2669. Thomas Robert Wm. born 22 July 1985
  2668. Jhona Lee (f)   born 22 July 1985

2507. JOHN ALLEN-11 ECKELMAN, son of Ellen Amelia-10 DRISKO (Henry William-9 DRISKO; George Augustus-8 ; Captain George Washington-7; Captain John-6; Joseph-5; 4; John-3; 2) and John Henry ECKELMAN, MD, was born 17 Dec 1938 at Syracuse, Onondaga County, New York. He married Anne Marie BINGLE on 8 Feb 1959 at Carthage, Jefferson County, NY. She was the daughter of Harry BINGLE and Genevieve WISNER, and was born 27 Aug 1941.

Children of John Allen-11 ECKELMAN and Anne BINGLE:
    Surname ECKELMAN
+ 2670. TAMARA JOAN born 8 Aug 1959 Carthage, Jefferson Co., NY
            married Andrew NORRIS 12 Sept 1981 1st Baptist Church, Lowville, NY (divorced 1987)
+ 2671. ALAN JEFFERY born 16 July 1960 Carthage, NY
            married Christina THOMAS 13 Feb 1988 Lowville, NY (divorced)
  2672. Brian Todd   born 8 June 1963 Hudson, NY

2508. BERNARD CARL-11 ECKELMAN, brother of above, was born 31 July 1940 at Harrisville, Lewis County, New York. He married first to Sharon Marie SAYER on 28 Feb 1959 at Carthage, Jefferson County, NY. She was the daughter of Colin B. SAYER and Ruth Ella LENNOX, and was born 27 July 1939; died 25 Nov 1991 at Hamilton, Ohio (cancer). She is buried at Carthage, NY. His second marriage, on 6 June 1992, was to Paula Marie HENDRICK at Hamilton, Ohio. She was the daughter of Ronald A. HENDRICK and ____ HOOPER of Carthage, Jefferson Co., NY., and was born 15 May 1957.

Children of Bernard Carl-11 ECKELMAN and Sharon SAYER:
    Surname ECKELMAN
+ 2673. MICHAEL VON   born 17 Sept 1959 Carthage, NY; married Cheryl RIEHLE Sept 1990
+ 2674. COLIN PATRICK born 10 Aug 1961 Troy, NY; married Anna SENORA 3 Aug 1991 Peoria, AZ
+ 2675. JOHNNA LYNN   born 17 Aug 1963 Seattle, WA; married John LARKIN 2 Feb 1990 Albany, NY

2509. WILLIAM DWIGHT-11 ECKELMAN, brother of above, was born 4 Dec 1942 at Harrisville, Lewis County, New York. He married Carol Marie KNAPP on 28 Apr 1962. She was the daughter of Harold A. KNAPP and Cora V. HEWITT, and was born 18 Jan 1942. At Carthage, NY. William-11 (Bill) was a New York State Trooper, retiring 1999.

Children of William-11 ECKELMAN and Carol KNAPP:
    Surname ECKELMAN
+ 2676. LISA JANE   born 16 June 1963 Denver, Colorado; 1m. Jeffrey CLAVETTE 13 Nov 1982
                       (he son/o Roger CLAVETTE and Jeanette __?__) divorced 1985 no issue
                       2m. Charles STOCKS 27 Sept 1985 (he born 16 Aug 1953; divorced)
                       3m. James D. THOMAS 14 Aug 1995
  2677. David Harold   born 22 Mar 1974 Oneonta, NY
                       married Stephanie TATEM on 22 May 1999; resides Glendale, CA

2513. DANA STERLING-11 DRISKO, son of George Dolbey-10 DRISKO (Henry W.-9; George A-8; Captain George W.-7; Captain John-6; Joseph-5; 4; John-3; 2) and Frances Jean STERLING, was born 29 July 1958 at Syracuse, Onondaga Co., NY. He graduated from North Syracuse Central High School, Class of 1976; where he was a member of the National Honor Society. He played several Varsity sports – Baseball (4 yr) Soccer (3 yr) and Basketball (1 yr). He was a 2-time High School All-American in Baseball.

He graduated from Cornell University, Ithaca, NY, class of 1980, with a degree in Personal Finance. In Dec 1980 he entered the Law Enforcement profession, working for a short period with the North Syracuse Police Dept., then transferring to the Onondaga County Sheriff's Dept. in Sept 1982. In 1984 he was made Detective, working mainly on forgery and fraud cases. In 1990 he worked in the Budget and Finance division of the department, transferring in 1995 to the Community relations division to become a D.A.R..E. instructor to the area fifth graders. He retired from the Sheriff's Department in 2000.

He married Jennifer Lynn " Jenny " REYNOLDS on 17 Sept 1983 at Andrews Memorial Methodist Church, No. Syracuse, NY. She was the daughter of John REYNOLDS and Patricia DAIR, and was born 23 Apr 1961 at Syracuse, NY.

Children of Dana S-11 DRISKO and " Jenny " REYNOLDS:
   Surname DRISKO   (born Syracuse, N Y)
  2678. Zachory John " Zack "   born 25 Mar 1987
  2679. Maximiliam Dair " Max " born 10 May 1991

2517. MELVILLE ANSON-11 DRISKO, JR. , son of Melville Anson-10 DRISKO, Sr. (William H-9; Augustus Melville-8; Jeremiah-7; Joseph-6; 5; 4; John-3; 2) and Margaret Marie RENNIX, was born 26 July 1935 at Chicago, IL. He married Alice Jane SAUNDERS on 8 June 1958 at the Cadet Chapel, West Point , NY. She was the daughter of Walter Ellis SAUNDERS and Mary Jewell SMITH, and was born 10 Mar 1936 at Roanoke, Virginia.

Children of Melville-11 DRISKO and Alice SAUNDERS: *Dana Sterling-11 DRISKO*
   Surname DRISKO
+ 2680. MELISSA ANNE born 23 Sept 1959 Fort Bragg, North Carolina
                    married Philip David KOSMACKI 2 Aug 1986 Old Post Chapel, Ft. Myer. VA
   2681. Melinda Alison   born 24 Oct 1961 Okinawa, Japan
                    married John James DANIELS 16 July 1988 Pohick Church, Fairfax, VA
           One child: Margaret Jane-13 DANIELS born 23 Sept 1994 Midlothian, VA
   2682. Melville A., III   born 26 Oct 1963 Ft. Benning, Georgia
                    married M. Jodi GINSBURG 1 Apr 1989 Denver, Colorado
   2683. Michael David   born 12 Aug 1968
      Saunders   marr. Caroline Elizabeth IHLENBURG 23 Apr 1994 West Point, New York

2518. RICHARD WILLIAM-11 DRISKO, brother of above, was born 5 May 1938 at Davenport, Iowa. He married first to Joyce WALDROP ca 1962. She was the daughter of _____ WALDROP, and was born 27 July 1942; died July 1974. He married 2nd to Brenda _?_ ca 1975. He married 3rd to Florence _?_ ca 1981.
  Children of Richard W-11 DRISKO and Joyce WALDROP:
  Surname DRISKO   2684. Robin   born July 1963 Panama Canal Zone
  2685. Diane   born ca 1965 Panama Canal Zone   2686. Stacy   born ca 1967 Fort Benning, GA

2519. MARY MARGARET-11 DRISKO, sister of above, was born 29 Sept 1944 at Troy, NY. She married Robert L. McCALL, III on 2 Sept 1967 at Fort Benning, Georgia. He was the son of Robert McCALL, Jr.
  Children of Mary Margaret-11 DRISKO and Robert McCALL, III:
  Surname McCALL
  2687. Stephanie Ann born 19 July 1969 Peoria, IL; married Forrest MUELLER 19__ AZ
             Two children: Forrest-13 MUELLER born July 1993 and Micah-13 MUELLER
  2688. Jennifer   born 24 June 1972 CA   2689. Charlie   born 17 Nov 1977 Phoenix, AZ

2527. RICHARD LINDSAY-11 DRISKO, son of Richard Burton-10 DRISKO (Harold P-9; Alonzo-8;

Oramander-7; Jeremiah-6; Joseph-5;4; John-3;2) and Elizabeth GRAY, was born 6 Nov 1954. He married Debbie Artha KNEER ____ . She was born 11 Dec 1960.

Children of Richard Lindsay-11 DRISKO and Debbie KNEER:
  Surname DRISKO
  2690/2691. Lindsay and Kimberly (twins) born 8 July 1987   2692. Jennifer Helen born 1 Dec 1991

2528. KATHERINE-11 DRISKO, sister of above, was born 4 July 1956. She married Marc/Mark METIVIER on ____ . He was born 27 Dec 1954.

Children of Katherine-11 DRISKO and Mark METIVIER:
  Surname METIVIER   2693. Marilla born 12 Feb 1987   2694. William Nolin born 7 July 1985

2529. JOHN THOMPSON-11 DRISKO, brother of above, was born 14 Apr 1958. He married Cynthia A. BOOTHBY on 20 July 1984. She was born 10 Nov 1954.

Children of John T-11 DRISKO and Cindy BOOTHBY:
  Surname DRISKO
  2695. Katelyn Boothby born 8 May 1985   2696. John Thompson   born 14 July 1993

2530.   LLOYD HARRY-11 DRISKO, son of Harry E-10 DRISKO (George C-9; Eri H-8; Chandler Robbins-7; Jonathan-6; Samuel G-5; Joseph-4; John-3; 2) and Lillian WORCESTER, was born 26 Sept 1900 at Machias, Washington County, Maine. He married first to Dorothy B-8 STROUT on 16 Dec 1922. She was the daughter of Sidney-7 STROUT (Nehemiah-6; Isaac-5; Joseph-4; 3; 2; Christopher-1) and Frances MITCHELL, and was born 1903; died 20 Aug 1939. His second wife, whom he married on 23 July 1941, was Juanita L. ROBINSON, daughter of Curtis ROBINSON and Lillian JONES. She was born 20 June 1925 at Milbridge, Maine; still living 12/96. Lloyd-11 DRISKO died 11 June 1995 at Columbia, ME.

Children of Lloyd Harry-11 DRISKO and Dorothy STROUT:
  Surname DRISKO
+ 2697. JOYCE   born 18 July 1923; married Calvin BAGLEY 12 July 1941 Cherryfield, ME.
      LILLIAN   (he born 19__; died 7 Jan 1996)
+ 2698. DONNA FRANCES   born 31 May 1926; married Willard ACKLEY 26 Sept 1946
+ 2699. MYRNA LA VERNE born 8 July 1931; married Wallace A. CHIPMAN 6 Sept 1952
+ 2700. AVONNE ESTELLE born 25 Feb 1935; 1m. Fred W. FAULKINGHAM 25 June 1954 (div)
                      2m. Charles BROWN   (he born 15 July 19__)
+ 2701. SYLVIA DOROTHY born 15 Aug 1939; 1m. Kenneth L. MANN 1 June 1960 (div)
                      2m. _____ WYMAN

2531. OTHELLO-11 DRISKO, brother of above, was born ca 1904. He married Kathleen PLUMMER 4 July 1925. She was the daughter of Oscar PLUMMER and Alta __?__ of Harrington, ME.; and was born 29 July 1903; died 13 Jan 2000, Haverhill, MA. Othello-11 DRISKO died 26 Mar 1957 at Haverhill, MA.

Children of Othello-11 DRISKO and Kathleen PLUMMER:
  Surname DRISKO
  2702. Eloise   born 4 Oct 1925; married Al THOMPSON
  2703. Adriann   born 4 Feb 1928; 1m. Ray BATEMAN (div); 2m. Donald ADAMS
            One child: Terry-13 ADAMS born 19__
  2704. Alan H.   born 2 June 1930

2533. KEITH CLARK-11 DRISKO, called " Babe ", son of Joseph Willard-10 DRISKO (George C-9; Eri H-8; Chandler-7; Jonathan-6; Samuel G-5; Joseph-4; John-3; 2) and Queen B. WORCESTER, was born 28 June 1912 at Tibbettstown, Maine. He married Donna A. RAMSDELL on 7 Mar 1941. Keith " Babe " DRISKO attended the Maine School of Commerce (Husson College) and was a minor league pitcher for several years. In 1980 he was inducted into the Maine Baseball Hall of Fame, and to the Husson College Sports Hall of Fame. He was a high school baseball coach, an active Methodist, school board member, trustee of the Milbridge Medical Center and served on the Board of Directors on the FHA. He was a blueberry and tree farmer, residing at Columbia Falls at the time of his death on 21 Oct 1996.

Children of Keith-11 DRISKO and Donna RAMSDELL:
   Surname DRISKO
2705. Hugh E.   born 19__; married Junita A. LAWRENCE 1 June 1963; res Orrington, ME.
         2 ch: 1. Keith-13 DRISKO
              2. Melissa Elaine-13 DRISKO who married Randy Michael DAY 23 July 1994

2706. Karen D.   born 19__; married Larry N. PINEO 1 Apr 1960 ; resided East Corinth, ME
      Two children: 1. Troy-13 PINEO (married Barbara ?)
                2. Todd-13 PINEO (married Laura ?)
2707. Sharon Lee   born 19__; married Lyle ROLFE; resided Milbridge, Maine
      Two children: Jonathan-13 ROLFE and Toby-13 ROLFE

2535. JOSEPH W-11 DRISKO, JR., son of Joseph W-10 DRISKO (George Camelo-9; Eri Hathaway-8; Chandler-7; Jonathan-6; Samuel G-5; Joseph-4; John-3;2) and Queen B-9 WORCESTER, was born 16 Jan 1919. He married Almeda BEAL on 5 June 1940. He died 10 Jan 1973 at Columbia Falls, Maine.

Children of Joseph W-11 DRISKO, Jr. and Almeda BEAL:
   Surname DRISKO
2708. Michael L.   born 19__; married Lynn R. ALLEY 24 June 1978
2709. Kevin Lewis   born 19__; 1m. Linda BAGLEY 9 Sept 1983; 2m. Mary B. REED 12 Aug 1995

2539. WILLIAM HENRY-11 DRISKO, son of Clarence Holmes-10 DRISKO (William Pitt-9; Joseph W-8; Chandler-7; Jonathan-6; Samuel G-5; Joseph-4; John-3; 2) and Almira MORRIS, was born 7 May 1925 at Bangor, Maine. He married Carolyn A. WORCESTER of Columbia, Maine on 12 Aug 1948. She was the daughter of Alden WORCESTER and Laura MAWHINNEY, and was born 19__.

Children of William H-11 DRISKO and Carolyn WORCESTER:
   Surname DRISKO
2710. Charlene   born 4 Aug 1949 Machias, ME; died 18 June 1995 Smyrna Falls, Maine
      Worcester 1m. James LITTLETON; 2m. Alton GRAY; 3m. Donald D. NODINE 25 Mar 1983
         3 children: Barbara Ann-13 LITTLETON; Amy A-13 GRAY and A. Andrew-13 GRAY
2711. Myra Mabel   born 15 June 1951 Elmandorf AFB, AK; married Charles WHARTON
        2 children: Michael-13 WHARTON and Mathew-13 WHARTON
2712. William Stephen born 27 Sept 1956 Machias, ME; married Kelley SMITH
        1 child: Stephanie-13 DRISKO born 19__

2540. CHANDLER ROBBINS-11 DRISKO, brother of above, was born 12 Aug 1927 at Jonesport, ME. He married Ramona STROUT on 11 July 1955. She was the daughter of Carroll STROUT and Ida WORCESTER, and was born 19__.

Children of Chandler-11 DRISKO and Ramona STROUT:
   Surname DRISKO
2713. Cynthia Lynn   born _ June 1956 Niagara Falls, NY; married Stephen GIBSON
        1 child: Jennifer-13 GIBSON born 19__
2714. Carol Ann   born 19__; married Mark MILLER (2 ch: Rachel-13 & Christopher-13 MILLER

2541. MARILYN IDA-11 DRISKO, sister of above, was born 3 Oct 1930 at Bangor, Maine. She married Verrill R. WORCESTER, Jr. on 15 Sept 1950. He was the son of Verrill WORCESTER, Sr. and Erma WHITE, and was born ___.

Children of Marilyn-11 DRISKO and Verrill WORCESTER, Jr.:
  Surname WORCESTER
  2715. Deyanne   born   9 June 1951 Bangor, Maine
+ 2716. CATHY   born 31 Oct 1952 Ft. Campbell, KY; married Edward MARSHALL 1 June 1974
  2717. Sandra   born 14 Nov 1954 Ft. Campbell, KY; married Mark POTTER 7 Aug 1976
              1 child: Andrew Cole-13 POTTER born 19__
+ 2718. KYMM   born   8 June 1956 Munich, Germany; married Stephen LANGE 31 May 1982
+ 2719. PAMELA   born 19 Aug 1958 Munich, Germany; married David HULL 31 Oct 1982
  2720. Gayle   born 28 May 1960 Ft. Bragg, NC; 1m. Michael BAILEY; 2m. Arthur CORBETT
              2 children: Carrie Deyanne-13 BAILEY and Heather Lynn-13 BAILEY
+ 2721. CRAIG DRISKO born 23 Feb 1963 Ft. Bragg, NC; married Sally VOSE 19 Feb 1982

2542. SHAPLEIGH MORRIS-11 DRISKO, brother of above, was born 10 Aug 1932 at Columbia Falls,
Maine. He married Barbara L. BARRON on 28 Aug 1955. She was the daughter of the Rev Dr. Ralph J.
BARRON and Lucille VOLZ, and was born _____.

Children of Shapleigh-11 DRISKO and Barbara BARRON:
  Surname DRISKO
  2722. Shapleigh Chandler born 26 Dec 1956 Nuremberg, Germany; married Cecelia PERUSSE
              2 children: Kimberly Margaret-13 DRISKO and Christopher-13 DRISKO
  2723. Jennifer Elizabeth   born 7 Aug 1958 Bad Cannstatt, Germany
  2724. James Coburn   born 20 Apr 1960 El Paso, TX; married Mary Jane McGUIGAN
              1 child: Sarah-13 DRISKO born 19__
  2725. Jonathan Tabbutt   born 10 Nov 1962 West Point, NY; married Laura ROSS
              1 child: Joshua Tabbutt-13 DRISKO born 19__

2548. MARY PAMELA-11 HALL, daughter of Mary/Mamie-10 DRISKO (William Pitt-9; Joseph W-8;
Chandler-7; Jonathan-6; Samuel G-5; Joseph-4; John-3; 2) and Marvin HALL, was born 19 Sept 1932 at
Washington, DC. She married William E. HUTH on 11 Aug 1962. He was the son of ?_HUTH and was
born 26 July 1930. Pamela-11 was an artist, and her husband was an attorney. They res. in Fairfield , CT.

Children of Pamela-11 HALL and William HUTH:
  Surname HUTH
  2726. Katherine   born 22 June 1967; married Bret PALMER 18 Sept 1994
                          (they are both attorneys, residing New York City 1997)
  2727. Alan   born 20 Nov 1973; attending college in Daytona, FL 1997

2549. DAVID DRISKO-11 HALL, brother of above, was born 8 July 1936 at Washington, DC. He
married Diane LONG on 24 Sept 1960. She was the daughter of Hugh LONG (19__-1970) and Hilda
JARMAN (19__- 8 Oct 1988); and was born 11 May 1938. They were divorced. David-11 HALL
(1997) was a Professor of Early American Religious History at Harvard University Divinity School.
He resided in Arlington, MA.

Children of David Drisko-11 HALL and Diane LONG:
  Surname HALL
  2728. John Greenwood born 9 May 1961
  2729. Jeffrey Drisko   born 9 May 1963 New Haven, CT.
  2730. Hugh Franklin   born 31 Mar 1967; married Debbie VOLKER

2557. CHARLES GILBERT-11 TRACY, JR., son of Charles Gilbert-10 TRACY (John Franklin-9; Amos
L-8; Abigail-7 DRISKO; Jonathan-6; Samuel G-5; Joseph-4; John-3;2) and Maggie LEITH, was born 15
Nov 1916 at Kamsack, Saskatchewan Province, Canada. He married first to Gay WILLIAMS on 30 June
1937. His second marriage was to Rowena Jean SMITH 28 Dec 1946 at Whitehorse, Yukon Territory,
Canada. He died 8 Mar 1986 at Fort. St. John, British Columbia.

Child of Charles –11 TRACY, Jr. and Gay WILLIAMS
  Surname TRACY
+ 2731. CHARLES VICTOR born 11 Nov 1939 Winnipeg, Manitoba; married Heather Ann ?
Children of Charles-11- TRACY, Jr. and Rowena SMITH:
  Surname TRACY
+ 2732. THOMAS   born 17 Nov 1947 Edmonton, Alberta, Canada
        LEIGH   1m. Brenda Ann MORRISON 30 May 1980 Trail, BC, Canada
                        2m. Floy Marie SHANTZ 14 Apr 1990 Edmonton, Alberta, Canada
+ 2733. GARY   born 30 Nov 1948 Whitehorse, Yukon Territory, Canada
        GILBERT   married Carol Marlene HELM 10 Oct 1970 Fort St. John, British Columbia
+ 2734. GLORIA DENE   born 1 Oct 1950 Wetaskiwin, Alberta, Canada; married Keith PATEY
+ 2735. PARTICIA ANN   born 7 Apr 1956 Edmonton, Alberta; 1m. ?; 2m. Robert DERKACH
  2736. Donald Craig   born 18 July 1959 Edmonton, Alberta, Canada
+ 2737. SHAWN GLEN   born 22 Aug 1962 Edmonton, Alberta, Canada
                        married Sandy Jo FRITA 10 Dec 1994 Canmore, Alberta, Canada

2559.. JOHN WILLIAM FRANKLIN-11 (*FRANK*) TRACY, brother of above, was born 5 June 1921 at Kamsack, Saskatchewan, Canada. He married Dora Katherine RHEAULT 21 July 1945 at Redditt, Ontario, Canada. John Franklin-11 died Feb 1978 at Coons Rapid, Minnesota.

Children of John Franklin-11 TRACY and Dora RHEAULT:
  Surname TRACY
  2738. Charles Gilbert born 8 Dec 1948 Kenora, Ontario, Canada; died ____ Alberta, Canada
+ 2739. ANN LOUISE   born 13 Apr 1946 St. Boniface, Manitoba, Canada; married Robert DYKE
  2740. Jacqueline Rose born 23 June 1951 Port Arthur, Ontario, Canada; married Derek KEEPING
                         (Child: Linda Tracy-13 KEEPING born ____)

2560. DOROTHY MAUDE-11 TRACY, sister of above, was born 19 Apr 1923 at Kamsack, Saskatchewan, Canada. She married first to Gordon SKINNER ____ British Columbia. She married second to Josiah THARP on 20 June 1942 at Winnipeg, Manitoba, Canada.

Children of Dorothy-11 TRACY and Josiah THARP:
  Surname THARP
+ 2741. KENNETH   born 17 Jan 1943; 1m. Sandy __?__
        JOSIAH   2m. Catherine Ann MEADOWS 17 July 1971 at Huntington Park, CA
  2742. Judith   born 30 Sept 1945; married Bill SWITZER ____
+ 2743. CAROL ANNE   born 14 Dec 1946; 1m. Ken FAWCETT; 2m. Eric Jayne PERRIN
+ 2744. DIANE   born 26 Aug 1947; married Norman CHARLES 20 Nov 1965

2561. LEIGH ALLEN (AMOS)-11 TRACY, brother of above, was born 14 Jan 1926 at Kamsack, Saskatchewan, Canada. He married Mary WASYLYNCHUK on 17 Feb 1951 at Edmonton, Alberta .

Children of Leigh Allen-11 TRACY and Mary WASYLYNCHUK:
  Surname TRACY
+ 2745. KAREN LEIGH   born 15 Apr 1952 Edmonton, Alberta Canada
                      married Graham John SICKLER 22 June 1874 Edmonton, Alberta, Canada
  2746. Patrick Allen   born 2 Mar 1956 Edmonton, Alberta; married Rhonda ALTON 1 Oct 1983
              Child: Kieran Leigh James Patrick Alton-13 TRACY born 18 July 1995
  2747. Matthew James   born 3 July 1966 Edmonton; married Bernadette NAPRAWA ____ Edmonton
              Child: Spencer Allen Leigh-13 TRACY born __ ___ 1996
        Note: They adopted 2 girls: Dorothy Darlene born 12 Oct 1947; Marlene Deborah born 22 Aug 1948

2562. VICTOR SAMUEL-11 TRACY, brother of above, was born 20 July 1928 at Winnipeg, Manitoba, Canada. He married Katherine " Cassie " WESELOWSKI 30 June 1951 at Winnipeg. She was the daughter of Teodor WESELOWSKI and Petrunela URBANOWSKI, and was born 24 Jan 1932. Victor-11 TRACY died 29 July 1974 at Burnaby, British Columbia, Canada.

Children of Victor Samuel-11 TRACY and Katherine WESELOWSKI:
Surname TRACY
2748. Victor Leigh   born 24 June 1956 Vancouver, British Columbia
2749. Sandra Cassie   born 10 Nov 1959 Vancouver, BC
                           married Antonio DE STEFANO 26 Sep 1983 Rome Italy
                           (he son /o Angelo DE STEFANO and Felicia CRISPINO)
                 Child: Michele-13 DE STEFANO born 9 Mar 1988

2563. SHARON ROSIE-11 TRACY, sister of above, was born 5 May 1937 at Winnipeg, Manitoba, Canada. She married first to John SHYMKIW on 5 June 1954. She married second to William James JOHNSTONE on 30 Dec 1972 at Burnaby, British Columbia. She married her third husband , Ralph PARLIN on 8 Sept 1990 at Long Beach, Los Angeles Co., CA.

Children of Sharon-11 TRACY and John SHYMKIW:
Surname SHYMKIW
2750. Debra Joan   born 23 Feb 1957 Winnipeg, Manitoba, Canada
                         1m. Denny YOUNG 25 June 19__; 2m. Kenneth VANDERBEEK Aug 1975
                         3m. Gary AGNEW 16 Mar 1991 Calgary, Alberta, Canada
+ 2751. JANICE HOLLY   born 30 Dec 1961 St Boniface, Manitoba, Canada
                         1m.Michael SUTHERLAND 27 June 1979 Burnaby, BC
                         2m. Gary FONTAINE 8 Aug 1992 Vancouver, BC
+ 2752. BRENDA LEE   born 17 June 1960 St. Boniface, Manitoba
                         married John Charles ROSS 27 Oct 1984 Edmonton, Alberta

2569. WINONA VICTORIA-11 TRACY, daughter of Victor Thurlow-10 TRACY (John Franklin-9; Amos-8; Abigail-7 DRISKO;Jonathan-6; Samuel G-5; Joseph-4; John-3;2) and Fidelia Jane GREENLAW, was born 7 June 1922 at Portland, Maine. She married first to Larry GARVEY ca ____. She married second to Frank E. ALEXANDER on 21 Nov 1942.

Children of Winona-11 TRACY and Frank ALEXANDER:
Surname ALEXANDER   2753. Janet   born 19___   2754. Judy   born 19__

2570. NETTIE ISABEL-11 TRACY, sister of above, was born 5 July 1923 at Calais, Maine. She married first to _____GORMAN/GOHRMAN, and second to Clifford G. HOLDEN on 17 Aug 1952.

Children of Nettie-11 TRACY and _____ GORMAN:
Surname GORMAN/GOHRMAN   2755. Stanley born 19__   2756. Doreen   born 19__

2572. GWENDOLYN CAROLINE-11 TRACY, sister of above, was born 11 Oct 1926 at Woodland, Maine. She married Raymond Howard SHAW on 17 Feb 1946 at South Portland, Maine. He was the son of Howard SHAW and Exemia GRENIER.

Children of Gwendolyn-11 TRACY and Raymond SHAW:
Surname SHAW
2757. Caroline Jane   born 25 Nov 1946 Bath, Maine; 1m. Paul ?; 2m. Robert MONIN
+ 2758. GLORIA JEAN   born 25 Oct 1948 Portland, ME; 1m. Craig WORTHING ca 1967
                         2m. Kenneth COLLIER
2759. Nancy Ellen   born 25 Feb 1950 Sanford, ME; married Dean ECKHOFF
2760. David Howard   born 10 Oct 1951 Sanford, ME; married Janet KOPYLIC
2761. Dennis Raymond   born 24 Mar 1953 Philadelphia, PA; married Anna Maria MC GREE
2762. Susan Marie   born 10 Apr 1956 So. Portland, ME: married Kenneth __?__

Children of Gwendolyn-11 TRACY, continued:
    Surname SHAW
    2763. Karen Rae   born 20 Jan 1959 South Portland, ME.
                                 married Bernard R. LA POINTE 10 Oct 1981 Westbrook, ME.
    2764. Craig Stephen/   born 26 July 1960 South Portland
          Steven   married Mary Elizabeth MICHAUD 23 Jan 1991 Portland, Maine

2574. CONRAD THURLOW-11 TRACY, brother of above, was born 16 Aug 1933 at Baileyville; Maine. He married first to Rhonda Margaret THURLOW; no issue.. He married second to Alice May HAGLEY on 5 Sept 1954. Conrad-11 THURLOW worked for Philco Ford in Greenland tracking satellites.

Children of Conrad-11 TRACY and Alice HAGLER:
    Surname TRACY
    2765. Kathie   born 19__   2767. Pamela   born 19__
    2766. Thomas   born 19__   2768. Mark   born 19__

2575. ALGERNON PETER -11 TRACY, brother of above, was born 12 Jan 1935. He married Alicia M. EMERY on 1 Apr 1960. (Spelling of his name varies Aljernon and Aljnon).

Children of Algernon-11 TRACY and Alicia EMERY:
    Surname TRACY
    2769. Michael   born 19__   2771. Allen   born 19__
    2770. Cheryl Anne   born 19__   2772. Cynthia   born 19__

2576. SYLVIA DESMA-11 TRACY, sister of above, was born 26 Dec 1936. She married Fred KEYS.

Children of Sylvia-11 TRACY and Fred KEYS:
    Surname KEYS
    2773. Brenda   born 19 __   2775. Denise   born 19__
    2774. Freddy   born 19__   2776/77. Unnamed twins born ca 1970

2580. AMOS PETER-11 TRACY, JR, son of Amos Peter-10 TRACY (John Franklin-9; Amos-8; Abigail-7 DRISKO; Jonathan-6; Samuel G-5; Joseph-4; John-3;2) and Priscilla BURGESS, was born 3 Nov 1937 at Calais, Maine. He married Bernice V. MC CURDY on 1 Dec 1959. She was the daughter of Horace MC CURDY and Matty PRESTON.

Children of Amos-11 TRACY, Jr. and Bernice MC CURDY:
    Surname TRACY   (all born Calais, Maine)
    2778. Wayne Allen   born 26 Nov 1960   2780. Terry Amos   born 8 June 1965
    2779. Bryant Lee   born 27 Dec 1962

2581. MARY E-11 TRACY, sister of above, was born 9 Dec 1938 at Woodland, Maine. She married Denys/Dennis L. ROBBINS on 7 Dec 1957 at Calais, Maine. He was the son of William ROBBINS and Dorothy HARRIMAN.

Children of Mary E-11 TRACY and Denys/Dennis ROBBINS:
    Surname ROBBINS   (both born in Skowhegan, Maine)
    2781. Deborah Lorraine born 25 Dec 1963
    2782. Roberta   born 4 Mar 1966; married Troy Allen WHITTEMORE 24 Dec 1990
                            (both resided Skowhegan, Maine)

2584. ELIZABETH I-11 FITZSIMMONS, daughter of Harriette-10 TRACY (John Franklin-9; Amos-8; Abigail-7 DRISKO; Jonathan-6; Samuel G-5; Joseph-4; John-3;2) and John Russell FITZSIMMONS, was born 22 Mar 1924, possibly at Jonesboro, Maine. She married ____ FITZSIMMONS ca 19__ .

Children of Elizabeth-11 FITZSIMMONS and _____ FITZSIMMONS:
    Surname FITZSIMMONS
    2783. David   born ca 1944   2785. Merry Sue   born ca 1947
    2784. Walter   born ca 1946   2786. Warren   born ca 1950

2595. ANNE RAQUET-11 CURTIS, daughter of Edward Gilman-10 CURTIS (Mary Augusta-8 WILSON; Aphphatha-7 NASH; Mary-6 DRISKO; Samuel G-5; Joseph-4; John-3;2) and Mary Helen SEELBACH, was born 21 Oct 1925 in New York City, NY. She was a graduate of Vassar College. She married J. Wayne FREDERICKS on 19 Jan 1952 at Bronxville, NY. He was the son of William Jennings FREDERICKS and Flossa Esther WALTER; and was born 26 Feb 1917 in Wakarusa, IN. He was a graduate of Purdue University. He worked in the State Department under President John F. KENNEDY. He worked for the FORD Foundation, and was an expert on Africa. He received an honorary LLD degree from the University of Witwatersrand in Johannesburg, South Africa.

Children of Anne Raquet-11 CURTIS and J. Wayne FREDERICKS:
    Surname FREDERICKS
    2787. Maria Loring   born 6 Feb 1956 Battle Creek, MI; a book conservator
                          1m. William Hudson HARPER June 1979; divorced 1984
                          (he son/o Paul Church HARPER and Eleanor EMERY)
                          (he born Oct 1950 ; PhD in Music from Eastman School of Music)
                          2m. _____; divorced
    2788. William Curtis born 3 July 1961 Washington, DC; an attorney
                          married Ivy LINDSTROM
             Ch: 1. Charlotte-13 FREDERICKS born Jan 1995
                 2. Thomas Curtis FREDERICKS born Feb 1997

2596. ELEANOR COLSON-11 CURTIS, sister of above, was born 18 Nov 1926 at New York City, NY. She was a graduate of Wellesley College, and an artist. She married Jan Samuel Francois van HOOG-STRATEN on 4 July 1953 in Hengelo, the Netherlands. He was the son of Francois van HOOGSTRATEN and Alida Maria Hendrika WIGMAN; and was born 22 May 1922 in Zaltbommel, the Netherlands. They resided in Thompson, CT.

Children of Eleanor Colson-11 CURTIS and Jan van HOOGSTRATEN:
    Surname van HOOGSTRATEN
    2789. David   ++   born 17 Dec 1954 Bronxville, NY
                          married Michelle Irene KAYON
                          (she dau/o Moreno KAYON and Ella STUMES)
                          (she born 12 Oct 1955, NY)
             2 ch: 1. Daniel Dirck-13 born 26 Nov 1986 NYC; and 2. Julia-13 born ____
         ++ David was a graduate of the University of Pennsylvannia. He had a law degree from the University
                     of Wisconsin. Resides in Washington, DC, where he works for the State Department
    2790. Nicholas Frans born 9 Dec 1956 Bronxville, NY; a theatrical producer in NYC
                          married Sarah BROCUS

2597. EDWARD MOREY-11 CURTIS, brother of above, was born 18 Aug 1930 at Bronxville, NY. He was a Harvard graduate and an attorney. He married Margaret Gwendolyn KELLER on 22 Sept 1962 at Bronxville. She was the daughter of Arthur Charles KELLER and Margaret Devers McHALE; and was born 12 Oct 1935. Edward Morey-11 CURTIS committed suicide on 22 Sept 1984 at Bronxville,

Children of Edward Morey-11 CURTIS and Margaret KELLER:
    Surname CURTIS
    2791. Morey McHale   born 14 Jan 1964 Bronxville, NY – an artist
                           twice married and divorced
                           Ch: Tor _____ born _____

Children of Edward Morey-11 CURTIS, continued:
  Surname CURTIS
  2792. Whitney Devers   born 10 Nov 1966 Bronxville, NY
                          married

2598. MARIAN-11 FOSTER see CROCKER section # 804 and # 966 for descendants

The Twelfth American Generation

2670. TAMARA JOAN-12 ECKELMAN, daughter of John Allen-11 ECKELMAN (Ellen Amelia-10 DRISKO; Henry William-9; George Augustus-8; Captain George Washington-7; Captain John-6; Joseph-5; 4; John-3; 2) and Anne Marie BINGLE, was born 8 Aug 1959 at Carthage, Jefferson County, New York. She married Andrew John NORRIS on 12 Sept 1981 at the First Baptist Church, Lowville, Jefferson County, NY. He was the son of James NORRIS and Jan __?__, and was born ____. They divorced 1987.

Children of Tamara-12 ECKELMAN and Andrew NORRIS:
  Surname NORRIS   (children born Watertown, Jefferson Co., NY)
  2793. Angela Sue   born 29 June 1983   2794. Tara Nicole   born 30 Mar 1985
Child of Tamara-12 ECKELMAN and __?__:
  Surname ECKELMAN   2795. Nicholas   born __ ___ 1996 Jefferson Co., NY

2671. ALAN JEFFERY-12 ECKELMAN, brother of above, was born 16 July 1960 at Carthage, Jefferson County, New York. He married Christina THOMAS on 13 Feb 1988 at Lowville, New York. She was the daughter of Kenneth E. THOMAS and Bonnie __?__, and was born 13 Apr 1969. They divorced 199_.

Children of Alan Jeffery-12 ECKELMAN and Christina THOMAS:
  Surname ECKELMAN   (children born at Lowville, NY)
  2796. Sasha Elizabeth   born 9 Oct 1988   2797. Daniel Francis   born 12 Dec 1991

2673. MICHAEL VON-12 ECKELMAN, son of Bernard Carl-11 ECKELMAN (Ellen Amelia-10 DRISKO; Henry William-9; George Augustus-8; Captain George W-7; Captain John-6; Joseph-5; 4; John-3; 2) and Sharon SAYER, was born 17 Sept 1959 at Carthage, Jefferson County, New York. He married Cheryl RIEHLE on 22 Sept 1990 at Cincinnati, Ohio. She was the daughter of Arthur L. RIEHLE and Christine ____, and was born 12 Aug 19__.

Children of Michael-12 ECKELMAN and Cheryl RIEHLE:
  Surname ECKELMAN
  2798. Alexander Cole born 29 Sept 1994 Cincinnati, OH   2799. Camille Elise born 12 Mar 1998

2674. COLIN PATRICK-12 ECKELMAN, brother of above, was born 10 Aug 1961 at Troy, Albany County, New York. He married Anna Marie SENORA on 3 Aug 1991 at Peoria, Arizona. She was the daughter of Jose' SENORA and Esther MEDINA, and was born 3 Apr 19__.

Children of Colin-12 ECKELMAN and Anna SENORA:
  Surname ECKELMAN   (children born San Diego., CA)
  2800. Corey Joseph   born 14 Feb 1992   2801. Ian Patrick born 29 Sept 1994

2675. JOHNNA LYNN-12 ECKELMAN, sister of above, was born 17 Aug 1963 at Seattle, Washington. She married John LARKIN on 2 Feb 1990 at Albany, New York. He was the son of John LARKIN and Florence HEMRICK, and was born 21 Feb 1960.

Children of Johnna-12 ECKELMAN and John LARKIN:
  Surname LARKIN
  2802. Matthew John   born 14 Mar 1986   2804. Casey Edward   born 10 Oct 1993
  2803. John Hemrick   born 27 Apr 1992   2805. child   born __ Feb 1999

2676. LISA JANE-12 ECKELMAN, daughter of William Dwight-11 ECKELMAN (Ellen Amelia-10 DRISKO; Henry William-9; George Augustus-8; Captain George W-7; Captain John-6; Joseph-5;-4; John-3; 2) and Carol Marie KNAPP, was born 16 June 1963 at Denver, Colorado. She married first to Jeffery CLAVETTE on 11 Nov 1982 at Elkton, MD. He was the son of Roger CLAVETTE and Jeanette __?__, and was born 19 May 1963 at Harbison, DE. They were divorced, without issue, in Feb 1985. She married second to Charles STOCKS, Jr. on 27 Sept 1985. He was the son of Charles W. STOCKS and Marjorie BOOTH, and was born 16 Aug 1953. They divorced June 1992. She married her third husband, James D. THOMAS, on 14 Aug 1995 at Dover, DE. He was the son of James THOMAS, and was born 12 Dec 1952.

Children of Lisa-12 ECKELMAN and Charles STOCKS:
   Surname STOCKS   (children born at Dover AFB, Dover, Delaware)
   2806. Christina Michelle born 12 Aug 1987   2807. William Charles   born 21 July 1989

2680. MELISSA ANNE-12 DRISKO, daughter of Melville Anson-11 DRISKO (Melville-10; William Herbert-9; Augustus-8; Jeremiah-7; Joseph-6; 5; 4; John-3; 2) and Alice Jane SAUNDERS, was born 23 Sept 1959 at Fort Bragg, NC. She married Philip David KOSMACKI on 2 Aug 1986 at the Old Post Chapel, Fort Myer, VA.

Children of Melissa-12 DRISKO and Philip KOSMACKI:
   Surname KOSMACKI   (children born at Alexandria, Virginia)
   2808. Alison Grace   born 26 Nov 1991   2809. Rachel Anne   born 2 May 1995

2697. JOYCE LILLIAN-12 DRISKO, daughter of Lloyd Harry-11 DRISKO (Harry E-10; George-9; Eri H-8; Chandler-7; Jonathan-6; Samuel G-5; Joseph-4; John-3; 2) and Dorothy STROUT, was born 18 July 1923 at Columbia, Maine. She married Calvin BAGLEY on 12 July 1941 at Cherryfield, Maine. He was the son of _____ BAGLEY and was born 15 July 1920; died 7 Jan 1996 at Robbinsdale, Minnesota.

Children of Joyce-12 DRISKO and Calvin BAGLEY:
   Surname BAGLEY
+ 2810. CAROL ELAINE born 5 June 1942 Harrington, ME; married Ervin BERGEMANN 28 Aug 1960
   2811. Gareth Dale   born 27 Sept 1944; died at birth
   2812. Larry Wayne   born 12 Dec 1946; died 27 June 1987 (murdered) unmarried
   2813. Linda Sue   born 12 Oct 1949 unmarried
   2814. Douglas Winthrop born 26 May 1953 unmarried
+ 2815. RONDA MARIE born 12 May 1955; married Peter HARRITY 15 Oct 1983 (he born 19 Feb 1953

2698. DONNA FRANCES-12 DRISKO, sister of above, was born 31 May 1926 at ____, Maine. She married Willard Omar ACKLEY 21 Sept 1946. He was the son of Clayton ACKLEY and Virginia E. REED; and was born 24 Jan 1924.

Children of Donna-12 DRISKO and Willard O. ACKLEY:
   Surname ACKLEY
   2816. Clayton Carl   born   ; married Nora Kewana FORBES
            children: Robert Clayton-14 and Melissa Ann-14 ACKLEY
   2817. Wayne Carl   born 19 July 1947 unmarried
   2818. Susan Lois   born   ; 1m. David J. SMITH; 2m. Allen Francis CUST
            children: Kimberly Lynn-14; Kelly Marie-14; and Jeffery Alan-14 CUST
   2819. Paula Louise   born
   2820. Scott Lloyd   born 5 June 1959 Whitneyville, ME
            married Sabrina WIDDICOMBE 28 Oct 1978 (div)
            Ch: Jessyca Joye-14 ACKLEY born 7 June 1977

2699. MYRNA LAVERNE-12 DRISKO, sister of above, was born 8 July 1931 at __, Maine. She married Wallace CHIPMAN 6 Sept 1952. He was the son of _____ CHIPMAN, and was born ____.
   Children of Myrna LAVERNE-12 DRISKO and Wallace CHIPMAN:
   Surname CHIPMAN
+ 2821. MILTON LLOYD   born 13 July 1953; married Beverly WEITZEL (she born 11 Oct 1956)
+ 2822. DAVID HAROLD   born 23 May 1955; 1m. June THOMPSON (divorced)
            2m. Victoria POMEROY 14 Nov 1978

Children of Myrna Laverne-12 DRISKO, continued:
  Surname CHIPMAN
+ 2823. DOROTHY ANN   born 29 Dec 1956; married Mark Allen BLUMS/BLOMS
                    (he born 1 Dec 1954)
+ 2824. DIANE MARIE   born 4 Oct 1961; 1m. Timothy Robert GROTE 29 Dec 1979
                    (he born 18 July 1961)   2m. Randy Lee MEYER
   2825. Donald   born 22 Sept 196_

2700. AVONNE ESTELLE-12 DRISKO, sister of above, was born 25 Feb 1935 at ___, Maine. She married first to Fred W. FAULKINGHAM 25 June 1954. They divorced. She married second to Charles BROWN.
  Children of Avonne-12 DRISKO and Fred FAULKINGHAM:
    Surname FAULKINGHAM
+ 2826. ROGER   born 28 Oct 1957; married Vicky Lynn MITCHELL 25 Mar 1978
      WILLIAM   (she born 16 June 1957;   )
+ 2827. AUSTIN LEROY born 31 May 1961; married Elizabeth Ann KLICK 22 Sept 19__
                    (she born 19 Sept 1959;   )

2701. SYLVIA DOROTHY-12 DRISKO, sister of above, was born 15 Aug 1939 at ____, Maine. She married Kenneth L. MANN 1 June 1960.
  Children of Sylvia-12 DRISKO and Kenneth MANN:
    Surname MANN
+ 2828. CATHY LYNN   born 5 June 1961; married Raymond BAILEY, Jr. 28 Feb 1981
                    (he born 21 Feb 19__;   )
+ 2829. SUSAN DAWN   born 16 June 1965; married Steven Allen BAKER 3 May 1986
                    (he born 17 Aug 1956;   )

2716. CATHY-12 WORCESTER, daughter of Marilyn Ida-11 DRISKO (Clarence H-10; William Pitt-9; Joseph Whitney-8; Chandler-7; Jonathan-6; Samuel G-5; Joseph-4; John-3; 2) and Verrill WORCESTER, Jr., was born 31 Oct 1952 at Fort Campbell, KY. She married Edward Phillip MARSHALL on 1 June 1974
  Children of Cathy-12 WORCESTER and Edward MARSHALL:
    Surname MARSHALL
    2830. Edward Phillip, Jr.born ____   2832. Meghan Ashley   born ____
    2831. Benjamin Mathes born ____

2718. KYMM-12 WORCESTER, sister of above, was born 8 June 1956 at Munich, Germany. She married Stephen LANGE on 31 May 1982 at _____. He was the son of ____ LANGE, and was born _____.
  Children of Kymm-12 WORCESTER and Stephen LANGE:
    Surname LANGE
    2833. Whitney Michelle born _____   2835. Kelsey Elizabeth   born ____
    2834. Alexandra Nicole born _____

2719. PAMELA-12 WORCESTER, sister of above, was born 19 Aug 1958 at Munich, Germany. She married David HULL on 31 Oct 1982 at _____.
  Children of Pamela-12 WORCESTER and David HULL:
    Surname HULL
    2836. Sarah Elizabeth born ____   .   2838. Jonathan David   born ____
    2837. Katie Lynn   born ____

2721. CRAIG DRISKO-12 WORCESTER, brother of above, was born 23 Feb 1963 at Fort Bragg, North Carolina. He married Sally VOSE on 19 Feb 1982 at ____.
Children of Craig-12 WORCESTER and Sally VOSE:
    Surname WORCESTER
    2839. Ryan Craig born ____   2840. Cory David born ____   2841. Curtis James born ____

2731. CHARLES VICTOR-12 TRACY, son of Charles Gilbert-11 TRACY, Jr (Charles Gilbert-10; John Franklin-9; Amos-8; Abigail DRISKO-7; Jonathan-6; Samuel- G-5; Joseph-4; John-3;2) and Gay WILLIAMS, was born 11 Nov 1939 at Winnipeg, Manitoba, Canada. He married Heather Ann __?__.

Children of Charles V-12 TRACY and Heather Ann __?__:
    Surname TRACY
    2842. Heather Colleen   born 11 June 1964   2843. Shannon Kimberly   born 13 Apr 1969

2732. THOMAS LEIGH-12 TRACY, half brother of above, son of Charles Gilbert-11 TRACY, Jr. and his second wife Rowena SMITH, was born 17 Nov 1947 at Edmonton, Alberta, Canada. He married first to Brenda Ann MORRISON on 30 May 1980 at Trail, British Columbia. His second wife was Floy Marie SHANTZ. They were married 14 Apr 1990 at Edmonton, Alberta, Canada.

Child of Thomas L-12 TRACY and Brenda MORRISON:
    Surname TRACY   2844. Ryan Leonard George Maunier   born 23 July 1982

2733. GARY GILBERT-12 TRACY, brother of above, was born 30 Nov 1948 at Whitehorse, Yukon Territory. He married Carol Marlene HELM on 10 Oct 1970 at Fort St. John, British Columbia.

Children of Gary-12 TRACY and Carol HELM:
    Surname TRACY   (born at Fort St. John, British Columbia)
+ 2845. RHONDA   born 29 Dec 1970
      CHARLENE   married Michael Andrew FEDORUK 29 July 1993 Nisku, Alberta, Canada
    2846. Cara Dene   born 23 Apr 1974; married Dennis Scott LIZEE 5 Sept 1998
                          Ch: MacKenzie Charlene-14 LIZEE born 29 Mar 1997

2734. GLORIA DENE-12 TRACY, sister of above, was born 1 Oct 1950 at Wetaskiwin, Alberta, Canada. She married Keith PATEY ca 19___.

Children of Gloria-12 TRACY and Keith PATEY:
    Surname PATEY   (born Victoria, British Columbia, Canada)
    2847. Ashley Nicole   born 12 Mar 1976   2849. Natalie Regan   born 14 Mar 1979
    2848. Ryan Shane   born 23 Dec 1977

2735. PATRICIA ANN-12 TRACY, sister of above, was born 7 Apr 1956 at Edmonton, Alberta, Canada. She married first to ___?__. Her second husband was Robert/Bob DERKACH.
    Child of Patricia-12 TRACY:
    Surname TRACY   2850. Brandon Leigh   born 8 Mar 1977 Fort St. John, British Columbia
    Child of Patricia-12 TRACY and Bob DERKACH:
    Surname DERKACH   2851. Kyla   born 20 March 1987

2737. SHAWN GLEN-12 TRACY, brother of above, was born 22 Aug 1962 at Edmonton, Alberta, Canada. He married Sandy Jo FRITA on 10 Dec 1994 at Canmore, Alberta, Canada.
    Children of Shawn-12 TRACY and Sandy Jo FRITA:
    Surname TRACY
    2852. Cole Glen   born 18 May 1995   2853. Jessie Jo   born 24 Jan 1997

2739. ANN LOUISE-12 TRACY, daughter of John Franklin-11 TRACY (Charles Gilbert-10; John F-9; Amos-8; Abigail-7 DRISKO; Jonathan-6; Samuel G-5; Joseph-4; John-3;2) and Dora RHEAULT, was born 3 Apr 1946 at St. Boniface, Manitoba, Canada. She married Robert DYKE.

Children of Ann LOUISE-12 TRACY and Robert DYKE:
    Surname DYKE   (born Montreal, Quebec, Canada)
    2854. Robert Leighton   born 22 Aug 1967   2855. Dana Louanne   born 8 Aug 1968

2741. KENNETH JOSIAH-12 THARP, son of Dorothy Maude-11 TRACY (John Franklin-11; Charles G-10; John Franklin-9; Amos-8; Abigail-7 DRISKO; Jonathan-6; Samuel G-5; Jospeeh-4; John-3;2) and Josiah THARP, was born 17 Jan 1943. He married first to Sandy __?__ (no issue). He married second to Catherine MEADOWS on 17 July 1971 at Huntington Park, CA.

Children of Kenneth-12 THARP and Catherine MEADOWS:
   Surname THARP
   2856. Marci/Marcy Ann born 18 Nov 1968 Bellflower, CA
   2857. Kenneth Jason   born 2 Jan 1973 Orange, Orange Co., CA

2743. CAROL ANNE-12 THARP, sister of above, was born 14 Dec 1946. She married first to Kenneth FAWCETT. She married second to Eric Jayne PERRIN.
Children of Carole-12 THARP and Eric PERRIN:
   Surname PERRIN
   2858. Ken(neth)   born 6 May 1964 Manitoba, Canada
   2859. Tammy   born 1 May 1966 Winnipeg, Manitoba, Canada
   2860. Scott   born 26 Nov 1968 Collingwood, Ontario, Canada
   2861. Jennifer   born 6 Sept 1971

2744. DIANE-12 THARP, sister of above, was born 26 Aug 1947. She married Norman CHARLES on 20 Nov 1965.
Children of Diane-12 THARP and Norman CHARLES:
   Surname CHARLES
   2862. Vincent Lloyd   born 16 June 1966   2863. Gilbert Joseph   born 23 Nov 1968

2745. KAREN LEIGH-12 TRACY, daughter of Leigh Allen-11 TRACY (Charles G-10; John Franklin-9; Amos-8; Abigail-7 DRISKO; Jonathan-6; Samuel G-5; Joseph-4; John-3;2) and Mary WASLYLNCHUK, was born 15 Apr 1952 at Edmonton, Alberta, Canada. She married Graham John SICKLER on 22 June 1974 at Edmonton.

Children of Karen-12 TRACY and Graham SICKLER:
   Surname SICKLER   (born at Fort St. John, British Columbia, Canada)
   2864. Graham Luke   born 15 Dec 1978   2865. Joshua John   born 8 Dec 1981

2751. JANICE HOLLY-12 SHYMKIW, daughter of Sharon Rosie-11 TRACY (Charles Gilbert-10; John Franklin-9; Amos-8; Abigail-7 DRISKO; Jonathan-6; Samuel G-5; Joseph-4; John-3;2) and John SHYKMIW, was born 20 Dec 1961 at St. Boniface, Manitoba, Canada. She married first to Michael SUTHERLAND on 27 June 1979 at Burnaby, British Columbia. She married second to Gary FONTAINE on 8 Aug 1992 at Vancouver, British Columbia, Canada.

Child of Janice-12 SHYKMIW and Michael SUTHERLAND:
   Surname SUTHERLAND   2866. Tammie Marie born 15 June 1984 Burnaby, British Columbia

Children of Janice-12 SHYKMIW and Gary FONTAINE:
   Surname FONTAINE   (born Burnaby, British Columbia)
   2867. Cristine Elizabeth born 16 Aug 1993   2868. Ashley Nicole   born 24 May 1995

2752. BRENDA LEE-12 SHYKMIW, sister of above, was born 17 June 1960 at St. Boniface, Manitoba, Canada. She married John Charles ROSS on 27 Oct 1984 at Edmonton, Alberta, Canada.

Children of Brenda-12 SHYKMIW and John ROSS:
   Surname ROSS   (born Edmonton, Alberta, Canada)
   2869. Meaghan Leith   born 20 Aug 1988   2871. Kelsey Christina   born 7 June 1993
   2870. Carl Amos Wm.   born 31 May 1991

2758. GLORIA JEAN-12 SHAW, daughter of Gwendolyn-11 TRACY (Victor Thurlow-10; John Franklin-9; Amos-8; Abigail-7 DRISKO; Jonathan-6; Samuel G-5; Joseph-4; John-3;2) and Raymond SHAW, was born 25 Oct 1948 at Portland, Maine. She married first to Craig WORTHING ca 1967, and second to Kenneth COLLIER.

Children of Gloria-12 SHAW and Craig WORTHING:
  Surname WORTHING
  2872. Tracy Lara   born 8 Jan 1969   2873. Terry Shawn   born 7 July 1970

The Thirteenth American Generation

2810. CAROL ELAINE-13 BAGLEY, daughter of Joyce-12 DRISKO (Lloyd H-11; Harry E-10; George C-9; Eri H-8; Chandler-7; Jonathan-6; Samuel G-5; Joseph-4; John-3; 2) and Calvin BAGLEY, was born 5 June 1942 at Cherryfield, Maine. She married Ervin BERGEMANN, Jr. on 28 Aug 1960 at ___. He was the son of Ervin BERGEMANN and _____ ____, and was born 15 Aug 1938.

Children of Carol Elaine-13 BAGLEY and Ervin BERGEMANN, Jr. :
  Surname BERGEMANN
  2874. Kimberly Jolene   born 27 Dec 196_; married Jamie OWENS
          Children: Tyler James-15 OWENS born 20 July 1984
                Logan William-15 OWENS born 20 Dec 1985, and 2 adopted sons
  2875. Kenneth James   born 12 Oct 1975

Note: Carol Elaine adopted Kathryn Joyce (_____) Bergemann born 22 June 1962.
    (Kathryns' mother was Ardis ULLMAN, father unknown) ; married Brett OSBORNE, had 2 ch

2815. RONDA MARIE-13 BAGLEY, sister of above, was born 12 May 1955 at _____. She married Timothy Peter HARRITY ca 19__. He was the son of ____ HARRITY, and was born 19 Feb 1953.

Children of Ronda Marie-13 BAGLEY and Timothy HARRITY:
  Surname HARRITY
  2876. Joseph Lawrence born 1 June 1989   2877. Timothy William   born 28 Jan 1994

2821. MILTON LLOYD-13 CHIPMAN, son of Myrna-12 DRISKO (Lloyd-11; Harry-10; George-9; Eri-8; Chandler-7; Jonathan-6; Samuel-5; Joseph-4; John-3; 2) and Wallace CHIPMAN, was born 13 July 1953. He married Beverly WEITZEL on 29 Aug 1974. She was the daughter of _____ WEITZEL, and was born 11 Oct 1956.

Children of Milton-13 CHIPMAN and Beverly WEITZEL:
  Surname CHIPMAN
  2878. Jason Michael   born 22 Aug 1974; died 15 Aug 1995 (suicide)
  2879. Tracy Lynn   born 17 Nov 1979

2822. DAVID HAROLD-13 CHIPMAN, brother of above, was born 21 May 1955 at ____. He married first to June THOMPSON ca 197_. They divorced and he married second to Victoria POMEROY on 14 Nov 1978. She was the daughter of ____ POMEROY, and was born 11 June 19__.

Child of David-13 CHIPMAN and June THOMPSON:
  Surname CHIPMAN
  2880. Andrea Lea   born 21 Sept 1974

Children of David-13 CHIPMAN and Victoria POMEROY:
  Surname CHIPMAN
  2881. Helen Joan   born 30 May 1978   2883. Ian Thomas   born 13 Feb 1983
  2882. Patrick Neil   born 27 July 1980

2823. DOROTHY ANN-13 CHIPMAN, sister of above, was born 29 Dec 1956 at ____. She married Mark Allen BLUMS/BLOMS on 15 Oct 1977. He was the son of ____ BLUMS/BLOMS, and was born 1 Dec 1954.

Children of Dorothy-13 CHIPMAN and Mark BLUMS/BLOMS:
  Surname BLUMS/BLOMS
  2884. James Allen   born 19 Oct 1980   2885. Christine Anne   born 4 Feb 1982

2824. DIANNE MARIE-13 CHIPMAN, sister of above, was born 4 Oct 1961 at ____. She married first to Timothy Robert GROTE on 29 Dec 1979 at ____. He was the son of ____ GROTE, and was born 18 July 1961. They were divorced and she married second to Randy Lee MEYER. He was the son of ____ MEYER and was born 8 May 1955.

Children of Dianne Marie-13 CHIPMAN and Timothy GROTE:
    Surname GROTE
  2886. Michael Timothy born 15 Dec 1980   2887. Matthew Robert   born 7 July 1985
Child of Dianne-13 CHIPMAN and Randy Lee MEYER:
    Surname MEYER
  2888. Amy Kristine   born 18 Sept 1989

2826. ROGER WILLIAM-13 FAULKINGHAM, son of Avonne Estelle-12 DRISKO (Lloyd-11; Harry-10; George-9; Eri-8; Chandler-7; Jonathan-6; Samuel-5; Joseph-4; John-3; 2) and Fred FAULKINGHAM, was born 28 Oct 1957 at ____. He married Vicky Lynn MITCHELL on 25 Mar 1978.

Children of Roger-13 FAULKINGHAM and Vicky Lynn MITCHELL:
    Surname FAULKINGHAM
  2889. Melissa May   born 8 July 1980   2890. Matthew William   born 9 July 1983

2827. AUSTIN LEROY-13 FAULKINGHAM, brother of above, was born 31 May 1961 at ____. He married Elizabeth Ann KLICK on 22 Sept 197_ at _____. She was the daughter of ____ KLICK, and was born 19 Sept 1959.

Children of Austin-13 FAULKINGHAM and Elizabeth KLICK:
    Surname FAULKINGHAM
  2891. Brooke Amber   born 17 Sept 1980   2893. Erin Beth   born 20 Mar 1987
  2892. Dustin Jorden   born 1 Sept 1984

2828. CATHY LYNN-13 MANN, daughter of Sylvia Dorothy-12 DRISKO (Lloyd-11; Harry-10; George-9; Eri-8; Chandler-7; Jonathan-6; Samuel-5; Joseph-4; John-3; 2) and Kenneth MANN, was born 5 June 1961 at ____. She married Raymond BAILEY, Jr. on 28 Feb 1981. He was the son of Kenneth BAILEY, and was born 21 Feb 19__.

Children of Cathy Lynn-13 MANN and Raymond BAILEY:
    Surname BAILEY
  2894. Michael Ray   born 22 Jan 1988   2895. Jessica Lynn   born 22 Feb 1990

2829. SUSAN DAWN-13 MANN, sister of above, was born 16 June 1965 at ____. She married Steven Allen BAKER on 3 May 1986 at _____. He was the son of _____ BAKER, and was born 17Aug 1956.

Children of Susan Dawn-13 MANN and Steven BAKER:
    Surname BAKER
  2896. Cory Steven   born 2 June 1986   2897. Jessica   born __ ___ 1990

2845. RHONDA CHARLENE-13 TRACY, daughter of Gary Gilbert-12 TRACY (Charles Gilbert-11; 10; John Franklin-9; Amos-8; Abigail-7 DRISKO; Jonathan-6; Samuel G-5; Jospeh-4; John-3;2) and Carol HELM, was born 29 Dec 1970 at Fort St. John, British Columbia. She married Michael Andrew FEDORUK on 29 July 1993 at Nisku, Alberta, Canada.

Children of Rhonda-13 TRACY and Michael FEDORUK:
    Surname FEDORUK   (all born Leduc, Alberta, Canada)
  2898. Jennifer Ashley born 5 Nov 1987   2900. Matthew Cameron born 29 Nov 1991
  2899. Stephanie Anne born 8 July 1989

UNATTACHED DRISKO FAMILIES

(The DRISKO surname was adopted by at least one family residing in Maine.)

The First American Generation

1. TIMOTHY-1 DRISCOLL, born ca 1817, emigrated from Ireland to Jonesport, Maine ca 1840. He married, at Jonesport, to Rachel-3 CUMMINGS Skinner ca 1841. She was the daughter of _____ CUMMINGS, and the widow of Justin SKINNER. She was born ca 1817; died ____.

Rachel-3 had four children from her first marriage, surname SKINNER : 1. Elizabeth, born ____; married George Alvin-8 DRISKO (# 1125 , pp. 82; 126) 2. Nancy born ____; married Moses-_ LEIGHTON; 3. Austin born ___ and 4. William SKINNER born ____.

Timothy-1 DRISCOLL died ca 1886. At least four of his children used the DRISKO spelling.

Children of Timothy-1 DRISCOLL and Rachel-3 CUMMINGS:
    Surname DRISCOLL/DRISKO

+ 2. MATILDA J.	born Apr 1842 Jonesport, Maine
(Drisko)	married Langdon S-8 LEIGHTON 29 Nov 1860 at Addison, Maine
	(he son/o Enoch-7 LEIGHTON and Susanna EMERSON)
	(he born 29 May 1837; died 19 Nov 1900, Michigan)
	died 1920 Escanaba, Michigan
3. John	born ca 1845
4. David (twin)	born ca 1848
5. Morey (twin)	born ca 1848; married Augusta KELLEY; resided Kansas City, KS
6. Christiana E.	born Apr 1852 Jonesport
(Drisko)	married George M-8 EMERSON 15 July 1870 Columbia Falls, Maine
	(he born Mar 1846; died 1 Jan 1880 Brazil)
	died 29 Dec 1935 Escanaba, Michigan no issue EOL
7. George Dewey	born 1 Aug 1853 Jonesport
(Drisko)	married Mary C-8 WASS 31 Mar 1877 Addison, Maine
	(she dau/o David M-7 WASS and Jane Dyer MOORE)
	(she born 25 June 1857; died 7 Mar 1934)
	died 12 May 1921 West Haven, CT.
+ 8. AARON EMERSON	born Feb 1856 Jonesport, Maine; died 1927
(Drisko)	married Alice E. EMERSON, intentions published 24 Aug 1881
	(she dau/o Joseph D-7 EMERSON and Eliza M. WAKEFIELD)
	(she born Aug 1859; died 30 Aug 1921)

Reference: 1850 and 1860 Census Addison, ME; Clarence Holmes DRISKO (deceased)

The Second American Generation

2. MATILDA J-2 DRISCOLL (DRISKO), daughter of Timothy-1 DRISCOLL and Rachel CUMMINGS Skinner was born ca Apr 1842 at Jonesport, Maine. She married Langdon Shorey-8 LEIGHTON on 29 Nov 1860 at Addison, Maine. He was the son of Enoch-7 LEIGHTON and Susanna EMERSON, and was born 29 May 1837; died 19 Nov 1900 in a railroad accident at Escanaba, Michigan. Matilda-2 died there ca 1920.

Children of Matilda-2 DRISCOLL/DRISKO and Langdon-8 LEIGHTON:
  Surname LEIGHTON
  9. Byron Alton   born Feb 1864 Addison, Maine
                            married Harriet VAN VALKENBURG 10 Jan 1894 Escanaba, Michigan
                            (she born June 1874; died ____ ; CA)
                            died ca 1918 Rochester, Minnesota
+ 10. MILDRED   born ca June 1870
       CHRISTIANA   married Loveatus Plummer-9 NORTON (# 1796) 1891 Michigan
                            (he son/o Ackley E. NORTON and Priscilla-8 DRISKO (# 1124)
                            (he born ca 1861 Addison; died 1932 Michigan)
                            died 1924 Manistique, Michigan

8. AARON EMERSON-2 DRISCOLL/DRISKO, brother of above, was born ca Feb 1856 at Jonesport, Maine. He married Alice E-8 EMERSON on ____; intentions published 24 Aug 1881. She was the daughter of Joseph D-7 EMERSON (Eusebius-6) and Eliza M. WAKEFIELD, and was born Dec 1863 at Addison; died there 30 Aug 1921. Aaron-2 DRISCOLL/DRISKO, a sardine canner and farmer, died at Addison, Maine ca 1927.

Children of Aaron-2 DRISCOLL/DRISKO and Alice EMERSON:
  Surname DRISKO
  11. Margaret E.   born 25 Feb 1882; died 20 Jan 1969 Milbridge, ME (unmarried) EOL
  12. Sumner Stinson   born 11 Nov 1883 Addison, died 5 Sept 1963 Ellsworth, ME
                            married Mercy Ellen " Mertie " McDONALD Tibbetts
                                  5 May 1908 St. Stephen, NB (her 2nd marriage)
                            (she dau/o Alexander-1 McDONALD and Elizabeth J. CROWLEY)
                            (she born 23 Mar 1860; died 29 Dec 1940)
                            (she 1m. Leonard A. TIBBETTS ca 1880)
                            died 5 Sept 1963 Addison/Ellsworth, Maine
  13. Fred M.   born 21 Oct 1886; died Apr 1967 Waverly, Tioga County, NY
+ 14. MERRILL F.   born 16 Feb 1890; married Hope F. DRESSER 5 Oct 1912
                            (she born 7 Feb 1889 Milbridge, ME; died 24 Nov 1970 Addison)
                            died 3 Nov 1972 Addison, Maine

Reference: Census 1900/1910/1920 Addison, Maine; LEIGHTON Genealogy; Social Security Death Index

The Third American Generation

10. MILDRED CHRISTIANA-3 LEIGHTON   see LOVEATUS PLUMMER-9 NORTON
        # 1796 Drisko Section – Page 156

14. MERRILL F-3 DRISKO (DRISCOLL), son of Aaron-2 DRISKO (Timothy-1 DRISCOLL) and Alice EMERSON, was born 16 Feb 1890 at Addison, Maine. he married Hope Frances DRESSER on 5 Aug 1912 at Milbridge, Washington Co., Maine. She was the daughter of Alvin Emerson DRESSER and Mary Letitia WALLACE; and was born 7 Feb 1889 at Milbridge, Maine; died 24 Nov 1970 at Addison, Maine. Merrill F-3 DRISKO died 3 Nov 1972 at Machias, Maine.

Children of Merrill-3 DRISKO and Hope DRESSER:
  Surname DRISKO
+ 15. FRANCES   born 23 Nov 1913 Addison, ME
       BARBARA   married Eugene Stanley LOOK 23 June 1934 Columbia Falls, Maine.
+ 16. ARNOLD W.   born 6 June 1915 Addison, ME; died 30 Jan 1990 So. Portland, ME.
                            married Hilda Muriel HERITAGE 25 Dec 1940 Addison
                            (she born ca 1909; died 19 Dec 1986)
  17. Ruth E.   born ca 1916 (no further information)

The Fourth American Generation

15. FRANCES BARBARA-4 DRISKO, daughter of Merrill F-3 DRISKO (Aaron-2; Timothy-1 DRISCOLL), was born 23 Nov 1913 at Addison, Maine. She married Eugene Stanley LOOK 23 July 1934 at Columbia Falls, Maine. He was the son of Walter LOOK and Alice NASH, and was born 27 Feb 1913; died 20 Mar 1984 at Blue Springs, MO.

Children of Frances Barbara-4 DRISKO and Eugene LOOK:
   Surname LOOK
   18. Lorraine   born 8 Feb 1935 Addison, Maine
                      1m. Kenneth THOMPSON 2 Sept 1951 Blue Springs, MO.
                      2m. Kenneth HENDRIX 16 Dec 1958 Nashville, TN
             Children : 1st husband   surname THOMPSON
                        i. Bonnie S-6   born 19__
                        ii. Mark E-6   born 19__
            Children 2nd husband   surname HENDRIX
                        iii. Lou Ann-6   born 19__
                        iv. Jay S-6   born 19__
                        v. Jennifer L-6 born 19__

   19. Marilyn   born 17 Feb 1938 Machias, Maine
                      1m. Robert PHILLIPS 19 Aug 1956 Independence, MO
                      2m. Terry SMITH
           2 children: surname PHILLIPS
                        i. Michael Allen-6 born 12 Sept 1957 Independence, MO
                        ii. Holly Susan-6   born 23 Feb 1960; married Robert COOK

16. ARNOLD-4 DRISKO, brother of above, was born 6 June 1915 at Addison, Washington Co., Maine. He married Hilda Muriel HERITAGE on 25 Dec 1940 at Addison. She born 13 June 1909, ME; died Dec 1986 at South Portland, Cumberland, Maine. Arnold-4 DRISKO died 30 Jan 1990, ME.

Children of Arnold-4 DRISKO and Hilda HERITAGE:
   Surname DRISKO
   20. Aaron Douglas   born 2 Jan 1942 South Portland, Cumberland, Maine
                        married Arlene G. PARE Aug 1966
   21. Marcia Hope   born 27 Jan 1944 South Portland, Maine
                        married Robert SAVOY

UNPLACED DRISKO INFORMATION

Social Security Death Index (SSDI)

DRISKO, Adalaide	born 16 Feb 1909, CA; died 31 Aug 1987 Santa Rosa, CA
, Anna	born 20 Apr 1903, ME; died Mar 1974 Milford, MA
, Bernice	born 17 Jan 1917, CA; died 11 May 1996 Beaverton, Washington Co., Oregon
, Betty	born 28 May 1914, MO; died 26 Apr 1997 Angleton, Brazoria, TX
, Chester E.	born ca 1898; died 29 Dec 1961 So. Portland, ME.
, Colby R.	born 17 Oct 1990, ME; died Apr 1993 Jonesboro, Washington, ME
, Edith	born 21 Apr 1890, FL; died Aug 1981
, Eleanor Mae	born 9 Aug 1887, CA; died 8 Dec 1982 Clute, Brazoria, TX
, Elizabeth	born 21 Apr 1915, NY; died 18 Apr 1994 Yonkers, NY
, Elwood	born 7 Feb 1905, ME; died Nov 1977 Beals, Maine
	married Maggie SEAVEY 23 Nov 1929
, Emily	born 24 Apr 1908, NY; died July 1969 Bronx, NYC, NY
, George	born 9 Mar 1911, PA; died Aug 1966
, Gertrude	born 5 Jan 1889, MA; died Nov 1967
, Gladys	born 25 Jan 1895, MA; died 25 Sept 1994 Milbrook, NY
, Harrison M.	born 10 Dec 1888, ME; died Oct 1970 Augusta, Kennebec, Maine
	married May SMITH 9 Dec 1945
, Helen	born 29 July 1917, MA; died Mar 1976 Maynard, Middlesex, MA
, Janet	born 3 Aug 1915, OR; died 2 July 1994 Concord, CA
, Joan	born 25 Jan 1932, MA; died 17 Apr 1997 Milford, Worcester, MA
, John William	born ____; died 3 Jan 1987 Brazoria, TX
, Paul	born 4 Mar 1932; died 27 Dec 1999 Northborough, MA
, Walter A.	born ca 1829; died 10 Nov 1855 Staten Island, NY
, William	born 28 June 1950, ME; died Aug 1978 Addison, Washington, ME

MAINE MARRIAGES

DRISKO, Donald A. of Salem , MA., married Elizabeth J. SULLIVAN of Ipswich, MA 27 Feb 1942	
, Dorothy D.	married Roy KILNER 14 May 1926 Waterville, Maine
, George V.	married Barbara L. PERLEY Nov 1965
, Vestin	married Mabel NORTON 13 July 1950 Beals, Maine

MISCELLANEOUS UNPLACED INFORMATION
Indiana Census   1850 Parke County (Microfilm # M432-164) P. 0298 b.txt

DRISKO, Esquire	DRISKO, Isabella
, Henry	, Louisa
, Patsy	, Nancy
, Anna	, Patsy
, David	, Susan
, Henry W.	

Northern CA. Bounty Land Grantees (Page 228) mentions " people who served in Capt. DRISKO'S Company, MA Militia – **War of 1812**."

Cambridge, MA Blue Book (page 200) lists Mrs. L. M. DRISKO , 51 Brattle

DRISKO, Barbara   born 3 Dec 1915 Los Angeles, CA; died 28 Sept 1997 Spokane, WA
                         married Marcel Jacob De LOTTO

MACHIAS, MAINE REGISTERS AND ENROLLMENTS
DRISKO CAPTAINS

DRISKO, A. J.	Schooner *O. SAWYER* of Jonesport	no date
DRISKO, ALAMON R.	Schooner *ADA BARKER* of Jonesport	1882-83
(# 1282)	Schooner *ORRIE V. DRISKO*	1883
	Schooner *JAMES WARREN* of Addison	no date
	Schooner *J. C. READ* of Harrington	no date
DRISKO, BENJAMIN F.	(# 463)	
DRISKO, EDGAR	Schooner *ORRIE V. DRISKO* of Machias	1881
EVERSON	Schooner *ADA BARKER* of Jonesport	1882
(# 1283)	Schooner *ISAAC CARLTON* of Machias	1885
	(built Columbia Falls 1883)	
	Schooner *HENRY* of Jonesport	1889
	Schooner *JOSEPH B. THOMAS* of Thomaston	1903
DRISKO, EDMUND	Schooner *MARY & FRANCES* of Columbia	1852
CURTIS	Schooner *S & B SMALL* of Columbia	1854-58
(# 450)	Brig *J & H CROWLEY* of Addison	1865
	Schooner *FLORILLA* of Milbridge	1871
DRISKO, GEORGE B.	Schooner *MARY* of Columbia Falls	1869
(# 503)	Schooner *GERTRUDE PLUMMER* of Columbia Falls	1871
	(he master and builder)	
DRISKO, GEORGE	Schooner *CYPRUS*	1845-46
WASHINGTON	Schooner *B A TUFTS* of Machiasport	1845
(# 427)	Schooner *ALBERT H. WAITE*	1873
	(also the master of vessels at Belfast, ME and Boston, MA)	
DRISKO, HIRAM	Schooner *ELVIRA* of Cutler	1865
CROWLEY	Brig *PROTEUS* of Cutler	1867
(# 1262)	Schooner *MORO* of Jonesport	1877
	Schooner *YREKA* of Machias	1879
DRISKO, JOEL	Schooner *MARY E GAGE* of Columbia	1852
WILSON	Schooner *CRYSTAL PALACE* of Columbia	1854
(# 456)	Schooner *CATHERINE* of Swan's Island	1854
	Schooner *J W DRISKO* of Columbia Falls	1856-63
	(built 1856)	
	Schooner *O. SAWYER* of Jonesport	1868-70
	Brig *ADELINE RICHARDSON* of Addison	1875
	(principal owner Leander A. KNOWLES)	
	Schooner *NETTIE P DOBBIN* of Jonesport	1878
	Schooner *JOSIE* of Machias	1879
	Schooner *JAMES WARREN* of Machias	1883
	Schooner *ELVIRA* of Machias	1883
DRISKO, JOHN	Schooner *ELIZA* of Addison	1801
(# 132)	(41 ton; 46' long; 2-masted)	
	Schooner *ONLY DAUGHTER* of Addison	1830
	Note: " Fisherman's Memorial and Record Book " page 13 states –	
	" Schooner *ONLY DAUGHTER* was run down and sunk off	
	Cape Canso (NS) July 18th 1845. Crew saved. "	
DRISKO, JOHN J.	Schooner *PIONEER* of East Machias	1848
(# 356)		
DRISKO, JOSIAH	Schooner *LIVELY* of Jonesboro	1828
	Schooner *DOVE* of Addison	1835
DRISKO, JUDAH	Schooner *LIVELY* of Jonesboro	1827
(# 118)		

DRISKO Captains continued:

DRISKO, JUDAH (2)	Schooner *J A WEBSTER* of Machiasport	1876-77
DRISKO, ORREN W.	Schooner *BAT* of Jonesport	1889-90
(# 1292)		
DRISKO, PERRIN C.	Brig *HENRY BROOKS* of Addison	1854
(# 466)		
DRISKO, RALPH	Schooner *F T DRISKO* of Machias	1888-90
BURTON	Schooner *DRISKO*	1891
(# 1928)	_____ *DEERING*	1892
	Schooner *CAMILLA MAY PAGE* of Bath	1905
	Schooner *ELWOOD SMITH* of New Haven	1905
	Schooner *ELLA PIERCE THURLOW* of Rockland	1918
	Barkentine *CECIL P STEWART* of Thomaston	1919

DRISKO, RALPH B.,JR	Schooner *MARY STUART* of Phippsburg	
	Steamship *LILLIAN LUCKENBACK*	1924
(#1928 a)	Note: He died 11 March 1924, when he was swept over the *LILLIAN LUCKENBACK* on passage from New York to San Francisco.	

DRISKO, THOMAS	Schooner *IDA MAY* of Jonesport	1866-72
ARTHUR	Schooner *SPEEDWELL* of Jonesport	1872
(# 1265)	Schooner *ORRIE V DRISKO* of Machias	1873-74
	Schooner *YREKA* of Machias	1877
	Schooner *F T DRISKO* of Machias	1882-91
	Schooner *DRISKO* of Jonesport	1888
	Schooner *TWILIGHT* of Jonesport	1889
	Schooner *T A DRISKO* of Jonesport	1891

DRISKO, THOMAS	Schooner *A K McKENZIE* of Addison	1853-55
CROWLEY	(173 ton; 92' long; 2-masted)	
(# 453)	Brig *J & H CROWLEY*	1859
	Schooner *MARY E GAGE* of Columbia	1861-62
	Schooner *SARAH* of Jonesport	1862
	Schooner *PULASKI* of Jonesport	1866
	Schooner *JOHN S MOULTON* of Addison	1867
	(159 ton; 103' long; 2-masted) Alonzo NASH owner)	
	Schooner *JAMES WARREN* of Addison	1867-72
	(11 ton; 98'; 2-masted) owner George FARNSWORTH	

DRISKO, ZIMRI T.	Schooner *WIGWAM* of Cherryfield	1881-86

DRISKO / DRISCO CAPTAINS Portsmouth, NH

DRISCO, James, Jr	Sloop *DOLPHIN*	1792.
(# 178)	Schooner *BETSEY*	1793-95
	Schooner *RISING SUN*	1794-99
	Schooner *RANGER*	1794-1800
	Brig *CAMILLUS*	1799-1800
	Sloop *EAGLE*	1802-1803
	_____ *HAMPDEN AND SIDNEY*	1803-1807
	_____ *VENUS*	1807-1812
	_____ *FLY FISH*	
DRISCO, James, Sr.	Sloop *DOLPHIN*	1792
(# 62)	Schooner *BETSEY*	1793-95
	Sloop *SALLY*	1794-99
	Brig *RANGER*	1798
	Brig *ORLAND*	1800-1802
	Sloop EAGLE	1802-1803
	____ *HAMPDEN AND SIDNEY*	1803-1807
	____ *FLY FISH*	1808-1812
DRISCO, Joshua	# 574	

The following owned shares in vessels in the Machias (ME) district:
Alexander DRISKO; C. DRISKO; C A DRISKO; C T DRISKO; Catherine W. DRISKO; Charles A. DRISKO; Gertrude E. DRISKO; Edmund DRISKO; Eva A. DRISKO; F T DRISKO; F. Jasper DRISKO; Francesca T. DRISKO; Frances J. DRISKO; Jeremiah DRISKO; Joseph DRISKO; Levi DRISKO; Mayhew DRISKO; O H DRISKO; Oramander DRISKO; Ralph B. DRISKO; Samuel DRISKO; Sewall M. DRISKO; T A DRISKO; Thomas DRISKO; W H DRISKO; Mr/Mrs. W J DRISKO; W P DRISKO.

DRISKO SHIPBUILDERS
Builder: Jeremiah DRISKO # 139

Year built	Type/Class Vessel name	Dimensions	Master
1812	Schooner *REBECCA* of Addison	26 ton; 42'	Jonas WASS
1817	Schooner *NANCY* of Columbia		
1819	Brig *MOUNT HOPE* of Addison	206 ton; 85'	
1820	Schooner *WILLIAM/WITHAM* of Columbia	40 ton; 50'	James CROWLEY
1820	Schooner *STRANGER* of Jonesboro		
1821	Schooner *STEVEN JONES* of Jonesboro		
1826	Schooner *MARY* of Addison	105 ton	
1826	Brig *GEORGE WASHINGTON* of E. Machias		
1827	Schooner *VOLANT* of Columbia		
1827	Schooner *ST MICHAEL* of Columbia		
1837	Brig *WASHINGTON* of Addison	176 ton; 83'	Henry TRUE, Jr
1838	Brig *COMMODORE HALL* of Jonesport		
1840	Brig *WAMPANOAG* of Addison	180 ton; 68'	Moses NORTON
1845	Schooner *JOSEPH CRANDON* of Columbia		
1849	Schooner *J A HOBART* of Addison	149 ton; 82'	
1852	Schooner *NORTHERN LIGHT* of Rockland		

Shipbuilder: George B. DRISKO # 503

Year built	Type/Class Vessel name	Master
1866	Schooner + *FANNY and MAY* of Columbia Falls	Fred A. BUCKNAM
1869	Schooner *MARY* of Columbia	
1871	Schooner *GERTRUDE PLUMMER* of Columbia	
1872	Schooner *MODOC* of Columbia Falls	

+ The *FANNY and MAY*, built 1866 at Columbia Falls, Maine, was a 2-masted Schooner, with one deck, a square stern, and a billethead. It weighed 136.93 tons, and was 89.5 feet long, 26.5 feet wide and 8.2 feet deep. It was enrolled # 40, on 22 Aug 1866 at Machias, Washington County, Maine. The principal owners, Captain Frederick A. R. BUCKNAM and his brother George Little BUCKNAM each owned 1/8th of the vessel.

Richard ALLEN, Hillman ALLEN, James L. BUCKNAM, F H PETERSON, Truman WILSON, Thomas TABBUT/TIBBETTS, James CURTIS, J P WASS, A S HATHAWAY, William BUCKNAM, Robert William BUCKNAM, E R BUCKNAM, all of Columbia Falls, each owned a 1/16th share of the vessel.

This vessel, enrolled 12 Sept 1867 at Machias, with Captain Fred A. BUCKNAM as the master, sailed from Fortress Monroe, Virginia on 25 Nov 1867 – bound for Kittery, Maine with a cargo of oak. It was never heard from again. Captain BUCKNAM (# 977), and a cousin, the son of William BUCKNAM, were from Columbia Falls. The remainder of the crew were from Addison, Maine including Frederick BISHOP, the son of the Rev Thomas BISHOP and his wife Jane. Other crew members were Fletcher WHITE and Arthur RAMSDELL.

> Note: Frederick BISHOP, was the uncle of Marion SCHOPPEES' grandfather. Marion SCHOPPEE, of Machias, Maine, was most helpful in securing vessel information for this book.

Shipbuilder and Owner DRISKO, Captain John # 132

Year Built	Type/Class	Vessel name	Master
1830	Schooner	*ONLY DAUGHTER* of Addison	John DRISKO

Shipbuilder DRISKO, Samuel Gatchell, Jr. # 146
Shipyard was at Columbia, Maine, on the Branch Stream

18__	*SAMUEL TRAIN*	18__	*WAVE*

RICKER, Andrew # 272 Shipbuilder – Nova Scotia
ROGERS, Alton V. # 1806 Shipbuilder at Jonesport

MARITIME OCCUPATIONS – OTHER THAN SEA CAPTAINS

DRISKO, Abdon R.   (# 1122) Seaman
    , Alexander Milliken   (# 1259) Assistant Lighthouse Keeper, Jonesport, Maine
    , Augustus W (# 1135) Seaman   Addison, Maine
    , Benjamin Franklin   (# 463) Ships' carpenter
    , Caleb Haskell   (# 352) Ships' carpenter
    , Charles A.   (# 506) Keeper of the Libby Island Lighthouse
    , Everett W.   (# 1167) Ships' carpenter   Addison, Maine
    , Francis Marion   (# 951) Ships' carpenter   Addison
    , George Alvin   (# 1125) Seaman   Addison
    , Henry Brooks   (# 1313) Seaman

MARITIME OCCUPATIONS – OTHER THAN SEA CAPTAINS

DRISKO, Horatio	(# 958)	Seaman	
, James Parker	(# 430)	Seaman	Addison
, Jason Clapp	(# 428)	Ships' carpenter	Addison and Jonesboro
, Jeremiah Norton	(# 1260)	Seaman and fisherman	Head Harbor Island
, John Jeremiah	(# 356)	Master ships' caulker	
, John Perkins	(# 955)	Seaman	
, Judah Johnson	(# 942)	Master ships' caulker	Addison
, Louraine/Lorrain	(# 429)	Seaman	Addison
, Oramander H.	(# 464)	Ships' carpenter	Addison
, Mayhew C.	(# 424)	Ships' carpenter	Addison
, Philo Lewis ++	(# 361)	Ships' caulker	
, Thomas	(#)	Seaman	
, Walter Harris	(# 504)	Ships' carpenter	
, William Johnson	(# 351)	Assistant Lighthouse Keeper	
, Zimri Tabbut	(# 448)	Seaman	Milbridge

++   Philo Lewis- 7 DRISKO, worked in Leander KNOWLES shipyard. According to John Bucknam-9 DRISKO (# 1702), grandson of Philo Lewis DRISKO, " Leander KNOWLES was a prominent shipbuilder who lived next door to my grandfather in Addison, and his lot was part of one of the original grants of land to DRISKOS' in the then Township # 6, East – now Addison. "

Vessels built at Addison, Maine by Leander KNOWLES
(He was principal owner of all, and Master of some)

| Schooner *SEA GULL* | 160 ton; 85' long; 2-masted; built 1864/46, Horatio PLUMMER, master |
| Bark *NELLIE CHAPIN* | 566 ton; 133' long; 3-masted; built 1866 |

(this vessel, with Warren WASS as Master, took the Adams Colony to Jaffa, Palestine

Brig *ADELINE RICHARDSON*	223 ton, 107' long; 2-masted, built 1867
Schooner *H. KNOWLES*	177 ton; 97' long; 2-masted , built 1868
Schooner *Melona N. KNOWLES*	205 ton; 105' long; 2-masted, built 1869
Schooner *TARRY NOT*	246 ton; 112' long; 2-masted; built 1870
Schooner *SPEEDWELL*	418 ton; 127' long; 3-masted; built 1872, Thomas DRISKO, master
Schooner *J & H CROWLEY*	240 ton; 106' long; 2-masted; Joel CROWLEY, master
Brig *ELLEN MUNROE*	built 1876

CAPTAINS - ALLIED LINES

BARTMAN, Albert   2nd husband of # 1124
BARTON, John H.   husband of # 462
BATSON, Adrian Abbot   # 1151
BATSON, Franklin Jones   # 1153
BATSON, John Drisko   # 1152
BUCKNAM, Benjamin Franklin   father-in-law of # 974

Master	1862	Bark *ANNIE L. MORSE*; 500 ton; built 1862 Eastport by C S HUTTON
Master	1863	Bark *ZELINDA*; 539 ton; built Eastport 1863 by C S HUTTON
Master	1864	Schooner *J W DRISKO* of Columbia Falls; built 1856 Columbia
Master	1867	Brig *CALLAO* of Columbia Falls ; built 1867; also part owner

BUCKNAM, Frederick A. R.   # 977
CATES, Joseph Willard   husband of # 967
COFFIN, Charles Everett   # 1393
COFFIN, Charles F.   # 1406
COFFIN, Eugene Amos   # 1405
COFFIN, Herbert W.   # 1394
COFFIN, Samuel Moody   # 1404
COFFIN, Temple Cook   husband of # 944

Master	1864-65	Schooner *JULIA* of Harrington; built there 1864; also part owner
Master	1868	Brigantine *GOODWIN* of New York; built 1866 Harrington
Master	1872	Brig *DIRIGO* of Harrington; built there 1862; also part owner

COLSON, Gilman   2nd husband of # 1340
DAVIS, Galen W.   # 1355 sea captain Addison, ME
DORR, Joseph Patten, Jr.   # 1275; also shipbuilder
DUNBAR, Horace Marston   husband of # 1908
DYER, John Wass   husband of # 954

| Master | 1854-55 | Schooner *KORET* of Saco; built 1821 Haddam, CT; also part owner |

FOSTER, Warren   husband of # 1148
GOODWIN, Jedediah   husband of # 44
GOODWIN, Reuben   husband of # 293
KELLEY, John   husband of # 442; sea captain at Addison
LEIGHTON, Gilbert H.   husband of # 1730

CAPTAINS – Allied Lines continued:

LEIGHTON, Harris H.	# 1138		
LEIGHTON, Jason Drisko	# 1140		
Master 1868	Brig *RAVEN*	Brig *G F BUCKNAM*	
	Bark *I. SARGENT*	Brig *J W SAWYER*	
	Schooner *CRYSTAL PALACE*	Brig *MARY E LEIGHTON*	
LOOK, Bert Sidney	# 1740		
LOOK, Oscar William	# 1738		
LOOK, Silas Hillman	husband of # 385		
LORING, Joseph B.	1st husband of # 1340		
NASH, Holmes	husband of # 141		

       Master and part owner (except where noted *)

1800	Schooner *UNION* of Addison; built there 1800; 99 tons; 2-masted
1800	Schooner *POLLY* of Addison, built there 1801
1815	Brig *ANTELOPE* of Columbia; built there 1815
1819	Brig * *MOUNT HOPE* of Addison; built there 1819; Jeremiah DRISKO, owner (206 tons; 85' long; 2-masted)
1823	Schooner *BELLISLE* of Addison; built Camden. ME 1815
1827	Schooner * *NEW YORK*; Nathaniel NASH, owner (109 tons; 78' long; 2-masted)
1832	Schooner * *SUPERIOR*; Levi SMALL, owner (153 tons; 82' long; 2-masted)
1833	Schooner * *BILLINGS*; Levi SMALL, owner (154 tons; 83' long; 2-masted)
	Schooner *SIDNEY* of Addison; built there 1835

NORTON, Ackley Ezra	husband of # 1124	
Master 1863	Schooner *ELVIRA CONANT*	
PLUMMER, Amos B., Jr.	# 937	
PLUMMER, Bryce T.	Father-in-law of # 503 (Captain George B-7 DRISKO)	
Master 1837	Brig *SARAH & ELIZABETH* of Addison	
Master 1841-42	Brig *ARCTURUS* of Addison (owner Jeremiah DRISKO)	
Master 1848	Bark *COLUMBIA* of Addison; also owner ; 230 tons	
PLUMMER, Robert Perkins	husband of # 962	
PLUMMER, William Wilmot	# 909	
PLUMMER, Voranus Coffin	# 938	
RICKER, Benjamin	# 104	
RICKER, Ebenezer	# 101 reportedly the master./part owner of the 1st square rigged sailing vessel from Yarmouth, Nova Scotia. After the War of 1812, he was a shipbuilder.	
RICKER, Nathaniel	# 108	
RICKER, Paul	# 47	
RICKER, Robert	# 109 (son of above)	
SAWYER, Oliver	husband of # 443 (also a shipbuilder at Jonesport)	
SMITH, Andrew	husband of # 285	
STROUT, George V.	# 1828	
TREFETHEN, William	husband of # 179	
WASS, Holmes Nash	husband on # 347	
WASS, Warren	husband of # 1378	
WHITE, Warren M.	husband of # 1412 Sea captain	
WHITEHOUSE, Benjamin	husband of # 291	

OTHER MARITIME OCCUPATIONS

BEAL, Reuben S.	husband of # 1235 - Seaman
COFFIN, John Bartlett	# 1409 Marine Engineer
COLSON, Gilman-9	# 2036 Ship's cook and sailor
DAVIS, David-2	husband of # 477 ships' carpenter
DAVIS, George Adams	# 1661 Seaman
DINSMORE, Daniel W.	husband of # 489 Ship builder
LIBBY, Jonathan-7	# 542 Sailor/ fisherman
NOYES, Daniel	husband of # 1166 Seaman Jonesboro
PLUMMER, Amos B.	# 349 - ships' carpenter
PLUMMER, Milton E.	# 1671 Sailor Harrington, ME
PLUMMER, Moses 4th	# 346 - ships' steward
PLUMMER, Walter W.	# 1676 Lighthouse keeper Addison, ME
RICKER, Andrew	# 272 - Shipbuilder Nova Scotia
RICKER, Paul	# 107 - sailor (see page 19 for more about this sailor , and the next two)
RICKER, Sylvanus	# 105 - sailor
RICKER, William	# 106 - sailor

OTHER MARITIME OCCUPATIONS, CONTINUED

RICKER, William   # 278 - shipbuilder Nova Scotia
SARGENT, Daniel   husband of # 277 shipbuilder Nova Scotia
SAWYER, Ebenezer   husband of # 440 ships' carpenter   Jonesport
SAWYER, Luther   husband of # 941 ships' caulker
SIMMS, Robert   husband of # 271 shipbuilder Nova Scotia
SMALL, Levi   husband of # 353 ship owner
TABBUT, Benjamin Franklin   # 402   sailor
TABBUT, David   # 377   ships' carpenter
TIBBETTS, Leslie   # 1037   seaman
WILSON, John Drisko   # 326   shipbuilder, Brewer, Maine

CLASSIFICATIONS OF VESSELS

BRIG/BRIGANTINE   A two-masted ship with the main mast fore-and-aft rigged; and the foremast
                        square rigged.

BARQUE/BARK/   Any sailing ship; especially a small one; a sailing vessel with its mast square
    BARKENTINE   rigged and its two other masts rigged fore and aft.

BARGE   A large; usually flat bottomed boat for carrying heavy freight on rivers,
                        canals, etc.

LIGHTER   A large open barge used chiefly in loading or unloading large ships wherever
                        shallow water prevents these from coming to the shore.

SCHOONER   A ship with two or more masts; rigged fore and aft.
SLOOP   A small one masted vessel; originally rigged fore and aft with a jib; mainsail
                        And often topsails and staysails.

SHIP   1. Any vessel of considerable size navigating deep water and not propelled
                        By oars, paddles or the like.
                        2. A sailing vessel with bow sprit and at least three square rigged masts –
                        each composed of lower, top and topgallant members.

STEAMER   Something operated by steam power; a steamship.

TUGBOAT   A small – sturdily built, powerful boat – designed for towing or pushing ships,
                        barges, etc.

Two-masted Schooner

VESSELS and CAPTAINS

VESSEL NAME	TYPE	CAPTAIN	YEAR
ABIGAIL	Sloop	AMES, Isaac	1816-18
		CROCKER, James	1819
		AMES, Isaac	1820-21
ADA BARKER	Schooner	DRISKO, Alamon R.	1882-83
		DRISKO, Edgar E.	1882
ADDIE B LAWRENCE	Schooner	CROCKER, W H	1912
ADELINE RICHARDSON	Brig	DRISKO, Joel W	1875
A K MC KENZIE	Schooner	DRISKO, Thomas	1853-55
ALAMO	Brig	CHANDLER, Aaron W	1875-76
ALBERT H. WAITE	Schooner	DRISKO, George W	1873

> Note: Built in the WILDER yard at Pembroke, Maine for Captain George DRISKO, it later became part of the Winslow Fleet at Portland, and foundered 1887

VESSEL NAME	TYPE	CAPTAIN	YEAR
ALCORA	Schooner	FOSTER, William H	1865
ANNA E J MORSE	Schooner	CROCKER, Charles W	1900
ANNIE L MORSE	Bark	BUCKNAM, Benjamin F	1862
ANN LOUISA	Schooner	TABBUTT, Thomas S	1838
ANTELOPE	Brig	NASH, Holmes	1815
ARCTURUS	_____	PLUMMER, Bryce T	

> Note: May 1866 – the Schooner ARCTURUS, in the Georges fishery, struck L'Hommedieu Schoal and was sunk. The crew was saved. The wreckage of the ARCTURUS was abandoned by the Insurnace Underwriters, but was later raised and sold. It was owned by James MANSFIELD and Co. Captain, at the time, was Eben DAVIS. When it was sunk the vessel was valued at $ 2400, and was insured for $ 2250.

VESSEL NAME	TYPE	CAPTAIN	YEAR
ARTHUR C WADE	Schooner	CROCKER, William G	1902
		FOSTER, John William	1832
BAT	Schooner	DRISKO, O W	1889-90
B A TUFTS	Schooner	DRISKO, George W	1845
		BARTER, Jacob	1852-53
		FOSTER, Nathan, Jr.	1856
BELLISLE	Schooner	NASH, Holmes	1823
BETSEY	Schooner	DRISCO, James, Jr.	1793-95
		DRISCO, James, Sr.	1793-95
		AMES, Isaac	1810
BILLINGS	Schooner	NASH, Holmes	1833
BOSTON	Schooner	FOSTER, William H	1835
BOUNAPARTE	Brig	FOSTER, James M	1852
		FOSTER, Nathan, Jr	1853
		CROCKER, A	1868
BOUNDARY	Schooner	CLARK, Quincy A	1861
	(built Eastport, Maine)		
CALLAO	Brig	BUCKNAM, Benjamin F	1867
CAMILLA MAY PAGE	Schooner	DRISKO, Ralph B	1905
CAMILLUS	Brig	DRISCO, James Jr.	1799-1800
CAROLINE	Schooner	FOSTER, Paul C	1844
CAROLINE & NANCY	Schooner	FOSTER, Nathan	1818
		CROCKER, James Jr.	1823
CARROLL	Schooner	CROCKER, Jacob Barter	1861-64
CATHERINE	Schooner	DRISKO, Joel W	1854
CECIL	Steamer	CROCKER, C H	1903
CECIL P STEWART	Bark	DRISKO, Ralph B	1919
CHAMPION	Packet Schooner	FOSTER, John William	1833
	(built Eastport, Maine)		
CHARLES E BALCH	Schooner	CROCKER, Edward H	1889
		CROCKER, William G	1900
CHARLES L DAVENPORT	Schooner	CROCKER, James B	1900
CHARLES R FARWELL	?	CROCKER, John	1854
CHARLES HOLMAN	?	CROCKER, Robert	
CHEVIOT	Schooner	CHANDLER, Aaron W	1862
CONEANT	Barge	CROCKER, Cyrus P	19__
CONSTELLATION	Schooner	FOSTER, Nathan	1824
		AMES, Abraham	1826
		CROCKER, Benjamin	1833

VESSEL NAME	TYPE	CAPTAIN	YEAR
CRYSTAL PALACE	Schooner	DRISKO, Joel W	1854
		LEIGHTON, Jason D	18__
CRUSOE	Schooner	FOSTER, William H	1856
CYPRUS	Schooner	CROCKER, Paul Jr.	1838
		DRISKO, George W	1845-46
DEA VOLENTE	Tug	CROCKER, W W	1888
DEERING	Schooner	DRISKO, Ralph B	1892
DELIGHT (Nova Scotia)	Schooner (Privateer)	RICKER, Ebenezer	1780
DENMARK	Brig	RONEY, John	1848
		CROCKER, Robert	1841
DIRIGO	Brig	AMES, Isaac	1821-22
		COFFIN, Temple C	1872
DOLPHIN	Schooner	FOSTER, Nathan Jr.	1856
	(built Eastport 1852 – 17 ton)		
DOLPHIN	Sloop	DRISCO, James Jr.	1792
		DRISCO, James Sr.	1792
DOROTHY PALMER	Schooner	CROCKER, William G	1914
DOVE	Schooner	RICKER, Ebenezer	1809
		RICKER, Joseph	1809
		RICKER, William	1809
		RICKER, Abbott	1809
		DRISKO, Josiah	1835
DRISKO	Schooner	DRISKO, Thomas A	1888
		DRISKO, Ralph B	1891
EAGLE	Sloop	DRISCO, James Jr.	1802-03
		DRISCO, James Sr.	1802-03
EDINBURG	Brig	CROCKER, John	1840
EDWARD D/G PETERS	Schooner	BARTER, Jacob	1832-34
ELIA	Schooner	CROCKER, John L	1865-67
ELIZA	Schooner	DRISKO, John	1801
	(built 1797 Pembroke – 108 ton)	CROCKER, James	1819
		CROCKER, Matthias	1851
ELIZA ANN	Schooner	WESTON, Timothy Jr.	1818
		CROCKER, Paul Jr.	1833
		LONGFELLOW, Stephen	1835
ELIZABETH	Brig	CROCKER, James Jr.	1834
ELIZABETH	Schooner	CROCKER, Paul Jr.	1833
ELIZA HUPPER	Schooner	FOSTER, Zebedee	
ELLA PIERCE	Schooner	DRISKO, Ralph B	1918
ELVIRA	Schooner	DRISKO, Hiram C	1865
		DRISKO, Joel W	1883
ELVIRA CONANT	Schooner	NORTON, Ackley Ezra	1863
ELWOOD SMITH	Schooner	DRISKO, Ralph B	1905
EVERGREEN	Schooner	BARTER, Jacob	1827-28
EXPRESS	Schooner	RICHARDS, James H	1862
FAIR AMERICA	Schooner	BARTER, Jacob	1827-28
		CROCKER, James	1827
FALKS	Yacht	CROCKER, E W	1903
FAME	Schooner	AMES, Isaac Jr.	1835
FANNY & MAY	Schooner	BUCKNAM, Fred A	1866-67
FAVORITE	Schooner	FOSTER, Nathan	1818
FLORILLA	Schooner	DRISKO, Edward C	1871
FLY FISH	?	DRISCO, James Jr.	1808-12
		DRISCO, James Sr.	1808-12
FRANKLIN	Schooner	CROCKER, James Jr.	1839-41

(built Eastport 1833 – 73 tons)
Reported to be " one of the sturdiest small vessels ever built, even in Eastport ". The FRANKLIN
followed the whaling industry for 60 years. (Page 89 Vessels " Way Down East " by Joyce KINNEY)

FREDERICK REED	Schooner	FOSTER, William H	1841
FREEDOM	Schooner	CROCKER, James L	1856-57
F T DRISKO	Schooner	DRISKO, Thomas A	1882-91
		DRISKO, Ralph B	1889-90
GENERAL CATES	Schooner	FOSTER, Nathan	1816

VESSEL NAME	TYPE	CAPTAIN	YEAR
GENERAL JACKSON	Schooner	BARTER, Jacob	1828
		FOSTER, Nathan Jr.	1832
		FOSTER, William H	1832
		CROCKER, James	1832
		CROCKER, Paul Jr	1832

Note: Oct 1858 – Captain CALLIGAN of the Brig OLIVE, reported passing the wreck of the *GENERAL JACKSON* of Jonesport about 60 miles off Cape Cod. (KINNEY page 96)

VESSEL NAME	TYPE	CAPTAIN	YEAR
GEORGE EVANS	Schooner	FOSTER, William H	1846
GEORGE WASHINGTON	Brig	FOSTER, Nathan	1826
GERTRUDE PLUMMER	Schooner	DRISKO, George B	1871
G F BUCKNAM	Brig	LEIGHTON, Jason D	18__
GIRARD	Brig	CROCKER, James Jr.	1832
GOODWIN	Brig	COFFIN, Temple C	1868
G W BRINCKERHOFF	Brig	CROCKER, James	1848
HAMPDEN AND SIDNEY	?	DRISCO, James Jr.	1803-07
		DRISCO, James Sr.	1803-07
HANNAH	Schooner	FOSTER, Nathan Jr.	1841-43
HARRIET AND FANNY	?	DRISCO, James Jr.	1805
		DRISCO, James Sr.	1805
HARRIET B SHIEBLY	Lighter	CROCKER, C H	1903-06
HENRY	Schooner	FOSTER, Robert	1818
HENRY	Schooner	DRISKO, Edgar E	1889
HENRY BROOKS	Brig	DRISKO, Perrin C.	1854
HENRY CLAY	Schooner	HOLWAY, John Jr.	1832
		FOSTER, Nathan Jr.	1840-42
HENRY P HAVENS	Schooner	CROCKER, Nelson	1807
HUNTER	Schooner	FOSTER, Nathan	1834
IDA MAY	Schooner	DRISKO, Thomas A	1866-72
INDEPENDENCE	Schooner	CROCKER, James	1821
INDUSTRY	Schooner	TREFETHEN, William	1793
ISAAC CARLTON	Schooner	DRISKO, Edgar E	1885
JACOB & WILLIAM	Schooner	BARTER, Jacob	1846-47
JACOB LONGFELLOW	Schooner	BARTER, Jacob	1848-49
		FOSTER, Nathan Jr	1849
JAMES & CAROLINE	Schooner	CROCKER, James	1829
JAMES POWER	Schooner	CHANDLER, Aaron W	1863
JAMES R TALBOT	Schooner	CROCKER, Jacob B	1874-79
		CROCKER, James B	1876 & 1889
		CROCKER, Edward H	1880-85
JAMES WARREN	Schooner	DRISKO, Thomas	1867-72
		DRISKO, Alamon R	
		DRISKO, Joel W	1883
JAMES W ELWELL	Schooner	CROCKER, William G	1903
J A WEBSTER	Schooner	DRISKO, Judah (2)	1876-77
J C READ	Schooner	DRISKO, Alamon R	
JENNIE BEAL	?	CROCKER, John	1859
J & H CROWLEY	Brig	DRISKO, Edmund C	1865
		DRISKO, Thomas	1859
JOHN F RANDALL	Schooner	CROCKER, Edward H	1902
JOHN S MOULTON	Schooner	DRISKO, Thomas	1867
JOSEPH E RAY	Schooner	CROCKER, James B	1901
JOSEPH B THOMAS	Schooner	DRISKO, Edgar E	1903
JOSIE	Schooner	DRISKO, Joel W	1878
JULIA	Schooner	COFFIN, Temple C	1864-65
JULIET	Schooner	BARTER, Jacob	1856-59
(built Calais, Maine 1856 – 74 ton)			
JUNO (Nova Scotia)	Schooner	CROCKER, Abram	1795
J W DRISKO	Schooner	DRISKO, Joel W	1856-63
		BUCKNAM, Benjamin F	1864
J W SAWYER	Brig	LEIGHTON, Jason D	18__
KEOKUK	Schooner	CROCKER, Jacob B	1872-73
		CROCKER, James B	1872-73

VESSEL NAME	TYPE	CAPTAIN	YEAR
KORET	Schooner	DYER, John B.	1854-55
		CROCKER, Jacob B	1869-70
LAVINIA	Schooner	CROCKER, Benjamin	1826
LAVINIA F WARREN	Schooner	CROCKER, William G	1888
LILLIAM LUCKENBACK	Steamship	DRISKO, Ralph B., Jr.	1924
LIVELY	Schooner	DRISKO, Judah	1827
		DRISKO, Josiah	1828
LOUISA	Schooner	FOSTER, Francis	1862
LUCY WATTS	Schooner	RONEY, John	1852
MARINER (Nova Scotia)	Brig	CROCKER, Simeon	1840
MARION	Tug	CROCKER, W. W.	1889
MARTHA	Schooner	FOSTER, Paul C.	1838
MARTHA ANN	Brig	FOSTER, Nathan Jr.	1837
MARY OF CUSHING	Schooner	MAYHEW, Zebedee	1817
		CROCKER, James	1818
		DRISKO, George B.	1869
MARY & ELIZABETH	Schooner	BARTER, Jacob	1841-44
MARY & FRANCES	Schooner	DRISKO, Edmund C.	1852
MARY E GAGE	Schooner	DRISKO, Joel W.	1852
		DRISKO, Thomas	1861-62
MARY E LEIGHTON	Brig	LEIGHTON, Jason D.	18__
MARY HELEN	Schooner	CROCKER, Charles W.	1876
		CROCKER, James B.	1881-84
MARY H KENDALL	Bark	CROCKER, John	1846
MARY ROBINSON	?	CROCKER, F.	1854
MARY SPEAR	Schooner	FOSTER, Nathan Jr.	1834
		CROCKER, Benjamin	
		CROCKER, Zebedee M.	1837-40
MARY STUART	Schooner	DRISKO, Ralph B, Jr.	
MATTIE J ALLEN	Schooner	CROCKER, George	1911
MAYFLOWER	Schooner	FOSTER, James M.	1846
MECHANIC	Schooner	CLARK, Quincy A.	1853-54
		FOSTER, James M.	1858
MORO	Schooner	DRISKO, Hiram C.	1877
MOUNT HOPE	Brig	NASH, Holmes	1819
NANCY	Sloop	CROCKER, Paul	1802
NELLIE CHAPIN	Bark	WASS, Warren	1866
NETTIE P DOBBIN	Schooner	DRISKO, Joel W.	1878
NEW ENGLAND	Brig	CROCKER, James, Jr.	1841
NEW YORK	Schooner	NASH, Holmes	1827
NORTH AMERICA	Brig	FOSTER, Nathan Jr.	1852
NORTHLAND	Aux Schooner	CROCKER, Cyrus P	19__
OCEAN (Nova Scotia)	Schooner	RICKER, Ebenezer	1818
OLD HUNDRED	Schooner	LONGFELLOW, Stephen	1832
OLIVE	Schooner	WESTON, Timothy Jr.	1812
ONLY DAUGHTER	Schooner	DRISKO, John	1830
OREGON	Schooner	LONGFELLOW, Stephen	1837
		CROCKER, James, Jr.	1837
ORLAND	Brig	DRISCO, James, Sr.	1800-02
ORION	Brig	AMES, Isaac	1824
ORRALLOO	Schooner	CHANDLER, Aaron W.	1868
ORIENTAL	Schooner	CROCKER, Jacob B .	1866
ORRIE V DRISKO	Schooner	DRISKO, Thomas A.	1873-74
		DRISKO, Edgar E.	1881
		DRISKO, Alamon R.	1883
O SAWYER	Schooner	DRISKO, A. J.	
		DRISKO, Joel W.	1868-70
PATRIOT	Schooner	AMES, Isaac Jr.	1838-41
PILGRIM	Schooner	TABBUTT, Thomas S.	1829-47
PIONEER	Schooner	DRISKO, John J.	1848

VESSEL NAME	TYPE	CAPTAIN	YEAR
PLEIADES	Schooner	FOSTER, Nathan	1825-26
POLLY	Schooner	NASH, Holmes	1802
POLYANTHUS	Schooner	DRISKO, George W.	1849
(built Pembroke by George RUSSELL – 1849)			
PRESIDENT	Schooner	AMES, Isaac	1825-27
		FOSTER, John William	1840
PROTEUS	Brig	DRISKO, Hiram C.	1867
PULASKI	Schooner	DRISKO, Thomas	1866
RAMBLER	Launch	CROCKER, L A	1905
RANGER	Brig	DRISCO, James Sr.	1798
RANGER	Schooner	DRISCO, James Sr.	1794-1800
		FOSTER, Nathan	1812-14
(built Denneysville 1797 – 110 ton)			
RAVEN	Brig	LEIGHTON, Jason D.	1868
RENO	Schooner	FOSTER, William H.	1866, 1868-72 1875-77
RESOLUTION	Schooner	CROCKER, Paul	1801-04
RESOLUTION	Brig	CROCKER, Paul	1807
		MAYHEW, Zebedee	18__
RIO	Schooner	CHANDLER, Aaron W.	1858-61
RIPLEY	Schooner	RICKER, Nathaniel	1832
(built Eastport- 98 ton)			

Note: This vessel was owned by Spencer TINKHAM and Jonathan BUCK of Eastport, Maine. It was chartered by John James AUDUBON ,the naturalist, in 1833 for a trip to the coast of Labrador.   (Reference: " Vessels of Way Down East ", KINNEY; page 97)

VESSEL NAME	TYPE	CAPTAIN	YEAR
RISING SUN	Schooner	DRISCO, James Jr.	1794-99
SALLY	Sloop	DRISCO, James Sr.	1794-99
SALLY ANN	Brig	WESTON, Timothy Jr.	1815
SARAH	Schooner	DRISKO, Thomas	1862
S & B SMALL	Schooner	DRISKO, Edmund C.	1854-58
SEA GULL	Schooner	CROCKER, James Jr.	1836
SEGUIN	Tug	CROCKER, W. W.	1888
SHENANGO	Barge	CROCKER, Cyrus P.	1903
SIDNEY	Schooner	NASH, Holmes	1835
SINGLETON PALMER	Schooner	CROCKER, William G.	1915
SPEEDWELL	Schooner	DRISKO, Thomas A.	1872
SUPERIOR	Schooner	NASH, Holmes	1832
SUSAN	Schooner	AMES, Abraham	1819 & 1823-25
		CROCKER, James Jr.	1825
T A DRISKO	Schooner	DRISKO, Thomas A.	1891
THREE BROTHERS	Schooner	WESTON, Timothy Jr.	1806
THREE SALLYS	Schooner	WESTON, Timothy Jr.	1805
		AMES, Isaac	1806
TWILIGHT	Schooner	DRISKO, Thomas A.	1891
TWO BROTHERS	Schooner	AMES, Isaac	1811-15
		AMES, Abraham	1817-19
		CROCKER, Benjamin	1829
		AMES, Isaac	1840
UNION	Schooner	NASH, Holmes	1800
VANCOUVER	Schooner	CROCKER, Timothy B.	1847-54
VENUS	?	DRISCO, James Jr.	1807-12
VIRGINIA	Bark	LONGFELLOW, Stephen	1852
WASHINGTON	Schooner	WESTON, Timothy Jr.	1812
WATCHMAN	Schooner	CROCKER, John	1832
WILLIAM & JOHN	Schooner	HOLWAY, John Jr.	1833
WILLIAM POPE	Schooner	FOSTER, William H.	1846, 1848, 1851
WILLIAM PENN	Schooner	FOSTER, James M.	1840
WILLOW	Schooner	RONEY, John	1844-47
WINFIELD S SCHUSTER	Schooner	CROCKER, William G.	1905

VESSEL	TYPE	CAPTAIN	YEAR
WINIFRED IN	Steamer	CROCKER, Cyrus P.	19__
YREKA	Schooner	DRISKO, Thomas A.	1877
		DRISKO, Hiram C.	1879
ZELINDA	Bark/Barque	BUCKNAM, Benjamin F.	1863

Note: The *ZELINDA* was built in 1863 by C. S. HUSTON at Eastport, Maine - Captain BUCKNAM was the first Master.

The Eastport Sentinel described the vessel as " a beautiful Barque, finished and furnished in the very best manner ".

It was launched 26 Sept 1863 and made the passage from Eastport to Boston in 27 hours. It was burned by the " pirate " *FLORIDA* off the Delaware Capes in July 1864. The vessel was valued at $ 40,000.

BICKFORD, Elizabeth	18	
, Helen Marie	164	
, Inez	133	
, Justus W.	133	
, Melinda E.	94	
, Nettie Wallace	139, 164	
BICKNER,	70	
BINGLE, Anne Marie	181, 195	
, Harry	181	
BIRD, Mary	87	
, Thomas	87	
BISHER, Jennie	137, 162	
BISHOP, Frederick,	219	
, James	18	
, Rev Thomas	219	
BLACK, Geraldine	179	
, Lloyd Evan	156, 179	
, Lois E.	179	
, Maurice G.	123, 156	
BLACKINGTON, Charles	94	
, Clarence	94	
BLACKMAN, George A.	60	
BLAISDELL, Ada Elizabeth	108	
, Alonzo E.	108	
, Esther	28	
, Hannah	41	
, Ida May	108	
, Mary Ella	108	
, Thomas	55, 108	
BLAKE, Edward	87	
, Hannah M.	68	
, Jane	87	
, John	118	
, Mehitable	118	
BLANCHARD, Mary	46	
, Sewall	51	
BLOCKER, James A.	111, 151	
, James A., Jr.	151	
BLOMS/BLUMS, Christine A.	211	
, James Allen	211	
, Mark Allen	207, 211	
BLOOM, David	192	
BLOUIN, Leon	104, 148	
, Marie Louise	104, 148	
BLUNT, Calcida/Cassie A.	82	
, Thomas	82	
BOGART, Emma Ann	74, 121	
BOLO, Sarah	56	
BOOTH, Marjorie	206	
BOOTHBY, Cynthia A.	183, 197	
BORHO, Alexander	115	
, James S.	115	
BOUDWAY, Edward Frank	155	
BOWEN, Charlotte	30,58	
, Louisa	36	
, Nathan	58	
, William	36	
BOWLES, George H.	145, 173	
, Helen	173	
, John	173	
BOWLEY, George W.	76	
BOYD, Mary	50	
BOYNTON, Amos	46	
, Dale L.	178	
, David	46	
, Joshua	46	
, Polly	46	
, William	46	
BOYORAK, David Brent	193	
, John G.	192	
, John Matthew	193	
, Mark Anthony	179, 192	
, Robert Philip	193	
BRACEY, Ida	130	
BRACKETT, Benjamin	157	
, Vernon Kelley	157	
BRACY, Minnie L.	82	
BRADSHAW, Benjamin V.	114	
, Clarence D.	114	
, Edgar R.	114	
, Leonard T.	114	
, Vaughan V.	114	
BRAGDON, Alonzo	57	
, Betsey P.	57	
, Hannah Lois	57	
, Ivory	29	
, James	29, 57	
, William	5 7	
BRAGG, Frederick	63	
BRANCH, Sophronia	30, 59	
BRENDEL, Clara Norine	180	
BRIDGHAM, Alden	144	
, Alvin	144	
, Andrew	97, 144	
, Blanche	171	
, Calla	171	
, Carl	171	
, Claire	171	
, Clara	143, 171	
, Dana	144	
, Emma	79	
, George	144	
, James	80	
, Joseph	80	
, Levi	144	
, Lorenzo	97, 144	
, May	144	
, Murray	144	
, Rev Milton F.	79	
, Ruth E.	171	
, Willie	144	
, Wilson	144, 171	
BRIGGS, Annis	27, 53	
, Lydia	49	
BRIGHTMAN, Omer W.	172	
BROOKS, Hannah	32, 63	
, John	188	
, Lila Curtis	188	
BROUGHTEN, Pearl	153, 177	
BROWN, Ben O.	120, 155	
, Charles	60, 197	
, Edwin Albert	59	
, Elizabeth	25, 72	
, Eunice D.	120	
, Frederick	112	
, George E.	100	
, Grace E.	60	
, Henry L.	100	
, James	100	
, Jane	155	
, Louisa	59, 111	
, Mary L.	60	
, Prudence	132	
, Sharon	193	
, Susanna	100, 147	
, Wilton	147	

DRISKO, Donna Frances	197, 206	DRISKO, Frank Eugene	184
, Dorothy	162, 183, 216	, Fred Howard	95, 141
, Dr. Elliot H.	167	, Fred M.	119, 154, 214
, Earl Winfield	120, 155	, Frederick	183
, Edgar	163	, Gennetta Leighton	184
, Edith	216	, George	216
, Edmund	20, 23, 46, 138, 217	, George Alvin	82, 84, 126, 213, 219
, Edmund C.	85, 128	, George Augustus	87, 132
, Edmund W.	93, 137	, George B.	73, 126, 219
, Edna	141, 169, 185	, George Camelo	124, 142, 166, 183
, Edwin Irwin	142, 166	, George Dewey	213
, Effie M.	167	, George Dolbey	160, 181
, Eleanor	216	, George Thomas	138
, Eliza Evelyn	136	, George Todd	94
, Eliza N.	42, 90	, George W.	12, 83, 96
, Eliza V.	95, 141	, Georgia Anne	136
, Elizabeth	6, 10, 14, 21, 166, 216	, Georgianna	155, 179
, Elizabeth Maria	91	, Gerald Perrin	142
, Elizabeth N.	42, 90	, Gertrude	163, 216
, Ella	23, 96, 163	, Gertrude B.	103, 148
, Ellen Amelia	160, 181	, Gertrude E.	218
, Ellen E.	138	, Gladys	161, 216
, Ellis	88, 136	, Grace D.	94, 137
, Elmira	36, 71, 92	, Grace E.	142
, Eloise	196	, Grace Plummer	142, 166
, Elton B.	137, 162	, Guy C.	137, 162
, Elwood	216	, Hannah	22, 42, 43, 167
, Emily	216	, Harold Philbrick	141, 165
, Emma Bigelow	44, 96	, Harriet R.	87
, Eri Haskell	142, 167	, Harrison	216
, Eri Hathaway	75, 97, 122, 142	, Harry	138, 162
, Ernest H.	135	, Harry E.	166, 183
, Esquire	216	, Harry Lee	155, 178
, Esther Ruth	143, 168	, Harry M.	148
, Ethel	142	, Harvey McKenzie	94, 138
, Ethel May	135	, Hattie	133, 167
, Ethel Whitney	131	, Helen	141, 161, 162, 166, 216
, Eugene Cyrus	143, 167	, Henry	216
, Eugene Sanborn	153, 177	, Henry A.	127
, Eulalia F.	138	, Henry B.	92, 142
, Eunice Parker	43, 91	, Henry B., 3rd	137
, Eva A.	219	, Henry Brooks	96, 141, 219
, Eva Frances	132, 159	, Henry W.	216
, Evelyn Salome	138	, Henry William	132, 159, 160
, Evelyn Winifred	162	, Hiram C.	43
, Everard Irving	87, 131	, Horatio	72, 220
, Everett	86	, Howard Perrin	95, 141
, Everett W.	88, 133, 219	, Hubert	87
, F. T.	219	, Hugh E.	198
, Faith E.	178	, Hugh R.	166
, Fannie/Fanny	87, 130	, Hughene R.	183
, Fanny M.	72	, Ida Frances	93, 137
, Faustina W.	94	, Inez	166
, Feah Parker	42, 47, 90	, Iona D.	160
, Felice A.	171	, Irene Frances	142
, Fellows E.	160, 182	, Irene H.	138
, Fern	161	, Irving L.	94
, Flora	136	, Isabel	135
, Florence	139, 163	, Isabella	216
, Frances	36, 37, 72, 74	, James Coburn	199
, Frances Barbara	214, 215	, James Hamilton	88
, Frances Bucknam	73	, James Parker	41, 88, 220
, Frances J.	218	, James Walker	143, 171
, Frances M.	72, 119, 183	, Jane Barfield	137
, Francesca T.	218	, Jane W.	88
, Francis Eugene	169	, Janet	216
, Francis Jasper	91, 135, 218	, Jason Clapp	41, 87, 88, 220
, Francis Marion	71, 119, 219	, Jasper Thomas	191

GODFREY, Jonathan	118	
GOLLINGER, Terry	181, 194	
GOMM, Bernard J.	188	
GONZALES, Norma Hortense	111	
GOOCH, Ann	34	
GOODALE, Zachariah	3, 5	
GOODWIN, Anna	137, 162	
, Aubrey	113	
, Augusta B.	65	
, Byron M.	65	
, Capt. Jedediah	220	
, Capt. Reuben	32, 65, 22	
, Clara E.	65	
, Daniel	9	
, Edwin A.	56	
, Ezra A.	113	
, Henry	18	
, Irving W.	56	
, Jedediah	10, 18, 19	
, John	9	
, Joseph R.	33, 62, 113	
, Letitia H.	113	
, Lindsey B.	65	
, Mansfield	65	
, Moses	17	
, Sarah B.	120, 155	
, Sarah Emma	113	
, William	9, 32, 113	
, Willoughby	9	
GORDON, Earl	108	
GORE, Etta	121	
GORMAN,	187, 201	
GOSS, Betsey Ann	51	
, Samuel	51	
GOWEN, Flora M.	59, 112	
GRACE, Leonice Gertrude	91, 134, 160	
, William B.	91, 134	
GRAFF, Emma S.	74	
GRAFFAM, Robert	148	
GRAHAM, Daniel	42	
GRANT, Alden	156	
, Babe	109	
, Calvin	77	
, Capt. Daniel	17, 28	
, Caroline	55, 109, 137	
, Carrie	109	
, Cinda Ella	56, 110	
, Clara B.	79	
, Clayton	122	
, Daniel	55, 109	
, Delia Ann	55	
, Dependance	28, 55	
, Edward	122	
, Elsie	76	
, Emma	109	
, Ephraim	75, 77	
, Flora A.	109	
, Forester P.	122	
, Francena	108	
, Frank	107, 108, 109	
, Geneva Helen	111, 152	
, Gilbert Leslie	122	
, Harry Linden	109	
, Joanna	28, 56	
, John	55, 109	
, John Billings	122	
, Joseph H.	58, 111	
, Laura	122, 172	

GRANT, Leander	124	
, Lettie Lee	172	
, Lewis	55, 108	
, Lillian May	109	
, Lois	55	
, Lorey Worcester	122	
, Lucy	28, 55	
, Marguerite M.	124	
, Maria/ Mercy	55, 109	
, Martha	28, 55	
, Mary	55, 109	
, Mary Jane	123, 156	
, Moses Ricker	28	
, Pluma A.	109	
, Polly	28	
, Rufus Meserve	122	
, Samuel	28	
, Solomon	55, 108	
, Susan Elizabeth	55	
, William G.	122	
GRAVES, Roscoe	59	
GRAY, A. Andrew	198	
, Abigail Crowley	97, 145	
, Alton	198	
, Amy A.	198	
, Clara J.	137	
, Elizabeth	165, 182	
, Eugene W.	79	
, Jeremiah	137	
, Katherine	165, 183	
, Mary	7, 102	
, Reginald F.	163	
, William	97, 145	
GREEN, Abigail	34, 69	
, Amelia A.	87, 132, 133	
, Emily M.	164	
, Henry, Jr.	87, 132, 133	
, J. D.	159	
, John	69	
, Julia K.	57	
, Roy G.	155, 179	
, Sandra	179	
, Sarah	118	
GREENLAW, Charles	173, 187	
, Fidelia Jane	173, 187	
, Keith	187	
, Kenneth C.	186	
GREIN, Philip	53	
GRENIER, Exemia	200	
GRIFFIN, Cynthia	180, 194	
, Elias Burt	130	
, John W.	130	
, William Joseph	180, 194	
GRIGGS, Augustus	30	
, Reuben	30	
, Rufus	27	
GROSS, Betty Jane	193	
GROSSMAN, Marty	192	
GROTE, Matthew Robert	212	
, Michael Timothy	212	
, Timothy Robert	207, 212	
GROVER, Edna E.	103	
, Edwin Albert	59	
, William	14, 59	
GULLIVER, Ella	65, 114	
, Mary Adams	98, 146	
GUPTILL, Martha A.	95, 140	
HADDON, Georgia	172	

RICKER, Eleanora J.	61, 113		RICKER , Isabel Harkins	61
, Eli R.	27, 54		, Isabella	31, 53
, Elias	18, 29		, Isaiah	30, 58
, Elijah	17, 27, 53		, James	32
, Eliphalet	18, 30, 63		, James A.	28, 56, 113
, Eliza	18		, James D.	65
, Elizabeth	5, 9, 19, 30, 31, 53, 58, 62, 113		, James E.	110
, Ella	53, 61		, James H.	62
, Ellen S.	56		, James Linden	110
, Elmira	54, 55, 108		, James Malcolm	151
, Emma Caroline	55		, James O'Connor	111
, Ephraim	9, 17, 30		, James Orren	112
, Eri S.	53		, James W.	32, 33
, Ernest Leroy	112		, Jan Violet	112
, Esther	18, 29, 57		, Jason	29
, Eunice	31, 62, 64		, Jedediah	17, 28
, Evelena	32, 65		, Jennie	56, 112
, Everett Giles	114		, Jennie Phoebe	58, 111
, Ezekiel	17, 28, 55		, Jennie Sabrina	58, 111
, Ezra Kimball	29, 57		, Jeremiah	18, 32
, Fannie/ Fanny	54, 56, 58		, Jessica Marcia	151
, Florence A.	62, 113, 115		, Jessie Curtis	65
, Forrester	65		, Joanna	17, 28
, Frances	33, 114, 152		, John	5, 9, 18, 29, 30, 33
, Francis B.	58		, John Hanson	30, 60
, Frank	61, 64		, John Knox	19, 33
, Franklin H.	31		, John M.	59, 151
, Fred Harold	112		, John Romaine	110
, Frederick	64, 110, 112, 151		, Joseph G.	60
, Freeman Dennis	58		, Josephine Romaine	110
, George	5, 9, 27, 30, 54, 61		, Josephine Theresa	110
, George Alex	107		, Julia	56, 60, 61, 109, 110
, George B.	56		, Karen Ella	153
, George Dexter	31, 61		, Kerry	112
, George E.	56		, Larry Gene	152
, George F.	61, 110		, Lawrence Herbert	153
, George H.	55		, Lee	66
, George Jackson	62		, Lemuel	9, 17
, George M.	33		, Leonard	28, 56, 60
, George S.	30		, Leslie Alfred	151
, George Valentine	113		, Levi B.	58
, George W.	30, 31, 59, 61, 63		, Lewis	54, 108
, Georgia Anna	59		, Lewis Downs	27, 54
, Georgianna	59		, Lewis W.	112
, Gertrude	61		, Lillian Adeline	107
, Giles	65, 114		, Lilly	33, 66
, Gladys M.	56		, Lizzie	107
, Grace	66, 108, 110, 115		, Lloyd Eugene	113
, Hannah	9, 17, 18, 27, 29		, Lois	29
, Hannah Clementine	53		, Lorana	27, 54
, Hannah Elizabeth	58		, Lorenzo D.	58
, Hannah M.	30		, Loretta	53
, Harriet W.	56		, Lottie	108
, Harry Phillips	59		, Louisa Ann	28, 56
, Hazel F.	111, 151		, Lovina B.	58
, Helen S.	30, 113		, Lucinda	33
, Henry	17, 53, 115		, Lucy	18, 19, 29, 31, 32, 57, 64
, Herbert	56, 110		, Lydia	10, 18, 32, 55, 64
, Hiram	28, 114		, Mabel	66, 110, 112, 115
, Horace	30		, Maetta Rose	151
, Horatio	33		, Margaret	19, 32, 58
, Hortense Higgins	110		, Maria	27, 32, 62, 64
, Ida May	56		, Mark H.	31
, Idella Augusta	54		, Martha	31, 54, 56, 59, 63, 107, 108, 114
, Imogene	56		, Mary	19, 32, 107
, Ina Rosalina	53		, Mary A.	55, 58
, Inez Isabell	110		, Mary C.	60
, Isaac	54, 107		, Mary E.	33, 53, 59, 111, 115

The First American Generation

Where this family originated – and who the immigrant ancestor was, are questions that many have pondered over for generations. Numerous researchers have shared information and theories and one fact seems to be clear, this line does not appear to be descended from William CROCKER of Barnstable.

1. PELETIAH/ PELETIA/ PEL/PAUL –1 CROCKER, most likely the progenitor of this CROCKER line, was born ca 1695-1700 at a place as yet undetermined.

He married Joanna/ Johannah/Joannah-3 GOWING/GOWINGE/GOWEN on 23 Feb 1724/25 at Lynn, Essex County, MA. (Lynn, MA VR, Vol.2, Marriages page 110) Joanna was the daughter of John-2 GOWING (Robert-1) and his wife Johanna (possibly) DARLING, and was born 30 Aug 1699 at Lynn, MA. (Lynn, MA VR; Vol.1, Births and Deaths, page 166).

The *ESSEX GENEALOGIST*, August 1988, page 143 – states " Peletiah CROCKER was assessed at Lynnfield (MA) in 1729."

Peletiah/Paul-1 CROCKER died possibly before 1759. Records show that his widow Johannah CROCKER and Jonas FLETCHER of Groton had marriage intentions published 9 Mar 1759 at Groton; and married 1 May 1759.

Baptismal records confirm that James-2; John-2; and Paul-2 are children of this couple. While no records have been found regarding Joanna-2 and Timothy-2 CROCKER – it is believed that they are also children of this pair.

Paul-2 CROCKER was at Windham, Maine in 1748; Timothy-2 CROCKER was at Gorham, Maine in 1754, and John-2, Timothy-2; James-2 and Paul-2 (along with Daniel AUSTIN and Thomas GOWING) were all at Annapolis, Nova Scotia in 1759.

John-2 CROCKER, who married second to the widow Jane FREEMAN Berry; and Timothy-2 CROCKER who married Hannah- 4 MESERVE, moved to Machias, Maine ca 1768. Published accounts in that area stated that " they were brothers who had came from Nova Scotia to that place. "

Children of Peletiah-1 CROCKER and Joanna GOWING:
  Surname CROCKER

+ 2. JAMES	born 7 July 1726 Lynn, Essex, MA (VR); baptized 30 Nov 1729 Reading, MA
	1m. Rebecca COLE 7 Nov 1751; int pub 6 July 1751 North Yarmouth, Maine
	(she dau/o Ephraim COLE and Susanna WASTE)
	(she born 28 Nov 1729; died possibly 1758)
	2m. Anna GRIFFIN, intentions published 8 Oct 1785
+ 3. CAPTAIN PAUL	born ca 1727 poss Lunenburg, MA; bapt 30 Nov 1729 Reading, Middlesex, MA
	1m. Lydia AUSTIN 4 June 1750 Lunenberg, Worcester, MA
	(she dau/o Daniel AUSTEN/AUSTIN and Priscilla STEVENS)
	(she born 3 June 1729; died 1 Sept 1794)
	2m. Mary FAULKNER Hovey (widow)
	died 27 Apr 1814 Lunenberg, MA
+ 4. JOHN	born ca 1729, MA; bapt 30 Nov 1729 Reading, MA
	1m. Mary DEXTER 18 June 1751 Stoneham, Middlesex, MA
	(she dau/o John DEXTER and Joanna GREEN)
	(she born 23 Apr 1730 Stoneham; died before 1768 poss Nova Scotia)
	2m. Jane FREEMAN Berry (widow) ca 1768 at Machias, Maine

Children of Peletiah-1 CROCKER, continued:
Surname CROCKER

5. Elizabeth	born ca 1730/31; bapt 22 Aug 1731 Reading, Middlesex, MA
+ 6. TIMOTHY	born ca 1732/33
	married Hannah-4 MESERVE 16 Nov 1754 at Gorham, Maine
	(she dau/o Clement-3 MESERVE and Sarah DECKER)
	(she born 17__; bapt 7 May 1736 Scarboro, Maine)
7. Johannah/Joanna	born ca 1745/35; married Samuel LARRABEE, int pub 18 Sept 1758 Lunenberg

Note: According to " Old Times in Yarmouth, Maine " page 642, there is a reference to Captain Samuel
LARRABEES' Tavern.

The Second American Generation

2. JAMES-2 CROCKER, son of Peletiah/Pel/Paul-1 CROCKER and Joannah-2 GOWING, was born 7 July 1726 at Lynn, Essex County, MA. He was baptized 30 Nov 1729 at Reading, Middlesex County, MA

His marriage intentions to Rebecca-3 COLE were published on 6 July 1751 at North Yarmouth, Maine. The marriage took place there 7 Nov 1751. (" Old Times in North Yarmouth ", page 658)

Rebecca-3 COLE was the daughter of Ephraim-2 COLE and his 2ⁿᵈ wife Susanna WASTE. She was born 28 Nov 1729, and died before 1785. (Ephraim-2 COLE was the son of Nathaniel-1 COLE and Sarah ? of Duxbury, MA, and was born 14 June 1688; died 1756; moved to North Yarmouth ca 1753). James-2 CROCKER married second to Anna GRIFFIN – intentions published 8 Oct 1785.
Reference: (Maine Historical and Genealogical Register, page 81).

James-2 CROCKER (255 1ˢᵗ Church – April 15, 1770 – discharged to Freeport (ME) 13 Dec 1789). He was a Corporal in the **Revolutionary War.** Vol.9, page 81, MH&GR states " James CROCKER (North Yarmouth) a Private in Captain Richard MAYBERRYS' Company from Cumberland County, ME. "

Children of James-2 CROCKER and Rebecca-3 COLE:
Surname CROCKER

8. Mary	born ca 1752; baptized 13 Dec 1752
+ 9. JOHN GOWEN	born 17 May 1754; baptized 14 July 1754
	married Margaret PARKER, int pub 21 Jan 1755 (N Yarmouth VR 1:599)
10. Ruth	born 8 Mar 1756; baptized 25 Apr 1756; died 16 Jan 1771 (N. Yarmouth VR)
11. Nancy	born 12 Feb 1758; baptized 2 Apr 1758
	married Samuel WESCOT(T) 14 Feb 1776 (int pub 20 Jan 1776)

3. CAPTAIN PAUL-2 CROCKER, brother of above, was born ca 1727 at ____, MA. He was baptized 30 Nov 1729 at Reading (Wakefield), Middlesex, MA.

He married first to Lydia-3 AUSTIN on 4 June 1750 at Lunenberg, Worcester County, MA. She was the daughter of Daniel-2 AUSTIN ++ and his wife Priscilla STEVENS, and was born 3 June 1729 at Lunenberg, MA; died there 1 Sept 1794. She is buried at the South Burial Ground, Lunenberg, MA He married second to the widow Mary FAULKNER Hovey (1737-1823). Paul-2 CROCKER died 27 Apr 1814 at Lunenberg, MA.

Children of Paul-2 CROCKER and Lydia-3 AUSTIN:
Surname CROCKER

+ 12. MARY	born 30 Mar 1751 Lunenberg, MA; baptized 19 May 1751 Lunenberg
	married John-6 CHUTE, Jr. (# 292 FOSTER Section)
	(he son/o John-5 CHUTE and Judith-5 FOSTER)
	(he born 9 Apr 1752 Hampstead, NH; died 8 Mar 1841 Digby Joggins, NS)
	died 8 Aug 1829 Digby Joggins, Digby County, Nova Scotia
+ 13. PAUL, JR	born ca 1755-56 Lunenberg, MA
	married Thankful-5 GATES ca 17__ at Aylesford, Nova Scotia
	(she dau/o Oldham-4 GATES and Thankful ADDAMS)
	(she born 9 July 1760; died 1811 Kingston, NS)
	died 1811 Kingston, Nova Scotia

++ Ancestry of Lydia-3 AUSTIN
THOMAS-1 AUSTIN, the immigrant, was born ca 16__ at ____. He married Hannah FOSTER ca ____. Their son Daniel-2 AUSTIN was born 7 Aug 1698 at Andover, Essex County, MA. He married Priscilla STEVENS ca ____. They were the parents of nine children: (the first 3 born Andover, MA; the rest born Lunenberg, MA) 1. Priscilla born 26 July 1723, died young; 2. Daniel born 1 Oct 1724, died young; 3. Priscilla (2) born 11 Feb 1725/26; 4. Daniel (2) born 13 Apr 1727; 5. LYDIA born 3 June 1729; 6. Timothy born 2 Mar 1731; 7. Ruth born 1 Apr 1733; 8. Hannah born 2 Feb 1735; and 9. Phoebe born 24 Oct 1736.

4. JOHN-2 CROCKER, brother of above, was born was born ca 1729 , MA. He was baptized 30 Nov 1729 at Reading, Middlesex County, MA. He married first to Mary DEXTER on 18 June 1751. She was the daughter of John DEXTER and Joanna GREEN ++, and was born 23 Apr 1730; died before 1768.

> Reference : DEXTER Genealogy 1642-1904 by Orrando Perry DEXTER, pub 1904; page 48)
> and Essex Genealogist, Feb 1988 (GOWING/GOWEN).

John-2 CROCKER married second ca 1768, to Jane FREEMAN Berry, daughter of _____ FREEMAN, widow of Westbrook BERRY at Bristol, Maine. (Westbrook BERRY, the son of Elisha BERRY and Mary BABB, was born 12 Jan 1735; married Jane FREEMAN 2 Jan 1755 at Scarboro, ME; died ca 1766).

John-2 CROCKER enlisted 16 Sept 1775 in Captain Stephen SMITHS' Seacoast Company; discharged 31 Dec 1775. He also served in Captain Joseph LIBBYS' 9th Company; Colonel Benjamin FOSTERS' (Lincoln County) Regiment- enlisted 23 June 1777; discharged 16 July 1777 – ordered on defense of Machias and adjacent rivers when the BRITISH ship *AMBRUSCADE* lay in Machias Harbor. He also served in Captain Stephen SMITHS' Company, Colonel FOSTERS' Regiment 16 July 1777 – 10 Oct 1777 at Machias when British ships lay in the harbor during the **Revolutionary War**. Other services through 1780. John-2 CROCKER died ca 1787 at Marshfield, Washington County, Maine.

Children of John-2 CROCKER and Mary DEXTER:
       Surname CROCKER   (all born Nova Scotia)
+ **14.** JAMES   born Dec 1763; married Rebecca BERRY 3 Dec 1785 Machias, ME
       WHEELER   (she dau/o Westbrook BERRY and Jane FREEMAN)
                          (she born Jan 1766 Machias, ME; died 12 Jan 1818 Marshfield, ME)
    15. Betsey/Elizabeth   born ca 17__; married Henry BAKER
    16. Paul   born ca 17__; remained in Nova Scotia
Children of John-2 CROCKER and Jane FREEMAN Berry:
       Surname CROCKER
+ **17.** SIMEON   born after 1768 Machias, ME; married Katherine WATERHOUSE 29 May 1796
                          (she born ca 1777; died ____)
    18. Mary/Molly   born ca 1774 Machias; died 5 Apr 1797 (childbirth)
                          married Captain William–5 SANBORN ++ 21 Feb 1796
       One child: Mary-4 SANBORN born 5 Apr 1797; died ____; unmarried Machiasport, ME
              (he 2m. Priscilla MAYHEW – she born 1773; died 1845)
                          ++ See SANBORN Ancestry page 325-326

6. TIMOTHY CROCKER, brother of above, was born ca 1730-32 possibly at Lynn, MA. He married Hannah-4 MESERVE ++ on 16 Nov 1754. She was the daughter of Clement-3 MESERVE and Sarah-3 DECKER +++, and was born ca 1736; baptized 7 May 1736 at Scarboro, Maine. Timothy-2 and Hannah-4 were both from Gorham, Maine at the time of their marriage. (NEH&GR Vol. 14, page 224).

Timothy-2 CROCKER and his wife resided at Pearsontown (later Standish) Maine. Timothy-2 was one of only eight men who served at the Fort at Standish 1755. (History of Gorham, ME, page 69)

Timothy-2 CROCKER, listed as CROOKER, of Gorham, Maine was named on page 195 " History of Annapolis County, Nova Scotia ". It was on a list of names of persons who applied for grants of land there in 1759. It also listed their " former place of residence in New England ".

> AUSTIN, Daniel..................... Lunenberg, MA (brother of Lydia)
> CROCKER, John .... Lunenberg, MA
> CROCKER, James .... Narragansett (Goreham, ME)
> CROOKER, Timothy .... Goreham, Maine

" A grant passed 27 June 1759 to consist of 200 shares of 500 acres each " (138 conveyed on that date and 19 others conveyed 16 Aug 1759). The above mentioned four were in the original group.

" By Dec 1760 the Townships of Annapolis and Granville, Nova Scotia were occupied by 30 of the proprietors and the remainder were expected to arrive by spring, with their families. "

Timothy-2 CROCKER was a resident of Machias, Maine ca 1768; Bristol, Me ca 1771; and later at Cushing, ME- as listed on the 1790 Census.

Timothy-2 CROCKER was a soldier in the **Revolutionary War.** " Soldiers, Sailors and Patriots of the Revolutionary War, Maine " by FISHER, page 169 states " CROCKER, Timothy, MA; resided St. George, Captain PLUMMERS' Company; married Hannah MESERVE Crocker ". Also CROCKER, Timothy, MA in Captain TURNERS' Company.

" MA Soldiers, Sailors of the War of the Revolution ", pages 126-127 states: " CROCKER, Timothy, Pvt., Captain Caleb TURNERS' Company; enlisted 13 July 1775, service to 31 Dec 1775, 6 mo. 3 days in defense of the seacoast. Roll sworn to at Bristol; also same Company enlisted 26 Mar 1776 – service to 10 Sept 1776; 5 mo. 15 days; rolls dated at Bristol. Also same Company service from 10 Sept to 7 Dec 1776; 2 mo. 27 days, at Boothbay.

Children of Timothy-2 CROCKER and Hannah-4 MESERVE:
    Surname CROCKER   (first 4 born at Pearsontown/Standish, Maine)
+ 19. MARY/MOLLY   born 1755; married Josiah BEAN
                         (he son/o Jonathan BEAN and Abigail GORDON)
+ 20. CAPTAIN JAMES born 1757; married Peggy COOK
+ 21. MARGARET   born 1759; married Abraham FLETCHER
+ 22. CAPTAIN PAUL   born ca 1761/62; died 12 Jan 1829 Machias, Maine
                         married Nancy MARTIN, int pub 23 Aug 1783 Bristol, ME
       (she dau/o Thomas MARTIN and Sarah GOODWIN) (she born ca 1765; died 28 Sept 1841)
+ 23. SUSAN   born ca 1763; married Eben (ezer) FOSTER
+ 24. HANNAH   born ca 1764 Bristol, ME
                         married William RICHARDS the 3rd on 17 Oct 1785 Bristol
                         (he son of William RICHARDS,2nd and Ruth BRYANT)
                         (he grandson of William RICHARDS and Hannah SIMMONS)
                         died 1843 Round Pond, Maine; buried Maple Grove Cemetery
+ 25. SALLY/SARAH   born ca 1766; baptized 28 July 1771 Pearsontown/Standish, ME
                         married William CLARK, int pub 9 Oct 1785 Bristol, ME
   26. Abigail/Nabby   born ca 1768; baptized 28 July 1771 Pearsontown
                         married William MARTIN 10 Nov 1789 (int pub 23 Aug 1789 Bristol, ME)
                         (he born 1765; died 1845 Bremen, Maine)
   27. Eliza/Elizabeth   born 1770/71; baptized 28 July 1771 Pearsontown
                         married William HENDERSON, intentions published 19 Jan 1791

References: History of Machias, page 390; Bristol, Maine VR; Records of Old Bristol and Nobleboro, ME., Volumes 1 and 2; Records of Old Falmouth (now Portland); NEH&GR Vol. 14, page 224; Early Marriages of Machias 1767-1827 JOHNSON; Early Records of Cushing, ME; Soldiers, Sailors and Patriots of the Rev War, page 169; Early Settlers of Standish, ME by Albert SEARS; First Baptist Church, St. George, ME. lists members as : Paul, Nancy, and Sally CROCKER; Abraham FLETCHER; Mary FLETCHER; and Thomas MARTIN.

Records of Cushing list: Timothy CROCKER – elected a " road surveyor "at a 1797 Town meeting
Paul CROCKER – elected as a " road surveyor " at 1798 and 1799 Town meetings.

Records of the Proprietors of Narragansett Township # 1 (now the Town of Buxton, York County, Maine) From 1 Aug 1733 – 4 Jan 1811. Published 1871 by William F. GOODWIN – gives the following information:
        Narragansett # 7 (later Gorham, Maine)
        A Muster Roll of the Company in His Majesty's Service under the command of
        Joseph WOODMAN, Captain (viz)

Total of 50 men listed as follows:

     1st Column   Man's name: # 48 TIMOTHY CROCKER   aL1:6:8
     2nd Column   Of what Town: Persontown (later Standish, Maine)
     3rd Column   Time of entrance into service: 1757, May 2
     4th Column   Until what time in service: 1757, Sept 28 (21 weeks, 3 days)
     5th Column   The whole wage due this man: 7 pounds, 2 shillings, 9 pence
     6th Column   What each rec'd at the Commissary & c: 3 pounds, 10 shillings, 8 pence
     7th Column   Balance due each man: 3 pounds, 12 shillings, 1 pence
     Examined 7 Dec 1757, signed by Jo. WHEELRIGHT   (from the MA Archives)

Other records regarding Timothy-2 CROCKER: Saco Valley Settlements – pages 121 and 128
" 1755 – April 16 in Standish; 1771 moved to Bristol "

MA Historical Society – Volume 1, page 144
" 1788 to receive deed from Henry KNOX for land in St. George "

++ Ancestry of Hannah-4 MESERVE

The surname MESERVE/MESERVEY is believed to be of Norman French ancestry. They are known to have been residents of the Isle of Jersey in the Channel Islands. Records going back to GREGOIRE (F) MESSERVEY, born about 1490, show that he resided at Anneville, St. Martin's Parish. His son RICHARD (E) MESSERVEY, born at Anneville ca 1511; married Marie deGOUCHY. Richard later moved to Gorey, Grouville, where he died 1554.

THOMAS (D) MESSERVEY, son of Richard, was born at Gorey ca 1530. He married an Elizabeth FALLE, daughter of Jean FALLE. Thomas died ca 1580 and is believed to have been a farmer in the very fertile Grouville Valley. THOMAS (C) MESSERVEY, son of Thomas, born ca 1559 at Gorey, married an Elizabeth PAYN, daughter of Anthony PAYN; and died Nov 1623. His son CLEMENT (B) MESSERVEY, born Aug 1595 at Gorey; married Suzanne PERCHARD on 22 June 1614. Clement-B died 1631. JEAN (A) MESSERVEY, son of Clement, was born June 1615 at Gorey; and married in 1635 to Marie MACHON. He died possibly ca 1664/65.

CLEMENT-1 MESERVE/MESSERVEY, the immigrant, was the son of Jean, and was born ca 1645 at Gorey, Grouville. He was a farmer and raised cattle until he left the Isle of Jersey in 1670 to settle at Portsmouth, NH. For a time he was a herdsman for Richard CUTTS. Clement-1 MESERVE was a taxpayer in Portsmouth, and took the oath of allegiance in 1685. He married Elizabeth _?_, of Welch or Welchman's Cove, Kittery, Maine. They had 7 children including CLEMENT-2 born 1678.

CLEMENT-2 MESERVE was a joiner and finish carpenter by trade. He married first to Elizabeth JONES on 24/26 Sept 1702. She was the daughter of Jenkin JONES and Abigail-3 HEARD ++). He married second to Mrs. Sarah Stone of Scarboro, Maine. In 1717 Clement-2 sold land in NH and purchased 100 acres at Scarboro, Maine. They had 9 children including CLEMENT-3 MESERVE who was born ca 1703. He married Sarah-3 DECKER on 13 Oct 1726. She was the daughter of John-2 DECKER (John-1 DECKER and Mary-2 SCOTT) and Sarah-2 BENNETT. She was the granddaughter of Margaret STEVENSON-1 Scott +++ and Benjamin SCOTT.

CLEMENT-3 MESERVE and Sarah DECKER resided at Scarboro in 1727, where probably all of their 7 children were born. HANNAH-4 MESERVE born ca 1736; baptized 7 May 1736, married Timothy-2 CROCKER. In addition to her lineage, I have included an account of two of her notable ancestors, and the stories of their bravery in a time when women were often overlooked and sometimes persecuted.

These two women, Elizabeth-2 HULL Heard ++ and Margaret STEVENSON Scott +++ have been well-documented in History books. Elizabeth-2 was praised, for her deeds, in the HULL Family Genealogy and the Magnalia Christi Americana by Cotton MATHER. Margaret STEVENSON Scott must be remembered for her courage and the injustice she suffered before her hanging at Salem, MA.

++ Elizabeth-2 HULL Heard, the daughter of the immgrant Rev. Joseph-1 HULL and his first wife, Joanna COFFIN (sister of Tristam COFFIN) was born ca 1628 at Northleigh, Devon, England. She came to America with her father in 1635. He had gathered over a 100 persons from Somerset, Dorset, England – and sailed on an unnamed vessel, arriving in Boston on 6 May 1635.

Elizabeth-2 HULL married John-2 HEARD. He arrived on the same vessel. He was the son of Luke-1 HEARD (Edmund-A) and Sarah-1 WYATT (John-A), and was born ca 16__, England; died 17 Jan 1689 at Dover, NH. Elizabeth-2 HULL died there 30 Nov 1706.

Elizabeth-2 HULL Heard was the mother of 16 children including Abigail-3 who was born 2 Aug 1651 at

York, Maine, who married Jenkin JONES (for descendants see Timothy-2 CROCKER); and Samuel-3 born 4 Aug 1663 Dover, NH who married Experience OTIS (for descendants see Nathan-6 FOSTER).

A WOMAN'S COURAGE

" Elizabeth-2 HULL Heard holds a high rank among the heroic gentlewomen of that period, and is deserving of more space than can be given in this volume, but the story of her experience on an exposed outpost, where for a long time she was surrounded by hostile savages, has been told in detail by MATHER, WILKINSON, BELKNAP and WHARTON – all of whom bear testimony to her heroism and devotion. One incident in her remarkable career will have to suffice in this connection. "

" During the unprovoked and cruel massacre of Indians by whites in 1676, she saved the life of a young Indian by concealing him until his would-be slayers had left her house, and then aided him to escape. Twelve years later she fell into the hands of savages and was enabled to escape unharmed by the aid of this same Indian. "

Reference: HULL Family Genealogy, published 18__; page 252
Further detailed accounts can be read in the Magnalia Christi Americana, page 591.

+++ THE SALEM WITCH HYSTERIA AND MARGARET STEVENSON-1 SCOTT

For centuries, people believed that " witches " had evil powers. When Christianity began to encompass most of Europe, people who broke religious laws, or the accepted moral conduct, were accused of being " witches ". Historians estimate that as many as 300,000 women were put to death between 1484 and 1782. Women were accused much more often than men. They were tortured until they confessed, in order to put an end to their pain.

Historian Samuel Eliot MORISON, Harvard Professor, stated " Almost everybody in the Western World, including divines and men of science, then believed a person could make a bargain with the devil, by virtue of which he could visit good or ill on friends or enemies. "

The Rev Cotton MATHER, called the " boy wonder of the New England clergy ", wrote a book titled *MEMORABLE PROVIDENCES* which described a case of alleged witchcraft in Boston for which a poor old woman was executed. He related how he had handled the accusing children in order to prevent a " witch-hunting epidemic." He produced another book, a sort of how-to-do-it edition; with data on how the " possessed " were expected to behave. It described broomstick rides, flying saucers, witches' sabbaths, sexual relations with the devil, and " everything witches were supposed to do." Unfortunately, that book fell into the hands of a group of young girls in Salem.

These girls may have thought it was a harmless prank – when in Feb 1692, they (the daughter and niece of the Rev Samuel PARIS of Salem) accused a female half-Indian, half-Negro servant girl named *Tituba* of being a witch by pinching, pricking and tormenting them. The girls said *Tituba* was visible to them, when others could not see her – and the family physician stated that he thought " they were under an evil hand. "

Tituba was beaten by her master until she falsely confessed; at which time she accused two respectable ' goodwives' as being her accomplices. The young girls liked the attention they had attracted and persisted in their charges, for fear their prank would be found out. This event would start a chain reaction. Innocent people who were accused – implicated others, to save themselves.

Thomas GAGE, in his book the " History of Rowley (MA)", published at Boston 1840 (pages 167-178) states that in May of 1692, when Sir William PHIPS was appointed Governor of MA; he found the province in a " distressed condition ". Many people, especially those in the County of Essex, were " dreadfully distracted " by what they referred to as the *" Salem Witchcraft "*.

Complaints and accusations increased until 2 June 1692 when an Oyer and Terminer Court was convened.

(Oyer and Terminer was a term used to designate the higher criminal courts) This special court only made matters worse, because the chief justice, William STOUGHTON, and his colleagues were not trained in the use of evidence and became " panic-stricken " themselves.

The *Salem " Witch Trials "* were often kept secret by family members – and to this day some people are reticent to admit that they are descended from a *Salem " witch "*.

The hangings began on 10 June 1692 and ended on 22 Sept 1692, the day that Margaret STEVENSON Scott and eight others were hanged on Gallows Hill, Salem MA. Each hanging was carried out after a very brief trial in which their accusers read statements. Shortly thereafter a sentence was rendered. None of the accused, to that date, had been found innocent.

A book titled " The Trial of Mrs. Elizabeth Howe, the Witchcraft Delusion " page 28, states " Those who suffered were a remarkable company of men and women. They came from the humble walks of life, but most of them were old in experience and solidified in character and sentiments. "

In GAGES' History of Rowley, pages 169-175 are recorded the depositions of several people who made complaints against Margaret STEVENSON Scott. She is believed to be the only person from Rowley to fall victim to that terrible fate.

One of the complaints, was made by a 19 year old girl by the name of Mary DANIEL. From the wording of the deposition it seems likely that she may have suffered from epilepsy, and that Margaret Scott and others may have been trying to come to her aid during ' grand mal ' seizures. Another deposition was from a neighbor who had borrowed money from her and had never paid it back.

Margaret STEVENSON Scott was in her 70's , probably set in her ways, and may have appeared eccentric to some. That certainly did not make her a " witch" or justify the taking of her life. She will always be in that small group of individuals who " though they were posted as criminals, taunted with aspersions, forbidden counsel in law and religion, and had every word of defense twisted into a semblance of condemnation, yet they exhibited the true nobility of life in truth and righteousness; they counted their lives not dear to them, could they only reach the goal of their hope in God the Savior."

Gravestone of Margaret STEVENSON Scott   Salem, MA

The Third American Generation

9. JOHN GOWEN-3 CROCKER, son of James-2 CROCKER and Rebecca COLE, was born 17 May 1754; baptized 14 July 1754 at North Yarmouth, Maine. He married Margaret PARKER ca ____, intentions published 21 Jan 1775 at North Yarmouth. (VR 1:599).

Children of John Gowen-3 CROCKER and Margaret PARKER:

Surname CROCKER	(order of birth uncertain)
28. Warren	born 17__; baptized 22 Sept 1791 North Yarmouth, ME
+ 29. TIMOTHY	born ca 1785; baptized 22 Sept 1791
	married Mary HALL, intentions published 12 Apr 1806 (No. Yarm. VR 2:22)
30. John	born ____; baptized 22 Sept 1791; died 1833 – lost at sea
31. William	born ____; baptized 22 Sept 1791
32. Jacob	born ____; baptized 22 Sept 1791
	married Mehitabel DENNET 27 June 1818 Corinth, Penobscot, ME
33. James	born ____; baptized 22 Sept 1791
34. Miles Davis	born ____; baptized 22 Sept 1791
35. Lee	born ____; baptized 22 Sept 1791
	married Betsey P. WHITTIER 3 Apr 1827 Corinth, Penobscot, ME
36. Sarah	born ____; baptized 9 May 1793

Note: Margaret PARKER Crocker, # 415 1st Church North Yarmouth,ME., discharged to Cumberland, Maine 9 Nov 1794.

12. MARY-3 CROCKER, daughter of Captain Paul-2 CROCKER and Lydia AUSTIN, was born 30 Mar 1751, baptized 19 May 1751 at Lunenberg, MA.

She married John-6 CHUTE, Jr. before 1772. He was the son of John-5 CHUTE (Lionel-4; James-3;2; Lionel-1) and Judith-5 FOSTER, and was born 9 Apr 1752 at Hampstead, NH. John CHUTE, Jr. was taken to Nova Scotia by his parents in 1759. He moved from Granville, Annapolis County, Nova Scotia to Digby Joggins, Digby County, Nova Scotia in 1799 where he lived as " a good honest farmer, Captain of the Militia, pious Deacon of the Baptist church " . He died 8 March 1841, his funeral being attended by the Rev Charles RANDALL . The sermon was taken from II Corinthians, Verse 1. Mary-3 CROCKER died 8 Aug 1829.   (Reference: CHUTE Family in America by William E. CHUTE, Salem, MA 1894.)

Children of Mary-3 CROCKER and John-6 CHUTE, Jr.:

Surname CHUTE	(all children born Annapolis County, Nova Scotia)
+ 37. JOANNA	born 9 July 1772; died 1836
	1m. Timothy BROOKS (he born ca 1765; died June 1823 – age 58)
	2m. John HARVEY ca 1825; moved to Lower Canada ca 1827
	(he born ca 1775; died 1837 – age 62)
38. Crocker	born 23 Jan 1774; married Cynthia DODGE 1797 Granville Twsp,
	(she born ca 1782 Granville, NS)
+ 39. ELISABETH P.	born 18 Apr 1776; died Apr 1813
	married Richard CHANDLER of Yorkshire, Eng. ca 1792
40. George Washington	born 27 Apr 1778; married Anna BATHRICK 1797
41. Daniel Austin	born 16 Mar 1780; died 1796 unmarried EOL
42. Paul	born ca 1782; married Bethia BETTS 5 Aug 1804 Digby Joggins, NS
+ 43. MARY (twin)	born 19 Apr 1785; died Nov 1856
	1m. Solomon FARNSWORTH 23 May 1801 (he born ____; died 1812)
	2m. John ELLIS 15 Feb 1813
+ 44. LYDIA (twin)	born 19 Apr 1785; married Samuel-7 FOSTER ++ 17 Mar 1805 Granville, NS
+ 45. PETER PRESCOTT	born 27 May 1787; married Lucy RANDALL ca 1808; died 1865 NS
+ 46. ELEANOR	born 11 July 1789; married James ADAMS; died 1868
+ 47. JOHN 2nd	born 14 Oct 1790; married Abigail JONES

Children of Mary-3 CROCKER, continued:
   Surname CHUTE
+ 48. LEAH FOWLER   born 7 Apr 1793; died 6 Mar 1875; married Robert WOODMAN ca 1814
                           (he son/o Jacob WOODMAN and Mary CHESLEY of Durham, NH)
  49. Joseph Fowler   born 21 Feb 1795; married Susan Harris PELHAM
              ++ Samuel-7 FOSTER (# 506 FOSTER Section) page 394

13. PAUL-3 CROCKER, Jr., brother of above, was born ca 1755-57, probably at Lunenberg, Worcester County, MA. He married Thankful-5 GATES ++ ca _____. She was the daughter of Captain Oldham-4 GATES and Thankful ADDAMS, and was born 7 July 1760 at Spencer, MA. She and Paul-3 both died 1811 at Kingston, Nova Scotia.

Children of Paul-3 CROCKER, Jr. and Thankful-5 GATES:
   Surname CROCKER   (all born Aylesford, Nova Scotia)
  50. Mary   born _____; married Samuel VAN BUSKIRK
  51. Elizabeth   born _____; 1m. Thomas CLARK 8 Jan 1818 at Wilmot, Annapolis, NS
                           (he born 1784; died _____); 2m. John STEVENSON
  52. Mehitable/Hettie   born _____; married William GOUCHER (he born 1785)
                           (he son/o Stephen GOUCHER and Mary GAGE)
+ 53. JOHN   born 28 Mar 1797; died 28 Mar 1876 Tremont, NS
                         married Eliza Ann CHESLEY 31 May 1820 Wilmot, NS
                         (she born 4 July 1803; died 27 Dec 1880)
  54. Susanna   born _____; married Barnard CAREY (brother of Charles, below)
  55. Ruth   born _____; married Charles CAREY 19 Nov 1829 Aylesford, NS
+ 56. ANN G./ ANNA   born 1803; died 1890 Greenwood Square, Kings County, NS
        married Jacob Beach SPINNEY, Sr. 26 Jan 1826 Aylesford, NS (he born 1799; died 1879)
+ 57. JAMES   born 1806; died 1890 Kings County, NS
                   1m. Abigail TUPPER 14 May 1827 Aylesford, NS (she born 1803; died 1828)
                   2m. Jane SPINNEY ca 1831 (she born 8 Nov 1810; died 1 Feb 1869)
                   (she dau/o Samuel McClure SPINNEY and Elizabeth BEACH)

Note: Re: Eliza CHESLEY: " Stephen GATES of Hingham and Lancaster, MA " lists John CROCKER as marrying Eliza BANKS, daughter of Timothy BANKS. Researchers state that this is an error. Judy WHITE of Scottsdale, Arizona, a descendant, relates that Margaret BASS (not BARSS) did marry Timothy BANKS. However, Eliza was not his daughter, but a child conceived by the rape of Margaret by a Colonel William CHESLEY (a British soldier). Eliza was born 1803. Margaret BASS did not marry Timothy BANKS until ca 1809 at Meadowvale, Nova Scotia. She had two other children: Caroline BANKS who married Parker BAKER and John BANKS who married Ann SPINNEY (Joseph).

++Ancestry of Thankful-5 GATES

STEPHEN-1 GATES (Thomas-A; Peter-B; Geoffrey-C), the immigrant ancestor, was born ca 1600 at ++ Hingham, England. He married Ann VEARE of Hingham on 5 May 1628. She was born ca 1603; died possibly 19 Feb 1682 at Marlborough, MA. Stephen-1 GATES died 1662 at Cambridge, MA.

SIMON-2 GATES, born 16__; baptized 3 May 1646 at Hingham, MA ; married Margaret BARSTOW ca Nov 1670. She was the daughter of George BARSTOW and Susan MARRETT, and was born 16__; baptized 24 Feb 1649/50 at Scituate, MA; died 13 Apr 1707 at Brookline, MA. Simon-2 GATES died 26 Aug 1692 at Muddy River (now Brookline), MA. AMOS-3 GATES, born ca 1680/81 at Cambridge, MA; married Hannah-3 OLDHAM. She was the daughter of Samuel-2 OLDHAM (Richard-1) and Hannah DANA, and was born 10 Oct 1681; died before 24 Jan 1763. Amos-3 GATES died 22 July 1754 at Framingham, MA.

CAPTAIN OLDHAM-4 GATES, born 3 Sept 1716; was baptized 30 Sept 1716 at Cambridge, MA. He married Thankful ADDAMS of Spencer, MA, as his 3rd wife, on 5 Sept 1759. Captain Oldham-4 GATES became a resident of Annapolis County, NS ca 1760, and was commissioned as Captain of the Militia in 1763. (History of Annapolis County, page 513). He died ca 1800 at Wilmot, NS.

14. JAMES WHEELER-3 CROCKER, son of John-2 CROCKER and Mary DEXTER, was born Dec 1763 at _____ , Nova Scotia. He married Rebecca BERRY +++ 3 Dec 1785 at Machias, ME. She was the daughter of Westbrook BERRY and Jane FREEMAN, and was born Jan 1766; died 12 July 1818. James W-3 CROCKER died 16 Oct 1840 at Marshfield, Maine.

Children of James W-3 CROCKER and Rebecca BERRY:
  Surname CROCKER
+ 58. JOHN, JR.   born 30 Sept 1786 Machias, ME; married Sally/Sarah BERRY
             (she born 1788; died ____) (both living 1850)
             (she dau/o Jonathan BERRY and Hannah KNIGHT)
+ 59. BETSEY   born 9 Dec 1788 Machias; married Henry LYON 14 July 1809
             (he son/o James LYON and Martha HOLDEN)
+ 60. CAPTAIN OTIS born 9 Dec 1790 Machias; Sarah F. O'BRIEN
+ 61. SALLY (twin) born 20 Apr 1795 Machias; married Henry THAXTER 14 May 1817
+ 62. POLLY (twin) born 20 Apr 1795; 1m. Ephraim WHITNEY
             2m. Stephen-6 BOYNTON (as his 4th wife) no issue
+ 63. KATHERINE/   born 19 Dec 1797; married Colonel William BURNHAM 4 Aug 1816
    CATHERINE (twin)(he son/o Job BURNHAM and Mary O'BRIEN) (he 2m. Mary SPROUL)
+ 64. OLIVE (twin) born 19 Dec 1797; died 1868 (age 70)
             married William F. PENNIMAN 1 Sept 1818 Machias
      (he son/o Jacob PENNIMAN and Mary O'BRIEN) (he born 1784; died 1874 (age 90)
        (Note: 1860 census lists his age as 64; which would make his birthdate 1794)
+ 65. MARINER GREEN born 31 Aug 1800 Machias; died 10 Aug 1872 Machias, Maine
             married Martha-6 LONGFELLOW (she born 8 Aug 1800; died 29 Aug 1893)
+ 66. CALEB STRONG born 27 May 1804 Machias; married Cynthia-6 LONGFELLOW
             (she 2m. Harrison G-5 CROCKER # 209)
+ 67. HANNAH   born 3 Dec 1806 Machias ; died ca 1834/35
             married Amos LONGFELLOW (he 2m. Nancy P. BAKER before 1836)
  68. George Ulmer   born 28 Mar 1809 Machias; a farmer; died before 1864 no issue EOL
      1m. Agnes L. SPEAR of Thomaston, ME. (she born 18 Jan 1807; died 12 Apr 1887)
        (she 2m. Jotham LIPPINCOTT 29 Apr 1864)

+++ Ancestry of Rebecca BERRY
ELISHA BERRY, father of Westbrook BERRY, was born ca 1705; and died after 1756. His first wife, Mary BABB, was born ____; died before 1744. WESTBROOK BERRY, was one of the " Original 16 " who settled Machias, Maine. He was a member of the association formed during the winter of 1763, for the purpose of building a double sawmill, to be owned in as many shares. Thirteen of the members, including Westbrook BERRY, went to Machias from Scarboorough – a district known as Black Point. WEST-BROOK BERRY, was born 16 Dec 1734; baptized 12 Jan 1735 at Scarborough (ME). He married Jane FREEMAN ++ there on 2 Jan 1755; and died ca 1766 at Machias. Jane FREEMAN Berry married second to John-2 CROCKER ca 1768.

++ SAMUEL-1 FREEMAN, the immigrant, was born ca ___, England. He came to America with his wife Apphia _?_ ca ____. He returned to England on a business trip and died there ca 1639. DEACON SAMUEL-2 FREEMAN, born ca ____; married Mercy SOUTHWORTH. They were the parents of CONSTANT-3 FREEMAN, who was born 31 Mar 1669; and married Jane TREAT on 11 Oct 1694. JONATHAN-4 FREEMAN was born 9 June 1710 at Truro, MA; and married Rebecca BINNEY on 23 Sept 1731. JANE-5 FREEMAN and Westbrook BERRY had five children including Jonathan whose daughter Sally married John-4 CROCKER, Jr.; and Rebecca BERRY, born 1766, who married James W-3 CROCKER (above).

17. SIMEON-3 CROCKER, son of John-2 CROCKER and Jane FREEMAN Berry, was born after 1768 at Machias, Washington County, Maine. He married Katherine WATERHOUSE on 29 May 1796 at Machias., by George STILLMAN, Esq. She was the daughter of Enoch WATERHOUSE and Abigail WEST, and was born 20 Oct 1777; died ____ (still living 1850). Simeon-3 died 7 July 1818.

Children of Simeon-3 CROCKER and Katherine WATERHOUSE:
  Surname CROCKER
  69. Oliver Wiles   born 10 Apr 1797; married Lucinda CHALONER (she born 1805)
    (she dau/o Ebenezer CHALONER and Betsey HILL)(granddau/o Dr. William CHALONER of RI)
+ 70. STEPHEN   born 20 Dec 1798 Machias, Maine
    BURGAIN   married Jane STARRETT 4 July 1833
             (resided on the S. LIBBY Farm, North Warren, Maine)
+ 71. JANE FREEMAN born 28 Nov 1800; died 26 Oct 1879
             1m. Obed HOLMES (he son/o James HOLMES and Sarah Berry LYONS
             2m. Rufus FOSS (he son/o William FOSS and Lydia FLYNN)

Children of Simeon-3 CROCKER, continued:
    Surname CROCKER

+ 72. MARTHA G.   born 2 July 1803; died 24 May 1886
                       married Levi BOWKER, Jr. (he son/o Levi BOWKER and Betsey WATTS)
+ 73. ABAGAIL   born 7 Mar 1806; married William FLYNN
  74. Elvira   born 9 Jan 1808; 1m. Sherburne HUSE; 2m. Thomas NASON
+ 75. GEORGE   born 20 Nov 1810 Machias; married Lucinda HARMON
    WATERHOUSE   (she dau/o Samuel Japhet HARMON and Mercy FISHER)
                      (she born Oct 1813; died 18 Jan 1889, 76-3 gs)
+ 76. ENOCH SIMEON   born 17 Oct 1812/13 Machias; died 21 Mar 1894 Marshfield, ME
                      married Adaline P. JORDAN 22 May 1842
                      (she dau/o James JORDAN and Bethia-3 CATES (Samuel-2)
                      (she born 1 Dec 1824; died 25 Feb 1887 Marshfield, ME)
+ 77. MARY   born 20 Sept 1817
    CATHERINE   married John F. HARMON (brother of Lucinda, above)
        References: History of Machias, Maine by George W. DRISKO; Earliest Records of Machias, ME by JACKMAN;
            Machias Union newspaper 14 June 1881; Annals of Warren, ME, page 531; Census

19. MARY/MOLLY-3 CROCKER, daughter of Timothy-2 CROCKER and Hannah-4 MESERVE, was born ca 1755, probably at Pearsontown (later Standish), Maine. She married Josiah-5 BEAN ca 1771/72 at Standish, ME. He was the son of Jonathan-4 BEAN and Abigail GORDON; and was born 17 Oct 1748 at Kingston, NH; died, by his own hand, in 1832. He was the great great grandson of John-1 BEAN, an emigrant from Scotland, who settled early in Exeter, NH. Josiah-5 BEAN purchased land at Bethel, ME. 1780.

Children of Mary/Molly-3 CROCKER and Josiah-5 BEAN:
    Surname BEAN

  78. Dolly   born 14 May 1773; married Francis KEYES of Rumford, Maine
+ 79. TIMOTHY   born 8 June 1775; married Hannah KIMBALL (she dau/o Asa KIMBALL)
  80. Amos   born 15 Apr 1778; married Huldah KIMBALL (she dau/o Samuel KIMBALL)
+ 81. LUTHER   born 23 Apr 1781 St. George, ME.
                      married Lydia KIMBALL (she sister of above)
+ 82. EDMUND   born 12 Aug 1786; married Emma KIMBALL ca 1812
                      (she born 4 Jan 1795; died _____) (she dau/o Asa KIMBALL)
                      died 16 Feb 1875, age 91; resided Rumford, Maine
+ 83. JOSHUA   born 27 Apr 1789; married Betsey BARTLETT; died 19 May 1871 (age 83)
  84. Mary/Molly   born 27 Jan 1792; married Moses F. KIMBALL of Rumford
  85. Hannah   born 29 June 1794; died 19 Feb 1884 Bethel, ME.; 1m. Israel COLBY of Gray
            2m. Captain Timothy HASTINGS (he born 31 Oct 1790/91 Fryeburg, Oxford, Maine)
                      (he son/o Amos HASTINGS and Elizabeth WILEY)
            Child: Timothy-5 HASTINGS, Jr. born 1 Oct 1814 Bethel, Maine
  86. Abigail   born 1 Dec 1797 Bethel, ME.; married Phineas FROST ca 1815 Bethel
                      (he son/o Thomas FROST and Abigail YORK) resided Anoka, MN
                      (he born 18 Feb 1794 Berwick, ME)
            Child: Phineas Howard-5 FROST born 7 Apr 1828 Bethel, Oxford, Maine

20. CAPTAIN JAMES-3 CROCKER, brother of above, was born ca 1757 at Pearsontown/Standish, Maine. He married Peggy COOK ca 17__.

Children of Captain James-3 CROCKER and Peggy COOK:
    Surname CROCKER

  87. Mary E.   born 17__; married Steven SPRAGUE 1 Aug 1819 Machiasport, Maine
  88. Hannah   born 1801; died 28 Apr 1837 Machiasport (unmarried)
  89. Captain James, Jr.   born 1804; married Eliza H. _?_ (she born 10 Jan 1810; died 4 Sept 1849)
  90. John   born ca 1806/07   + 91. CAPTAIN TIMOTHY   born ca 1809

21. MARGARET-3 CROCKER, sister of above, was born 1759 at Standish, Maine. She married Abraham FLETCHER ca ____. He was born ca 1757 at Machias, Maine.

Children of Margaret-3 CROCKER and Abraham FLETCHER:
   Surname FLETCHER
   92. James   born ____; poss marr Sally LIBBY 10 June 1818 Machias, ME
   93. Timothy C. born ____; married Rebecca HOLMES (ch: Crocker Paul FLETCHER)
   94. William   born ____; marr Lydia HOLMES (ch: Sarah, Lucinda, Miranda, Asa FLETCHER)
   95. Abraham   born ____;
   96. Ephraim   born ____; marr Amelia/Aurilla GETCHELL (ch: Abbie and Amanda FLETCHER)
   97. Asa   born ____

22. CAPTAIN PAUL-3 CROCKER, brother of above, was born ca 1761/62 at Standish, Cumberland County, Maine. He married Nancy-4 MARTIN ++, intentions published 23 Aug 1783 at Bristol, Maine. She was the daughter of Thomas-3 MARTIN and his 2nd wife Sarah GOODWIN, and was born 17__; baptized 28 Feb 1765, probably at Marblehead, MA.

In 1803, Captain Paul-3 CROCKER moved to Machias, Maine. In 1804 as part owner and master, he sailed the Schooner *RESOLUTION*, the first vessel to be sailed as a packet from Machias to Boston. In 1807, Zebedee MAYHEW (his son-in-law) became part owner and master of the vessel; and in 1817 was the master of the *MARY OF CUSHING*. Captain Paul-3 CROCKER died 12/13 Jan 1829 (aged 67 gs) at Machias, Maine. The Republican Journal published his obituary 13 Feb 1829. The obituary stated he was " long known as a coaster and skillful pilot along the eastern shore. "

Nancy-4 MARTIN died 28 Sept 1841, age 76 years, 3 months. She and her husband are buried at Machiasport, ME. – behind the church – where the Machias River meets the Atlantic Ocean, a most beautiful and fitting spot for a sea captain. The gravestone of Captain Paul-3 CROCKER reads " Stop travelers as you pass by, As you are now so once was I. As I am now soon you may be, Prepare to die and follow me. " His wife's gravestone reads   " Dearest Mother thou hast left us, Here thy loss we deeply feel. But 'tis God that has bereft us, How can all our sorrows heal. "

Children of Captain Paul-3 CROCKER and Nancy-4 MARTIN:
   Surname CROCKER
+ 98. SARAH G/ SALLY born ca 1785 Bristol, ME; married Nathan-7 FOSTER 20 Aug 1803
            (he son of Nathan-6 FOSTER and Amy THOMPSON) (see Foster section – page ___)
                        died 5 Feb 1858 (age 72) buried Machiasport, Maine
+ 99. HANNAH   born 1786; died 1849 East Machias, Maine
                      married Captain Zebedee MAYHEW 21 Nov 1806 Machias
                      (he son of Nathan MAYHEW **) (he born 1782; died 1834)
         ** Note: Nathan MAYHEW of Martha's Vineyard was a direct descendant of Sir Thomas MAYHEW, the first governor
            of Martha's Vineyard. He was the master of the Schooner *MARY* (1817) The vessel was built at Warren, Maine 1803.
   100. Benjamin   born 1787/88; married Catherine WEBSTER
+ 101. POLLY   born 1794/95; married Captain Jacob BARTER 15 Sept 1816 Machias
                      (he born 1793 St. George, Maine) (sea captain Machiasport 1850)
   102. Lucy   born Jan 1799; married John MAYHEW 24 Oct 1817 Machias
                      died 2 Feb 1868, buried East Machias
   103. Mayhew   born ca 1801-03
+ 104. CAPTAIN PAUL, born ca 1805; died before 1850
            JR.   married Jane BARTER 22 Oct 1828 St. George, Maine
                      (she born ca 1809; died 16 Sept 1891 Newburg, Maine)
                      (she 2m. Francis BUSSEY of Newburg 6 Sept 1852)
   105. Nancy M.   born ca 1810; married James Gooch WHITTEMORE ca 1829
                      (he son /o William WHITTEMORE and Deborah GOOCH ***)
                      (he born 27 Mar 1805; died 30 Mar 1853 NY, NY)
                      died 9 Apr 1849 East Machias, Maine
         *** Deborah GOOCH was the dau/o James GOOCH and Anna CATES

References: Early Machias Marriages by Beulah JOHNSON; History of Machias by DRISKO, pages 390- 91; Old Bristol and Nobleboro, ME VR to 1892, Vol. 2; Earliest records of Machias.

This researcher has three original documents relating to this family:

1. " Bristol June the 29th day of 1780   Mr. Arunah WESTON   Sir   please to pay Mr. Paul CROCKER the sum of one pound eighteen shillings   and nine pense lawful money   and in so doing you will oblige your friend William RICHARDS the 3rd. "

2. " Marblehead   Dec 1 , 1790 For value received of Capt. Charles LeBALLISTER, I promise to pay him or his order, thirteen pounds   fourteen shillings   lawful money in six months from this date   and interest after that time. Witness my hand , signed Paul CROCKER "

" 18 April 1791 A credit (or payment on) of the within note, three pounds on account of Paul CROCKER, signed Charles LeBALLISTER. "

3. Calais (Maine) 24 May 1810 " Captain Paul CROCKER   Sir please pay Capt Daniel WESTON order the sum of eight dollars. It being do me for labour   and you will oblidge yours truly   Samuel CHUSER "

++ Ancestry of Nancy-4 MARTIN

ROBERT-1 MARTIN, was born ca 1633 at ____. His son THOMAS-2 MARTIN was born ca 1675 at ____, MA. Thomas-2 married Eleanor KNOTT 28 Apr 1701 at Marblehead, MA. Eleanor was born 1683, baptized 18 June 1687 (age 4 years) at Marblehead, MA.

CAPTAIN THOMAS-3 MARTIN was born ca 17__; baptized 8 Oct 1721 at Marblehead, MA. He married first to Mary GORDON/ GORDEN/GOURDEN. She was the daughter of Henry GOURDEN and _?_. They were married 20 Nov 1746; and she died before 1750. He married his second wife Sarah GOODWIN on 27 Feb 1750. She was the daughter of William GOODWIN and Jane _?_; and was born 10 July 1726 at Marblehead, MA. Captain Thomas-3 MARTIN died 8 Feb 1807 at Bristol, ME, and is buried there.

Child of Thomas-3 MARTIN and his 1st wife Mary GORDON:
1. Richard-4 born ca 1747 at Marblehead, MA. He married 1st to Hannah CROWELL/CROW (Thorndike Genealogy); and 2nd to Sarah LeBALLISTER 4 Aug 1778. His 3rd wife was Mary McCARTER – who survived him. Richard-4 MARTIN died 18 Oct 1799 at St. George, Maine.

Children of Thomas-3 MARTIN and Sarah GOODWIN:
2. Hannah baptized 3 Feb 1751; married Charles LeBALLISTER 13 June 1769
3. Samuel baptized 29 Oct 1752; married Mary FOOT 26 Aug1780 Lynn, MA; died 1823 Marblehead, MA.
4. Mary baptized 18 Aug 1754; married James FULLER 11 Dec 1774 Marblehead, MA
5. Sarah/Sally bapt 23 Apr 1758 Marblehaead. MA; married Arunah –4 WESTON 4 Feb 1777 at Bristol, ME., and died 20 Jan 1814.
        Arunah-4 WESTON (Eliphas-3; John-2; Edmund-1) was born 4 Feb 1746; died 17 Jan 1831. He removed from
        Duxbury,   MA before the Revolutionary War and settled at Bristol, ME. He was widely known and extensively
        engaged in business.
6. Eleanor bapt 15 Apr 1759 Marblehead; married Timothy KIMBALL 15 Jan 1778 at Bristol, ME.
7. RACHEL bapt 18 Oct 1761 Marblehead, MA; married Timothy WESTON, int pub 23 May 1779 Bristol, ME.
        (She is probably the widow WESTON who married Nathan-6 FOSTER 18 May 1790 (see FOSTER Section # ____).
        Timothy WESTON was a privateer in the Revolutionary War, and was lost in the Bay of Fundy while cruising
        there before the end of the war. They had one child Timothy, born 17 June 1780; married Ann GOOCH
        13 June 1802 ; resided Machias, Maine.
8. Elizabeth bapt 15 jan 1764; died young
9. NANCY-4 bapt 24 Feb 1765 Marblehead, MA; married CAPTAIN PAUL-3 CROCKER (# 22), int pub 23 Aug 1783
        Bristol, Maine. She died 23 Sept 1841 at Machiasport, Maine.
10. Elizabeth/Betsey bapt 2/8 Aug 1767 at Marblehead, Ma.; married Joshua WEBBER 26 Jan 1791 Bristol; died 12 Nov 1841 Bristol.
11. Lucy bapt 15 July 1770 Marblehead, MA; 1m. Charles MARTIN 3 Feb 1793; 2m. __?__ SMITH

References: Marblehead, MA VR; Bristol, Maine VR; Old Bristol and Nobleboro; Thorndike Genealogy; Lincoln County, Maine Probate Records 1760-1800, page 343; Descendants of Edmund WESTON; Priscilla Waters, Westbrook, Maine; Joyce Sykes, South Bristol, Maine; Reginald FRENCH, Waldoboro, Maine.

23. SUSAN-3 CROCKER, sister of above, was born ca 1763 at Gorham , Maine. She married Ebenezer FOSTER on ____ . He was the son of _____ FOSTER and _____ ___, and was born ____; died ____. Susan-3 CROCKER died _____.

Children of Susan-3 CROCKER and Ebenezer FOSTER:
   Surname FOSTER
   106. Betsey/ Elizabeth   born ____; married Charles EMERSON
   107. Susan   born ____; married John EMERSON   108. Eben (ezer) born ____

24. HANNAH-3 CROCKER, sister of above, was born ca 1764 at Gorham, Maine (VR). She married William-7 RICHARDS,III on 1/17 Oct 1785 at Bristol, Maine. he was the son of William-6 RICHARDS,II ++ and Ruth BRYANT; and was born 1764; died 1846 at Round Pond, Maine. Hannah-3 CROCKER died ____. They are both buried at Maple Grove Cemetery, Round Pond, Maine.

Children of Hannah-3 CROCKER and William-7 RICHARDS, III:
   Surname RICHARDS   (order of birth uncertain)
+ 109. ISAAC   born 22 Dec 1793; married Charity HOLMES Clark
        (she dau/o James HOLMES and Sally BERRY Lyons) (she wid/o Charles CLARK)
+ 110. CAPTAIN   born 1796 Bristol, Maine; died 13 Aug 1856
     JAMES   married Hannah Keyes HARRIMAN 30 Aug 1820 Prospect, ME.
        (she born 3 Jan 1799; died 1 Oct 1878 Bristol)
   111. Un-named child   born ____
   112. William, IV   born ____; married Diademia HARRIMAN, int pub 2 July 1827

Ancestry of William-7 RICHARDS, III

JOHN-1 ALDEN, born 1599, England; married Priscilla MULLINS before 1624. Priscilla, who reportedly said " Speak for yourself John ", when he asked for her hand in marriage for Miles STANDISH; was born ____; died after 1650. John-1 ALDEN died 22 Sep 1687 at Duxbury, MA. He was one of the founders of the Massachusetts Bay Colony. He was in Captain Miles STANDISH'S Duxbury Company, 1643. He was a Governor's Assistant, 1639-40-50-86. A Deputy to the General Court of MA, 1641-2-4-49. A member of the Council of War 1646. Acting Deputy Governor 1644-77. Treasurer 1655-59. Assistant 1632-33-34-40-50-1686.

ELIZABETH-2 ALDEN, the daughter of John-1 (the 7th signer of the Mayflower Compact) was born ca 1624 at Plymouth, MA. She married William PABODIE/PEABODY on 26 Dec 1644 at Plymouth. He was born ca 1620; died 3 Dec 1707 at Little Compton, RI. Eizabeth-2 ALDEN died 2 May 1717.

MERCY-3 PABODIE/PEABODY was born 2 Jan 1649; married John-3 SIMMONS 16 Nov 1669 at Duxbury, MA. John SIMMONS was born ____; died 8 Feb 1713. BENJAMIN-4 SIMMONS, son of Mercy-3, was born ca 1678; married Priscilla DELANO; and died 7 Feb 1748. Duxbury, MA HANNAH-5 SIMMONS, dau/o Benjamin-4, was born 16 June 1718; and married William –5 RICHARDS,I on 7 Sept 1738 at Pembroke, MA. He was born 1696 at Bristol, ME. WILLIAM-6 RICHARDS, II was born 23 Mar 1742; and married Ruth BRYANT on 16 May 1765 at Scituate, MA. She was born 5 Aug 1744; died 1837. They had 2 sons: Lemuel-7 RICHARDS, and WILLIAM-7 RICHARDS,III who married Hannah-3 CROCKER, above.

References: The McCUTCHEON Records and Allied Families Ancestry by Florence McCUTCHEON McKEE, 1931; Mayflower Descendants, Vol 1, 3, 16; ALDEN Genealogy; Duxbury VR; PABODIE Genealogy; SIMMONS Family Genealogy (Elizabeth SIMMONS Desc); RICHARDS Genealogy (The Family of Emery RICHARDS of Round Pond, Maine); Muscongus Cemetery Gravestones; History of Gorham, Maine

25. SALLY-3 CROCKER, sister of above, was born ca 1766; baptized 28 July 1771 at Pearsontown, Standish, Maine. She married William CLARK , intentions published 9 Oct 1785 at Bristol, Maine. He was born 9 May 1769; died ____. Sally-3 died _____.

Children of Sally-3 CROCKER and William CLARK:
   Surname CLARK
   113. Benjamin   born ____
+ 114. CHARLES   born ____; married Charity HOLMES (she born 14 Sept 1797; died ___)
      (she dau/o James HOLMES and Sally BERRY Lyons)(she 2m. Isaac- 4 RICHARDS, # 111)
+ 115. ABIGAIL   born Apr 1786; died 1 Mar 1866
      married Captain Isaac AMES
      (he son/o Mark AMES and Priscilla HOWLAND)
      (he born ca 1788; died 22 Dec 1844)
   116. Hannah   born ____; married John QUINBY

Children of Sally-3 CROCKER, continued:
    Surname CLARK
+ 117. SALLY/SARAH   born ca 1795; died 13 Mar 1864 Machiasport, ME.
                        married John COLBETH 28 Jan 1816 Machiasport, ME
                        (he born 5 Nov 1789; died 7 Nov 1856 Machiasport)
                        (he son/o Peter COLBETH/COOLBROTH++ and Hannah LIBBY)

           ++ Note: Peter COLBETH served in the Revolutionary War.

    118. Susan   born ____; married Captain Abraham AMES
                        (he 2m. Hannah Day; 3m. Olive WATERHOUSE
    119. Nancy   born ____; married Abial HOLMES
+ 120. TEMPERANCE   born 1804; married James F. HOLMES
    121. Eliza   born ____; married Salem LAFLIN 21 May 1815

The Fourth American Generation

29. TIMOTHY-4 CROCKER, son of John Gowen-3 (James-2) and Margaret PARKER, was born 179_; baptized 22 Sept 1791 at North Yarmouth, Maine. He married Mary HALL on 4 May 1806 at North Yarmouth, Cumberland County, ME; intentions published 12 1806.

Children of Timothy-4 CROCKER and Mary HALL:
    Surname CROCKER   (all children born at No. Yarmouth, Maine)
    122. John   born 22 Oct 1807   123. William   born 7 Nov 1810   124. Mary   born 7 Oct 1815

37. JOANNA-4 CHUTE, daughter of Mary-3 CROCKER (Captain Paul-2) and John-6 CHUTE, Jr., was born 9 July 1772 at Granville, Annapolis County, Nova Scotia. She married first to Timothy BROOKS. He was born ca 1765; died June 1823 (age 58). She married second to John HARVEY ca 1825. They moved to Lower Canada ca 1827. He was born ca 1775; died 1837 (age 62). Joanna-4 CHUTE died 1836.

Children of Joanna-4 CHUTE and Timothy BROOKS:
    Surname BROOKS
    125. Mary   born 2 May 1801; died 1819
  + 126. TIMOTHY   born 2 Dec 1802; married Susan RHODES ; died 7 May 1888
    127. John   (1)   born 11 Jan 1805; died 1808
    128. John   (2)   born 4 Nov 1808; married Susan GRIMES Lubec, Maine
    129. Thomas   born 9 Nov 1812; married Phebe Ann ELLIS 29 Dec 1836

39. ELIZABETH P-4 CHUTE, sister of above, was born 18 Apr 1776 at Granville, Annapolis County, Nova Scotia. She married Richard CHANDLER ca 1792 at Chute's Cove, Annapolis, NS. He was from Yorkshire, England. Elizabeth-4 CHUTE died Apr 1813.

Children of Elizabeth-4 CHUTE and Richard CHANDLER:
    Surname CHANDLER
  + 130. FANNY   born 1793; married John LINGLEY
    131. Sarah   born 1795; married David M. CHUTE
  + 132. MARY   born 1797; married John HARVEY
  + 133. ELEANOR   born 1800; married James MILLER 14 Dec 1821; died ca 1879

43. MARY-4 CHUTE, sister of above, was born 19 Apr 1785 at Granville, Annapolis Co., NS. She married first a Solomon FARNSWORTH on 23 May 1801 at Chute's Cove, Annapolis, NS. He was the son of Solomon FARNSWORTH and Lucy FARNSWORTH, and was born ca 1781; died 1812. She married second to John ELLIS on 15 Feb 1813. Mary-4 CHUTE died Nov 1856.

Children of Mary-4 CHUTE and Solomon FARNSWORTH:
    Surname FARNSWORTH
    134. Benjamin   born 1 Feb 1802; died 1880
                         married Anna Matilda ELLIS 1822 Granville Twsp. NS
    135. Peter   born 9 July 1803; married Mary HOLDEN; died 1882
    136. John Chute   born 11 Oct 1805; died 11 Sept 1884
                         married Mary Cecelia PACK 15 Feb 1826 Hampton, NS
    137. Mary   born 1807; married William HALL 29 Apr 1827 Granville, NS
    138. Solomon   born 9 Oct 1809; died ca 1888
                         married Anna B. CUMMINGS 19 Nov 1834 Granville, Twsp. NS
              Child: Solomon-6 FARNSWORTH born 11 Nov 1837 Granville Twsp. NS

139. Margaretta	born ca 1814	142. Phoebe	born 12 July 1820
	married Robert SHERRAR	143. Abigail	born 16 Aug 1822
140. Sarah	born ca 1816; died 1836		married Joseph BOGERT
141. Edward	born ca 1818; died 1834	144. William	born ca 1824

References: History of Annapolis, NS; FARNSWORTH Family History by Fanny FARNSWORTH Trull, Marlboro, MA

44. LYDIA-4 CHUTE, twin sister of above, was born 19 Apr 1785 at Granville, Annapolis Co., NS. She married Samuel FOSTER -7++ on 17 Mar 1805 at All Saints Anglican Church, Granville Twsp., NS. He was the son of Benjamin-6 FOSTER and Elizabeth RICHARDSON, and was born 9 Sep 1783 Granville, NS; died 29 July 1879 at Hampton, Granville Twsp, Annapolis Co., NS. Lydia-4 CHUTE died ____.

Children of Lydia-4 CHUTE and Samuel-7 FOSTER:

Surname FOSTER   (all born Granville Twsp. Annapolis, Nova Scotia)

145.Thomas	born ca 1807; died 1818	151. Abigail	born 1 Feb 1819
146. Samuel, Jr.	born 22 Apr 1808; died 1881	152. Stephen Thorne born 20 Oct 1821	
147. John Van Buren	born 17 Feb 1811; died 1913		died 1857
148. Lucy	born 30 Sep 1814	153. Abner born 3 Mar 1823; died 1894	
149. Harris Miller	born 28 June 1815; died 1902	154. Susannah Ann born 9 Feb 1825	
150. Ruby Ann	born 12 Apr 1817	155. Jacob born 29 Feb 1828; died 1893	

++ For ancestry of Samuel-7 FOSTER # 506 (Benjamin-6; Isaac-5; Benjamin-4; Jacob-3; Isaac-2; Reginald/Renold-1) see FOSTER SECTION page 394.

45. PETER PRESCOTT-4 CHUTE, brother of above, was born 27 May 1787 at Granville, Annapolis County, Nova Scotia. He married Lucy RANDALL ca 1808. She was the daughter of David RANDALL and Amy PAYSON, and was born 19 Nov 1787 Aylesford, Kings County, NS; died 21 Apr 1854 at Bridgetown, Annapolis, NS. Peter-4 CHUTE died ca 1865 at Bridgetown, Annapolis Co., NS.

Children of Peter-4 CHUTE and Lucy RANDALL:

Surname CHUTE   (all children born Annapolis, Nova Scotia)

156. Alexander	born 24 Feb 1809	158. George	born 24 Apr 1814; died 11 Oct 1821
157. Charles	born 19 Apr 1811	159. Gilbert R. born 13 Sep 1817	

46. ELEANOR-4 CHUTE, sister of above, was born 11 July 1789 Annapolis County, Nova Scotia. She married James ADAMS ca 1808 at Digby County, Nova Scotia.

Children of Eleanor4 CHUTE and James ADAMS:

Surname ADAMS

160. James (Jr.)	born ca 1809; died Dec 1828 (drowned in the Bay of Fundy) NS
161. Mary A.	born 10 Mar 1811; married Thomas O'CONNOR; died Dec 1860
162. Lydia	born 22 Feb 1813; married Edward MIDDLETON 4 Dec 1831
163. Austin D.	born ca 1815; married Nancy O'CONNOR
164. Robert	born ca 1818; married Augusta CAMPBELL
165. Maurice	born 15 Sep 1820; 1m. Eliza A. CAMPBELL 16 Dec 1842
	2m. Eliza Jane PINKNEY 12 Nov 1856
166. Susan	born 2 Apr 1822; married Eleazer WOODWORTH
167. Lovina	born ca 1824; married William CRONK
168. John	born ca 1826; married Mary Ann MORRISON
169. Sarah	born ca 18828; married John BROWN
170. Matilda	born ca 1830; married John MIDDLETON

47. JOHN-4 CHUTE, 2nd, brother of above, was born 14 Oct 1790 at Annapolis County, Nova Scotia. He married Abigail JONES ca 18__. She was the daughter of ____ JONES, and was born ca 17__.

Child of John-4 CHUTE and Abigail JONES:

Surname CHUTE

+ 171. ELIZABETH   born 8 Apr 1820; 1m. John Balser-4 RICE Dec 1837 (as his 3rd wife)
(he son of Jonas-3 RICE (Ebenezer-2;1) and __?__) (he born ca 1810; died 14 June 1852)
2m. the 2nd son of Silas RICE ca 1852/3

48. LEAH FOWLER-4 CHUTE, sister of above, was born 7 Apr 1793 at Granville, Annapolis County, Nova Scotia. She married Robert WOODMAN ca 1814. He was the son of Jacob WOODMAN and Mary CHESLEY, and was born 1792 Durham, NH; died 10 Mar 1853, NS. Leah-4 CHUTE died 6 Mar 1875.

Children of Leah-4 CHUTE and Robert WOODMAN:

Surname WOODMAN	(all children born at Durham, NH)
172. Mary Elizabeth	born 21 Apr 1815; died 21 Dec 1837
173. Miles Chesley	born 26 May 1816; married Caroline RICE 22 Jan 1846 Hillsburgh, NS
174. James Edward	born 26 Sep 1817; married Lucy J. PATCH ca 1849; died Dec 1884
175. Capt Jacob Crocker	born 23 May 1819; married Eliza COSSETT ca 1850 (she born ca 1819)
	(she dau/o Frank E. COSSETT and Bessie NICHOLS)
176. Agnes Jane	born 28 Sep 1820; 1m. William Henry RANDALL
	2m. Benjamin SEELY 14 Nov 1854
177. Sarah Selina	born 5 Apr 1822; married John COSSETT; died 7 Aug 1881
178. Robert George	born 20 Dec 1823; died 30 Dec 1824
179. Bethia Matilda	born 21 Sep 1825; married James T. HINXMAN 25 Dec 1854; died 4 Jan 1892
180. Robert George (2)	born 1 May 1827; married Maria BIRSTEAD; died 3 June 1864
	(died at the Battle of Cold Harbor – **Civil War**)
181. Cynthia Anna	born 28 June 1829; married John GABEL ca 1859; died 27 June 1888
+ 182. JOHN CHUTE	born 9 May 1831; married Mary Elizabeth RICE ca 1852
183. Henry Austin	born 10 Apr 1833 (went to sea – sailor)
184. Israel Potter	born 24 Mar 1835; died 12 Feb 1875 ; 1m. Sarah Jane BUSKIRK ca 1865
	2m. Sophronia Ann NICHOLAS ca 1869
185. Victoria Selinda	born 8 Apr 1837; died 26 Apr 1855
186. Mary Amoret	born 9 July 1839; died 24 Dec 1844

Reference: CHUTE Family Genealogy: 29; LDS-IGI

53. JOHN-4 CROCKER, son of Paul-3 CROCKER, Jr. (Captain Paul-2) and Thankful GATES, was born 28 Mar 1797 at Aylesford, Nova Scotia. He married Eliza Ann CHESLEY (Banks) on 31 May 1820/21 at Wilmot, Nova Scotia. Eliza Ann was erroneously given as Eliza Ann BANKS in the CHUTE Genealogy. Her mother was Margaret BASS ++ (Not BARSS), as stated but her father was not Timothy BANKS. Eliza was a child of the rape of Margaret BASS by a Colonel William CHESLEY, a British officer. The family history relates that " the BASS family was away from their farm – leaving Margaret there alone. She was attacked in the barn by Col. CHESLEY."

Eliza Ann CHESLEY was born 4 July 1803. Her mother married Timothy Saunders BANKS 8 Jan 1809 at Meadowvale, Nova Scotia. She probably used the name of BANKS, thus causing some confusion. She died 27 Dec 1880, age 77 (gs). John-4 CROCKER died 28 Mar 1876 at Tremont, Nova Scotia, age 79.

Children of John-4 CROCKER and Eliza Ann CHESLEY:

Surname CROCKER	
187. William	born 13 Mar 1820/21,NS; married Maria BANKS; died 16 Jun 1896 Tremont, NS
188. Susan Eliza/	born 6 June 1825 poss Meadowvale, NS; married William M. BROWN
Elizabeth	died 22 Dec 1908 Tremont, Nova Scotia
+ 189. ABIGAIL	born 6 Apr 1827 Wilmot, NS; died 17 June 1905 Margaretsville, NS
	married Captain Richard Pirl ALDRED 17 May 1851
	(he son/o John ALDRED and Mary PEARL/PIRL) (he born ca 1817; died 1872)
+ 190. JAMES	born 26 May 1829/30; married Mary Etta LANGLEY ca 1850
	(she dau/o Will LANGLEY and Ann WILSON) (she born 29 Jul 1832; died 22 Feb 1909)
	died 18 Feb 1899 Meadowvale, NS
+ 191. ALDEN BASS	born 16 May 1832; married Jessie Idella McMASTER
	(she dau/o Thomas McMASTER and Margaret McQUARRIE)
192. Margaret Ann	born 11 Sep 1834; died 8 Apr 1887
	1m. Franklin A. ROBLEE; 2m. Thomas McMASTER

Children of John-4 CROCKER, continued:
  Surname CROCKER
  193. Simeon   born 14 Feb 1836/37 Tremont, NS; married Mary Lavinia BANKS
                              died 3 Jan 1899, Tremont, Nova Scotia
  194. John Dexter   born ca 1840; married Amelia MESSENGER
  195. Ruth Ella   born 23 Mar 1841; married Thomas McMASTER; died 8 Apr 1929
  196. Israel   born ca 18__; died at age 17   EOL
  197. Nellie Wilhemina   born ca 24 Mar 1848 Tremont, NS; married John McMASTER
                              died 21 Aug 1918 Tremont, Nova Scotia

++   Ancestry of Margaret BASS

SAMUEL-1 BASS, the immigrant and father of John-2, was born ca 1600 in England. He married Ann-1 RAWSON. She was born ca 1600 in England; died 16 Sep 1693. Samuel-1 BASS died 10 Jan 1695. JOHN-2 BASS was born 1632 at Roxbury, MA; married RUTH-2 ALDEN on 2 Feb 1657 at Duxbury, MA. Ruth-2 was the daughter of John-1 ALDEN ++ and Priscilla MULLINS; and was born 1634; died 1674 at Braintree, MA. John-2 BASS died 12 Sept 1716 at Braintree.

JOSEPH-3 BASS was born 6 Dec 1655 at Braintree; married Mary-3 BELCHER on 5 June 1688. She was the daughter of Moses-2 BELCHER (Gregory-1) and was born 8 July 1668; died 2 Nov 1705 at Boston, MA. Joseph-3 BASS died 22 Nov 1733/34 at Boston. JOSEPH-4 BASS was born 1 July 1692 at Braintree, MA. He married Elizabeth-4 BRECK on 14 Sept 1715 at Dorchester. She was the daughter of Edward-3 BRECK (John-2; Edward-1) and Susanna-3 WISWELL (Enoch-2; Thomas-1) and was born 30 Apr 1700 at Dorchester; died 21 June 1751 Dorchester.

JOSEPH-5 BASS, who was born 23 Sept 1723 Dorchester; died 15 Jan 1797. He married Lydia-3 SEARLE on 8 Mar 1747. She was the daughter of Jabez-2 SEARLE and Patience-3 TOPLIFF; and was born 17 May 1723; died 1789 at Dorchester. ALDEN-6 BASS, the son of Joseph-5; was born July 1750 at Dorchester, MA. He married Christine BURNS ca ____ at Nicteaux, Nova Scotia, and died there ca ____. Margaret-7 BASS, born ca 1785 at Nicteaux, baptized 24 Dec 1785; married Timothy Saunders BANKS 8 Jan 1809 at Meadowvale/Wilmot, NS. Timothy BANKS was the son of Moses BANKS and Judith SAUNDERS and was born 9 Dec 1783 at Wilmot, NS; died 26 Feb 1853.

++ JOHN-1 ALDEN (George-A) was born 1599 in England; married Priscilla-1 MULLINS (William) John-1 ALDEN died Sept 1686/87. (Note: William-7 RICHARDS, III; page 285 CROCKER section is also a descendant of John-1 ALDEN .)

56. ANN/ANNA G-4 CROCKER, sister of above, was born ca 1803 at Aylesford, N. Scotia. She married Jacob Beach SPINNEY on 26 Jan 1826 at Aylesford. He was the son of Samuel SPINNEY and Elizabeth BEACH, and was born ca 1799; died 1879. Anna died 1890 at Greenwood Square, Kings Co., NS.

Children of Ann/Anna-4 CROCKER and Jacob SPINNEY:
  Surname SPINNEY
+ 198. AUSTIN   born 1827; married Elizabeth Jane MORSE; died 1891
       WELTON   (she born 1828; died 1904)
+ 199. JACOB   born 1829; married Jane R. DUNCANSON; died 1907
       BEACH, Jr   (she born 1831; died 1910)
+ 200. HARDING   born 1831; married Helen F. BARTEAUX; died 1877
       THEODORE   (she born 1834; died 1906)
+ 201. DEACON   born 1833; married Parnie BARTEAUX; died 1906
       CALEB   (she born 1840; died 1921)
  202 Harriet Ann   born 1836; married Stephen C. BANKS; died 1865 (he born 1823; died 1918)
                                     One son: Clark-6 BANKS born ____
+ 203. BERIAH B.   born 1838; married Mary Jane WHITMAN; died 1923
                            (she born 1843; died 1869)
+ 204. ENOCH   born 1840; married Phebe BOWLBY; died 1907 (she born 1845; died 1922)
  205. Maria Elizabeth   born 1843; died 1847   EOL
+ 206. CLARK THOMAS born 1846; married Orinda SLOCUM; died 1926   (she born 1855; died 1944)

57. JAMES-4 CROCKER, brother of above, was born 1806 at Aylesford, N S. He married first Abigail TUPPER on 14 May 1827 at Aylesford. She was born 1803; died 1828. His 2nd marriage was to Jane SPINNEY ca 1831. She was born 8 Nov 1810; died 1 Feb 1869. James –4 CROCKER died 1890 at Kings County, Nova Scotia.

Child of James-4 CROCKER and Abigail TUPPER:
    Surname CROCKER
+ 207. CALVIN   born 1828; married Catherine SAUNDERS; died 1899
                     (she born 1834; died 1902)
Child of James-4 CROCKER and Jane SPINNEY:
    Surname CROCKER
+ 208. JOHN M.   born 23 Dec 1836 Aylesford, NS; died 12 Jan 1915 Harmony, Kings Co., NS
                     married Mary Adelaide BRENNAN 7 Oct 1865 (she born 1846; died 1925)

58. JOHN-4 CROCKER, son of James Wheeler-3 CROCKER (John-2) and Rebecca BERRY, was born 30 Sept 1786 at Machias, Washington County, Maine. He married Sarah/Sally BERRY ca ____. She was the daughter of Jonathan BERRY and Hannah KNIGHT, and was born ca 1788; died ____. (Note: They were both still living 1850; and had a Hannah HANSCOM, age 12, residing with them)

Children of John-4 CROCKER and Sally BERRY:
    Surname CROCKER
+ 209. HARRISON G.   born 8 Aug 1809; married Cynthia-7 LONGFELLOW
                     (she born ca 1807; died ____) (she 1m. Caleb S-4 CROCKER # 66)
                     lumberman; resided Marshfield, Washington Co., Maine
+ 210. SAMUEL   born 20 Jan 1811; married Susan H-7 LONGFELLOW Lyon 19 Oct 1848
      GOULD   (she dau/o Jonathan LONGFELLOW and Sally BOYNTON)
                     (she born ca 1816; died ____) (she 1m. James C. LYON)
  211. John   born 30 June 1813; died young
+ 212. MARY   born 16 Feb 1815; married Alfred GARDNER; died before 1850
                     (he son/o Thomas GARDNER and Sarah BERRY) (he born 16 July 1812)
+ 213. REBECCA   born 30 Dec 1820; married Hiram GARDNER 27 July 1843; died 1902
                     (he born 18 June 1819; brother of Alfred GARDNER, above)
  214. Thomas born 1825   215. Nathan born 1827   216. John W.   born 1832

59. BETSEY-4 CROCKER, sister of above, was born 9 Dec 1788 at Machias, Washington County, Maine. She married Henry LYON on 14 July 1809. He was the son of the Rev James LYON and Martha HOLDEN, and was born ____; died ____. Betsey-4 CROCKER was residing with her son Albert; according to the 1850 Census, Marshfield, ME.   (Note: Albert # 217, was the only sibling still living in 1881)

Children of Betsey-4 CROCKER and Henry LYON:
    Surname LYON
  217. Albert   born 1811 Marshfield, ME; married Caroline CLARK ca 1835 Machias; (she born 1821)
  218. James born 18__   219. Rebecca   born 18_   220. Hannah   born 18__
  221. Ludlum   born ca 1818 Machias, ME
+ 222. WILLIAM   born 1818; married Sarah GETCHELL; (she born 1827; died ____)
      PENNIMAN   (she dau/o Simeon-3 GETCHELL and Betsey BOWKER)
+ 223. WARREN   born ca 1824; married Phyzannah NORTON
+ 224. AMELIA   born ca ____; married Bryant GATES ca 1842
+ 225. CYRUS   born ca ____; married Inez COTA
+ 226. SANFORD   born 1832; married Annie T. HANSCOM after 1860

60. CAPTAIN OTIS-4 CROCKER, brother of above, was born 9 Dec 1790 at Machias, Maine. He married Sarah F. O'BRIEN on ____. She was born ca 1796; died ____. Captain Otis-4 CROCKER, later a merchant at Machias, ME., died ____. Note: 1850 Census (Machias) shows Otis CROCKER listed as a merchant. His daughters, all single, were residing with him.

Children of Captain Otis-4 CROCKER and Sarah O'BRIEN:
    Surname CROCKER
  227. Lewis born 18__; d y + 228. HELEN J/G born 1828; married Ladwick-5 HOLWAY 23 Oct 1851

Children of Captain Otis-4 CROCKER, continued:
  Surname CROCKER
  229. Annette/Antoinette born 1830   230. Henrietta   born 1832   231. Sarah E.   born 1836

61. SALLY-4 CROCKER, sister of above, was born 20 April 1795 at Machias, Maine. She married Henry THAXTER on 14 May 1817 at Machias. He was the son of ____ THAXTER and ____ ____; and was born _____; died ____. Sally-4 CROCKER died ____.

Children of Sally-4 CROCKER and Henry THAXTER:
  Surname THAXTER
  232. Harry   born ____; poss marr Lucy DREW   236. Laura E.   born ____
  233. John D.   born ____; died young   + 237. A. WALLACE born ____
  234. Robert   born ____   married Mary BURNHAM
+ 235. LEVI B.   born ca 1822 Machias   238. Jane   born ____
                   married Susan BURNHAM

62. POLLY-4 CROCKER, twin sister of above, was born 20 Apr 1795 at Machias, Maine. She married first to Ephraim WHITNEY 20 June 1813, Machias. He was the son of ____ WHITNEY and _____ _____; and was born ___; died 1828. She married 2nd to Stephen-6 BOYNTON, as his 4th wife, on ____. He was the son of Amos-5 BOYNTON and his 2nd wife Lucy LORING, and was born ca 1787. He married 1st to Hannah JEWETT; 2nd to Myra BROWN, 3rd to Hannah BOWKER. No issue from those unions.

Children of Polly-4 CROCKER and Ephraim WHITNEY:
  Surname WHITNEY
  239. Otis   born 27 Apr 1814; resided Machias, Me. 1840; removed to MN ca 1850
  240. Emma Olive   born 1 July 1816   242. Ephraim (twin)   born 4 Mar 1823
  241. Arathusa Brigham   born 16 Nov 1817   243. Hannah (twin)   born 4 Mar 1823
                          Reference: Machias, ME VR p. 22-28-41

63. KATHERINE/CATHERINE-4 CROCKER, sister of above, was born 19 Dec 1797 at Machias, Washington Co., Maine. She married Colonel William BURNHAM on 4 Aug 1816 at Machias. He was the son of Job BURNHAM ++ and Mary O'BRIEN.

 Col. William BURNHAM married second to Mary SPROUL and had 8 more children: George; William F. Oscar; Alonzo; Gilbert; Amanda; Mary and Ella BURNHAM.

++ Job BURNHAM was the first of the name to settle in Machias according to the History of Machias by George W. DRISKO, published 1904. He went to the area in 1770; and built a house that year which was known for over a century as the BURNHAM TAVERN. It was the site of a meeting 10/11 June 1775 where they discussed the feasibility of attacking the British war vessel, the MARGARETTA. Their actions resulted in the First Naval Battle of the **Revolutionary War.** BURNHAMS' TAVERN was used as a hospital for the wounded after the engagement and the capture of the MARGARETTA. Job BURNHAMS' wife was Mary O'BRIEN, the daughter of Morris O'BRIEN (a native of Cork, Ireland) and his wife Mary KEAN/KEEN. Mary KEAN was the only child of Captain KEAN, a sea captain.

Children of Katherine-4 CROCKER and William BURNHAM:
  Surname BURNHAM
  244. Lewis   born ca 1820; married Martha W. WASS 6 Oct 1845 (she born ca 1825; died ____)
  245. Job   born ____
  246. Rebecca   born ____
  247. Alfred P. born ____; married Clara V. ORCUTT Nash 12 June 1865 (she 1m. _?_ NASH)
  248. Hannah born _____ 249. Catherine born ____   250. Sarah born ____   251. Susan born _____

64. OLIVE-4 CROCKER, twin sister of above, was born 19 Dec 1797 at Machias, Washington County, Maine. She married William F. PENNIMAN on 1 Sept 1818 at Machias. He was the son of Jacob P. PENNIMAN and Mary-3 O'BRIEN (Gideon-2; Morris-1) , and was born ca 1784; died 1874 (age 90). Olive-4 CROCKER died 1868, age 70.

Children of Olive-4 CROCKER and William PENNIMAN:
Surname PENNIMAN

252. Moses	born ____	255. Sarah B.	born ____
253. Laura U.	born ____	256. Mary Olive	born ___; married Jacob LONGFELLOW
254. Jacob	born ___		1 child: Mary O-6 LONGFELLOW born 1845
married Mary Jane-7 TENNEY 1848/49		257. Elizabeth L.	born ____
(she # 991 DRISKO section)		258. Hannah C.	born ____

65. MARINER GREEN-4 CROCKER, brother of above, was born 31 Aug 1800 at Machias, Washington County, Maine. He married Martha-6 LONGFELLOW ++ ca 1820-21. She was the daughter of Jonathan-5 LONGFELLOW and Sally-6 BOYNTON, and was born 8 Aug 1800, died 29 Aug 1893, age 93. Mariner G-4 CROCKER, a lumberman, died 10 Aug 1872. He is buried at Machias, Maine.

Children of Mariner G-4 CROCKER and Martha-6 LONGFELLOW:
Surname CROCKER

+ 259. MERCY   born 14 May 1822; married Abel CURTIS of Fairlee, VT.; died 1907
LONGFELLOW   (he born 4 July 1814; died 22 May 1882)
     (he son/o Abel CURTIS and Lucy MOREY)
260. Jane Thaxter   born 4 Apr 1824; poss married Henry ALBEE
     moved to St. Stephen, New Brunswick
+ 261. ALVIN GREEN   born 1826; married Julia A-8 FOSTER 2 Sept 1849 (# 982 FOSTER)
     (she dau/o Lewis-7 FOSTER and Julia PINEO)
262. Martha Jane   born Dec 1827; died 8 Feb 1870 (42yr4mo) Machias. ME (gs)
263. Hannah   born 14 Mar 1830; married Captain Joseph STRATTON after 1860
Longfellow   died 22 Aug 1906; buried Machias, ME
         One child: Freddy-6 STRATTON born June 1863; died 1868   EOL
+ 264. CYRUS   born 1832; married Martha H. Peach-8 SMITH 6 Jan 1855
STRONG   (she born ca 1834; died June 1908)
265. Frank B. (Handy)   born 1834
+ 266. SUSAN AMELIA   born 1836; married Flavius Josephus MOORE ca Aug 1869
     (he born 6 Jan 1829 St. David, New Brunswick; died ____)
     (he son/o Witter Davison MOORE and Penelope Hunt MABEE)
267. Betsey A.   born 12 Feb 1838; died 27 Apr 1852 (14-2-15) gs Machias
268. Francis B.   born 1840; 1m. ___ WILDER (no issue); 2m. Emily FARRAR
+ 269. NEWELL W.   born ca 1844; married Antoinette CATES 5 Apr 1869
     divorced 19 Mar 1886; moved to Amador, CA

++ Ancestry of Martha-6 LONGFELLOW

WILLIAM-1 LONGFELLOW, the immigrant, was the 2nd son of WILLIAM-A LONGFELLOW and Elizabeth THORNTON, and was born ca 1650/51 at Yorkshire, England. He went to Newbury, MA ca 1676, and settled in a part known as the FALLS. He married Ann SEWELL on 10 Nov 1678. She was the daughter of Henry SEWELL and Jane DUMMER, and was born 3 Sept 1662 at Newbury; died ____.

In 1690 William-1 LONGFELLOW, who was an Ensign in the Newbury Company, was one of the officers on an expedition to Quebec. On the return voyage he was aboard a vessel which was met by a violent storm. He, and 9 others, drowned near the island of Anticost. William-1 LONGFELLOW had at least 3 sons: Lt. Stephen; William; and NATHAN-2 LONGFELLOW who was born ca 1689/90 at Newbury, MA. He married Mercy GREEN on 28 May 1713. She was the daughter of Jacob GREEN and Sarah ?, and was born 17 Apr 1693; died ____. Nathan-2 LONGFELLOW died Jan 1731.

JONATHAN-3 LONGFELLOW, was the eldest son of Nathan-2; and was born 23 May 1714 at Hampton Falls, NH. He married Mercy CLARK 29 Oct 1731. She was the daughter of Henry Clark and Elizabeth GREENLEAF; and was born 26 Dec 1714; died 29 Apr 1797 at Cornwallis, Nova Scotia. Jonathan-3 LONGFELLOW died 1774 at Machias. Jonathan-3 LONGFELLOW went to Machias in 1767, and built a house thereafter kept as a Tavern by his son David-4. Jonathan-3 LONGFELLOW was the first Justice of the Peace in Maine; East of the Penobscot River. NATHAN-4 LONGFELLOW, son of Jonathan-3, was born 30 Dec 1743, poss NH; and married Margaret BIGELOW on ____. She was the daughter of Isaac BIGELOW and Abigail SKINNER, and was born 2 Aug 1747 at Colchester, CT; died 29 Jan 1842 at Machias, ME. JONATHAN-5 LONGFELLOW, son of Nathan-4, was born 6 Sept 1770, poss at Cornwallis, NS., died 8 Jan 1835; and married Sally BOYNTON 11 Dec 1797. She was the daughter of Amos BOYNTON and Mary LIBBY, and was born 22 Dec 1777 at Machias, Maine. She died there 3 Oct 1843.

66. CALEB STRONG-4 CROCKER, brother of above, was born 27 May 1804 at Machias, Maine. He married Cynthia-7 LONGFELLOW on ____. She was the daughter of Isaac-6 LONGFELLOW (Jonathan-5) and Polly-6 BOYNTON (Amos-5), and was born ca 1807; died ____. Caleb-4 CROCKER died ____. Cynthia-7 married 2nd to Harrison G-5 CROCKER (# 209), son of John-4 CROCKER and Sally BERRY.

Children of Caleb Strong-4 CROCKER and Cynthia-7 LONGFELLOW:
    Surname CROCKER

270. Julia A.	born ca 1824; married Levi B. GETCHELL		
	(he son of Simeon-3 GETCHELL and Betsey BOWKER)		
	(he born ca 1820, Marshfield, ME; died Oct 1900 Machias, ME)		
271. Caroline	born ____	272. Olive	born ca 1833

67. HANNAH-4 CROCKER, sister of above, was born 3 Dec 1806 at Machias, Washington County, Maine. She married Amos B-7 LONGFELLOW, a lumberman, on ____. He was the son of Jonathan-6 LONGFELLOW and Sally-6 BOYNTON, and was born 20 Mar 1803 at Machias.; died ____. Hannah-4 CROCKER died ca 1834/35. Amos B-7 LONGFELLOW married second to Nancy P. BAKER and had 8 children; i. Arodell (d y); ii. Amelia born 1836, married Henry R. TAYLOR: iii. Nancy; iv. Hannah born 1839, married Jared CRANE; v. Jonathan A. born ca 1840, married Emeline SMITH; vi. Tristam (d y); vii. Harriet born ca 1847, married Silas SMITH and viii. Zena B. LONGFELLOW.

Child of Hannah-4 CROCKER and Amos-7 LONGFELLOW:
    Surname LONGFELLOW

+ 273. LYDIA	born ca 1827/28; married Isaac HEATON (a lumberman)
GOODHUE	(he born 17 Dec 1820, Hillsboro, NH; died ____)

70. STEPHEN BURGAIN-4 CROCKER, son of Simeon-3 CROCKER (John-2) and Katherine/ Catherine WATERHOUSE, was born 20 Dec 1798 at Machias, ME. He married Jane S. STARRETT on 4 July 1833. She was the daughter of Isaac STARRETT (Thomas; William; Robert) and Mary SPEAR, and was born 9 Mar 1799 at Warren, Knox County, ME. They resided on the S. LIBBY farm at North Warren, ME..

Children of Stephen Burgain-4 CROCKER and Jane STARRETT:

Surname CROCKER	Reference: Annals of Warren, Maine
274. David S.	born 8 Mar 1837; died 13 Apr 1837
275. David (2)	born 22 June 1838; died 18 Nov 1855
+ 276. SAMUEL S.	born 7 Nov 1839; married Lizzie ANGIER 1 Nov 1862
277. Edward	born 8 Apr 1847; 1m. Ella LINDLEY Nov 1869
	2m. Eugenia R. JEWETT 17 Aug 1876 (she from Clinton, MA)

71. JANE FREEMAN-4 CROCKER, sister of above, was born 28 Nov 1800 at Machias, Maine. She married Obed (iah) HOLMES, son of James HOLMES and Sarah/Sally BERRY Lyons. He was born 21 Apr 1806, Machias, died ____. She married second to Rufus FOSS on ____. He was the son of William FOSS and Lydia FLYNN, and was born ____; died ____. Jane-4 CROCKER died ____.

Children of Jane F-4 CROCKER and Obed HOLMES:
    Surname HOLMES

278. William	born ____	279. Fannie	born ____
280. Martin	born ____married Melissa FRYE (res Kennebec 1850)		
+ 281. ADDIE A.	born ____ married Samuel W. HILL		
	(he son/o Warren HILL and Maria B. SHAW (he born 1858; died ____)		

72. MARTHA G-4 CROCKER, sister of above, was born 2 July 1803 at Machias, Maine. She married Levi BOWKER, Jr. on 22 May 1822 at Machias, Maine. He was the son of Levi BOWKER, Sr. ++ and Elizabeth/Betsey WATTS; and was born 20 Aug 1795 Machias; died ___ (still living June 1881). Levi BOWKER, Jr. was in the Fort at Machiasport on Aug 1814. He was a drummer boy and an Orderly

Sergeant under the command of Colonel MORSE (Machias Union Newspaper , 14 June 1881). Levi BOWKER, Jr. was a land Surveyor, and resided at Marshfield, Maine according to the 1850 Census.

Children of Martha G-4 CROCKER and Levi BOWKER, Jr.:
Surname BOWKER

282. Simeon	born 182_	283. Wellington	born 182_
+ 284. NATHAN	born 15 May 1826; died 18 July 1910		
STEPHEN	married Mary Abigail-8 BERRY ca 1850		
+ 285. FERDINAND	born ca 1830; died 1852; married Lucy-3 BOYNTON 2 Oct 1850 Machias		
	(she dau/o Stephen-2 BOYNTON and Hannah JEWETT) (she 2m. Albert MOORS)		
286. Warren	born 8 Mar 1832	+ 289. MARTHA A.	born 4 Apr 1837
287. George W.	born ca 183_		married Roscoe-3 BOYNTON
288. Enoch E.	born ca 183_	290. Hannah	born ca 183_

++ Major Levi BOWKER, Sr. was born 25 July 1763 at Scituate, MA. He married Elizabeth/Betsey WATTS, daughter of Samuel WATTS of Haverhill, MA. She was born 1764; died 23 Feb 1854. Major BOWKER enlisted in the army on Mar 1781, and served until 18 Dec 1783 under Captain KING and Colonel TUPPER. Major BOWKER died on 28 Aug 1850 at Machias, Maine.

73. ABIGAIL-4 CROCKER, sister of above, was born 7 Mar 1806 at Machias, Maine. She married William FLYNN ca ____. He was born ca 1804/05. He was a millman, and resided at Cherryfield, ME.

Children of Abigail-4 CROCKER and William FLYNN:
Surname FLYNN

+ 291. GEORGE W.	born ca 1828/31; died 1860
	1m. Mary J. LONGFELLOW (she born 1832; died ____)
	2m. Thirza-5 GETCHELL (she dau/o Marshfield-4 GETCHELL and Martha J. HOLMES)
+ 292. ABAGAIL C.	born ca 1833; married Arthur R. NASH (he born ca 1827; a shoemaker)
293. Mary A.	born ca 1839; died ____ unmarried EOL
294. Horace W.	born ca 1840/41; 1m. Abbie TRACY
	2m. Dora GETCHELL (no issue) (she 2m. Thomas DENNISON)

75. GEORGE WATERHOUSE-4 CROCKER, brother of above, was born 20 Nov 1810 at Machias, Maine. A lumberman, he married Lucinda HARMON ca 183_. She was the daughter of Samuel Japhet HARMON and Mercy FISHER, and was born 8 Oct 1812/13; died 18 Jan 1889 (86 yr 3 mo). She and her husband are buried at Machias, Maine. George-4 CROCKER died 24 July 1870 (59 yr 8 mo) at Machias.

Children of George W. CROCKER and Lucinda HARMON:
Surname CROCKER

+ 295. SOPHIA H.	born 1835; married Thomas WILLIAMSON
+ 296. DELIA A.	born 1 June 1837; married Horace T. GARDNER 1 Sept 1853
	(he born 11 May 1830; died ____) (a successful lumberman at Machias)
297. George S. (twin)	born Apr 1840; died 11 Dec 1868 (28yr8mo) buried Machias, Maine

Note: George S. CROCKER was a member of Co C., 6th Regt, MA Volunteers in the Civil War, and was engaged in the riot of Baltimore, MD on 19 Apr 1861.

298. Georgianna (twin)	born Apr 1840; died 26 June 1858 (18yr3mo) buried Machias, ME.
299. Anson	born 1843; married Ellen G. ESTEY; died 1913 (no issue) EOL
	(she born 1851; died 1933)

Note: Anson CROCKER was a member of Co B, 11th Maine Regt of Volunteers, Civil War

300. Frank	born ___; died ___ unmarried EOL
301. Major Andrew	born 1846/47; died ____ Note: Served 1 year with the US Army in Mexico
302. Amanda	born 1848/49; died ____
303. Mercy T.	born June 1850; died ____
304. Junette/Junie	born ca 1854; 1m. William H. ALLEN
	2m. Alberto-7 LONGFELLOW 18 Dec 1878
	(he son/o Gates-6 LONGFELLOW (Issac-5; Nathan-4; Jonathan-3; Nathan-2; William-1)(he born 2 Apr 1849)
305. Cyrus	born 185_; died young

76. ENOCH SIMEON-4 CROCKER, brother of above, was born 17 Oct 1812/13 at Machias, Washington County, Maine. He married Adaline JORDAN on 22 May 1842. She was the daughter of James JORDAN and Bethia CATES, and was born 1 Dec 1824; died 25 Feb 1887. Enoch Simeon-4 CROCKER was a seaman, residing at Marshfield, Maine (1850 Census). He died 21 Mar 1894 at Marshfield, Maine.

Children of Enoch S-4 CROCKER and Adaline JORDAN:
   Surname CROCKER
   306. Simeon E.   born 1844   307. Adaline A.   born 1846

77. MARY CATHERINE-4 CROCKER, sister of above, was born 20 Sept 1817 at Machias, Maine. She married John F. HARMON on ____. He was the son of Samuel Japhet HARMON and Mercy FISHER, and was born 6 Apr 1816, Machias, ME.; died ____. John F. HARMON was the brother of Lucy (above) who married George Waterhouse-4 CROCKER (# 75). They resided at Marshfield, Maine.

Children of Mary Catherine-4 CROCKER and John F. HARMON:
   Surname HARMON

308. Fidelia	born 1840/41; married William H. ALBEE (as his 2nd wife); died ____ CA

308. Fidelia   born 1840/41; married William H. ALBEE (as his 2nd wife); died ____ CA
                    (he son/o John C. ALBEE and Hannah GUPTILL)
                    (he 1m. Deborah LONGFELLOW; she died 1857)
309. Sophia   born ca 1842/43; married ____ CUNNINGHAM
           Child: Mary-6 CUNNINGHAM born ____; married Fred W. BOWKER

310. Lauretta   born 1846; married Magloir/ Magliore MAYNARD (of St. George, NB)
311. Lorenzo   born Apr 1850 Marshfield, Maine
+ 312. IDA   born born 185_; married Deola C-5 GETCHELL
                    (he son/o Marshfield-4 GETCHELL (John-3; Joseph-2;1)
313. Seymour   born 185_; died young

79. TIMOTHY-4 BEAN, son of Mary/Molly-3 CROCKER (Timothy-2; Peletiah-1) and Josiah-5 BEAN, was born 8 June 1775, possibly at Standish, Maine. He married Hannah KIMBALL ca 1795 Bethel, ME. She was the daughter of _____ KIMBALL, and was born ca 1779 at Bethel, Maine.

Children of Timothy-4 BEAN and Hannah KIMBALL:
   Surname BEAN   Reference: LDS-IGI
314. James Crocker   born 11 May 1807 Bethel, Oxford, Maine
                    married Eleanor Douglass BARTLETT (she born 22 Jan 1807 Bethel)
                    (she dau/o Thaddeus BARTLETT and Sybil Gibbs POWERS)
+ 315. TIMOTHY   born 6 Apr 1813 Bethel
                    1m. Lovina D. RUSSELL 30 Apr 1842 Bethel, Maine
                    2m. Elizabeth E. SWIFT 12 Mar 1846 Bethel

81. LUTHER-4 BEAN, brother of above, was born 23 Apr 1781 at St. George, Maine. He married Lydia KIMBALL ca 1816. She was the daughter of Samuel KIMBALL, and was born ca 1797.

Children of Luther-4 BEAN and Lydia KIMBALL:
   Surname BEAN
316. Stephen   born ca 18__
+ 317. LUCINDA   born ca 1817 Rumford, Oxford, Maine
                    married Hezekiah HUTCHINS ca 18__ (he born ca 1813 Rumford, Maine)
318. Edmund   born 29 Dec 1824 Standish, Oxford, Maine

82. EDMUND-4 BEAN, brother of above, was born 12 Aug 1786, probably at Bethel, Maine. He married Emma KIMBALL ca 1812. She was the daughter of Asa KIMBALL, and was born 4 Jan 1795; died ____. Edmund-4 BEAN died 16 Feb 1875 (age 91) at Rumford, Maine.

Children of Edmund-4 BEAN and Emma KIMBALL:
    Surname BEAN
+ 319. ELIPHAZ   born 25 July 1813 Bethel, ME.
                         married Sarah B. FARNUM 27 May 1838 Bethel, Oxford, Maine
        (she daughter of David Hall FARNUM and Maria BARTLETT; she born ca 1820 Rumford, ME)
+ 320. ZACHARIAH   born 16 Feb 1815 Bethel, Oxford, Maine
       HANNAFORD   married Emeline FARNUM 17 Jan 1841 Bethel, Oxford, Maine
                         (she sister of above) (she born ca 1823 Rumford, ME; died ___)

83. JOSHUA-4 BEAN, brother of above, was born 27 Apr 1789, probably at Bethel, Maine. He married
Betsey BARTLETT ca 18__. She was the daughter of Reuben BARTLETT(Enoch; Ebenezer; Joseph, Jr.;
Joseph) and Lydia FROST (Moses; Wm.; James; Wm.), and was born 20 Feb 1794 at Bethel, Oxford
Co., Maine. Joshua-4 BEAN died 19 May 1871 (age 83).

Children of Joshua-4 BEAN and Betsey BARTLETT:
    Surname BEAN   (all children born at Bethel, Maine)
    321. Francis Cushman born 21 Nov 1815   325. Phineas Frost   born 7 June 1824
    322. Mary C.   born 23 May 1818   326. Joshua   born 2 Mar 1828
    323. Josiah   born 28 Apr 1820   327. Lydia   born 11 Sept 1830
    324. Reuben Bartlett born 11 July 1822

+ 328. DOLLY KIMBALL born 27 May 1833; marr Moses Foster KIMBALL ca 1855
                     died 28 Jan 1892 at Bethel, ME

91. CAPTAIN TIMOTHY-4 CROCKER, son of James-3 CROCKER (Timothy-2) and Peggy COOK,
was born ca 1809 at ____, Maine. He married ___?___. She was born ____; died poss before 1860.
Timothy-4 CROCKER, a master mariner, was residing at East Machias, Maine in 1860 (family # 413).

Children of Timothy-4 CROCKER and ? :
    Surname CROCKER
    329. James L.   born ca 1831, ME.; married Ann __?__; (she born ca 1837)
                         One child: Mary E-6 CROCKER born 1859
    330. Edwin F.   born 1835 – a sailor   331. Abigail M.   born 1840/41

98. SARAH G-4 CROCKER, daughter of Captain Paul- 3 CROCKER (Timothy-2) and Nancy MARTIN,
was born ca 1785 at Bristol, ME. She married Captain Nathan-7 FOSTER (# 457 FOSTER section) on 20
Aug 1803 at Bristol. He was the son of Nathan-6 FOSTER (Nathan-5; Caleb-4;3; Abraham-2; Reginald-
1) and Amy/Anna THOMPSON. He was born Jan 1783; died 16 Apr 1837. Sarah G-4 CROCKER died 5
Feb 1858 (age 72). She and her husband are buried at Machiasport, Maine.

Children of Sarah-4 CROCKER and Nathan-7 FOSTER:
    Surname FOSTER   (all children born Machiasport, Maine)
+ 332. CAPTAIN   born 3 Jan 1806; married Eliza MESERVE 7 Aug 1825/26
       NATHAN O.   (she born 30 Jan 1807; died 11 Mar 1864)
                         (she dau/o Joseph MESERVE and his 2nd wife Susanna SMALL)
                         died 28 Apr 1889 Machiasport, Maine
+ 333. CAPTAIN   born 26 July 1808; married Susan McKELLER 4 Aug 1836 Machiasport
       JOHN WM.   (died 6 June 1844 (age 36) gs)
+ 334. CAPTAIN   born ca 1809/10; married Eliza G. MAVION 24 Dec 1835 Machiasport
     WM. HENDERSON   (she born 1812/13; died 24 Mar 1869 (age 56)
                         died 26 July 1877; buried East Machias, Maine
+ 335. CAPTAIN JAMES   born 13 Oct 1811; 1m. Mary Ann LIBBY 14 Nov 1833 Machiasport
       MADISON   (she born 1812/13; died 24 Mar 1869 , 56 yr)
                         2m. Clarissa (poss) BURNHAM (she born 1813; died 9 May 1891 (age 78 gs)

Children of Sarah G-4 CROCKER, continued:
  Surname FOSTER
  336. Nancy B.   born 17/20 Mar 1813
+ 337. CAPTAIN PAUL   born ca 1814; married Mary Jane-5 BARTER 19 Dec 1839; died 15 Mar 1861
     CROCKER   (she born 1821) (she dau/o Jacob BARTER and Polly-4 CROCKER # 101)
+ 338. ZEBEDEE M.   born 11 Apr 1817; married Louise-5 BARTER 14 Nov 1839
                          (she sister of Mary Jane-5, above) (see FOSTER # 766)
+ 339. MARGARET G.   born 1819; 1m. George W. GARDNER 26 Sept 1841
                          (he son/o John GARDNER and Susan BERRY)
                          2m. Captain George Washington-7 DRISKO 19 Sept 1855 (# 427 DRISKO)
                          (he son/o Captain John-6 DRISKO and Eunice PARKER)
                          died 12 Aug 1909 Syracuse, Onondaga County, NY
+ 340. SARAH G.   born Apr 1820; married William HOLWAY, Jr. 21 Jan 1836
                          died 5 Nov 1874 Machiasport (typhoid fever)
                          buried East Kennebec Cemetery, Machias, Maine
+ 341. HANNAH M.   born Apr 1824; 1m. Leonard LIBBY 18 Dec 1842
                          2m. Henry A. LIBBY 1852 (bro/o above)
                          (he born 8 Jan 1817; died 19 Mar 1900 (83-2-11))
                          For descendants of this family – See FOSTER Section # 760-# 769; pp. 427-430.

99. HANNAH-4 CROCKER, sister of above, was born ca 1786 at Bristol, Maine. She married Captain Zebedee MAYHEW on 21 Nov 1806. At Machias, Maine. He was the son of Nathan MAYHEW and __?_ of Martha's Vineyard, MA; and was born there 1782; died 1834 at East Machias, Maine. He was descended from Sir Thomas MAYHEW, the 1st Governor of Martha's Vineyard. Hannah-4 CROCKER died at East Machias 1849. The are both buried there.

Children of Hannah-4 CROCKER and Zebedee MAYHEW:
  Surname MAYHEW
  342. Mary C.   born 18 June 1807
  343. Captain Thomas M. born 3 June 1810; married Jane KELLAR (dau/o Capt. Josiah KELLAR)
                         died Aug 1877 Brooklyn, NY; buried Greenwood Cemetery, Brooklyn
       Captain Thomas MAYHEW became a member of the firm of MAYHEW, TALBOT and Co., lumber commission
       merchants and dealers in East Machias, Maine. (Possibly has a son Thomas, Jr. born 1834, resided East Machias, with wife
       Elizabeth (born 1838) and a son John H. MAYHEW, born 1857.   (Family # 399) 1860 Census.
  344. Captain Zebedee,Jr. born 30 July 1814; married Augusta BROWN
                         died 5 Dec 1865 Brooklyn, NY; buried Greenwood Cemetery
  345. Hannah   born 19 Aug 1820; died 9 July 1822   EOL

Note: Captain Zebedee Mayhew, Jr. moved to New York City, where he married Augusta BROWN. In 1848, with his brother Thomas, he became a member of the firm of SIMPSON, MAYHEW and CO., commission merchants and wholesale dealers in lumber. That firm was succeeded by SIMPSON, CLAPP and CO., of which his son Zebedee was a member in 1904.

101. POLLY-4 CROCKER, sister of above, was born ca 1794/95, probably at Bristol, Maine. She married Captain Jacob BARTER on 15 Sept 1816 at Machias, Maine. He was the son of _____ BARTER and ____ ____; and was born ca 1793 at St. George, ME.; died ____. They resided at Machiasport, ME. (1850)

Children of Polly-4 CROCKER and Jacob BARTER:
  Surname BARTER
+ 346. MARY JANE   born ca 1821; married Captain Paul Crocker-8 FOSTER (# 765 FOSTER)
+ 347. LOUISE   born ca 1822; married Captain Zebedee-8 FOSTER   (# 766 FOSTER)

104. PAUL-4 CROCKER, JR., brother of above, was born ____ at Bristol, Maine. He married Jane BARTER of St. George, Maine on 22 Oct 1828 there. She was the daughter of _____ BARTER and and was born ca 1809; died 16 Sept 1891 (age 82) at Newburg, Maine. Paul-4 CROCKER died before 1850. Jane BARTER married 2nd to Francis BUSSEY on 6 Sept 1852 at Machias.

Children of Paul-4 CROCKER, Jr. and Jane BARTER:
    Surname CROCKER   (all children born _____, Maine)
  348. Antoinette Emma   born ca 1830/31; married James Francis-8 FOSTER 24 Sept 1851 (# 1182)
     (he son of Nathan O-7 FOSTER and Eliza MESERVE; he born ca 1829; a sailor; died 19 Dec 1918)
+ 349. CAPTAIN   born ca 1832; married Lucinda KENNEY
    JACOB BARTER   (resided Machiasport, Maine)
  350. Charles F.   born ca 1836; 1m. Josephine HOYT 16 Aug 1854 Machiasport, ME
              (she born 1837; died 1859 East Machias, ME)
              2m. Julia HOLMES (she dau/o Ebenezer HOLMES and Susan DENNISON)
      Note: Charles may have died before 1900. His wife was listed as Head of Household on the Census.
        Children born between 1881-1900 (at least 1 son and 1 daughter)

109. ISAAC-4 RICHARDS, brother of above, was born 22 Dec 1793. He married Charity HOLMES Clark ca ___. She was the daughter of James HOLMES and Sally BERRY Lyon, the widow of Charles CLARK, and was born 14 Sept 1797 Machiasport, ME; died there 13 May 1869. Isaac-4 RICHARDS served in the War of 1812, and died 11 June 1893 at Bristol, Lincoln County, Maine.

Children of Isaac-4 RICHARDS and Charity HOLMES Clark:
    Surname RICHARDS
+ 351. ABIGAIL G.   born ca 1840; married Albert Nelson INGALLS
              (he born 4 Oct 1838 Grand Manaan, Washington Co., Maine)

110. CAPTAIN JAMES-4 RICHARDS, son of Hannah-3 CROCKER (Timothy-2) and William-7 RICHARDS, III, was born ca 1796 at Bristol, Maine. He married Hannah Keyes HARRIMAN, intentions published 30 Aug 1820 at Bristol. She was the daughter of Joshua Jewett HARRIMAN (Asa) and Betsey KEYS/KEYES of Prospect (Ferry), Maine. She was born 3 Jan 1799; died 1 Oct 1876/78 at Bristol, Maine. Captain James-4 RICHARDS died 13 Aug 1856. (Ref: Gravestones of Muscongus Cemetery ; LDS-IGI)

Children of Captain James-4 RICHARDS and Hannah Keyes HARRIMAN:
    Surname RICHARDS   (children born Bristol, Maine)
+ 352. DIODEMA   born 10 Jan 1821; married Richard Heagan KILLMAN 8 Sept 1841
    HARRIMAN   (he born 10 May 1818; died 22 Oct 1889) (she died 22 May 1903)
  353. Captain James H. born July 1834; married Elizabeth/Mary M. PERKINS 6 June 1858 Bristol
             (she born Apr 1838; died 7 Jul 1867; buried Maple Grove Cemetery)

114. CHARLES-4 CLARK, son of Sally-3 CROCKER (Timothy-2) and William CLARK, was born ___, poss at Machias, Maine. He married Charity HOLMES ca ____. She was the daughter of James HOLMES and Sally BERRY Lyons, and was born 14 Sept 1797; died 13 May 1869. She married second to Isaac-4 RICHARDS (# 109). Charles CLARK died ____.

Children of Charles-4 CLARK and Charity HOLMES:
    Surname CLARK
+ 354. CAPTAIN   born ca 1823; married Jane HOLMES after 1860
    QUINCY A.   (she dau/o Jonathan HOLMES and Abigail AMES)
              (1860 he was single; a master mariner; residing Machiasport, ME)
  355. John   born ____
  356. James   born ____; married Lucinda FLETCHER;
      (she dau/o William FLETCHER (# 94) and Lydia HOLMES) (she 2m. Elijah HUNTLEY)
        2 children : Adelbert-6 and William-6 CLARK

115. ABIGAIL-4 CLARK, sister of above, was born ca Apr 1786 probably at Bristol, Maine. She married Captain Isaac AMES on ____. He was the son of Mark AMES and Priscilla HOWLAND, and was born ca 1785; died 12 Mar 1854 (age 69). Abigail-4 CLARK died 1 Mar 1866. They are both buried at the Baptist Church Cemetery, East Machias, Maine.

Children of Abigail-4 CLARK and Captain Isaac AMES:
   Surname AMES
   357. Captain Isaac, Jr.   born ____; 1m. Hannah STEVENS (she born Feb 1806; died 5 May 1838)
                             2m. Thankful HOLMES (she born 1807; died 11 Sept 1842)
                             (resided at East Machias, Maine)
                Child of Captain Isaac-5 AMES and his 2nd wife:
                         Thankful-6 AMES born ____; married ____ BARTER

358. CAPTAIN ALFRED	born ____		361. Charles	born ____
married Mary KELLER/KELLAR			married Charlotte MARSTON	
359. Benjamin	born ____		362. Warren	born ____
360. Priscilla	born ____		363. Susan	born ____
married Charles SMITH			married Morrill MARSTON ca 1846	
			(he born 5 Dec 1820 Machiasport, ME)	

117. SARAH/SALLY-4 CLARK, sister of above, was born ca 1795 at _____. She married John COL-
BETH on 28 Jan 1816 at Machiasport, Maine. He was the son of Peter COOLBROTH/COLBETH and
Hannah LIBBY, and was born 5 Nov 1789 ____, ME.; died 7 Nov 1856 at Machiasport. Sarah-4 CLARK
died 13 Mar 1864 at Machiasport.

Children of Sarah-4 CLARK and John COLBETH:
   Surname COLBETH (all children born at Machiasport, Washington Co., ME)
   364. John   born ca 1819; married Abigail S. LIBBY ca 1840; died 1903
                 (she dau/o Luther C. LIBBY and Mary McCALEB)(she born ca 1820; died 1900)
   365. Charles   born ca 1819
   366. Albert B.   born ca 1822
   367. Dan(iel)   born ca 1823
   368. Mary E.   born May 1823/24; 1m. Elisha Coffin GRAY (he born ca 1824; died 27 May 1886)
                 2m. Horace-8 FOSTER (# 759) ca 1892; she died 7 Apr 1901
   369. Richard   born ca 1827; married Pamelia PHINNEY ca 1848
   370 Henderson   born ca 1829; married Margret HARMON 14 Aug 1858 Machiasport, ME
   371. William Austin born ca 1831; married Emmeline Augusta MITCHELL 26 June 1859
+ 372. CHARITY   born 16 Apr 1832; died 26 Oct 1916
      ELIZABETH   married Andrew Gauld JOHNSON ca 1853
   373. Thomas Jefferson born ca 1833; died 25 Dec 1885
                 1m. Hannah PROCTOR; 2m. Elizabeth H. CLARK
   374. George   born ca 1834

120. TEMPERANCE-4 CLARK, sister of above, was born ca 1804 at Machias, Maine . She married James
F. HOLMES ca ____ . He was the son of James HOLMES and Sarah/ Sally LYONS; and was born 14 May
1804; died 1874. Temperance-4 CLARK died ca 1864. They are buried at the Calais Cemetery, Calais, ME.

Children of Temperance-4 CLARK and James HOLMES:
   Surname HOLMES   (1st 2 children born Machias, ME; others born at Calais, ME)

+ 375. JAMES FRANCIS	born 1829	378. Lenora A.	born 1839; died 1843
married Mary Emeline SMITH		379. Ann Louisa	born 2 Jul 1844; died 1866
376. Charles	born 1833	380. Salem Laflin	born 25 Jun 1846; died 1849
377. Gilbert	born 1835; died 1911	381. Everett	born 1851; died 1870

The Fifth American Generation

126. TIMOTHY-5 BROOKS, Jr., son of Joanna-4 CHUTE (Mary-3 CROCKER; Captain Paul-2) and Timothy BROOKS, was born 2 Dec 1802 at Annapolis County, Nova Scotia. He married first to __?__ ; before 1833. He married second to Susan RHODES ca 1838. She was the daughter of John RHODES, and was born ____; died ___. Timothy-5 BROOKS, Jr. died 7 May 1888.

Children of Timothy-5 BROOKS, Jr. and ___?__ :
   Surname BROOKS
+ 382. ISRAEL   born Dec 1833; married Julia A. STEADMAN ca 1854; died ca 1869
+ 383. MARY ANN   born 12 July 1835; married John Eber CHUTE
   384. Elizabeth E.   born 11 Oct 1837; married Foster BROOKS ca 1857
Children of Timothy-5 BROOKS, Jr. and Susan RHODES:
   385. Phoebe R.   born 15 Sept 1842 ; married John Edward FARNSWORTH ca 1860
   386. John Fletcher   born 11 July 1845; married Julia BROWN 10 Apr 1874
   387. Joanna A.   born 3 Dec 1850; married George WHITMAN 9 Mar 1887
   388. Lloyd D.   born 16 Dec 1854; married Hattie SNOW

130. FANNY-5 CHANDLER, daughter of Elizabeth P-4 CHUTE (Mary-3 CROCKER; Captain Paul-2) and Richard CHANDLER, was born ca 1793 at Annapolis County, Nova Scotia. She married John LINGLEY ca 18__. He was the son of ____ LINGLEY, and was born ca 17__; died 18__.

Children of Fanny-5 CHANDLER and John LINGLEY:
   Surname LINGLEY
+ 389. CHARLES   born ca 1829; married his cousin Eliza MILLER (# 393); died ca 1873
   390. Elizabeth   born ca 18__   391. Frances Ellen   born ca 18__

132. MARY-5 CHANDLER, sister of above, was born ca 1797 at Annapolis County, Nova Scotia. She married John HARVEY ca 18__. He was the son of ____ HARVEY born ca 18__.

Child of Mary-5 CHANDLER and John HARVEY:
   Surname HARVEY
   392. James Richard   born ca 1820 , MA; 1m. Mary CLARK; 2m. Louise D. MILLER (# 400 below)

133. ELEANOR-5 CHANDLER, sister of above, was born ca 1800 at Annapolis County, Nova Scotia. She married James MILLER 14 Dec 1821 at ____. He was the son of ____ MILLER, and was born ____; died ca 18__. Eleanor-5 CHANDLER died ca 1879.

Children of Eleanor-5 CHANDLER and James MILLER:
   Surname MILLER
   393. Eliza   born ca 1822; married Charles LINGLEY (# 389 above)
   394. Catherine   born ca 1824; died ca 1837
   395. Ann   born ca 1827; 1m. Jacob BOGART; 2m. Charles MILLS
   396. James E.   born Jan 1829; married Horatia D. STEADMAN Nov 1852
   397. Weston   born ca 1831; married Almaretta SAUNDERS
   398. Lois   born ca 1834; married David TUCKER
   399. Joseph   born ca 1840; died ca 1842
   400. Louise D.   born ca 1836; married James Richard HARVEY (her cousin # 392 above)

171. ELIZABETH-5 CHUTE, daughter of John-4 CHUTE, 2nd (Mary-3 CROCKER; Captain Paul-2) and Abigail JONES, was born 8 Apr 1820 at Annapolis County, N S. She married John Balser-4 RICE (as his 3rd wife) ca Dec 1837 at Annapolis Co., NS. He was the son of Jonas-3 RICE (Ebenezer -2;1); and was born ca 1810; died 14 June 1852. Elizabeth-5 CHUTE married 2nd to _____ RICE, son of Silas RICE ca 1852.

Children of Elizabeth-5 CHUTE and John-4 RICE:
   Surname RICE   (all children born Annapolis County, NS)
  401. Augusta   born 16 Oct 1840; married George COSSETT
                   Child: George Ambrose –7 COSSETT born 13 Sept 1867 Hillsburgh, Digby, NS
  402. Phebe Ann   born ca 1842; died ca 1859
  403. Eliza Ann   born ca 1845; married William LEE
  404. Dorothy   born ca 1847; married John MAILING
  405. John   born ca 1852; married Jessie Maria CHUTE \
                   (dau /o Joseph CHUTE and Maria __?__) (she born ca 1856)

182. JOHN CHUTE-5 WOODMAN, son of Leah-4 CHUTE (Mary-3 CROCKER; Captain Paul-2) and Robert-9 WOODMAN (Jacob-8; Archelaus-7; Joshua-6; Jonathan-5; John-4; Edward-3;2; Thomas-1), was born 9 May 1831 at Digby, Digby, Nova Scotia. He married Mary Elizabeth RICE ca 1852. She was the daughter of Henry RICE and Zebudah RICE, and was born ca 18__; died ___. John Chute-5 WOODMAN died 16 Nov 1897.

Children of John Chute-5 WOODMAN and Mary Elizabeth RICE:
   Surname WOODMAN
+ 406. JOHN EDWARD   born 28 June 1854 Smith Cove, Digby, NS; died there Jan 1932
                   married Lydia Mae WARNE (she dau/o Hiram WARNE and Jane GAVEL)
  407. Clarence Edgar   born 12 Oct 1863 Joggin Bridge, Digby, NS; died 22 Sept 1934
  408. George W.   born ca 1865 Joggin Bridge, NS; died 6 July 1896 Worcester. MA
  409. Arthur Gordon   born ca 1867

189. ABIGAIL-5 CROCKER, daughter of John-4 CROCKER (Paul-3; 2; Pel/Paul-1) and Eliza Ann CHESLEY (Banks), was born 5/6 Apr 1827 at Wilmot, N.S. She married Captain Richard Pirl ALDRED ca 1850/51. He was the son of John Aldred and Mary PIRL/PEARL, and was born 6 Sept 1819 in England; died 22 July 1870 Nova Scotia. Abigail-5 CROCKER died 17 June 1905 at Margaretsville, Nova Scotia.

Children of Abigail-5 CROCKER and Captain Richard Pirl ALDRED:
   Surname ALDRED   (all children born Margaretsville, NS)
+ 410. JOHN   born 5 May 1852; married Lizzie Emma McMASTER 18 May 1880
    MORTIMER   died 30 June 1922 Rockville Notch, NS
+ 411. MARY   born 17 Apr 1854
    ELIZA(BETH) married William Henry MILLS 17 Nov 1882
+ 412. MARGARET A.   born 11 Sept 1855; died 19 May 1940 Hingham, MA
                   married George Thomas NOWLIN 12 Nov 1877 Boston,MA
       (he son/o Robert NOWLIN and Arminella EAGLES) (he born 1850; died 1918 Everett, MA)
  413. Richard William born 13 Jan 1857; died young   EOL
  414. Abby Elizabeth   born 15 Jul 1858; died 21 Jan 1860
+ 415. JAMES DEXTER born 21 Sept 1860; died 23 Jan 1938
                   married Jennie Mabel GORDON 3 Feb 1891
  416. Joseph Pirl   born 15 Jul 1862; married Isabelle SIMONDS 1 Jan 1908
                   died 6 Feb 1934 Kingston, NS
  417. Susan Ellen   born 31 Mar 1864; died 13 Dec 1936
                   1m. John W. SERVICE 14 Feb 1893 Nashua, NH; 2m. Joseph A. SULLIVAN
  418. Frank   born 21 Oct 1869; married Hattie ARMSTRONG
+ 419. JUDITH   born 17 Aug 1870
ELIZABETH ALBERTA married Elias Russell HIGGINS/HUGHES/HUDGINS 26 May 1891 Boston
     Reference: ALDRED Family Bible (Judith A. WHITE, Ithaca, NY. descendant); Dorothy GOULD, Rushforth, FL

190. JAMES-5 CROCKER, brother of above, was born 26 May 1829/30 at Meadowvale, Nova Scotia. He married Mary Etta LANGLEY ca 1850, at Aylesford, NS. She was the daughter of Will LANGLEY and Ann MESSINGER, and was born 29 July 1832; died 22 Feb 1909 at Rockville, NS.

Children of James-5 CROCKER and Mary Etta LANGLEY:
Surname CROCKER

+ 420. IDA MAE   born 15 May 1856 Meadowvale, NS; died 19 Feb 1945 Kingston, NS
married James Albert GOULD 2 Apr 1880
(he son/o Leonard GOULD and Nancy CAREY) (he born 3 Nov 1856; died 17 Aug 1904)

421. Anna Maria   born 26 Nov 1858, NS; died 15 Jan 1936, NS
1m. Biard BANKS; 2m. John Banks BARTEAUX

422. Charles Renfrew   born ca 1861, NS; died ca 1929 NS
1m. Nell Banks VanBUSKIRK; 2m. Ella Mae VanBUSKIRK

+ 423. MINNIE ETTA   born 27 May 1871 Hyde Park, MA; died 1952 Kingston, NS
(married Edward McMASTER 25 Dec 1894) (he born ca 1856; died 1954)

191. ALDEN BASS-5 CROCKER, brother of above, was born 16 May 1832 at Meadowvale, NS. He married Jessie Idella McMASTER on ____. She was the daughter of Thomas McMASTER and Margaret McQUARRIE, and was born ____; died ____. Alden-5 CROCKER died 25 Oct 1890 at Tremont, NS.

Children of Alden-5 CROCKER and Jessie McMASTER:
Surname CROCKER

424. Ina born __   425. Henry Elwood born _____   426. Lloyd George born ____
427. Maurice born ____   428. Thomas   born ____

198. AUSTIN WELTON-5 SPINNEY, son of Ann G-4 CROCKER (Paul-3, Jr.; Captain Paul-2) and Jacob Beach SPINNEY, was born 14 Sept 1826 Greenwood, Kings Co., Nova Scotia. He married Elizabeth Jane MORSE on 24 July 1846 at Harmony, Kings, NS. She was the daughter of _____ MORSE, and was born 1828; died 12 Nov 1904. Austin-5 SPINNEY died 18 Jan 1891. They are buried in the Greenwood (NS) Union Church Cemetery.

Children of Austin-5 SPINNEY and Elizabeth MORSE:
Surname SPINNEY

+ 429. ELIZABETH   born 1846; married Thomas Cornelius STEELE; died 7 Sept 1886 NS
     MARIA   (he born 1839; died 1920)

+ 430. MELISSA ANNIE born 1848; married Alfred Parker SAUNDERS (he born 1831)

431. Jacob Church   born 1850; died 1857   EOL

432. Charlotte Lavinia born 1851; died 1853   EOL

433. Zilpha Sophia   born 1853; died ____ unmarried   EOL

434. Jonathan Moore   born 1856; died ____ unmarried   EOL

+ 435. MINNIE SALOME born 1857; married James William JEFFERSON (he born 1853)

436. Austin Spurr   born 1859; died ____; unmarried EOL

437. Eunice Harriet   born 1862; died 1865   EOL

438. Caleb Snow   born 15 July 1865; died 1931 Harmony, Kings, NS

439. Noble Joshua   born 1867; died 1878   EOL

440. Ida Odessa   born 1871; died 1877   EOL

199. JACOB BEACH-5 SPINNEY, JR, brother of above, was born ca 1829. He married Jane R. DUNCANSON ca ____. She was born 1831; died 1910. Jacob-5 SPINNEY, Jr. died ca 1907.

Children of Jacob-5 SPINNEY, Jr. and Jane DUNCANSON:
Surname SPINNEY

441. Jacob C.   born ____; died ____ unmarried EOL

+ 442. WILLIAM G.   born 1854; married Flora Belle HUTCHINSON; died 1935
(she born 1861; died 1922)

443. Anna Irene   born 1858; married Arvard POTTER; died 1935 (he born 1863; died 1922)

444. Eliza   born 1860; died 1861   EOL

445. Harriet   born 1866; married Ernest NEILY; died 1955 (he born 1867; died 1952)

200. HARDING THEODORE-5 SPINNEY, brother of above, was born ca 1831. He married Helen F. BARTEAUX on ____. She was born 1834; died 1906. Harding-5 SPINNEY died ca 1877.

Children of Harding-5 SPINNEY and Helen BARTEAUX:
   Surname SPINNEY
   446. Ruby Lavinia   born 1857; married Albert BENSON
 + 447. JAMES BARTEAUX   born 1860; married Mary E. FITCH; died 1921
                                  (she born 1865; died 1960)
   448. Ingram Judson   born 1862; died 1862   EOL
   449. Anna Elizabeth   born 1863; married Isaiah BRUCE; died 1897
   450. Parney Samantha   born 1865; married Charles B. WILLIAM
   451. Rowena Salome   born 1870; married Noble J. LYONS

201. DEACON CALEB-5 SPINNEY, brother of above, was born ca 1833 at Aylesford, NS. He married Parnie BARTEAUX ca ____. She was born ca 1840; died 1921. Deacon Caleb-5 SPINNEY died ca 1906.

Children of Deacon Caleb-5 SPINNEY and Parnie BARTEAUX:
   Surname SPINNEY
   452. Flora Belle   born 1861; died 1934   unmarried   EOL
   453. Bertha Maude   born 1863; married Avery BANKS; died 1939 (he born 1867; died 1944)
   454. Ulysses Grant   born 1865; died 1865   EOL
 + 455. EDWARD   born 1867; married Bessie WEBBER; died 1961
        MANNING   (she born 1868; died 1962)
   456. Mary Jane   born 1870; married Herbert BURKE
   457. Julia Etta   born 1872; married Reuben SMILEY
   458. Helen Amanda   born 1874; married _____ GRAVES

203. BERIAH B-5 SPINNEY, brother of above, was born ca 1838. He married Mary Jane WHITMAN ca ____. She was the daughter of _____ WHITMAN, and was born 1843; died 1869. Beriah-5 died ca 1923.

Children of Beriah-5 SPINNEY and Mary Jane WHITMAN:
   Surname SPINNEY
 + 459. MELBOURNE E. born 1864; married Harriet SMALL; died 1928   (she born 1862; died 1952)

204. ENOCH-5 SPINNEY, brother of above, was born ca 1840. He married Phebe BOWLBY ca ____. She was the daughter of ____ BOWLBY, and was born 1845; died 1922. Enoch-5 SPINNEY died 1907.

Children of Enoch-5 SPINNEY and Phebe BOWLBY:
   Surname SPINNEY
   460. Lily Blanche   born 1863; died 1865   EOL
   461. Blanche Lily   born 1865; married ___ JEFFERSON; died 1908
   462. Everett Lamont   born 1868
   463. George Elburn   born 1870; died 1924
   464. Harry Atwood   born 1874; married Bertha __?__ ; died 1901
 + 465. LELAND   born 1875; married Agnes Georgeanna HARRIS; died 1950
        TEASDALE   (she born 1877; died 1952)

206. CLARK THOMAS-5 SPINNEY, brother of above, was born 20 June 1846 at Greenwood, Kings Co., N S. He married Orinda SLOCUM ca ____. She was born 1855; died 1944. Clark-5 SPINNEY died 1926.

Children of Clark-5 SPINNEY and Orinda SLOCUM:
   Surname SPINNEY
   466. Annas/Annis W.   born 1874; died 1894 unmarried   EOL
   467. Althea L.   born ____; married Everett SMITH (2 ch: Everett and Laura SMITH)

Children of Clark-5 SPINNEY, continued;
   Surname SPINNEY
+ 468. BURPEE A.   born 1883; married Maria Leona STEELE; died 1969
                         (she born 1891; died 1974)
  469. Georgia E.   born 1887; died 1936

207. CALVIN-5 CROCKER, son of James-4 CROCKER (Paul-3; Captain Paul-2) and his 1st wife Abigail TUPPER, was born ca 1828, Nova Scotia. He married Catherine SAUNDERS ca ____. She was the daughter of _____ SAUNDERS, and was born ca 1834; died 1902. Calvin-5 CROCKER died 1899.

Children of Calvin-5 CROCKER and Catherine SAUNDERS:
   Surname CROCKER
  470. James H. born 1859   471. William M. born 1862   472. Martha A.   born 1872

208. JOHN M-5 CROCKER, half-brother of above, son of James-4 CROCKER and his 2nd wife Jane SPINNEY, was born 23 Dec 1836 at Aylesford, Kings County, Nova Scotia. He married Mary Adelaide BRENNAN on 7 Oct 1865 at Aylesford. She was the daughter of Patrick BRENNAN and Catherine HUDGINS, and was born 21 May 1846; died 10 May 1925 at Greenwood, Kings County, NS. John-5 CROCKER died 13 Jan 1915 at Greenwood.

Children of John-5 CROCKER and Mary Adelaide BRENNAN:
   Surname CROCKER   (all children born Harmony, Kings County, Nova Scotia)
+ 473. ROULOF W.   born 29 Aug 1865; died 20 Dec 1934 Westboro, Worcester Co., MA
                     married Charlotte A. JACKSON 7 June 1892 at Millville, Kings, NS
                     (she born 1871; died 1933)
+ 474. AMORET JANE   born 15 Nov 1866; married Albert Ralph CHARLTON 1 July 1887
                     (he born 4 Aug 1862; died 24 May 1933, MA)
                     (he son/o Solomon Simpson CHARLTON and Mary Elizabeth DELONG)
                     died 15 June 1943 Worcester, MA
  475. Mary Ann   born 29 Aug 1867; died 1940
                     married Judson A. MONROE 26 Sept 1888 at Kingston, Kings, NA
                     (he born 1866; died ____) (2 ch: Lizzie B. born 1889; Ernest born 1890)
  476. Nellie N.   born Feb 1872; died Apr 1960
                     married Stephen COLLINS 2 Dec 1897 (he born 1868)
  477. Katherine E.   born 4 July 1874; married Owen BANKS 14 Feb 1902 Harmony, NS
                     died 18 Feb 1952 Waterville, NS
+ 478. LAMERT   born 3 Aug 1880; died 14 Dec 1956 Kentville, Kings, NS
     STEPHEN   married Agnes E. WINOTT 6 Nov 1907 Harmony, NS
                     (she born 1882; died 1987)
  479. Charlotte Blanche born Dec 1886; died 20 Feb 1887   EOL
  480. Harriet Blanche born 1889; married Percy Berwell EWING 5 June 1911; died 7 Jan 1983
            Child: Mildred-7 EWING born ____; married ____ BENSON (resided MA)

209. HARRISON G-5 CROCKER, son of John-4 CROCKER (James Wheeler-3; John-2) and Sally BERRY, was born 8 Aug 1809 Machias, ME. He married Cynthia-7 LONGFELLOW ca ____. She was the daughter of Jonathan-6 LONGFELLOW and Sally BOYNTON, and was born ca 1807; died ____. She married 2nd to Caleb-S-4 CROCKER (# 66). Harrison-5, a lumberman, died ____.

Children of Harrison G-5 CROCKER and Cynthia-7 LONGFELLOW:
   Surname CROCKER
  481. Lewis born ca 1837   482. Edward born ca 1841   483. Hanford   born ca 1845

210. SAMUEL GOULD-5 CROCKER, brother of above, was born 20 Jan 1811 at Machias, Maine. He was residing at Marshfield, Maine when he married Susan H-7 LONGFELLOW Lyon on 19 Oct 1848 at

Machias, the Rev Amos BROWN officiating. She was the daughter of Jonathan-6 LONGFELLOW and Sally BOYNTON, and was born ca 1816; died ____. She was married 1st to James H. LYON, by whom she had: i. Julia M B LYON, born 1839, married Watts Henry BOWKER; ii. Henrietta LYON, born 1843, married George W. CAMPBELL; iii. James H. LYON, Jr. born 1845, married Emma DREW; and iv. Levi T. LYON, born 1847.   Samuel-5 CROCKER, a lumberman at Machias, Maine died ____.

Children of Samuel G-5 CROCKER and Susan-7 LONGFELLOW:
   Surname CROCKER
+ 484. GILBERT   born June 1850; married Martha WRIGHT
   485. Calista   born 1853; married John E. HARMON
        Ch: Orris V-7 HARMON born ____; married May BURROWS; Ernest –7 HARMON born ___
   486. Betsey   born 1857/58

212.   MARY-5 CROCKER, sister of above, was born 16 Feb 1815 at Machias, ME. She married Alfred GARDNER ca ____. He was the son of Thomas GARDNER and Sarah BERRY/BARRY, and was born 16 July 1812; died ____. Mary-5 CROCKER died before 1850, and Alfred GARDNER married 2nd to Hannah M. FOSS (she born 1833, Maine). They had 3 children: William born 1852; Lyman B. born 1854; and Frederick H. born May 1860. Alfred Gardner married 3rd to Lizzie M. HARMON on 2 Feb 1862. He was a farmer at Hadley's Lake, Maine – on the farm where he was raised.

Children of Mary-5 CROCKER and Alfred GARDNER:
   Surname GARDNER
   487. Peter Harris   born 4 Mar 1838; died 3 Mar 1840
   488. Henry Lyons   born 5 Dec 1839; died 2 Feb 1840
   489. Jacob William   born 27 Mar 1841; married Sophia BURTON 19 Apr 1868; res. Eureka, CA
+ 490. MARY   born 26 May 1843; died 31 Dec 1885;   1m. James T. GARDNER 1858
        ELIZABETH   (he son/o James A. GARDNER and Almira KILTON) served in the **Civil War**
                          2m. Daniel Webster-5 HARMON
                          (he son/o Hiram-4 HARMON and Mary GARDNER) (he born 19 May 1852)
   491. Olive Catherine   born 9 Jan 1846; died 14 Feb 1849
   492. Delia   born 17 Feb 1848; died July 1880; married Morton D. HARMON 2 Oct 1867
                          (he son/o Henry HARMON and Mary Jane WHITTEMORE)

213. REBECCA-5 CROCKER, sister of above, was born 30 Dec 1820 at Machias, Maine. She married Hiram GARDNER on 27 July 1843. He was the brother of Alfred GARDNER (above) who married Rebecca's sister Mary (# 212). He was a successful lumberman and resided Machias, ME. Hiram Gardner was born 18 June 1819; died ____. Rebecca-5 CROCKER died 1902. 1860 resided Marshfield, Maine.

Children of Rebecca-5 CROCKER and Hiram GARDNER:
   Surname GARDNER
+ 493. AMELIA   born 9 June 1844; married Gilbert LaFayette-5 HARMON 31 May 1869
                          (he son/o Hiram-4 HARMON and Mary GARDNER) (he born 1840, a **Civil War** Veteran)
   494. Donna Viola   born 23 Feb 1846; died 1899
   495. George E.   born 10 Feb 1849; died 24 Dec 1868
   496. Morey   born 15 Apr 1852; married Susan N. LYNCH 28 Nov 1872
   497. Emma Lucy   born 17 July 1854; died 9 Sept 1879
   498. Addie Rosa   born 9 Dec 1858; died 28 Mar 1872
   499. Angelica M.   born 24 Dec 1861; died 15 Jul 1877
                  Reference: GARDNER Family of Machias and Vicinity by Charles ANDREWS, Augusta, ME.

222. WILLIAM PENNIMAN-5 LYON, son of Betsey-4 CROCKER (James Wheeler-3; John-2) and Henry LYON, was born ca 1818, probably at Machias, Maine. He married Sarah-4 GETCHELL ca ____. She was the daughter of Simeon-3 GETCHELL and Betsey BOWKER, and was born ca 1827; died ___. William-5 LYON died before 1881.

Children of William-5 LYON and Sarah-4 GETCHELL:
    Surname LYON
+ 500. GEORGE M.   born 1846; married Jennie BERRY
+ 501. WILLIAM   born 1848; married Josephine Ermina-8 LEIGHTON
      HENRY   (she dau/o Joseph-7 LEIGHTON and Susan VOSE)
  502. Amelia G.   born 1850
+ 503. SIMEON G.   born 1852; married Hannah SEDGLEY
  504. Sanford P.   born 1854; married Sarah ELLISON ca 1877 Machias, Maine
                          2 children: Marion-7 LYON and George-7 LYON
  505. Lizzie/Eliza   born 1857; married Willis BLOOD (3 ch: Fred, Charles and Leon-7 BLOOD)
+ 506. ANDREW G.   born May 1860, Marshfield, ME; married Catharine CLARK

223. WARREN-5 LYON, brother of above, was born ca 1823/24 at Machias, Maine. He married
Phyzannah NORTON ca ____. She was the daughter of _____ NORTON, and was born ca 1832/33.
(1850 Census Marshfield, ME listed Warren LYON as a laborer; in 1860 he was listed as a farmer.)

Children of Warren-5 LYON and Phyzannah NORTON:
    Surname LYON
+ 507. OTIS   born June 1850; married Marjery BUTLER
  508. Anna/Hannah   born 1853   510. Cyrus   born 1857
  509. Herbert   born 1854   511. Edwin   born 1859

224. AMELIA-5 LYON, sister of above, was born ___ at Machias, Maine. She married Bryant GATES
ca 1842. He was the son of _____ GATES, and was born ca 1818 Machias, Maine; died ____.

Children of Amelia-5 LYON and Bryant GATES:
    Surname GATES
  512. Adalida   born 1843/44
  513. Banning   born ca 1845; married Melissa HANSCOM ca 1869 Machias, ME.
                    2 children: Austin B-7 GATES; and George D-7 GATES

225. CYRUS-5 LYON, brother of above, was born ___ at Machias, Maine. He married Inez/Ynez COTA
ca ____. She was the daughter of ___ COTA , and was born ____; died ___, CA. Cyrus-5 LYON died ____
CA, and is buried at the Evergreen Cemetery in Los Angeles, CA.

Children of Cyrus-5 LYON and Inez/Ynez COTA:
    Surname LYON
  514. Irene Rebecca   born ____; married Don Juan RHODA
  515. Alice Ophelia   born ____; married Charles FREEMAN
  516. Cyrus, Jr.   born ca 1855; married Lela CALVERT/CALAVERT
  517. Robert Merrill   born ____;
  518. Anna   born ____; died in infancy
  519. Arthur Edward   born ____; married Eva Mabel HALL (child: Arthur-7 LYON, Jr.)

226. SANFORD-5 LYON, brother of above, was born ca 1832 at Machias, Maine. He married Annie T.
HANSCOM after 1860. She was the daughter of _____ HANSCOM, and was born ___; died ____.

Children of Sanford-5 LYON and Annie HANSCOM:
    Surname LYON
  520. Lewis H.   born ____; married Ida J. MYERS (Child: Carrie/ Carolyn-7 LYON born __)
  521. Carrie   born ____; married Charles DENENDOR (2 ch: Frank –7 and Charlie-7)
  522. Annie Betsey   born ____; married Lewis R. TARR (2 ch: Harold –7 and Floyd-7 TARR)
  523. Addie Warren   born ____; married ____ STEVENS (Child: Edith-7 STEVENS)
  524. Frank   born ____; died at age 6

228. HELEN J/G-5 CROCKER, daughter of Captain Otis-4 CROCKER (James Wheeler-3; John-2) and Sarah O'BRIEN, was born ca 1828 at Machias, ME. She married Ladwick-5 HOLWAY on 23 Oct 1851 at Machias, the Rev G. BACHELLER officiating. Ladwick-5 was the son of John-4 HOLWAY ++ (Ladwick-3; Martha O'BRIEN-2; Morris-1) and Leonice H. CROCKER, and was born 27 July 1822, died ____. ++ John-4 HOLWAY married Leonice CROCKER 9 June 1816. They had 3 children: i. William Crocker HOLWAY born 5 Dec 1817; ii. Elizabeth born 29 Jan 1820 and LADWICK-5 (above)

Children of Helen-5 CROCKER and Ladwick HOLWAY:
    Surname HOLWAY
    525. Lewis   born ____   526. Gertrude   born ____

235. LEVI B-5 THAXTER, son of Sally-4 CROCKER (James Wheeler-3; John-2) and Henry THAXTER, was born ca 1822 at Machias, Maine. He married Susan BURNHAM ca ____. She was the daughter of George BURNHAM (grandson of Job) and Mary LONGFELLOW (Isaac) , and was born ca 1824/25; died ____. Levi-5 THAXTER, a ships' carpenter, died ____.

Children of Levi-5 THAXTER and Susan BURNHAM:
    Surname THAXTER
+ 527. GEORGE W/H   born 1848/49   530. Hattie M.   born 1858
                  married Sabrina COOK   531. Fred   born ca 1859; died young
    528. Laura E.   born 1852   532. Levi, Jr.   born Jan 1860
    529. Delia E. born 1854; married Alden G. DAVIS

237. A. WALLACE-5 THAXTER, brother of above, was born ca ___, Maine. He married Mary BURNHAM ca ____. She was the sister of Susan BURNHAM who married Levi B THAXTER.

Children of A. Wallace-5 THAXTER and Mary BURNHAM:
    Surname THAXTER
    533. Henry   born ____   534. Clara   born ____

259. MERCY LONGFELLOW-5 CROCKER, daughter of Mariner Green-4 CROCKER (James Wheeler-3; John-2) and Martha-6 LONGFELLOW, was born 14 May 1822 at Machias, Maine. She married Abel CURTIS ca ___. He was the son of Abel CURTIS, Sr. ++ and Lucy MOREY, and was born 4 July 1814 Fairlee, VT; died 22 May 1882 at Machias, Maine. Mercy-5 CROCKER died 18 Apr 1907 at Machias.

Children of Mercy-5 CROCKER and Abel CURTIS (Jr):
    Surname CURTIS
    535. Charles Bissell   born 1844; married Elvie JAMES, OR
                              (1 ch: Edna-7; married Geo. TRULLINGER)
    536 George Morey   born 1846; died 1846   EOL
+ 537. LUCY MOREY   born 10 Mar 1851'; married James Henry-10 BAILEY 1 Feb 1873
+ 538. EDWARD   born 20 Feb 1853, Machias, ME; married Mary Augusta COLSON
         BISSELL   (she dau/o Captain Gilman COLSON and Mary Elizabeth WILSON)
                            (she born 11 Aug 1865 Lexington, MA; died 9 Dec 1951 Machias, ME)
                            died 15 Apr 1927 Machias, ME
    539. Martha/Mattie   born 1861; died ____ unmarried   EOL
         Crocker
    540. Daniel A.   born 1863; married Annie M. PERRY
                ++ Note: Abel CURTIS, Sr. was born 15 July 1782 at Hanover, NH; died 20 Sept 1863.

261. ALVIN G-5 CROCKER, brother of above, was born ca 1826 at Machias, Maine. He married JULIA A-8 FOSTER (# 982) on 2 Sept 1849 at Machias., John C. ADAMS officiating. She was the daughter of Lewis-7 FOSTER (Elias-6; Woodin-5; Benjamin-4;3; Isaac-2; Reginald-1) and Julia PINEO, and was born ca 1831/32; died ____. Alvin-5 CROCKER, a lumberman, died ___.

Children of Alvin G-5 CROCKER and Julia A-8 FOSTER:
  Surname CROCKER
   541. Lewis   born Apr 1850
   542. Everett   born 185_; married Martha THERIN (1 ch: Edna-7 CROCKER)
 + 543. DR. FRANK H.   born 1852; married Lucy H. CRANE; died June 1903 Gardiner, ME
        (FRANCIS)   (she dau/o Abijah CRANE and Lydia T. GILPATRICK)
   544. Elizabeth   born 1854; married Frank GLESSNER (2 ch: Agnes and Alvin-7 GLESSNER)
   545. George   born 1856; married Mary AVERILL (1 ch: Lewis-7 CROCKER)
 + 546. FANNIE   born Jan/Feb 1860; married Fred WILLEY
   547. Ellen   born 186_; married George MARTIN (no issue) EOL

264. CYRUS STRONG-5 CROCKER, brother of above, was born ca 1832 at Machias, Maine. He
married Martha H. Peach-8 SMITH on 6 Jan 1855. She was the daughter of Moses-7 SMITH and Mary
CARLETON, and was born ca 1834 at Jonesboro, Maine; died June 1908. Cyrus-5 CROCKER died
_____. Martha married second to George F. HANSCOM of Machias.

Children of Cyrus-5 CROCKER and Martha-8 SMITH:
  Surname CROCKER
   548. Charles   born _____   +550. ANNA/ANNIE M. ++   born _____
   549. Frederic   born _____

266. SUSAN AMELIA-5 CROCKER, sister of above, was born ca 1836 at Machias, ME. She married
Flavius Josephus MOORE ca 1869. He was the son of Witter Davison MOORE and Penelope Hunt
MABEE, and was born 6 June 1829 at St. David, New Brunswick, Canada.

Child of Susan-5 CROCKER and Flavius MOORE:
  Surname MOORE + 551. ELLA F. born 187_; married Harry L. GILSON 14 Oct 1896 Machias, ME

269. NEWELL W-5 CROCKER, brother of above, was born ca 1844 at Machias, Maine. He married
Antoinette CATES on 5 Apr 1869 at Machias. She was the daughter of Atkins S. CATES ++ and Susan
PALMER, and was born 18__. They divorced 19 Mar 1886 at Machias. Newell-5 CROCKER moved to
Amador, CA.   ++ Note: Atkins S. CATES, a ship master, was the son of Henry CATES and Betsey MARSTON (Samuel)
of Machiasport, ME. He was born 1813. Susan PALMER was the daughter of Daniel PALMER and Mary ALBEE (Lt. William)

Child of Newell-5 CROCKER and Antoinette CATES:
  Surname CROCKER
   552. Czarina Henry   born _____; married Fred Marston SWITZER 27 July 1898 Machias, ME
        (he was a native of Chelsea, MA; res. Halifax, NS)   2 ch: Katherine-7 and Harl-7 SWITZER

273. LYDIA GOODHUE-5 LONGFELLOW, daughter of Hannah-4 CROCKER (James Wheeler-3;
John-2) and Amos LONGFELLOW, was born 1828 at Machias, Maine. She married Isaac HEATON,
a lumberman, ca _____. He was the son of Isaac HEATON (James) +++ and Lois STARRETT, and was
born 17 Dec 1820 Hillsborough, NH; died _____. (Isaac HEATON was listed on the Census as a boom
master) According to the Webster's Dictionary – the term, in lumbering, refers to i. a barrier across a river,
or around an area of water, to prevent logs from dispersing; and ii. the area in which logs are confined.)
         +++ NOTE: James HEATON born 20 Nov 1748; married Susanna __?__ ca 17__; died 11 Apr 1811.
      Susanna was born 16 Dec 1758; died 3 Dec 1823. Their son Isaac HEATON (Sr.) was born 9 July 1794; died 8 Feb 1867.

Children of Lydia Goodhue-5 LONGFELLOW and Isaac HEATON:
  Surname HEATON   (all children born Machias, Washington Co., Maine)
   553. Hannah L.   born 1848   556. Mary E.   born _____
   554. Emily A.   born Sept 1849   557. Amos S.   born _____
 + 555. SARAH   born 7 Feb 1852   558. Hattie M. born _____
        LONGFELLOW   married Horace-8 LEIGHTON

276. SAMUEL S-5 CROCKER, son of Stephen-4 CROCKER (Simeon-3; John-2) and Jane STARRETT, was born 7 Nov 1839 at Warren, Maine. He married Lizzie ANGIER on 1 Nov 1862. She was the daughter of ____ ANGIER, and was born ___; died ___. She was from Royalston, MA.

Children of Samuel-5 CROCKER and Lizzie ANGIER:
Surname CROCKER   (all children born Marlboro, MA)

559. Jennie	born 13 Feb 1864	561. Albion M.	born 5 Mar 1871
560. Charles	born 2 Oct 1869		died 31 Aug 1871 EOL

281.   ADDIE A-5 HOLMES, daughter of Jane-4 CROCKER (Simeon-3; John-2) and Obed (iah) HOLMES, was born ca ____ at Machias, Maine. She married Samuel W. HILL ca ____. He was the son of Warren HILL + (Obadiah, Jr; Obadiah) and Maria B. SHAW, and was born 1858 at Machias; died ____.
+ NOTE: Warren Hill, born 1827; married Maria SHAW of Gouldsboro, Maine. She was born ca 1830. Children were SAMUEL; Walter; Sarah P.; and Edwin. 1860 they resided Machias. Obadiah HILL, Jr , son of Obadiah, Sr. and Sara HARRIS, was born 8 Aug 1786 at Machias, and married Sally PIERCE Pope.

Children of Addie-5 HOLMES and Samuel HILL:
Surname HILL

		564. Jeanette M.	born ____
562. Charles F.	born ____	565. Warren M.	born ____
563. Carrie E.	born ____		married Grace S. MORRISON 9 July 1917 ME

284. NATHAN STEVEN-5 BOWKER, son of Martha G-4 CROCKER (Simeon-3; John-2) and Levi BOWKER, Jr., was born 15 May 1826. He married Mary Abigail-8 BERRY ca 1850. She was the daughter of Stephen-7 BERRY (John-6; 5; Elisha-4; Joseph-3; 2; William-1) and Rebecca BERRY, and was born 28 Nov 1827; died 16 Sept 1911. Nathan-5 BOWKER died 18 July 1910.

Children of Nathan S-5 BOWKER and Mary Abigail BERRY:
Surname BOWKER

+ 566. SIMEON	born 20 Jan 1851; married Keziah J. HOLMES 2 Mar 1872; died 1 May 1907		
OSCAR	(she dau/o Tristam HOLMES and Hannah Knight BERRY)		
+ 567. FERDINAND B.	born ca 185_; married Lillie PALMER ca 1882 Marshfield, ME		
568. Stephen	born ca 18__	570. Ada F.	born ca 18__
569. Samuel C.	born ca 18__		married Dayton W. SMITH 26 May 1897

285. FERDINAND-5 BOWKER, brother of above, was born ca ____. He married Lucy L-3 BOYNTON 2 Oct 1850. She was the daughter of Stephen-2 BOYNTON ++ (Amos-1) and Hannah JEWETT. Ferdinand-5 BOWKER died 1852.
++ Stephen-2 BOYNTON was born 10 June 1787 at Machias, Maine. Still living 1860; residing with (2nd) wife Mary, plus Lucy BOWKER (d-i-l), Mary BOYNTON 17; and Levi BOWKER 9. Amos-1 BOYNTON was the first BOYNTON settler in Machias.

Children of Ferdinand-5 BOWKER and Lucy-3 BOYNTON:
Surname BOWKER   (children born Machias, Maine)

571. Levi	born 20 May 1851; 1m. ____ MUNSON of Milltown, ME; (2 ch) div
	2m. _____; she from New York State
572. Child	born ____; died young

289. MARTHA A-5 BOWKER, sister of above, was born 4 Apr 1837 at Machias, Maine. She married Roscoe Green-3 BOYNTON ca ____. He was born 13 July 1836 Machias, ME. died ___.

Children of Martha-5 BOWKER and Roscoe-3 BOYNTON:
Surname BOYNTON

573. Almira	born 1862; died 1884	576. George B. *	born 1870, living 1904
574. Annie	born 1865; died 1880		Machias
+ 575. EMILY J.	born ca 1867/68		
	married Bradford ESTEY	* He was a clerk and later manager of the Machias branch of the Eastern Trust & Banking Co.	

291. GEORGE W-5 FLYNN, son of Abigail-4 CROCKER (Simeon-3; John-2) and William FLYNN, was born ca 1828/31 at Cherryfield, Washington County, Maine. He married first to Mary J. LONG-FELLOW ca ____. She was born ca 1832; died ___. He married second to Thirza J-5 GETCHELL ca ___. She was the daughter of Marshfield-4 GETCHELL (John-3; Joseph-2;1) and Martha J. HOLMES, and was born ____. No issue. She was the sister of Dora-5 GETCHELL, who married Horace W. FLYNN.

Child of George W-5 FLYNN and Mary J. LONGFELLOW:
 Surname FLYNN
 577. Ella J.   born ca 1856; married Albert CROWELL
        2 children: Cora A-7 and Martha G-7 CROWELL

292. ABAGAIL C-5 FLYNN, sister of above was born ca 1833 at Cherryfield, Maine. She married Arthur R. NASH , a shoemaker, ca ____. He was the son of William Bingham NASH (John) and Triphena LEIGHTON, and was born ca 1827, Cherryfield; died ____. Abigail-5 died ____.

Child of Abagail-5 FLYNN and Arthur R. NASH:
 Surname NASH
 578. Emma born ca 1855; married Arthur HUTCHINSON (1 dau: Emma-7 HUTCHINSON)

295. SOPHIA H-5 CROCKER, daughter of George Waterhouse-4 CROCKER (Simeon-3; John-2) and Lucinda HARMON, was born ca 1835 at Machias, Maine. She married Thomas WILLIAMSON ca ____.

Children of Sophia-5 CROCKER and Thomas WILLIAMSON:
 Surname WILLIAMSON
+ 579. MARY D. born ____; 1m. Captain A Lee WATERHOUSE; 2m. John WHITTEMORE
 580. Amanda born ____; married Charles W. SMITH (1 ch: Walter-7; marr Lena GRAVES)
 581. Lucinda born ____; married Osmer A. CASE (2 ch: Maurice-7 and Hillman-7 CASE)
 582. John   born ____; married _____ BISHOP (2 ch: Alfred-7 and Sophia-7 BISHOP)

296. DELIA A-5 CROCKER, sister of above, was born 1 June 1837 at Machias, Maine. She married Horace T. GARDNER, a very successful lumberman, at Machias, on 1 Sept 1853. He was the son of Thomas GARDNER +++ (Ebenezer) and Sarah BERRY, and was born 11 May 1830; died ____.
  +++ Thomas GARDNER was born 10 Oct 1783 at Machias; 1m. Sarah BERRY 1 Dec 1808 (she daughter of
    Jonathan BERRY and Hannah KNIGHT) Thomas GARDNER died 17 Dec 1872.

Children of Delia-5 CROCKER and Horace T. GARDNER:
 Surname GARDNER   Reference: GARDNER Genealogy, page 249
 583. Albert   born 22 Dec 1854; died 31 Dec 1854
 584. Ella M.   born 21 Nov 1856; died 24 Nov 1856
 585. William E. born 18 Apr 1859; married Harriet CROWLEY 25 Dec 1879
       2 children: Angelia-7 GARDNER and Ethel –7 GARDNER
 586. Evelyn S. born 20 Dec 1864; died 20 Aug 1865

312. IDA BELL-5 HARMON, daughter of Mary Catherine-4 CROCKER (Simeon-3; John-2) and John Fisher HARMON, was born 23 June 1856 Marshfield, ME. She married Deola C-5 GETCHELL ca ____. He was the son of Marshfield-4 GETCHELL (John-3; Joseph-2;1) and Martha J. HOLMES, and was born 6 Aug 1851. Originally, Deola-5 GETCHELL was engaged in the grain trading business with his father. They had a mill at Marshfield, Maine. Later, he built a mill at Machias, equipped with all the facilities for handling grain. It was said to be the best grist mill in the county. In 1904 his business had grown in production, and produced 40 - 50,000 bushels annually.

Children of Ida-5 HARMON and Deola-5 GETCHELL:
 Surname GETCHELL (children all born Marshfield, Maine)

587. Maude	born 15 Mar 1875; d y	590 Thomas	born 1 May 1881
588. Mina/Nina	born 4 Mar 1876	591. Mary	born ca 1883
589. Guy	born 28 Oct 1877		

315. TIMOTHY-5 BEAN, son of Timothy-4 BEAN (Mary/Molly-3 CROCKER; Timothy-2; Peletiah-1) and Hannah KIMBALL, was born 6 Apr 1813 at Bethel, Maine. He married first to Lovina D. RUSSELL on 30 Apr 1842 at Bethel. He married second to Elizabeth E. SWIFT on 12 Mar 1846 at Bethel.

Children of Timothy-5 BEAN and _?_:
Surname BEAN	Reference: JORDAN Memorial by Tristam JORDAN, pages 108-09; published 1882
592. Ella H.	born ca 184_ Greenwood, Oxford Co., Maine
	married Cushman-10 JORDAN 4 May 1870
	(he was a spoolmaker; they resided Waterford, Maine)

(he was the son/o John-9 JORDAN (Abraham-8; Humphrey-7; Joseph-6; Robert-5; John-4; Robert-3; Edward-2; Thomas-1)
Child: Harry E-7 JORDAN born Feb 1871, another child born 1 Sept 1878

317. LUCINDA-5 BEAN, daughter of Luther-4 BEAN (Molly/Mary-3 CROCKER; Timothy-2; Peletiah-1) and Lydia KIMBALL, was born ca 1817 at Rumford, Oxford Co., ME. She married Hezekiah HUTCHINS ca ___. He was the son of _____ HUTCHINS, and was born ca 1813 Rumford, Maine.

Child of Lucinda-5 BEAN and Hezekiah HUTCHINS:
Surname HUTCHINS	
593. Jane M.	born 20 July 1839 Rumford, Oxford Co., Maine
	1m. Nathan Clifford KNAPP ____ Rumford, Maine
	(he born 11 Feb 1840 Rumford, ME: died 7 Nov 1863 Rumford)
	2m. Charles W. KIMBALL ca 1864 Rumford, Maine

319. ELIPHAZ-5 BEAN, son of Edmund-4 BEAN (Mary/Molly-3 CROCKER; Timothy-2; Peletiah-1) and Emma KIMBALL, was born 25 July 1813 at Bethel, Oxford, Maine. He married Sarah B. FARNUM 27 May 1838 at Bethel. She was the daughter of David Hall FARNUM and Maria BARTLETT, and was born ca 1820 at Rumford, Maine.

Children of Eliphaz-5 BEAN and Sarah FARNUM:
Surname BEAN	(all children born at Bethel, Oxford County, Maine)
594. Loretta P.	born 9 Sept 1839
	married James Osgood BROWN 28 Oct 1860 Bethel (he born ca 1835 Bethel)
595. Emma Maria	born 20 July 1841; married Edmund MERRILL, Jr. 4 Mar 1860
	(he son/o Edmund MERRILL and Relief F. FROST)
	(he born 12 May 1834 Bethel, ME; died ____)
596. Freeborn G.	born 25 May 1844; died 3 Aug 1873 Portland Harbor, Cumberland, ME
597. Edmund D.	born 17 Aug 1855
	married Imogene PERRY ca 1879 Bethel, Maine (she born ca 1857)
598. Fred C.	born 28 Mar 1858; married Tavis BARTLETT 11 May 1884 Bethel, ME

(she dau/o Harry Russell BARTLETT and Sophronia GLINES) (she born 28 Dec 1855 Bethel, ME)

320. ZACHARIAH HANNAFORD-5 BEAN, brother of above, was born 16 Feb 1815 at Bethel, Oxford County, Maine. He married Emeline FARNUM on 17 Jan 1841 at Bethel. She was the daughter of David Hall FARNUM and Maria BARTLETT, and the sister of Sarah (above). Emma was born ca 1823.

Children of Zachariah-5 BEAN and Emma FARNUM:
Surname BEAN	(all children born Bethel, Oxford, Maine)
599. Catherine Maria	born 16 Sept 1843
	married Humphrey B. HOLT 4 Mar 1866 Bethel (he born ca 1839 Bethel)
600. Frances Kimball	born 25 Mar 1846
	married Arthur M. BEAN ca 1868 Bethel (he born ca 1842 Bethel)
601. Sarah Ellen	born 1 Jan 1849
	married James Frank RICH ca 1871 Bethel, ME (he born ca 1845 Bethel)
602. Emma Etta	born 7 Oct 1856

328. DOLLY KIMBALL-5 BEAN, daughter of Joshua-4 BEAN (Mary/Molly-4 CROCKER; Timothy-2; Peletiah-1) and Betsey BARTLETT, was born 27 May 1833 at Bethel, Oxford, Maine. She married Moses Foster KIMBALL ca 1855 at Bethel. He was the son of Asa KIMBALL and Abigail BARTLETT, and was born 29 Sept 1824 at Bethel; died at NYC, NY. Dolly K-5 BEAN died 28 Jan 1892 at Bethel, Maine.

Children of Dolly Kimball-5 BEAN and Moses Foster KIMBALL:
   Surname KIMBALL   (all children born at Bethel, Oxford, Maine)
  603. Charles C. born 27 July 1856   604. Arabella born 16 Jul 1859   605. Ellen F. born 21 Sep 1863

332-341. See FOSTER section   pages 427 -430 (# 760-769)
346. MARY JANE-5 BARTER   see FOSTER # 765
347. LOUISE-5 BARTER   see FOSTER # 766

349. CAPTAIN JACOB BARTER-5 CROCKER, son of Captain Paul-4 CROCKER, Jr. (Paul-3; Timothy-2) and Jane BARTER, was born ca 1832, ME. He married Lucinda KENNEY ca 1852. They resided Machiasport, ME. Captain Jacob-5 CROCKER died 14 May 1904, Portland, ME (obituary in the *Bath Daily Times*). All of his sons were ships' captains.

Children of Captain Jacob-5 CROCKER and Lucinda KENNEY:
   Surname CROCKER
  606. Captain Edward H. born ca 1854, Machias; 1m. ? (1 son); 2m. ? (2 dau); died 17 Feb 1902
       Note: He was lost at sea 17 Feb 1902 on the Schooner *JOHN F RANDALL*. His son, by his first wife, was lost
         with him. He was survived by his widow, 2 daughters and five brothers " all six-footers ".
  607. Captain James B.   born ca 1856; married Celia H. GRATTO 25 Apr 1881 Philadelphia, PA
  608. Captain Charles W. born 1858
Children of Captain Jacob-5 CROCKER and his 2nd wife:
   Surname CROCKER
  609. Captain William G. born ca 1871   610. son born _____   611. son born ca 1877

351. ABIGAIL G-5 RICHARDS, daughter of Isaac-4 RICHARDS (Hannah-3 CROCKER; Timothy-2) and Charity HOLMES Clark, was born ca 1840. She married Albert Nelson INGALLS ca 18__. He was born 4 Oct 1838 at Grand Manaan, Washington County, Maine.

Children of Abigail-5 RICHARDS and Albert Nelson INGALLS:
   Surname INGALLS   (children born East Machias, Maine)
  612. Abigail E.   born 13 Apr 1857; married George CATES
  613. Margaret A.   born 22 Dec 1859 ; married Edgar HOLMES
  614. Cynthia   born 4 Apr 1862; married Charles CROCKER
  615. Nelson, Jr.   born 23 June 1864; married Cora STEWART
  616. Nina P.   born 16 June 1866; married George Fred HIGGINS
+ 617. FLORENCE H.   born 8 Apr 1869; married Hiram Elbridge MOAN ca 1886 E. Machias
  618. John Newton   born 4 Dec 1871; married Alice Julia HANSCOM 13 May 1893 E. Machias
  619. Charles Howard born 13 July 1876; married Addie V. BAGLEY 16 May 1896 E. Machias, ME

352. DIADEMA HARRIMAN-5 RICHARDS, daughter of Captain James-4 RICHARDS (Hannah-3 CROCKER; Timothy-2) and Hannah Keyes HARRIMAN, was born 10 Jan 1821 at Bristol, Maine. She married Richard Heagan KILLMAN on 8 Sept 1841. He was the son of _____ KILLMAN, and was born 10 May 1818; died 22 Oct 1889. Diadema-5 RICHARDS died 22 May 1903.

Children of Diadema-5 RICHARDS and Richard KILLMAN:
   Surname KILLMAN   Ref: McCUTCHEON Family Records by McKEE 1931
+ 620. NANCY   born 11 Dec 1848 Prospect, ME; died Jan 1922 Bangor, Maine
     FRANCES   married James Francis GERRITY 11 Dec 1881 at Stockton, Maine
                 (he born 9 Oct 1856 Roxbury, MA; still living 1931 Bangor, Maine)

354. CAPTAIN QUINCY A-5 CLARK, son of Charles-4 CLARK (Sally-3 CROCKER; Timothy-2) and Charity HOLMES, was born ca 1823. He married Jane HOLMES ca ____ (after 1860). She was the daughter of Jonathan HOLMES and Abigail AMES, born ___; died ____. He was a master mariner.

Children of Captain Quincy-5 CLARK and Jane HOLMES:
Surname CLARK

621. Sarah	born ____		624. Emily	born ___; married Peter DURGAN
622. William	born ____; died young		625. George	born ____
623. William (2) born ____; res Jonesport			626. Annie	born ____; married Maurice HOLMES

358. CAPTAIN ALFRED-5 AMES, son of Abigail-4 CLARK (Sally-3 CROCKER; Timothy-2) and Captain Isaac AMES, was born ca ____ , Maine. He married Mary KELLER ca ____ .

Children of Captain Alfred-5 AMES and Mary KELLER:
Surname AMES
+ 627. JOHN KELLER   born ____; married Sarah Albee SANBORN
                (she dau/o Cyrus SANBORN and Susan GARDNER) (she born 17 Sept 1833)
+ 628. BENJAMIN F   born ____; married Mary ELLISON
  629. Napoleon B.   born ____; died young
  630. Martha   born ____; unmarried   EOL
+ 631. MARIA LOUISA born ____; married George FURBER

372. CHARITY ELIZABETH-5 COLBETH, daughter of Sarah-4 CLARK (Sally-3 CROCKER; Timothy-2) and John COLBETH, and was born 16 Apr 1832 at Machiasport, ME. She married Andrew Gauld JOHNSON ca 1853. He was the son of Joseph Brookins JOHNSON and Nancy WESCOTT, and was born 18 May 1826 Machias, ME; died 12 Feb 1904 Machiasport. Charity died there 26 Oct 1916.

Children of Charity Elizabeth-5 COLBETH and Andrew JOHNSON:
Surname JOHNSON   (all children born at Machiasport, ME)
632. Esmeralda Essie   born Oct 1854; married Herbert ROBINSON; died 1 Apr 1936
633. William Andrew   born 20 Oct 1858; married Alice Octavia WOODWARD; died 6 Jan 1930
634. Elizabeth   born 20 Oct 1858; married Edmund D. ROBBINS; died 16 Aug 1919
635. Ulmer   born 12 Feb 1860; married Melinda PRESLEY; died 18 Nov 1943
636. Mary S.   born 20 Mar 1864; married Frank BEAL 20 Dec 1884; died 6 Mar 1941
637. Carrie Belle   born 14 Feb 1868; married George JOHNSON 18 Sep 1889; died 18 Feb 1945
638. Lucy Emma   born 31 July 1870; married Charles W. DAVIS 6 Jan 1889; died 25 Jan 1954

375. JAMES FRANCIS-5 HOLMES, son of Temperance-4 CLARK (Sally-3 CROCKER; Timothy-2) and James F. HOLMES, was born ca 1829 at Machias, Maine. He married Mary Emeline SMITH on 28 Oct 1856 at Calais, Maine. She was the daughter of Stewart SMYTH/SMITH and Charity CALDWELL, and was born 8 July 1833 at Calais; died 1886. James Francis-5 HOLMES died 1886. They are both buried at Calais Cemetery, Calais, Maine.

Children of James-5 HOLMES and Mary E. SMITH:
Surname HOLMES   (all children born Calais, Maine)
639. Lucy T.   born ca 1857; married C. F. CRAIG
640. Mary Alice   born 15 June 1860; married Edwin BROWN
641. Lillian Marie   born 29 Sept 1861; died 15 May 1943
+ 642. FRANK   born 18 Oct 1866; married Hannah Elzina JELLISON 2 June 1891
    WILLARD   (she dau/o Sylvanus JELLISON and Lydia BROWN)
            (she born 3 Oct 1872, Princeton, ME; died 3 Aug 1935 Grand Lake Stream, ME)
            died 14 Sept 1949 Calais, Maine
643. Edith Charity   born 1868; died 1953 (poss marr Fred H. WOODMAN 20 Oct 1899)

The Sixth American Generation

382. ISRAEL-6 BROOKS, son of Timothy-5 BROOKS, Jr. (Joanna-4 CHUTE; Mary-3 CROCKER; Captain Paul-2) and __?__, was born Dec 1833 at Annapolis County, Nova Scotia. He married Julia A. STEADMAN ca 1854. She was the daughter of ___ STEADMAN, and was born 18__; died ___. Israel-6 BROOKS died ca 1869.

Children of Israel-6 BROOKS and Julia STEADMAN:
  Surname BROOKS

644. Susan D.	born ca 18__	647. Laura	born ca 18__
645. Charles B.	born ca 18__	648. Florence	born ca 18__
646. Norman	born ca 18__	649. Euphemia	born ca 18__

383. MARY ANN-6 BROOKS, sister of above, was born 12 July 1835 at Annapolis County, Nova Scotia. She married John Eber CHUTE ca 185_. He was the son of Handley-7 CHUTE (James-6; Samuel-5; Lionel-4; James-3; 2; Lionel-1) and Martha PINNEY/PHINNEY, and was born 20 Oct 1833; died 18__.

Children of Mary Ann-6 BROOKS and John Eber-7 CHUTE:
  Surname CHUTE

650. Jesse D.	born 5 June 1858
651. Aledia J.	born 29 Sep 1859
652. Traverse Brinton	born 5 Feb 1862; died 18 Nov 1894
+ 653. CAPTAIN EATON	born 2 Dec 1864; married Emily Agnes HUDSON; died ca 1908
654. Jessie A.	born 29 June 1867
655. HENRY DUNN	born 1 Aug 1869; died ca 1925
(twin)	1m. May CLATON/CLAYTON; 2m. Maude POOLE
656. Ida May (twin)	born 1 Aug 1869
657. Hannah D.	born 21 Apr 1871; married Oliver PARKER
658. MYRTLE R.	born 24 Sep 1874; married Burpee ARMSTRONG; died 1943
659. REUBEN P.	born 2 Apr 1876; married Clara SIMMS; died 1941
660. EFFIE	born 13 May 1878; married Bradford POOLE; died 1945

389. CHARLES-6 LINGLEY, son of Fanny-5 CHANDLER (Elizabeth-4 CHUTE; Mary-3 CROCKER; Captain Paul-2) and John LINGLEY, was born ca 1829 at Annapolis Co., N S. He married his cousin, Eliza-6 MILLER ca 18__. She was the daughter of Eleanor-5 CHANDLER (Elizabeth-4 Chute; Mary-3 CROCKER; etc.) and James MILLER, and was born ca 1822. Charles-6 LINGLEY died ca 1873.

Child of Charles-6 LINGLEY and Eliza-6 MILLER:
  Surname LINGLEY   661. Elizabeth Ann   born ca 1853; died ca 1873 (age ca 20)

406. JOHN EDWARD-6 WOODMAN, son of John Chute-5 WOODMAN (Leah-4 CHUTE; Mary-3 CROCKER; Captain Paul-2) and Mary Elizabeth RICE, was born 28 June 1854 at Smith Cove, Digby County, N S. He married first to Lydia Mae WARNE ca 187_. She was the daughter of Hiram WARNE and Jane GAVEL, and was born ca 1856 and died at the age of 24 (1880). He married 2nd _?_ ca 1881.

Children of John Edward-6 WOODMAN and Lydia Mae WARNE:
  Surname WOODMAN   Note: Perhaps there were several other children of this marriage

662. Bernard	born ca 187_	664. Lillian May	born Oct 1878
663. Clarence	born ca 187_	665. Annie Dora	born 16 Jan 1880

Children of James Edward-6 WOODMAN and 2nd wife :
  Surname WOODMAN

666. Byron Edward	born 4 Nov 1881 Joggin Bridge, NS; married Edith __; died 15 July 1959
667. Ada Bell	born 27 Sep 1883 Smith Cove, NS; died 15 May 1967
	married Nelson Charles MOREHOUSE 9 Nov 1899 Digby, NS

410. JOHN MORTIMER-6 ALDRED, son of Abigail-5 CROCKER (John-4; Paul-3;2; Peletiah-1) and Captain Richard Pirl ALDRED, was born 8 July 1852 at Margaretsville, Annapolis County, Nova Scotia. He married Elizabeth/Lizzie Emma McMASTER on 16 May 1880 at Hillsboro, Nashua County, NH. She was the daughter of Robert McMASTER and Mary Caroline SIMONDS, and was born 19 Jan 1858 at Wilmot, Annapolis Co., NS; died 10 July 1932 at Tremont, Annapolis Co., NS. John-6 ALDRED died 30 June 1922 at Rockville Notch, Annapolis, NS.

Children of John M-6 ALDRED and Lizzie McMASTER:
Surname ALDRED   (1st seven children born Rockville, NS; others born Tremont, NS)
668. Augusta May   born 14 Mar 1881; died 30 Dec 1953 Atascadero, San Luis Obispo, CA
                          married Simon Blanchard HAGER 22 Sept 1903 Kings Co., NS
669. William Lionel   born 23 Dec 1882; married Priscilla Alden HAGER 14 Nov 1906
                          died 19 Dec 1952 Concord, MA
670. Charles Henry   born 20 July 1884; died 29 Sept 1901 Rockville Notch, NS   (EOL)
671. Alvin Earl   born 13 Mar 1886; married Frances DRUMMOND 27 Jan 1910 NH
672. Russell Pirl   born 10 Oct 1890; died 27 Aug 1962 West Newton, MA
                          married Ruth Elizabeth McMASTER 7 May 1912 Meadowvale, NS
+ 673. JESSIE   born 27 Dec 1892; died 6 July 1967 No. Reading, MA
      MARGUERITE   1m. BURTON THOMAS-7 GOULD, Sr. 26 Feb 1912 Framington, NS
                          2m. Henry Richard CLARKE
674. Robert Lionel   born 9 May 1896; died 10 Sept 1961 Boxboro, MA
                          married Pearl Gertrude McKNIGHT 13 Sept 1919 St. John, New Brunswick
675. Richard Wylie   born 14 Nov 1901; died 21 Mar 1973 Kingston, NS
                          married Marion Hettie SAUNDERS 1933 So. Framington, MA
676. Georgianna   born 16/18 May 1904; died 2 Mar 1977 Lusk, Wyoming
     Elizabeth Simonds   married Frederick William SULLIVAN 20 Nov 1920 Kentville, NS

411. MARY ELIZA(BETH)-6 ALDRED, sister of above, was born 17 Apr 1854 at Margaretsville, NS. She married William Henry MILLS on 17 Nov 1882 at Boston, MA. Mary E-6 died ___ at Everett, MA.

Children of Mary E-6 ALDRED and William MILLS:
Surname MILLS
677. Richard Henry   born ____   679. Gladys Alberta born Sept 1890; marr. Joseph O'BRIEN
678. William James   born 31 Aug 1885   680. Mabel Pearl   born 17 Nov 1906, MA

412. MARGARET ANN-6 ALDRED, sister of above, was born 11 Sept 1855 at Margaretsville, NS. She married George Thomas NOWLIN on 12 Nov 1877 at Boston, MA. He was the son of Robert NOWLIN and Arminella EAGLES, and was born 1850; died 1918 at Everett, MA. Margaret-6 ALDRED died 19 May 1940 at Hingham, MA.

Children of Margaret Ann-6 ALDRED and George NOWLIN:
Surname NOWLIN
+ 681. AUGUSTA   born 7 Apr 1878; married Francis P. MATHEWS 11 July 1905
      ARMINELLA   died 5 June 1962 Oxford, NY
682. Edith May   born 20 Sept 1879; married Rupert G. STRONACH 14 Nov 1901 IL
                          (he son of George L. STRONACH and Susan MARGESON)
683. Alice Abigail   born 14 July 1883; married True Herbert FILES 28 Mar 1906
                          died ca 1975 Hingham, MA
684. Phoebe Josephine   born 24 Aug 1885; died 11 July 1911, unmarried   EOL
685. George Robert   born 10 July 1887; died 1964 CA
686. Georgie Etta   born 25 May 1891

415. JAMES DEXTER-6 ALDRED, brother of above, was born 21 Sept 1860 at Margaretsville, Nova Scotia. He married Jennie Mabel GORDON on 3 Feb 1891 at Margaretsville. She was the daughter of John

GORDON/GORDEN and ___ ____; and was born 19 June 1869; died 17 Dec 1931 at Margaretsville. James-6 ALDRED died there 23 June 1939.

Children of James-6 ALDRED and Jennie GORDON:
    Surname ALDRED   (children born Margaretsville, NS)
    687. Kenneth Pirl   born 9 Mar 1891   688. Gordon Richard born 15 Aug 1897

419. JUDITH ELIZABETH ALBERTA-6 ALDRED, sister of above, was born 17 Aug 1870 at Margaretsville, N S. She married Elias Russell HIGGINS/HUDGINS on 26 May 1891 at Boston, MA. He was the son of ? HIGGINS/HUDGINS, and was born ____. Judith-6 ALDRED died ____ at Dorchester, MA.

Children of Judith-6 ALDRED and Elias HIGGINS/HUDGINS:
    Surname HIGGINS/HUDGINS
    689. Eva Maude   born____   691. Dorothy Viola   born ____
    690. Susan Pearl born ____; married William EDWARDS

420. IDA MAY/MAE-6 CROCKER, daughter of James-5 CROCKER (John-4; Paul-3; Paul-2; Peletiah-1) and Mary Etta LANGLEY, was born 15 May 1856 at Meadowvale, Nova Scotia. She married James Albert GOULD on 2 Apr 1880 at Meadowvale, NS. He was the son of Leonard GOULD and Nancy CAREY, and was born 3 Nov 1856 at Aylesford, Cornwallis, NS.; died there 17 AUG 1904. Ida Mae-6 CROCKER died 19 Feb 1945 at Kingston, Nova Scotia.

Children of Ida Mae-6 CROCKER and James GOULD:
    Surname GOULD   (children born at Aylesford, Nova Scotia)
+ 692. BURTON   born 22 Jan 1881; died 19 Apr 1953 Torbrook Mines, NS
       THOMAS   married JESSIE MARGUERITE-7 ALDRED 28 Feb 1912 (she # 673)
    693. Ethelyn Elizabeth born 10 Feb 1885; died 1 May 1985 Shelburne, NS (age 100-3)

         Note: She adopted a child in 1899. His name was Walter GOULD, born 13 Feb 1897. He married Evelyn
                        Ann BENT ca 1933; died Dec 1961 at Scarborough, Ontario, Canada.

423. MINNIE ETTA-6 CROCKER, sister of above, was born 27 May 1871 at Hyde Park, MA. She married Edward McMASTER on 25 Dec 1894 at Aylesford, NS. He was born 1856; died 1954.

Children of Minnie-6 CROCKER and Edward McMASTER:
    Surname McMASTER
    694. Clifford   born ____; married Rosie McMASTER
    695. Clayton   born ____; married Elsie CROUSE
    696. Lewis Rutherford born ____; married Hazel Irene SAUNDERS; died 1987 Kingston Village, NS

429. ELIZABETH MARIA-6 SPINNEY, daughter of Austin Welton-5 SPINNEY (Ann-4 CROCKER; Paul-3;2) and Elizabeth Jane MORSE, was born ca 1846/47. She married Thomas Cornelius STEELE ca ____. He was the son of _?_ STEELE, and was born 1839; died 1920. (Possibly the grandson of Isaac STEELE and Martha ____). Elizabeth-6 SPINNEY died 7 Sept 1886.

Children of Elizabeth-6 SPINNEY and Thomas STEELE:
    Surname STEELE
    697. Elmera Amelia   born 1864   700. Annis Sophia   born 1871; died 25 Sep 1879
                          died 24 Sep 1879   701. Harris Atwood   born 1875 (twin)
    698. Church Morse   born 1866   702. Harry Franklin born 1875 (twin)
    699. Burpee Clarke   born 1867   died 14 Aug 1885

430. MELISSA ANNIE-6 SPINNEY, sister of above, was born 1848. She married Alfred Parker SAUNDERS ca ____. He was born 1831; died ____. Melissa-6 SPINNEY died ____.

Children of Melissa-6 SPINNEY and Alfred SAUNDERS:
    Surname SAUNDERS

703. Martha Jane	born 1873	706. Alfred Noble	born ____
704. Mary Elizabeth	born 1874; died 1881	707. Helen Irene	born ____
705. Arthur Church	born 1876	708. Bertha Odessa	born ____

435. MINNIE SALOME-6 SPINNEY, sister of above, was born ca 1857. She married James William JEFFERSON ca ___. He was the son of _?_ JEFFERSON, and was born 1853; died ___.

Children of Minnie-6 SPINNEY and James JEFFERSON:
    Surname JEFFERSON

709. Arthur Spurgeon	born 1880	710. Burpee Seymour	born 1882; died 1886

442. WILLIAM G-6 SPINNEY, son of Jacob Beach-5 SPINNEY, Jr. (Ann-4 CROCKER; Paul-3;2; Pelatiah-1) and Jane DUNCANSON, was born ca 1854; died ____. He married Flora Belle HUTCH-INSON ca ____. William-6 SPINNEY died ca 1935.

Children of William-6 SPINNEY and Flora HUTCHINSON:
    Surname SPINNEY

+ 711. EVA	born 1889; married Samuel GRIFFIN; died 1976
	(he born 1894; died 1954)
712. Milton	born 1904; married Ruby PEARL; died 1981

447. JAMES BARTEAUX-6 SPINNEY, son of Harding Theodore-5 SPINNEY (Ann-4 CROCKER; Paul-3; 2; Peletiah-1) and Helen BARTEAUX was born ca 1860. He married Mary E. FITCH ca ____. She was the daughter of ____FITCH, and was born ca 1865; died 1960. James B-6 SPINNEY died 1921.

Children of James-6 SPINNEY and Mary FITCH:
    Surname SPINNEY

713. Leroy Howard	born 1890; died 1894 EOL
+ 714. HELEN LUCY	born 1895; married John GRIFFIN; died 1981 (he born 1897; died 1974)
+ 715. LAURA	born 1897; married MAYNARD-7 SPINNEY (# 717)
BLANCHE	(he born 1897; died 1978)
716. Anna Myra	born 1902; married Lorimer WOODBURY; died 1967

455. EDWARD MANNING-6 SPINNEY, son of Deacon Caleb-5 SPINNEY (Ann-4 CROCKER; Paul-3;2; Peletiah-1) and Parnie BARTEAUX, was born 1867. He married Bessie WEBBER ca ____. She was the daughter of ___ WEBBER, and was born 1868; died 1962. Edward-6 SPINNEY died 1961.

Children of Edward-6 SPINNEY and Bessie WEBBER:
    Surname SPINNEY

+ 717. MAYNARD	born 1897; married LAURA B-7 SPINNEY (# 715); died 1978
+ 718. LESLIE	born 1898; married BEATRICE-7 SPINNEY (# 726); died 1982
MANNING	(she born 1899; died ____)
719. Zelda Hope	born 1904; married Arnold ETTER (2 sons: John and David-8 ETTER)
+ 720. ALBERT W.	born 1908; married Daisie MARSHALL (she born 1912; died ____)

459. MELBOURNE E-6 SPINNEY, son of Beriah B-5 SPINNEY (Ann-4 CROCKER; Paul-3;2; Peletiah-1) and Mary Jane WHITMAN, was born ca 1864. He married Harriet SMALL ca ____. She was born 1862; died 1952. Melbourne-6 SPINNEY died 1928.

Children of Melbourne-6 SPINNEY and Harriet SMALL:
    Surname SPINNEY

+ 721. HORACE LESTER born 1887; married Gladys KEDDY; died 1951

Children of Melbourne-6 SPINNEY, continued:
 Surname SPINNEY
 722. Edith Adelaide   born 1889; married Wilfred GROSS; died 1975
                              (2 children : Clyde-8 and Norma-8 GROSS)
 723. Loring Victor   born 1890; married Cora JACQUES; died 1957
                              (she born ____; died 1963) (1 dau: June Rose-8 born 1929)
 724. Ralph Whitman   born 1892; died 1967 unmarried EOL
+ 725. HOWE BELL   born 1894; married Bessie PARKER; died 1965 (she born 1893; died 1975)
+ 726. BEATRICE   born 1899; married LESLIE MANNING-7 SPINNEY (# 718)

465. LELAND TEASDALE-6 SPINNEY, son of Enoch-5 SPINNEY (Ann-4 CROCKER; Paul-3;2;
Peletiah-1) and Phebe BOWLBY, was born 1875. He married Agness Georgeanna HARRIS ca ____.
She was the daughter of ____ HARRIS, and was born 1877; died 1952. Leland-6 SPINNEY died 1950.

Children of Leland-6 SPINNEY and Agness HARRIS:
 Surname SPINNEY
+ 727. WINTHROP HARRIS   born 1900; married Marjorie Eunice WHITAKER; died 1950
+ 728. KINGSLEY SELLAR   born 1902; married Evelyn PALMER; died 1973
+ 729. VERA BELLE   born 1904; married Cecil PALMER; died 1951
+ 730. EARLE WINFRED   born 1914; married Flora MORSE; died 1980
+ 731. FRANCIS LELAND   born 1915; married Leonore BRYDEN; died 1979
 732. Margaret Louise   born 1919

468. BURPEE A-6 SPINNEY, son of Clark T-5 SPINNEY (Ann G-4 CROCKER; Paul-3;2; Peletiah-1)
and Orinda SLOCUM, was born 1883 at ____. He married Maria Leona STEELE ca ____. She was the
daughter of ____ STEELE, and was born 1891; died 1974. Burpee-6 SPINNEY died 1969.

Children of Burpee-6 SPINNEY and Maria STEELE:
 Surname SPINNEY
+ 733. BURPEE CLYDE   born 18 Aug 1912; married Bertha Maud CHAMBERS 30 Nov 1935
 734. Marjorie   born ____   735. Lloyd   born ____
 736. Ella   born ____   737. Leroy   born ____   738. Louis   born ____

473. ROULOF W-6 CROCKER, son of John M-5 CROCKER (James-4; Paul-3;2; Peletiah-1) and Mary
Adelaide BRENNAN, was born 29 Aug 1865 at Harmony, Kings County, Nova Scotia. He married
Charlotte A. JACKSON on 7 June 1892 at Millville, Nova Scotia. She was the daughter of _?_ JACKSON,
and was born 1871; died 1933. Roulof-6 CROCKER died 20 Dec 1934 at Westboro, MA.

Child of Roulof-6 CROCKER and Charlotte JACKSON:
 Surname CROCKER   + 739. VICTOR born 1887; marr. BLANCHE ETHEL-7 CHARLTON (# 743)

474. AMORET JANE-6 CROCKER, sister of above, was born 15 Nov 1866 at Harmony, Kings County,
Nova Scotia. She married Albert Ralph CHARLTON on 1 July 1887 at Harmony. He was the son of
Solomon Simpson CHARLTON and Mary Elizabeth DELONG, and was born 4 Aug 1862 Milford; died
24 May 1933 at Westboro, MA. Amoret Jane-6 CROCKER died 15 June 1943 at Worcester, MA. They are
buried at Pine Grove Cemetery, Westboro.

Children of Amoret Jane-6 CROCKER and Albert R. CHARLTON:
 Surname CHARLTON
 740. Almon Henry   born 1 Aug 1888 Harmony, NS; married Clara WARREN; died 18 Aug 1914
+ 741. GRACE MAY   born 18 Dec 1890 Harmony, NS; died 27 June 1986 Worcester, MA
                           married Ellwood Irving TEMPLE 10 Dec 1910 at Holyoke, MA
                           (he born 4 Feb 1888, Pittsburgh, PA; died 18 Jan 1940 Worcester, MA)
                           (he son/o George Irving TEMPLE and Flora L. WOOD)

Children of Amoret Jane-6 CROCKER, continued:
    Surname CHARLTON
    742. Merle Welton   born 23 Nov 1901 Westboro, MA; died 29 July 1924 Rutland, MA   EOL
  + 743. BLANCHE   born 15 Sept 1906 Westboro, MA; 1m. VICTOR-7 CROCKER (# 739)
        ETHEL   2m. Jack FAYERS
                            died 28 Dec 1980 Uncasville, New London, CT.
    744. Marion Crocker   born 13 Apr 1910 Westboro, MA; died 1 July 1933
                            married Murray E. STOKES, Sr. (he born 1902; died 1943)
            Children: Murray-7 STOKES, Jr born 1931; died 1943 - and an unnamed son born 1933; dy

478. LAMERT STEPHEN-6 CROCKER, brother of above, was born 3 Aug 1880 at Harmony, Kings
County, Nova Scotia. He married Agnes E. WINOTT on 6 Nov 1907 at Harmony. She was the daughter of
_____ WINOTT, and was born 1882; died 1978. Lamert-6 CROCKER died 14 Dec 1956 at Kentville, NS.

Children of Lamert-6 CROCKER and Agnes WINOTT:
    Surname CROCKER
  + 745. MAYFRED   born 1909; married Kenneth Earl SPINNEY
        DELILAH   (he born 1906; died _____)
    746. Horace Vaughan   born 1910; married Ellen SPROULE; died 1983   (she born 1913)
                    One daughter: Beverly Ann-8 CROCKER born 1943; married Donald KEEFE
  + 747. LORNA   born 1913; married Vernon Hadley PALMER
        MARGUERITE   (he born 1911; died _____)
  + 748. NOLA BEATRICE   born 1915; married Vincent David HILTZ (he born 1913); died 1975
    749. Francis Opal   born 1918; died 1918
    750. Theodore Bernard   born 1919; married Gladys Beatrice EDDY
                    One child: Deanna Mae-8 CROCKER born 1943; married Herman MAILMAN
  + 751. ELSIE PAULINE   born 1920; married Hubert Osborne STEELE (he born 1921)
    752. Elvin Lorris   born 1923; 1m. Wava JODREY (born 1929); 2m. Jeanette BARNES

484. GILBERT L-6 CROCKER, son of Samuel Gould-5 CROCKER (John-4; James W-3; John-2;
Peletiah-1) and Susan LONGFELLOW, was born ca 1850. He married Martha WRIGHT ca _____.

Children of Gilbert-6 CROCKER and Martha WRIGHT:
    Surname CROCKER
    753. Melville M. born _____; married Julia M. ALLEN 26 Dec 1898 Machias , ME
        2 ch: Catharine-8 and Marion-8 CROCKER   756. Florence born _____
    754. Harold   born _____   757. Gilbert born _____
    755. Carroll N. born _____; marr Florence M. ACKLEY 10 Nov 1912   758. Louis   born _____

490. MARY ELIZABETH-6 GARDNER, daughter of Mary-5 CROCKER (John-4; James-3; John-2;
Pelatiah-1) and Alfred GARDNER, was born 26 May 1843 at Machias, Maine. She married first to
James T. GARDNER ca 1858. He was the son of James A. GARDNER and Almira KILTON, and was
born _____; died _____. He served in the **Civil War**. Her second marriage was to Daniel Webster-5
HARMON. He was the son of Hiram-4 HARMON and Mary GARDNER, and was born 19 May 1852.
Mary-6 GARDNER died 31 Dec 1885. Daniel W-5 HARMON married second to Mary BARSTOW.

Child of Mary E-6 GARDNER and James T. GARDNER:
    Surname GARDNER
  + 759. ALMIRA R.   born _____ ; married Loring A. HOLMES

493. AMELIA-6 GARDNER, daughter of Rebecca-5 CROCKER (John-4; James W-3; John-2;
Peletiah-1) and Cynthia-7 LONGFELLOW, was born 9 June 1844. She married Gilbert LaFayette-5
HARMON 31 May 1869. He was the son of Hiram-4 HARMON and Mary GARDNER, and was born ca
1840; served in the **Civil War**; died _____.

Child of Amelia-6 GARDNER and Gilbert L-5 HARMON:
 Surname HARMON
 760. Ray E.   born ____; married Phebe/Phoebe H. WHITNEY 30 Nov 1899 Machias, ME
        2 children: Dorris-8 HARMON and
        Edwin-8 HARMON born ___; married Birdie E. ELLIS 24 Dec 1919 E. Machias

500. GEORGE M-6 LYON, son of William-5 LYON (Betsey-4 CROCKER; James W-3; John-2; Peletiah-1) and Sarah GETCHELL, was born ca ____. He married Jennie BERRY ca ____.

Children of George-6 LYON and Jennie BERRY:
 Surname LYON
 761. Sarah   born ____
 762. Phyzannah born ____; married Simon B. ELWELL 14 Sept 1893
       2 ch: George-8 ELWELL and Herbert-8 ELWELL
 763. Irving   born ____; married Lottie GOOCH
 764. Roscoe   born ____; unmarried   EOL
 765. Willard   born ____; married Ada M. ANDREWS 26 July 1899
       2 ch: Melvin-8 LYON and Dorris-8 LYON
 766. Effie   born ____; married Enoch A. HOWIE 25 June 1896 of Whitneyville, ME
       3 ch: John-8 HOWIE; Mellus-8 HOWIE; and Calista-8 HOWIE
 767. Anna/Annie born ____; married Willie E. ACKLEY 10 Nov 1896
      4 ch: Cora-8 ACKLEY; George-8 ACKLEY; Marion-8 ACKLEY; and Clayton-8 ACKLEY
 768. Josie   born ____;
 769. Lizzie B.   born ____; married Walter B. CLOW 15 Oct 1902 (he of Eastbrook, ME)
 770. Walter   born ____   771. Millie   born ____;
 772. Mary A.   born ____; married Uriah T. CROSBY 28 Sept 1920 (he of E. Machias, ME)
 773. Carrie C.   born ____; married Henry T. MILES 19 May 1906 (he of Princeton, ME)

501. WILLIAM / WILLIE HENRY-6 LYON, brother of above, was born ca ____ at Machias. ME. He married Josephine Ermina-8 LEIGHTON on 3 July 1869 at Machias. She was the daughter of Joseph-7 LEIGHTON and Susan VOSE, and was born 21 May 1854; died 12 Dec 1901.

Children of William-6 LYON and Josephine-8 LEIGHTON:
 Surname LYON   (all children born Machias, Maine)
 774. William Henry born 14 Feb 1871; married Mildred ROGERS
 775. Horace Carroll born 24 Jan 1872; died Aug 1892 Minneapolis, MN
 776. Leila Ethel   born 29 Apr 1874; died Aug 1886, MN

503. SIMEON G-6 LYON, brother of above, was born ca ____. He married Hannah SEDGELY ca ____.
Children of Simeon-6 LYON and Hannah SEDGELEY:
 Surname LYON
 777. James   born ____   780. Grace   born ____
 778. Fred   born ____   781. Mignonette born ____
 779. Albert B. born ____; poss married Mabel SPRY of Freeport, ME 14 Mar 1924

506. ANDREW G-6 LYON, brother of above, was born ca ____. He married Catherine CLARK ca ____.
Children of Andrew-6 LYON and Catherine CLARK:
 Surname LYON
 782. Avoid   born ____   786. Bradford born ____
 783. Leda   born ____   787. Percie   born ____
 784. Willie   born ____   788. Ruby   born ____
 785. Sadie   born ____   789. Aubrey   born ____

507. OTIS-6 LYON, son of Warren-5 LYON (Betsey-4 CROCKER; James W-3; John-2; Peletiah-1)

and Phyzannah NORTON, was born ca ____. He married Marjery BUTLER ca ____.
Children of Otis-6 LYON and Marjery BUTLER:
   Surname LYON
   790. Samuel   born ____; wife unknown; 2 children: Wilfred-8 and Herbert-8 LYON
   791. Annie   born ____   792. Ida M.   born ____
   793. Lillian   born ____; married William HARNE; 2 ch: Alice-8 and Lillian-8 HARNE

527. GEORGE W / H-6 THAXTER, son of Levi-5 THAXTER (Sally-4 CROCKER; James W-3; John-2;
Pelatiah-1) and Susan BURNHAM, was born ca 1848/49. He married Sabrina COOK ca ____.
Children of George-6 THAXTER and Sabrina COOK:
   Surname THAXTER
   794. Adelaide   born ____; dy   796. Amy   born ____
   795. F. Jay   born ____   797. Roy   born ____

537. LUCY MOREY-6 CURTIS, daughter of Mercy-5 CROCKER (Mariner Green-4; James W-3; John-2;
Peletiah-1) and Abel CURTIS, Jr., was born 10 Mar 1851. She married James Henry-10 BAILEY on
1 Feb 1873 at Machias. He was the son of Henry-9 BAILEY and Jerusha WILSON, and was born 16 Sept
1845; died 22 Mar 1901 at Machias. Lucy-6 CURTIS died ____.

Children of Lucy-6 CURTIS and James H-10 BAILEY:
   Surname BAILEY
   798. Ralph C.   born ____; married Mary E. STERRITT 2 Mar 1915 Machias, ME
   799. Marcia C.   born ____; married Frederick G. MARSH (of Framingham, MA) 18 Oct 1905
   800. Henry   born ____   801. Alice   born ____   802. Clara   born ____

538. EDWARD BISSELL-6 CURTIS, brother of above, was born 20 Feb 1853 at Machias, Maine. He
married Mary Augusta COLSON 31 Dec 1885 Somerville, MA. She was the daughter of Captain Gilman
COLSON + and Mary Elizabeth WILSON Loring, and was born 11 Aug 1865 at Lexington, MA; died
9 Dec 1951 at Machias, ME. Edward-6 CURTIS died 15 Apr 1927 at Machias.
                    + Note: Gilman COLSON was the illegitimate son of Mary COLSON and an unknown
                       father. He was born 16 May 1813 at Addison, ME; died 17 May 1879.
Children of Edward-6 CURTIS and Mary COLSON:
   Surname CURTIS
   803. Edward Gilman   born 7 Dec 1886   805. Mary   born 24 July 1892
 + 804. JOSEPHINE   born 6 Apr 1889 Cambridge, MA; married William Silliman FOSTER
      NASH   (he born 15 Oct 1886 Water Mill, LI,NY; died 2 Jan 1926 Minneapolis, MN)
                       died 3 July 1941 Minneapolis, MN (see DRISKO section pages 188-189)

543. DR. FRANK/FRANCIS H-6 CROCKER, son of Alvin G-5 CROCKER (Mariner Green-4; James
W-3; John-2; Peletiah-1) and Julia FOSTER, was born ca 1852 at Machias, Maine. Frank-6 studied
medicine; and practiced his profession in Boothbay, Machias and Gardiner, Maine. He married Lucy H.
CRANE ca ____. She was the daughter of Abijah CRANE and Lydia KILPATRICK, and was born ____;
died ____. Frank-6 died June 1903 at Gardiner, Maine.

Children of Dr. Frank-6 CROCKER and Lucy CRANE:
   Surname CROCKER   806. Julia   born ____   807. David   born ____

546. FANNIE-6 CROCKER, sister of above, was born ca ____. She married Frank WILLEY ca ____.
Children of Fannie-6 CROCKER and Frank WILLEY:
   Surname WILLEY   They resided Gardiner, Maine.
   808. John born ____   809. Paul born ___   810. Florence born ____   811. Elizabeth born ____

550. ANNA/ANNIE M-6 CROCKER, daughter of Cyrus Strong-5 CROCKER (Mariner Green-4; James
W-3; John-2; Peletiah-1) and Martha H. Peach-8 SMITH, was born ca 186_. She married Willis/Willie-9

PARLIN on 31 Aug 1885. He was the son of George Albert-8 PARLIN + (Amos-7; Stephen-6; Silas-5; John-4;3;2; Nicholas-1) and Mary Elizabeth HANSCOM ++, and was born 2 June 1861 at Machias, Maine.

+ Note: George Albert-8 PARLIN was an editor and proprietor of the Machias Union newspaper for many years. He married ++ Mary Elizabeth HANSCOM on 29 Aug 1860 at Machias. She was the daughter of Ellis HANSCOM ** (Isaac; Aaron) and Sarah/Sally BOWKER, granddau/o Levi BOWKER and Betsey WATTS.   Ref. Descendants of Nicholas PARLIN of Cambridge, MA 1913.
** Ellis HANSCOM born 15 Apr 1802; died 14 Apr 1883 at Machias, Maine.

Children of Annie M-6 CROCKER and Willis-9 PARLIN:
  Surname PARLIN
  812. Earl Colby   born 24 Dec 1886; died 2 Nov 1963 Machias, ME
                             married Florence G. DURGIN 21 Nov 1906 Machias, ME
  813. Samuel Fletcher   born 21 Feb 1891; died 19 Aug 1982 Machias, ME
                             1m. Marcella S. HATT 27 Oct 1909 (she born ca 1893; died 16 May 1968)
                             2m. Amy B. COOPER of Machiasport, ME on 13 Apr 1917
                             (she born ca 1893; died 28 June 1992 Machias, ME)
  814. Alice   born 24 June 1895
  815. Ellis H.   born 1 May 1897; died 9 Sept 1982 Machias, ME
                             married Annie E. BROWN 11 Oct 1924 (she of West Pembroke, ME)
  816. Rebecca G.   born 31 Jan 1899; died 5 Jan 1988 Winthrop, ME
                             married John P. VOSE of Machias on 10 Apr 1918
                             (he born ca 1888; died 23 Apr 1975 (age 87) Winthrop, ME)
  817. Donald   born 9 Sept 1901   818. Francis   born 12 Dec 1903

551. ELLA-6 MOORE, daughter of Susan-5 MOORE (Mariner Green-4 CROCKER; James W-3; John-2; Peletiah-1) and Flavius Josephus MOORE, was born ca 187_. She married Harry L. GILSON 14 Oct 1896.

Children of Ella-6 MOORE and Harry L. GILSON:
  Surname GILSON
  819. Agnes   born ____; married Harold E. COOMBS 18 Dec 1915 Portland, ME
  820. William P.   born ___   821. Roger   born _____

555.   SARAH LONGFELLOW-6 HEATON, daughter of Lydia-5 LONGFELLOW (Hannah-4 CROCKER; James W-3; John-2; Peletiah-1) and Isaac HEATON, was born 7 Feb 1852 at Machias, Maine. She married Horace Newell-8 LEIGHTON ++ at Machias ca ____. He was the son of Joseph-7 LEIGHTON and Susan Adelaide-8 VOSE, and was born 1853, Machias.

Children of Sarah-6 HEATON and Horace N-8 LEIGHTON:
  Surname LEIGHTON (1st child born Machias, ME; the others at Minneapolis, MN)
  822. Mabelle Ermina   born 28 July 1875
  823. Addie L.   born 7 June 1879
  824. Maude Alice   born 30 June 1882
                             married Edward S. LEIGHTON of Milbridge, ME on 17 Apr 1901
  825. Elizabeth Amelia   born 14 Apr 1884; died 3 Nov 1906
  826. Lewis Leroy   born 28 Sept 1886; died 13 Sept 1965
                             married Ethel W. HULIT 3 Oct 1906 Westbrook, ME (she born ca 1885; died 3 Mar 1981)
  827. George Everett   born 20 June 1888; married Garnet STONE 4 June 1913
  828. Sarah Lydia   born 30 Jan 1891; married John H. ZARFOS 11 Jan 191_

++ Ancestry of Horace N-8 LEIGHTON
THOMAS-1 LEIGHTON, born ca 1604, England; married Joanna __?__; came to America on ____; and died at Dover, NH on 22 Jan 1671. His son, THOMAS-2 LEIGHTON was born ca 1642 at Dover; married Elizabeth NUTTER ca ___; and died ca 1677 at Dover. THOMAS-3 LEIGHTON, born Dover 1671; married Deborah __?__; and died at Newington, NH ca 1744.

HATEVIL-4 LEIGHTON, born Newington ca ___; married Sarah TRICKEY ca ___; died ____. Their son, HATEVIL-5 LEIGHTON was born 28 Feb 1750 at Newington, NH. He married Martha DENBOW at Dover ca 1772. CLEMENT-6 LEIGHTON, son of Hatevil-5, was born at Dennyville, ME ca 1790. He married first to Mary WILDER on 4 Oct 1812 at Dennyville. She was the

daughter of Zenas WILDER. He married twice more and died ca ___ at Trescott, Maine. JOSEPH HATEVIL-7 LEIGHTON, son of Clement-6, was born 30 March 1831 at Trescott, Maine. he married Susan Adelaide-8 VOSE +++ on 2 Aug 1851, the Rev Thomas B. TUPPER, officiating. She was the daughter of Ebenezer-7 VOSE and Mary BAKER, and was born 8 May 1836 at Machias; died 29 Apr 1925 at Minneapolis, MN. They are buried in Court Street Cemetery, Machias, ME
          +++ Susan-8 VOSE descended from an early family who were natives of Kingfield, Franklin County, Maine.

They had eight children: HORACE NEWELL-8 who married Sarah-6 HEATON (above); Josephine Ermina-8 who married William Henry LYON (#501) ; Eben Everett; Mary Addie; George Addi; Frederick Arba; Joseph Leroy; and Carroll-8 LEIGHTON.

Horace Newell-8 LEIGHTON, after finishing school, became a carpenter in Machias. In 1876 he moved to Minneapolis, MN and worked his trade there until 1881. He returned to Machias where he opened the contracting firm of H.N.LEIGHTON & Co. with his brother Eben E. LEIGHTON. In 1891 he, his brother, and their brother-in-law William Henry LYON – incorporated as stockholders, to form the H.N.LEIGHTON PRINTING CO. He a prominent businessman, and also served as an Alderman from 1898-1902.

ROBERT-1 VOSE, the immigrant, was born 1599, and came to America from England in 1635. He settled at Milton, MA; and died 1683. His son, THOMAS-2 VOSE (1641-1708); married Maria W. WYATT (1645-1727). Their son, THOMAS-3 VOSE was born 1667; and married Hannah BABCOCK in 1695. JONATHAN-4 VOSE, born 1704; married Mary __?__.

Their son, JESSE-5 VOSE born 1742, married Mary DURFEE and had EBENEZER-6 VOSE who was the father of EBENEZER-7, father of Susan-8 (above).

566. SIMEON OSCAR-6 BOWKER, son of Nathan Stephen-5 BOWKER (Martha G-4 CROCKER; Simeon-3; John-2) and Mary Abigail BARRY, was born 20 Jan 1851. He married Keziah J. HOLMES on 2 Mar 1872. She was the daughter of Tristam HOLMES and Hannah Knight BERRY, and was born 19 May 1851; died 8 Apr 1906. Simeon-6 BOWKER died 1 May 1907.

Children of Simeon-6 BOWKER and Keziah HOLMES:
    Surname BOWKER
    829. Leslie S.   born ca 1873; died 1901
  + 830. SEYMOUR   born 29 Mar 1875; died 26 June 1939
           HARMON   married Lillie Mabel GETCHELL 8 July 1896
    831. Gertrude E.   born ca 1879; died 1905
    832. Simeon, Jr.   born ca 1882; died 1932   834. Clarence   born ca 18__
    833. Elizabeth   born ca 1887; died 1887   835. Nathaniel   born ca 18__

567. FERDINAND-6 BOWKER, brother of above, was born ca 185_. He married Lillie PALMER ca 1882 at Marshfield, Maine.

Children of Ferdinand-6 BOWKER and Lillie PALMER:
    Surname BOWKER   836. Harlan L.   born ca 18__; marr Eva L. GETCHELL 4 Dec 1909
    837. Samuel   born ca 18__   838. Oras / Horace T.   born ca 18__

575. EMILY J-6 BOYNTON, daughter of Martha-5 BOWKER (Martha-4 CROCKER; Simeon-3; John-2; Pelatiah-1) and Roscoe-3 BOYNTON, was born ca 1867/58. She married Bradford ESTEY ca ____.

Children of Emily-6 BOYNTON and Bradford ESTEY:
    Surname ESTEY   839. Cora A.   born ____   840. Martha   born ____

579. MARY D-6 WILLIAMSON, daughter of Sophia-5 CROCKER (George W-4; Simeon-3; John-2; Peletiah-1) and Thomas WILLIAMSON, was born ca ____. She married first to Captain A. Lee WATER-HOUSE ca ____. He was the son of __ WATERHOUSE, and was born ___; died ____ (killed in a railroad accident). Mary-6 WILLIAMSON married second to John T. WHITTEMORE ca ____.

Children of Mary-6 WILLIAMSON and Captain A. Lee WATERHOUSE:
    Surname WATERHOUSE
    841. Frances/Fanny R.   born ____ married Frank A. RYDER of Lynn, MA 2 Oct 1901
                           1 son: Frank-8 RYDER born ____
    842. Mary L.   born ____; married Charles H. CLIFFORD of Lynn, MA 2 Jan 1905

617. FLORENCE HUNTLEY-6 INGALLS, daughter of Abigail-5 RICHARDS (Isaac-4; Hannah-3 CROCKER; Timothy-2; Peletiah-1) and Albert Nelson INGALLS, was born 8 Apr 1869 at Machiasport, Maine. She married Hiram Elbridge MOAN ca 1886. He was the son of Thomas MOAN and Eliza BASSETT, and was born 30 Oct 1866 at Lubec, Maine; died 4 Aug 1916 at East Machias, ME. Florence-6 INGALLS died 22 July 1954 at Jacksonville, Maine.

Children of Florence-6 INGALLS and H. Elbridge MOAN:
   Surname MOAN   (all children born East Machias, Maine)
   843. Etta Cynthia   born 25 Dec 1887; died 16 June 1972 Machias, ME
                     married Jasper Curtis CATES 21 Nov 1914
    (he son/o Obed Willard CATES and Elletta BRYANT; born 9 Dec 1884; died 16 Oct 1966 Cutler, ME)
   844. Jennie/Jane   born 11 Feb 1889; died 7 Dec 1956
                     married Cecil PATTERSON (he born ca 1888 East Machias, ME)
   845. Ada Vianna   born 14 Jan 1891; died 19 Feb 1955
                     married Foster L. HIGGINS 23 Feb 1914 (he born ca 1887 E. Machias, ME)
   846. Leroy Wesley   born 24 Apr 1893; died 15 Feb 1975 West Hartford, CT.
   847. Ralph Thomas   born 15 July 1897; married Kathleen Van BRUNT (she born ca 1901)

620. NANCY FRANCES-6 KILLMAN, daughter of Diadema-5 RICHARDS (Captain James-4; Hannah-3 CROCKER; Timothy-1; Peletiah-1) and Richard KILLMAN, was born 11 Dec 1848 at Prospect, Waldo County, Maine. She married James Francis GERRITY on 11 Dec 1881 at Stockton, Waldo County, Maine. James GERRITY was the son of _____ GERRITY, and was born 9 Oct 1856 at Roxbury, MA; died____ (was still living 1931 at Bangor, Maine) Nancy-6 KILLMAN died Jan 1922 at Bangor.

Children of Nancy-6 KILLMAN and James GERRITY:
   Surname GERRITY
+ 848. JOE WARREN   born 14 Dec 1886 Prospect, Waldo, ME.; died Apr 1967, MA
                     married Florence Margaret McKEE 5 Jan 1914
    (she born 21 May 1891, Grand Rapids, MI; died 7 July 1989); resided Newton, MA 1931

627. JOHN KELLER-6 AMES, son of Captain Alfred-5 AMES (Abigail-4 CLARK; Sally-3 CROCKER; Timothy-2; Peletiah-1) and Mary KELLER/KELLAR, was born 2 Nov 1831 at East Machias, ME. He married Sarah Albee-7 SANBORN ++ 7 Oct 1855. She was the daughter of Cyrus-6 SANBORN and Susan GARDNER, and was born 17 Sept 1833; died _____. John-6 AMES died 22 Mar 1901 Machias, ME.
" Mr. AMES was one of the leading merchants of Machias, and was largely interested in navigation and timberlands. He was a selectman of his town for thirty years; state senator from 1893–96, and at the time of his death was collector of customs at the port in Machias. "   Reference: SPRAGUE"S Journal of Maine History (Vol. VIII, No. 1, page 52; June 1920)

Children of John-6 AMES and Sarah-7 SANBORN:
   Surname AMES
   849. Edwin Gardner   born ca 1857; married Maude WALKER (she from Port Gramble, WA)
   850. Anna Mary   born ca 1859; married Fred H. PEAVEY (he from Sioux City, IA)
+ 851. JULIA POPE   born ca 18__; married R. Clinton FULLER (he from Providence, RI)
   852. Frank Sanborn   born ca 18__
   853. Alfred Kellar   born 4 Sep 1866; married Nellie E. HILL on 4 Sep 1900 (she from Calais, ME)
   854. Lucy Talbot   born ca 18__; died before 1920

++ Ancestry of Sarah Albee-7 SANBORN

Lieutenant JOHN-1 SANBORN/SANBORNE, the immigrant, probably the son of WILLIAM-A SANBORNE of Brimpton, Berks, England, and Anne BACHILLER (dau/o Rev Stephen, Jr.) was born ca 1620 in England. He came to America with his brothers John and Stephen, along with their grandfather, the Rev BACHILLER , in 1632. Lt. John-1 SANBORNE married twice; 1st to Mary TUCK (dau/o Robert). She was born _____; died 30 Dec 1668. He married 2nd to Margaret PAGE Moulton (dau/o Robert PAGE); widow of William MOULTON.

JOHN-2 SANBORNE/SANBORN, his eldest son, was born ca 1649. John-2 married Judith COFFIN (dau/o Tristam COFFIN of Newbury) on 19 Nov 1674. They had 10 children including ENOCH-3 SANBORNE/SANBORN, who was born ca 1685.

ENOCH-3 SANBORNE married twice; 1st to Elizabeth DENNETT ca 1709. She was the daughter of Alexander DENNETT of Portsmouth, NH. His 2nd wife was Mehitable BLAKE Godfrey. They married 1 Apr 1736. She was the daughter of John BLAKE of Hampton, NH and the widow of Jonathan GODFREY.   ENSIGN ENOCH-4 SANBORN, was born at Hampton Falls, NH ca ____; baptized there 28 June 1724. Reportedly, he was an Ensign in the British Army at the capture of Cape Breton. He lived in Hampton Falls, Epping and Machias, Maine. He was married 4 times: 1. Mary MORRILL; 2. Sarah GREENE Sanborn; 3. Phebe SANBORN and 4. the widow Hannah Day in 1772.

CAPTAIN WILLIAM-5 SANBORN, the son of his 4th wife, was born 8 Oct 1773. He married first to Mary-3 CROCKER (# 18) on 21 Feb 1796; and 2nd to Priscilla MAYHEW on 4 Nov 1798. He died 31 Mar 1846. He lived all of his life in Machias, Maine. CYRUS-6 SANBORN, a blacksmith, the son of William-5 and his 2nd wife, was born 28 Nov 1801. He married Susan GARDNER on 11 Sept 1823 at East Machias. Susan was born ca 1804; died ____. They were the parents of SARAH ALBEE-7 SANBORN, born 1833. Other children were: Thomas M born 1834; Caroline born 1841; and Frank born 1844. They resided East Machias, Maine.

628. BENJAMIN F-6 AMES, brother of above, was born ca ____. He married Mary ELLISON ca ____. .

Children of Benjamin-6 AMES and Mary ELLISON:
   Surname AMES
   855. Charles E.   born ____
   856. Jennie M.   born ____; married Charles H. YOUNG
                                 3 children: Maybell-8; Ethel-8; and Ruth-8 YOUNG
   857. Benjamin, Jr.   born ____; married Kate G. LORD
   858. Maria Louisa   born ____; married Arthur STEVENS
                                 2 children: Arthur-8 and Benjamin-8 STEVENS
   859. Susan   born ____; married Lewis A. STEVENS
   860. Isabel   born ____; married James Dillon GILBERT (1 child: Alice-8 GILBERT)
   861. John McDougal   born ____   863. Alfred   born ____
   862. Eunice Carr   born ____   864. George   born ____

631. MARIA LOUISA-6 AMES, sister of above, was born ca ___. She married George FURBER ca ____.
Children of Maria Louisa-6 AMES and George FURBER:
   Surname FURBER
   865. George Pope   born ____; married Laura PARKER
                                 2 children: Edward P-8 and Harold P-8 FURBER
   866. Jane   born ____
   867. William Henry   born ____; married Mabel HOLDEN (1 child: Holden-8 FURBER)

642. FRANK WILLARD-6 HOLMES, son of James Francis-5 HOLMES (Temperance-4 CLARK; Sally-3 CROCKER; Timothy-2; Peletiah-1) and Mary Emeline SMITH, was born 18 Oct 1866 at Calais, Washington County, Maine. He married Hannah Elzina JELLISON on 2 June 1891 at Princeton, Washington County, Maine. She was the daughter of Sylvanus JELLISON and Lydia BROWN, and was born 3 Oct 1872 Princeton, Maine; died 3 Aug 1935 at Grand Lake Stream, Washington Co., ME. Frank Willard-6 HOLMES died 14 Sept 1949 at Calais, ME. They are buried at Grand Lake Stream Cemetery.

Children of Frank W-6 HOLMES and Hannah JELLISON:
   Surname HOLMES
   868. Phillip Franklin   born 13 Jul 1906 Grand Lake Stream, ME.
                           died 14 Mar 1971 Hampden, ME; buried Locust Grove Cemetery there
   869. Olive Evelyn   born 23 Mar 1892 Calais, Maine; died 17 Mar 1912
   870. Grace Emmerline   born 27 Jan 1894 Calais; died 24 Mar 1932
   871. Blanche Mildred   born 8 Aug 1896 Calais; died 14 Jan 1958
   872. James Arthur   born 1 June 1891 Calais; died 11 Jul 1922
   873. Charles Arnold   born 18 Oct 1900 Grand Lake Stream; died 8 July 1901
   874. Allison May   born 6 Mar 1905 Grand Lake Stream; died 8 Sep 1905
   875. child   born _____
   876. child   born _____
   877. Kenneth Neal   born 3 June 1914 Grand Lake Stream; died ca 1915

The Seventh American Generation

653. CAPTAIN EATON-7 CHUTE, son of Mary Ann-6 BROOKS (Timothy-5; Joanna-4 CHUTE; Mary –3 CROCKER; Captain Paul-2; Peletiah-1) and John Ever CHUTE, was born 2 Dec 1864, Nova Scotia. He married Emily Agnes HUDSON ca 18__. She was the daughter of David HUDSON and Jane GUEST, and was born ____. Captain Eaton-7 CHUTE died ca 1908, after falling aboard ship.

Children of Captain Eaton-7 CHUTE and Emily HUDSON:
    Surname CHUTE   (all children born Nova Scotia)
    878. Harold David   born 6 July 1893
    879. Nellie Elma   born 25 Sept 1895; married Lewis LANGDON
    880. Morris Winfred   born 1 Jan 1899; died 27 July 1974 Waterville, ME.

655. HENRY DUNN-7 CHUTE, brother of above, was born 1 Aug 1869, Nova Scotia. He married first to Maude POOLE before 1900. She was born ___; died ___. He married 2nd to May CLATON/CLAYTON before 1913. Henry-7 CHUTE died ca 1925.

Children of Henry-7 CHUTE and Maude POOLE:
    Surname CHUTE
    881. Mary Anne   born 21 Jan 1900   883. Achsah   born 7 Nov 1904
    882. Mark Henry   born 7 Apr 1901; married Edith PIERCE
Children of Henry-7 CHUTE and May CLAYTON:
    Surname CHUTE
    884. Addie Pearl   born 5 Feb 1913   887. Maude   born 12 Nov 1920
    885. Ida Pauline   born 14 Oct 1914   married Joseph HALL
    886. Reginald   born 7 Sept 1918

658. MYRTLE ROBERTA-7 CHUTE, sister of above, was born 24 Sept 1874, Nova Scotia. She married Burpee ARMSTRONG ca ____. Myrtle-7 CHUTE died ca 1943.

Children of Myrtle-7 CHUTE and Burpee ARMSTRONG:
    Surname ARMSTRONG
    888. Clara   born ca 1901   890. Morgan   born ca 1905
    889. Lloyd   born ca 1903   891. Melbourn   born ca 1908

659. REUBEN PERKINS-7 CHUTE, brother of above, was born 2 Apr 1876, Nova Scotia. He married Clara SIMMS ca ____. He died ca 1941.

Children of Reuben-7 CHUTE and Clara SIMMS:
    Surname CHUTE
    892. Gordon Osmun   born 9 Jan 1904   894. Clifford Robert   born 23 Jan 1909
    893. Lawrence Fred   born 19 Nov 1907   895. Floyd Barry   born 23 Oct 1922

660. EFFIE-7 CHUTE, sister of above, was born 13 May 1878, Nova Scotia. She married Bradford POOLE ca ____. She died ca 1945.

Children of Effie-7 CHUTE and Bradford POOLE:
    Surname POOLE
    896. Leta Marion   born ca 1898   900. Elvin Israel   born ca 1906
    897. Vaughn Eber   born ca 1900   901. Mildred   born ca 1908, d y
    898. Kathleen Dorcas   born ca 1902   902. Harvey Bradford   born ca 1910
    899. Alyce Susanne   born ca 1905   903. Minnie Myrl   born ca 1913
            married Harold PALMER EOL   904. Myrna Doris   born ca 1915

673. JESSIE MARGUERITE-7 ALDRED   see # 692 BURTON THOMAS-7 GOULD

681. AUGUSTA ARMINELLA-7 " Nellie " NOWLIN, daughter of Margaret-6 ALDRED (Abigail-5 CROCKER; John-4; Paul-3;2; Peletiah-1) and George T. NOWLIN, was born 7 Apr 1878 at South Boston, MA. She married Francis P-7 MATHEWS on 11 July 1905 at Everett, MA. He was the son of George Harvey-6 MATHEWS ++ and Selina H-6 SWETT ++; and was born 27 Sept 1878 at Everett, MA.; died 7 Oct 1968 at Norwich, NY. Augusta A-7 NOWLIN died 6 June 1962 at Oxford, NY. They resided at Boston and Williamstown, MA.; and Rotterdam Junction and Pattersonville, NY

Children of Augusta A-7 NOWLIN and Francis-7 MATHEWS:
  Surname MATHEWS
+ 905. RUTH LUCILLE   born 17 June 1906 Everett, MA; died 30 July 1972 Ithaca, NY
                        married James Justin WHITE 19 May 1928 Geneseo, NY
                        (he son/o James Edward WHITE and Susan HAWKINS)
                        (he born 20 Jan 1897; died 15 Aug 1951)
  906. Evelyn Audrey   born 2 Dec 1907 Williamstown, MA; married Lawrence HARDING
  907. Helen Barbara   born 3 May 1909 Rotterdam Junction, NY; married Walter KING
  908. Robert Harvey   born 24 Sept 1910 Rotterdam Junction; 1m. Margaret SARGEANT
                        2m. Roberta THOMAS
  909. Margaret Edith   born ca 1913 Pattersonville, NY; died 1952

++ Ancestry of George Harvey-6 MATHEWS

CALEB-2, the son of the immigrant CALEB-1 MATHEWS (1675-1755) and Elizabeth HOTCHKISS (1684–1736), was born 18 Dec 1703 at New Haven, CT. He married Ruth-2 MERRIAM on 9 May 1733 at Wallingford, CT. She was the daughter of William-1 MERRIAM and Ruth WEBB, and was born 12 Nov 1713 at Lynn, MA.; died 3 Nov 1785 at Bristol, CT. Caleb-2 MATHEWS died 7 Apr 1786 at Bristol, CT.

JOHN-3 MATHEWS, son of Caleb-2, was born 24 Apr 1750 at East Plymouth, CT. He married Olive-3 ROYCE (Abel-2; Samuel-1) on 30 Nov 1769 at Bristol, CT. Olive was born 12 June 1749 at Farmington, CT; died ca 1815. John-3 MATHEWS died ca 1840 at Norwich, CT.

JOHN P-4 MATHEWS, son of John-3, was born 31 May 1781 at Bristol, CT. He married Cynthia-4 BRADLEY ca 1814 at Norwich, VT. Cynthia-4 was the daughter of Jonathan-3 BRADLEY (Jonathan-3; Nehemiah-2; Joseph-1) and Hannah HAZELTINE, and was born 7 Oct 1790 at Claremont, NH; died 27 June 1868 at Norwich, VT.

PHILANDER-5 MATHEWS, son of John-4, was born 30 Apr 1831 at Norwich, VT. He married Matilda HUNTOON; and died 28 Dec 1908 at Everett, MA. GEORGE HARVEY-6 MATHEWS, son of Philander-5, was born 7 Dec 1857 at Roxbury, MA. He married Selina H-6 SWETT ca ____. She was the daughter of Joseph-5 SWETT (Joseph- 4; 3; Noah-2; Benjamin-1) and Betsey R. SMITH, and was born 11 Feb 1859; died 28 July 1944 at Somerville, MA.

692. BURTON THOMAS-7 GOULD, son of Ida May-6 CROCKER (James-5; John-4; Paul-3;2; Peletiah-1) , was born 22 Jan 1881 at Aylesford, Nova Scotia. He married his cousin JESSIE MARGUERITE-7 ALDRED (# 673) on 28 Feb 1912 at Farmington, Nova Scotia. She was the daughter of John Mortimer-6 ALDRED and Elizabeth McMASTER, and was born 27 Dec 1892 at Rockville, NS; died 6 July 1967 at North Reading, MA. Burton Thomas-7 GOULD died 19 Apr 1953 at Torbrook Mines, Nova Scotia.

Children of Burton T-7 GOULD and Jessie-7 ALDRED:
   Surname GOULD   (1st child born Meadowvale, NS; the others at Boston, MA)
  910. Donald Addison born 24 1915; married Dorothy Theresa GRAY 17 Mar 1952
  911. James Earl   born 3 July 1916; died 25 Dec 1990 Port Richey, FL
                       married Ruth Marion BENNETT 17 Aug 1952 N. Reading, MA
  912. Burton T. Jr.   born 2 Nov 1919; died 16 July 1991 Brockton, MA
                       married Marion Louise MAHER 3 July 1944
+ 913. DOROTHY MAE   born 31 Dec 1920
                       married Alvah Albertus RUSHFORTH 19 June 1943 Dorchester, MA
  914. John Mortimer   born 17 Jan 1925; died 30 Oct 1989
                       married Virginia Lee FRANCE 26 Feb 1946 KY

711. EVA-7 SPINNEY, daughter of William G-6 SPINNEY (Jacob Beach-5; Ann-4 CROCKER; Paul-3; 2; Peletiah-1) and Flora HUTCHINSON, was born ca 1889. She married Samuel GRIFFIN ca 1914. He was born ca 1894; died 1954. Eva-7 SPINNEY died ca 1976

Children of Eva-7 SPINNEY and Samuel GRIFFIN:
    Surname GRIFFIN

+ 915. LLOYD	born ca 19__; married Ethel PIERCE	917. Vivian	born ca 19__
916. Hazel	born ca 19__; married Percy CHUTE		

714. HELEN LUCY-7 SPINNEY, daughter of James-6 SPINNEY (Harding Theodore-5; Ann-4 CROCKER; Paul-3; 2; Peletiah-1) and Mary FITCH, was born ca 1895. She married John GRIFFIN ca 1924. He was born ca 1897; died 1974. Helen Lucy-7 died 1981.

Children of Helen Lucy-7 SPINNEY and John GRIFFIN:
    Surname GRIFFIN
+ 918. ELSIE MAY   born ca 1928; married Earl FOSTER ca 1946
+ 919. CURTIS JAMES   born ca 1930; married Evelyn CRAWFORD ca 1958

715. LAURA BLANCHE-7 SPINNEY, daughter of James Beach-6 SPINNEY (Harding T-5; Anna G-4 CROCKER; Paul-3;2; Peletiah-1) and Mary FITCH, was born ca 1897 at ____. She married MAYNARD-7 SPINNEY (# 717) ca ____. He was the son of Edward M-6 SPINNEY and Bessie WEBBER, and was born 1897; died 1978. Laura B-7 SPINNEY died 1977.

Children of Laura B-7 SPINNEY and Maynard-7 SPINNEY:
    Surname SPINNEY
920. Gerald Edward   born ca 1928; married Ann FORTIN
921. Marina Blanche   born ca 1935; 1m. James CLARK; 2m. Del CHRISTIANSON

717 MAYNARD-7 SPINNEY   see # 715 LAURA BLANCHE-7 SPINNEY

718. LESLIE MANNING-7 SPINNEY, son of Edward H-6 SPINNEY (Caleb-5; Ann G-4 CROCKER; Paul-3; 2; Peletiah-1) and Bessie WEBBER, was born ca 1898 at ____. He married BEATRICE-7 SPINNEY (# 726) ca ____. She was the daughter of Melbourne-6 SPINNEY and Harriet SMALL, and was born ca 1899; died ____. Leslie-7 SPINNEY died 1982.

Children of Leslie-7 SPINNEY and Beatrice-7 SPINNEY:
    Surname SPINNEY
922. Frances   born ca 1929; married Keith HATT
923. Constance   born ca 1939; married Robert McMAHON

720. ALBERT W-7 SPINNEY, brother of above, was born ca 1908 at ____. He married Daisie MARSHALL ca ____. She was the daughter of ____ MARSHALL, and was born ca 1912; died ____.

Children of Albert-7 SPINNEY and Daisie MARSHALL:
    Surname SPINNEY

924. Ena Ewen	born ca 1945; married David JONES	925. Brenda L.	born ca 1951

721. HORACE LESTER-7 SPINNEY, son of Melbourne-6 SPINNEY (Beriah-5; Ann G-4 CROCKER; Paul-3; 2; Peletiah-1) and Harriet SMALL, was born ca 1887. He married Gladys KEDDY ca ____. She was the daughter of ____ KEDDY, and was born ____; died ____. Horace-7 SPINNEY died 1951.

Children of Horace-7 SPINNEY and Gladys KEDDY:
    Surname SPINNEY
926. Neil   born ca 1912; married Eva WORTHINGTON
927. Allston   born ca 1914; married Myrtle CLATTENBURG

725. HOWE BELL-7 SPINNEY, brother of above, was born ca 1894. He married Bessie PARKER ca ____. She was born 1893; died 1975. Howe-7 SPINNEY died 1965.

Children of Howe-7 SPINNEY and Bessie PARKER:
    Surname SPINNEY
+ 928. ELLIS   born 1927; marr Irene HERGET   930. Clare * born 1935; marr J. FARNSWORTH
   929. Mary Ellen born 1929; marr Edgar NORMAN   * 1 ch: Thomas Howe-9 SPINNEY born 1956

726. BEATRICE-7 SPINNEY see # 718 LESLIE MANNING-7 SPINNEY
727. WINTHROP HARRIS-7 SPINNEY, son of Leland-6 SPINNEY (Enoch-5; Ann G-4 CROCKER; Paul-3; 2; Peletiah-1) and Agnes D. HARRIS, w as born ca 1900. He married Marjorie Eunice WHITAKER ca ____. She was born ca 1911; died ____. Winthrop-7 SPINNEY died ca 1950.

Children of Winthrop-7 SPINNEY and Marjorie WHITAKER:
    Surname SPINNEY
   931. Charlotte Cynthia   born 1936
+ 932. JAMES LELAND   born ca 1940; married Janis E. BROWN
+ 933. WINTHROP WARREN   born ca 1945; married Patricia A. COOPER

728. KINGSLEY SELLAR-7 SPINNEY, brother of above, was born 23 July 1902. He married Evelyn PALMER ca 19__. He died 22 March 1973.

Child of Kingsley-7 SPINNEY and Evelyn PALMER:
    Surname SPINNEY
+ 934. PHYLLIS MAE   born 15 June 1935; married Ervin Clifford WARD 22 Sept 1954

729. VERA BELLE-7 SPINNEY, sister of above, was born 26 Mar 1904. She married Cecil PALMER on 15 Dec 1925. She died 27 Apr 1951 at Nicholsville, Nova Scotia.

Children of Vera Belle-7 SPINNEY and Cecil PALMER:
    Surname PALMER
+ 935. GERALD EUGENE   born 12 Oct 1931; married Joan CLARK June 1951 Harmony, NS
+ 936. JOYCE AGNES   born 5 May 1936; 1m. Howard JOHNSON 19 June 1963
                            2m. Leonard MacINNIS 3 July 1965
+ 937. ALFARETTA B.   born 6 Nov 1937; married Almon Lawrence MORSE 30 Sept 1958

730. EARLE WINFRED-7 SPINNEY, brother of above, was born 12 Jan 1914. He married Flora MORSE ca 19__. He died 28 April 1980.

Children of Earle-7 SPINNEY and Flora MORSE:
    Surname SPINNEY
+ 938. SANDRA LOUISE   born 3 Nov 1939, NS; married James THAIN 19 Dec 1959 NS
+ 939. DELMA PEARL   born 4 Dec 1942; married Jeffrey Oliver NEWMAN 12 Mar 1960 NS

731. FRANCIS LELAND-7 SPINNEY, brother of above, was born 15 Aug 1915. He married Leonore Muriel BRYDEN / BRYDON on 20 Apr 1946 at Black Rock, Nova Scotia. Francis-7 SPINNEY died 28 Aug 1979.

Children of Francis Leland-7 SPINNEY and Leonore BRYDON:
    Surname SPINNEY
+ 940. PHILIP VANCE   born 15 Nov 1946; married Phyllis Donna PARSONS 11 Nov 1967
+ 941. DORIS AGNES   born 17 Jan 1948; married Marshall Hedley SCHOFIELD 14 Oct 1967
+ 942. VERA ANNE   born 16 Oct 1953; married Jordan YARN 25 Mar 1972
   943. Catherine Frances born 9 Dec 1961

733. BURPEE CLYDE-7 SPINNEY, son of Burpee-6 SPINNEY (Clark T-5; Ann G-4 CROCKER; Paul-3; 2) and Maria STEELE, was born 18 Aug 1912. He married Bertha Maud CHAMBERS on 30 Nov 1935.

Children of Burpee-7 SPINNEY and Bertha CHAMBERS:
    Surname SPINNEY
    944. Alden Clark born ca 193_   945. Carole Grace born ca 19__; married Wm. S. SPINNEY

739. VICTOR-7 CROCKER, son of Roulof-6 CROCKER (John M-5; James-4; Paul-3 2; Peletiah-1) and Charlotte JACKSON, was born ca 1887. He married BLANCHE ETHEL-7 CHARLTON (# 743) ca ____. She was the daughter of Albert R. CHARLTON and Amoret Jane-6 CROCKER, and was born 15 Sept 1906; died 28 Dec 1980. Victor-7 died ____.

Child of Victor-7 CROCKER and Blanche-7 CHARLTON:
    Surname CROCKER
+ 946. GERALDINE   born 1928; married Jack DEMPSEY (he born 1928)

741. GRACE MAY-7 CHARLTON, daughter of Amoret-6 CROCKER (John M-5; James-4; Paul-3; 2; Peletiah-1) and Albert Ralph CHARLTON, was born 18 Dec 1890 at Harmony, Nova Scotia. She married Ellwood Irving TEMPLE on 10 Dec 1910 at Holyoke, MA. He was the son of George Irving TEMPLE and Flora Levina WOOD, and was born 4 Feb 1888 at Pittsburg, PA; died 18 Jan 1940 at Worcester, MA. Grace May-7 died 27 June 1986.

Children of Grace May-7 CHARLTON and Ellwood Irving TEMPLE:
    Surname TEMPLE
+ 947. IRVINE   born 9 Mar 1912 Hartford, Hartford, CT
       CHARLTON   married Frank Sydney ANDREWS 17 June 1931 Nashua, NH
                       (he born 18 May 1911 Essex,MA; died ____)
+ 948. MARJORY JANE born 1920; married David Ernest TAYLOR (he born 1921)

743. BLANCHE ETHEL-7 CHARLTON   see # 739 VICTOR-7 CROCKER
745. MAYFRED DELILAH-7 CROCKER, daughter of Lamert-6 CROCKER (John M-5; James-4; Paul-3; 2; Peletiah-1) and Agnes WINOTT, was born ca 1909. She married Kenneth Earl SPINNEY ca ____.

Children of Mayfred-7 CROCKER and Kenneth SPINNEY:
    Surname SPINNEY
+ 949. GERALDINE DELORES   born 1932; married Donald F. SMITH
  950. Philip Kenneth   born 1938; married Marth HILL
                           (2 children: Karen-9 and Stephen-9 SPINNEY)

747. LORNA MARGUERITE-7 CROCKER, sister of above, was born ca 1913. She married Vernon Hadley PALMER ca ____. He was the son of ____ PALMER, and was born 1911.

Children of Lorna-7 CROCKER and Vernon PALMER:
    Surname PALMER
  951. Milton LaVerne   born 1939; married Mary Phyllis / Phillis WALSH
  952. Linda Evelyn   born 1946; married Chesley SHANE

748. NOLA BEATRICE-7 CROCKER, sister of above, was born ca 1915. She married Vincent David HILTZ ca ____. He was the son of ____ HILTZ, and was born 1913; died ____. Nola-7 died 1975.

Children of Nola-7 CROCKER and Vincent HILTZ:
    Surname HILTZ
  953. Barbara Ann   born 1939; married Keith CUMMINGS
  954. Betty Jean   born 194_; married Charles David Freeman LUSBY

Children of Nola-7 CROCKER, continued:
    Surname HILTZ
  955. Lawrence T.   born 194_; married Linda Foster CAREY
  956. Bernice   born 19__; married Fred CLARKE
  957. Gordon David   born 19__; married Linda CARVER

751. ELSIE PAULINE-7 CROCKER, sister of above, was born ca 1920. She married Hubert Osborne STEELE ca ____. He was the son of ____ STEELE, and was born 1921.

Children of Elsie-7 CROCKER and Hubert STEELE:
    Surname STEELE
  958. Elaine Gwenda   born 1946; married Lewis Ervin TURNER
         2 children: Kimberly Darlene-9 (born 1965) and Crystal Lynn –9 (born 1966) TURNER
  959. Garth Hubert   born 1951; married Joan Marie McKINNON
         3 ch: Angela –9 (born 1980); Darren Wayne-9 (born 1982); and Ashley Jane-9 STEELE

759. ALMIRA-7 GARDNER, daughter of Mary E-6 GARDNER (Rebecca-5 CROCKER; John-4;3;2; Peletiah-1) and James T. GARDNER, was born ca ____. She married Loring A. HOLMES ca _____.

Children of Almira-7 GARDNER and Loring HOLMES:
    Surname HOLMES

960. Edna	born ____	963. Emma	born ____
961. Thomas S.	born ____	964. Cora	born ____
962. Nellie E.	born ____	965. U. Grant *	born ____

                     Note: U. Grant-8 HOLMES was a trader in Cherryfield, Maine

804. JOSEPHINE NASH-7 CURTIS, daughter of Edward-6 CURTIS (Mercy-5 CROCKER; Mariner G-4; James W-3; John-2; Peletiah-1) and Mary COLSON, was born 6 Apr 1889 at Cambridge, MA. She married William Silliman-7 FOSTER ++ 22 July 1918 at Machias, ME. He was the son of William Carlos-6 FOSTER ++ and Katherine Frances LANGDON, and was born 15 Oct 1886 at Water Mill, Long Island, New York; died 2 Jan 1926 at Minneapolis, MN. Josephine N-7 CURTIS died 3 July 1941 at Minneapolis.

Children of Josephine N-7 CURTIS and William S. FOSTER:
    Surname FOSTER
+ 966. MARIAN   born 2 July 1922 Minneapolis, MN
      AUGUSTA   married Alexander Stuart FRASER Aug 1953
                     (he born 18 March 1923 Minneapolis, MN)
  967. Harriet Wilson   born 24 Apr 1925 Minneapolis, MN; unmarried

                  ++ Ancestry of William Silliman-7 FOSTER
BENJAMIN HALSEY-4 FOSTER (Matthew-3; Stephen-2; 1) was born 21 Dec 1795 at Southampton, New York. He married Fanny-4 SAYRE , daughter of Rufus-3 SAYRE (Joshua-2; Nehemiah-1). She was born 3 Jan / June 1806; died 7 Aug 1890 at Water Mill, Long Island, NY. Benjamin-4 died 22 Nov 1863 at Southampton, Long Island, NY.

WILLIAM SAYRE-5 FOSTER, son of Benjamin-4, was born 13 Nov 1828 at Water Mill, LI,NY. he married Harriet SILLIMAN 9 Dec 1857. She was the daughter of Samuel Carlos SILLIMAN and Harriet L'HOMMEDIEU, and was born 22 June 1837 at Chester, CT; died 18 Apr 1877 at Water Mill, LI, NY. William-5 FOSTER died 4 Sep 1885 at Water Mill.

WILLIAM CARLOS-6 FOSTER was born 28 Sept 1858 at Chester, CT. He married Katherine Frances LANGDON 26 / 28 Nov 1885. She was the daughter of William J. LANGDON and Catherine F. HAYNES, and was born 8 June 1858 at Brooklyn, NY; died 22 Oct 1942 at Water Mill, LI. William C-6 FOSTER died 2 Aug 1927 at Southampton, NY. William Silliman-7 FOSTER, the son of William-6, married Josephine Nash-7 CURTIS (above).

830. SEYMOUR HARMON-7 BOWKER, son of Simeon-6 BOWKER (Nathan S-5; Martha G-4 CROCKER; Simeon-3; John-2) and Keziah HOLMES, was born 29 Mar 1875. He married Lillie Mabel GETCHELL on 8 July 1896. She was the daughter of Jacob GETCHELL and Josephine BERRY, and was born 24 Jan 1877; died 13 Jan 1938. Seymour-7 BOWKER died 26 June 1939.

Children of Seymour-7 BOWKER and Lillie GETCHELL:
   Surname BOWKER

+ 968. ESTHER LILLIE	born 23 Sept 1897; died 16 Apr 1969 MA	
	married Lee Martin GETCHELL, Jr. 16 June 1921	
969. Hazel	born 10 Mar 1899; married Carl THOMPSON; died 26 Feb 1993 RI	
970. Oscar	born 25 Sept 1900; married Leona COOPER; died 27 Mar 1994 MA	
971. Mabel	born 16 May 1904; died June 1986	
	married William I. HANSCOM 16 June 1925	
	(he born 11 Apr 1903; died June 1977	
972. Leslie (Sr)	born 20 Jan 1906 ; died 16 Aug 1996 MA	
	married Etta M. LARKIN 24 June 1931	
973. Alvin (Sr.)	born 20 June 1907; died Mar 1968	
	married Etta M. GARDNER 24 June 1931	
974. Gertrude E.	born 31 Mar 1912; died 25 May 1997 Marshfield, ME	
	married Eldon LYON(S), Sr. 8 July 1935 Marshfield, ME	
	(he born 13 Jan 1913; died 8 Jul 1990)	

848. JOE WARREN-7 GERRITY, son of Nancy Frances-6 KILLMAN (Diadema-5 RICHARDS; Captain James-4; Hannah-3 CROCKER; Timothy-2; Peletiah-1) and James GERRITY, was born 14 Dec 1886 at Prospect, Maine. He married Florence Margaret-11 McKEE on 5 Jan 1914. She was the daughter of ____ McKEE and Florence Elfreda McCUTCHEON, and was born 21 May 1891 at Grand Rapids, MI; died 7 July 1989 (98 yr). She was a 1913 graduate of Vassar College. (Maine State Archives Certificate # 8905779) They resided Newton, MA. Joe Warren –7 GERRITY died Apr 1967 Suffolk, MA.

Children of Joe Warren-7 GERRITY and Florence McKEE:
   Surname GERRITY

975. Robert McCutcheon	born 25 Jan 1915; died 20 Aug 1915
976. Joseph Warren	born 14 Aug 1916
977. James Francis II	born 3 Dec 1918

851. JULIA POPE-7 AMES, daughter of John Keller-6 AMES (Captain Alfred-5 AMES; Abigail-4 CLARK; Sally-3 CROCKER; Timothy-2; Pelatiah-1) and Sarah Albee SANBORN, was born ca ____. She married Rufus Clinton FULLER 5 Oct 1856 at Providence, RI. He was the son of Frederick FULLER, and Mary L. SMITH, and was born ____; died ____. He was from Providence, Rhode Island.

Children of Julia Pope-7 AMES and Rufus Clinton FULLER:
   Surname FULLER

978. Margaret Ames	born ____	980. Rufus Clinton, Jr.	born ___
979. Harriet A.	born ____		

The Eighth American Generation

905. RUTH LUCILLE-8 MATHEWS, daughter of Augusta A-7 NOWLIN (Margaret-6 ALDRED; Abigail-5 CROCKER; John-4; Paul-3; 2; Peletiah-1) and Francis MATHEWS, was born 17 June 1906 at Everett, MA. She married James Justin-4 WHITE on 19 May 1928 at Geneseo, New York. He was the son of James Edward-3 WHITE and Susan HAWKINS, and was born 20 Jan 1897 at Rochester, NY.; died 15 Aug 1951 at Lansing, NY. Ruth L-8 MATHEWS died 30 July 1972 at Ithaca, Tompkins County, NY.

Children of Ruth L-8 MATHEWS and James J. WHITE:
   Surname WHITE
   981. Joyce Justine   born 1930; married Alex CIMA, Jr.
   982. Judith Anne   born 1937

913. DOROTHY MAE-8 GOULD, daughter of Burton Thomas-7 GOULD (Ida Mae-6 CROCKER; James-5; John-4; Paul-3; 2; Peletiah-1) and Jessie-7 ALDRED, was born 31 Dec 1920 at South Boston, MA. She married Alvah Albertus " Bert " RUSHFORTH, Jr. on 19 June 1943 at Dorchester, MA. He was the son of Alvah A. RUSHFORTH, Sr. and Ethel Melissa EAGER, and was born 23 Mar 1916; died 21 Apr 1949 at Eaton, Weld County, Colorado.

Children of Dorothy-8 GOULD and Alvah RUSHFORTH, Jr.:
   Surname RUSHFORTH
   983. Janice Lee   born 15 Aug 1944 Boston, MA; unmarried 1996
                  (changed name to REVELL)
   984. Bruce Alan, Sr.   born 8 Feb 1947; married Aurelia Alice ESTY 24 Nov 1965 at Hingham, MA

915. LLOYD-8 GRIFFIN, son of Eva-7 SPINNEY (William G-6; Jacob Beach-5; Ann-4 CROCKER; Paul-3; 2) and Samuel GRIFFIN, was born ca 19__. He married Ethel PIERCE.

Children of Lloyd-8 GRIFFIN and Ethel PIERCE:
   Surname GRIFFIN
   985. Harold   born ca 19__; married Pamela MEISNER
   986. Roy   born ca 19__; married Muriel HILTZ
   987. Veloria   born ca 19__; married Richard/Rick GIBSON

918. ELSIE MAY-8 GRIFFIN, daughter of Helen Lucy-7 SPINNEY (James-6; Harding T-5; Ann-4 CROCKER; Paul –3;2) and John GRIFFIN, was born ca 1928. She married Earl FOSTER ca 1946.

Children of Elsie May-8 GRIFFIN and Earl FOSTER:
   Surname FOSTER
   988. Marguerite Ann   born ca 1946; married William RIUTTA
   989. David Earl   born ca 1951; married Shelley MONK
   990. George Vernon   born ca 1957; married Jocelyn GOULD

919. CURTIS JAMES-8 GRIFFIN, brother of above, was born ca 1930. He married Evelyn CRAWFORD ca 1958.

Children of Curtis-8 GRIFFIN and Evelyn CRAWFORD:
   Surname GRIFFIN
   991. Linda Marie   born ca 1959   993. Susan Marie   born ca 1963
   992. Eric James   born ca 1961

928. ELLIS-8 SPINNEY, son of Howe Bell-7 SPINNEY (Melbourne-6; Beriah-5; Ann G-4 CROCKER; Paul-3; 2; Peletiah-1) and Bessie PARKER, was born ca 1927. He married Irene HERGET ca ____. She was the daughter of ____ HERGET, and was born ____.

Children of Ellis-8 SPINNEY and Irene HERGET:
   Surname SPINNEY

994. Janice	born 1958	996. Glenna	born 1963
995. Allen	born 1959	997. Wynne	born 1966

932. JAMES LELAND-8 SPINNEY, son of Winthrop-7 SPINNEY (Leland-6; Enoch-5; Ann G-4 CROCKER; Paul-3; 2; Peletiah-1) and Marjorie WHITAKER, was born 16 July 1940 at Worcester, MA. He married Janis Elizabeth BROWN on 12 Oct 1963 at Westboro, MA.

Children of James Leland-8 SPINNEY and Janis BROWN:
   Surname SPINNEY   (all children born Miami, FL)

998. Jean Marjorie	born 31 Aug 1964	1000. James Winthrop born 29 May 1968
999. Jean Elisabeth	born 14 June 1966	

933. WINTHROP WARREN-8 SPINNEY, brother of above, was born 19 Mar 1945 at Milford, MA. he married Patricia Ann COOPER on 15 Apr 1967 at Marlboro, MA.

Children of Winthrop W-8 SPINNEY and Patricia COOPER:
   Surname SPINNEY

1001. Winthrop James	born 1 June 1970 Rantoul, IL	1003. Cathryn Jean	born 27 Jan 1977
1002. Jennifer Marie	born 26 Apr 1973 Sumter, SC		Tampa, FL

934. PHYLLIS MAE-8 SPINNEY, daughter of Kingsley –7 SPINNEY (Leland-6; Enoch-5; Ann G-4 CROCKER; Paul-3; 2; Peletiah-1) and Evelyn PALMER, was born 15 June 1935. She married Ervin Clifford WARD on 22 Sept 1954.

Children of Phyllis-8 SPINNEY and Ervin WARD:
   Surname WARD

1004. Barbara Louise	born 13 Dec 1955; married Michael ROSS
1005. Carolyn	born 6 Aug 1958
1006. Kathleen	born 27 Aug 1961; married Michael SCHMEISSER

935. GERALD EUGENE-8 PALMER, son of Vera Belle-7 SPINNEY (Leland-6; Enoch-5; Ann-4 CROCKER, Paul-3;2; Peletiah-1) and Cecil PALMER, was born 12 Oct 1931. He married Joan CLARK June 1951 at Harmony, Nova Scotia.

Children of Gerald-8 PALMER and Joan CLARK:
   Surname PALMER

1007. Deborah Lynn	born 14 June 1952
1008. Patricia Joy born 23 Feb 1954	

936. JOYCE AGNES-8 PALMER, sister of above, was born 5 May 1936. She married first to Howard JOHNSON on 19 June 1953. She married second to Leonard McINNIS on 3 July 1965.

Children of Joyce-8 PALMER and Howard JOHNSON:
   Surname JOHNSON

1009. Gary A.	born 17 Mar 1954	1011. Kim	born 18 July 1956
1010. Wayne	born 28 June 1955		

Children of Joyce-8 PALMER and Leonard McINNIS:
   Surname McINNIS

1012. Peter	born 10 May 1968	1013. Dwight born 1 May 1971

937. ALFARETTA BLANCHE-8 PALMER, sister of above, was born 6 Nov 1937 at Harmony, Nova Scotia. She married Almon Lawrence MORSE on 20 Sep 1958 at Aylesford, Nova Scotia.

Children of Alfaretta-8 PALMER and Almon MORSE:
  Surname MORSE
  1014. Heather   born 15 May 1965   1016. Dianna   born 27 Mar 1969
  1015. Sheila   born 23 Jan 1968   1017. Anthony   born 13 Nov 1970

938. SANDRA LOUISE-8 SPINNEY, daughter of Earle Winfred-7 SPINNEY (Leland-6; Enoch-5; Ann-4 CROCKER; Paul-3; 2; Peletaih-1) and Flora MORSE, was born 3 Nov 1939 at Middleton, Nova Scotia. She married James THAIN on 19 Dec 1959 at Greenwood, NS.

Children of Sandra-8 SPINNEY and James THAIN:
  Surname THAIN   (1st four children born Middleton, NS; last 2 born Ottawa, Ontario, Canada)
  1018. Kimberly Ann   born 5 Dec 1960   1022. Steven Earle   born 30 Sept 1968
  1019. Lisa Carol   born 30 Dec 1961   1023. Tasha Marie   born 23 Apr 1970
  1020. James   born 25 June 1963   married Larry GALLANT
  1021. Susan Louise   born 10 Feb 1965

939. DELMA PEARL-8 SPINNEY, sister of above, was born 4 Dec 1942 at Middleton, Nova Scotia. She married Jeffrey Oliver NEWMAN on 12 Mar 1960 at Greenwood, Nova Scotia

Children of Delma-8 SPINNEY and Jeffrey NEWMAN:
  Surname NEWMAN   (1st three born Middleton, NS; last 2 born Edmonton, Alberta, Canada)
  1024. Debra Pearl   born 10 Nov 1960
  1025. Jacqueline Margaret   born 19 Nov 1961
                                 married Ivan Raymond LOVELY 3 Mar 1981 Mission, BC
  1026. John Thomas   born 15 Oct 1963
  1027. Pamela Helen " Tammi " born 15 Dec 1968; married Mark Victor LUSK 26 Aug 1989 Mission
  1028. Randall Jeffrey   born 27 Mar 1971

940. PHILIP VANCE-8 SPINNEY, son of Francis Leland-7 SPINNEY (Leland-6; Enoch-5; Ann-4 CROCKER; Paul-3; 2; Peletiah-1) and Leonore BRYDEN/BRYDON, was born 15 Nov 1946. He married Phyllis Donna PARSONS on 11 Nov 1967.

Children of Philip-8 SPINNEY and Phyllis PARSONS:
  Surname SPINNEY
  1029. Stephanie   born ca 1968/69   1031. Jennifer Dawn   born 8 Nov 1971
  1030. Candace Nadine   born 29 Apr 1970   1032. Justin Philip   born 28 Jan 1979; d y

941. DORIS AGNES-8 SPINNEY, sister of above, was born 17 Jan 1948. She married Marshall Hedley SCHOFIELD on 14 Oct 1967.

Children of Doris-8 SPINNEY and Marshall SCHOFIELD:
  Surname SCHOFIELD
  1033. Denise Jeanette   born 28 July 1972   1034. Dwayne Marshall   born 23 Feb 1978

942. VERA ANNE-8 SPINNEY, sister of above, was born 6 Oct 1953. She married Jordan YARN on 25 Mar 1972.

Children of Vera-8 SPINNEY and Jordan YARN:
  Surname YARN
  1035. Lucinda Kelley   born May 1978   1036. Philip Jordan   born 6 Oct 1980

946. GERALDINE-8 CROCKER, daughter of Victor-7 CROCKER (Roulof-6; John M-5; James-4; Paul-3;2; Peletiah-1) and Blanche CHARLTON, was born ca 1928. She married Jack SWEENEY ca ____. He was the son of _____ SWEENEY, and was born ____.

Children of Geraldine-8 CROCKER and Jack SWEENEY:
   Surname SWEENEY

1037. Vickie	born 1949	1039. John Francis	born 1954
married Albert E. SKULCZYCK		1040. Michael James	born 1956
1038. Robert John	born 1950		married Joanne MEEK

947. IRVINE CHARLTON-8 TEMPLE, daughter of Grace May-7 CHARLTON (Amoret-6 CROCKER; John M-5; James-4; Paul-3;2; Peletiah-1) and Ellwood Irving TEMPLE, was born 9 Mar 1912. She married Frank Sydney ANDREWS on 17 June 1931 at Nashua, NH. He was the son of Frank Albert ANDREWS and Lavinia Wells GODDARD, and was born 18 May 1911 at Essex, Essex County, MA.

Children of Irvine-8 TEMPLE and Frank S. ANDREWS:
   Surname ANDREWS

+1041. SYDNEY BYRON born 22 Sept 1932 Framingham, Middlesex County, MA
                   1m. June Margaret LANG 14 July 1951 (divorced) (she born 1934)
                   2m. Doris GATES Inman 24 June 1960 (divorced)
+1042. SHIRLEY MAE   born 10 Oct 1934 Worcester, Worcester County, MA
                married Donald Edwin WARE, Jr. 26 Sept 1953 Westboro, MA (he born 1935)
+1043. CAROLE JOAN born 8 Sept 1938 Worcester, MA
                1m. Nelson Richard NEDDE 7 Sept 1958 (divorced)
                (he born 1936; died 1990)
                2m. Allen ERLER 13 Feb 1981 (he born 1943)
+1044. BETTY ELAINE born 1 Feb 1943 Worcester, MA
                married James David STOREY 18 Mar 1967 Pittsburgh, Allegheny, PA
                (he born 1939; died 1992)

948. MARJORY JANE-8 TEMPLE, sister of above, was born 13 Nov 1920 at Grosse Isle, Wayne County, MI. She married David Ernest TAYLOR on 6 June 1942 at Worcester, MA. He was the son of Harry TAYLOR and Harriet Edith CHATTERTON, and was born 9 Dec 1921 Ashland, Middlesex County, MA.

Children of Marjory-8 TEMPLE and David TAYLOR:
   Surname TAYLOR

+ 1045. DAVID   born 2 Mar 1943 Framingham, MA
      ELLWOOD   married Abbie Dingley AUSTIN 3 May 1975 at Vineyard Haven, Dukes, MA
                (she born 30 May 1949 , Farmington, Maine)
  1046. Gregory Allen born 30 Jan 1949 Marlborough, MA
                married Rita FAIRCLOTH 27 June 1976 at Knoxville, TN
          (she dau/o Jefferson FAIRCLOTH and Arlene REAVES) (she born 1 Feb 1949, AL)
          1 child: Matthew Allen-10 TAYLOR born 16 Feb 1979 Dahran, Saudi Arabia

949. GERALDINE DELORES-8 SPINNEY, daughter of Mayfred-7 CROCKER (Lamert-6; John M-5; James-4; Paul-3; 2; Peletiah-1) and Kenneth SPINNEY, was born ca 1932. She married Donald F. SMITH ca ____. He was the son of ___ SMITH, and was born ____.

Children of Geraldine-8 SPINNEY and Donald SMITH:
   Surname SMITH

1047. Susan	born ____	1050. Christopher	born ___
1048. Deborah June	born ____		married Paula THEODORE
married Philip Anthony TROPASSO		1051. Douglas	born ____
1049. Pamela Gail	born ____; married Mike PERRY		

966. MARIAN AUGUSTA-8 FOSTER, daughter of Josephine Nash-7 CURTIS (Edward-6; Mercy-5 CROCKER; Mariner G-4; James W-3; John-2; Peletiah-1) and William FOSTER, was born 2 July 1922 at Minneapolis, MN. She married first to Oliver Sinclair OSTERBERG on 21 Dec 1946. They divorced Apr

1949, no issue. She married second to Alexander Stuart FRASER Aug 1953. He was the son of Stuart Hugh FRASER of London, England and Aida SCHLEIER of Bahia, Brazil. He was born 18 Mar 1923 Bahia, Brazil.

Children of Marian-8 FOSTER and Alexander FRASER:
    Surname FRASER
+ 1052. ALEXANDRA MARY   born 5 April 1955 Salvador, Bahia, Brazil
                              married Joaquim Antonio de Oliveira PORTELA 10 Feb 1979
+ 1053. ELIZABETH   born 1 Nov 1957
        KATHERINE   married Gerferson Santana LIMA 9 Jan 1982 ; divorced
                              companion of Richardo Ribeiro da SILVA

967. ESTHER LILLIE-8 BOWKER, daughter of Seymour-7 BOWKER (Simeon-6; Nathan-5; Martha G-4 CROCKER; Simeon-3; John-2; Peletiah-1) and Lillie GETCHELL, was born 23 Sept 1897. She married Lee Martin GETCHELL, Jr. on 16 June 1921. He was the son of Lee Martin GETCHELL and Lucinda Smith BERRY, and was born 18 Nov 1897 at Marshfield, Maine; died 4 May 1958 at Bridgewater, MA. Esther Lillie-8 BOWKER died 16 Apr 1969 at Bridgewater, MA.

Children of Esther Lillie-8 BOWKER and Lee GETCHELL, Jr.
    Surname GETCHELL
    1054. Josephine L.   born ca 192_; died young
    1055. Stanley Austin   born 24 Nov 1928, MA; married Norma Anna FILLIPPINI 27 Jan 1950, MA
    1056. Walter Lee   born 16 Nov 1935; married Susan DOLBER (she born 18 Apr 1937)
    1057. Kenneth Paul   born 12 Nov 1939; married Joyce CHILDS   (she born 28 May 1940)

The Ninth American Generation

1041. SYDNEY BYRON-9 ANDREWS, son of Irvine-8 TEMPLE (Grace May-7; Amoret-6 CROCKER; John M-5; James-4; Paul-3; 2; Peletiah-1) and Frank S. ANDREWS, was born 22 Sept 1932 at Framingham, MA. He married June Margaret LANG on 14 July 1951. She was the daughter of Richard LANG and Agnes __?__, and was born 24 May 1934 New Britain, CT. They were divorced. His second wife was Doris GATES Inman. They were married 24 June 1960. She was the daughter of J S GATES, and was born ____ at Westboro, MA. They were divorced.

Children of Sydney-9 ANDREWS and June M. LANG:

Surname ANDREWS	(all children born at Worcester, MA)
+ 1058. ROBERT BYRON	born 19 June 1954
	married Jeanne Marie HANSEN 3 Jan 1976 at Chicago. IL
+ 1059. WENDY LOU	born 27 Aug 1955
	married James Nelson CYR 17 July 1976 at West Brookfield, MA
+ 1060. THOMAS MARK	born 15 Sept 1957
	married Takae KANAI 13 Mar 1984 Tokyo, Japan
	(she dau/o Yutaka KANAI and Keiko NISHIWAKI)
	(she born 1960 Tokyo, Japan)

Child of Sydney-9 ANDREWS and Doris GATES:

Surname ANDREWS	
1061. Kathleen Louise	born 16 Nov 1960; married Gilliam CIOPPA
	1 child: Gilliam (Jill) born 1979

1042. SHIRLEY MAE-9 ANDREWS, sister of above, was born 18 Oct 1934 at Worcester, MA. She married Donald Edwin WARE, Jr. on 26 Sept 1953 at Westboro, MA. He was the son of Donald E. WARE, Sr. and Margaret Ethel TROCHELMAN, and was born 25 Sept 1935 at Chicago, IL.

Children of Shirley-9 ANDREWS and Donald E. WARE, Jr.:

Surname WARE	(all children born Worcester, MA)
1062. William Michael	born 28 Oct 1954;
	1 child: Keith Guy-11 CUMMINGS-WARE born 19 July 1985
	(mother was Laurie CUMMINGS)
1063. Linda Margaret	born 26 Nov 1965; died 22 June 1966
+ 1064. SUSAN ELAINE	born 10 Apr 1960
	1m. John Alden CLARKE 28 Feb 1981 at LaPorte, TX (divorced)
	2m. David E. BROWN 4 Aug 1990

1043. CAROLE JOAN-9 ANDREWS, sister of above, was born 8 Sept 1938. She married first to Nelson Richard NEDDE on 7 Sept 1958 at Wilmette, IL. He was the son of William NEDDE, Sr. and Eleanor __?__, and was born 27 Sept 1936 at Beaver Falls, PA.; died 26 Sept 1990 at North Attleboro, MA. They were divorced. Her second marriage was to Allen ERLER on 13 Feb 1981.

Children of Carole-9 ANDREWS and Nelson NEDDE:

Surname NEDDE	
1065. Deborah Lynn	born 15 Feb 1960 Decatur, IL
+ 1066. ELLEN MARIE	born 31 Aug 1961 Decatur, IL
	married William McKay SHIPP 16 June 1984 at Dranesville, Fairfax, VA
1067. David Nelson	born 5 Sept 1965; married Yuhong ZHANG Feb 1995

1044. BETTY ELAINE-9 ANDREWS, sister of above, was born 1 Feb 1943 at Worcester, MA. She married 18 Mar 1967 to James David STOREY at Pittsburgh, PA. He was the son of William Ryan STOREY and Maxine Anita McCULLOUGH, and was born 29 Oct 19939 at Butler, PA; died 17 Sept 1992 at Lee Township, Allegan, Michigan.

Children of Betty-9 ANDREWS and James David STOREY:
   Surname STOREY
   1068. Laura Elaine   born 6 Oct 1971 Racine , Wisconsin
                           baptized 4 June 1980 Whithall Park Lutheran Church, Hales Corners , WI
   1069. David Ryan   born 6 May 1973 Milwaukee, Wisconsin
                           baptized 4 June 1980 Whithall Park Lutheran Church

1045. DAVID ELLWOOD-9 TAYLOR, son of Marjory Jane-8 TEMPLE (Grace May-7 CHARLTON; Amoret-6 CROCKER; John M-5; James-4; Paul-3;2; Peletiah-1) and David Ernest TAYLOR, was born 2 Mar 1943 at Framingham, Middlesex, MA. He married Abbie Dingley AUSTIN on 3 May 1975 at Vineyard Haven, Dukes County, MA. She was the daughter of _____ AUSTIN, and was born 30 May 1949 at Farmington, Maine.

Children of David-9 TAYLOR and Abbie AUSTIN:
   Surname TAYLOR
   1070. Jane Elizabeth   born 5 Dec 1980   1071. Emily Allison   born 15 July 1986
                       Hyannis, MA   Dover, NH

1052. ALEXANDRA MARY-9 FRASER, daughter of Marian-8 FOSTER (Josephine Nash-7 CURTIS; Edward-6 CURTIS; Mercy-5 CROCKER; Mariner Green-4; James W-3; John-2; Peletiah-1) and Alexander FRASER, was born 5 April 1955 at Salvador, Bahia, Brazil. She married Joaquim Antonio de Oliveira PORTELA on 10 Feb 1979 at the beach house in Mar Grande, on the island of Itaparica, across the bay from Salvador. He was the son of Boa Ventura Nabor Lima PORTELA and Durvalina Cerqueira de OLIVEIRA; and was born 25 March 1954 in Salvador, Bahia, Brazil.

Alexandra was a graduate of the Pan-American School in Brazil, and attended the Philadelphia College of Art. She worked for Dow Chemical in Brazil. In 2000 they resided in Singapore.

Children of Alexandra-9 FRASER and Joquim PORTELA:
   Surname PORTELA
   1072. Bianca Fraser   born 19 June 1980 Boston, MA
       “ Bibi ”   2000 – Junior at Boston University
   1073. Caroline Fraser   born 29 March 1983 Bahia, Brazil
                       2000 – Senior at the International High in Singapore
   1074. Felipe Alexandre born 28 Nov 1984 Amarillo, TX.
       Fraser   2000 – Sophomore at Canadian School in Singapore

1053. ELIZABETH KATHERINE-9 “ Puni ” FRASER, sister of above, was born 1 November 1957 at Bahia, Brazil. Elizabeth-9 graduated from Florida Southern College in Lakeland, FL. She married Gerferson Santana LIMA, an architect and photographer, on 9 Jan 1982 . He was the son of Paulo Silva LIMA and Maria Fonseca de SANTANA; and was born 13 Aug 1947. They divorced. She resided with Richardo Ribeiro “ Rhatto ” da SILVA. He was born 16 Sep 1961; and was a Physical Education teacher.

Child of Elizabeth-9 FRASER and Gerferson LIMA:
   Surname LIMA
   1075. Ian Fraser   born 17 Sept 1983 Bahia, Brazil
                       2000 – High school Sophomore – Brazil

Children of Elizabeth-9 FRASER and Richardo da SILVA:
   1076. Luiz Ricardo Fraser born 21 Oct 1995 Salvador, Brazil
   1077. dau   born   Nov 2000

The Tenth American Generation

1058. ROBERT BYRON-10 ANDREWS, son of Sydney-9 ANDREWS (Irvine-8 TEMPLE; Grace May-7 CHARLTON; Amoret-6 CROCKER; John M-5; James-4; Paul-3; 2; Peletiah-1) and June M. LANG, was born 19 June 1954 at Worcester, MA. He married Jeanne Marie HANSEN on 3 Jan 1976 at Chicago. IL.

Children of Robert B-10 ANDREWS and Jeanne HANSEN:
   Surname ANDREWS
   1078. Christopher Robert   born 15 Mar 1979 Chicago. IL
   1079. Lauren Michelle   born 29 Aug 1980 Chicago

1059. WENDY LOU-10 ANDREWS, sister of above, was born 27 Aug 1955 at Worcester, MA. She married James Nelson CYR on 17 July 1976 at West Brookfield, MA.

Children of Wendy Lou-10 ANDREWS and James CYR:
   Surname CYR
   1080. Sara June   born 21 July 1977   1082. Matthew James   born 20 feb 1983
   1081. Jill Lee   born 1 Apr 1981

1060. THOMAS MARK-10 ANDREWS, brother of above, was born 15 Sept 1957 at Worcester, MA. He married Takae KANAI on 13 Mar 1984 at Tokyo, Japan. She was the daughter of Yutaka KANAI and Keiko NISHIWAKI, and was born 16 Oct 1960 at Tokyo, Japan.

Children of Thomas-10 ANDREWS and Takae KANAI:
   Surname ANDREWS
   1083. Rie Kanai   (f)   born 26 Aug 1985 Yokosuka, Japan
   1084. Motoyasu Kanai   (m)   born 18 Dec 1986 Misawa, Japan

1064. SUSAN ELAINE-10 WARE, daughter of Shirley Mae-9 ANDREWS (Irvine-8 TEMPLE; Grace May-7 CHARLTON; Amoret-6 CROCKER; John-5; James-4; Paul-3;2; Peletiah-1) and Donald WARE, was born 10 Apr 1960 at Worcester, MA. She married first to John Alden CLARKE on 28 Feb 1981 at LaPorte, Texas. He was the son of Gerald CLARKE and Dorothy __?__, and was born 22 Mar 1960 at ___ Alabama. They divorced. She married second to David E. BROWN on 4 Aug 1990.

Children of Susan-10 WARE and John A. CLARKE:
   Surname CLARKE
   1085. Timothy Alden   born 7 July 1983 Bryan, Brazos County, TX
   1086. Adam Keith   born 29 Oct 1985 Bryan, Texas

1066. ELLEN MARIE-10 NEDDE, daughter of Carole-9 ANDREWS (Irvine-8 TEMPLE; Grace-7 CHARLTON; Amoret-6 CROCKER; John-5; James-4; Paul-3;2; Peletiah-1) and Nelson EDDE, was born 31 Aug 1961 at Decatur, Macon County, Illinois. She married William McKay SHIPP on 16 June 1984 at Dranesville, Fairfax County, VA. He was the son of Thomas SHIPP and Winona Jacqueline SHREVE, and was born 26 Apr 1960 at Washington, DC

Children of Ellen M-10 NEDDE and William SHIPP:
   Surname SHIPP
   1087. Nora Rose   born 12 Nov 1992 Washington, DC
   1088. Lillian Mae   born 5 Sept 1995 Washington, DC

MISCELLANEOUS CROCKER INFORMATION

CROCKER, Abby, born ___; married George Washington COBB ca 1822. He was the son of Gen. David COBB (Thomas) and Eleanor BRADISH; and was born 14 Jan 1790; died 27 Feb 1832 at Gouldsboro, Maine.   Reference: Early Families of Gouldsboro (Maine)

CROCKER, Alfreda Mary born 30 Dec 1891 Milbridge, ME (dau George CROCKER and Effie LEIGHTON) married Walter Lewis STROUT ++ (as his 2nd wife) ; died 20 Jan 1956 Milbridge, ME Children: 1. Everett Barnard STROUT born 26 Aug 1912, married Annie Belle KELLEY; died 28 Jan 1998 Milbridge, ME. And 2. Lawrence Walter STROUT born ca 19__, married Sylvia Lozina TIBBETTS. ++ Walter STROUT born 30 Mar 1885, married 1st Ethel ROBINSON; and died 28 July 1962 Sullivan, ME

CROCKER, Charles; married Julia HOLMES (dau/o Ebenezer HOLMES and Susan DENNISON)

CROCKER, Charles A. of Machias, Maine; married Elizabeth M. SMITH 12 Aug 1844, the Rev J A MILLIKEN officiating. (Marriage Records of Washington Co., Maine) He was a Postmaster, born ca 1822; wife Elizabeth was born ca 1826. Children: Charles M. born 1846; Eliza F. born ca 1848 and Harriet born 1859

CROCKER, David   lost at sea – died 18 Nov 1855 New Orleans, Louisiana
CROCKER, George W., born 13 Dec 1849 Bucksport, Hancock, Maine; the son/o Benjamin CROCKER and Mary Ann WHITTEMORE. (LDS-IGI)
CROCKER, John G.   married Sally LIBBY 11 May 1825 Pownal, Cumberland Co., Maine

CROCKER, J. W. of Rockland, Maine; married Annie SPEAR 25 May 1863. He was the Deputy Collector of Customs at Rockland (1871).

CROCKER, Margaret K., born 27 Oct 1817 at Machias, Washington, Maine; the dau/o William Allen CROCKER and Elizabeth Lowell ALLINE; married Stacy FOWLER 2 Dec 1855 at Machias, Maine.

CROCKER, MATHIAS T. born ca 1823; married Elizabeth BABB 1 Apr 1853. She born ca 1837; still living 1910; Ch: Hiram D. CROCKER born ca 1864 ; married Annie L. __?_; she born ca 1876.
                    Reference: 1910 Federal Census East Machias, Maine (ED 290)
CROCKER, Mathias; married Katherine HOLMES (dau/o James HOLMES and Sarah BERRY Lyons)

CROCKER, Nathaniel   married Laura-9 HANSCOM 3 June 1855
          (she dau/o Otis Pineo-8 HANSCOM (Isaac-7; Aaron-6; Thomas-5;4;3;2; John-1)
                    she born 6 Feb 1824 Machias, Maine
CROCKER, Nathaniel of Dixmont, Maine; married Laura HANSCOM (dau/o Isaac HANSCOM and Lydia BOWKER) (Reference History of Machias, Maine pages 466, 468)

CROCKER, Nellie R. of Marshfield, ME married Harry W. ALBEE 28 Dec 1895 (he of Northfield, ME)

CROCKER, Solomon   married Sarah-9 HANSCOM
          (she dau/o Joseph-8 HANSCOM (Nathaniel-7; Jos-6; Samuel-5; Thomas-4;3;2; John-1)
CROCKER, William A.   merchant at Machias, ME; was born ca 1793. His 2nd wife was Julia __?
(she born ca 1806) Children: Sarah B. born 1820; Eliza born 1824; Samuel S. born 1826 (shoemaker); Margaret K. born ca 1828; Leonice H. born ca 1830 (Ref: Census 1850)

CROCKER, William B. of Bath Maine; married Hannah TUFTS of New York

DEED (3 Oct 1794) of Thomas and Eunice THORP to Samuel ELLIS (Conveying their property on Buck's Harbor (ME) " to which they are entitled as 'squatters down' prior to 1784 " ----
          States " Eunice was Eunice CROCKER, married to Reuben CROCKER "

MACHIAS, MAINE REGISTERS AND ENROLLMENTS
AND MUSEUM CAPTAINS LIST

CROCKER CAPTAINS

CROCKER, A.	Brigantine *BOUNAPARTE* of Machias	1868
CROCKER, BENJAMIN	Schooner *LAVINIA* of Machias	1826
	Schooner *MARY SPEAR* of Machias	no date
	Schooner *TWO BROTHERS* of Machias	1829
	Schooner *CONSTELLATION* of Boston	1833
CROCKER, C. H.	Steamer *CECIL*	1903
(of Bowdoinham ,ME)	Lighter *HARRIET B SHIELBY*	1903 & 1906
CROCKER, CHAS. W.	Schooner *MARY HELEN* of Machias	1876
(# 608)	Schooner *ANNA E J MORSE* of Portland	1900
CROCKER, CYRUS P.	Barge *SHENAGO*	1903
	Barge *CONEANT*	no date
	Auxiliary Schooner *NORTHLAND*	no date
	Steamer *WINIFRED IN*	1903

Note: Cyrus P. CROCKER, born 1854 Prospect, Maine; 1st married Sarah SHUTE of Bucksport, ME; 2nd married Mrs. Abby Wiley of Roxbury, MA. he came from TX in 1903 in the Steamer WINIFRED IN.

CROCKER, EDWARD H.	Schooner *JAMES R TALBOT* of Machias	1880-85
	Schooner *CHARLES E BALCH* of Bath	1889
(# 606)	Schooner *JOHN F RANDALL*	1902

Note: Captain Edward H. CROCKER was lost at sea 17 Feb 1902 on the JOHN F RANDALL. His son (by his 1st wife) was lost with him. He was survived by his 2nd wife, 2 daus; and 5 brothers who it is said were " all six-footers ".

CROCKER, E. W.	Yacht *FALKS*	1903
CROCKER, F.	Ship *MARY ROBINSON*	1854
CROCKER, GEORGE	Schooner *MATTIE J ALLEN*	1911
	Note: he from Milbridge, Maine	
CROCKER, JACOB BARTER (# 349)	Schooner *CARROLL* of East Machias	1861-64
	(vessel built 1857 at E. Machias, Maine)	
	Schooner *ORIENTAL* of Machias	1866
	Schooner *KORET* of Machias	1869-70
	Schooner *KEOKUK* of Machias	1872-73
	Schooner *JAMES R TALBOT* of Machias	1874-79
	(vessel built 1874 East Machias, Maine)	
CROCKER, JAMES (# 20)	Schooner *MARY* of Machias	1818
	Schooner *ELIZA* of Machias	1819
	Sloop *ABIGAIL* of Machias	1819
	Schooner *INDEPENDENCE* of Machias	1821
	Schooner *CAROLINE AND NANCY* of Machias	1823
	Schooner *SUSAN* of Machias	1825
CROCKER, JAMES, JR. (# 89)	Schooner *GENERAL JACKSON* of Machiasport	1832
	Brig *GERARD* of Saco	1832
	Brig *ELIZABETH* of Machias	1834

CROCKER CAPTAINS, continued:

CROCKER, JAMES,	Schooner *SEA GULL* of Westport	1836
JR. (cont'd) (# 89)	Schooner *OREGON* of Machias	1837
	Schooner *FRANKLIN* of Machiasport	1839-41
	Brig *NEW ENGLAND* of Machias	1841
	Brig *WILLIAM* of Machias	1842
	Brig *G W BRINKERHOFF* of Machias	1849
CROCKER, JAMES	Schooner *JAMES R TALBOT* of East Machias	1876
BARTER (# 607)	Schooner *MARY HELEN* of Machias	1881-84
	Schooner *JAMES R TALBOT* of Machias	1889
	Schooner *CHARLES L DAVENPORT* of Thomaston	1900
	Schooner *JOSEPH E RAY* of Thomaston	1901
CROCKER, JAMES L.	Schooner *FREEDOM* of Machiasport	1856-57
CROCKER, JOHN	Schooner *WATCHMAN* of Thomaston	1832
	Brig *EDINBURG* of Thomaston	1840
	Bark *MARY H KENDALL* of Thomaston	1846
	Ship *CHARLES R FARWELL* of Rockland	1854
	Ship *JENNIE BEAL* of New York	1859

CROCKER, JOHN L.	Schooner *ELIA* of Rockland	1865-67
CROCKER, LEONARD A. Launch *RAMBLER*		1905

Note: Leonard CROCKER, born ___; married _?_ 25 May 1854 at Monteville, ME.
Had a daughter Hannah R. CROCKER, born ___; married Daniel STEVENS

CROCKER, MATHIAS T. Schooner *ELIZA* of East Machias   1851
Note: Mathias T. CROCKER, born 1823; married Elizabeth BABB 1 Apr 1853 E. Machias, ME.

CROCKER, NELSON	Schooner *HENRY P HAVENS* of Bucksport	1807
CROCKER, PAUL	Sloop *NANCY* of Machias	1802
(# 21)	Schooner *RESOLUTION* of Machias	1801-04
	Brig *RESOLUTION* of Machias	1807
	(vessel 70'1'' long; 21'8" wide; 7'8" deep)	

Note: The Brig RESOLUTION, later had Paul CROCKERS' son-in-law Zebedee MAYHEW as Master.
In 1817 Captain MAYHEW was the Master of the MARY OF CUSHING.
Owners of the RESOLUTION were Moses, Elias, James and John W. FOSTER of Machias;
John McCLAINE of Bristol, ME; and John HOWE of Boston, MA.

CROCKER, PAUL, JR.	Schooner *GENERAL JACKSON* of East Machias	1832
(# 104)	Schooner *ELIZABETH* of Machias	1833
	Schooner *ELIZA ANN*	1833
	(vessel 77' long; 23' wide; 8' deep; built 1819)	
	Schooner *CYPRUS* of Machias	1838

CROCKER, ROBERT   Ship *CHARLES HOLMAN* of Rockland   no date

CROCKER, TIMOTHY B. Schooner *VANCOUVER* of Machiasport   1847-54
(# 91)

CROCKER, W W	Tug *SEGUIN*	1888
(he of W. Bath, ME)	Tug *DEA VOLENTE*	1888
	Tug *MARION*	1889

Note: W. W. CROCKER, born Apr 1850 Woolwich, ME; died West Bath, ME 4 Mar 1911;
aged 60 years 11 mo. Commanded Tugboats on the Kennebec.

CROCKER CAPTAINS, continued:

CROCKER, WM. B.	(he of Bath, MAINE; married Hannah TUFTS of New York)	
CROCKER, WM. G.	Schooner *LAVINIA F WARREN* of Machiasport	1888
(# 609)	Schooner *CHARLES E BALCH* of Bath	1900
	Schooner *ARTHUR C WADE* of Bath	1902
	Schooner *JAMES W ELWELL*	1903
	Schooner *WINFIELD S SHUSTER* 1905	
	Schooner *DOROTHY PALMER* of Waldoboro	1914
	Schooner *SINGLETON PALMER* of Portland	1915
CROCKER, ZEBEDEE M. (# 315)	Schooner *MARY SPEAR* of East Machias	1837-40

CROCKERS WHO OWNED SHARES IN VARIOUS VESSELS IN THE MACHIAS DISTRICT:

Mr/Mrs A. E. CROCKER; Alvin G. CROCKER; A. J. CROCKER; Antoinette CROCKER; Catherine CROCKER; Flora B. CROWLEY Crocker; Frank CROCKER (poss Dr. Frank H.) ; George Ulmer CROCKER; Joel CROCKER; Mariner Green CROCKER; Oliver Wiles CROCKER; Samuel Gould CROCKER; Sarah F. O'BRIEN Crocker and her husband Otis CROCKER; Stephen Burgain CROCKER; William A. CROCKER and William C. CROCKER.

CAPTAINS – SURNAMES RELATED TO THE CROCKER LINE

AMES, ALFRED (# 341)		
AMES, ABRAHAM (husband of # 118)	Schooner *TWO BROTHERS* of Machias (built 1811 Machias, Maine)	1817-19
	Schooner *SUSAN* of Machias (built 1819 Machias)	1819; 1823-25
	Schooner *CONSTELLATION* (built 1824 E. Machias)	1826
AMES, ISAAC (husband of # 115)	Sloop *THREE SALLYS* of Machias (built 1796 Bristol)	1806
	Schooner *BETSEY* of St. George (built 1801 Warren, ME)	1810
	Schooner *TWO BROTHERS* (built 1811 Machias) Note: listed as part owner of this vessel in 1823	1811-15
	Sloop *ABIGAIL* of Machias (built 1816 Machias) Note: also listed as Part owner of this vessel	1816-18; 1820-21
	Brig *DIRIGO* of Machias (built 1821 Machias)	1821-22
	Brig *ORION* of Machias (built 1824 Machias)	1824
	Schooner *PRESIDENT* of Machias (built 1825 Machias)	1825-27
	Schooner *TWO BROTHERS* of Machiasport 1840 (built 1829 Manchester, MA)	
AMES, ISAAC, JR. (# 340)	Schooner *FAME* of East Machias (built 1828 Sullivan)	1835
	Schooner *PATRIOT* of Machias (built 1838 Machias) (Master and part owner of the above vessels)	1838-41
BARTER, JACOB (husband of # 101)	Schooner *FAIR AMERICA* of Machias (built 1816 Warren, ME)	1822-24
	Schooner *EVERGREEN* of Machias (built 1818 Newcastle)	1827-28
	Schooner *GENERAL JACKSON* of East Machias (built 1826 East Machias, Maine)	1828
	Schooner *EDWARD D PETERS* of Machias (built 1832 Trescott, Maine)	1833-34

CAPTAINS - CROCKER ALLIED LINES

BARTER, JACOB (cont'd)	Schooner *MARY & ELIZABETH* of Machiasport	1841-44
	(built 1841 Machias)	
	Schooner *JACOB & WILLIAM* of Machias	1846-47
	(built 1846 Machiasport, ME) (he part owner of this vessel)	
	Schooner *JACOB LONGFELLOW* of Machias	1848-49
	(built 1848 Machias; also part owner of this vessel)	
	Schooner *B A TUFTS* of Machiasport	1852-53
	(built 1846 Machiasport; also part owner of this vessel)	
	Schooner *JULIET* of St. George	1854-59
	(built 1849 Waldoboro; also part owner of this vessel)	

CLARK, QUINCY A.	Schooner *MECHANIC* of Machiasport (built 1833)	1853-54
	Schooner *BOUNDARY* of Machiasport	1861
	(built 1825 Eastport, Maine)	

MAYHEW, THOMAS M. # 320

MAYHEW, ZEBEDEE   (husband of # 99)

MAYHEW, ZEBEDEE, JR. # 321

RICHARDS, JAMES   # 109

| RICHARDS, JAMES H. | Schooner *EXPRESS* of Bristol (built 1858 Bristol) | 1862 |

The First American Generation

1. REGINALD/ REINOLD/RENOLD-1 FOSTER/FORSTER, the immigrant, possibly the son of Thomas-A FOSTER/ FORSTER and his 2nd wife Elizabeth JANE CARR, was born ca 1595 at Brunton, England.

He married 1st to Judith WIGNOL ca 1619 at Theydon-Garnon; Essex, England. She was born ca 1597-1602; died Oct 1664. Reginald-1 FOSTER and Judith came to America in 1638 and settled at Ipswich, MA. She was the mother of all of his children. His 2nd wife was the widow Mrs. Sarah WHITE Martin of Ipswich, MA. They married on 19 Sept 1665 (American Marriages Before 1699, page 77). Reginald-1 FOSTER died ca 1681 at Ipswich, MA.

Children of Reginald/Renold-1 FOSTER and Judith WIGNOL:
    Surname FOSTER   (all children born at Exeter, Devonshire, England)

+ 2. MARY	born 1618/19; 1m. Daniel WOOD ca 1638 Exter, Devon, England
	(he born ca 1615; died 27 Mar 1642)
	2m. Lt. Francis PEABODY May 1642
	(he born 1614; died Feb 1697/98)
	died 9 Apr 1705 Topsfield, Essex Co., MA
+ 3. SARAH	born 15 Oct 1620 Exeter, England; died 1681
	married William-1 STOREY ca 1640
	(immigrant) (he born 1614; died 1702/03)
+ 4. ABRAHAM	born ca 1622 Exeter, Devon, England; died 25 Jan 1711 Ipswich, MA
	married Lydia BURBANK ca 1655
	(she dau/o John BURBANK and his 2nd wife Jemima __?__)
	(she born 7 Apr 1624; died 29 Mar 1692 ,MA)
+ 5. ISAAC	born ca 1630; died Feb 1691/92 Ipswich, MA
	1m. Mary JACKSON 5 May 1658 (she born __; died 27 Nov 1677)
	(she dau/o William JACKSON of Rowley)
	2m. Hannah DOURING/DOWNING 25 Nov 1678
	3m. Martha HALE/HALL 16 Mar 1680
6. William	born ca 1633; married Mary _____
7. Deacon Jacob	born ca 1635; died 9 July 1710
	1m. Martha KINSMAN 12 Jan 1659/60 (dau/o Robert KINSMAN)
	(she born 1636; died 15 Oct 1665/6) 4 ch
	2m. Abigail LORD 26 Feb 1667 (she dau/o Robert LORD and Mary WAITE)
	(she born ca 1640; died 4 June 1729)
+ 8. REGINALD/	born ca 1636; died ca 1707/08
RENOLD	married Elizabeth-2 DANE ca 1652 Ipswich, MA
	(she dau/o John-1 DANE, Jr. and Eleanor CLARK of Ipswich)
	(she born ca 1636 Exeter, England; died 21 Jan 1692/93)

Reference: FOSTER GENEALOGY by Frederick Clifton PIERCE contains the early FORESTERS;
American Marriages Before 1699, p 77; LDS-IGI

Reginald/ Renold-2 FOSTER was the third signer of a petition in favor of John PROCTOR and his wife Elizabeth, who had been sentenced to death for " witchcraft " at Salem, MA. It was to no avail, however, as John Proctor was hanged 19 Aug 1692. His wife, who was about eight months pregnant, was saved by her condition, and gave birth to a child about two weeks after his death.

The Second American Generation

2.   MARY-2 FOSTER, daughter of Reginald/Renold-1 FOSTER, was born ca 1618-19 at Exeter, Devonshire, England. She married first to Daniel WOOD ca 1638. He was the son of Richard WOOD, and was born 23 Mar 1615 at Bedford, England; died ca 27 Mar 1642. She married 2nd to Lt. Francis-1 PEABODY ca May 1642 at Framingham, Middlesex County, MA. He was the son of John PEABODY / PAYBODY / PABODIE and Isabell HARPER, and was born ca 1613-14 St. Albans, Hertfordshire, England; died 19 Feb 1698 Topsfield, Essex, MA. Mary-2 FOSTER died 9 Apr 1705 Topsfield, MA

Child of Mary-2 FOSTER and Daniel WOOD:
   Surname WOOD
+ 9. JUDITH   born ca 1641/42, Topsfield, MA ; married Thomas DORMAN 16 Mar 1662
                             (he son/o Thomas DORMAN and Ellen HADLEY (?)
                             (he born ca 1615; died 27 Mar 1643)
Children of Mary-2 FOSTER and Lt. Francis-1 PEABODY:
   Surname PEABODY
   10. John   born ca 1643; married Hannah ANDREWS
   11. Joseph   born ca 1644; married Bethia BRIDGES
   12. William   born ca 1646; married Hannah HALE
   13. Isaac   born ca 1648
+14. SARAH   born ca 1650; marr. Abraham HOWE 26 Mar 1678; died 29 Sep 1732 Ipswich
+15. HEPZIBAH   born ca 1652; married David REA/RAY 10 Apr 1678 Salem, MA
   16. Lydia   born ca 1654; married Jacob PERLEY 3 Dec 1696 Topsfield, MA
+ 17. MARY   born ca 1656; married John DEATH,III ca 1670 Topsfield, MA; died after 1690
   18. Ruth   born 22 Mar 1658 Topsfield, MA; married Daniel AVINS; died before 1698
   19. Damaris   born 21 June 1660; died young
   20. Samuel   born 4 June 1662, Topsfield; died 1677
+ 21. JACOB   born 28 July 1664; died 24 Nov 1689 Topsfield, MA
                             married Abigail TOWNE 12 Jan 1686
   22. Hannah   born 8 May 1668, Topsfield; died before 1698
                             married Daniel ANDREWS 1689 Topsfield, MA
                             (he born 2 Sept 1667 Topsfield; died 6 Feb 1717 Topsfield
   23. Nathaniel   born 29 July 1669, Topsfield, MA; married Frances HOYT (?) 1701

3. SARAH-2 FOSTER, sister of above, was born 15 Oct 1620 at Exeter, Devon, England. She married William-1 STOREY, the immigrant, ca 1640 at Ipswich, Essex, MA. He was the son of Andrew STOREY, and was born ca 1614 at Norwich, Norfolk, England; and died 20 Jan 1702 at Ipswich, Essex, MA. Sarah-2 FOSTER died ca 1681 at Ipswich, MA.

Children of Sarah-2 FOSTER and William-1 STOREY:
   Surname STOREY   (all children born at Ipswich, MA)
   24. Hannah   born 19 Aug 1642; died 1658
   25. Sarah (twin)   born 13 Dec 1645; died 29 May 1723 Ipswich
   26. Seth (twin)   born 13 Dec 1645; died 9 Oct 1732 Ipswich, MA
   27. Samuel   born ca 1647; died young
   28. William   born ca 1650; died 20 Jul 1721 Brookline, Norfolk, MA
   29. Abigail   born ca 1654; died 1658
   30. Samuel (2)   born ca 1660; died 1726 Norwich, New London, MA
   31. Hannah (2)   born 19 Aug 1662; died 20 July 1721 Brookline, Norfolk, MA
   32. Susannah Clark   born 4 Mar 1664; died 9 Jan 1734 Boxford, Essex, MA
   33. Mary   born ca 1666

4. ABRAHAM-2 FOSTER , son of Reginald-1 FOSTER, was born ca 1622 at Exeter, Devonshire, England He married Lydia BURBANK 7 Feb 1644. She was the daughter of John BURBANK + and Jemima __?__

of Rowley, MA., and was born ca 1624 Rowley, MA; died 29 Mar 1692. Abraham-2 came from England with his father, when he was 16 years of age (1638). He located at Ipswich, MA. Abraham-2 FOSTER joined the church , in full communion, on 12 Apr 1664. He was 76 years of age, on 26 Sept 1698, when he gave a deposition concerning the Rev John NORTONS' property. He was a yeoman. There was no will or administration of his estate, as he distributed it among his family by deed, 21 Dec 1698. (Deeds, Essex Deeds, lib 13 P. 206). Abraham-2 FOSTER died 25 Jan 1711 at Ipswich, MA.

+ John-1 BURBANK, father of Lydia, was made a freeman at Rowley (MA) on 13 May 1640; and in his will (dated 6 Apr 1681) he mentions his wife Jemima, and children John, Caleb and Lydia.

Children of Abraham-2 FOSTER and Lydia-2 BURBANK:
Surname FOSTER   (children born Ipswich, MA)

+ 34. EPHRAIM   born 9 Oct 1657; married Hannah EAMES ca 1677 Andover, MA
                     (she dau/o Robert EAMES and Rebecca BLAKE)
+ 35. ABRAHAM   born 16 Oct 1659; died 22 May 1741
                     married Mary ROBINSON 13 July 1681 Andover, MA
                     (she dau/o Robert ROBINSON and Mary SILVER)
  36. James   born 12 Jan 1662; died before 1698
  37. Isaac   born ca 1663; died poss 13 Feb 1717
                     Ch: Ebenezer-4 FOSTER, born ca 1690 Ipswich, MA
  38. unnamed child born 27 Dec 1668; died the same day
  39. Benjamin   born ca 1670; married Ann _?_ ca 1692 Ipswich, MA; died 12 Sept 1735
            Ch: Benjamin; Amos; Deborah; Kezia; Gideon; Jemima, d y ; Isaac ; and Jemima (2).
  40. Ebenezer   born 15 July 1672; died 25 Feb 1718
                     married Mary BROWN/BORMAN 23 June 1705 (she born ca 1684; died 19 June 1716)
                     Children: Jemima bpt 1706, d y ; Ruth born 23 Jan 1709/10, marr Jacob WILDES;
                     and Moses born 5 Oct 1713, married Hannah ANDREWS.
  41. Mehitable   born 12 Oct 1675; married Ebenezer AVERILL 31 Dec 1700; died ca Nov 1740
                     (he son/o William AVERILL and Hannah JACKSON)
  42. Samuel   born 29 Oct 1676
+ 43. CALEB   born 9 Nov 1677; died 25 Jan 1766 Ipswich
                     married Mary SHERWIN 2 June 1702 Ipswich, MA
                     (she dau/o John Sherwin and Frances LOOMIS)
  44. Ruth   born 18 Apr 1680; married Jeremiah PERLEY 16 Apr 1702
                     (he son of John PERLEY and Mary HOWLETT)
                     (he born 10 July 1677 Boxford,MA; died 16 June 1758)

5. ISAAC-2 FOSTER, brother of above, was born ca 1630, probably at Exeter, Devon, England. He came to America with his father at age 8 and resided at Ipswich, MA. He married three times: first to Mary JACKSON on 5 May 1658, Ipswich, MA. She was the daughter of John JACKSON and Kathryn _?_; and was born 8 Dec 1639, England; died 27 Nov 1677. He married 2nd to Hannah DOURING/ DOWNING on 25 Nov 1678; and 3rd to Martha HALE/HALL, who survived him. Isaac-2 died ca March 1692 at Ipswich.

Children of Isaac-2 FOSTER and Mary JACKSON
Surname FOSTER   (all children born Ipswich, MA)

  45. Jonathan   born 9 Jan 1659 ; died 15 May 1661
  46. Mehitable   born 19 Sept 1660; died Feb 1661
+ 47. JACOB   born 9 Feb 1662; die ca 1745 Topsfield, MA
                     1m. Sarah WOOD 12 Sept 1688 Topsfield, MA
                     (she dau/o Isaiah WOOD and Mercy THOMPSON)
                     (she born 26 Dec 1665; died 27 Sept 1697 Topsfield, MA)
                     2m. Mary EDWARDS 20 May 1700 Ipswich, MA
+48. BENJAMIN   born June 1665, MA; married Mary JOHNSON ; died ca 1700 Scarboro, ME

Children of Isaac-2 FOSTER, continued;
    Surname FOSTER

49. Elizabeth	born 20 Apr 1667
50. Mary	born 26 June 1669; married Richard GRANT 27 Feb 1686/88 Ipswich, MA
+ 51. DANIEL	born 14 Nov 1670; married Katherine FREESE 2 Mar 1693
	2m. Mary DRESSER 4 Dec 1696 Rowley, Essex, MA
	died Nov 1753 Lebanon, New London, CT.
+ 52. MARTHA	born 1 Aug 1672; married Thompson WOOD 8 Dec 1691
53. Ruth	born 20 Feb 1674; died ca 1749 Ipswich, MA
	married Samuel GROVE/ GROW 25 Apr 1694 Topsfield, MA
	(he son of John GROVE/GROW and Hannah LORD)
	(he born 3 Dec 1671 Ipswich, MA; died ca 1745)

Child: Samuel GROVE/GROW born 31 Aug 1696 Ipswich, MA

+ 54. PRUDENCE	born 23 May 1675; died 28 Oct 1755 Ipswich, MA
	married Joseph BORMAN 17 Feb 1696/97 Ipswich, MA
	(he born ca 1675; died ____)
55. Hannah	born 24 Oct 1676; died before 1681

Children of Isaac-2 FOSTER and Hannah DOURING/DOWNING:
    Surname FOSTER

56. Hannah	born 16 Feb 1681		
57. Eleazer	born Apr 1684; married Eliza FISKE	58. Sarah	born 19 Mar 1687

8. REGINALD/RENOLD-2 FOSTER, brother of above, was born ca 1636 at Exeter, Devon, England. He married Elizabeth-2 DANE ca 1652 at Ipswich, Essex, MA. She was the daughter of John-1 DANE, Jr. and Eleanor CLARK, and was born ca 1636 Exeter, England; died ____. Reginald-2 FOSTER died ca 1707/08 Ipswich.

Child of Reginald-2 FOSTER and Elizabeth-2 DANE:
    Surname FOSTER

59. Isaac	born ca 1656 Ipswich; died 11 Apr 1741 Ipswich.
	married Abigail __?__ 25 Nov 1676, MA (she born ca 1657; died 4 Oct 1749)

The Third American Generation

9. JUDITH-3 WOOD, daughter of Mary-2 FOSTER (Reginald/Renold-1) and Daniel WOOD, was born ca 1641/42 at Topsfield, Essex County, MA. She married Thomas DORMAN (Jr.) on 16 Mar 1662 at Topsfield. He was the son of Thomas DORMAN (Sr.) and Ellen HADLEY, and was born ca 1644 at Topsfield, died 1715/16. Judith-3 WOOD died 7 June 1725 at Topsfield.

Children of Judith-3 WOOD and Thomas DORMAN, Jr.:
  Surname DORMAN
+ 60. MARY   born 18 Dec 1667 Boxford, Essex, MA; died before 1695
                           married John ESTEY 31 May 1688
                           (he son/o Isaac ESTEY and Mary TOWNE) (he born 2 Jan 1662; died 1720)
  61. Hannah   born 2 Dec 1674 Boxford, MA;
                           married Thomas ROBINSON (he born 16 Mar 1671)
          Child: Hannah-5 ROBINSON born 6 Sept 1696; died 7 Dec 1777 Ashford, CT.

14. SARAH-3 PEABODY, daughter of Mary-2 FOSTER (Reginald/Renold-1) and Francis-1 PEABODY, was born ca 1650 at Ipswich, Essex County, MA. She married Abraham HOWE on 26 Mar 1677/78 at Ipswich. He was the son of James HOWE/HOW and Elizabeth DANE , and was born 28 Mar 1655 (?) Ipswich, MA; and died 21 Jan 1717. Sarah-3 PEABODY died 29 Sept 1732 at Ipswich.

Children of Sarah-3 PEABODY and Abraham HOWE:
  Surname HOWE   (children born Ipswich, MA)
  62. Love/Lore   born 15 Jan 1678; died 9 Aug 1762
  63. Increase   born 12 Apr 1680
  64. Sampson   born 13 Nov 1682; died 3 Sept 1736
  65. Abraham (Jr)   born 27 June 1686; died 6 Mar 1770 Ipswich, MA

15. HEPZIBAH-3 PEABODY, sister of above, was born ca 1652 at Ipswich, Essex, MA. She married David REA/RAY 10 Apr 1678 at Salem, Essex, MA. He was the son of Joshua REA/RAY and Sarah WATERS, and was born 30 Mar 1654 at Salem, MA; died 5 Mar 1714 at Boxford, Essex, MA. Hepzibah-3 PEABODY died before 1708.

Children of Hepzibah-3 PEABODY and David REA/RAY:
  Surname REA/RAY   (all children born Salem, Essex, MA)
  66. Jemima   born 29 Dec 1680   70. Elizabeth (twin) born 4/14 Aug 1687
  67. Daniel   born 23 Nov 1682   71. Lemuel   born 1689; died 1749
  68. Zerobabel   born 12 May 1684;   72. Uzziel   born Mar 1693; died Nov 1754
                   died 22 Jan 1739   73. Pilgrim   born 30 Nov 1695
  69. Hepzibah (twin) born 4/14 Aug 1687; died 9 Apr 1716

17. MARY-3 PEABODY, sister of above, was born 22 May 1656. She married John DEATH, II (John I) ca 1670 at Topsfield, Essex, MA. He was the son of John DEATH, I and Abigail TURNER, and was born ca 1651 at Framingham, MA; died _____ at Sherburn, MA. She died after 1690.

Children of Mary-3 PEABODY and John DEATH:
  Surname DEATH
  74. Oliver   (twin)   born May 1670 Topsfield, MA; died 3 Mar 1705 Framingham, Middlesex, MA
                           married Martha FAIRBANKS Apr 1697
  75. Thomas (twin)   born May 1670
+ 76. MARY   born ca 1673; married Samuel EAMES Jan 1688
+ 77. JOHN, III   born 2 Jan 1675/76 Sherburn, Middlesex Co.,MA; died Dec 1754
                           1m. Waitsill VOSE; 2m. Elizabeth BARKER
 +78. HEPZIBAH   born June 1680 Sherburn; married David HOW/HOWE; died 15 Apr 1769

Children of Mary-3 PEABODY, continued:
   Surname DEATH
+79. LYDIA   born Mar 1682 Sherburn; married Jonathan LAMB
  80. Samuel   born Sept 1684 Sherburn, MA   81. Ruth   born July 1688 Sherburn, MA

21. JACOB-3 PEABODY, brother of above, was born 28 July 1664 at Topsfield, Essex, MA. He married Abigail TOWNE on 12 Jan 1686 at Topsfield. She was the daughter of Edmund TOWN/TOWNE and Mary BROWNING; and was born 6 Aug 1664 Chebacco, Ipswich, Essex, MA; died 14 Feb 1712 at Chebacco. Jacob-3 PEABODY died 24 Nov 1689 at Topsfield.

Children of Jacob-3 PEABODY and Abigail TOWNE:
   Surname PEABODY
  82. Sarah (twin)   born 15 Jan 1687 Topsfield, MA
+ 83. MERCY/MARCY   born 15 Jan 1687
           (twin)   married Richard DRESSER 29 June 1708 Topsfield, MA
  84. Jacob   born 1688 Topsfield, MA

34. EPHRAIM-3 FOSTER, son of Abraham-2 FOSTER (Reginald / Renold-1) and Lydia BURBANK, was born 9 Oct 1657 at Ipswich, Essex County, MA. He married Hannah EAMES ca 1677 at Andover, MA. She was the daughter of Robert EAMES ++ and Rebecca BLAKE, and was born 18 Dec 1661 Andover, MA; died 8 July 1731 at Andover. Ephraim-3 FOSTER died 21 Sept 1746 at Boxford, MA
           ++ Robert EAMES, born 1630 MA; died 22 July 1693 at Boxford, Essex, MA. He married
                Rebecca BLAKE ca ____. She was born Feb 1641, MA; died 8 May 1721, MA.

Children of Ephraim-3 FOSTER and Hannah EAMES:
   Surname FOSTER   (all children born Andover, Essex, MA)
  85. Rose   born 9 May 1679; died 25 Feb 1693 Andover
  86. Hannah   born 28 May 1682; died 1684
  87. Jemima   born 25 Feb 1686; died 14 Feb 1706 Haverhill, Essex, MA
+ 88. EPHRAIM   born 12 Mar 1687; married Abigail POOR 11 Jan 1716; died 8 Apr 1738
+ 89. JOHN   born 26 Mar 1690; married Rebeckah REA 7 Jan 1713/14; died 18 Oct 1778
  90. Hannah (2)   born 25 May 1694; married _?_ 5 Mar 1701

35. ABRAHAM-3 FOSTER, brother of above, was born 16 Oct 1659 at Ipswich, Essex , MA. He married Mary ROBINSON 13 July 1681 at Andover, MA. She was the daughter of Robert ROBINSON and Mary SILVER. Abraham-3 FOSTER died 22 May 1741.

Child of Abraham-3 FOSTER and Mary ROBINSON:
   Surname FOSTER
+ 91. ABRAHAM   born 12 Jan 1692 Ipswich; died 23 Apr 1767
             married Sarah DUNNELL 5 Apr 1716/18 (she born ca 1696; died 10 Apr 1732)

43. CALEB-3 FOSTER, brother of above, was born 9 Nov 1677 at Ipswich, Essex, MA. He married Mary SHERWIN 2 June 1702 at Ipswich. She was the daughter of John-2 SHERWIN++ and Frances LOOMIS (Edward), and was born ____. In 1700 Caleb-3 FOSTER had a seat assigned to him " behind ye pu(l)pit " in the meeting house; " then recently built." Caleb-3 FOSTER died 25 Jan 1766 at Ipswich. In deeding his property to his sons (1766) he did not mention his son John He is presumed to have died before that date.

Children of Caleb-3 FOSTER and Mary-3 SHERWIN:
   Surname FOSTER   (all children born Ipswich, MA)
+ 92. LYDIA   born 14 May 1703; baptized 16 May 1703 Ipswich, MA
             married Nathan DRESSER intention published 21 Apr 1724
             (he son/o John DRESSER and Mercy DICKINSON)
             (he born 11 Apr 1700 Rowley, MA; bapt 13 Apr 1701)

Children of Caleb-3 FOSTER , continued:
Surname FOSTER
93. Jonathan   born 30 Nov 1704 ; baptized 3 Dec 1704
                       1m. Jemima JENNINGS 1 Jan 1733 Topsfield, MA
        Child: Philemon-4 FOSTER born 17 Feb 1737 Ipswich; MA; married _?_ 8 Sep 1767 Ipswich;
        died 10 May 1818 Linebrook, Essex, MA;   2m. Dorcas PORTER 17 Dec 1751 Ipswich, MA.

94. Sarah   born 3 Sept 1706; baptized 8 Sept 1706; died young
+ 95. CALEB, JR.   born 5 June 1708; died 25 Jan 1766
                       married Priscilla-4 BUXTON 4 Nov 1729 Rowley, MA
                       (she dau/o John-3 BUXTON and Priscilla LYNN)
96. Stephen   born 24 Apr 1710, baptized 30 Apr 1710; died 19 Dec 1780
                       married Rebecca PEABODY ca 1740 (she born 1710)
97. Mary   born 25 Dec 1711; died unmarried 19 Dec 1780
98. Philemon   born 2 June 1713; baptized 6 June 1713; died 1737
99. Sarah (2)   born 1715; baptized 11 Sept 1715; admitted to Topsfield Church 27 June 1736
100. John   born 1717; baptized Nov 1717; presumed died before 1766

47. JACOB-3 FOSTER, son of Isaac-2 FOSTER (Reginald-1) and Mary JACKSON, was born 9 Feb 1662
at Ipswich, Essex, MA. He married first to Sarah WOOD on 12 Sept 1688 at Topsfield, MA. She was the
daughter of Isaiah WOOD and Mercy THOMPSON, and was born 26 Dec 1665; died 27 Sept 1697 at
Topsfield, MA. His second wife was Mary EDWARDS. They married on 20 May 1700 at Topsfield, MA.

Children of Jacob-3 FOSTER and Sarah WOOD:
Surname FOSTER   (children born Topsfield, Essex, MA)
+101. BENJAMIN   born 6 Oct 1689; married Sarah WOODWARD 15 Mar 1725 Ipswich, MA
                         (she dau/o Ezekiel WOODWARD and Abigail _?_ of Granville Twsp, Nova Scotia
                          (she born 10 Mar 1703 Gloucester, MA; died 1805 Granville, NS)
102. Mary   born 13 May 1691; married __?__ 10 Feb 1715; died 16 Feb 1770

48. BENJAMIN-3 FOSTER, brother of above, was born ca June 1665 at Ipswich, MA. He married Mary
JOHNSON ca 16__; and died ca 1700. The administration of his estate was granted to his brother Daniel-3
(# 51 below) on 20 Nov 1700.

Child of Benjamin-3 FOSTER and Mary JOHNSON:
Surname FOSTER
+103. BENJAMIN I.   born ca 1699 Ipswich; died ca 1763 Scarboro, Maine
                       married Wilmot GRIFFITH 1 Nov 1716 (she born ca 1701 Scarboro, ME; died 1776)

51. DANIEL-3 FOSTER, brother of above, was born 14 Nov 1670 at Ipswich, Essex, MA. He married 1st to
Katherine FREESE on 2 Mar 1693 (she born ____; died ca 1696, possibly childbirth). He married 2nd to
Mary DRESSER on 4 Dec 1696 at Rowley, MA. She was the daughter of Samuel DRESSER and Mary
LEAVER, and was born 16 June 1670 at Rowley, MA; died CT. Daniel-3 FOSTER died Nov 1753, CT.

Child of Daniel-3 FOSTER and Katherine FREESE:
Surname FOSTER
104. Katherine   born 21 Aug 1696 Topsfield, MA

Children of Daniel-3 FOSTER and Mary DRESSER:
105. Mary   born 23 Jan 1698   110. Jeremiah   born 16 June 1707
106. Hepzibah   born 7 May 1700   married Mary SKINNER ca 1730 Lebanon, CT
107. Mehitable   born 16 Oct 1701   (she dau/o Nathaniel SKINNER/ Mary GILLETT)
108. Phineas   born 16 July 1703   111. Asa   born 15 Nov 1710
109. Hannah   born 29 Apr 1705; died 1746

52. MARTHA-3 FOSTER, sister of above, was born 1 Aug 1672 at Ipswich, Essex, MA. She married Thompson WOOD 8 Dec 1691. He was the son of Michael WOOD and Mary HARLOW, and was born ca 1650; died ca 1725.

Children of Martha-3 FOSTER and Thompson WOOD:

Surname WOOD	(last three children born at Framingham, Middlesex, MA)		
112. Jemima	born 18 May 1693 Ipswich; dy	115. Hezekiah	born 29 May 1701, MA
113. Martha	born 4 July 1696	116. Thomas	born 20 Nov 1704
114. Mercy	born 15 Nov 1698 Concord, MA	117. Hannah	born 20 Jan 17077

54. PRUDENCE-3 FOSTER, sister of above, was born 23 May 1675 at Ipswich, Essex, MA. She married Joseph BORMAN/ BOREMAN/ BOARDMAN 17 Feb 1696 at Ipswich, MA. He was the son of Daniel BOREMAN/ BOARDMAN and Hannah HUTCHINSON, and was born ca 1663 Ipswich, MA; died 18 May 1737 at Ipswich. Prudence-3 FOSTER died 28 Oct 1755 at Ipswich.

Children of Prudence-3 FOSTER and Joseph BORMAN/BOARDMAN:

Surname BORMAN/BOARDMAN	(children born Topsfield, Essex, MA)
118. Abigail	born 8 Sep 1700; married _?_ 8 Mar 1717; died 5 Oct 1771 Ipswich
119. Hannah	born 16 Aug 1703; married _?_ 5 Dec 1721; died 27 Apr 1783 Topsfield

The Fourth American Generation

60. MARY-4 DORMAN, daughter of Judith-3 WOOD (Mary-2 FOSTER; Reginald-1) and was born 18 Dec 1667 at Boxford, Essex, MA. She married John ESTEY 31 May 1688. He was the son of Isaac ESTEY and Mary TOWNE, and was born 2 Jan 1662; died ca 1720. Mary-4 DORMAN died before 1695.

Children of Mary-4 DORMAN and John ESTEY:
Surname ESTEY
120. Mary   born 1692; bapt 31 Jul 1692
+ 121. HANNAH   born 1693; bapt 24 Dec 1693; died 30 Sep 1730
                 married Jonathan RUSSELL 10 Apr 1718 Salem, Essex, MA
                 (he son/o William RUSSELL and Elizabeth NOURSE/NURSE)

76. MARY-4 DEATH, daughter of Mary-3 PEABODY (Mary-2 FOSTER, Reginald-1) and John DEATH, II (John, I) was born ca 1673. She married Samuel EAMES ca Jan 1688.

Children of Mary-4 DEATH and Samuel EAMES:
Surname EAMES

122. Samuel	born Sept 1692 Sherburn, MA; died June 1775		
+ 123. LYDIA	born Oct 1694; died June 1722 Woburn, MA		
	married Ebenezer BUCK Nov 1713 Woburn, MA		
124. Daniel	born Jan 1696; married Abigail HARNDON Mar 1719 Reading, MA		
125. Jacob	born July 1699	128. Caleb	born Mar 1707
126. Hepzibah	born Mar 1701	129. Elizabeth	born Mar 1711
	married Joseph EAST Feb 1731	130. Abigail	born Apr 1714
127. Joshua	born May 1705; died Aug 1775	131. Jonathan	born Aug 1716

77. JOHN-4 DEATH, III, brother of above, was born 2 Jan 1675/ 76 at Sherburn, MA. He married first to Waitsill VOSE 3 July 1717 at Milton, Norfolk, MA. She was the daughter of Henry VOSE and Elizabeth BABCOCK/BADCOCK , and was born 29 July 1688 Milton, MA; died 22 June 1750, MA. He married second to Elizabeth BARKER. He died 14 Dec 1754 at Sherburn, MA.

Children of John-4 DEATH, III and Waitsill VOSE:
Surname DEATH   (all children born Sherborn, Middlesex, MA)
132. Henry   born 22 Sep 1714
133. Mary   born 10 Oct 1716; died 27 May 1795
               married Daniel LELAND 25 May 1737 Sherborn, MA
               (he son/o Hopestill LELAND and Mary BULLARD)
134. John   born 4 Dec 1718; died 21 July 1721 Sherborn
135. Ruth   born 20 Apr 1721; married John WESSON 22 Jan 1740, MA
                  Child: Samuel-6 WESSON born 14 July 1741, MA
+ 136. ABIGAIL   born 3 Oct 1723; died 1 Oct 1814
               married William GREENWOOD 14 Feb 1744 Sherborn, MA
137. John (2) born 27 May 1726; died 29 Apr 1797
138. Waitsill   born 27 Oct 1728; died 12 June 1764
139. Hepzibeth born 27 July 1731; died 7 May 1762

78. HEPZIBAH-4 DEATH, sister of above, was born 5 June 1680 at Sherborn, MA. She married David HOW/HOWE on 25 Dec 1701 at Sudbury, Middlesex, MA. He was the son of Samuel HOWE and Martha BENT, and was born 2 Nov 1674 at Sudbury, MA; died 3 Aug 1759. Hepzibah-4 DEATH died 15 Apr 1769 at Sudbury.

Children of Hepzibah-4 DEATH and David HOWE:

Surname HOWE	(all children born Sudbury, Middlesex, MA)
140. Thankful	born 15 Dec 1703; died 25 Jan 1766 Hopkinton, Middlesex, MA
	married Peter HOWE 9 Apr 1723 Sudbury, MA
+ 141. HEPZIBAH	born 1 Oct 1706; died 15 Apr 1792 Shrewsbury, Worcester, MA
	married Cyprian KEYES 15 Dec 1729 Sudbury, MA
142. Eliphalet	born ca 1710; died ca 1785 Rutland, MA
	1m. Hepzibah MORSE 1733; 2m. Sarah NICHOLS 9 Nov 1765
+ 143. ISRAEL	born 6 May 1712; died 23 June 1748 Rutland, MA
	married Elizabeth HUBBARD 24 Mar 1740
144. Ruth	born 23 Feb 1714; died 2 Aug 1809 Auburn, Worcester, MA
	1m. Hezekiah STONE ca 1735 Sudbury, MA
	2m. David BANCROFT 14 Oct 1779 Auburn, MA
+ 145. DAVID	born 3 June 1717; died 14 Nov 1802
	married Abigail HUBBARD 15 Mar 1742 Concord, Middlesex, MA
146. Ezekiel	born 5 Apr 1720; died 15 Oct 1796 Sudbury, MA
	1m. Bathsheba STONE 19 Jan 1744; 2m. Rebecca RUGGLES 22 Dec 1772

79. LYDIA-4 DEATH, sister of above, was born 25 Mar 1682 at Sherborn, Middlesex, MA. She married Jonathan LAMB 9 July 1708 at Framingham, Middlesex, MA. he was the son of Abial LAMB, II and Elizabeth CLARK, and was born 11 Nov 1682 at Roxbury, Suffolk, MA; died 23 Sep 1749 at Spencer, Worcester, MA.

Children of Lydia-4 DEATH and Jonathan LAMB:
Surname LAMB

147. Lydia	born 21 Dec 1710; died 1736	150. Dorothy	born 3 Feb 1717; died 1753
148. Mary	born 8 Nov 1712; died 1750	+151. JOSHUA born 19 Jan 1719; died 1793
149. Jonathan	born 26 Feb 1715; died 9 Apr 1760	152. Elizabeth born ca 1721

83. MERCY/MARCY-4 PEABODY, daughter of Jacob-3 PEABODY (Mary-2 FOSTER; Reginald-1) and Abigail TOWNE, was born 15 Jan 1687 Topsfield, Essex, MA. She was the twin of Sarah-4. She married Richard DRESSER 29 June 1708 at Topsfield, MA. He was the son of John DRESSER and Martha THORLEY, and was born 24 June 1679 at Rowley, MA; died 14 July 1728 at Thompson, Windham, CT.

Children of Mercy/Marcy-4 PEABODY and Richard DRESSER:

Surname DRESSER	(all children born Woodstock, Windham, CT)		
153. Jacob	born 14 Nov 1710	156. Asa	born 8 Feb 1720
154. Richard (Jr)	born 22 Sept 1714; died 27 Aug 1797	157. Abigail	born 25 Oct 1723
+ 155. JOHN	born 8 Dec 1716; bapt 27 Jan 1717	158. Benjamin	born 16 May 1725
	died 9 Jan 1789 Charlton, MA		

88. EPHRAIM-4 FOSTER, son of Ephraim-3 FOSTER (Abraham-2; Reginald-1) and Hannah EAMES, was born 12 Mar 1687 at Andover, MA. He married Abigail POOR 11 Jan 1716. She was born ___; died 28 Aug 1747. Ephraim-4 FOSTER died 8 Apr 1738 at Andover. Abigail married second to Captain _?_ FRYE. (Only one of their children reached adulthood)

Children of Ephraim-4 FOSTER and Abigail POOR:

Surname FOSTER					
159. Pamela	born 17__	160. Theodore	born 17__	161. Theophilus	born 17__
162. Abigail	born 17_	163. Dwight	born 17__	164. Peregrine	born 17__

+ 165. JEDEDIAH   born 10 Oct 1726 Andover, MA; died 17 Oct 1779 Brookfield, MA
    married Dorothy DWIGHT 18 May 1749 (she dau/o Brig Gen Joseph DWIGHT)
Note: He was a graduate of Harvard University – Class of 1744

89. JOHN-4 FOSTER, brother of above, was born 26 Mar 1690 at Andover, Essex, MA. He married Rebeckah REA 7 Jan 1713/14 . She was born ca 1694 at Boxford, MA. John-4 FOSTER died 18 Oct 1778.

Children of John-4 FOSTER and Rebeckah REA:
Surname FOSTER

+ 166. STEPHEN	born 14 Aug 1720 Andover, MA; died ca 1787
	married Abigail SMITH 28 Jan 1744 Salem, Essex Co., MA
	(she dau/o Walter SMITH and Ruth FULLER) (she born 20 Dec 1722 MA)

91. ABRAHAM-4 FOSTER, son of Abraham-3 (Abraham-2; Reginald-1) and Mary ROBINSON, was born 12 Jan 1692 at Ipswich, Essex, MA. He married Sarah DUNNELL ca 1716. She was born ca 1696; died 10 Apr 1732. Abraham-4 FOSTER died 23 Apr 1767.

Child of Abraham-4 FOSTER and Sarah DUNNELL;
Surname FOSTER

+ 167. ABRAHAM	born 4 May 1719 Topsfield, MA; died 27 Oct 1796
	married Priscilla TODD 10 May 1744
	(she dau/o Abner TODD and Elizabeth _?_; she born 16 Jan 1724, MA)

92. LYDIA-4 FOSTER, daughter of Caleb-3 FOSTER (Abraham-2; Reginald-1) and Mary SHERWIN, was born 14 May 1703; baptized 16 May 1703 at Ipswich, Essex, MA. She married Nathan-4 DRESSER, intentions published 21 Apr 1724 at Andover, MA. He was the son of John-3 DRESSER (Lt. John-2; John-1) and Mercy DICKINSON, and was born 11 Apr 1700 Rowley, MA; baptized 13 Apr 1701; died ____.

Children of Lydia-4 FOSTER and Nathan DRESSER:

Surname DRESSER   (1ˢᵗ 2 children born Rowley, MA; last 4 born Boxford, MA)

+ 168. JONATHAN	born ca 1724 Rowley, MA; died 12 Oct 1800/06		
	married Sarah- FOSTER 24 Nov 1748 Andover, Essex, MA		
169. un-named	born ca 1727 Rowley	+172. JOHN	born 9 July 1735
170. Mercy	born 28 Mar 1728/29	marr Jane HARRIMAN 19 Mar 1761 Ipswich	
171. Mary	born 20 June 1731	173. Lydia	born 24 Apr 1737

95. CALEB-4 FOSTER, JR, brother of above, was born 5 June 1708 at Ipswich, Essex, MA. He married Priscilla-4 BUXTON ++ 4 Nov 1729 at Rowley, MA. She was the daughter of John-3 BUXTON and Priscilla LYNN, and was born ____, baptized 26 May 1706 (CR .10) ; died ____. Caleb-4 FOSTER, Jr. died 25 Jan 1766. Note: Caleb-4 FOSTER, Jr. and wife Priscilla made a deed to Thomas FOSTER, Ipswich on 14 Jan 1763.

Children of Caleb-4 FOSTER, Jr. and Priscilla-4 BUXTON:
Surname FOSTER

+ 174. NATHAN	born ca 1730 Ipswich, MA; married Miriam NORWOOD; died 19 Apr 1806
	(she born 14 Feb 1725; died ___) res Pigeon Hall, Ipswich, MA (Rockport)
175. Reginald	born ca 1732; married __?__ CONANT ca 1762 (she born 1736 Rowley)
+ 176. JOHN	born ca 173_; bapt 30 May 1760;1m. ____ KILMER ca 1764; 2m ?; 3m. ?

Reference: Maine (LM 28 ABL, Vol. 4) page 164 states " no record of children of Ipswich, but three are credited "

Ancestry of Priscilla-4 BUXTON

ANTHONY-1 BUXTON, the immigrant, was born ca 1610 in England. He came to America on the MARY AND JOHN before 1643 when he married Elizabeth __?__ at Salem, MA. Elizabeth was born ca 1623; died ca 1713. Anthony-1 BUXTON died 1684 at Salem. They were the parents of 12 children; 1. JOHN-2; 2. Elizabeth; 3. Lydia; 4. Mary; 5. Sarah; 6. Anthony-2; 7. Samuel; 8. James; 9. Thomas; 10. Joseph; 11. Hannah; and 12. Rachel BUXTON.

JOHN-2 BUXTON, the eldest son of Anthony-1, was born ca 1644. His first marriage was to Mary SMALL on 30 Mar 1668 at Salem, MA. Mary was the daughter of John SMALL and Ann_?_; and was born ____; died 27 Jan 1676. His second wife was Elizabeth HOLTON, daughter of Joseph HOLTON. They were married on 7 Oct 1677. John-2 BUXTON died 16 May 1715, age 71. Children of John-2 BUXTON and his 1ˢᵗ wife were: Mary; Elizabeth; and JOHN-3. He and his 2ⁿᵈ wife had 11 more children: Joseph; Sarah; Anthony; Hannah; Rachel; Ebenezer, Lydia; Benjamin; James, Amos and Jonathan BUXTON.

JOHN-3 BUXTON was born 29 Nov 1675 at Salem, MA. He married Priscilla LYNN on 26 Nov 1700. Her parents are not known. John-3 BUXTON had three children: John-4; Stephen-4; and PRISCILLA-4, who married Caleb-4 FOSTER, Jr. (above)

101. BENJAMIN-4 FOSTER, son of Jacob-3 FOSTER (Isaac-2; Reginald-1) and Sarah WOOD, was born 6 Oct 1689 at Topsfield, Essex, MA. He married Sarah WOODWARD 15 Mar 1725 at Ipswich. She was the daughter of Ezekiel WOODWARD and Abigail _?_ of Granville Twsp, Nova Scotia; and was born 10 Mar 1703 at Gloucester, MA; died 1805 at Granville, NS. Benjamin-4 FOSTER died ca 1790 Granville.

Child of Benjamin-4 FOSTER and Sarah WOODWARD:
   Surname FOSTER

+ 177. JUDITH	born 20 Mar 1728, MA; died Nov 1808 Granville, Annapolis, NS.
	married John-5 CHUTE 26 Nov 1745 Timberland, Hampstead, NH
+ 178. ISAAC	born 20 Mar 1728, MA; died 29 Jan 1819 Granville, Annapolis, Nova Scotia
	married Mehitable WORTHING 31 Oct 1754 Granville, NS
	(she dau/o Samuel WORTHEN and Mehetabel HEATH)
	(she born 12 Oct 1733, Bridgton, NS; died ca 1826 Granville, NS)
+ 179. EZEKIEL	born ca 1730; died 29 Jan 1819 Annapolis, NS
	married Mary ROBERTS 31 Oct 1754 Hampstead, NH
+ 180. ELIZABETH	born ca 1733; married Francis Barclay LeCAIN ca 1761 Annapolis, NS
181. Jeremiah	born ca 1733; died young
182. Sarah	born 28 Sept 1739 Andover, MA; married Abel WHEELOCK
183. Jeremiah (2)	born ca 1740; married Jemima KENT

103. BENJAMIN I-4 FOSTER, son of Benjamin-3 FOSTER (Abraham-2; Reginald-1) and Mary JOHNSON, was born ca 1699 at Ipswich, Essex, MA. He married Wilmot GRIFFITH 1 Nov 1716 at Portsmouth, NH. She was born ca 1701 Scarboro, Maine; died 1776 at East Machias, Maine. They were both members of the Greenland (NH) Church in 1722. He removed to Scarborough by 1737, and is presumably the Benjamin FOSTER who, with Robert HASTY, bought 100 acres in Scarborough in 1731. Benjamin-4 FOSTER died ca 1763 at Scarborough, Maine.

Children of Benjamin-4 FOSTER and Wilmot GRIFFITH:
   Surname FOSTER

184. Hannah	born 1724; baptized 1724; died ca 1799
	married John SCAMMON 11 Nov 1741 Scarboro
+ 185. COL. BENJAMIN	born 1726; baptized 1726; died 4 July 1818; buried E. Machias, ME
JR.	1m. Abigail MILLIKEN 26 Nov 1747 Scarborough, ME
	(she dau/o Edward MILLIKEN and Abigail NORMAN)
	2m. Elizabeth SCOTT 29 Jan 1750 Scarborough (she born 1734 Greenland, NH; died 1805)
	Note: He was the **Revolutionary War** hero of Machias
186. Sarah	born ___; baptized 29 May 1729; died young
+ 187. WOODEN/	born 1730; baptized 1730; died 2 Feb 1810 East Machias, ME
WOODIN	married Frances SCOTT 28 May 1753
	(she dau/o Sylvanus SCOTT and Sarah MOSES)
188. Sarah (2)	born ___; baptized 1733; died ca 1808
	married Joseph MILLIKEN 17 May 1750 (he 2m. ____ BERRY)
	(he was a Grantee of Trenton on Union River 1763) (he born 1729 Scarboro)
+ 189. ISAIAH	born 18 Jul 1734; baptized 1735; died ca 1809 Machias, Maine
	married Lydia FOGG 18 Jul 1754 Scarborough
	(she born 5 Apr 1734 Scarborough, ME)(she dau/o Seth FOGG and Mary PICKERNELL)
+ 190. EZEKIEL	born 1737; baptized 2 Oct 1737; ca 1799 Machias, ME
	married Mary Pickernell FOGG 17 Nov 1757 Scarborough
	(she dau/o Seth FOGG and Mary PICKERNELL) (he born 11 Oct 1738 Scarborough, ME)

References: DAR Vol. 14-16-25-31-118-268; Pierces' FOSTER Genealogy; Maine Historical Magazine

The Fifth American Generation

121. HANNAH-5 ESTEY, daughter of Mary-4 DORMAN (Judith-3 WOOD; Mary-2 FOSTER; Reginald-1) and John ESTEY, was born ca 1693, baptized 24 Dec 1693 probably at Boxford, MA . She married Jonathan RUSSELL ++ on 10 Apr 1718 at Salem, Essex, MA. He was the son of William RUSSELL and Elizabeth NOURSE/NURSE, and was born 19 Aug 1682 at Salem, MA; died ca 1730 at Salem. Hannah-5 ESTEY died 30 Sept 1730. Note: Jonathan RUSSELL probably a descendant of Rebecca NOURSE, one of the women who was hung as a " witch " at Salem in 1692.

Children of Hannah-5 ESTEY and Jonathan RUSSELL:
    Surname RUSSELL   (all children born at Salem, MA)

+ 191. SUSANNAH   born 11 Feb 1719; died 15 Jun 1779   +193. JONATHAN born 7 Feb 1724
    192. Hannah   born 12 Nov 1721   194. John   born 19 July 1730

123. LYDIA-5 EAMES, daughter of Mary-4 DEATH (Mary-3 PEABODY; Mary-2 FOSTER; Reginald-1 and Samuel EAMES, was born Oct 1692/94 at Woburn, MA. She married Ebenezer BUCK Nov 1713 at Woburn, MA. He was the son of Ephraim BUCK and Sarah BROOKS; and was born 20 May 1689; died 1752 Woburn. She died June 1722 at Woburn.

Children of Lydia-5 EAMES and Ebenezer BUCK:
    Surname BUCK   (children born Woburn, MA)
    195. Ebenezer   born 22 Feb 1716/17
+ 196. JONATHAN   born 20 Feb 1718; died 1795; married Lydia MORSE Oct 1742 Haverhill, MA

136. ABIGAIL-5 DEATH, daughter of John-4 DEATH, III (Mary-3 PEABODY; Mary-2 FOSTER; Reginald-1) and Waitsill VOSE, was born 3 Oct 1723 at Sherborn, Middlesex, MA. She married William-3 GREENWOOD on 14 Feb 1744 at Sherborn, MA. He was the son of William-2 GREENWOOD (Thomas- 1) and Abigail WOODWARD (John; George); and was born 4 Nov 1721 at Sherborn, MA; and died 28 June 1782 New Ipswich, NH. Abigail-5 DEATH died 1 Oct 1814 Sherborn, MA.

Children of Abigail-5 DEATH and William GREENWOOD:
    Surname GREENWOOD   (children born Sherborn, Middlesex, MA)
    197. Waitsill   born 17 Nov 1745; died 11 June 1788
                      married Ebenezer TWITCHELL 4 June 1767 Sherborn
    198. John Death   born 24 Sep 1747; died 13 Oct 1758 Sherborn, MA
    199. Daniel   born 1 Oct 1749; married Rebecca CHURCH (she born ca 1753 Sherborn)
    200. Eli   born 30 Sep 1751; died 8 Oct 1827
    201. Elizabeth   born 8 Apr 1754; died 5 Apr 1827
                      married Moses GREENWOOD 27 Aug 1771/72 Watertown, MA
    202. Joshua   born 11 Oct 1755; died 1 Dec 1827
    203. William   born 25 June 1758; died 30 Aug 1830
    204. Miriam   born 6 Nov 1760; died 4 Apr 1763 Sherborn, MA
+ 205. HEPSIBETH   born 10 Oct 1763; married James ROLLINS 4 Nov 1779 Rutland, VT
    206. Abigail   born 1766; died 17 Sep 1852
                      married Joseph ROLLINS 6 Oct 1785 Dublin, Cheshire, NH

141. HEPZIBAH-5 HOWE, daughter of Hepzibah-4 DEATH (Mary-3 PEABODY; Mary-2 FOSTER; Reginald-1) and David HOWE, was born 1 Oct 1706 at Sudbury, Middlesex, MA. She married Cyprian KEYES on 15 Dec 1729 at Sudbury. He was the son of Deacon Thomas KEYES and Elizabeth HOWE. He was born 15 Sept 1706 Shrewsbury, MA; died 18 Jan 1802 Boylston, MA. Hepzibah-5 died 15 Apr 1792 .

Children of Hepzibah-5 HOWE and Cyprian KEYES;

   Surname KEYES   (all children born Shrewsbury, Worcester, MA 0

207. Hepzibah	born 9 Nov 1730	210. Lavina born 2 Feb 1737; died 19 Jan 1756
208. Elizabeth	born 17 Aug 1732	211. Persis born 22 Jan 1739
	died 3 May 1805	212. David born 20 Aug 1741; died 11 Sept 1745
209. Cyprian (Jr) born 9 Jan 1735; died ca 1805		

143. ISRAEL-5 HOWE, brother of above, was born 6 May 1712 at Sudbury, Middlesex, MA. He married Elizabeth HUBBARD 24 Mar 1740. She was the daughter of Joseph HUBBARD and Rebecca BULKLEY/ BUCKLEY, and was born 23 Sept 1720 at Concord, Middlesex, MA; died 12 May 1802. Israel-5 HOWE died 23 June 1748 at Rutland, Worcester, MA.

Children of Israel-5 HOWE and Elizabeth HUBBARD:

   Surname HOWE   (children born Rutland, Worcester, MA)

213. Israel (Jr)	born 24 Aug 1742; died 13 June 1745	
214. Lucy	born 3 June 1743; died 6 Aug 1819	
215. Elizabeth	born 12 Nov 1744; died 6 Apr 1820 Lexington, MA	
216. Ruth	born 7 Nov 1746	217. Rebecca born 20 Jan 1748

145. DAVID-5 HOWE, brother of above, was born 3 June 1717 at Sudbury, Middlesex, MA. He married Abigail HUBBARD on 15 Mar 1742 at Concord, Middlesex, MA. She was the sister of Elizabeth HUBBARD (above) , and was born 20 Feb 1725 Concord; died 23 Feb 1812 at Sudbury, MA. David-5 HOWE died 14 Nov 1802

Children of David-5 HOWE and Abigail HUBBARD:

   Surname HOWE   (all children born Sudbury, Middlesex, MA)

218. Persis	born 18 Dec 1743; died 7 May 1806 Framingham, MA
219. Buckley	born 23 July 1746; died 1 Nov 1789
220. Israel	born 13 Mar 1749; died 29 Dec 1789
221. Abigail	born 8 Oct 1751; died 14 Apr 1829
222. David	born 12 Mar 1754; died 16 Mar 1755
223. David (2)	born 7 Jan 1756; died 13 Oct 1803
224. Joseph	born 1 Dec 1760; died 27 Jan 1808
225. Alice	born 12 July 1763; died 6 Apr 1834
226. Rebecca	born 20 Aug 1766; died 17 Apr 1854
227. Lucy	born 3 June 1769; died 3 Oct 1784

151. JOSHUA-5 LAMB, son of Lydia-4 DEATH (Mary-3 PEABODY; Mary-2 FOSTER; Reginald-1) and Jonathan LAMB, was born 19 Jan 1719 at Framingham, Middlesex, MA. He married Sarah WILSON on 19 Mar 1741 at Leicester, Worcester, MA. She was the daughter of James WILSON, Jr. and Mehitable LEAVENS, and was born ca 1720 Killingly, Windham, CT; died ____. Joshua-5 LAMB died 18 Jan 1793 at Spencer, Worcester, MA.

Children of Joshua-5 LAMB and Sarah WILSON:

   Surname LAMB   (all children born Leicester, MA)

228. Joshua (Jr)	born 3 July 1741; married Sarah COLEIGH (she born ca 1743 Leicester)
229. Samuel	born 4 July 1743; died 27 July 1796; married Elizabeth DAVIS 16 Apr 1756
	Child: Josiah Quincy-7 LAMB born 5 Mar 1776 Leicester, MA; died there 3 Jan 1819
+ 230. DAVID	born 24 May 1745; died 11 Nov 1823
	married Sarah CLARK 2 Sep 1767 Spencer, Worcester, MA
231. Sarah	born 24 Aug 1747; married Isaac RICE 14 Jan 1771; died 4 Mar 1816
	(he born ca 1745 Spencer, Worcester, MA)
232. Mary	born 8 Aug 1749; died 24 Aug 1754
233. Benjamin (twin)	born 8 Apr 1752; died 12 Aug 1754

Children of Joshua-5 LAMB, continued:
    Surname LAMB
    234. Lydia   (twin)   born 8 Apr 1752; died 7 Aug 1754
    235. Jonas   born 24 June 1755; married Mehitable PIERCE; died 3 Sept 1822
                                 (she born ca 1759 Spencer, Worcester, MA)

155. JOHN-5 DRESSER, son of Mercy/ Marcy-4 PEABODY (Jacob-3; Mary-2 FOSTER, Reginald-1)
and Richard DRESSER, was born 8 Dec 1716 at Woodstock, Windham, CT. He married Sarah SCOTT
on 9 Jan 1740 at Dudley, Worcester, MA. She was the daughter of Joseph SCOTT and Hannah PRIOR,
and was born 21 Dec 1722 at Brookline, Suffolk, MA; died 27 June 1782 at Charlton, Worcester, MA.
John-5 DRESSER died Jan 1789 at Charlton.

Children of John-5 DRESSER and Sarah SCOTT:
    Surname DRESSER   (children born at Charlton, Worcester, MA)
    236. Sarah   born 20 Dec 1740   241. Joseph   born 5 July 1750
    237 Hannah   born 9 Oct 1742   242. Benjamin   born 5 Sept 1752
    238. John   born 7 Sept 1744   243. Prudence   born 13 Aug 1754
    239. Asa   born 6 May 1746   244. David   born 31 Aug 1756
    240. Abigail   born 3 July 1748   245. Isaac   born 5 Sept 1752

165. JEDEDIAH-5 FOSTER, son of Ephraim-4 FOSTER (Ephraim-3; Abraham-2; Reginald-1) and
Abigail POOR, was born 10 Oct 1726 at Andover, Ma. He married Dorothy DWIGHT 18 May 1749.
She was the daughter of Brigadier General Joseph DWIGHT and Mary PYNCHON; and was born 13
Nov 1729; died 12 Jan 1818 Brookfield, Worcester, MA.

Child of Jedediah-5 FOSTER and Dorothy DWIGHT:
    Surname FOSTER
+ 246. THEOPHILUS   born 16 Mar 1754 Brookfield, MA; died ___ Wilmington, VT
                      married Susanna PACKARD 22 June 1775 Brookfield, MA
              (she dau/o Captain Joseph PACKARD and Sarah JOHNSON; she born ca 1755)
    247. Peregrine   born 28 Dec 1759 Brookfield, MA

166. STEPHEN-5 FOSTER, son of John-4 FOSTER (Ephraim-3; Abraham-2; Reginald-1) and Rebeckah
REA, was born 14 Aug 1720 at Andover, MA. He married Abigail SMITH 28 Jan 1744 at Salem, Essex,
MA. She was the daughter of Walter SMITH and Ruth FULLER, and was born 20 Dec 1722 at Salem, MA
Stephen-5 FOSTER died ca 1787 .

Children of Stephen-5 FOSTER and Abigail SMITH:
    Surname FOSTER   (all children born at Andover, Essex, MA)
    248. David   born 5 Mar 1745; married Ruth PEABODY 31 Dec 1767 Boxford, MA
                       (she born ca 1748 Boxford, MA)
    249. Rebecca   born 11 Mar 1746; married William RUNNELS 3 May 1768 Andover, MA
                       (he born 9 Sept 1739 Boxford; died 10 July 1822 Boxford)
    250. Abigail   born 23 Aug 1749; married Phineas BARKER 23 June 1774 Andover
                       (he born ca 1745 Andover, MA; died ___)
    251. Stephen   born 3 July 1751; married Rebecca WOOD 3 Aug 1775 Bradford, MA
                       (she born ca 1755 Bradford; died ____)
    252. Eunice   born 15 Apr 1753
                       married Jeremiah PERLEY/ PEARLEY 14 July 1778 Boxford, MA
                       (he born ca 1749 Andover, MA; died 4 June 1784 Boxford, MA)
    253. Simeon   born 14 Aug 1755 ; died 21 Sept 1831 Andover, MA
                       married Mary HARRIMAN 9 Oct 1828 Boxford, MA
                       (she born ca 1759)
    254. Elizabeth   born 9 Aug 1757; died 27 June 1843 Andover, MA

Children of Stephen-5 FOSTER, continued:
    Surname FOSTER

255. John	born 10 Dec 1759; died 30 Nov 1837
	married Sally INGALLS 25 Nov 1788 Metheun, MA (she born ca 1763)
+ 256. NATHAN	born 23 Nov 1761; died 12 July 1844 Andover, MA
257. Daniel	born 26 Apr 1765; died 3 Jan 1821
	married Hannah SWAN 20 Oct 1797 Andover, MA (she born ca 1769)

167.   ABRAHAM-5 FOSTER, son of Abraham-4 FOSTER (Abraham-3; 2; Reginald-1) and Sarah DUNNELL, was born 4 May 1719 at Topsfield, MA. He married Priscilla TODD on 10 May 1744. She was the daughter of Abner TODD and Elizabeth _?_, and was born 16 Jan 1724, MA; died __. Abraham-5 FOSTER died 27 Oct 1796.

Child of Abraham-5 FOSTER and Sarah DUNNELL:
    Surname FOSTER

+ 258. ABIJAH	born 12 Sept 1762 Topsfield, MA; died 2 Apr 1822 Keene, NH
	married Artemesia BLAKE 16 Feb 1797

(she dau of Dr. Obadiah BLAKE and Zipporah HARRIS)(born 5 Dec 1765; died 8 Jan 1837, Keene, NH)

168. JONATHAN-5 DRESSER, son of Lydia-4 FOSTER (Caleb-3; Abraham-2; Reginald-1) and Nathan DRESSER, was born ca 1724 at Rowley, MA. He married Sarah- FOSTER on 24 Nov 1748 at Andover, MA. Jonathan-5 DRESSER died 12 Oct 1800/ 06. They moved to Fryeburg, Maine ca 1777.

Children of Jonathan-5 DRESSER and Sarah FOSTER:
    Surname DRESSER   (all children born at Andover, MA)

259. Sarah	born 17 Sept 1750; married Job EASTMAN ++ (int pub 23 Jan 1776) Gorham, ME
	(he son/o Deacon Richard EASTMAN and Mary LOVEJOY; he born 26 Jul 1754 Pembroke, NH)
260. Elizabeth	born 23 July 1752
+ 261. STEPHEN	born 25 Oct 1754 died 28 Sept 1829 Lovell, ME
+ 262. JONATHAN	born 14 Sept 1757 died 13 Apr 1814 Fryeburg, ME
263. Simeon	born 21 Feb 1759 (served in the **Revolutionary War** from Andover, MA)
264. Levi	born 24 Feb 1761 (served in the **Revolutionary War** from Fryeburg, ME)
265. Mary	born 1 Nov 1762
266. Chloe	born 15 Dec 1765 267. Benjamin born 6 Jan 1768

  ++ Job EASTMAN, a native of Pembroke, NH. Resided at Fryeburg in 1776 when his marriage intentions to Sarah DRESSER were published. He had an innkeeper's license in Standish (ME) in 1788, and was taxed there for property in 1789. He removed to Norway, ME ca 1792, and was there in 1798, when he sold land. The death date of Sarah-6 DRESSER is unknown, but he was married 2nd to a Jane G. _?_ Jackson. She was the widow of a Joseph JACKSON, and was born ___; died after 1852. Job EASTMAN died 28 Feb 1845. He and Sarah DRESSER may have had 2 children; but they may have pre-deceased him.

172. JOHN-5 DRESSER, brother of above, was born 9 July 1735 at Boxford, MA. He married Jane HARRIMAN on 19 Mar 1761 at Ipswich, Essex, MA. She was the daughter of John HARRIMAN and Jane BAILEY, and was born 27 Mar 1741 at Rowley, MA; died ____.

Children of John-5 DRESSER and Jane HARRIMAN:
    Surname DRESSER   (all children born Boxford, Essex, MA)

268. Thomas	born 7 Aug 1762	274. Molly	born 2 May 1776
	married Hannah HAZEN 15 Nov 1791	275. Mercy	born 21 Aug 1778
269. Jane	born 31 Dec 1764	276. Nathaniel	born 14 Aug 1781
270. Lydia	born 24 Apr 1767	277. Mehitable	born Aug 1783
271. Rebeckah	born 22 Aug 1770	278. Sally	born 15 Feb 1786
272. John	born 29 Aug 1772	279. Eunice	born 18 Mar 1788
+ 273. ENOCH	born 9 June 1774; died 7 Oct 1824 Georgetown, MA		

174. NATHAN-5 FOSTER, son of Caleb-4 FOSTER, Jr. (Caleb-3; Abraham-2; Reginald –1) and Priscilla-4 BUXTON, was born ca 1730 at Rockport (Ipswich), MA; baptized as an adult on 30 Mar 1760, Rockport, MA. He married Miriam-3 NORWOOD ++ ca 1747/48 at Ipswich. She was the daughter of Joshua-2 NORWOOD and Elizabeth ANDREWS, and was born 14 Feb 1725, possibly died after 1806.

Children of Nathan-5 FOSTER and Miriam NORWOOD:
  Surname FOSTER

+ 280. ELINOR   born ca 1748; baptized 30 Mar 1760; married Joshua GAMAGE 27 Dec 1764

  281. Jemima   born ca 1749/50; baptized 30 Mar 1760

  282. William   born ca 1750/51; baptized 30 Mar 1760
      Note: he is possibly the Sgt. William FOSTER; born 5 Feb 1750 Gloucester, MA who was a **Revolutionary War**
      soldier under the command of Col. BRIDGE's Regiment; and was wounded in the left wrist by a musket ball,
      in action at Bunker Hill 1775. He died at Bristol, Maine.

+ 283. NATHAN   born ca 1753; baptized 30 Mar 1760
                         1m. Anna/Amy THOMPSON 23 Nov 1773
                         (she dau/o Thomas THOMPSON and Abigail SMITH)
                         (she baptized 20 Mar 1755 So. Berwick, ME; died ____)
                         2m. Rachel MARTIN Weston (widow) 18 May 1790
                         died 8 Apr 1819 St. George, Maine; buried there in Clark's Hill Cemetery

+ 284. EBENEZER   born ca 1754; baptized 30 Mar 1760
                         1m. Mary LANCASTER 12 Feb 1782 Rowley, MA
                         (she dau/o Paul LANCASTER and Mary GAGE)
                         2m. Susanna KENNY of Bristol, Maine

+ 285. JOHN   born ca 1756; baptized 30 Mar 1760
                         married Susannah ROBINSON (of Plymouth, MA) 25 Dec 1779 Bristol, ME
      Note: Resided St. George, Maine. Enlisted in the Continental Army (**Revolutionary War**) at Weymouth, MA 1778

  286. Miriam   born ca 1758; baptized 30 Mar 1760 ; died 1828
      Note: She possibly the Miriam FOSTER who married Miles THOMPSON, brother of Amy (above)
      He was baptized 21 Sept 1746; married 15 May 1777 at Bristol, ME; died ca 1815

  287. ZABUD/   born ca 1760/61; baptized 21 Mar 1762 Rockport, MA (**Rev War veteran**)
       ZEBARD   married Hannah STONE int pub 20 Oct 1787 Bristol, ME
                        (she dau/o William STONE and Elizabeth THOMPSON)
                        (she born ca 1770; died 17 Dec 1859)
                        died 12 Nov 1831 (age 71) Montville, Maine; buried Halldale Cemetery

++ Ancestry of Miriam-3 NORWOOD

FRANCIS-1 NORWOOD, the immigrant, was born before 1636, the son of THOMAS-A NORWOOD of Leckhampton Parish, Cheltenham, Gloucestershire, England. Francis-1 NORWOOD built his house (1662) at the entrance of Lobster Cove (now Hyatt House). He married Elizabeth COLDOM 13 Oct 1662 at Gloucester, MA. She was the daughter of Clement COLDOM, and was born ___; died 3 Aug 1711. Francis-1 NORWOOD died 4 Mar 1708/09. Their children (all born Gloucester, MA) were: Thomas; Francis-2; Elizabeth; Mary; Stephen; Deborah; Hannah; JOSHUA-2; Caleb and Abigail NORWOOD.

JOSHUA-2 NORWOOD was born 27 Feb 1683; married Elizabeth ANDREWS of Chebacco, intentions published 25 Sept 1704. Elizabeth ANDREWS was the daughter of Ensign William ANDREWS and Margaret WOODARD, and was born ca 1684; died 1 Nov 1774. She was the granddaughter of Lieutenant John ANDREWS and Jane JORDAN. Joshua-2 NORWOOD died 1762 at Gloucester. Joshua-2 NORWOOD and Elizabeth ANDREWS had 15 children: Elizabeth; Joshua; dau/dy; Sarah; Stephen; Hannah; Mary (who married Nathaniel GAMAGE); Susannah, dy; Francis; Abigail; MIRIAM-3; Susannah (2); Rachel; Patience and Caleb NORWOOD. MIRIAM-3 NORWOOD was born 14 Feb 1725 at Gloucester, MA. She married Nathan-5 FOSTER (above)

176. JOHN-5 FOSTER, son of Caleb-4 FOSTER, Jr. (Caleb-3; Abraham-2; Reginald-1) and Priscilla-4 BUXTON, was born ca 173_; baptized 30 May 1760 probably at Ipswich, Essex, MA. He married three times: first to __?_ KILMER ca 1764. His second and third wives names are unknown.

Children of John-5 FOSTER and __?__ KILMER:
  Surname FOSTER
  288. Thomas D.   born 17__   289. Ebenezer   born 17__

177. JUDITH-5 FOSTER, daughter of Benjamin-4 FOSTER (Jacob-3; Isaac-2; Reginald-1) was born

20 Mar 1728, MA. She married John-5 CHUTE 26 Nov 1745 at Timberlane, Hampstead, Rockingham County, NH. He was the son of Lionel-4 CHUTE and Anna/Hannah CHENEY, and was born June 1720 at Byfield Parish, Essex County, MA.; died Nov 1791 at Granville, Annapolis, Nova Scotia. Judith-5 FOSTER died Nov 1808 at Granville, NS.

Children of Judith-5 FOSTER and John CHUTE:

Surname CHUTE	(1st 6 children born Hampstead, NH; last 4 born Granville, NS)
290. Samuel	born 16 Feb 1746; died 12 Nov 1786 drowned Annapolis River, NS
291. John (Jr)	born 7 Apr 1748; died 7 May 1748
292. Hannah/Anna	born 16 Sept 1749; died 1 Nov 1749
293. John (Jr.) (2)	born 9 Apr 1752; died 8 Mar 1841 Digby-Joggins, Nova Scotia
	married Mary-3 CROCKER (# 12 CROCKER Section)
294. Benjamin	born 27 Sept 1754
295. Thomas	born 13 Mar 1757; died 13 June 1838
296. Sarah	born 3 Nov 1758; died Aug 1836
297. James	born 22 Jan 1762
298. Hannah (2)	born 25 Dec 1764; died 1841 Nova Scotia
299. Susan	born 10 Dec 1767; died 1 July 1858 Granville, NS

178. ISAAC-5 FOSTER, brother of above, was born ca 1728, MA. He married Mehitable WORTHEN/ WORTHING 31 Oct 1754 at All Saints Anglican Church, Granville Twsp., Nova Scotia. She was the daughter of Samuel WORTHEN/ WORTHING and Mehitable HEATH, and was born 12 Oct 1733 at Bridgton, Granville Twsp, NS; died ca 1826 Granville, NS. Isaac-5 FOSTER died 29 Jan 1819 Granville Township, Nova Scotia.

Children of Isaac-5 FOSTER and Mehitable WORTHEN/WORTHING:

Surname FOSTER	(1st 8 ch born Granville Twsp.; NS ; last one born Hampstead, NH)		
300. Jacob	born 1757; died 1759	305. Samuel	born 1 Oct 1770
301. Sarah	born 15 Oct 1760	+ 306. OLIVER	born 1 May 1773
302. Isaac	born 24 Aug 1763		died 1827
	died 1852	+ 307. ASA	born 24 Nov 1776; died 20 Sep 1854
303. Mehitable	born 23 Mar 1766	+ 308. BENJAMIN	born 25 May 1755
304. Elizabeth	born 17 Dec 1768		married Elizabeth RICHARDSON

179. EZEKIEL-5 FOSTER, brother of above, was born ca 1730, MA. He married Mary ROBERTS 31 Oct 1754 at Hampstead, NH. She was the daughter of ___ ROBERTS, and was born ca 1733, Nova Scotia. Ezekiel-5 FOSTER died 29 Jan 1819 at Annapolis, NS.

Children of Ezekiel-5 FOSTER and Mary ROBERTS:

Surname FOSTER	(1st 3 children born NH; last 3 born Nova Scotia)		
309. Sarah	born ca 1756; died 1760	312. Ezekiel	born 30 Mar 1763
310. Martha	born 13 Aug 1757	313. Joseph	born 18 Oct 1771
311. John	born 29 Mar 1760		died 19 June 1848 Annapolis, NS
	died 29 Sep 1827	314. Ezra	born 1 Aug 1773

180. ELIZABETH-5 FOSTER, sister of above, was born ca 1733. She married Francis Barclay LeCAIN ca 1761 at Annapolis Twsp, Annapolis, NS. He was the son of __?__ LeCAIN and was born ca 1720/21 on the Isle of Jersey; died ca 1806 at Annapolis Royal, Annapolis, NS. Elizabeth-5 FOSTER died ____.

Children of Elizabeth-5 FOSTER and Francis LeCAIN:

Surname LeCAIN	(all children born Annapolis Royal, Annapolis Twsp, Annapolis, NS)		
315. Francis B. Jr.	born ca 1762	317. Nicholas	born ca 1765
316. Benjamin	born ca 1764	318. William	born ca 1767; died 1830, NS

185. COLONEL BENJAMIN-5 FOSTER, son of Benjamin-4 FOSTER (Benjamin-3; Abraham-2; Reginald-1) and Wilmot GRIFFITH, was born ca 1726; baptized 1726 at Greenland, New Hampshire. He married first to Abigail MILLIKEN on 26 November 1747 at Scarborough, Maine. She was the daughter of Edward MILLIKEN and Abigail NORMAN, and was born 6 June 1731; died before 1750. His second wife was Elizabeth SCOTT. They were married on 29 Jan 1750 at Scarborough. She was the daughter of ___ SCOTT, and was born ca 1734 at Greenland, NH; died ca 1805. Colonel Benjamin-5 FOSTER died 4 July 1818. He and his wife are buried at East Machias, Maine. His monument there reads: " The Chief Leader in the Capture of the Schooner MARGARETTA. " (**Revolutionary War**)

Child of Colonel Benjamin-5 FOSTER and Abigail MILLIKEN:
    Surname FOSTER
319. Abigail   born 23 Jan 1749 Scarborough, ME; married _?_ 11 Dec 1766; died 1807
Children of Colonel Benjamin-5 FOSTER and Elizabeth SCOTT:
    Surname FOSTER   (order of birth uncertain)
+ 320. JACOB   born 1750; 1m. Anna/Pamelia JONES; died 25 Feb 1824 Trenton, ME
     (poss dau/o Nathan JONES of Gouldsboro) (she born 23 May 1763)
     2m. Mrs Mary ____ Curtis of Boston ca Apr 1800
321. Daniel   born 1752; died young
+ 322. JOHN   born 1754; married Phebe BURR (she of Trenton, Maine)
+ 323. BENJAMIN, Jr.   born ca 1755; bapt 28 Mar 1756 Scarborough, ME
     married Ruth SCOTT 20 Apr 1777 Machias, ME (she dau/o Samuel SCOTT)
+ 324. ABIJAH   born ca 1760; married Apphia TALBOT 12 Dec 1790 Machias, ME
     (she dau/o Peter TALBOT and Lucy HAMMOND)
325. Elizabeth   born 1764; died young
+ 326. LEVI   born ca 1765; married Sally BEAL (dau of Edward BEAL of Union River)
+ 327. BETSEY   born 1766; 1m. Joshua BURR/BURNHAM 9 Oct 1796 (removed to Trenton)
     2m. Asa-7 FOSTER (son/o Benjamin-6 FOSTER (# 323) and Ruth SCOTT)
328. Asa   born 17__; (before 1770)
+ 329. DEACON   born ca 17__; married Comfort SCOTT 5 Jun 1792
     SAMUEL   (dau/o Sylvanus SCOTT) (she born ca 1774; died 3 May 1860 (age 86)
     died 17 May 1860 (age 83) East Machias, ME
330. Daniel (2)   born ca 1769; married Hannah GARDNER 12/30 Mar 1797
     (she dau/o Ebenezer GARDNER and Damaris MERRILL)
     (she born 3 May 1774, Cumberland Co., NS; died 1 Sept 1858)
+ 331. GEORGE   born 17__; married Cynthia CHASE 14 July 1799; died 1855 Presque Isle
     KELLEY   (she dau/o William CHASE and Lucy SMITH)

187. WOODEN/WOODIN-5 FOSTER, brother of above, was born ca 1730; baptized 1730 at Scarborough, Maine. He married Frances SCOTT on 28 Feb 1753. She was the daughter of Sylvanus SCOTT +++ and Sarah MOSES, and was born ca 1733; died 1822. She was the sister of Samuel and Sylvanus SCOTT, Jr. Woodin-5 FOSTER enlisted in 1777 as a Private in Captain James SEVEY"S Co., Colonel Benjamin FOSTER'S Regiment for the Defense of Machias (**Revolutionary War**). Woodin-5 FOSTER died at East Machias on 2 Feb 1810. +++ Note: Sylvanus SCOTT and Sarah MOSES were married 21 Oct 1714.

Children of Woodin-5 FOSTER and Frances SCOTT:
    Surname FOSTER
+ 332. JOHN WOODIN   born 29 Sept 1754; married Lucy CHASE
     (she dau/o William CHASE (Ephraim) and Lucy SMITH)
+ 333. SARAH   born 17__; married Stephen MUNSON
     (he son of Joseph MUNSON and Sarah MORSE)
+ 334. MOSES   born 17__; married Drusilla WEST 22 May 1787
335. Jennie   born 17__; died young
+ 336. PAUL   born 17__; married Betsey WEBBER 22 July 1792
+ 337. JOEL   born 17__; 1m. Mary WEST (she dau/o Jabez WEST and ____) ; 2m. _?_

Children of Woodin-5 FOSTER, continued:
    Surname FOSTER
+ 338. RUTH   born 17__; married Nathan HANSCOM
           (he son/o Aaron HANSCOM and Sally SEVEY) (he born 176_; died after 1810)
+ 339. ELIAS   born 17__; 1m. Mary / Molly GOOCH Aug 1793
                     2m. Lucy DORMAN 15 July 1810; 3m. Lydia MILLER
+ 340. JAMES   born 1779; died 21 Feb 1848 East Machias, ME
          1m. Lucy GOOCH 7 Dec 1800 (she born 17__; died 24 Oct 18__ (age 47)
          2m. Hannah LONGFELLOW Simpson (she born 1779; died 29 Oct 1854 (age 75)

189. ISAIAH-5 FOSTER, brother of above, was born 18 July 1734; baptized 1735 at Greenland, NH. He married Lydia FOGG on 17 Nov 1757 at Scarborough, Maine. She was the daughter of Seth FOGG and Mary PICKERNELL of Scarborough; and was born 5 Apr 1734; died ca 1809. Isiaiah-5 FOSTER moved to Machias in 1766, but only remained there a few years. His entire family removed from Machias before the Revolution. He died ca 1809, Maine.

Children of Isaiah-5 FOSTER and Lydia FOGG:
    Surname FOSTER
  341. Ezekiel   born ca 1758
+ 342. WILMOT   born Aug 1759 Scarborough, ME; died 9 Oct 1838 (79-2) Newburgh
        married John CROXFORD 12 Oct 1783 (he born 17__; died 26 Dec 1820 Newburgh, ME.)
+ 343. BENEN/   born 14 Nov 1760 Scarborough, ME; died 24 Oct 1843 Wakefield, NB
     BENNING   married Deborah KINNEY 20 May 1782 Oromocto, NB
  344. Daniel   born 17__

345. Mary	born 17__	349. Lydia	born 17__
married John HODSDON		350. Isaiah	born 17__
346. Dorothy	born 17__	351. Benjamin	born 17__
married James GOULD		352. Hannah	born 17__
347. Sarah	born 17__		married Thomas PARSONS

+ 348. KEZIAH   born ca 1769; died 20 Jan 1831
        married Boardman JOHNSON 10 Jan 1792 (he son/o Benjamin JOHNSON and _____)

190. EZEKIEL-5 FOSTER, brother of above, was born 17__; baptized 2 Oct 1737 at Scarboro, Maine. He married Mary Pickernell FOGG on 17 Nov 1757 at Scarborough. She was the daughter of Seth FOGG and Mary PICKERNELL, and the sister of Lydia (above). She was born 11 Oct 1738 Scarborough, ME; died ____. Ezekiel-5 FOSTER was a member of the Crown Point Expedition in 1758. He was a Lieutenant in WHITCOMB'S MA. Regiment in 1775 (**Revolutionary War**), and was a participant in the attempt to take Fort Cumberland, Nova Scotia.

Children of Ezekiel-5 FOSTER and Mary FOGG:
    Surname FOSTER
  353. Esther   born ca 1756, MA; died 4 Nov 1844 (age 88) Grand Manaan, NB
         married Turner FISHER ca 17__   Child: Wilford-7 FISHER born ca 17__; NB
  354. Daniel   born ca 1760
  355. Benjamin   born ca 1762; married Hannah BARTLETT Oct 1797 Limerick, ME
  356. Isaiah   born ca 1765 , ME; died before 1855 Carleton Co., NB
         Child: Mary-7 FOSTER born ca 1804 , NB
+ 357. SARAH   born ca 1769 Machias, ME; died 1813 Wakefield, Carleton, NB
+ 358. SETH   born ca 1770 Machias, ME; died May 1830 Millstream, Studholm, Kings , NB
         married Elizabeth DANIELS ca 1805 Kings Co., NB
+ 359. MARY   born ca 1772 Machias, ME; died 20 Apr 1855 Studholm, Kings, NB
         married William McLEOD, Jr.
+ 360. EZEKIEL, Jr.   born ca 1776 Machias, ME; died 20 May 1849 Studholm, Kings, NB
         married Mary BUNNELL ca 1805 Kings Co., NB

The Sixth American Generation

191. SUSANNAH-6 RUSSELL, daughter of Hannah-5 ESTEY (Mary-4 DORMAN; Judith-3 WOOD; Mary-2 FOSTER; Reginald-1) and Jonathan RUSSELL, was born 11 Feb 1719 at Salem, Essex County, MA. She married Ebenezer RUSSELL, Jr. on 10 Sept 1735 at Salem. He was the son of Ebenezer RUSSELL and Deborah HUBBARD, and was born 21 Feb 1714 at Reading, MA; died 5 Aug 1791 at Wilbraham, MA. Susannah-6 RUSSELL died 15 June 1779.

Children of Susannah-6 RUSSELL and Ebenezer RUSSELL, Jr.:

Surname RUSSELL	(all children born Windsor, CT)		
361. Susannah	born 14 Mar 1736	365. Jonathan	born 1 May 1748
362. Anna	born 29 Oct 1739	366. Lucy	born 20 July 1749
	died 18 Dec 1804	367. Jerusha	born 21 June 1751
363. Ebenezer (III)	born 3 June 1741	368. John	born 27 Aug 1755
364. Hannah	born 16 Mar 1745; died 25 Jun 1822		

193. JONATHAN-6 RUSSELL, brother of above, was born 7 Feb 1724 at Salem, MA. He married Hannah FLINT on 14 Feb 1745 at Middleton, MA. She was the daughter of Stephen FLINT and Hannah MOULTON, and was born 3 Dec 1727 at Middleton, Essex County, MA; died ____. Jonathan-6 RUSSELL died ca ____ at Windsor, VT.

Children of Jonathan-6 RUSSELL and Hannah FLINT:

Surname RUSSELL	(children born Danvers (?), MA)		
369. Jonathan	born ca 1746	372. Eli	born ca 1755
370. Daniel	born ca 1746	373. Asa	born ca 1758
371. William	born ca 1750; died 29 Apr 1802	+374. JOHN	born ca 1760; died 1820 VT

196. JONATHAN-6 BUCK, son of Lydia-5 EAMES (Mary-4 DEATH; Mary-3 PEABODY; Mary-2 FOSTER; Reginald-1) and Ebenezer BUCK, was born Feb 1718. He married Lydia MORSE ca ____.

Children of Jonathan-6 BUCK and Lydia MORSE:

surname BUCK	(all children born at Haverhill, MA)		
375. Ebenezer	born Mar 1742	376. Asa	born Aug 1744; died Sept 1744
377. Lydia	born Apr 1746; died Sept 1753 Haverhill		
+ 378. JONATHAN	born 3 Apr 1748; married Hannah GALE 27 July 1768 Buckfield, ME		
+ 379. MARY	born Sept 1750; died July 1827 Candia, NH		
	married Moses DUSTIN July 1767 Haverhill, MA		
380. Amos	born 24 July 1754	382. Lydia (2)	born Oct 1761
381. Daniel born Sept 1756; marr Mary SEWALL (Ch: Jonathan-8 BUCK born ca 1793 Haverhill, MA			

205. HEPSIBETH-6 GREENWOOD, daughter of Abigail-5 DEATH (John-4,III; Mary-3 PEABODY; Mary-2 FOSTER; Reginald-1) and William GREENWOOD, was born 10 Oct 1763 at Sherborn, Middlesex, MA. She married James ROLLINS/RAWLINGS 4 Nov 1779 at Rutland, VT. He was the son of James ROLLINS/RAWLINGS and Abigail DOWNING, and was born 22 Aug 1760 Dublin, Cheshire County, NH.; died 10 Aug 1849 at Parkerstown, Mendon, VT. Hepsibeth-6 GREENWOOD died 28 Nov 1848 at Parkerstown, VT.

Children of Hepsibeth-6 GREENWOOD and James ROLLINS:

Surname ROLLINS	(children born Dublin, Cheshire County, NH)		
383. Ebenezer	born 22 Apr 1780	388. Polly	born ca 1794
384. William	born ca 1782	389. Henry	born ca 1796
385. Abigail	born 7 June 1785	390. James	born 30 June 1798; died 1880 UT
386. Sarah	born ca 1787	391. Hepsibeth	born 14 Sept 1800
387. Julia	born ca 1790	392. Martha	born ca 1802

230. DAVID-6 LAMB, son of Joshua-5 LAMB (Lydia-4 DEATH; Mary-3 PEABODY; Mary-2 FOSTER; Reginald-1) and Sarah WILSON, was born 24 May 1745 at Leicester, MA. He married Sarah CLARK on 2 Sept 1767 at Spencer, Worcester County, MA. She was the daughter of Matthias CLARK(E) and Lydia EATON, and was born 25 Apr 1746 at Spencer, MA; died ____. David-6 LAMB died 11 Nov 1923 .

Children of David-6 LAMB and Sarah CLARK:
Surname LAMB

393. Olive	born 4 Nov 1767 Spencer, MA	397. Sally (twin) born 30 July 1777
394. Jonas	born 28 July 1772	398. Chloe (2) born 13 Feb 1780
395. Enos	born 21 Feb 1774	399. Lydia born 28 Sept 1785
396. Chloe (twin)	born 30 July 1777, died young	

246. THEOPHILUS-6 FOSTER, son of Jedediah-5 FOSTER (Ephraim-4; 3; Abraham-2; Reginald-1) and Dorothy DWIGHT, was born 16 Mar 1754 at Brookfield, Worcester, MA. He married Susanna PACKARD 22 June 1775 at Brookfield. She was the daughter of Captain Joseph PACKARD and Sarah JOHNSON, and was born ca 1755; died ____. Theophilus-6 FOSTER died ____ Wilmington, VT.

Child of Theophilus-6 FOSTER and Susanna PACKARD:
Surname FOSTER

+ 400. ELIJAH D. born 12 June 1791 Brookfield, MA; died 28 Aug 1874 Lowell, Lake, IN
married Ruth NICHOLS Cady 5 Oct 1823 Greenbrush, NY
(she born 12 Oct 1794; died 29 Nov 1850 West Creek Twsp. Lake, IN

256. NATHAN-6 FOSTER, son of Stephen-5 FOSTER (John-4; Ephraim-3; Abraham-2; Reginald-1) and Abigail SMITH, was born 23 Nov 1761 at Andover, Essex, MA. He married Susanna BARKER on 16 Mar 1790 at Andover, MA. She was the daughter of Samuel BARKER and Susanna FOSTER, and was born 30 Aug 1770, Andover; died there 10 Feb 1842. Nathan-6 FOSTER died 12 July 1844 at Andover.

Children of Nathan-6 FOSTER and Susanna BARKER:
Surname FOSTER   (all children born Andover, Essex, MA)

401. Susanna born 4 Apr 1791; died 4 July 1838 Andover, MA
married Amos KIMBALL 24 May 1828 Andover (he born ca 1787 Andover)
402. Elizabeth Barker born 10 Dec 1792; died 10 Dec 1872
403. Samuel born 10 May 1794; died 4 Jan 1812 Andover, MA
404. Abigail born 28 July 1796; married Reuben REED 14 Nov 1819 Andover
(he son of Amos REED and Lydia SYMONDS; he born 5 Mar 1795; died 3 Apr 1833
Child: Edward-8 REED born ca 1821
405. Nathan born 4 Sept 1798; died 25 Nov 1877
married Hannah BERRY 25 Dec 1832 Andover, MA (she born 1802 Andover)
406. Sally born 14 Oct 1800; married Silas BURNHAM 11 May 1817 Andover, MA
407. Rebecca born 9 Aug 1804; died 21 Oct 1895
+ 408. MARY BRIDGES born 19 Aug 1807; died 13 Sep 1867 Andover, MA
married Enoch FRYE 30 Dec 1830 Andover, MA

258. ABIJAH-6 FOSTER, son of Abraham-5 FOSTER (Abraham-4; 3; 2; Reginald-1) and Priscilla TODD, was born 12 Sept 1762 Topsfield, MA. He married Artemesia BLAKE 16 Feb 1797. She was the daughter of Dr. Obadiah BLAKE and Zipporah HARRIS, and was born 5 Dec 1765; died 8 Jan 1837 Keene, NH. Abijah-6 FOSTER died 2 Apr 1822 at Keene, NH.

Child of Abijah-6 FOSTER and Artemesia BLAKE:
Surname FOSTER

+ 409. HARRIETTE born 12 June 1805 Keene, NH; died 18 Jan 1872 Clarendon, NY
married Mortimer Delville-6 MILLIKEN 17 May 1836
(he son/o Edward-5 MILLIKEN and Julia-5 BIXBY; born 11 May 1805 Peterboro, NH; died 5 Feb 1900

261. STEPHEN-6 DRESSER, son of Jonathan-5 DRESSER (Lydia-4 FOSTER; Caleb-3; Abraham-2; Reginald-1) and Sarah- FOSTER, was born 25 Oct 1754 at Andover, MA. He married Abigail-5 ABBOTT 9 Sept 1777 at Lovell, Cumberland, ME. She was the daughter of Job-4 ABBOTT and Sarah _?_; and was born 15 July 1758 at Suncook, NH; died 1 May 1845 at Fryeburg, Cumberland, ME. Stephen-6 DRESSER died 28 Sept 1829 at Lovell, Maine.

Children of Stephen-6 DRESSER and Abigail ABBOTT:
    Surname DRESSER   (all children born at Lovell, Cumberland, ME)
410. Betsey   born 8 May 1790 ; died 10 Sep 1807
411. Stephen (Jr)   born 8 Apr 1781; married Abigail-4 KILGORE 6 Apr 1802
                         (she dau/o James-3 KILGORE (Joseph-2;1) and Abigail LORD)
                         (she born 18 Aug 1785; died 25 Aug 1817)

412. Sarah   born 1 Feb 1783; died 9 Mar 1783
413. Nabby (Abigail)   born 24 Apr 1785; died 1 May 1845
                        married James-4 KILGORE (Jr. ?) (he born 1781 Lovell, ME)
414. Job Abbott   born 5 Mar 1787; died 24 Apr 1882
                        married Hannah HALL 1 Oct 1810 (she born 24 Oct 1791 Lovell, ME)
415. Mary/Polly   born 8 May 1790; died 10 Sept 1807
416. Sarah (2)   born 6 Aug 1792   419. Emelia   born 30 Jul 1799
417. Jonathan Foster   born 19 July 1794   420. Chloe   born 18 Aug 1801;
418. Susanna   born 10 July 1796   died 2 Oct 1835

262. JONATHAN-6 DRESSER, brother of above, was born 14 Sept 1757 at Andover, Essex, MA. He married Elizabeth WALKER ca 1784. She was the daughter of Joseph WALKER and Elizabeth _?_; and was born 6 Sept 1760 at Billerica, Middlesex, MA; died 13 May 1849 Portland, Cumberland, ME. Jonathan-6 DRESSER died 13 Apr 1814 at Fryeburg, Maine.

Children of Jonathan-6 DRESSER and Elizabeth WALKER:
    Surname DRESSER   (all children born Fryeburg, Oxford, Maine)
421. Sarah Foster   born 28 Aug 1785   427. Harriet   born 15 Apr 1795
422. Elizabeth Walker   born 17 Oct 1786   428. Jonathan (Jr)born 7 Aug 1797
423. Nancy   born 30 Dec 1787   429. William F.   born 2 Aug 1799
424. John   born 1 Mar 1790; dy   430. Zilpha   born 13 Feb 1801
425. John Foster   born 15 Jan 1792;   431. Joseph   born 14 Feb 1803
                        died 19 Mar 1861   432. Louisa   born 3 Oct 1805
426. Nehemiah Charles   born 20 Feb 1793

273. ENOCH-6 DRESSER, son of John-5 DRESSER (Lydia-4 FOSTER; Caleb-3; Abraham-2; Reginald-1) and Jane HARRIMAN, was born 9 June 1774 at Boxford, Essex, MA. He married Elizabeth B. BRIDGES 30 Oct 1800. She was the daughter of John BRIDGES and Ann LAMBERT, and was born 26 Aug 1779, MA; died 26 June 1864, MA. Enoch-6 DRESSER died 7 Oct 1824 at Georgetown, MA.

Children of Enoch-6 DRESSER and Elizabeth BRIDGES:
    Surname DRESSER   (children born Rowley, Essex, MA)
433. Thomas   born 1801; died 11 Sep 1802
434. Eliza C.   born 17 Jul 1803; died 30 May 1879 Groveland, Essex, MA
435. Silena/Selena   born 28 Aug 1805; died 22 Nov 1892
436. Mahaliah   born 11 Nov 1807; died 23 Dec 1891 Georgetown, Essex, MA
437. Elbridge Gerry   born 3 Jan 1810; died 16 Dec 1896
438. Thomas Newman   born 1 Dec 1811; died 23 Aug 1876 Haverhill, Essex, MA
439. William Otis   born 9 Oct 1815; died 13 Oct 1892
440. Leonard P.   born 11 Sep 1816; died 1 May 1867
441. Mary Jane   born 18 Mar 1821

280. ELINOR-6 FOSTER, daughter of Nathan-5 FOSTER (Caleb-4;3; Abraham-2; Reginald-1) and Miriam-3 NORWOOD (Joshua-2; Francis-1), was born ca 1748 probably at Rockport/Ipswich, MA. She married Joshua-5 GAMAGE 27 Dec 1764, MA. He was the son of Nathaniel-4 GAMAGE (Joshua-3; John-2) and Mary-3 NORWOOD (sister of Miriam-3), and was born 3 Jan 1741 Cambridge, MA.

Children of Elinor-6 FOSTER and Joshua GAMAGE:

Surname GAMAGE	(all but last child born at Cambridge, Essex, MA)	
+ 442. JOSHUA (Jr)	born ca 1766; baptized 2 Feb 1766 Gloucester, Essex, MA; died 18 Apr 1838 married Sarah WEBSTER (she born 11 May 1766; died 4 Sept 1853)	
443. Elinor	born 29 Nov 1767	
444. Ruth	born 11 Mar 1770	
+ 445. NATHANIEL	born 1 Dec 1771; died 16 Jan 1840 South Bristol, ME married Mary M. DAVIS ca 1793	
446. Jenny	born 6 Mar 1774	
447. William	born 19 Nov 1775; dy	
448. William (2)	born 31 May 1778	
449. Jemima	born 2 Jul 1780; died 12 Jan 1870 Edgecomb, ME 1m. ___ McFARLAND; 2m. Ebenezer POOL	
450. Samuel	born 22 May 1783	452. Stephen born ca 1787
451. Daniel	born ca 1785; died 1814	453. Jane born ca 1789 Gloucester, MA

283. NATHAN-6 FOSTER, brother of above, was born ca 1753 at Rockport, MA; baptized there 30 Mar 1760. He married 1st to Anna/Amy-4 THOMPSON ++ 23 Nov 1773 at Bristol, ME. She was the daughter of Thomas-3 THOMPSON and Abigail SMITH, and was born ____; baptized 20 Mar 1755 at South Berwick, ME., died before 1790. (marriage record listed her as Amey THOMPSON). He married 2nd to the widow Rachel MARTIN Weston 18 May 1790. (she was married 1st to Timothy WESTON, Sr., and had a son Captain Timothy WESTON, Jr., born 17 June 1780; who married Ann GOOCH 13 June 1802; and resided Machias, ME) Nathan-6 FOSTER died 8 Apr 1819 at St. George, Maine, and is buried there in the Clark's Hill Cemetery. (a **Revolutionary War** grave marker).

He enlisted 26 Mar 1776 at Bristol, Maine, and served in Captain Caleb TURNER'S Company at Boothbay (ME). His will was presented for probate on 22 May 1819. His widow, Rachel Foster, was the Executrix. The will dated 3 Apr 1819 listed 13 children.

Children of Nathan-6 FOSTER and Anna/Amy-4 THOMPSON:

Surname FOSTER	
454. Ebenezer	born ca 1774
455. Betsey	born ca 1776; married __?__ McKILLAN
+ 456. FRANCIS	born 14 Apr 1778 Bristol, ME; married Sarah TRAIN/TRANE (she born 14 Mar 1777; died 29 Oct 1847 Machiasport, ME) died 26 May 1826 St. George, Maine (served in the **War of 1812**)
+ 457. CAPTAIN NATHAN	born 16 Dec 1782 Bristol; died 16 Apr 1837 (54-4) Machiasport, ME married Sarah G-4 CROCKER 20 Aug 1803 Machias, ME (she dau/o Captain Paul-3 CROCKER and Nancy MARTIN (# 98)
458. James	born ca 1784; purchased land near Donut Point
459. Abigail	born ca 1785/86; married James MARSHALL ca 1806 (he son/o Samuel MARSHALL of Boothbay, Maine)
460. Peter/Robert	born ca 1787; married Eunice ___?__; (buried near his father at Clark's Hill Cemetery) Child: Maria-8 FOSTER born ca 1833; died 4 Sept 1849 (age 16)
461. Richard	born 10 Jan 1789 Served in the MA Volunteer Militia in the **War of 1812**. Was a member of Captain KENNEY"S Company from Sept 3-9 and Nov 2-5 1814. Raised at ST. George, service at Thomaston

Children of Nathan-6 FOSTER and Rachel MARTIN Weston:

Surname FOSTER	
462. Jeremiah (twin)	born ca 1794 (Served in the same Company (**War of 1812**) as his brother (above)
463. Amy/ Annie (twin)	born ca 1794; married ____ BARTER

Children of Nathan-6 FOSTER , continued:
Surname FOSTER

464. Lucy   born 1 Apr 1796; married Joshua WESTON 5 July 1818
> Possibly Joshua Martin-4 WESTON, son/o Arunah-3 WESTON (Eliphas-2; John-1) and
> Sally MARTIN , born 22 Sept 1794 Bristol, ME.

465. Sally   born ca 1798/99   466. Mary   born ca 1802

NATHAN-6 FOSTER , Private, on Muster, and on Payroll of Captain Caleb TURNER'S Company; enlisted 13 July 1775 to 31 Dec 1775; service 6 months, 3 days. Autograph signature for one months pay – dated Bristol 18 Nov 1775.

On Muster and Payroll; enlisted 26 Mar 1776 to 10 June 1776; service 2 months 15 days; also 3 months service between 10 June and 10 Sept 1776; and from 10 Sept 1776 to 7 Dec 1776; service 2 months 27 Days. Stationed at Boothbay – Seacoast Defense; all rolls dated Bristol (ME).

Gravestone Clark's Hill Cemetery, St. George, Maine
Revolutionary War Marker
Inscription reads:

**SACRED TO THE MEMORY
OF
MR. NATHAN FOSTER
8 APRIL 1819
AGE 66 YRS.**

**Here dust to dust in solemn
trust convey'd
The mortal part of
Nathan Foster laid
Possess'd of true philanthropy
And love
A plant celestial
For the field above**

++ Ancestry of Amy/Anna-4 THOMPSON

Reference: Old Kittery and Her Families, by Everitt S. STACKPOLE: published 1903;
Lewiston, Maine provides the following information on pp 764-66.

MILES-1 THOMPSON, baptized 1614; died possibly 1708. He was mentioned in the Court records of Boston 27 May 1642. He was a carpenter, and was living on the first lot North of Thompson's Brook in South Berwick (ME) in 1655, and had a grant of land there 15 July 1656. His wife Ann, probably Ann TETHERLY (daughter of William TETHERLY and Christian THORNE), was born ca 1632; and died 19 Sep 1717 (Aged 85). Children of Miles-1 THOMPSON were: Miles-2; John; Bartholomew; THOMAS-2; Amy; Sarah; Mary and Ann.

THOMAS-2 THOMPSON was born ca 1672/73 at Kittery, ME. He married Sarah FURBISH/FURBUSH (dau/o William) ca 1698. Thomas-2 THOMPSON died ca 1715. He had the following children: Miles; Sarah; Anne; Mehitable; and THOMAS-3.

THOMAS-3 THOMPSON was born 24 May 1712 at Kittery. He married Abigail-3 SMITH +++ , daughter of John-2 SMITH and Elizabeth-3 HEARD. She was born 18 Sept 1719 at Berwick, ME. Thomas-3 THOMPSON had 7 children, all baptized at South Berwick, Maine. They were: Dorcas and Sarah (twins); Thomas-4, Jr. ; Miles who married Miriam FOSTER; Joshua who married Martha COOMBS on 29 Sep 1782; Abigail; AMY/ANNA who married Nathan-6 FOSTER (above)

Thomas THOMPSON (Jr) of Bristol, Lincoln County, ME deeded the following parcel of land to Nathan-6 FOSTER for the consideration of " 12 shillings lawful money ". (dated 24 June 1772; witnessed by Thomas THOMPSON and Thomas STEWARD).

He " sold , set over and delivered unto the said Nathan FOSTER, his heirs and Executors, administrators all my right to a certain Tract of land on Rutherford's Island, so called in the Town of Bristol, aforesaid, beginning on the western side of Christmas Cove, so called, at a stake and heap of stones at the mouth of the brook that runs into the head of said Cove, then running northwardly by said brook to John's Bay, so called, on the shore side, then by the shore southerly as the shore runs to Nathan FOSTER'S corner line and then westerly by the said FOSTER'S line to the first mentioned bounds containing acres more or less. "

Recorded in the Lincoln County Registry of Deeds, Book 9; page 125

Ancestry of Abigail-3 SMITH

JAMES-1 SMITH, was born ca 16__ in England. He was living at Berwick, Maine in 1668; and was granted 50 acres of land there in 1669. He married Martha-2 MILLS by 25 Apr 1671. She was the daughter of Thomas-1 MILLS + and Mary WADLEIGH/WADEL; and was born/bapt 18 Jan 1653 at Saco, Maine. They had 4 children: James-2 who married Martha BRAGDON and settled in York, Maine; Mary; Elizabeth; and ELDER JOHN-2 SMITH who was born 26 July 1685 at Berwick and married Elizabeth-4 HEARD ++ by 1707. James-1 SMITH died ca 1687, and his wife married 2nd to Christopher GRANT.

JOHN-2 SMITH and Elizabeth-4 HEARD had 11 children: Elizabeth who married Caleb MADDOX; Martha; Experience; Captain John, Jr. who married Elizabeth LIBBY; Mary; ABIGAIL-3 who was born 18 Sep 1719 at Berwick and married Thomas-3 THOMPSON; Joshua; Ichabod who married Sarah CHADBOURNE; Ruth who married Joshua ROBERTS; Jane who married Tobias LORD; and Dorcas who married Philip YEATON.

+ Thomas-1 MILLS was from Exeter, England. His wife Mary was the daughter of John WADLEIGH and Mary _?_, and was born ca 1630 at Bristol, England.
++ Elizabeth-4 HEARD was the daughter of Samuel-3 HEARD and Elizabeth OTIS.

284. EBENEZER-6 FOSTER, brother of above, was born ca 1754 probably at Rockport, MA; baptized there 30 Mar 1760. He married first to Mary LANCASTER on 12 Feb 1782 at Rowley, MA. She was the daughter of Paul LANCASTER and Mary GAGE; and was born ca 17__; died ____. He married second to Susanna KENNY of Bristol, Maine. Ebenezer-6 FOSTER, a yeoman, died ____.

Child of Ebenezer-6 FOSTER and Mary LANCASTER:
    Surname FOSTER   Reference: Nancy C. Hayward, Wilmington, MA.
    467. Elinor   born 14 May 1785; married Nathaniel GARDNER 22 Aug 1803; died 8 Sept 1882

285. JOHN-6 FOSTER, brother of above, was born ca 1756; baptized 30 Mar 1760 at Rockport, MA. He married Susannah ROBINSON of Plymouth, MA 25 Dec 1779 at Bristol, Maine. She was the daughter of Alexander ROBINSON and Abigail WHITE, and was born ca 1759 Plymouth, MA; died ca 1842 at Bristol, Maine. John-6 FOSTER died ca 1837 at Bristol.

Children of John-6 FOSTER and Susannah ROBINSON:
    Surname FOSTER   (all children born Bristol, Maine)
    468. Sarah   born ca 1781; married John THURSTON 29 Jul 1802; died 26 Nov 1847
    469. Nancy   born 12 Feb 1783; married William THURSTON 24 Dec 1800; died 11 June 1852
    470. Abigail/Abby   born ca 1785; married John STINSON ca 1815
    471. Susannah   born ca 1787; married James SPROUL 6 Dec 1804; died 2 Oct 1817 Bristol
    472. Thomas   born 16 July 1789; married Jane SPROUL 24 Dec 1812
            died 12 Apr 1882 Ellsworth, Maine
+473. ALEXANDER born 25 June 1792; ; died 10 Sept 1864
      ROBINSON married Betsey THURSTON 30 Oct 1806
    474. John (Jr)   born ca 1794; married Mary MANN ca 1824

287. ZEBARD/ZABUD-6 FOSTER, brother of above, was born ca 1760/61; baptized 21 Mar 1762 at Rockport, MA. He married Hannah STONE, intentions published 20 Oct 1787 at Bristol, Maine. She was the daughter of William STONE and Elizabeth THOMPSON, and was born ca 1770; died 17 Dec 1859 (age 89). Zebard/Zabud-6 FOSTER died 12 Nov 1831 at Montville, Maine and is buried in Halldale Cemetery. Zebard-6 FOSTER was a " **Revolutionary** (War) soldier prest on board an English Man-o-war for several years, and was taken back by John Paul JONES." Ref: Republican Journal, Belfast, ME 17 Nov 1831.

Children of Zebard/Zabud-6 FOSTER and Hannah STONE:
    Surname FOSTER   (all children born Montville, Maine)
    475. Martha/Hattie   born 6 May 1789; died 15 Dec 1879 Montville
           married Job CLEMENTS 7 Jan 1808 (he born 15 Nov 1785; died 4 Apr 1832)
    476. Betsey   born 25 June 1793; died 16 Oct 1865
           married William THOMPSON 17 Feb 1811 Bristol, ME
    477. William (twin ?) born ca 1795; died 1870 USC age 74
    478. Miriam (twin ?) born ca 1795; died 14 Dec 1846; married John POLAND 22 Sept 1814

Children of Zebard/Zabud-6 FOSTER, continued;

Surname FOSTER	Reference: Faye W. SPROUL, Augusta, Maine 04330
479. Sarah	born 5 Mar 1800; died 5 Oct 1882 (82-7-0)
	married Benjamin SMITH 11 Aug 1821 (he born 14 May 1790; died 7 June 1860)
480. Zebard,, Jr.	born 7 Oct 1802; died 4 Mar 1894
	1m. Mary THOMPSON 14 Apr 1823 Freedom, ME
	(she born 28 Sep 1804; died 28 Mar 1833, 28-6-0)
	2m. Abigail SAWYER 24 Apr 1834 Montville, ME
481. Hannah	born ca 1808; died 25 June 1870 (62 yrs Halldale Cemetery)
	1m. Ephraim HALL, intentions published 12 Oct 1827
	2m. Nelson ALLEN (after 14 June 1862)
482. Thomas Stone	born 7 Aug 1809; died 6 Aug 1887 (gs) Montville, ME.
	married Caroline A. SPROUL 1 Dec 1840
483. Job C.	born 28 Feb 1813; married Achshah Sears BUMPS 8 May 1836
	(she dau/o Benjamin BUMPS and Hannah KELLOCH of Thorndike)
	(she born 10 Aug 1816; died 22 Aug 1880)

306. OLIVER-6 FOSTER, son of Isaac-5 FOSTER (Benjamin-4; Jacob-3; Isaac-2; Reginald-1) and Mehitable WORTHING, was born 1 May 1773 at Granville Twsp., Annapolis, NS. He married Cynthia FELLOWS on 13 Nov 1796 at Granville. She was the daughter of Benjamin-5 FELLOWS and Jemima __?__, and was born 12 Apr 1775 at Granville, NS; died 13 Nov 1813.

Children of Oliver-6 FOSTER and Cynthia-6 FELLOWS:

Surname FOSTER	(all children born Granville Twsp., Annapolis, NS)		
484. David	born 19 June 1797	+ 489. JERUSHA	born 19 May 1809
485. Cynthia	born 24 Mar 1799		married Henry RUFFEE 16 July 1829
486. Archibald Marsden	born 14 Apr 1801	490. Robert H.	born 5 Mar 1812
487. Anne	born 1 July 1803	491. Susan	born 8 Nov 1813
488. Maria	born 23 Aug 1807; died 25 Apr 1822		

307 ASA-6 FOSTER, brother of above, was born 24 Nov 1776 at Granville Twsp., Annapolis, Nova Scotia. He married Rhoda HICKS 26 July 1798 at Granville, NS. She was born 26 Jan 1785 Annapolis Twsp, NS; died ___. Asa-6 FOSTER died 20 Sept 1854.

Children of Asa-6 FOSTER and Rhoda HICKS:

Surname FOSTER	(1st four ch born Granville,NS; last 7 born Bridgetown, NS)
492. Harriet	born 26 Apr 1799
493. Irene	born 17 Mar 1802
494. Avicia	born 12 Oct 1804
495. William Worthing	born 15 Aug 1806; married Harriet CALVERT ca 1837; died 20 Jul 1873
496. Susan Ann	born 16 Sep 1808; married Jacob-7 FOSTER 23 Dec 1835 Granville, NS (# 791
	Child: James N-8 FOSTER born ca 1844/45; married Mary B _?_ Dec 1870 Bridgetown, NS
497. Louisa Jane	born 4 May 1811
+ 498. MINETTA	born 7 Feb 1813; married Israel FOSTER ca 1848 Granville, NS
499. Oliver G.	born 11 Dec 1816; died 1894 Bayham, Ontario, Canada
500. S. Matilda	born 16 Dec 1818 501. Leah born 27 Jan 1820 502. Eliza born 5 Mar 1823

308. BENJAMIN-6 FOSTER, brother of above, was born 25 May 1755 at Hampstead, NH. He married Elizabeth RICHARDSON on 23 Jan 1776 at Granville Twsp., Annapolis, NS. She was born ca 1758 at Granville Twsp; died 28 Nov 1828. Benjamin-6 FOSTER died 13 Nov 1842 at Granville Twsp, NS.

Children of Benjamin-6 FOSTER and Elizabeth RICHARDSON:

Surname FOSTER	(all children born Granville Twsp., Nova Scotia)
503. Mehitable	born 6 May 1778
504. Elizabeth	born 1 Sept 1780; died 9 Mar 1888

Children of Benjamin-6 FOSTER, continued:
   Surname FOSTER

+ 505. BENJAMIN   born 2 Aug 1782; died 5 Aug 1882 Cornwallis, Kings, NS
                       married Mary RANDALL 1804 All Saints Anglican Church, Granville, NS

+ 506. SAMUEL   born 9 Sep 1783; died 29 July 1879 Hampton, Granville, Annapolis, NS
                       married Lydia-4 CHUTE 17 Mar 1805 Granville, NS (she # 44 CROCKER)

   507. Susanna   born 31 Aug 1786

   508. Mary   born 29 Dec 1788   511. Lucy   born 24 May 1795

   509. Isaac   born 9 Apr 1791   +512. SOLOMON F.born 3 Aug 1797
                  died 19 Nov 1867 Granville, NS   513. Philip   born 3 July 1799

   510. Abner   born 9 May 1793; died 12 Aug 1875 Granville, NS

320. JACOB-6 FOSTER, son of Colonel Benjamin-5 FOSTER (Benjamin-4;3; Isaac-2; Reginald-1) and Elizabeth SCOTT, was born ca 1750 at Scarborough, ME. He married 1st to Pamela JONES ca 17__. She was the daughter of Nathan JONES ++ and Sarah SEAVERNS of Gouldsboro, ME, and was born 23 May 1763; died before 1801. Jacob-6 FOSTER, who resided at Trenton, ME, married 2nd to Mrs. Mary Curtis of Boston (MA) on 19 Apr 1801. Jacob-6 died at Trenton on 25 Feb 1824.
                      ++ Nathan JONES was an original grantee of Gouldsboro, Maine

Children of Jacob-6 FOSTER and Pamela JONES:
   Surname FOSTER

   514. Howard   born 178_

   515. Nahum   born 16 Feb 1783; was the Town Clerk of Trenton, ME in 1807

   516. Charles   born 7 Aug 1785; died 17 June 1801

   517. Harriet   born 28 May 1787; married William C. NORRIS 20 Dec 1816

+ 518. LOUISA   born 11 May 1788; died 30 Jan 1873
      HOLDEN   married William CHALONER (as his 2nd wife) resided Lubec, ME
      (he son/o Dr. William CHALONER and Mary DILLOWAY) (he born July 1775; died 16 Sept 1868)

   519. Daniel   born 10 Mar 1792   520. Sally born 10 Sept 1794; married _?_ SOMES

322. JOHN-6 FOSTER, brother of above, was born ca 1754 at Scarborough, Maine; baptized 23 Feb 1754 Scarborough. He married Phoebe BURR/ BURNHAM of Trenton, Maine . She was born ___; died ___.

Children of John-6 FOSTER and Phoebe BURR/BURNHAM:
   Surname FOSTER

   521. Susan   born 23 Aug 1783; married Moses HOVEY 1804 (int pub 9 Sept 1804) Machias

   522. William   born 14 Sept 1786 (poss married Wilma FOSTER 21 Nov 1813)

+ 523. MARY   born 15 Nov 1788; died 31 May 1858; married John Coffin TALBOT 27 Oct 1809/10
               (he son/o Peter TALBOT and Lucy HAMMOND) (he born __; died 18 Dec 1861)

   524. Henry   born 23 Oct 1791; married __?__ BURR

   525. Emma/Emily Caroline born 4 Mar 1796; died 27 Dec 1819

323. BENJAMIN-6 FOSTER, brother of above, was born ca 1755 at Scarborough, Maine; baptized 28 Mar 1756. He married Ruth SCOTT on 20 Apr 1777 at Machias, Maine. She was the daughter of ___ SCOTT.

Children of Benjamin-6 FOSTER and Ruth SCOTT:
   Surname FOSTER

+ 526. SIMEON/ SUMNER born 17__; married Katherine FARNSWORTH 27 Feb 1803
                  (she dau/o Jonas FARNSWORTH and ____)

   527. Asa   born 17__; married Bestey-6 FOSTER Burr (# 327)

   528. Thankful born 17__; married Tristam MOORE

   529. Lettice/ Lettie born 17__; married Lawrence WILLIAMS of Waterville, Maine

+ 530. JEREMIAH born 16 Sept 17__; died 16 Feb 1878
                  married ELIZA-7 FOSTER 21 Jan 1818 (# 535)
     (she dau/o Abijah-6 FOSTER and Apphia TALBOT) (Abijah-6 FOSTER resided St. David, New Brunswick)

Children of Benjamin-6 FOSTER, continued:
    Surname FOSTER
    531. Susan   born ____; married Samuel BURNHAM 532. Sally born ____; married ? WA(I)DE

324. ABIJAH-6 FOSTER, brother of above, was born ca 1760; baptized 4 May 1760 at Scarborough, ME. He married Apphia TALBOT 12 Dec 1790 at Machias, ME. She was the daughter of Deacon Peter TAL-BOT and Lucy HAMMOND, and was born Apr 1772; died 13 Oct 1860. Abijah-6 died 4 Mar 1823.

Children of Abijah-6 FOSTER and Apphia TALBOT:
    Surname FOSTER

533. Abigail Talbot	born 5 Nov 1791; died 1812 unmarried
534. Lucy Hammond	born 3 Aug 1793; died 1876 unmarried (g s)
+ 535. ELIZA/	born 7 Dec 1795; died 2 Mar 1824
ELIZABETH	married JEREMIAH-7 FOSTER (# 530 above)
536. Harriet	born 22 Feb 1797; died 2 Mar 1824
537. Apphia	born 25 Oct 1799 EOL
538. Charlotte	born 16 Oct 1802; died 2 Jan 1809
+ 539. MARY COFFIN	born 7 Aug 1804; married PHINEAS-7 FOSTER (# 595), as his 2nd wife
	(he son/o Moses-6 FOSTER and Drusilla WEST)
540. Frederic W.	born 24 Feb 1809; died 9 Jan 1819
541. Stephen Talbot	born June 1812; died 2 Sept 1887 (75-3) E. Machias, ME EOL

326. LEVI-6 FOSTER, brother of above, was born ca 1766 . He married Sally BEAL ca ____. She was the daughter of Edward BEAL of Union River, and was born ca 17__; died __. Resided East Machias, ME.

Children of Levi-6 FOSTER and Sally BEAL:
    Surname FOSTER

542. Susan/Sukey	born 3 July 1786; died by drowning ca ____
+543. BETSEY/	born 6 Aug 1788; 1m. George Halleburton AVERY
ELIZABETH	(he born 14 Oct 1782) (he son/o James AVERY and Rebecca EDES)
	2m. Charles EMERSON 1 May 1817
544. Edward	born 30 June 1793; 1m. Fannie CILLEY

           Ch: George Warren-9 born 20 June 1825; Edward Augustus-8 FOSTER born 10 Aug 1830 Machias, ME

	2m. Emeline SMITH
+ 545. PHEBE	born 4 Jan 1799; married Luther HALL
	(he born 28 July 1792; died 19 May 1867 Machias, ME)
546. George	born 10 Nov 1803; 1m. Sally LIBBY; 2m. Caroline DeWOLFE
547. Warren	born 17 Jan 1805; died 17 July 1811

327. BETSEY-6 FOSTER, sister of above, was born ca 1766 at East Machias, Maine. She married first to Joshua BURR/BURNHAM, and second to Asa-7 FOSTER (# 527) , son of Benjamin-6 FOSTER, Jr.

Children of Betsey-6 FOSTER and Joshua BURR/BURNHAM:
    Surname BURR/BURNHAM

548. Mary	born 17 Apr 1798	549. Eveline	born 25 Sept 1800

329. DEACON SAMUEL-6 FOSTER, brother of above, was born ca 1767 at E. Machias, ME. He married Comfort SCOTT ca 1792. She was the daughter of Samuel SCOTT, and was born ca 1774; died 3 May 1860 (86 yr) (gs). Dea Samuel-6 FOSTER died 17 May 1860 (93 yr). They are buried at E.Machias, ME

Children of Deacon Samuel-6 FOSTER and Comfort SCOTT:
    Surname FOSTER

+ 550. BENJAMIN	born 28 Apr 1793; married JOAN WEST-7 FOSTER 23 Aug 1817
	(she dau/o Moses-6 FOSTER and Drusilla WEST) (she # 594)

Children of Deacon Samuel-6 FOSTER, continued:
   Surname FOSTER

551. Nancy	born 29 Nov 1794; died 1 Dec 1794
+ 552. ALFRED	born 18 Dec 1795; married REBECCA WEST-7 FOSTER (# 617)
	(she dau/o Joel-6 FOSTER and Mary _?_)
+ 553. MEHITABLE	born 17 Feb 1798; died 7 Nov 1822
	married NATHAN WEBBER-7 FOSTER (# 602)
554. Clarissa	born 3 Mar 1800; married S. Clark FOSTER of Pembroke; no issue EOL
+ 555. SUSAN	born 17 June 1802; married William MARSH
556. Horatio N. ++	born 25 Nov 1804; died 14 Mar 1881 East Machias, ME (unmarried)
557. Elizabeth	born 10 Jan 1807; married Elijah WILDER (Child: Laura-8 WILDER)
558. Samuel Freeman	born 1 July 1809; married Jane P. FLETCHER; res. Crystal Lake, IL (EOL)
559. John Andrew	born 25 Sept 1811; died 15 Dec 1888 East Machias, ME
	1m. Hannah O. SMITH 29 July 1841 at Machias (by the Rev S D WARD)
	2m. Irene M. POPE (she born Jan 1823; died 29 Aug 1904)
560. George Hanson	born 2 Feb 1814; died 1815 EOL
561. Jacob	born 6 Dec 1818; died 4 Mar 1901, buried East Machias, ME
	1m. Deborah SMITH (she born 1824; died 1847 East Machias)
	2m. Margaret BOWKER (she dau/o Watts BOWKER and Lydia STICKNEY)
	(she born 8 Aug 1818; died 30 May 1896)

++ Horatio N. FOSTER , a deaf mute, must have battled adversity all of his life. His younger brother Jacob made a home for him, and when Horatio died he tried to pay him back for his kindness by leaving his " estate " to Jacob. The following is a record of the Probate Court which took place 2 Aug 1881.

From an article which appeared in the 9 Aug 1881 issue of the Machias Union :
" Probate Court was held in Machias August 2, (1881) continuing nearly two days, most of the time being occupied with the ' Foster Will Case ' . The parties belong at East Machias. "

" In March last, Mr. Horatio N. FOSTER; a deaf mute, died leaving a Will bequeathing to his brother Jacob FOSTER his entire property. H. N. had always lived with Jacob; though deprived of the two faculties he had intelligence sufficient to do chores and ordinary work. "

Mr. S. W. MARSH, an heir at law (a nephew) *** contested the Will; Hon. John C. TALBOT and A. McNICHOL, Esq appearing for Mr. MARSH; and Herbert W. HEATH, Esq. County Atty for Kennebec, appeared for Jacob FOSTER.

" The points raised were ' Incompetency to make a Will ' and no knowledge of values or correct idea of making, signing and executing a Will. Six of eight witnesses were examined and the merits of the case pro et con generally presented."

Judge MILLIKEN decided in favor of Mr. MARSH, on the ground of " lack of knowledge of the value of money, and not duly understanding the nature of the execution of the Will. "

" It is understood the amount involved is $6000 to $7000, that there are or may be seven heirs, though no one appeared in the case but Messrs. MARSH and FOSTER. Counsel for the respondent gave notice that an appeal would be taken. We understand that J. F. LYNCH has been retained as counsel with Mr.. HEATH. "

*** Note (S.W.) Samuel W. MARSH (# 864) was the son of Susan-7 FOSTER (# 555) and William MARSH.

331. GEORGE KELLEY-6 FOSTER, brother of above, was born ca 177_ . He married Cynthia CHASE on 14 July 1799 at Machias, Washington County, Maine. She was the daughter of William CHASE and Lucy SMITH, and was born ca 17__; died 18__. George-6 FOSTER died 18__.

Children of George Kelley-6 FOSTER and Cynthia CHASE:
   Surname FOSTER

562. Vashti (f)	born ca 1801	566. Hannah	born 18__
	married Samuel SCOTT	married ? CLOATMAN/ CLOUDMAN	
563. Josiah Harris	born 18__	of Waterville, ME	
564. Daniel (twin)	born 18__	567. Lydia	born 18__
565. Cynthia (twin)	born 18__ ; marr _?_ WHIDDEN	568. John	born 18__

332. JOHN WOODEN/WOODIN-6 FOSTER, son of Woodin/Wooden-5 FOSTER (Benjamin-4; 3; Isaac-2; Reginald-1) and Frances SCOTT, was born 29 Sept 1754. He married Lucy CHASE ca 1771 at Machias, Washington County, Maine. She was the daughter of William CHASE (Captain Ephraim and Lydia HATHEWAY) and Lucy SMITH; and was born ca 1752; died 1792. John W-6 FOSTER married second to Betsey BROWN on 27 Dec 1806. She was the daughter of Ellison BROWN and was born __; died __. She was the sister of Jesse BROWN. John-6 FOSTER died before 1822.

Children of John Wooden-6 FOSTER and Lucy CHASE:
    Surname FOSTER   (order of birth uncertain)
+ 569. JENNIE /JANE   born ca 1772; married Nathaniel BABB 4 June 1794; died before 1802
  570. Sally   born ca 177_; 1m. Joseph LARRABEE; 2m. Jacob CROSBY, Jr 10 Apr 1817
  571. Fannie/Fanny   born ca 177_; 1m. John WHITE 23 Apr 1797; 2m. _____ McLAUGHLIN
+ 572. JOHN   born 177_; married Mehitable-3 MESERVE 16 Apr 1803
      WOODEN, II   (she dau/o Solomon-2 (Daniel-1) MESERVE and Isabella JORDAN)
                   (she born 17__; baptized 26 Jan 1772)
+ 573. MERCY   born 15 Jan 1782; married PEARL HOWE May 1804
  574. Thankful   born ca 1783; married Amos ACKLEY Aug 1802
                   (he son/o Benajah ACKLEY and Anna HOLMES) (he born 5 Mar 1779)
  575. Charles   born ____
  576. Isaiah   born ____
+ 577. RUTH   born 178_; married Levi CHASE 12 May 1810
  578. Lucy   born 178_; married Moses ELMORE, Jr. 16 July 1814 at Machias, Maine
  579. Polly   born 17__; married _____ BUTLER

333. SARAH-6 FOSTER, sister of above, was born ca 1756/58. She married Stephen MUNSON ca 1781. He was the son of Joseph MUNSON and Sarah MORSE, and was born 31 Mar 1754 Scarborough, Maine; died before 1807. He married second to Sally HOIT ca 1799.

Children of Sarah-6 FOSTER and Stephen MUNSON:
  Surname MUNSON   (all children born Scarborough, Maine)
  580. Stephen   born ca 1782   585. Fanny   born ca 1794
  581. Robert   born ca 1785   586. John   born ca 1796
  582. Mark   born ca 1788   587. Moses   born ca 1798
  583. Paul   born ca 1790   + 588. SARAH/SALLY born 26 Aug 1806
  584. Foster   born ca 1792   married Ezra-7 FOSTER (# 630)

334. MOSES-6 FOSTER, brother of above, was born ca 176_. He married Drusilla WEST 22 May 1787 at Machias, Maine. She was the daughter of Jabez WEST and _____, and was born ____; died ____.

Children of Moses-6 FOSTER and Drusilla WEST:
  Surname FOSTER
  589. Wilmot/Wilma born 29 Oct 1787; married William FOSTER 21 Nov 1813
  590. Lydia   born 30 Mar 1789; died ____ unmarried   EOL
+591. JABEZ WEST   born 19 Sept 1790; married Drusilla CHASE 4 Mar 1816
                  (she dau/o William CHASE and Lucy SMITH)
+ 592. AARON MOSES born 17 May 1792; died 1 Oct 1836 ; buried East Machias, Maine
                  1m. Sally CHASE 17 Mar 1816 (sister of Drusilla)
                  (she born ca 1795; died 30 June 1841)
+ 593. CYRUS WOODIN born 29 Mar 1794; married Sally TURNER 9 May 1818
    (twin)   (she dau/o Silas TURNER and Jane SMITH)
                 (granddaughter of Captain Stephen SMITH) ++

++ Captain Stephen SMITH, born 30 May 1739 at Sandwich, MA – married Deborah ELLIS 23 Dec 1762; died 29 Sept 1806 at Machias, Maine. Deborah was the daughter of Jonathan ELLIS and Patience ___; and was born ____, ME; died 4 Mar 1825 at Machias. He was the Captain SMITH of **Revolutionary War** fame.

Children of Moses-6 FOSTER, continued:

Surname FOSTER

+ 594. JOAN WEST	born 29 Jan 1794; married BENJAMIN-7 FOSTER 23 Aug 1817 (# 550)
+ 595. PHINEAS	born 28 Mar 1796; died 15 Oct 1871 (age 75) Marion, Maine
	1m. Ruth RICH 25 Mar 1819 (she born ca 1797; died 30 May 1828 (age 31)
	2m. MARY COFFIN-7 FOSTER (# 539)
596. Ezra	born ca 1799
+ 597. DRUSILLA WEST	born 11 May 1802; married John Fairbanks HARRIS 6 Jan 1822
+ 598. CYNTHIA	born 18 May 1804; married Stephen T. HARRIS
+ 599. JEREMIAH	born 11 Sept 1807; married Lucy T. HARRIS

336. PAUL-6 FOSTER, brother of above, was born ca 17__ , probably at Machias, Maine. He married Betsey/Elizabeth WEBBER on 22 July 1792. She was the daughter of ____ WEBBER, and was born ___ .

Children of Paul-6 FOSTER and Betsey WEBBER:

Surname FOSTER

+ 600. MARTHA	born 7 Mar 1793; 1m. Titus Philbrick FOLSOM 7 Oct 1815
	2m. Henry CHASE (no issue)
+ 601. JAMES	born 6 Mar 1795; married Hannah HANSCOM 22 Feb 1819
	(she dau/o Nathan HANSCOM and Susan WESTON)
+ 602. NATHAN	born 11 May 1797; 1m. MEHITABLE-7 FOSTER (# 553)
WEBBER	2m. Hannah ELLIS (she dau/o Samuel ELLIS and Mary NYE)
	3m. Sophia HARDING
+ 603. ELIZA W.	born 9 Sept 1799; married Luther CARY 12 Sept 1818
	(he born 1794 North Bridgewater, ME; died 1886)
+ 604. JOEL	born 29 June 1802; married Olivia TOBIN
605. Hiram	born 18 July 1803; died ___ unmarried EOL

606. Sarah	born ____		
607. Jennie	born ____	610. Paul	born ____
608. Mary	born 4 July 1810	611. Eva	born ____
609. George	born ____	612. Grosvenor	born ____

Reference: Early Records of Machias, Maine

337. JOEL-6 FOSTER, brother of above, was born ca 17__ at Machias, Maine. He married first to Mary A. WEST ca ____ . She was the daughter of Jabez WEST and Ruth TUPPER, and was born ca 177_; died ___ .

Children of Joel-6 FOSTER and Mary WEST:

Surname FOSTER

613. Stephen	born 17 Mar 1793; died 3 Feb 1811	EOL
614. Joel (Jr)	born 17 Apr 1795; died 10 May 1801	EOL
615. Ezekiel	born 20 Oct 1797	
616. Stephen Clark	born 3 Dec 1799	
+ 617. REBECCA WEST	born 20 July 1801; married ALFRED-7 FOSTER (# 552)	

338. RUTH-6 FOSTER, sister of above, was born ca 17__ at Machias, Maine. She married Nathan HANS-COM ca 17__ . He was the son of Aaron HANSCOM (Thomas) and Sarah/ Sally SEAVEY (Captain Joseph,), and was born ca 1766 at Machias; died after 1810.

Children of Ruth-6 FOSTER and Nathan HANSCOM:

Surname HANSCOM   (children born Machias, Maine)

618. Susan/Susannah	born ca 179_	622. Rebecca	born 13 July 1804
619. Fannie	born 20 June 1793	married Joel SEAVEY, Jr. 9 Sep 1823	
620. John	born	(he born 3 Aug 1802)	
621. Joel	born 17 Sept 1801	(he son of Joel SEAVEY and Lorena HOLMES)	

Children of Ruth-6 FOSTER, continued:
  Surname HANSCOM
  623. Sarah   born 2 Jan 1807; married Hiram R. NASON 20 Feb 1827 Crawford, Washington, ME.
  624. William   born 4 Nov 1808

339. ELIAS-6 FOSTER, brother of above, was born 17__ at Machias, Maine. He married first to Molly GOOCH Aug 1793. She was the daughter of Benjamin GOOCH, Jr. and Molly NASH, and was born ca 1775 Machias, ME.; died before 1810. He married second to Lucy DORMAN on 15 July 1810. She was the daughter of Jabez DORMAN and Mary GODFREY, and was born 25 Oct 1783 Harrington, ME; died ____. Elias-6 FOSTER married third to Lydia MILLER ca __ at Machias by the Rev Marshfield STEELE.

Children of Elias-6 FOSTER and Molly GOOCH:
  Surname FOSTER
  625. Rebecca   born 24 Mar 1794; died 10 May 1797
+ 626. SARAH   born 30 Oct 1796; died 21 Feb 1843
                        1m. Robert Pagan-6 BUCKNAM 19 Dec 1816 (he of Columbia, ME)
                        (he son of John-5 BUCKNAM and Mary A. WILSON)
                        2m. Albert-6 KEENE 23 Oct 1836
+ 627. WOODIN   born 8 May 1799; married Amy MUNSON
  628. Mary   born 24 Aug 1801; died 20 Aug 1810
+ 629. JANE   born 21 July 1803; married George W. BLAKE
+ 630. EZRA   born 3 May 1805; married Sarah MUNSON (# 588)
+ 631. LEWIS   born 26 Mar 1807; married Julia PINEO
Children of Elias-6 FOSTER and Lucy DORMAN:
  Surname FOSTER
+ 632. MARY   born 14 May 1811; married Jacob DAY
  633. Gilbert/Guilbert born 2 Feb 1813
  634. Leonard C.   born ca 1817
+ 635. WILLARD W.   born ca 1819; 1m. Margaret BRIDGHAM; 2m. Mrs. Elizabeth Huckins
+ 636. ELISHA BARTON born ca 1821; married Mary Elizabeth NOYES (dau/o John)
  637. Stephen Harris   born ca 1823; died ___ (age 31) CA.
+ 638. ALMIRA   born ca 1825; married Albion P. WELLINGTON
+ 639. A. LORING   born ca 1827; married Lydia WILSON
                        (dau/o David WILSON and Lydia LONGFELLOW)

340. JAMES-6 FOSTER, brother of above, was born ca 1779 at Machias, Maine. He married first to Lucy GOOCH on 7 Dec 1800 at Machias. She was the sister of Molly GOOCH (above) and was born ca 1778, Machias; died 24 Oct 18__. He married second to the widow Hannah LONGFELLOW Simpson ca ___. She was born 1779; died 29 Oct 1854. James-6 FOSTER died 2 Dec 1848 at East Machias, Maine.

Children of James-6 FOSTER and Lucy GOOCH:
  Surname FOSTER
+ 640. CHARLES   born 10 Oct 1803; married Lavinia Pickett-5 CHASE
                        (she dau/o William CHASE and Lucy SMITH)
  641. Louisa   born 22 Nov 1805; died young
  642. Elizabeth Gooch born 7 Aug 1807; died young
+ 643 LOUISA (2)   born ca 1809; married Simeon CHASE (brother of Lavinia ,above)
+ 644. LUCY ANN   born 2 Dec 1811; married Captain Josiah P. KELLAR
  645. Olive Johnson   born 15 Nov 1813; died young
+ 646. FRANCES U.   born ca 1815; 1m. Captain David BROWN
                        (he son/o Jesse BROWN and Deborah WALLACE); 2m. James DWELLEY

342. WILMOT-6 FOSTER, daughter of Isaiah-5 FOSTER (Benjamin-4;3; Isaac-2; Reginald-1) and Lydia FOGG, was born Aug 1759 at Scarborough, ME. She married John CROXFORD on 12 Oct 1783, probably at Scarborough or Pearsontown, ME. John, a seaman, was born ca 1762, NH; died 6 Dec 1820 (age 68 yr) at Newburgh, ME. John CROXFORD was a native of New Hampshire, and served in the **Revolutionary War.** An enlistment record gave his age on 1 July 1781, as 24, which would change his birth date to 1757. He moved to Pearsontown ca 1782, and moved to Limerick, ME ca 1790. He later relocated to Jackson and then Newburgh, ME.

According to her obituary, Wilmot-6 FOSTER was the mother of 11 children, five of whom were living at the time of her death. She was also survived by 88 grandchildren. She died 9 Oct 1838 at the home of her son Ezekiel-7 FOSTER. She was 79 years and 2 months.

Children of Wilmot-6 FOSTER and John CROXFORD:
Surname CROXFORD (four children as yet un-identified)

647. Keziah Dolly	born ca 1785 Pearsontown, ME; died 19 June 1854 Owego, NY
	married John FENDERSON Jan 1801 Limerick, ME
	(he born 14 Oct 1777; died 1848 Old Town, ME)
	Child: John-8 FENDERSON, Jr. born ca 1803 Limerick, York, ME
648. Ezekiel	born 22 July 1787; died 22 Aug 1849 Newburgh, ME
	married Nancy GOODRIDGE 20 June 1808 Hampden, Penobscot, ME.
649. Isaiah	born ca 1789; died 8 Aug 1826 Newburgh, ME (crushed to death beneath a cart wheel)
650. John	born 25 Apr 1791 Limerick, ME; died 16 Nov 1864 Jackson, ME (73-6)
	married Wilmot FOGG, intentions published 20 Jan 1817
	(she born 8 Aug 1792 Buxton, ME ; died 28 Jan 1877 Jackson, ME)
651. Daniel F.	born 21 June 1793 Limerick; died 8 Jan 1833 (age 41) Newburgh, ME
	married Sophronia STANLEY 23 May 1823 Belfast, ME
652. child	born 179_; died 1796 Limerick
653. Thea/Thesis	born 18 June 1799 Limerick; married Portius-7 JOHNSON 25 Aug 1816

343. BENEN/BENNING-6 FOSTER, brother of above, was born 14 Nov 1760 at Scarborough, Maine. He married Deborah KINNEY 20 May 1782 at Oromocto, New Brunswick. She was the daughter of Israel KINNEY and Susannah HOOD, and was born ____, NB. Benen-6 died 24 Oct 1843 Wakefield, NB.

Children of Benen/Benning-6 FOSTER and Deborah KINNEY:
Surname FOSTER (1st nine children born Oromocto, NB; last 3 born Wakefield, NB)

654. Lois	born 21 Apr 1783; died 1811 Wakefield, NB
	married Lemuel CHURCHILL (he born 20 Feb 1777, NS; died 1859 ONT)
655. Lydia	born 15 July 1785; died 1880; married Advardus SHAW 19 Oct 1802
+ 656. MARY	born 17 Oct 1787; died 1868 Studholm, NB
	married Ulas HEINE (he born 25 Dec 1779, NY; died 19 May 1869, NB)
657. James	born 3 Nov 1789; married Mary BURTT 28 Nov 1811; died 1859
658. Benen	born 30 Sept 1792; died 1880
	married Isabella BLISS 17 Aug 1815 Oromocto, NB
659. Susannah	born 20 Sep 1794; married Enoch GALLOP; died 1882
660. Israel	born 14 Aug 1796; died 1840
661. Gideon	born 20 Aug 1798; died 1845
662. Elizabeth	born 19 Sep 1800; died 12 Nov 1885 Houlton, ME
	married Israel KINNEY 16 June 1819 Burton Parish, NB
	(he was born 1794, NB; died 6 Jul 1884 Houlton, ME)
663. Japhthah	born 23 Jan 1803 Wakefield, NB; died 1874 CA
	married Asenath HOVEY ca 1824 Oromocto, NB
	(she born 9 Nov 1808, NB; dau/o Aaron HOVEY and Dorothy PRICE)
664. John Moses	born 7 May 1805; married Sarah WHEELER
665. Aaron	born 15 Dec 1809; died 1809

348. KEZIAH-6 FOSTER, sister of above, was born ca 1769 at Scarborough, Maine. She married

Boardman JOHNSON 10 Jan 1792. He was the son of Benjamin JOHNSON (Asa) and Elizabeth ____ ; and was born 23 Sept 1769 at Canterbury, NH; died 13 Oct 1859 at Jackson, Maine. Keziah-6 FOSTER died 20 Jan 1831 at Jackson, Maine.

Children of Keziah-6 FOSTER and Boardman JOHNSON:

Surname JOHNSON   (all children born Jackson, Waldo, Maine)

666. Hannah   born ca 1793

667. Portius   born ca 1795/96; married Thea/Thesis-7 CROXFORD (# 653)
     Child: Harriet-8 JOHNSON born ____; resided Barre, MA

668 Charles   born ca 179_; married _?_
     Child: Melville-8 JOHNSON, Esq. born 18__; resided Macwahoc, ME.

+ 669. CYRUS   born 29 Dec 1799; died 4 May 1853 Vernon, CT
     married Hepzibah Hunt PAGE ca ____

670. Benjamin   born ca 1801; married _?_
     Child: Laura Maria –8 JOHNSON born 18__; resided Glencoe, IL

671 Mary Ann   born ca 1803

672. Laura Jane   born ca 1805

673. Augusta   born ca 1807; married _?_ GRAVES (Child: Perez-8 GRAVES born ca 18__)

+ 674. SAMUEL   born 23 Sept 1815; died 13 Feb 1884, Bangor, CA (a teacher)
     1m. Ann Mary UPTON 12 Dec 1844 (she born 31 Aug 1822; died 31 Oct 1846)
     2m. Abby CATES 25 Dec 1851 (she born 18__; died ca 1854)   3m. Marilla MANSON 20 Nov 1862

357. SARAH-6 FOSTER, daughter of Ezekiel-5 FOSTER (Benjamin-4;3; Isaac-2; Reginald) and Mary FOGG, was born ca 1769 at Machias, Washington County, Maine. She married William SIPPRELL ca 1790 at Studholm, Kings County, New Brunswick, Canada. He was born ca 1762 at Wyoming Valley, PA; died ca 1822 Carleton County, NB. Sarah-6 FOSTER died 18__ at Wakefield, Carleton, NB.

Children of Sarah-6 FOSTER and William SIPPRELL:

Surname SIPPRELL   (1st 8 Children born Studholm, Kings Co.,NB; last 2 at Brighton, Carleton, NB)

675. William, Jr.   born 22 July 1791; died 9 Nov 1851 Carholme, ONT
     married Caroline GRAY 12 Feb 1816 Fredricton, NB

676. Wilmot   born ca 1793

677. James F.   born 11 May 1795; died 10 Jan 1861 Ontario
     married Mary KINNEY 1 Feb 1816 Burton, Sudbury, NB

678. Margaret   born ca 1797; married William GRAY 10 Apr 1815 York Co., NB

679. Ezekiel   born 10 Aug 1799; died 9 Apr 1885 Somerville, NB
     married Letitia SHAW 3 Aug 1833 Wakefield, Carleton, NB
     (she born 16 Jul 1816 Northampton, NB ; died 7 Apr 1902, NB)

680. Seth   born 20 Aug 1801; died 22 Dec 1886 Somerville, NB
     married Lavinia SHAW ca 1833 Wakefield

+ 681. DEBORAH   born 28 Mar 1804; died 5 Nov 1875 Kings Co., NB
     married George GOOD 15 Mar 1825 Sussex, Kings, NB

682. Mary   born ca 1806; died 9 Oct 1871 Kings Co., NB
     married George A. MORTON 10 Feb 1825 Sussex, Kings, NB
     (he born ca 1802, NB; died 3 Jan 1875)

683. Henry   born 12 May 1810; died 5 Jan 1866 Monticello, Aroostook, ME.
     married Sophronia SHAW 9 Aug 1832

684. Sarah   born ca 1812; died ca 1847 St. John. NB
     married Stephen ORSER 2 Dec 1835 (he born ca 1801)

358. SETH-6 FOSTER, brother of above, was born ca 1770 , New Brunswick, Canada. He married Elizabeth DANIELS ca 1805 Kings County, NB. She was the daughter of Timothy DANIELS and _____ ; and was born ca 1776 _____ (US) ; died 17 June 1853 at Studholm, Kings County, NB. Seth-6 FOSTER died May 1830 at Millstream, Studholm, Kings County, NB.

Children of Seth-6 FOSTER and Elizabeth DANIELS;

Surname FOSTER	(all children born Kings County, New Brunswick, Canada)
+ 685. JOHN	born 29 June 1806; died 21 Nov 1888 Apohaqui, Kings, NB
	1m. Margaret HEINE 30 Nov 1827 Sussex, Kings, NB
	2m. Mary Ann PELOW 6 Oct 1852 Studholm, NB
686. Martha	born ca 1807; died 25 May 1859 Bridgewater, ME.
+ 687. JAMES	born ca 1811; married Mary __?__ ca 1844 , NB
+ 688. MARY	born ca 1811, died 16 May 1861, NB
	married John LESTER 25 Mar 1833 Sussex Parish, Kings, NB
+ 689. SETH, Jr	born ca 1816; died 23 Aug 1885 Sussex, Kings, NB
	1m. Elizabeth Ann WADE 19 Mar 1843; 2m. Maria ENGLISH 13 Oct 1849
690. Sarah	born ca 1820; died 19 Jan 1897 Kings Co., NB unmarried EOL

359. MARY-6 FOSTER, sister of above, was born ca 1772 at Machias, Washington County, Maine. She married William McLEOD, Jr. ca ____. He was the son of William McLEOD and Elizabeth __?__, and was born ca 1769 St. John's, Newfoundland,; died 2 Apr 1856 at Studholm, Kings Co., NB. Mary-6 FOSTER died 20 Apr 1855 at Studholm, NB.

Children of Mary-6 FOSTER and William McLEOD, Jr.:

Surname McLEOD	
691. Alex	born ____; married Maria FREEZE
692. Ezekiel	born ____
693. Isaiah	born ____; married Isabella McCREADY 19 Nov 1825
	(she born ca 1803; died 28 Nov 1882 Sussex, Kings, NB)
694. Jane	born ____; married Nelson MORTON 15 Mar 1821 Kings Co., NB
695. Robert	born ca 1798; died 24 Mar 1882 Kings Co., NB
	married Lydia PUGSLEY 20 Feb 1823 Sussex Parish, NB
	(she born ca 1805; died 9 Apr 1886 Kings Co., NB)
696. William	born ca 1802; died 27 Oct 1860 Kings Co., NB
	married Elizabeth SCOTT ____ (she born ca 1811; died 22 Jul 1891, NB)
697. John	born ca 1807

360. EZEKIEL-6 FOSTER, JR., brother of above, was born ca 1776 at Machias, Maine. He married Mary BUNNELL ca 1806 at Kings County, New Brunswick, Canada. She was the daughter of Isaac BUNNELL and Jerusha SHERWOOD, and was born ca 1775 at Newtown, Fairfield, CT; died after 1851 at Kings County, NB. Ezekiel-6 FOSTER, Jr. died 20 May 1849 at Studholm Parish, Kings County, NB.

Children of Ezekiel-6 FOSTER and Mary BUNNELL:

Surname FOSTER	(all children born Kings County, New Brunswick, Canada)
+ 698. LYDIA	born ca 1807 ; died 31 Dec 1853 Studholm, NB
	married Jonathan FENWICK 21 Mar 1825 Sussex Parish, Kings County, NB.
+ 699. SARAH	born ca 1811; died 23 May 1841 Studholm
	married Matthew McFARLAND ca 1827 Sussex Parish, NB
+ 700. HANNAH	born ca 1811; married William KELLY 12 Sep 1827; died after 1881
+ 701. ELIZABETH	born ca 1812; married Thomas LONG 27 Dec 1831; died after 1850 NB
+ 702. CLARISSA	born 23 Jul 1817; married Abraham GRAY 19 Mar 1835; died 11 Sep 1851

The Seventh American Generation

374. JOHN-7 RUSSELL, son of Jonathan-6 RUSSELL (Hannah-5 ESTEY; Mary-4 DORMAN; Judith-3 WOOD; Mary-2 FOSTER; Reginald-1) and Hannah FLINT, was born ca 1760 at Danvers (?), MA. He married Elizabeth HARTWELL on 17 Oct 1786 at Fitchburg, MA. She was the daughter of Josiah HART-WELL and Bethiah WOOD, and was born 22 Sept 1765 at Littleton, Middlesex, MA; died ca 1820 at Stowe, VT. John-7 RUSSELL died ca 1820 at Stowe, VT.

Children of John-7 RUSSELL and Elizabeth HARTWELL:
  Surname RUSSELL (children born Windsor, VT)

703. Ezra	born 20 Apr 1787	706. Flint	born 16 Mar 1793
704. Hartwell	born 25 Apr 1789	707. Stephen	born 1 June 1796
705. Josiah	born 5 Apr 1791		died 1 Sept 1860 Stowe, VT
	died 26 Nov 1867, Stowe,VT	708. Lorenzo	born 25 Nov 1799

378. JONATHAN-7 BUCK, son of Jonathan-6 BUCK (Lydia-5 EAMES; Mary-4 DEATH; Mary-3 PEABODY; Mary-2 FOSTER; Reginald-1) and Lydia MORSE, was born 3 Apr 1748 at Haverhill, Essex, MA. He married Hannah GALE on 27 July 1768 at Buckfield, Oxford, Maine. She was the daughter of Benjamin GALE and Hannah CLEMENTS, and was born 18 June 1851 at Haverhill, MA; died ____.

Children of Jonathan-7 BUCK and Hannah GALE:

Surname BUCK	(all children born Bucksport, Hancock, Maine)		
709. Benjamin	born 19 Nov 1768	712. Lydia	born 25 Oct 1777
710. John	born 27 Oct 1771	713. Amos	born 14 Oct 1782
711. Ruth	born 9 Aug 1775		

379. MARY-7 BUCK, sister of above, was born Sept 1750 at Haverhill, Essex, MA. She married Moses DUSTIN July 1767 at Haverhill. Mary-7 BUCK died July 1827 at Candia, Rockingham County, NH.

Children of Mary-7 BUCK and Moses DUSTIN:
  Surname DUSTIN

+ 714. JONATHAN born Jan 1768 Chester, NH; died 1848 Stanstead, QC, Canada
   1m. Mary ROBIE July 1787 Candia, NH
   2m. Mary BERRY ca 1806; 3m. Charlotte CLARK ca 1812
715. Lydia born Aug 1769 Chester, NH; married Joseph HALL; died Apr 1790
716. Polly born Dec 1771; died Feb 1791
717. Moses born Mar 1774; married Hannah DUSTIN Sept 1801; died Nov 1829
      Child: Mary-9 DUSTIN born 1802 Windham, NH; died 1809
718. Hannah born Nov 1778
719. George Washington born Nov 1781 Candia, NH; died Feb 1810
720. Nathaniel born Aug 1784 Candia, NH; died Nov 1810
721. Betsey (twin) born June 1786 Candia, NH; died July 1788
722. Sally (twin) born June 1786; died May 1840
723. Lydia (2) born Aug 1792 Candia, NH; died Feb 1815

400. ELIJAH D-7 FOSTER, son of Theophilus-6 FOSTER (Jedediah-5; Ephraim-4;3; Abraham-2; Reginald-1) and Susanna PACKARD, was born 12 June 1791 at Brookfield, MA. He married Ruth NICHOLS Cady on 5 Oct 1823 at Greenbrush, New York. She was the daughter of ___ NICHOLS, and was born 12 Apr 1794, Springfield, MA ; died 29 Nov 1850 at West Creek Township, Lake, IN. Elijah-7 FOSTER died 28 Aug 1874 at Lowell Lake, Indiana.

Child of Elijah D-7 FOSTER and Ruth NICHOLS:
    Surname FOSTER
    724. Eleanor   born 25 Mar 1832 Burlington, PA; died 1 Sept 1907 Lowell Lake, IN
                          married James BRANNON 17 May 1851
                          (he born 31 July 1819, Boston, MA ; died 7 Dec 1898 Lowell Lake, IN)
             Child: Lucina Cornelia-9 BRANNON born 23 June 1858, IN; died 3 Apr 1931 IN

408.   MARY BRIDGES-7 FOSTER, daughter of Nathan-6 FOSTER (Stephen-5; John-4; Ephraim-3; Abraham-2; Reginald-1) and Susanna BARKER, was born 19 Aug 1807 at Andover, Essex, MA. She married Enoch FRYE 30 Dec 1830 at Andover. He was the son of John FRYE and Elizabeth NOYES, and was born 23 Mar 1798 at Andover; died 26 Sept 1883. Mary-7 FOSTER died 13 Sept 1867 Andover, MA.

Children of Mary Bridges-7 FOSTER and Enoch FRYE:
    Surname FRYE   (all children born Andover, Essex, MA)
    725. Enoch Holton   born 24 Sept 1831; died 12 Oct 1834
    726. John   born 4 May 1833; died 18 Jul 1853
    727. Susan Foster   born 16 Mar 1835; died 6 Jan 1922, MA
    728. Mary Elizabeth born 18 Dec 1838; died 11 Oct 1840   729. Harriet Abby   born 19 Feb 1844

409.   HARRIETTE-7 FOSTER, daughter of Abijah-6 FOSTER (Abraham-5; 4; 3; 2; Reginald-1) and Artemesia BLAKE, was born 12 June 1805 at Keene, New Hampshire. She married Mortimer Delville-6 MILLIKEN on 17 May 1836. He was the son of Edward Alexander-5 MILLIKEN (Nathan-4; Joseph-3; 2; 1) and Julia-5 BIXBY, and was born 11 May 1805 at Peterboro, NH; died 5 Feb 1900. Harriette-7 FOSTER died 18 Jan 1872 at Clarendon, NY.

Children of Harriette-7 FOSTER and Mortimer Delville-6 MILLIKEN:
    Surname MILLIKEN
+ 730. WILLIAM   born 1 Mar 1837; died 29 June 1887
      DELVILLE   married Jennie NASON 17 Jan 1867
        Note: He enlisted and saw service in the **Civil War** as a member of the 4th NY Heavy Artillery; transferring later
    to the US Colored Regt as a 2nd Lt; he was mustered out in Dec 1865 – and suffered from ill health as a result of his service.
    731. George Ashley   born 29 June 1839 Keene, NH; died _____ unmarried
+ 732. MARY JULIA   born 17 July 1847 Clarendon, NY; died 18 Feb 1929 Canandaigua, NY
                      married Dallas Dudley COOK 30 Dec 1875 Clarendon, NY
+ 733. SARAH   born 18 Sep 1849 Clarendon, NY; died ____
      ARTEMESIA   married Frank H. MARTIN (he born 17 Oct 1852)

442.   JOSHUA-7 GAMAGE, Jr., son of Elinor-6 FOSTER (Nathan-5; Caleb-4; 3; Abraham-2; Reginald-1) and Joshua GAMAGE, was born ca 1766 at Gloucester, MA. He married Sarah WEBSTER ca ____. She was the daughter of Thomas WEBSTER and Deborah _?_, and was born 11 May 1766; died 4 Sept 1853. Joshua-7 GAMAGE, Jr. died 18 Apr 1838.

Children of Joshua-7 GAMAGE, Jr. and Sarah WEBSTER:
    Surname GAMAGE   (order of birth uncertain)
    734. Joshua (III)   born ca 1791; bapt 26 June 1791 Gloucester, MA
                      married Priscilla GRIFFIN 11 July 1811 (she born ca 1792 Gloucester)
    735. Sarah   born ca 1791; bapt 26 June 1791
    736. Jane   born ca 1793; marr Henry TIBBETTS 30 Dec 1819; died 23 Sept 1872
+ 737. THOMAS   born 20 Jan 1794 Gloucester, MA; died 27 Sept 1877 So. Bristol, ME
                      married Waity THOMPSON 31 Dec 1818 Bristol, ME
    738. Jemima   born ca 1795 Bristol, ME
+ 739. WILLIAM   born Apr 1796; Bristol, ME; marr Abigail THOMPSON; died 14 Dec 1862
    740. Hannah   born ca 1797 Bristol; marr George McFARLAND 12 Oct 1818; died 28 May 1872
                   Child: Lydia-9 McFARLAND born 24 May 1836; died 13 Nov 1923

Children of Joshua-7 GAMAGE, Jr., continued:
    Surname GAMAGE
    741. Samuel   born ca 1797 ; marr Deborah McFARLAND 5 Oct 1820; died 28 Aug 1887
    742. Martha   born ca 1801; marr James THOMPSON 16 Nov 1820
    +743. WEBSTER   born ca 1803; married Hannah POOL 5 May 1826; died 14 Dec 1862

445. NATHANIEL-7 GAMAGE, brother of above, was born 1 Dec 1771 at Cambridge, Essex Co., MA.
He married Mary M. DAVIS ca 1793. She was born ca 1771; died 19 Mar 1838. Nathaniel-7 GAMAGE
died 16 Jan 1840.

Children of Nathaniel-7 GAMAGE and Mary M. DAVIS:
    Surname GAMAGE   (all children born Bristol, Lincoln, ME)
    + 744. MARY   born ca 1795 ; married Benjamin R. THOMPSON 30 Dec 1819 Bristol
    745. Eleanor   born ca 1797; died Oct 1816
    + 746. NATHANIEL   born June 1798; married Mary THOMPSON 2 Dec 1826 Bristol, ME
    747. Martha   born ca 1801; died 25 July 1868
    748. Benjamin   born 15 Jul 1803; married Mary TARR 19 Nov 1830 Bristol
                         (she born 7 Feb 1813; died before 1860 Gloucester, MA)
                         Child: Alden Benjamin-9 28 Dec 1841 (unknown as to other children)
    749. Ruth   born ca 1807
    750. Daniel   born ca 1809; marr Eliza W. McCOORISON 25 Aug 1834; died 18 Apr 1837
    751. Oliver   born July 1811; marr Angeline TARR 29 Oct 1833 Bristol
    751a.Lucretia   born ca 1813
    752. Davis   born ca 1818; marr Margaret L-9 GAMAGE 3 Dec 1843 Bristol
                         (she dau/o Thomas-8 GAMAGE (# 737) and Waity THOMPSON)

456. FRANCIS-7 FOSTER, son of Nathan-6 FOSTER (Nathan-5; Caleb-4;3; Abraham-2; Reginald-1)
and Amy/Anna-4 THOMPSON, was born 14 Apr 1778 at Bristol, Maine. He was a farmer and a fisherman.
He married Sarah TRAIN/TRANE before 1800, ME. She was born 14 Mar 1777; died 29 Oct 1847 at
Machiasport, ME. They resided at Martinsville, Maine before 1800. In the will of Francis-7 FOSTER,
dated 11 May 1826 at St. George; probated 9 June 1826; he named all of the following children. (Probate
Records of Lincoln Co, ME). He died 26 May 1826 at St. George.

Francis-7 FOSTER served in the MA Volunteer Militia in the **War of 1812**. He was a member of Captain T. KENNEY'S Company;
raised at St. George, ME. Service at Thomaston from 3-9 Sept and 2-5 Nov 1814. (Reference: MA Records of Volunteer Militia of
1812; page 206)

Children of Francis-7 FOSTER and Sarah TRAIN/TRANE:
    Surname FOSTER
    753. Amy   born 9/19 Oct 1800; married John MARSHALL
    754. Elizabeth/Betsey born 12 July 1802; married Enoch NORTON
    + 755. MARY   born 11 Feb 1804; died 22 Sept 1871 White Head Island, St. George, ME
                        married Joseph P. NORTON (he born Dec 1800; died 6 Sept 1864 , age 63-9)
    756. John   born ca 1806/07; died ____ unmarried   EOL
    757. Rachel   born ca 1809/10; married Samuel-1 CROSBY
    758. Nancy   born 16 June 1813; married Lewis-7 ALBEE 6 Dec 1838; died 2 June 1885
                  (he son/o Arthur S-6 ALBEE and Betsey-6 BOYNTON; he born 30 July 1814; died 30 Aug 1896)
              Children: Horace F-9 ALBEE born ca Apr 1844; died 8 Dec 1863 in the **Civil War** at Morris Is, SC
              (He was a member of Co. C, 11th Maine Regiment) and Emma-9 ALBEE born June 1846, died 26 Mar 1872
                           (age 25-9) Buried Hadley Lake Cemetery

    + 759. HORACE   born 28 Mar 1817 Port Clyde, ME.; died 10 Apr 1900
                        1m. Nancy LIBBY 26 July 1840 Machiasport, ME.
              (she dau/o Timothy LIBBY and Susan MITCHELL Bateman; she born 19 Nov 1821; died 16 Jan 1887)
                        2m. Mary COLBETH Gray 28 Jan 1892

457. CAPTAIN NATHAN-7 FOSTER, brother of above, was born 16 Dec 1782 at Bristol, Maine. He married Sarah G-4 CROCKER (# 98 Crocker Section) on 20 Aug 1803 at Machias, ME, the Rev Marshfield STEELE, officiating. She was the daughter of Captain Paul-3 CROCKER and Nancy MARTIN, and was born ca 1785 at Bristol; died 5 Feb 1858 (age 72). Captain Nathan-7 FOSTER died 16 Apr 1837 at the age of 54 yr, 4 mos. According to the 1850 Census for Machiasport, Sarah G-4 CROCKER Foster was residing with her son James M. FOSTER, and his family. Both Sarah-4 and Nathan-7 FOSTER are buried at Machiasport, Maine.

Children of Nathan-7 FOSTER and Sarah G-4 CROCKER:

Surname FOSTER	(all children born at Machiasport, Washington Co., ME)
+ 760. CAPTAIN	born 3 Jan 1806; died 28 Apr 1889 Machiasport
NATHAN O.	married Eliza-5 MESERVE 7 Aug 1825/26
(she dau/o Joseph-4 MESERVE and Betsey BURNHAM) (she born 30 Jan 1807; died 11 Mar 1864)	
+ 761. CAPTAIN JOHN	born 26 July 1808; died 6 June 1844 (36 yr; gs)
WILLIAM	married Susan McKELLER 4 Aug 1836 Machiasport, ME
+ 762. CAPTAIN WM.	born ca 1810; died 26 July 1877 East Machias, ME
HENDERSON	married Eliza G. MAVION 24 Dec 1835 Machiasport
	(she born ca 1812; died 11 Jul 1898 Minneapolis, MN)
+ 763. CAPTAIN JAMES	born 13 Oct 1811; died 22/25 Apr 1889 Machiasport
MADISON	1m. Mary Ann LIBBY 14 Nov 1833 Machiasport
(she dau/o Ebenezer LIBBY and Pamela ANDREWS) (she born 25 Aug 1812; died 24 Mar 1869)	
	2m. Clarissa BURNHAM (she born ca 1813; died 9 May 1891; 78 yr)
764. Nancy B.	born 17 Mar 1813
+ 765. CAPTAIN PAUL	born ca 1814; died 15 Mar 1861; married Mary Jane BARTER 19 Dec 1839
CROCKER	(she dau/o Jacob BARTER and Polly CROCKER) (# 346 CROCKER)
+ 766. CAPTAIN	born 11 Apr 1817; died 12 May 1847
ZEBEDEE M.	married Louise BARTER 14 Nov 1839 (she born ca 1821, # 347)
+ 767. MARGARET G.	born ca 1819, ME; died 12 Aug 1909 Syracuse, Onondaga, New York
	1m. George W. GARDNER 26 Sept 1841
	2m. Captain George Washington –7 DRISKO 19 Sep 1855
+ 768. SARAH G.	born Apr 1820; died 5 Nov 1874 Machiasport (typhoid fever)
	married William HOLWAY, Jr. 21 Jan 1836
+ 769. HANNAH M.	born Apr 1824; died 14 Nov 1867 (age 43yr;7mo)
	1m. Leonard LIBBY 18 Dec 1842
	2m. Henry A. LIBBY ca 1852 (he son/o Ebenezer LIBBY and Pamela ANDREWS)
	(he born 8 Jan 1817; died 19 Mar 1900 (83-2-11)

473. ALEXANDER ROBINSON-7 FOSTER, son of John-6 FOSTER (Nathan-5; Caleb-4;3; Abraham-2; Reginald-1) and Susannah ROBINSON, was born 25 June 1785 at Bristol, Maine. He married Betsey Davis THURSTON 30 Oct 1806. She was the daughter of Ambrose THURSTON and Polly GAMAGE, and was born ca 1788 at Gloucester, MA; died 6 Sept 1870. Alexander-7 FOSTER died 10 Sept 1864.

Children of Alexander Robinson-7 FOSTER and Betsey THURSTON:

Surname FOSTER	
770. Ambrose	born ca 1807
771. Alexander	born ca 1809; married Margaret WENTWORTH
	Child: Ambrose-9 FOSTER born 1842 Bristol, Maine
772. Frederick	born ca 1811 married Olive POOL(E); died 16 Nov 1889
	Child: Edward Thorp-9 FOSTER born 10 Dec 1848 Bristol, ME)
773. Harriet Thorp	born ca 1814/15
774. Elijah	born ca Dec 1816; married Hannah A-9 GAMAGE 30 Sept 1847; died 16 Feb 1901
775. John Jackson	born ca 1818
776. Charlotte Trumbull	born ca 1822; married William CUNNINGHAM
777. Belinda	born ca 1822; married Simon MAR(S)DEN; died 2 Mar 1890

Children of Alexander Robinson-7 FOSTER, continued:
Surname FOSTER

778. Thomas	born ca 1825	779. Deborah Tarr	born ca 1828
+ 780. NANCY THURSTON	born 17 Oct 1829; died 27 Nov 1909 married Asa T-9 GAMAGE Sept 1847 (he born 1 Oct 1827; died 27 July 1903)		

489. JERUSHA-7 FOSTER, daughter of Oliver-6 FOSTER (Isaac-5; Benjamin-4; Jacob-3; Isaac-2; Reginald-1) and Cynthia FELLOWS, was born 19 May 1809 at Granville TWSP, Annapolis, Nova Scotia. She married Henry RUFFEE on 18 July 1829 at All Saints Anglican Church, Granville, NS. He was the son of ____ RUFFEE, and was born ca 1805 Wilmot Twsp, Annapolis, NS.

Children of Jerusha-7 FOSTER and Henry RUFFEE:
Surname RUFFEE   (all children born at Wilmot Twsp, Annapolis, Nova Scotia)

781. Louisa Maria	born ca 1830	784. Oliver	born ca 1836
782. Fanny Adelaide	born ca 1832	785. George	born ca 1839
783. Mary	born ca 1834	786. William	born ca 1842

498. MINETTA-7 FOSTER, daughter of Asa-6 FOSTER (Isaac-5; Benjamin-4; Jacob-3; Isaac-2; Reginald-1) and Rhoda HICKS, was born 7 Feb 1813 at Granville, NS. She married Israel FOSTER ca 1848. He was the son of Oliver FOSTER and Elizabeth SAUNDERS, and was born 22 Apr 1819.

Children of Minetta-7 FOSTER and Israel FOSTER:
Surname FOSTER   (children born Granville, NS)

787. Charles	born ca 1849/50	789. Henry R.	born 14 Jan 1855
788. E. Chipman	born ca 1851/52		died 4 May 1867

505. BENJAMIN-7 FOSTER, son of Benjamin-6 FOSTER (Isaac-5; Benjamin-4; Jacob-3; Isaac-2; Reginald-1) and Elizabeth RICHARDSON, was born 2 Aug 1782 at Granville Township, Nova Scotia. He married Mary RANDALL ca 1804 at All Saints Anglican Church, Granville, NS. Benjamin-7 died 5 Aug 1882 at Cornwallis, Kings County, NS.

Children of Benjamin-7 FOSTER and Mary RANDALL:
Surname FOSTER   (children born Granville, NS)
790. Isaac   born 27 Oct 1806
791. Jacob   born 27 Apr 1810; Susan Ann-7 FOSTER 23 Dec 1835 (# 496); died 1877

512. SOLOMON F-7 FOSTER, brother of above, was born 3 August 1797 at Granville Township, Annapolis, Nova Scotia. He married Susannah/Susan PHINNEY 1 Aug 1821 at Granville Twsp. She was the daughter of _____ PHINNEY, and was born 5 Sept 1802 at Phinney's Cove, Granville Twsp, Annapolis, NS., and died there Sept 1884. She is buried at Hampton Cemetery, Granville.

Children of Solomon-7 FOSTER and Susan/Susannah PHINNEY:
Surname FOSTER   (all children born Granville Twsp. Annapolis, Nova Scotia)
792. Ann   born 28 May 1822
793. Martha   born 24 Nov 1823
794. Zaccheus   born 8 Oct 1827; died 1858
795. Zeruah   born 15 Aug 1833; died 15 Aug 1858 NS

518. LOUISA HOLDEN-7 FOSTER, daughter of Jacob-6 FOSTER (Col. Benjamin-5; Benjamin-4; 3; Isaac-2; Reginald-1) and Anna/Pamelia JONES, was born 11 May 1788 at Trenton, Maine. She married William CHALONER, as his 2nd wife, on 15 July 1810. He was the son of Dr. William-1 CHALONER and Mary DILLOWAY (who came to Maine from Newport, Rhode Island). William-2 CHALONER was born 7 July 1775; died 16 Sept 1868. His first wife was Mary PRESCOTT. Louisa-7 FOSTER died 30 Jan 1873.

Children of LOUISA H-7 FOSTER and William-2 CHALONER:
  Surname CHALONER

+ 796. MARIA	born 18__	801. Mary	born 18__
married Winslow BATES ca 1831		802. Eliza	born 18__
797. William	born 18__	803. Charles	born 18__
798. Leonice	born 18__	804. Theodore	born 18__
799. Eben	born 18__	805. George	born 18__
800. James	born 18__	806. Ann	born 18__

523. MARY-7 FOSTER, daughter of John-6 FOSTER (Col. Benjamin-5; Benjamin-4;3; Isaac-2; Reginald-1) and Phoebe BURR/BURNHAM, was born 15 Nov 1788, Maine. She married John Coffin TALBOT on 27 Oct 1810. He was the son of Peter TALBOT and Lucy HAMMOND, and was born ____; died ca 1860. John Coffin TALBOT was a prominent citizen at East Machias, Maine. He filled many municipal offices and served as Representative in the Maine State House. He was a state Senator, president of the Senate, and served as a Judge of the Probate Court.

Children of Mary-7 FOSTER and John Coffin TALBOT:
  Surname TALBOT

807. Stephen Peter	born 23 Oct 1811		
+ 808. WILLIAM H.	born 20 Sept 1813; married Martha L. POOR of Andover, ME		
+ 809. JOHN COFFIN, JR.	born 3 Nov 1816 East Machias, ME; died 1899 (age 83) married Clara Antoinette WASS 10 Dec 1849; (she dau/o David WASS and Hadassah ?)		
+ 810. GEORGE FOSTER	born 15 Jan 1819 East Machias; still living 1903 1m. Elizabeth DeWitt NEIL May 1844 (she dau/o John G. NEIL) 2m. Elizabeth B. Lincoln		
811. Emily Caroline	born 18 Apr 1821		
812. Foster	born 18 Apr 1821	814. Susan H.	born 18__
813. Thomas Hammond	born 20 July 1823	815. Mary E.	born 18__

526. SIMEON/SUMNER-7 FOSTER, son of Benjamin-6 FOSTER (Col. Benjamin-5; Benjamin-4; 3; Isaac-2; Reginald-1) and Ruth SCOTT, was born ca 17__. He married Katherine FARNSWORTH on 27 Feb 1803. She was the daughter of Jonas FARNSWORTH and Sarah DELAP, and was born __; died ____.

Children of Simeon/Sumner-7 FOSTER and Katherine FARNSWORTH:
  Surname FOSTER

816. Benjamin Franklin	born 2 June 1803	820. Theodore Harding	born 21 Oct 1811
817. Albert Gallatin	born 31 Oct 1804	821. J. O. L., Esq.	born ____; a lawyer at Thomaston, Maine
818. Edwin	born 8 Jan 1807		
819. Henry Laurens	born 23 May 1809	822. Clarissa	born ____

530. JEREMIAH-7 FOSTER, brother of above, was born 16 Sept 17__. He married ELIZA-7 FOSTER (# 535) on 21 Jan 1818 at ____. She was the daughter of Abijah-6 FOSTER and Apphia TALBOT, and was born 7 Dec 1795; died 2 Mar 1824. They were 1st cousins. They resided at St. David, New Brunswick.

Children of Jeremiah-7 FOSTER and Eliza-7 FOSTER;
  Surname FOSTER

823. John F.	born 18__	826. Eliza born 18__; marr James CASTELLO
824. Benjamin	born 18__	Child: Frederic CASTELLO born ____
825. Apphia	born 18__	827. Flora born 18__; marr Asa BUTTERFIELD

535. ELIZA/ELIZABETH-7 FOSTER see JEREMIAH-7 FOSTER # 530
539. MARY COFFIN-7 FOSTER see PHINEAS-7 FOSTER # 595
543. BETSEY/ELIZABETH-7 FOSTER, daughter of Levi-6 FOSTER (Col. Benjamin-5; Benjamin-4;3; Isaac-2; Reginald-1) and Sally BEAL, was born 6 Aug 1788 at East Machias, ME. She married first to

George Halleburton AVERY ca Dec 1805 at Machias, ME. He was the son of James AVERY ++ and Rebecca EDES, and was born 14 Oct 1782. She married second to Charles EMERSON on 1 May 1817.

Children of Betsey-7 FOSTER and George H. AVERY:

Surname AVERY	(order of birth uncertain)
828. Sarah	born 18__; married Joseph LIBBY (George)
+ 829. SUSAN	born 18__; married James STUART
	(he poss son/o Asa STUART and Betsey ?; he born 14 Mar 1831 Scarboro, ME)
830. James	born 18__
+ 831. L. TRESCOTT	born 18__; married Sarah A. HOYT
832. Elizabeth/Betsey A	born 18__; married Atkins GARDNER (Child: Theophilus-9 GARDNER)
833. Rebecca	born 18__
+ 834. MARY H.	born 18__; married Joseph NILES
835. Caroline	born 18__
836. Levi	born 18__

Note: reportedly there were 11 children of this marriage (2 are unidentified)

+ JAMES AVERY, a native of Connecticut, was born 29 Nov 1758. He married Rebecca EDES on 15 Dec 1781. He was elected the first Town Clerk of Machias (ME) in 1784. He died in 1798, age 40. James AVERY had the following children: 1. GEORGE H. (above) ; 2. Rebecca; 3. James Edward; 4. John G W; 5. Sally; and 6. Elizabeth Carter AVERY. His widow married Major Lemuel TRESCOTT, and resided at Lubec, Me; dying there at the age of 75.

545. PHEBE-7 FOSTER, sister of above, was born 4 Jan 1799. She married Luther HALL 3 Feb 1820. He was born 28 July 1792 at Dorchester, MA; and died at East Machias, ME on 19 May 1867. He had a twin brother by the name of Elijah HALL. Luther Hall went to East Machias in 1811, and after a year walked back to MA (Boston) where he remained until 1813; then he returned to East Machias.

Children of Phebe-7 FOSTER and Luther HALL:

Surname HALL	(all children born Machias, Maine)
+ 837. ALBERT	born 28 Sept 1821; died 1899 Albert Lea, MN
	married Anna/Annie PARKER of Cutler, ME (born ____; died 1901)
838. Warren	born 9 Aug 1823; died 5 Sept 1823
+ 839. ELIZABETH A.	born 13 July 1825; married John A. HARRADEN of Portsmouth, NH
840. Miranda T.	born 2 Dec 1826
841. Augustus	born 19 Jan 1829; died Feb 1829
842. Oliver L.	born 9 Jan 1830; died May 1831
843. George Lyman	born 4 Feb 1832
844. Mary A.	born 6 Dec 1834; marr John WISEWELL
845. Orrin A.	born 12 Apr 1836
846. James A.	born 31 May 1838; marr Etta SETTLE (Ch: Lena and Oakley/James-9 HALL)
847. Jules	born 18_
848. Inez I.	born 20 May 1844

550. BENJAMIN-7 FOSTER, son of Deacon Samuel-6 FOSTER (Col. Benjamin-5; Benjamin-4;3; Isaac-2; Reginald-1) and Comfort SCOTT, was born 28 Apr 1793, probably at East Machias, Maine. He married JOAN WEST-7 FOSTER (# 594) on 23 Aug 1817. She was the daughter of Moses-6 FOSTER and Drusilla WEST and was born 29 Jan 1794; died ____. She was the twin of Cyrus Woodin-7 FOSTER.

Children of Benjamin-7 FOSTER and Joan West-7 FOSTER:

Surname FOSTER	
849. Emily Caroline	born 30 Dec 1819; died 29 Jan 1820
850. Eunice	born ca 1820; 1m. Edward WISEWELL/WISWELL; 2m. John ALLEN
+ 851. LYDIA URSULA	born 11 Oct 1821; married John WISWELL/WISEWELL
+ 852. JULIA EMELINE	born 2 June 1823; married Charles KILBY
+ 853. DRUSILLA	born ca 1825; married Charles HOBART
854 Joanna	born 18__; died at age 25
855. Benjamin	born 18__; died at age 17

552. ALFRED-7 FOSTER, brother of above, was born 18 Dec 1795. He married REBECCA WEST-7 FOSTER (# 617). She was the daughter of Joel-6 FOSTER and Mary WEST and was born 20 July 1800. Children of Alfred-7 FOSTER and Rebecca-7 FOSTER:

Surname FOSTER

856. Stephen C.	born ca 1820; married Signora Meced LUGO of Los Angeles, CA
	(he a graduate of Yale University – Class of 1840)
	Children: Stephen H-9 FOSTER and another un-named child (d y)
857. Fannie	born 18__; married William PATTANGALL
+ 858. REBECCA	born 18__; married Rev George INGRAHAM
859. Emeline	born 18__; died young
860. Samuel	born 18__; married Mary LINDEN (Child: Samuel-9 FOSTER – no info)
861. Julia	born 18__; died ____ unmarried
862. Clarissa	born 18__; died young 863. Mary born 18__; dy

553. MEHITABLE-7 FOSTER see NATHAN WEBBER-7 FOSTER # 602

555. SUSAN-7 FOSTER, sister of above, was born 17 June 1802. She married William MARSH ca 18__. He was the son of ____ MARSH, and was born 18__; died ____.

Children of Susan-7 FOSTER and William MARSH:

Surname MARSH

864. Samuel W.	born 18__; married Julia McQUILLAN	865. Hannah born 18__
(dau/o Abraham McQUILLAN and Almira CHALONER)		died unmarr EOL

569. JENNIE/JANE-7 FOSTER, daughter of Wooden-6 FOSTER (Wooden-5; Benjamin-4; 3; Isaac-2; Reginald-1) and Lucy CHASE, was born ca 1772. She married Nathaniel BABB on 4 June 1794 at Machias, ME. He was the son of Daniel BABB (James; Peter), and was born 1770-75 at E. Machias; died 11 Mar 1847 at Machias. Jennie-7 FOSTER died before 1802. He 2m. Ruth THOMPSON 29 Aug 1802. She dau/o George THOMPSON; she died ca 1815/16; and he married third to Mrs. Drusilla Babb.

Children of Jennie-7 FOSTER and Nathaniel BABB:

Surname BABB   (all children born at Machias, Washington Co., ME)

866. Daniel	born 20 Sept 1794
867. Sally	born 27 Mar 1796; married John SMITH Nov 1819 Dennysville, ME.
	(he born 1794 Dennysville, Washington, ME)
868. James	born 16 Apr 1798
869. Esther	born 15 Feb 1800 Child: Samuel Peleg Sprague-9 BABB born 25 Apr 1819 Machias

572. JOHN WOODIN-7 FOSTER, brother of above, was born ca 177_ . He married first to mehitable MESERVE on 16 Apr 1803. She was the daughter of Solomon MESERVE(Daniel) and Isabella JORDAN of Scarborough and Machias, ME. Mehitable was born ____; baptized 26 Jan 1772; died before 1806. John Woodin-7 FOSTER married second to Betsey BROWN on 27 Dec 1806. She was the daughter of Ellison BROWN, and the sister of Jesse BROWN (an early settler of what was to be the Town of Milbridge, ME.)

Children of John Woodin-7 FOSTER and Mehitable MESERVE:

Surname FOSTER

870. Susan/Susannah	born 24 Jan 1804
+ 871. SOLOMON M.	born 3 Sept 1805; married Elizabeth WILDER of Dennysville, Maine

Children of John Woodin-7 FOSTER and Betsey BROWN:

Surname FOSTER   872. John Woodin   born 29 Mar 1808

+ 873. ELIAS   born ca 1809; 1m. Hannah HANSON; 2m. Hannah LIBBY

573. MERCY-7 FOSTER, sister of above, was born 15 Jan 1782 probably at Machias, Maine. She married Pearl HOWE May 1804 at Machias. He was the son of Tilly HOWE and Susanna PUFFER, and was born ca 1782 at Keene, NH; died 14 May 1854 at East Machias, Maine. Mercy-7 FOSTER died ____.

Children of Mercy-7 FOSTER and Pearl HOWE:
    Surname HOWE
    874. Susan   born 3 Feb 1805; married John HALL (he born ca 1801)
    875. Joanna   born 21 Aug 1806; married Oran HALL (he born ca 1802)
+ 876. GILBERT D.   born 11 Nov 1808; died 9 Jul 1873 East Machias, ME
                       married Abigail W. KINGSLEY 21 Mar 1830 Whiting, ME
                       (she dau/o Samuel KINGSLEY, Jr and Elizabeth/Betsey WILSON)
                       (she born ca 1810; died 9 Feb 1880 East Machias)

577. RUTH-7 FOSTER, sister of above, was born ca 178_. She married Levi CHASE 12 May 1810.

Children of Ruth-7 FOSTER and Levi CHASE:
    Surname CHASE
    877. Cyrus   born 18__; married Sophronia ACKLEY
    878. Charles   born 18__; married Susan ACKLEY
    879. Cynthia   born 18__; married Parker DENNISON
    880. Lucille/Lucelle   born 18__
    881. Mary   born 18__; married John PARSONS
    882. Ethel/Esther   born 18__; 1m. Gilbert DENNISON; 2m. Ezra DENNISON
    883. Isaiah   born 18__; married Rebecca PIGEON
    884. Evaline/Evelyn born 18__; married Abner McGUIRE
    885. Amanda   born 18__; married William HUNTLY
    886. Deborah   born 18__; married Stephen PIGEON, moved to New York

588. SARAH/SALLY-7 MUNSON   see EZRA-7 FOSTER # 630
591. JABEZ WEST-7 FOSTER, son of Moses-6 FOSTER (Wooden-5; Benjamin-4;3; Isaac-2; Reginald-1) and Drusilla WEST, was born 19 Sept 1790. He married Drusilla CHASE 4 Mar 1816. She was the daughter of William CHASE and Lucy SMITH and was born ca 1792; died ____.

Children of Jabez-7 FOSTER and Drusilla CHASE:
    Surname FOSTER
    887. William Henry   born 10 Apr 1817; poss married Anna K. INGERSOLL
    888. Delia Seward   born 22 June 1819/21
    889. Eliza O.   born ca 1823; married Thomas WOOD
    890. Ruth   born ca 18___   891. Louisa   born ca 1834; married W. I. CRANE

592. AARON MOSES-7 FOSTER, brother of above, was born 17 May 1792. He married Sally CHASE (sister of Drusilla) on 17 Mar 1816 at Machias, Maine. She was born ca 1795; died 30 June 1841. Aaron Moses-7 FOSTER died 1 Oct 1836. They are buried at East Machias, Maine.

Children of Aaron Moses-7 FOSTER and Sally CHASE:
    Surname FOSTER
    892. Moses   born 18 July 1818   894. Deborah Caroline   born 10 May 1822
    893. Silas Herman   born 7 Feb 1820

593. CYRUS WOODIN-7 FOSTER, brother of above, and twin of Joan West-7 FOSTER, was born 29 Jan 1794 at Machias, Maine. He married Sally TURNER on 9 May 1818 at Machias. She was the daughter of Silas TURNER and Jane SMITH (Captain Stephen), and was born ca 1798 Machias; died ____. Cyrus W-7 FOSTER, a merchant, died ca ____. Resided East Machias, Maine.

Children of Cyrus Woodin-7 FOSTER and Sally TURNER:
    Surname FOSTER
+ 895. ELIZABETH OTIS TURNER   born 4 Mar 1819; married Josiah H. TALBOT
  896. Deborah Caroline   born 10 May 1822; died 1877; married James R. TALBOT (Edward)

Children of Cyrus Woodin-7 FOSTER, continued:
   Surname FOSTER

+ 897. HARRIET M.	born ca 1827; married Edgar WHIDDEN
898. Emma	born ca 1833
899. Eliza	born ca 1835/36; died poss before 1850
+ 900. REV EDGAR L.	born 7 Aug 1838 East Machias; died 16 Nov 1872
	married Mary BOYDEN 20 Aug 1867 (she of Chicago. IL)

594. JOAN WEST-7 FOSTER see BENJAMIN-7 FOSTER # 550

595. PHINEAS-7 FOSTER, brother of above, was born 28 Mar 1796 at East Machias, Maine. He married first to Ruth RICH on 25 Mar 1819. She was the daughter of ____ RICH, and was born ca 1797; died 30 May 1828 (age 31) at East Machias. Phineas-7 FOSTER married second to MARY COFFIN-7 FOSTER (# 539). She was the daughter of Abijah-6 FOSTER and Apphia TALBOT, and was born 7 Aug 1804 at Machias; died ____. Phineas-7 FOSTER died 15 Oct 1871 at Marion, Maine (age 75). He and his 1st wife, and four of their children, are buried at East Machias.

Children of Phineas-7 FOSTER and Ruth RICH:
   Surname FOSTER

901. Ezra Warren	born 18 June 1819; died 18 Sept 1838 (age 19; drowned in Cedar River, IA)
902. Joniz Talbot	born 25 Mar 1821
903. James Richard	born 27 Oct 1823; died 11 Jan 1850 San Francisco, CA
904. Ruth R.	born ca 1833; died 18 Apr 1857 (age 24) buried East Machias, ME
905. Alonzo F.	born Sept 1838; died 25 June 1864 (age 25)

                Note: He was a member of Company C, 6th Regiment, Maine (**Civil War**), and died
                at Andersonville Prison, Georgia. Buried East Machias, Maine.

597. DRUSILLA WEST-7 FOSTER, sister of above, was born 11 May 1802. She married John Fairbanks-5 HARRIS ++ on 6 Jan 1822 at East Machias, Maine. He was the son of Josiah-4 HARRIS and Lucy TALBOT, and was born 18 Oct 1797; died 30 Sept 1877. He was a Maine Senator from 1859-60. Drusilla-7 FOSTER died 2 Oct 1870 (age 68).

Children of Drusilla-7 FOSTER and John-5 HARRIS:
   Surname HARRIS

906. Eliza W.	born 7 Oct 1822		
+ 907. JOSIAH	born 21 Dec 1824	910. Charlotte F.	born 14 June 1833
	married Sarah TOBEY	911. Maria	born 5 Feb 1837; dy
908. Leonard A.	born 10 Mar 1827; died at age 15	912. Lucy	born 28 June 1841
+ 909. LAURA F.	born 4 Feb 1830; married N. Page PATTANGALL		

                ++ Ancestry of John Fairbanks-5 HARRIS

JOHN-2 HARRIS, of Charlestown, MA, the father of Samuel-3 HARRIS; married Amy-2 HILLS. She was the daughter of the immigrant, Joseph-1 HILLS and Rose-1 DUNSTER. They came to America in 1658 or earlier. Joseph-1 HILLS, a woolen draper by trade, later moved to Yarmouth where he was captured by Indians.

JOSIAH-4 HARRIS, the youngest son of Samuel-3 HARRIS and Sarah MORE of Boston, was born 27 Feb 1770. He went to Machias, Maine ca 1787, but returned to Charlestown,, MA a year later. In 1789 he returned to East Machias to work for Edward H. and Nathaniel ROBBINS, in the mercantile business. He later became a partner in the business.

Josiah-4 HARRIS married Lucy TALBOT 11 Dec 1796. They were the parents of JOHN FAIRBANKS-5 (above); Stephen T. HARRIS (below); George; LUCY T-5 (below); Sarah B; Peter T.; Betsey; and Samuel HARRIS. Lucy TALBOT was the daughter of Peter TALBOT and Lucy HAMMOND, and was born 8 Jan 1775; died 27 Dec 1861.

598. CYNTHIA-7 FOSTER, sister of above, was born 18 May 1804. She married Stephen T-5 HARRIS before 1827 at East Machias, ME. He was the son of Josiah-4 HARRIS and Lucy TALBOT, and was born 9 Sept 1800; died 30 Jan 1879. Stephen T. HARRIS was the brother of John F-5 HARRIS (above). Cynthia-7 FOSTER died 18 Oct 1856. Stephen-5 HARRIS married 2nd to Mrs. Joanna Chase, widow of Joel.

Children of Cynthia-7 FOSTER and Stephen-5 HARRIS:
    Surname HARRIS
+ 913. WILLIAM   born 30 June 1827; 1m. Lucinda-4 HANSCOM
                            2m. Mary-4 HANSCOM (both sisters of Elizabeth-4, below)
                            died 186_ ; killed in the **Civil War**
+ 914. SARAH E.   born 14 Mar 1829; married William Thomas-4 HANSCOM
                            (he brother of Elizabeth-4 HANSCOM (below)
+ 915. BENJAMIN F.   born 24 June 1831; married Elizabeth-4 HANSCOM
                            (she dau/o Luther-3 HANSCOM +++ and Mary A. BEDELL/BEADLE)
    916. Stephen T (1)   born Jan 1833; died young
    917. Stephen T (2)   born 13 Apr 1836; died 22 Sept 1859 (drowned at Columbia Falls) age 23
    918. Cynthia F.   born 20 July 1838
+ 919. CHARLES A.   born 6 Feb 1841; married Clara BRYANT
+ 920. BETSEY TALBOT born 17 Aug 1843; married Sylvanus DWELLEY
    921. Leonard A.   born 29 Nov 1845; married Elizabeth CURRAN (Ch: Mary-9 HARRIS)
        +++ Luther-3 HANSCOM was born 1809 E. Machias. Mary BEDELL/BEADLE was born 1815; died 1901 Milford, CT
    In addition to William-4 , Lucinda-4; Mary-4 and Elizabeth-4; they had Charles Alonzo-4 HANSCOM, born 2 Dec 1836, ME.

599. JEREMIAH-7 FOSTER, brother of above, was born 11 Sept 1807. He married Lucy Talbot-5
HARRIS ca ____ at East Machias, Maine. She was the daughter of Josiah-4 HARRIS and Lucy TALBOT,
and was born 4 June 1807. Jeremiah-7 FOSTER died 16 Feb 1878. He was a state representative from
1854-1857.

Children of Jeremiah-7 FOSTER and Lucy-5 HARRIS:
    Surname FOSTER
    922. Thomas   born 5 Feb 1835; died young
    923. Betsey H.   born 25 Oct 1836 ; died 4 Apr 1882 unmarried
+ 924.MARTHA H.   born 12 Aug 1838; married General John C. CALDWELL
    925. Gulian V.   born ca 1841; married Alice EVERLY (Ch: Herman-9 FOSTER born ca 1879)
    926. Orville   born 18__; died young

600. MARTHA-7 FOSTER, daughter of Paul-6 FOSTER (Woodin-5; Benjamin-4; 3; Isaac-2; Reginald-1)
and Betsey/ Elizabeth WEBBER, was born 7 Mar 1793 at Machias, Washington County, ME. She married
Titus Philbrick FOLSOM on 7 Oct 1815. The marriage was officiated by Josiah HARRIS, Esq. Titus
FOLSOM was the son of ____ FOLSOM, and was born ___; died ___. Martha-7 FOSTER married second
to Henry S. CHASE (no issue). Martha-7 FOSTER died ____.

Child of Martha-7 FOSTER and Titus FOLSOM:
    Surname FOLSOM
+ 927. PAUL F.   born 20 Feb 1820; 1m. Maria G. BROWN ca 1851
                           (she dau/o Jesse BROWN and Deborah WALLACE)
                           2m. Helen Sophia Farnsworth LIVERMORE ca 1853

601. JAMES-7 FOSTER, brother of above, was born 6 Mar 1795 at Machias, Maine. He married Hannah
HANSCOM on 22 Feb 1819 at Machias. She was the daughter of Nathan HANSCOM (Aaron) and his
second wife Susan WESTON (Josiah), and was born ____; died 31 Mar 1866, NB.

Children of James-7 FOSTER and Hannah HANSCOM:
    Surname FOSTER
+ 928. DEBORAH   born ____; married David E. STRONG
+ 929. SARAH J.   born ca 1831, ME ; married Chandler KEIVER 19 June 1861 Albert, NB
                           (he born ca 1836, NB)
+ 930. MARTHA A.   born ca 1833, NB; died ca 1872
                           married Rev. James ROGERS 1 Feb 1857 Albert, NB

Children of James-7 FOSTER and Hannah HANSCOM, continued:
　　Surname FOSTER
　931. Susan　　　　　　　born 18__; married Robert WRIGHT (2 ch: Albert-9 and Susan-9 WRIGHT)
　932. Hiram　　　　　　　born 18__; died young
+ 933. ALBERT　　　　　　born 18__; 1m. Joan LOCKE; 2m. Ruth ELLIOT
+ 934. LUCY ELLEN　　　　born June 1840; died 30 Jan 1916 Seattle, King Co., WA
　　　　　　　　　　　　married Alexander McRAE 5 Mar 1863 Albert, NB
+ 935. NATHANIEL　　　　born ca 1841; died 1893 Alma, Albert, NB
　　　HANSCOM(B)　　　married Mary A. SHIELDS
+ 936. HANNAH MARIAborn ca 1844; married William Sears CLEVELAND

602. NATHAN WEBBER-7 FOSTER, brother of above, was born 11 May 1797 at Machias, Maine. He married first to MEHITABLE-7 FOSTER (# 553) ca ____. She was the daughter of Deacon Samuel-6 FOSTER and Comfort SCOTT, and was born 17 Feb 1798; died 7 Nov 1822. His second marriage was to Hannah ELLIS ca ____. She was the daughter of Samuel ELLIS and Mary NYE of Sandwich, MA. His third marriage was to Sophia HARDING ca ____. Nathan W-7 FOSTER, a ship's carpenter, died ____.

Child of Nathan-7 FOSTER and Mehitable-7 FOSTER:
　　Surname FOSTER　　+ 937. ELIZABETH　　　born ca 1820/21; married Frederic DAVIS
Children of Nathan-7 FOSTER and Hannah ELLIS:
　　Surname FOSTER
　938. Samuel Calvin　　　born ca 1832, New Brunswick; married Jane F. LAMBERT
　　　　　　　　　　　　(she born ca 1834, Maine; died ____)
　939. Lemuel Carver　　　born 183_; died ____ unmarried (a sailor)
　940. Mary M.　　　　　　born 183_; married Loring Lucius KIETH (he born ____; died Feb 1897)
+ 941. ISABELLE　　　　　born ca 1839; married George Edwin MALOON
　942. James W/U　　　　　born ca 1844 NB; married Eunice DOYLE (Child: Emma-9 FOSTER)
　943. Sophia B.　　　　　born ____; died ___ (by drowning)
　944. Clara　　　　　　　born ____; married George W. HOOPER　　EOL

603. ELIZA W-7 FOSTER, sister of above, was born 9 Sept 1799 at Machias, Maine. She married Luther-5 CARY on 12 Sept 1818 at East Machias, Maine. he was the son of Jonathan-4 CARY (Jonathan-3; Recompense-2; Jonathan-1), and was born ca 1794 at North Bridgewater, Maine. He went to Machias in 1818, and later settled in Cooper, Maine, where he died in 1886 at the age of 92.

Children of Eliza W-7 FOSTER and Luther CARY:
　　Surname CARY　　　　(1st 2 children born E. Machias, ME; others born at Machias, ME)
+ 945. JAMES WEBBER born Aug 1819; married Annie/Anna E. ALLEN Oct 1857 Machias
　946. Eliza　　　　　　　born Apr　1822; died May 1827 East Machias, ME
　947. George William　　born Aug　1824; married Roxana DAMON ca 1855; died 1886 Cooper, ME
+ 948. DELIA F.　　　　　born June 1828; married Stephen J. GETCHELL Oct 1853 Machias
　949. Charlotte　　　　　born Dec 1830; married Henry L. FOSTER ca 1858 (he born Dec 1827)
+ 950. MARY E.　　　　　born Mar 1834; married Charles CARY of East Machias ca 1847
+ 951. MARTIN L.　　　　born Sept 1836; married Mary WATTLES
　952. Martha　　　　　　born Apr 1838; married W. S. HUMPHREYS; died 1894 Providence, RI
　　　　　　　　　　　　Child: Dr. Foster-9 HUMPHREYS born ____; resided Worcester, MA
　953. Hiram Foster　　　born Aug 1844

604. JOEL-7 FOSTER, brother of above, was born 29 June 1802 at Machias, ME. He married Olivia TOBIN ca ____. She was the daughter of ___ TOBIN, and was born ____; died ____.

Children of Joel-7 FOSTER and Olivia TOBIN:
　　Surname FOSTER
+ 954. JOHN　　　　　　　born ____; married Mary PULSIFER

Children of Joel-7 FOSTER, continued:
   Surname FOSTER
   955. Olivia   born ____; married Andrew KINNEY (no issue) EOL
+ 956. WILLIAM   born ____; married Annie SMITH
   957. Charles   born ____   958. Eliza   born ____
   959. Emeline   born ____; married David CONNOR (no issue) EOL
+ 960. HENRY   born ____; 1m. Alice STUART; 2m. Margaret ROSS

617. REBECCA WEST-7 FOSTER see ALFRED-7 FOSTER # 552

626. SARAH-7 FOSTER, daughter of Elias-6 FOSTER (Woodin-5; Benjamin-4;3; Isaac-2; Reginald-1) and Mary GOOCH, was born 30 Oct 1796 at Machias, Maine. She married first to Robert Pagan-6 BUCK-NAM on 6 Feb 1817 at Cooper, Washington, Maine. He was the son of John-5 BUCKNAM and Mary A. WILSON, and was born 28 Jan 1790 at Columbia Falls, ME; died 5 Nov 1827 at Columbia. Sarah-7 FOS-TER married second to Albert-6 KEENE on 23 Oct 1836 at Columbia Falls. He was the son of Ephraim-5 KEENE and Anna Shepard WILSON, and was born ca 1805; died 29 Jan 1862. Sarah-7 FOSTER died 21 Feb 1843 at Columbia Falls, Maine..

Children of Sarah-7 FOSTER and Robert Pagan BUCKNAM:
   Surname BUCKNAM   (all children born at Columbia Falls, Maine)
   961. Mary Frances   born 29 Nov 1817; died 2 Apr 1832
   962. Louisa Jane   born 27 Aug 1820; died 10 May 1853 unmarried
   963. Henry Laurens born 13 Dec 1824; died 26 Oct 1843 unmarried

Children of Sarah-7 FOSTER and Albert KEENE:
   Surname KEENE 964. Albert born 183_; d y   965. Sarah   born 183_; d y

627. WOODIN-7 FOSTER, son of Elias-6 FOSTER (Woodin-5; Benjamin-4;3; Isaac-2; Reginald-1) and and Molly GOOCH, was born 8 May 1799 at Machias, Maine. He married Amy MUNSON ca 18__.

Children of Woodin-7 FOSTER and Amy MUNSON:
   Surname FOSTER
   966. Sarah   born 18__   967. Eliza born 18__   968. Olive   born 18__
   969. Ambrose born 18__   970. Albert born 18__   971. Amy   born 18__

629. JANE-7 FOSTER, sister of above, was born 21 July 1803 at Machias, Maine. She married George Washington BLAKE ca 18__. He was the son of ___ BLAKE, and was born ____; died ____.

Children of Jane-7 FOSTER and George W. BLAKE:
   Surname BLAKE   (children born Cooper, Washington, Maine)
   972. Sarah   born 18__   974. Isabel   born 18__
   973. Bucknam   born 27 Mar 1829   975. George (Jr) born ca 1833
          married Hannah Abigail AVERILL 5 Oct 1850 Whitneyville, ME

630. EZRA-7 FOSTER, brother of above, was born 3 May 1805 at Machias, Washington County, Maine. He married his cousin SARAH-7 MUNSON (# 588) on 26 Aug 1825 at Machias. She was the daughter of Sarah-6 FOSTER and Stephen MUNSON, and was born 26 Aug 1806; died 15 Nov 1891.

Children of Ezra-7 FOSTER and Sarah-7 MUNSON:
   Surname FOSTER
   976. Andrew   born 18__   977. Stephen   born 18__   978. Lewis born 18__
   979. Benjamin Franklin born 18__   980. Uriah   born 18__

631. LEWIS-7 FOSTER, brother of above, was born 26 Mar 1807 at Machias, Maine. He married Julia PINEO ca 18__. She was the daughter of __ PINEO , and was born ____; died ____.

Children of Lewis-7 FOSTER and Julia PINEO:
   Surname FOSTER
   981. Caroline   born 18__; married Alvah HEWEY (no issue)
+ 982. JULIA A.   born 18__; married ALVIN G-5 CROCKER (# 261 CROCKER)

632. MARY-7 FOSTER, daughter of Elias-6 FOSTER and his second wife Lucy DORMAN, and half-sister of above, was born 14 May 1811 at Machias, Maine. She married Jacob-7 DAY ++ 9 Nov 1828 at Cooper, Maine. He was the son of Samuel-6 DAY and Mehitable GROVER, and was born 8 Mar 1799 at Leeds, Maine; died 3 Feb 1878. Mary-7 FOSTER died 25 Apr 1897.

Children of Mary-7 FOSTER and Jacob-7 DAY:
   Surname DAY   (1st 4 children born Wesley, ME; last 4 born Cooper, ME)
+ 983. JULIA   born 15 May 1830 Wesley, ME; married Sheldon GRAY
+ 984. ELIAS F.   born 24 Mar 1832 Wesley; married Joan STANCHFIELD
+ 985. HENRY   born 25 Sept 1835 Wesley; married Martha-8 FOSTER (# 994)
     GILBERT   (she dau/o Willard-7 FOSTER (# 635) and Margaret BRIDGHAM)
+ 986. LEWIS   born 12 Mar 1838; married Mary Melancy ELSEMORE 15 Jun 1862 Wesley,ME
     ELBRIDGE   (she born 2 Jan 1845 Wesley, ME; died 1 Jan 1929 Chico, CA)
+ 987. JOHN WILLARD born 4 June 1841 Cooper, ME; 1m. Josephine GUPTILL
                        2m. Eliza HOLMES
+ 988. JACOB LINCOLN born 19 Feb 1844 Cooper, ME; married Lizzie HOLLINSWORTH ca 1866
+ 989. ALBION JUDSON born 31 Jan 1848; married Martha Ella DAVIS 5 Jul 1873 Wesley Twsp, ME
+ 990. FRANK O.   born 8 May 1854 Cooper, ME; married Jessie DURLING

++ Ancestry of Jacob-7 DAY

ANTHONY-1 DAY, the immigrant, was born ca 1616, came to America ca 1635 from London, England on the ship *PAUL*. He married Susan MATCHETT/MATCBETT, and died 23 Apr 1707 at the age of 91. THOMAS-2 DAY, born ca 1651, married Mary LANGTON 30 Dec 1673, and died ca 1726. His wife and a daughter were killed by lightning in 1706. His son, THOMAS-3 DAY was born ca 1675, married unknown. He drowned while on a fishing voyage. JOSIAH-4 DAY, was the father of JACOB-5 DAY who was born ____; and married Bethany BLIFFITH 12 July 1764.

SAMUEL-6 DAY , born 17__, married Mehitable GROVER . They were the parents of Jacob-7 DAY, born 8 Mar 1799 at Leeds, ME. He went to Wesley, ME ca 1826. He married Mary—7 FOSTER on 9 Nov 1828.
          Reference: The DAY Family Genealogy, Anthony Day of Gloucester, MA , pub 1910

635. WILLARD W-7 FOSTER, brother of above, was born ca 18__. He married first to Margaret BRIDGHAM ca ____. She was the daughter of Alden BRIDGHAM and Margaret DOWNES, and was born ____; died ____. His second wife was the widow Mrs. Elizabeth ____ Huckins.

Children of Willard W-7 FOSTER and Margaret BRIDGHAM:
   Surname FOSTER
   991. Louise   born 18__; married Augustus BABCOCK (no issue)
   992. Horace   born 18__
   993. Frank   born 18__; married Etta CHALONER (no issue)
+ 994. MARTHA   born 18__; married HENRY GILBERT-8 DAY (# 985 above)
   995. Parris   born 18__

636. ELISHA BARTON-7 FOSTER, brother of above, was born ca 1823 at Machias, Maine. He married Mary Elizabeth NOYES ca 18__. She was the daughter of John NOYES, and was born 18__; died 18__.

Children of Elisha B-7 FOSTER and Mary Elizabeth NOYES:
   Surname FOSTER
+ 996. GEORGE HARRIS born ca 1845; married Sarah PENNELL (he a ship captain and/or owner)
+ 997. LUCY BARTON born 31 Mar 1847; married Joseph S-5 CRANDON 25 Jan 1868
   998. Eugene C.   born ca 1849; married Mary E. PENNELL (Ch: Ernest and Lewis-9 FOSTER)

638. ALMIRA-7 FOSTER, sister of above, was born ca 1825 at Machias, Washington County, Maine. She married Albion WELLINGTON ca 18__. He was born 26 Aug 1817 at Albion, Kennebec, Maine.

Children of Almira-7 FOSTER and Albion WELLINGTON:
Surname WELLINGTON

999. Arthur	born 18__	1001. Alice	born 18__
1000. Frank	born 18__	Note: All 3 children moved to the West Coast	

639. A. LORING-7 FOSTER, brother of above, was born ca 1827/28 at Machias, Maine. He married Lydia WILSON ca 18__. She was the daughter of David G. WILSON and Lydia LONGFELLOW of Jonesport, Maine. She was born ca 1836; died ____.

Children of A. Loring-7 FOSTER and Lydia WILSON:
Surname FOSTER   + 1002. HERBERT born 18__; married Elizabeth ELLIOT

640. CHARLES-7 FOSTER, son of James-6 FOSTER (Woodin-5; Benjamin-4;3; Isaac-2; Reginald-1) and Lucy GOOCH, a ship builder, was born 10 Oct 1803 at Machias or East Machias, Maine. He married Lavinia Pickett-5 CHASE ++ ca 18__. She was the daughter of William-4 CHASE and Lucy SMITH.

Children of Charles-7 FOSTER and Lavinia-5 CHASE:
Surname FOSTER

1003. James	born 18__; d y	1004. Warren	born 18__; d y	1005. Lucy	born 18__; d y

+1006. LAURA   born ca 18__; married George Ruggles CRANDON 30 May 1858
+1007. J. KELLAR   born 18__ ; married Augusta WHITTEMORE
+1008. FREDERIC   born 1822 Oct 1846 East Machias, Maine
          AUGUSTUS   1m. Abbie WESTON;   2m. Lizzie LORING

++ Ancestry of Lavinia-5 CHASE
WILLIAM-1 CHASE came to America with Governor WINTHROP and other Colonists. His son, ISRAEL-2 CHASE was born ca ____; married Wealthy KEAN/KANE, and were the parents of CAPTAIN EPHRAIM-3 CHASE, one of the early settlers of Machias, Maine. Ephraim-3 CHASE, born ____; married Lydia HATHEWAY, daughter of Silas HATHEWAY and Deborah CARLISLE. He went to Machias with David GARDNER, and built the first sawmill at Chases's Mill, East Falls. Ephraim-4 CHASE and his wife were the parents of the following: Cynthia; WILLIAM-4 ; Betsey; Appollos, Eleazer; Wealthy; Lydia; Cynthia (2); Deborah; Esther; Levi and Mark CHASE.   WILLIAM-4 CHASE, born ____; married Lucy SMITH. They were the parents of Henry; Drusilla; SIMEON (below) Sallie; Silas H.; William; Lucy; Eliza; LAVINIA-5, above; Elisha; Cynthia; and Joseph W. CHASE.

643. LOUISA-7 FOSTER, sister of above, was born ca 1809/10 at Machias, Maine. She married Simeon-5 CHASE ca 18__. He was the brother of Lavinia-5 (above) and was born ca 1797; still living 1880.

Children of Louisa-7 FOSTER and Simeon-5 CHASE:
Surname CHASE

+ 1009. J. LORING   born 18__; married Amanda ENNIS
+ 1010. OLIVE   born 18__; married James O. POPE
  1011. HELEN   born ca 1841; married Thomas M. SANBORN
          (he son/o Cyrus SANBORN and Susan GARDNER) (he born 31 Dec 1838; living 1897)

644. LUCY ANN-7 FOSTER, sister of above, was born 2 Dec 1811 at Machias or East Machias, Maine. She married Captain Josiah P. KELLAR before 1831. He was the son of __ KELLAR and was born ____.

Children of Lucy Ann-7 FOSTER and Josiah KELLAR:
Surname KELLAR

+1012. LUCY   born ca 1831; died 19 Nov 1895
          1m. Captain Ambrose BROWN +++ (he son/o Jesse BROWN and Deborah WALLACE)
          2m. Daniel F. GARDNER 8 Oct 1881 (he son/o Thomas GARDNER and Sarah BERRY)
                    (he born 25 Jan 1825; living 1895) (he 1m. Sarah S. LINCOLN (7 ch))
+++ Note: Captain Ambrose BROWN of Brooklyn, New York, died (of fever), about 6 months after his marriage, at Havana, Cuba.

646. FRANCES U-7 FOSTER, sister of above, was born ca 1815 at Machias or East Machias, Maine. She married first to Captain David BROWN +++ (brother of Captain Ambrose BROWN (above) ca 18__. He was born ____; died ____ (age 34). She married second to James DWELLEY ca 18__.

Children of Frances-7 FOSTER and Captain David BROWN:
    Surname BROWN
1013. Charles F.   born 18__; died 18__ by drowning at Machias (age 7)
1014. Jesse B. **   born 18__
        ** Jesse B. BROWN studied at Washington Academy and Colby University (ME). He was ordained, as a Baptist
        minister, at Machiasport, ME in May 1876. He was pastor of the Baptist Church there for many years.
1015. David, Jr.   born 18__; married Ida PEARL (dau/o Henry PEARL)
                          (he was a photographer and merchant)
1016. Frances C/Fannie   born 18__; married John B. CALLIGAN (4 children; all died young)
Child of Frances-7 FOSTER and James DWELLEY:
    Surname DWELLEY
+ 1017. CHARLES   born 18__; resided Franklin, Maine

+++ Captain David BROWN, son of Jesse BROWN, an early settler in Milbridge (ME), traveled to many foreign ports. He was the Master of a BARK built at E. Machias by his brother-in-laws Charles-7 FOSTER (# 640) and Josiah KELLAR (husband of # 644) After delivering the aforementioned vessel to a buyer in CA, he was returning to Maine via the Isthmus of Panama when he contracted a fever and died in New York.

656. MARY-7 FOSTER, daughter of Benen/Benning-6 FOSTER (Isaiah-5; Benjamin-4; 3; Abraham-2; Reginald-1) and Deborah KINNEY, was born 17 Oct 1787 at Oromocto, Sunbury, New Brunswick. She married Ulas HEINE ca 18__. He was the son of ____ HEINE, and was born 25 Dec 1779 NY; died 19 May 1869 at Millstream, Kings Co, NB. Mary-7 FOSTER died there ca 1868.

Children of Mary-7 FOSTER and Ulas HEINE:
    Surname HEINE   (children born at Millstream, Studholm, Kings County, NB)
+1018. MARGARET   born 25 Mar 1807; died 15 June 1850
                          married John FOSTER (# 685) on 30 Nov 1827 at Sussex, Kings Co, NB
                          (he son/o Seth FOSTER and Elizabeth DANIELS)
1019. Charlotte   born 27 May 1809   1020. James   born 28 Nov 1810
1021. Deborah   born 24 Apr 1812;married Matthew McLEOD; died 17 Mar 1864 NB
1022. Susannah   born 9 Jan 1814; married Joel FENWICK ca 1834; died 11 Feb 1840

669. CYRUS-7 JOHNSON, son of Keziah-6 FOSTER (Isaiah-5; Benjamin-4; 3; Abraham-2; Reginald-1) and Boardman JOHNSON, was born 29 Dec 1799 at Jackson, Maine. He married Hephzibah Hunt PAGE ca 1820/21. She was the daughter of Nathan PAGE and Hephzibah HUNT, and was born 24 Mar 1801 at Jackson, ME; died ca 1886 at Douglas, Ma. Cyrus-7 JOHNSON died 4 May 1853 at Vernon, CT.

Children of Cyrus-7 JOHNSON and Hephzibah Hunt PAGE:
    Surname JOHNSON
1023. Asa Foster   born 28 Oct 1823 Atkinson, ME
1024. Samuel Adams   born 16 Feb 1825 Atkinson, ME
1025. Erastus   born 20 Apr 1826; died 1909
1026. Henry   born 28 Feb 1828 Lincoln, ME; died 1894 Windham, VT
1027. Nathan Page   born 8 Mar 1829 Lincoln, Penobscot, ME
1028. Keziah   born 7 Jan 1831 Lincoln, ME; died after 1911
1029. William   born 8 May 1834 Lincoln, ME
1030. Charles P.   born 12 Feb 1836 Jackson, Waldo, ME
1031. James Brainard   born 30 May 1841 Jackson, ME.
1032. Mary Ann   born 17 Apr 1843 Jackson, ME
1033. Julia Augusta   born 27 Dec 1846 Jackson, ME
1034. George Meader   born 21 Apr 1839 Jackson, ME; died 21 Jan 1902 Seattle, WA

674. SAMUEL-7 JOHNSON, brother of above, was born 23 Sept 1815. He married first to Ann Mary UPTON on 12 Dec 1844. She was the daughter of __ UPTON, and was born 31 Aug 1822; died 31 Oct 1846. He married second to Abby CATES of Thorndike, Maine on 25 Dec 1851. She was born 18__; died 1854. He married third to Marilla MANSON on Unity, Maine on 20 Nov 1862. Samuel-7 JOHNSON, a teacher, died 13 Feb 1884 in Bangor, CA.

Child of Samuel-7 JOHNSON and Ann Mary UPTON:
    Surname JOHNSON
    1035. Nancy Hattie   born 29 Oct 1845; married John E. HASTINGS 4 Mar 1875
                       Child: Roland Johnson-9 HASTINGS born 16 Jan 1881
Child of Samuel-7 JOHNSON and Abby CATES:
    Surname JOHNSON
    1036. Arabella   born 18___; died 20 Nov 1854
Children of Samuel-7 JOHNSON and Marilla MANSON:
    Surname JOHNSON
    1037. Samuel Boardman born 14 Aug 1863 Jackson, ME
    1038. Ezra Abbott   born 6 Dec 1865 Jackson, ME
    1039. Abby Marilla   born March 1870

681. DEBORAH-7 SIPPRELL, daughter of Sarah-6 FOSTER (Benjamin-4;3; Isaac-2; Reginald-1) and William SIPPRELL, was born 28 Mar 1804 at Studholm, Kings County, NB. She married George GOOD 15 Mar 1825 at Sussex, Kings, NB. He was the son of Abraham GOOD, and was born 22 Dec 1800; died 27 Dec 1873 Kings Co., NB. Deborah-7 SIPPRELL died 5 Nov 1875 Kings Co., NB.

Children of Deborah-7 SIPPRELL and George GOOD:
    Surname GOOD   (all children born Kings County, NB)
    1040. Elizabeth born ca 1829   1041. Susan born ca 1834   1042. Hannah   born ca 1837

685. JOHN-7 FOSTER, son of Seth-6 FOSTER (Ezekiel-5; Benjamin-4;3; Isaac-2; Reginald-1) and Elizabeth DANIELS, was born 29 June 1806 at Kings County, New Brunswick, Canada. He married first to Margaret-8 HEINE (# 1018) on 30 Nov 1827 at Sussex, Kings, NB. She was the daughter of Mary-7 FOSTER and Ulas HEINE, and was born 25 Mar 1807; died 15 June 1850. He married second to Mary Ann PELOW on 6 Oct 1852 at Studholm, NB. John-7 FOSTER died 21 Nov 1888 at Apohaqui, Kings, NB.

Children of John-7 FOSTER and Margaret HEINE:
    Surname FOSTER   (all children born Wakefield, Carleton Co., NB)
    1043. Clarissa   born 18__; married Andrew CLARKE ca 1859 Wakefield, NB
    1044. Eunice   born 16 July 1830; died 24 Oct 1911 Kings Co., NB
                       married George Z. PARLEE, Jr (as his 2nd wife) 1 Jan 1861 Studholm, NB
    1045. Henry A.   born 2 Aug 1832 Wakefield, NB.
    1046. Elizabeth   born ca 1835; died 20 Apr 1860
                       married George Z. PARLEE, Jr. 29 Nov 1855 Studholm, NB
    1047. Sarah   born ca 1836
    1048. Rachel   born ca 1838   1051. Betsey   born ca 1844
    1049. Lois   born ca 1840   1052. George Eulas born 3 Sept 1847
    1050. Charles   born ca 1841   died 30 Dec 1931 Ottawa

687. JAMES-7 FOSTER, brother of above, was born ca 1811 at Kings County, NB. He married Mary _?_ ca 1844 in NB. She was born ca 1823.

Children of James-7 FOSTER and Mary _?_ :
    Surname FOSTER
    1053. Beverly   born ca 1845   1055. Wilford   born ca 1849
    1054. Seth   born ca 1846   died 1855 Wakefield, NB

688. MARY-7 FOSTER, sister of above, was born ca 1811 at Kings County, NB. She married John LESTER 25 Mar 1833 at Sussex Parish, Kings, NB. He was the son of Benjamin LESTER and Deborah OGDEN, and was born ca 1810 Kings Co., NB; died 4 Apr 1885, NB. Mary-7 FOSTER died 16 May 1861.

Children of Mary-7 FOSTER and John LESTER:
Surname LESTER   (all children born Kings County, NB)

1056. Enoch	born 16 Aug 1834	1059. Elizabeth	born ca 1844
1057. Elijah	born ca 1837	1060. Deborah	born 1846/47
1058. Mary Jane	born ca 1841	married David KELLY 5 Jul 1844 Collina, NB	
	married Thomas WILSON 13 May 1874, NB		

689. SETH-7 FOSTER, JR., brother of above, was born ca 1816 at Kings County, NB. He married first to Elizabeth Ann WADE on 19 Mar 1843 at ___, NB. He married second to Maria ENGLISH on 13 Oct 1849 at Studholm, NB. She was the daughter of Abel ENGLISH and Elizabeth CRAWFORD, and was born ca 1823; died 22 Mar 1882, Collina, Kings, NB.

Children of Seth-7 FOSTER, Jr. and Maria ENGLISH:
Surname FOSTER   (all children born Kings County, NB)

1061. Charles E. born ca 1850	1062. Hannah born ca 1852	1063. James W. born ca 1853
1064. Albert Brunswick born ca 1859	1065. Fanny M. born ca 1863	

698. LYDIA-7 FOSTER, daughter of Ezekiel-6 FOSTER (Ezekiel-5; Benjamin-4;3; Isaac-2; Reginald-1) and Mary BUNNELL, was born ca 1807 at Kings County, NB. She married Jonathan FENWICK on 21 Mar 1825 at Sussex Parish, Kings Co., NB. He was the son of Matthew FENWICK and Miriam FREEZE, and was born ca 1799 Southampton, NS; died 2 Sept 1851 Studholm, Kings, NB. Lydia-7 FOSTER died 31 Dec 1853 at Studholm, Kings, NB.

Children of Lydia-7 FOSTER and Jonathan FENWICK:
Surname FENWICK   (all born Kings County, NB)

1066. Hannah	born 27 July 1826	1070. Freeze	born ca 1835
1067. Matthew	born 10 May 1828	1071. Naomi	born ca 1839
1068. William	born ca 1831	1072. Alfred Jonathan born ca 1843	
1069. Ezekiel	born 17 Mar 1833		

699. SARAH-7 FOSTER, sister of above, was born ca 1811 at Kings County, New Brunswick. She married Matthew McFARLAND ca 1827 at Sussex Parish, Kings County, NB. He was the son of James McFAR-LANE He was born ca 1804 Dromore Co. Ireland; died 25 May 1865 at Studholm, NB.

Children of Sarah-7 FOSTER and Matthew McFARLAND:
Surname McFARLAND   (all children born Kings County, NB)

1073. James	born ca 1828	1076. Charles	born ca 1837
1074. Mary	born ca 1830		died 25 Jan 1904 Studholm, NB
1075. Foster	born Dec 1834	1077. Elizabeth	born ca 1839

700. HANNAH-7 FOSTER, sister of above, was born ca 1811 at Kings County, NB. She married William KELLY 12 Sept 1827 at Sussex Parish, Kings County, NB. He was the son of William KELLY and Abigail WHELPLEY, and was born ca 1804 Kings Co.,NB. Hannah-7 FOSTER died after 1881 Kings Co.,NB.

Children of Hannah-7 FOSTER and William KELLY:
Surname KELLY   (all children born Kings County, NB)

1078. Abigail	born ca 1828	1081. David	born ca 1836
1079. Ezekiel	born 12 May 1829	1082. Lydia	born ca 1843
	married Elizabeth A. KIRSTEAD ca 1853	1083. Sarah C.	born ca 1845
1080. Mary	born ca 1835		

701. ELIZABETH-7 FOSTER, sister of above, was born ca 1812 at Kings County, NB. She married Thomas LONG 27 Dec 1831 at Sussex Parish, Kings Co.,NB. He was born ca 1810 in Ireland. Elizabeth-7 FOSTER died after 1850 at Kings County, NB.

Children of Elizabeth-7 FOSTER and Thomas LONG:

Surname LONG (all children born Kings County, NB)

1084. John	born ca 1833	1086. Lydia A.	born ca 1846
1085. Edward	born ca 1841	1087. George	born ca 1849

702. CLARISSA-7 FOSTER, sister of above, was born 23 July 1817 at Sussex, Kings County, NB. She married Abraham GRAY on 19 Mar 1835 at Studholm, Kings County, NB. He was born 27 July 1807 at Springfield, Kings Co., NB.; died there 18 Feb 1883. Clarissa/Clarasa-7 FOSTER died 11 Sep 1851 at Kings Co., NB.

Children of Clarissa/Clarasa-7 FOSTER and Abraham GRAY:

Surname GRAY

1088. Hannah Sophia	born ca 1836	1091. Mary Ann	born ca 1845
1089. Lydia Jane	born ca 1839	1092. Abraham Sprague	born ca 1847
1090. Hiram	born ca 1842	1093. Ezekiel Isaiah	born ca 1850

The Eighth American Generation

714. JONATHAN-8 DUSTIN, son of Mary-7 BUCK (Jonathan-6; Lydia-5 EAMES; Mary-4 DEATH; Mary-3 PEABODY; Mary-2 FOSTER; Reginald-1) and Moses DUSTIN, was born Jan 1768 at Chester, New Hampshire. He married first to Mary ROBIE July 1787 at Candia, NH. He married second to Mary BERRY ca 1806; and third to Charlotte CLARK ca 1812. He died ca 1848 at Stanstead, Quebec, Canada.

Children of Jonathan-8 DUSTIN and Mary ROBIE:
    Surname DUSTIN   (all children born at Candia, New Hampshire)
    1094. Betsey   born Aug 1788; died Apr 1812
    1095. Lydia   born July 1790; died Feb 1810
    1096. Walter   born Mar 1792; died May 1867 North Hatley, Quebec, Canada
                         married Mary WILLCOCK Nov 1847   (12 children)
    1097. Moses   born Jan 1794; married Clarissa HACKETT
    1098. Jonathan   born Feb 1796; married Elizabeth HEATH
    1099. Infant   born Mar 1798; died Mar 1798
    1100. Sukey   born Mar 1799; died Jan 1820
    1101. Mary   born Feb 1801; married Thomas PERKINS Dec 1823; died Jan 1867
    1102. Hannah   born May 1803; died Apr 1807 Candia, NH
    1103. Robie   born July 1805; married Betsey EMERSON Nov 1831; died May 1836
Children of Jonathan-8 DUSTIN and Mary BERRY:
    Surname DUSTIN   (all children born Candia, NH)
    1104. Hannah   born Dec 1807; married Sherburn BROWN; died Dec 1855
    1105. Samuel   born June 1809; married Betsey Ann BAGLEY Mar 1835 Stanstead, QC,
        Children: Mary Jane; Betsey Ann; Samuel Newell; Harriet Newell; and Warren Perkins DUSTIN
Children of Jonathan-8 DUSTIN and Charlotte CLARKE:
    Surname DUSTIN   (all children born Stanstead, Quebec, Canada)
    1106. Infant   born Jan 1813; died Jan 1813
    1107. Sally   born Feb 1818; died Oct 1816
    1108. Lydia   born June 1815; married John French BAGLEY Sept 1837; died Jan 1878
    1109. Harriet   born Mar 1817; married George HUCKINS; died Mar 1893
    1110. George W.   born Oct 1818; married Angeline CUMMINGS; died 1873 Lowell, MA (6 ch)
    1111. William Sargent   born Dec 1820; died Aug 1896 Quebec, Canada
                         married Mary Bullock DYER Dec 1849 Grafton, NH (7 children)
    1112. Betsey   born Dec 1822; married George WILDER
    1113. Sewell   born Dec 1824; unknown after 1855
    1114. John   born Feb 1827; died Nov 1858
    1115. Freeman   born Jan 1829; married Ann _?_
                         Children: Lemuel-10 and Timothy Wilder-10 DUSTIN
    1116. Florinda   born May 1832; married Rodney TOWLE May 1853 Stanstead, QC.

730. WILLIAM DELVILLE-8 MILLIKEN, son of Harriette-7 FOSTER (Abijah-6; Abraham-5; 4; 3; 2; Reginald-1) and Mortimer Delville-6 MILLIKEN, was born 1 Mar 1837 at Keene, New Hampshire. He married Jennie NASON 17 Jan 1867. She was born 1 May 1846 at New London, CT. William-8 MILLI-KEN died 29 June 1887, at age 50.

Children of William D-8 MILLIKEN and Jennie NASON:
    Surname MILLIKEN
    1117. Delville Henry   born 16 Oct 1867; died 22 Sept 1889
    1118. Hattie Belle   born 5 May 1869 Clarendon, NY; married William G. WOODWORTH 3 Sep 1871
        Children: Grace-10 (born 1897) and Mortimer William-10 (born 1904) WOODWORTH
    1119. Laura L.   born 25 Apr 1871 MO; resided Buffalo, NY
    1120. Edguilla Katherine born 23 Feb 1873 Holden, MO; married Matthew McCLELLAN 28 June 1905
        Children: Reginald-10 (born 1907) and George Thomas-10 (born 1909) McCLELLAN

732. MARY JULIA-8 MILLIKEN, sister of above, was born 17 July 1847 at Clarendon, New York. She married Dallas Dudley COOK on 30 Dec 1875 at Clarendon. He was the son of DeWitt Clinton COOK and Celestia Cynthia BURR, and was born 18__; died 8 Sep 1917, NY.

Children of Mary Julia-8 MILLIKEN and Dallas D. COOK:
    Surname COOK
    1121. Arthur Mortimer   born 22 Mar 1877 Clarendon, NY; died 5 Apr 1957 Orleans, NY
                            married Esther Pamelia GATES 7 Aug 1898 at Hopewell, NY
            (she dau/o Daniel GATES and Mary MILCAH) (born 30 July 1877; died 11 Mar 1973)
            Children: Stanley/Stanleigh -10 (born 1907) and Evelyn Mary-10 (born 1911) COOK
    1122. Orline Sarah   born 16 Jan 1887 Clarendon, NY; died ca Oct 1948 NY unmarried

733. SARAH ARTEMESIA-8 MILLIKEN, sister of above, was born 18 Sep 1849 at Clarendon, NY. She married Frank H. MARTIN ca _____. He was born 17 Oct 1852, and was a merchant at Oakfield, NY

Children of Sarah-8 MILLIKEN and Frank MARTIN:
    Surname MARTIN
    1123. Grover Henry   born 28 Mar 1883; died 8 July 1883
    1124. Mildred Grace   born 19 Mar 1885; married Charles McCRUM

737. THOMAS-8 GAMAGE, son of Joshua-7 GAMAGE, Jr. (Elinor-6 FOSTER; Nathan-5; Caleb-4; 3; Abraham-2; Reginald-1) and Sarah WEBSTER, was born 20 Jan 1794 at Gloucester, MA. He married Waity/Waty THOMPSON on 31 Dec 1818 at Bristol, Lincoln County, Maine. She was the daughter of Joshua THOMPSON and Martha COOMBS, and was born 31 Oct 1798 Bristol, died 8 Nov 1861. Thomas-8 GAMAGE died 27 Sept 1877 at South Bristol, Maine.

Children of Thomas-8 GAMAGE and Waity THOMPSON:
    Surname GAMAGE   (children born Bristol, Lincoln County, Maine)
    1125. Thomas Webster   born 27 Aug 1819; died 13 Dec 1904
                            1m. Hannah T. STINSON 10 Nov 1841; 2m. Thankful TIBBETTS 24 Mar 1889
    1126. Margaret L.   born 7 Oct 1821; died ca 1910
                            1m. Davis GAMAGE 3 Dec 1843; 2m. Jonathan NORWOOD 22 Mar 1860
    1127. Hannah   born 23 Jan 1824; died 25 Nov 1876
                            married Elijah-8 FOSTER (# 774) 30 Sep 1847
+ 1128. ASA T.   born 1 Oct 1827; died 27 July 1903 Rockland, Maine
                            married Nancy Thurston-8 FOSTER (# 780) Sept 1847
    1129. Albion O.   born 5 Nov 1830; died 13 Feb 1908 Bristol, ME
                            1m. Amanda OTIS 22 Dec 1853; 2m. Alice BARKER after 1896
    1130. Menzies R.   born 30 Apr 1833 ; died 21 Aug 1918
                            married Clarinda FARRAR 31 Jan 1858
    1131. Libbeus A.   born 2 May 1836; died 8 Apr 1911 Bristol, ME
                            married Mary F. OTIS 17 Nov 1860
    1132. Ellen A.   born 6 Oct 1839; married Bradford THOMPSON 26 Jan 18858
    1133. Nelson W.   born 5 July 1843; died 12 Oct 1928 South Bristol, ME
                            1m. Clara M. GOUDY 25 Nov 1872; 2m. Mahala RUSSELL 23 Nov 1879

739. WILLIAM-8 GAMAGE, brother of above, was born April 1796 at Bristol, Lincoln County, Maine. He married Abigail THOMPSON 28 Oct 1819 at Bristol. She was the daughter of Joshua THOMPSON and Martha COOMBS, and was born 15 Apr 1796 Bristol, died 12 Nov 1864 Bristol, ME. William-8 GAMAGE died there 14 Dec 1862.

Children of William-8 GAMAGE and Abigail THOMPSON:
    Surname GAMAGE   (all children born Bristol, Maine)
    1134. Sylvanus   born 1819/20 ; died 27 Nov 1903

Children of William-8 GAMAGE, continued:
  Surname GAMAGE
  1135. William H.   born Feb 1821; died 6 Sep 1869   1141. Lois   born 26 Dec 1837;
  1136. Waity A.   born 9 Jul 1825; died 1919 Bristol   died 15 Nov 1927
  1137. Allen   born 8 Jul 1828; died 8 Jul 1917   1142. Julia A.   born 3 July 1839
  1138. Nancy Eleanor   born 16 Feb 1831
  1139. Louisa   born ca 1833; died 1873   + 1143. ALEXANDER born ca 1840
  1140. Caroline   born 15 Jul 1836; died 15 Jul 1906

743. WEBSTER-8 GAMAGE, brother of above, was born ca 1803 at Bristol, Maine. He married Hannah POOL 5 May 1826. She was the daughter of ____ POOL, and was born ca 1810/11.

Children of Webster-8 GAMAGE and Hannah POOL:
  Surname GAMAGE   (all children born Bristol, Maine)
  1144. Emily   born Jul 1830; married John OTIS 13 May 1852; died 11 Oct 1875
  1145. Webster   born ca 1833; married Lois GAMAGE 28 Dec 1854; died 28 Jan 1894
  1146. Joshua   born Aug 1835; married Lydia THOMPSON 22 Aug 1863; died 3 Dec 1870
  1147. Margaret   born ca 1837; died 1872   1151. Winfield S. born ca 1847; died 28 Apr 1902
  1148. Emeline   born 18 June 1840   1152. Reuben P. born Feb 1850; died 3 Sept 1870
  1149. Armstrong   born ca 1843   1153. Martha P.born ca 1852
  1150. Cordelia   born 22 June 1845; died 28 Apr 1902

744. MARY-8 GAMAGE, daughter of Nathaniel-7 GAMAGE and Mary M. DAVIS, was born ca 1795 at Bristol, Lincoln County, Maine. She married Benjamin R. THOMPSON on 30 Dec 1819 at Bristol. He was born ca 1795; died 14 Aug 1854.

Children of Mary-8 GAMAGE and Benjamin THOMPSON:
  Surname THOMPSON (all children born Bristol, Maine)
  1154. James W.   born ca 1820   1157. Benjamin   born ca 1829
  1155. Elinor   born ca 1821   1158. Mary   born 7 Apr 1834;
  1156. Lois   born ca 1823   died 27 June 1872

746. NATHANIEL-8 GAMAGE, brother of above, was born June 1798 at Bristol, ME. He married Mary THOMPSON on 2 Dec 1826 at Bristol. She was born 1805. Nathaniel-8 GAMAGE died 28 Dec 1884.

Children of Nathaniel-8 GAMAGE and Mary THOMPSON:
  Surname GAMAGE   (all children born Bristol, Maine)
  1159. Susan M.   born 15 Nov 1829   1163. Daniel G. born ca 1840;
  1160. Nathaniel born ca 1832; died 19 Apr 1875   died 12 Aug 1855
  1161. Joshua   born ca 1833; died 15 Nov 1907   1164. Mary E. born 24 Oct 1843
  1162. Joseph D. born ca 1835; died 18 Aug 1855   died 1912

755. MARY-8 FOSTER, daughter of Francis-7 FOSTER (Nathan-6; 5; Caleb-4; 3; Abraham-2; Reginald-1) and Sarah (poss) TRAIN/TRANE, was born 11 Feb 1804 at Martinsville, Maine. She married Joseph P. NORTON ca 18__. He was born Dec 1800; died Sept 1864 at White Head Island, Town of St. George, ME. Mary-8 FOSTER died there on 22 Sept 1871 " at 10 o'clock, AM " according to an entry in her son's diary. She was buried at the THORNDIKE Burying Ground; South Thomaston, Maine.

Children of Mary-8 FOSTER and Joseph P. NORTON:
  Surname NORTON
  1165. Francis Foster   born 30 Jan 1827; died 17 May 1845 (drowned on Nantucket Shoals)
  1166. Joshua   born 7 Mar 1829; died 5 May 1853
  1167. Enoch   born 3 May 1830; married Mary A. ROBINSON 26 June 1856; died 1 Apr 1865
                        Child: Joseph-10 NORTON born ca 18__; resided So. Thomaston, ME

Children of Mary-8 FOSTER, continued:

Surname NORTON

+ 1168. ELIZABETH	born 17 May 1832; 1m. Elisha SNOW; 2m. Henry METCALF; d. 30 Sep 1911
+ 1169. SARAH F.	born 5 Feb 1834; married Edgar MAKER
1170. Mary Melvina	born 22 Apr 1836; died 24 Nov 1854 unmarried
1171. Joseph, Jr.	born 15 Dec 1837; died 16 Dec 1861
	(of wounds suffered at the Battle of Bull Run in the **Civil War**)
1172. Ruth	born 24 Jan 1839; died 2 Apr 1925 unmarried
1173. Amy/Emma M.	born 28 Mar 1841; married Samuel PIERCE
+ 1174. HORACE	born 19 Mar 1843; died 29 Nov 1911
FOSTER	marr. Asenath ELWELL 18 Apr 1868 (she born 9 Apr 1848; died 1 Jan 1935)
+ 1175. RUBY ANN	born 9 July 1845; died 25 Apr 1920
	married the Rev Greenfield Harrison BOWIE

759. HORACE-8 FOSTER, brother of above, was born 28 Mar 1817 at Port Clyde, (St. George), Maine. He married first to Nancy-7 LIBBY ++ on 26 July 1840. She was the daughter of Timothy-6 LIBBY and Susan MITCHELL Bateman; and was born 19 Jan 1821 at Machiasport, ME; died 16 Jan 1887. He married second to Mary COLBETH Gray 28 Jan 1892 (she # 368 CROCKER section). She was the daughter of John COLBETH and Sarah CLARK, and was born May 1823; died 7 Apr 1901 at Bucks Harbor, Maine. Horace-8 FOSTER died 10 Apr 1900 at Machiasport, Maine. They are buried at Bucks Harbor Cemetery.

Children of Horace-8 FOSTER and Nancy-7 LIBBY:

Surname FOSTER	(all children born Machiasport, Washington Co., ME)
1176. Captain Francis	born 1 Aug 1842; married Almira ACKLEY
1177. Sarah J.	born 6 Nov 1843; died 27 Nov 1916 Marshfield, ME
	married Freeman RICE 6 Sept 1864 Machiasport
	(he son of Benjamin RICE and Jane LARRABEE)
	(born 4 Jan 1846; died 30 June 1933 Marshfield, ME)
1178. Mary Elizabeth	born 20 Oct 1845; married Henry ALBEE (he born 1855; died 1923)
1179. Horace, Jr.	born 18 Sep 1847; died 28 Feb 1849
+ 1180. SUSAN A.	born 11 Nov 1849; married Judah RICE 18 Jan 1868
	(he brother of Freeman RICE, above)(he born 18 Jan 1843; died 30 Mar 1922 Marshfield, ME)
1181. Lewis L.	born 18 Nov 1851; married Nettie SMITH
1182. Samuel	born 27 Nov 1853; died young
+ 1183. ANNIE M.	born 27 Sept 1855; married James Alvin FLYNN 3 June 1875
	(he born 27 Feb 1852; died 12 July 1938)
1184. Rose/Rosina	born 7 Aug 1857; 1m. Sanford HOLMES
M.	(child: Maud who marr Dean PALMER)
	(he son o/ Jonathan HOLMES and Abigail AMES
	2m. Captain Andrew Jackson-9 BEAL ca 1886
	(he son o/ Ephraim Kelley-8 BEAL and Esther W. JOHNSON)
	Note: he was a sea captain at Bucks Harbor; Machiasport, ME
1185. Olive	born 7 Jan 1860; married Chester CLARK

++ Ancestry of Nancy-7 LIBBY

JOHN-1 LIBBY, born in England ca 1636; married Agnes _?_, and settled in Scarborough, Maine.Their son DAVID-2 LIBBY, was born ca 1657 at Scarborough. He married Eleanor _?_; and died ca 1736.

DAVID-3 LIBBY was born before 1690 at Scarborough. He married Esther HANSCOM, daughter of Thomas HANSCOM and Alice _?_ of Kittery, Maine. She was born ____; died Mar 1761 at Scarborough.

TIMOTHY-4 LIBBY was born ca 1724 at Kittery, Maine. He married Sarah STONE on 9 Oct 1746. She was born ___, Scarborough; still living 1787. Timothy-4 LIBBY died Feb 1765.

OBADIAH-5 LIBBY, a farmer and Rev War veteran ,was born 1757 at Scarborough; married Mary/Polly HILL. She was born ___; died 28 Nov 1840. Obadiah-5 LIBBY died ca 1847. TIMOTHY-6 LIBBY, father of Nancy-7, was born 3 Apr 1786, probably at Machias, Maine.

The following is a poem written by the Rev Jesse BROWN. It was read at the funeral of Horace-8 FOSTER, (Apr 1900) and dedicated to him.

HORACE FOSTER

Once there dwelt in Bucks Harbor town
A preacher, whose name was Jesse BROWN.
While there he met both friend and foe
But among his friends he remembers those

Who did the most to cheer him on,
Encourage his heart when left forlorn,
And Horace FOSTER is the name
Of one who did that very same.

Who kept the faith, was staunch and true
And cared not what did they, or you.
But faithful proved unto the end,
And preacher on him could depend.

Though some did try to turn him round,
He listened not to word or sound.
But steadfast moved from day to day
And laughed at what they had to say.

Believing GOD was with the one
Who proved his claim by what he'd done.
He's gone to rest, that old man now
And o'er his grave we weeping bow.

But he will rise again some day
And we shall have somewhat to say.
Where meet we shall in a better land,
And grasp each other by the hand.

And Christ will say, " Well done; " to one
Who fed a servant of the son.
For what is done to the least of these
He says will Heavenly Father please.

760. CAPTAIN NATHAN O-8 FOSTER, son of Nathan-7 FOSTER (Nathan-6; 5; Caleb-4;3; Abraham-2; Reginald-1) and Sarah G-4 CROCKER, was born 3 Jan 1806 at Machiasport, Washington County, Maine. He married Eliza-5 MESERVE 7 Aug 1825/26. She was the daughter of Joseph-4 MESERVE ++ and Betsey BURNHAM, and was born 30 Jan 1807; died 11 Mar 1864. Nathan-8 FOSTER, a sea captain, died 28 Apr 1889 at Machiasport, Maine.

Children of Captain Nathan-8 FOSTER and Eliza MESERVE:

Surname FOSTER		Reference: 1850 Census Machiasport, Maine	
1186. William (twin)	born ca 1829	1189. Susan Antoinette	born ca 1836
1187. James Francis (twin)	born ca 1829	1190. Nathan O., Jr.	born ca 1838
married Antoinette CROCKER (# 348)		1191. Charles R.	born ca 1843
	died 1918	1192. George H.	born ca 1846
1188. Sarah	born 18__	1193. Gilbert L.	born ca 1848

++ Ancestry of Eliza-5 MESERVE

The MESERVE/MESERVEY family is said to have originally been residents of the Isle of Jersey (the Channel Islands) . They were Norman French. CLEMENT-1 MESERVE, the immigrant, son of JEAN-A MESERVEY and Marie MACHON, was born ca 1645 at Gorey-Grouville. He was a farmer, and left the Isle of Jersey to settle at Portsmouth, New Hampshire. He married an Elizabeth _?_, of Welchman's Cove, Kittery, Maine. They later resided at Newington, NH.

Clement-1 MESERVE had 7 children : John; Elizabeth; CLEMENT-2; Daniel; Tamson; Aaron and Mary MESERVE. CLEMENT-2 MESERVE/MESERVEY was born ca 1679 at Portsmouth, NH. He married first to Elizabeth-2 JONES ca 24/26 Sept 1802. She was the daughter of Jenkin-1 JONES and Abigail HEARD, and was born ca 1684, NH; died before 1738.

Clement-2 MESERVE and Elizabeth-2 JONES were the parents of 9 children: Elizabeth; Clement-3; Colonel Nathaniel; John; Abigail; George; Peter; DEACON DANIEL-3; and Joseph. DEACON DANIEL-3 MESERVE was born ca 1715 probably at Newington, NH. He married Mehitable BRAGDON on 24 Jan 1738. Deacon Daniel-3 MESERVE had : William; JOSEPH-4; and possibly others. JOSEPH-4 MESERVE was born ca 17__. He married Betsey BURNHAM , daughter of Job BURNHAM and Mary O'BRIEN. They were the parents of Eliza-5 MESERVE, who was born 30 Jan 1807 and married Nathan-8 FOSTER (above).

761. CAPTAIN JOHN WILLIAM-8 FOSTER, brother of above, was born 26 July 1808 at Machiasport, Washington County, ME. He married first to Susan McKELLER on 4 Aug 1836 at Machiasport. He married second to Clarissa O. BURNHAM. She was born ca 1811; died 17 Aug 1848. Captain John William-8 FOSTER died 6 June 1844. They are buried at Machiasport.

Child of Captain John W-8 FOSTER and Susan McKELLER:
Surname FOSTER
1194. Abbyetter   born July 1837; died 16 June 1839   EOL

762. CAPTAIN WILLIAM HENDERSON-8 FOSTER, brother of above, was born ca 1810 at Machiasport, Maine. he married Eliza G. MAVION on 24 Dec 1835 at Machiasport. She was the daughter of ___ MAVION and Abigail _?_, and was born ca 1812; died 11 July 1898 at Minneapolis, MN. William-8 FOSTER died 26 July 1877. They are buried at East Machias, ME. They resided at East Machias, ME, possibly moving to Minnesota after 1877.

Children of Captain William H-8 FOSTER and Eliza MAVION:
   Surname FOSTER
   1195. Philena/Flora   born ca 1845   1196. Frank U/A   born ca 1849; died 1923/24

763. CAPTAIN JAMES MADISON-8 FOSTER, brother of above, was born 13 Oct 1812 at Machiasport, ME. He married Mary Ann-7 LIBBY 19 Aug 1832 at Machias. She was the daughter of Ebenezer-6 LIBBY and Permelia/Pamela ANDREWS, and was born 25 Aug 1812; died 24 Mar 1869 (age 56). He married second to Clarissa _?_, born ca 1811; died 9 May 1891 (age 78). James-8 FOSTER died 25 Apr 1889 at Machiasport.

Children of Captain James-8 FOSTER and Mary Ann-7 LIBBY:
   Surname FOSTER
   1197. Napoleon M.   born 29 Nov 1834; died 17 Apr 1857 (22 yr 5 mo)
                (he was a sailor, and was lost from the Schooner *CRUSOE* on her passage from Havana to Machiasport)
                married Mary Ellen SMALL 19 May 1856
   1198. Mary Harriet   born ca 1838; died young
   1199. Amelia   born ca 18__; died young
   1200. James Andrew   born 7 Dec 1845 Machiasport, ME.; died 7 Jan 1915
                1m. Rhoda DAVIS 17 Aug 1867 (she of Cutler, Maine); 2m. Hannah SMITH
   1201. Cora Jane   born 18 May 1854
+ 1202. EBEN   born 27 Apr 1857 Machiasport; died 1952
                marr. Laura HUNTLEY 30 Dec 1882 (she born 20 Apr 1861; died 1 Apr 1915 E. Boston
                Reference: 1850 and 1860 Federal Census Machiasport, Maine

765. CAPTAIN PAUL CROCKER-8 FOSTER, brother of above, was born ca 1814 at Machiasport, ME. He married Mary Jane BARTER 19 Dec 1839. She was the daughter of Jacob BARTER and Polly CROCKER, and was born ca 1821. Captain Paul C-8 FOSTER, a sea captain, died 15 Mar 1861.

Children of Captain Paul C-8 FOSTER and Mary Jane BARTER:
   Surname FOSTER
   1203. Sarah E.   born ca 1844   1205. Crocker   born ca 1855
   1204. Zebedee   born ca 1847   1206. Lydia/Linda born ca 1859
                Reference: 1850 and 1860 Federal Census Machiasport, Maine

766. CAPTAIN ZEBEDEE M-8 FOSTER, brother of above, was born 11 Apr 1817 at Machiasport, Maine. he married Louise/Louisa BARTER on 14 Nov 1839. She was the sister of Mary Jane BARTER (above) and was born ca 1822; died ___. Zebedee-8 FOSTER died 12 May 1847. They are buried at Machiasport.

Children of Captain Zebedee-8 FOSTER and Louise BARTER:
   Surname FOSTER
   1207. Jerome   born ca 1840; married Henrietta _?_ ca 1860 (she born ca 1842)
   1208. Henrietta   born ca 1842/43   1209. Mary   born ca 1845/46

767. MARGARET G-8 FOSTER, sister of above, was born ca 1819 at Machiasport, Maine. She married first to George W. GARDNER on 26 Sept 1841 at Machiasport. He was the son of John GARDNER and Susan BERRY, and was born ___. He was the grandson of Ebenezer GARDINER and Susanna MERRILL. They were among the early settlers of Machias, Maine. George W. GARDNER, a ships' carpenter, died ____. (before 1855) . Margaret-8 FOSTER married second to Captain George Washington-7 DRISKO (as his 2nd wife) on 19 Sept 1855 at Machias, Maine. He was the son of Captain John-6 DRISKO and

Phebe PARKER, and was born 16 Aug 1810 at Addison, Maine; died 30 Nov 1878 at Syracuse, New York. Captain George W-7 DRISKO was married first to Mary S. KILTON of Jonesboro, Maine (intentions published 15 May 1833 Jonesboro). Margaret-8 FOSTER and her husband Captain George W-7 DRISKO moved to Syracuse, NY in the 1870's. Margaret died there on 12 Aug 1909, and is buried with her husband at Oakwood Cemetery, Syracuse, Onondaga County, New York.

Children of Margaret-8 FOSTER and George W, GARDNER:
Surname GARDNER
+ 1210. SARAH   born ca 1846/47 Machiasport, ME; died poss before 1900 NY
  JOSEPHINE   marr. Sewell C. TRAFTON (son/o Jos. TRAFTON and Temperance ACKLEY
+ 1211. MARIETTA/   born ca 1849/50 Machiasport, ME.; died poss before 1900 NY
  HENRIETTA   married George W. LOOMIS ca 1867 (he born ca 1848 Hudson, NY)

Children of Margaret-8 FOSTER and Captain George W-7 DRISKO
Surname DRISKO
+ 1212. GEORGE   born 19 July 1856 Machiasport, ME; died 30 Apr 1936 Syracuse, NY
  AUGUSTUS   married Amelia A. " Minnie" GREEN 1880 at East Syracuse, NY
  1213. Laura   born ca Dec 1859 Machiasport, ME; died Mar 1860
                       For descendants of # 1207 , see # 1164 DRISKO Section, page 132.

Margaret-8 FOSTER Gardner Drisko

768. SARAH G-8 FOSTER, sister of above, was born Apr 1820 at Machiasport, Washington County, Maine. She married William-4 HOLWAY, Jr. ++ on 21 Jan 1836. He was the son of William-3 HOLWAY and Mary LIBBY, and was born ca 1809/10, Maine; died ____ . Sarah G-8 FOSTER died 5 Nov 1874 (of typhoid fever) at Machiasport, and is buried at the East Kennebec Cemetery, Machias, Maine.

Children of Sarah G-8 FOSTER and William-4 HOLWAY, Jr.:
Surname HOLWAY
  1214. Marietta   born ca 1837
+ 1215. NATHAN FOSTER   born ca 1838 (a farmer); married Harriet A. MOORE
+ 1216. EMILY J.   born ca 1840; married J. Hamilton SCHOPPEE
  1217. Laura   born ca 1841
+ 1218. MARY E.   born ca 1842; married Charles A. HILL; res. Canton, MA
  1219. Abbie   born ca 1843/4; died young

Children of Sarah G-8 FOSTER, continued:
Surname HOLWAY

+ 1220. ELLA	born ca 1847; married Lowell CASWELL
+ 1221. SARAH HELEN	born ca 1848/49; married Charles H. SCHOPPEE
+ 1222. CAROLINE " Caddie "	born ca 1850; married Olin A. TUPPER
+ 1223. WILLIAM B. " Willie "	born ca 1853; married Isabel BRADEEN
1224. Martha	born ca 1855; married Frank MASON
1225. Fred A.	born ca 1857; married Mary ALBEE
+ 1226. FRANK H.	born after 1860; married Minerva BRYANT

++ Ancestry of William-4 HOLWAY, Jr.

MORRIS-1 O'BRIEN, born ca 1715 at Cork, Ireland, came to America ca 1740. He married a Mary KEEN, the daughter of a sea captain. She was a native of Kittery, Maine, and was born ca 1719; died at Machias ca 1805. Morris-1 O'BRIEN settled first at Dunstan's Corners, Scarboro, Maine. he was a tailor by trade. In 1765 he, and two sons Jeremiah and John (adults) and 7 minor children, moved from Scarboro to Machias, Maine. That same year he built a mill on the south shore of the " Falls." He died ca 1799.

Captain KEEN, father of Mary, died before she was born , of colic while on his vessel during a trip to England. Mary's mother died when she was very young, and she was raised by her aunt, a Mrs. BARTER/ BARKER. The children of Morris-1 O'BRIEN and Mary KEEN were all born at Scarboro. Their six sons, and probably all three son-in-laws, were in the Battle of the MARGARETTA.

MARTHA-2 O'BRIEN, born at Scarboro ca 1752; married first to a Daniel ELLIOT and had 6 children: Daniel; Isabelle; Mary; Simon; Frank; and James ELLIOT. She married second to LADWICK HOLWAY, and had 3 children: Martha; WILLIAM-3; and John (born 1780's) who married Leonice Howard CROCKER 9 June 1816 Machias. (Leonice –6 CROCKER, was the daughter of William-5 CROCKER (Josiah-4; 3; 2; and William-1) and Leonice HOWARD of Falmouth, ME, and was born ___ Taunton, ME.

WILLIAM-3 HOLWAY, born ca 1784, married Mary LIBBY ca 1806. She was the daughter of David LIBBY and Abigail FITTS, and was born 2 May 1785; died ____. They were the parents of : Martha; John; WILLIAM-4, JR born ca 1809 (above); J. Elliot; Mary; Abigail (who married Captain Arthur MOORE); Isabella; A. Nickels; Lucia; and Margaret HOLWAY (born ca 1832).

In 1817 William HOLWAY purchased timberland in East Kennebec; built a house, and moved his family there. In 1818 he built a sawmill and store, and became engaged in the lumbering business. He later built two more sawmills. In 1830 he built the Schooner HENRY CLAY at the shipyard of Edward O'BRIEN at Thomaston, Maine. Mr. O'BRIEN, a master carpenter, built the Schooner WILLIAM and JOHN there in 1832. In 1842 he built the Brig MARGARETTA in the yard of his homestead at Kennebec. The East Kennebec district was part of the original Machias. In 1826 it was set off as part of Machiasport.

769. HANNAH-8 FOSTER, sister of above, was born Apr 1824 at Machiasport, Maine. She married first to Leonard LIBBY on 18 Dec 1842. He was the son of Francis LIBBY +++ and Sally BURNHAM; and was born 13 July 1820; died before 1852. Hannah-8 FOSTER married second to Henry Allen-7 LIBBY on 20 Sept 1852. He was the son of Ebenezer-6 LIBBY and Pamela ANDREWS, and was born 8 Jan 1817.

+++ Francis LIBBY, by birth was a GETCHELL. He was adopted by Deacon Joseph LIBBY and Sarah MESERVE. He received the homestead of his adoptive father, a leading citizen of Machias. Francis LIBBY was a well-to-do farmer. His wife, Sally BURNHAM was the daughter of Job BURNHAM and Mary O'BRIEN.

Children of Hannah-8 FOSTER and Henry A-7 LIBBY:
Surname LIBBY

+ 1227. LEON A.	born 10 June 1853 (a seaman); married Lucy E. LIBBY 6 Aug 1874
1228. Albert N.	born 12 May 1856; married Rose E. BRIDGES 19 Sept 1880
	(she dau/o William BRIDGES of Sedgwick, Maine)
1229. Sarah P.	born 14 Dec 1858; died 17 Aug 1868
1230. Mary A.	born 12 Mar 1861; married Benjamin C. HUNTLY 12 Sept 1879
1231. George M.	born 29 Apr 1863 1232. Sadie A. born 8 July 1865; died 18 Sept 1876

780. NANCY THURSTON-8 FOSTER, daughter of Alexander Robinson-7 FOSTER (John-6; Nathan-5; Caleb-4; 3; Abraham-2; Reginald-1) and Betsey THURSTON, was born 17 Oct 1829 at Bristol, ME. She married Asa T-9 GAMAGE (# 1128) ca Sept 1847. He was the son of Thomas-8 GAMAGE (Joshua-7, Jr; Elinor-6 FOSTER; Nathan-5; Caleb-4; 3; Abraham-2; Reginald-1) and Waity THOMPSON, and was born 1 Oct 1827; died 27 July 1903 at Rockland, Maine. Nancy Thurston-8 FOSTER died 27 Nov 1909.

Children of Nancy Thurston-8 FOSTER and Asa T-9 GAMAGE
    Surname GAMAGE
    1233. John M.   born 10 May 1848; died 24 Nov 1865 (drowned)
    1234. Ambrose P.   born 28 May 1852 Bristol, ME; died 11 Dec 1916 Boston, MA **
                               married Nellie PHILBRICK 16 June 1880
          Children: Laura E-10 (born 21 Feb 1882; d y) and William J-10 GAMAGE (born 1884)
          ** Note: Reportedly he died of injuries suffered when he fell into the hold of a vessel that he was working on.
                   Reference: John M. Falla   Tenants Harbor, Maine
    1235. Mary E.   born ca 1854; 1m. Reuben P. GAMAGE 19 June 1870 (he died Sept 1870)
                               2m. Harvey OLIVER 13 Oct 1873
    1236. Etta H.   born ca 1861; married Lemuel K. STEVENS 13 Nov 1881; died after 1916
    1237. John Menzies   born ca May 1865 Boothbay, ME; 1m. Mary E. ADAMS 16 June 1892
                               2m. Aletha L. BUTLER 2 May 1915 Union, Maine

796. MARIA-8 CHALONER, daughter of Louisa-7 FOSTER (Jacob-6; Colonel Benjamin-5; Benjamin-4; 3; Isaac-2; Reginald-1) and William CHALONER, was born ca 18__. She married Winslow BATES, Esq. ca 1831. He was the son of ___ BATES, and was born ca 1805; died 1894. He was a lawyer at Eastport, Maine. Maria-8 CHALONER died before 1875. Winslow BATES married second to Sabrina A-7 GARDNER Tenney on 8 Nov 1875.

Children of Maria-8 CHALONER and Winslow BATES:
    Surname BATES
    1238. Maria L.   born ca 18__   1241. Henrietta C.   born ca 18__
  + 1239. WILLIAM H.   born ca 18__
  + 1240. JOSEPH C.   born ca 18__; married Augusta PEARSON of Boston, MA

808. WILLIAM HENRY-8 TALBOT, son of Mary-7 FOSTER (John-6; Colonel Benjamin-5; Benjamin-4;3; Isaac-2; Reginald-1) and John Coffin TALBOT, was born 20 Sep 1813 at E. Machias, ME. He married Martha L. POOR of Andover, ME ca 18__. She was the daughter of ____ POOR, and was born ____.

Children of William H-8 TALBOT and Martha POOR:
    Surname TALBOT
    1242. Emma   born ca 18__
  + 1243. JOHN F.   born ca 18__; married Georgie FISHER of MA.
    1244. William H., Jr. born ca 18__; married Olive __?__; resided Spokane, WA (no issue)
  + 1245. GEORGE A.   born ca 18__; married Ida GRAHAM
    1246. Mary   born ca 18__
  + 1247. MARTHA   born ca 18__; married Charles CUSHMAN
    1248. Peter   born ca 18__; married Eva STILES   (Child: Charles W-10 TALBOT)

809. JOHN COFFIN-8 TALBOT, JR, brother of above, was born 3 Nov 1816 at East Machias, Maine. He graduated from Washington Academy and Bowdoin College (Class of 1839). He was elected to Phi Beta Kappa, and gave the class valedictory address. He studied law with the Honorable J A LOWELL, and was admitted to the bar at Ellsworth, Maine in Oct 1840. He opened a law office in Lubec, Maine, where he practiced until 1862. John Coffin-8 TALBOT married first to Clara/Clarissa Antoinette-7 WASS on 10 Dec 1849 at Addison, ME. She was the daughter of David-6 WASS and Hadassah NASH of Addison, and was born ca 1827; died before 1870. His second marriage was to her sister, Esther Bernice-7 WASS. She was born 27 Nov 1835; died 30 June 1918. John C-8 TALBOT was active in civic and political affairs; was a Free Mason and belonged to the SAR (Sons of the American Revolution). He died ca 1899.

Children of John Coffin-8 TALBOT and Clara WASS:
    Surname TALBOT
  + 1249. MARY H.   born ca 18__; married Prentiss WOODMAN of Minneapolis, MN
    1250. Annie M.   born ca 18__; married the Rev Samuel V. COLE; resided Norton, MA (EOL)

Children of John Coffin-8 TALBOT, continued:
  Surname TALBOT
  1251. John C.   born ca 18__; died young   1253. William H. born ca 18__; d y
  1252. Frank M.   born ca 18__; married __?_   1254. Esther B. born ca 18__;
    Child: John C-10 TALBOT; resided Minneapolis, MN   a teacher in Minneapolis, MN

810. GEORGE FOSTER-8 TALBOT, brother of above, was born 15 Jan 1819 at East Machias, Maine. He graduated from Washington Academy and entered Bowdoin College (ME) (1835) at age 16, graduating in 1837. He taught school for a year and then became a law student in the office of the Honorable J A LOWELL in East Machias. In 1840 he went to Augusta, Maine to complete his law studies, and was admitted to practice in the Fall of that year. In the Spring of 1842 he opened a law office in Rockland, ME. where he was a trial lawyer. He married first to Elizabeth DeWitt NEIL in May 1844. She was the daughter of John G. NEIL and __?__, and was born ca 18__; died ____. His second marriage was to Elizabeth B. LINCOLN. George F-8 TALBOT was still living in 1903.

Children of George F-8 TALBOT and Elizabeth NEIL:
  Surname TALBOT
  1255. Elizabeth N.   born ca 18__   1256. Gilman T.   born ca 18__; d y
Children of George F-8 TALBOT and Elizabeth LINCOLN:
  Surname TALBOT
  1257. Jane T.   born ca 18__; dy   1261. Catherine P.   born ca 18__
+ 1258. THOMAS L.   born ca 18__   1262. Francis   born ca 18__
          married Alice B. SPRING   + 1263. FREDERIC F.   born ca 18__
  1259. Hannah L.   born ca 18__   married Mary FRANK
  1260. Walter   born ca 18__

829. SUSAN-8 AVERY, daughter of Betsey/Elizabeth-7 FOSTER (Levi-6; Colonel Benjamin-5; Benjamin-4; 3; Isaac-2; Reginald-1) and George Halleburton AVERY, was born ca 18__ at Machias, ME. She married first to James STUART ca 18__. He was possibly the son of Asa STUART and Betsey _?_, and was born 14 Mar 1831 Scarboro, ME; died ____. She married second to __?_, and resided CA.

Children of Susan-8 AVERY and James STUART:
  Surname STUART
  1264. Joseph   born ca 18__; moved to CA.
+ 1265. LUCINDA   born ca 18__; married Harlan P. SMITH
  1266. Edgar   born ca 18__
  1267. Elmer   born ca 18__   1268. Frank   born ca 18__

831. L. TRESCOTT-8 AVERY, brother of above, was born ca 18__. He married Sarah A. HOYT ca 18__.

Children of L. Trescott-8 AVERY and Sarah HOYT:
  Surname AVERY
  1269. Henderson   born ca 18__; married Maggie COSSEBOOM; removed to Franklin, MA
                          1 child: Henderson-10 AVERY born ca 18__; died ___ (lost at sea)
  1270. Miranda   born ca 18__; married Henry RAYMOND; resided White's Point, WI
  1271. George   born ca 18__
+ 1272. EDWINA   born ca 18__; married George W. POPE of East Machias, ME
                          (he born ca 1832; died 9 Dec 1875) (she was living 1903)

834. MARY H-8 AVERY, sister of above, was born ca 18__. She married Joseph NILES ca 18__.

Children of Mary-8 AVERY and Joseph NILES:
  Surname NILES
  1273. Joseph (Jr) born ca 18_   1274. Elmer born ca 18__   1275. Lizzie   born ca 18__

837. ALBERT-8 HALL, son of Phebe-7 FOSTER (Levi-6; Colonel Benjamin-5; Benjamin-4; 3; Isaac-2; Reginald-1) and Luther Hall, was born ca 18__. He married Annie/Anna PARKER of Cutler, Maine ca 18__. She was the daughter of ____ PARKER, and was born ca 18__; died 1901 at Albert Lea, MN. Albert-8 HALL died there ca 1899.

Children of Albert-8 HALL and Annie PARKER:
　　Surname HALL
　　1276. Albert born ca 18__　　1277. Ellen born ca 18__　　1278. Ada born ca 18__　　1279. Charles born ____
　　1280. Annie/Anna born ca 18__　　1281. Nellie   born ca 18__　　1282. Carrie/Caroline   born ca 18__

839. ELIZABETH-8 HALL, sister of above, was born ca 18__. She married John A. HARRADEN of NH.

Children of Elizabeth-8 HALL and John HARRADEN:
　　Surname HARRADEN
　　1283. Fred B.   born ca 18__married Jennie R. _?_　　　　1285. James O.　　　　born ca 18__; d y
　　1284. William born ca 18__; d y　　　　　　　　　　　　1286. Laura H.　　　　born ca 18__

851. LYDIA DRUSILLA-8 FOSTER, daughter of Benjamin-7 FOSTER (Deacon Samuel-6 ;Benjamin-5; 4; 3; Isaac-2; Reginald-1) and Joan West-7 FOSTER, was born 11 Oct 1821. She married John WISWELL ca 18__. He was the son of Edward WISWELL and Deborah MARSHALL, and was born 9 Dec 1820.

Children of Lydia U-8 FOSTER and John WISWELL:
　　Surname WISWELL　　(children born East Machias, Maine)
+ 1287. FRANK H.　　　　born ca 1846; married Antoinette CHALONER
　　1288. Julia E.　　　　born ca 1848　　　　　　1289. George E.　　　　born ca 1850

852. JULIA EMELINE-8 FOSTER, sister of above, was born 2 June 1823. She married Charles H. KILBY ca 18_. He was the son of Theophilus KILBY and Deborah WILDER, and was born ca 18__ Dennysville.

Children of Julia Emeline-8 FOSTER and Charles H. KILBY:
　　Surname KILBY
　　1290. Fred　　　　　　　　born ca 18__; died young
+ 1291. BENJAMIN FOSTER　　born 1 Mar 1852; married Lucy CORTHELL
+ 1292. CHARLES HENRY　　　born 3 July 1854; married Eliza COX
+ 1293. EMILY U.　　　　　　born 30 Oct 1856; married Henry Howard KILBY 7 June 1884
　　　　　　(he son of Benjamin KILBY and 1st wife Eliza RICE; he born 4 Feb 1855 Dennysville, ME)
　　1294. Herbert　　　　　　born 8 July 1860; married Hattie PIKE
　　　　　　　　(2 ch: Humphrey-10 KILBY born ___; d y and Lucy-10 KILBY)

840. DRUSILLA-9 FOSTER, sister of above, was born ca 1825. She married Charles HOBART ca 18__.

Children of Drusilla-8 FOSTER and Charles HOBART:
　　Surname HOBART
　　1295. Clara　　　　　　born ca 18__; married Frank P. DENNISON (Ch: Charles-10)
+ 1296. MARIA　　　　　　born ca 18__; married Oscar CHALONER
　　1297. Joanna　　　　　born ca 18__ EOL　　　　　　1298. Mary born ca 18__; d y

858. REBECCA-8 FOSTER, daughter of Alfred-7 FOSTER (Deacon Samuel-6; Benjamin-5;4;3; Isaac-2; Reginald-1) and Rebecca-7 FOSTER, and was born ca 18__. She married the Rev George INGRAHAM ca 18__. He was the son of ____ INGRAHAM, and was born ca 18__; died ____.

Children of Rebecca-8 FOSTER and George INGRAHAM:
　　Surname INGRAHAM
　　1299. Mary　　　　　　　born ca 18__　　　　　+1300. CLARA   born ca 18__; married ___ BELL

871. SOLOMON M-8 FOSTER, son of John Woodin-7 FOSTER (Wooden-6; 5; Benjamin-4; 3; Isaac-2; Reginald-1) and Mehitable MESERVE, was born 3 Sept 1805 at Dennysville, ME.. He married Elizabeth WILDER on 12 Aug 1828 at Dennysville. She was the daughter of Ebenezer Cushing WILDER and Abigail AYERS, and was born 11 Mar 1810 at Dennysville. Solomon M-8 FOSTER died there 13 Mar 1828.

Child of Solomon-8 FOSTER and Elizabeth WILDER:
Surname FOSTER
1301. Elijah	born 7 Nov 1828; died young		
1302. Eliza Hayward	born 29 June 1830; died 11 Feb 1846		
+ 1303. DEBORAH R.	born 21 Feb 1832 Dennysville, ME; died 3 Mar 1901		
	married Dr. Albert Robinson LINCOLN 11/19 Feb 1857 Dennysville, ME		
1304. Elijah (2)	born ca 1835	1307. Edward T.	born 12 Dec 1840
1305. Edward F	born ca 1836; d y		died 21 Oct 1860
1306. William H.	born ca 1838; d y	1308. William H.	born 21 Nov 1844

873. ELIAS-8 FOSTER, half-brother of above, son of John Woodin-7 FOSTER (Wooden-6; 5; Benjamin-4; 3; Isaac-2; Reginald-1) and Betsey BROWN, was born ca 1809. He married first to Hannah HANSON ca 18__. She was the daughter of ? HANSON, and was born ca 18__. He married 2nd to Hannah LIBBY ca 18__ at Stephen, New Brunswick. She was the daughter of __ LIBBY, and was born ca 18__; died _____.

Child of Elias-8 FOSTER and Hannah HANSON:
Surname FOSTER
+ 1309. ALMIRA/ELMIRA   born ca 18___ NB; married ? HANSON

876. GILBERT D-8 HOWE, son of Mercy-7 FOSTER (Wooden-6; 5; Benjamin-4; 3; Isaac-2; Reginald-1) and Pearl HOWE, was born 11 Nov 1808, Maine. He married Abigail W. KINGSLEY on 21 Mar 1830 at Whiting, ME. She was the daughter of Samuel KINGSLEY, Jr. and Elizabeth/Betsey WILSON, and was born ca 1810 at Trescott, ME; died 9 Feb 1880 at East Machias, ME. Gilbert-8 died there on 9 July 1873.

Children of Gilbert D-8 HOWE and Abigail KINGSLEY:
Surname HOWE   (all children born East Machias, Maine)
1310. Gilbert P.	born 8 Mar 1831; marr Caroline H. DAVIS 9 June 1855; died ca 1917 ME		
	(1 child: Charles A-10 HOWE born 24 Oct 1856 Maine)		
+ 1311. SAMUEL ALONZO born 23 Feb 1833; married Harriet Thompson SIMPSON 6 Jan 1851			
1312. William H.	born 12 Mar 1835; died 1 June 1857		
1313. Thaddeus S.	born 13 May 1838; died 18 Mar 1884 East Machias, ME		
1314. Betsey A.	born 14 Dec 1840; married Eric COOK 22 Mar 1860; died 9 Apr 1872		
	(he born ca 1836 East Machias; died _____)		
1315. Albert C.	born 11 May 1843	1316. Marcus A. Standford	born 7 Aug 1845
1317. Abigail Ursula	born 27 Jan 1848; married Alden COOK 1 Jan 1876 (he born 1844)		
1318. Lucy E.	born ca 1853	1319. Mary L. C.	born 17 Aug 1851

895. ELIZABETH OTIS TURNER-8 FOSTER, daughter of Cyrus Woodin-7 FOSTER (Moses-6; Woodin-5; Benjamin-4; 3; Isaac-2; Reginald-1) and Sally TURNER, was born 4 Mar 1819 at Machias, Maine. She married Josiah H. TALBOT ca 18__.

Children of Elizabeth Otis T-8 FOSTER and Josiah TALBOT:
Surname TALBOT
1320. Frank E.	born ca 18__; married Anna BRYANT (Ch: Walter-10 and Eliza-10 (d y)
1321. Charles C.	born ca 18__; married Eliza J. NORRIS
1322. Walter	born ca 18__; married Nettie HUBBARD (Ch: Edith-10 and Miriam-10)
1323. Eliza	born ca 18__; died young

897. HARRIET M.-8 FOSTER, sister of above, was born ca 1827. She married Edgar WHIDDEN ca 18__.

Children of Harriet-8 FOSTER and Edgar WHIDDEN:
 Surname WHIDDEN
 1324. Caroline born ca 18__   1325. Harriet born ca 18__   1326. Edgar born ca 18__
 1327. James   born ca 18__   1328. Amy H.   born ca 18__

900. REVEREND EDGAR L-8 FOSTER, brother of above, was born 7 Aug 1838 at East Machias, Maine. He was educated at Washington Academy, East Machias; graduating from Amherst College in 1864 with a BA degree. In June 1867 he graduated from the Bangor Theological Seminary, and began his preaching career at Milltown, New Brunswick. He married Mary BOYDEN of Chicago. IL. on 20 Aug 1867. Rev Edgar-8 FOSTER died 16 Nov 1872.

Children of Rev Edgar-8 FOSTER and Mary BOYDEN:
 Surname FOSTER
 1329. Willard   born ca 18__   1331. Emma   born ca 18__; d y
 1330. Lillie   born ca 18__; d y   1332. Edgar L   born ca 18__

907. JOSIAH-8 HARRIS, son of Drusilla West-7 FOSTER (Moses-6; Woodin-5; Benjamin-4;3; Isaac-2; Reginald-1) and John Fairbanks HARRIS, was born ca 18__ at E. Machias, ME. He married Sarah TOBEY

Children of Josiah-8 HARRIS and Sarah TOBEY:
 Surname HARRIS   1335. William Page   born ca 18__
 1333. Clara F.   born ca 18__   married Mary WORTHLEY of Boulton
 1334. Edward T.   born ca 18__   Ch: Clinton P-10 HARRIS
    married Cora BATCHELDER (Ch: Bertha C-10) 1336. Linnie   born ca 18__

909. LAURA F-8 HARRIS, sister of above, was born 4 Feb 1830. She married N. Page PATTANGALL (of Perry, Maine) ca 18__. He was the son of ____ PATTANGALL, and was born ca 18__; died ____ .

Children of Laura-8 HARRIS and N. Page PATTANGALL:
 Surname PATTANGALL
 1337. Lucy   born ca 18__   1342. Mary.   born ca 18__
 1338. Frances   born ca 18__   1343. Laura P.   born ca 18__
 1339. Eliza   born ca 18__   1344. Drusilla   born ca 18__
         married Frank C. LYON   1345. Susan M.   born ca 18__
      Ch: Laura P-10 and Marion-10 LYON   married H. Merton SNOW (EOL)
 1340. Katherine   born ca 18__   +1346. CHARLOTTE   born ca 18__
 1341. Nathan F/P   born ca 18__; unmarr   married George L. WHITTEN

913. WILLIAM-8 HARRIS, son of Cynthia-7 FOSTER (Moses-6; Woodin-5; Benjamin-4;3; Isaac-2; Reginald-1) and Stephen T-5 HARRIS, was born 30 June 1827 probably at East Machias, Maine. He married first to Lucinda-4 HANSCOM ca 18__. She was the daughter of Luther-3 HANSCOM and Mary BEDELL/BEADLE, and was born ca 18__; died ____ . His 2nd marriage was to her younger sister Mary-4 HANSCOM. She was born ca 18__; died ____ . William-8 HARRIS died 186_; killed in the **Civil War**.

Children of William-8 HARRIS and __?__ HANSCOM:
 Surname HARRIS
 1347. Kate   born ca 18__   1348. William   born ca 18__

914. SARAH E-8 HARRIS, sister of above, was born 14 Mar 1829 at East Machias, Maine. She married William Thomas-4 HANSCOM ca 18__. He was the brother of Lucinda-4 HANSCOM (above).

Children of Sarah-8 HARRIS and William-4 HANSCOM:
 Surname HANSCOM   Note: There were reportedly 2 un-named infants who died young
 1349. Lyman born 18_   1350. Arno born 18__   1351. Emma born 18__   1352. Ernest born 18__

915. BENJAMIN F-8 HARRIS, brother of above, was born 24 June 1831 at East Machias, Maine. He married Elizabeth-4 HANSCOM ++ ca 18__. She was the sister of William-4 HANSCOM (above).

Children of Benjamin-8 HARRIS and Elizabeth-4 HANSCOM:
Surname HARRIS

1353. Ida	born ca 18__; married Charles M. GRAY (Ch: Mary-10 and Alice-10 GRAY)			
1354. Fred O.	born ca 18__; married Marcia PETTINGILL (no issue) EOL			
1355. Hattie	born ca 18__; died young			
1356. Lucy	born ca 18__			
+ 1357. BENJAMIN F., JR	born ca 18__; 1m. Nettie HAMMOND; 2m. Jennie FIELD			
+ 1358. ELIZABETH	born ca 18__; married Fred B. TAYLOR			
1359. Warren J.	born ca 18__	1363. James	born ca 18__	
1360. Loring L.	born ca 18__	married Jennie WILSON (Ch: Benjamin F-10 HARRIS)		
1361. Stephen T	born ca 18__	1364. Arno	born ca 18__; married Mabel CHURCH	
1362. Ernest	born ca 18__	(Ch: Dorothy M. and Elizabeth G-10 HARRIS)		

++   Ancestry of Elizabeth-4 HANSCOM

AARON-1 HANSCOM, one of the early settlers in the Machias (ME) area, was born ca ___; died ____. He married Sally SEAVEY ca ____, and was the father of the following: Nathan who married Ruth FOSTER; Aaron; Abigail; Sally; Isaac; Joseph; Lois; SYLVANUS-2; Daniel; Thomas and Moses HANSCOM. SYLVANUS-2 HANSCOM was born ca ____; married Eda AVERILL. They had James; LUTHER-3; Phebe; Eliza; Alfred; and Mary-3 HANSCOM.   LUTHER-3 HANSCOM, born ca 1___; married Mary BEDELL. Their children were: LUCINDA-4 who married William-5 HARRIS; ELIZABETH-4 who married Benjamin F-8 HARRIS; Elsie E.; Loring L.; and Mary A HANSCOM.

919. CHARLES A-8 HARRIS, brother of above, was born 6 Feb 1841 at East Machias, Maine. He married Clara BRYANT ca 18__. She was the daughter of ____ BRYANT, and was born ca 18__; died ____.

Children of Charles-8 HARRIS and Clara BRYANT:
Surname HARRIS

1365. Elmer	born ca 18__; d y	1367. Charles	born ca 18__
1366. Arthur	born ca 18__	1368. Chester/Nathan	born ca 18__

920. BETSEY TALBOT-8 HARRIS, sister of above, was born 17 Aug 1843 at East Machias, Maine. She married Sylvanus DWELLEY ca 18__. He was the son of ____ DWELLEY, and was born ca 18__.

Children of Betsey-8 HARRIS and Sylvanus DWELLEY:
Surname DWELLEY

1369. Mary E. born ca 18__	1370. Bessie	born ca 18__	1371. Arthur	born ca 18__	

924. MARTHA H-8 FOSTER, daughter of Jeremiah-7 FOSTER (Moses-6; Woodin-5; Benjamin-4;3; Isaac-2; Reginald-1) and Lucy-5 HARRIS, was born 12 Aug 18838 at East Machias, Maine. She married General John C. CALDWELL ca 18__. He was the son of ____ CALDWELL, and was born ca 18__; died ____. His home was in Topeka, KS. He was US Consul to Costa Rica, Central America beginning in 1897.

Children of Martha-8 FOSTER and General John CALDWELL:
Surname CALDWELL

1372. Charles	born ca 18__
1373. Harriet	born ca 18__; married Henry Simpson MURCHIE of Calais, Maine
	(he son/o James MURCHIE and Margaret THORPE; he born 1 Oct 1862)
	Children: Ralph D-10 and Harris F-10 MURCHIE
1374. Harry	born ca 18__; he worked for the Santa Fe RR Co., in Coahiula, Mexico

927. PAUL F-8 FOLSOM, son of Martha-7 FOSTER (Paul-6; Woodin-5; Benjamin-4; 3; Isaac-2; Reginald-1) and Titus Philbrick FOLSOM, was born 29 Feb 1820. He married first to Maria G. BROWN ca 1851. She was the daughter of Jesse BROWN and Deborah WALLACE, and was born ca 18__ at East

Machias; died before 1853. His second marriage was to Helen Sophia Farnsworth LIVERMORE ca 1853.
Child of Paul-8 FOLSOM and Maria G. BROWN:
    Surname FOLSOM

1375. Martha	born ca 18__; 1m. Everett CUTTER; 2m. Henry S CHASE (no issue) EOL		

Children of Paul-8 FOLSOM and Helen Sophia Farnsworth LIVERMORE:

1376. Sarah	born ca 18__	1379. George	born ca 18__
1377. Jennie	born ca 18__	1380. Paul	born ca 18__
	married Harry S. BRAYTON	1381. Eva	born ca 18__
1378. Mary O.	born ca 18__	1382. Grosvenor	born 8 Aug 1872, MA

928. DEBORAH-8 FOSTER, daughter of James-7 FOSTER (Paul-6; Woodin-5; Benjamin-4;3; Isaac-2;
Reginald-1) and Hannah HANSCOM, was born ca 1822, possibly at Machias, ME. She married David E.
STRONG on 4 Oct 1841 at Harvey Parish, Westmoreland, New Brunswick. He was born ca 1820 at Corn-
wallis, Nova Scotia.

Children of Deborah-8 FOSTER and David E. STRONG:

Surname STRONG	(all children born Alma, Albert, New Brunswick)		
1383. Susan	born ca 1842	1387. Deborah	born ca 1854
1384. Rachel	born ca 1844	1388. Laura	born ca 1859
1385. Foster	born ca 1846	1389. Herbert	born ca 1861
+ 1386. MARILLA F.	born ca 1849 married Stephen Stiles HOAR 2 Feb 1885; died 6 Nov 1890 WI		

929. SARAH-8 FOSTER , sister of above, was born ca 1831. She married Chandler KEIVER 19 June
1861 at Albert, New Brunswick. He was born ca 1836, NB.

Children of Sarah-8 FOSTER and Chandler KEIVER:
    Surname KEIVER

1390. Ernest	born ca 18__; d y
1391. Bertie	born ca 18__; married Albert MITTEN (1 child: Ina-10 MITTEN)
1392. Rupert C.	born ca 18__; married Lillie ADKINS 23 Jan 1895 Lancaster, Nebraska

930. MARTHA A-8 FOSTER, sister of above, was born ca 1833. She married the Reverend James
ROGERS on 1 Feb 1857 at Albert, NB. He was the son of _____ ROGERS, and was born ca 18__.
Martha-8 FOSTER died ca 1872.

Children of Martha-8 FOSTER and Rev James ROGERS:
    Surname ROGERS

1393. Charles born ca 18__	1394. Talbot born ca 18__	1395. Albert born ca 18__

933. ALBERT-8 FOSTER, brother of above, was born ca 18__. He married first to Joan LOCKE ca 18__.
She was possibly the daughter of Nathaniel LOCKE and Charlotte STEVENS, and was born Oct 1835 at
Alma, St. John; Albert, New Brunswick; died _____. He married second to Ruth ELLIOT ca 18__.

Children of Albert-8 FOSTER and Joan LOCKE:
    Surname FOSTER

1396. Clark	born ca 18__; died _____ unmarried
1397. Laura	born ca 18__; married Alvin BRAY (no issue) EOL
1398. Clara	born ca 18__; married Thomas COLPITT (Ch: Marion and Clark COLPITT)
1399. Nathaniel	born ca 18__

Children of Albert-8 FOSTER and Ruth ELLIOT:
    Surname FOSTER

1400. Hiram	born ca 18__	1401. Jerome	born ca 18__
1402. Mary	born ca 18__	1403. Fern born ca 18__	1404. Lloyd born ca 18__

934. LUCY ELLEN-8 FOSTER, sister of above, was born June 1840 at Salmon River, Westmoreland, New Brunswick. She married Alexander McRAE 5 Mar 1863 at Albert, NB. He was the son of Alexander McRAE and Nancy TERRIS, and was born 10 Feb 1836, died ca 1904. Lucy-8 FOSTER died 5 Mar 1863.

Children of Lucy Ellen-8 FOSTER and Alexander McRAE:
Surname McRAE	(all children born Hopewell Parish, Albert, New Brunswick)		
1405. Laura J.	born ca 1863		
1406. Franklin A.	born Oct 1866; died 27 Sep 1942	1409. Lena	born ca 1872/73
1407. Ella	born July 1870; died 27 June 1871	1410. Howard F.	born ca 1877
1408. Fannie W.	born Sept 1871	1411. Fred L.	born ca Mar 1879

935. NATHANIEL-8 FOSTER, brother of above, was born ca 1841 Salmon River, Westmoreland, NB. He married Mary A. SHIELDS ca 18__. She was the daughter of ____ SHIELDS, and was born ca 18__; died ____. Nathaniel-8 FOSTER died ca 1893 at Alma, Albert, NB.

Children of Nathaniel-8 FOSTER and Mary A. SHIELDS:
Surname FOSTER			
1412. Zella	born ca 18__; d y	1418. Margaret	born ca 18__
1413. Myrtle	born ca 18__	1419. Robert	born ca 18__
1414. Laurel	born ca 18__	1420. Alice	born ca 18__
1415. Edna	born ca 18__	1421. Pearl	born ca 18__
1416. Nellie	born ca 18__	1422. Ralph	born ca 18__
1417. Arthur	born ca 18__	1423. Nathaniel	born ca 18_

936. HANNAH MARIA-8 FOSTER, sister of above, was born 15 Mar 1844 at Alma, Westmoreland, New Brunswick. She married William Sears CLEVELAND on 22 Oct 1872 at Alma, NB. He was the son of John-6 CLEVELAND (Nathan-5; Benj.-4; 3; Aaron-2; Moses-1) and Amy MARTIN, and was born 25 Nov 1841.

Children of Hannah Maria-8 FOSTER and William Sears CLEVELAND:
Surname CLEVELAND	(all children born Salem, Essex Co., MA)		
1424. Mabel	born 5 June 1874	1426. Grace	born 28 Aug 1881
1425. Everett	born 21 Jan 1878; married Annie McDONALD		

937. ELIZABETH-8 FOSTER, daughter of Nathan Webber-7 FOSTER (Paul-6; Woodin-5; Benjamin-4; 3; Isaac-2; Reginald-1) and Mehitable-7 FOSTER (Samuel-6; Benjamin-5; 4; 3; Isaac-2; Reginald-1), was born ca 1820/21. She married Frederic DAVIS ca 18__. He was born ca 18__; died ____.

Children of Elizabeth-8 FOSTER and Frederic DAVIS:
Surname DAVIS	
1427. Frederic W.	born ca 18__; died ____; unmarried
1428. Fannie M.	born ca 18__; married Theophilus BATCHELDER, M.D. of Machias, ME
1429. Edgar	born ca 18__; died young
1430. Rev Edgar F.	born ca 18__; married Almira/Elmira S. TALBOT (she born 12 Feb 1850) (she dau/o Samuel Hammond TALBOT, Jr. and Margaret SCOTT) Ch: Grace H-10 and Clara T-10 DAVIS who marr. Dr. Frank B. GRANGERS)

941. ISABELLE/ISABELLA-8 FOSTER, sister of above, was born ca 1839. She married George Edwin MALOON ca 18__. He was the son of ____ MALOON, and was born ca 18__; died ____.

Children of Isabelle/Isabella-8 FOSTER and George MALOON:
Surname MALOON			
1431. Mary R.	born ca 18__; married Andrew LOPEZ (Ch: Amy and Isabel-10 LOPEZ)		
1432. Howard	born ca 18__	1434. Minerva	born ca 18__
1433. Carolyn	born ca 18__		married George E. SIMPSON, M.D.

945. JAMES WEBBER-8 CARY, son of Eliza W-7 FOSTER (Moses-6; Woodin-5; Benjamin-4;3; Isaac-2; Reginald-1) and Luther CARY, was born Aug 1819 at East Machias, Maine. He married Annie/Anna E. ALLEN/ALLAN ca Oct 1857 at Machias, Washington County, Maine. She was the daughter of _ ALLEN/ALLAN, and was born ca 1822 East Machias, ME; died ____ .

Children of James Webber-8 CARY and Annie ALLEN:
> Surname CARY   (children born at Machias, Maine)
> 1435. Amelia   born Oct 1858   1436. John Allan   born Mar 1861(Ch: James A. and Alice-10 CARY)

948. DELIA F-8 CARY, sister of above, was born June 1828 at East Machias, Maine. She married Stephen J-4 GETCHELL ca Oct 1853 at Machias. He was the son of Benjamin-3 GETCHELL and Abigail LONG-FELLOW, and was born ca 18__; died ____ .

Children of Delia-8 CARY and Stephen-4 GETCHELL:
> Surname GETCHELL
> 1437. Carroll/Waldo   born ca 18__   + 1439. JENNIE   born ca 18__
> 1438. Helen   born ca 18__   married Harvey LEITH

950. MARY E-8 CARY, sister of above, was born Mar 1834 at East Machias, Maine. She married Charles CARY (of East Machias) ca 1847. He was the son of Caleb CARY ++ and Sarah J. TALBOT, and was born ca 1826 at East Machias; died 1884. Mary E-8 CARY died ca 1875. Charles CARY married second to Mrs. Phidelia-7 " Delia " COFFIN Marshman on 23 May 1877. She was born 30 Apr 1836; died 1921/22 at Bangor, Maine.

Children of Mary E-8 CARY and Charles CARY:
> Surname CARY   (all children born Machias, Maine)
> 1440. William   born ca 1858; d y   1443. George F. +++   born ca 18__
> 1441. Lucy T.   born ca 1860; d y   married Lottie COLEMAN of CT ca 1889
> 1442. Austin   born ca 18__   Child: Charles Austin-10 CARY

++ Caleb Cary was born ca 1788, was one of three brothers (Jonathan born 1791, Luther born 1794) who were born at North Bridgewater, MA, and went to East Machias, Maine. Caleb CARY married Sarah J. TALBOT, daughter of Peter TALBOT. They had CHARLES (above) who married his cousin Mary E.; and Lewis CARY. Caleb CARY died ca 1848; his wife died ca 1856.

+++ George F. CARY (# 1443) was a graduate of Bowdoin College. He was Treasurer of the Machias Savings Bank for several years, and was later a Trustee and President of the Machias Banking Company. He was also Treasurer of the Washington Academy.

951. MARTIN LUTHER-8 CARY, brother of above, was born Sept 1836 at East Machias, Washington County, Maine. He married May Maria WATTLES 17 Sept 1867 at Providence, RI. She was the daughter of Luther Ripley WATTLES and Mary Ann BISSELL, and was born 13 Nov 1847, Montville, CT; died 22 Jan 1906 at Providence, RI.

Children of Martin L-8 CARY and May Maria WATTLES:
> Surname CARY   (children born at Providence, Rhode Island)
> +1444. EDWIN FOSTER born 13 Apr 1869; married Clara Louise PERRY 14 Sept 1898 Reheboth, MA
> 1445. Walter Wattles   born 16 Sep 1874   1446. Alice   born ca 18__   1447. Helen   born ca 18__

954. JOHN-8 FOSTER, son of Joel-7 FOSTER (Moses-6; Woodin-5; Benjamin-4;3; Isaac-2; Reginald-1) and Olivia TOBIN, was born ca 18__. He married Mary PULSIFER ca 18__. She was the daughter of ____ PULSIFER, and was born ca 18__; died ____ .

Children of John-8 FOSTER and Mary PULSIFER:
> Surname FOSTER
> 1448. William   born ca 18__   1450. Eliza A.   born ca 18__
> 1449. Whitman   born ca 18__   married David FLOYD   (EOL)

956. WILLIAM-8 FOSTER, brother of above, was born ca 18__. He married Annie SMITH ca 18__. She was the daughter of _____ SMITH, and was born ca 18__; died ____.

Children of William-8 FOSTER and Annie SMITH:
　　Surname FOSTER
　1451. William　born ca 18__　　　1452. Frank　　born ca 18__　　　1453. Charles　born ca 18__

960. HENRY-8 FOSTER, brother of above, was born ca 18__. He married first to Alice STUART ca 18__. She was the daughter of __ STUART, and was born ca 18__; died ____. He married second to Margaret ROSS ca 18__. She was the daughter of ____ ROSS, and was born ca 18__; died ____.

Child of Henry-8 FOSTER and Alice STUART:
　　Surname FOSTER
　1454. Helen　　　　　　　born ca 18__

Children of Henry-8 FOSTER and Margaret ROSS:
　　Surname FOSTER
　1455. Earl　　born ca 18__　　　1456. Melvin　　born ca 18__　　　1457. Olive　　born ca 18__

982. JULIA-8 FOSTER　see ALVIN G-5 CROCKER　# 261　Crocker Section

983. JULIA-8 DAY, daughter of Mary-7 FOSTER (Elias-6; Woodin-5; Benjamin-4;3; Isaac-2; Reginald-1) and Jacob-7 DAY, was born 15 May 1830 at Wesley, Maine. She married Sheldon GRAY Aug 1847. He was the son of _____ GRAY, and was born ____; died 8 June 1902 Chico, CA. Julia-8 DAY died 1 Aug 1908 Chico. CA.

Children of Julia-8 DAY and Sheldon GRAY:
　　Surname GRAY
　1458. Frank　　　　　　born 8 Jan 1849; died 26 Feb 1851
　1459. Henry　　　　　　born 18 Nov 1851; died 18 Dec 1860
+ 1460. LAURA　　　　　born 11 Apr 1855; 1m. James Randolph BROTHERTON 5 Dec 1870
　　　　　　　　　　　　2m. Richard OLNEY
　1461. Minnie　　　　　born 28 Sept 1828; 1m. Samuel BLACK 20 Aug 1875
　　　　　　　　　　　　2m. Joseph SPAUL; 3m. A. J. PIDGEON

984. ELIAS FOSTER-8 DAY, son of Mary-7 FOSTER brother of above, was born 24 March 1832 at Wesley, Washington County, Maine. He married Joan STANCHFIELD 25 June 1854. She was the daughter of Ezra STANCHFIELD and Hannah BURBANK, and was born ca 18__.

Children of Elias-8 DAY and Joan STANCHFIELD:
　　Surname DAY　　　　　(all children born Wesley, Maine
+ 1462. HERBERT L.　　born 22 Apr 1855;　married Rebecca McCREA
+ 1463. HIRAM　　　　　born 17 Mar 1858; married Mary McCREA (Ch: Ada-10 DAY)
　1464. Henry A.　　　　born　Aug 1860; married Myra SMITH 6 Dec 1900 Milltown, NB
　　　　　　　　　　　　(she dau/o Albert SMITH and Ella BRIDGES)
　1465. Thomas J.　　　　born 23 Jan 1864; died 16 Dec 1865
+ 1466. SHELDON G.　　born　Apr 1866; married Ada/Ida M. FOSTER 8 Nov 1899 Machiasport, ME
+ 1467. MANLEY E.　　　born 17 Jul 1868; married Abbie M. WEBBER 20 Mar 1890 Houlton, ME
　1468. David L.　　　　born 2 Nov 1872; died 23 Feb 1877
　1469. Mary H.　　　　born 11 Dec 1878; unmarried; schoolteacher

985. HENRY GILBERT-8 DAY, brother of above, was born 25 Sept 1835 at Wesley, Washington County, Maine. He married MARTHA-8 FOSTER (# 994, below) on 29 March 1879. She was the daughter of Willard W-7 FOSTER and Margaret BRIDGHAM, and was born ca 18__.

Children of Henry Gilbert-8 DAY and Martha-8 FOSTER:
    Surname DAY   (children born at Wesley, Washington County, Maine)
    1470. Alice Louise   born 4 Sept 1880   1471. Harry Almon born   29 May 1884

986. LEWIS ELBRIDGE-8 DAY, brother of above, was born 12 Mar 1838 at Wesley, Washington Co., ME. He married Mary Melancy ELSEMORE 15 June 1862. She was the daughter of John ELSEMORE and Abigail AVERILL, and was born ____. Lewis Elbridge-8 DAY was a hotelkeeper at Chico, CA, where he died 3 Feb 1907.

Children of Lewis- E-8 DAY and Mary ELSEMORE:
    Surname DAY   (all children born Wesley, Maine)
+ 1472. JULIA ADELIA   born 9 Feb 1863; married Fred RICH 1 Nov 1879 Chico, CA
  1473. Laura E.   born 18 Jan 1865; married Edward NELSON ___ Chico, CA
                (1 child: Francis-10 NELSON born 14 June 1883 Chico, CA)
+ 1474. FANNIE B.   born 28 Nov 1867; married Fred LAKE 29 Nov 1888 San Francisco, CA
  1475. Ira E.   born 3 Jan 1869; died 29 Aug 1895 Chico, CA
  1476. Nellie G.   born 11 May 1876

987. JOHN WILLARD-8 DAY, brother of above, was born 4 June 1841 at Cooper, Maine. He married Josephine GUPTILL ca June 1860. She was the daughter of Elijah GUPTILL and Harriet SCHUMAN, and was born ca 18__; died 25 Dec 1875 (probably as a result of childbirth). He married second Eliza HOLMES 4 July 1880 at Cutler, Maine. She was born ___; died 18 Oct 1896. His third wife was Cynthia E. EDGERLY. They were married 12 Oct 1899.

Children of John Willard-8 DAY and Josephine GUPTILL:
    Surname DAY   (all children born Wesley, Maine)
+ 1477. LUCY E.   born 18 Aug 1866; died 31 Jan 1894
                married Charles DURLING 1 Oct 1883 Crawford, ME
+ 1478. ALTHEA M.   born 25 Apr 1867; married Tholmena BROOKS 28 June 1885 Steuben, ME
+ 1479. CORRIN J.(twin)born 19 Feb 1869; married Carrie GUPTILL 27 June 1891
                (she dau/o Alexander GUPTILL and Mehitable HOLMES)
  1480. Orrin E. (twin) born 19 Feb 1869; married Etta C. LEIGHTON of Columbia, ME on 1 Feb 1899
                (she dau/o Alphonso LEIGHTON and Jeanette WORCESTER)
+ 1481. HORACE A.   born 10 Oct 1873; 1m. Lynnie M. HANSCOM 22 Aug 1904 Crawford, ME
                (she dau/o Ellsworth HANSCOM and Angelina GRAY)
  1482. Nettie   born 18 Dec 1875; died 28 Dec 1875
Children of John Willard-8 DAY and Eliza HOLMES:
    Surname DAY   (all children born Wesley, Maine)
  1483. Erastus W.   born 19 Oct 1881 ; married Mary Ann CROW 22 Jul 1904 Colfax, WA
                (she dau/o Lewis C. CROW and Nancy M. McGOWEN)
        (2 ch: Everett Oren-10 DAY born 10 Aug 1906; and Lewis Willard-10 Day born 2 Dec 1907)
  1484. Charlie J.   born 18 May 1883; married Sarah E HUGHES 18 Dec 1904 Colfax, WA
                (she dau/o Harry I. HUGHES and Emma J. MOOD)
  1485. Nettie C.   born 5 Oct 1880   1487. Ivan   born 14 Sept 1891
  1486. Essie I.   born 11 Dec 1882   died 14 Oct 1891

988. JACOB LINCOLN-8 DAY, brother of above, was born 19 Feb 1844 at Cooper, Maine. He married Lizzie HOLLINSWORTH 11 Nov 1866 at Wesley, Maine. She was the daughter of James HOLLINS- WORTH and Elmira HARPER, and was born ____; died 22 Feb 1889 at Wesley, Maine. Jacob L-8 DAY served in the **Civil War** as a Private in the **11ᵗʰ Maine Regiment.**

Children of Jacob Lincoln-8 DAY and Lizzie HOLLINSWORTH:
    Surname DAY   (all children born Wesley, Maine)
+ 1488. LULU   born 10 Apr 1871; married Lincoln BRIDGHAM 11 Dec 1895

Children of Jacob Lincoln-8 Day, continued:
    Surname DAY
    1489. Charles Edward   born 22 Apr 1869; married Almeda MOODY 7 Jan 1896 Rochester, NH
            (2 ch: Irma E-10 DAY born 21 Mar 1908, NH; Kendrick-10 DAY born Dec 1908, NH)
    1490. Mamie L.   born 24 June 1873; married Harvey E. MORRISON 15 Feb 1908
    1491. Josephine   born 10 Mar 1876; died 31 Mar 1879
    1492. Grace M.   born 24 July 1878; married Leroy PITKIN 26 Sept 1903
            (2 ch: Leroy-10 PITKIN born 1 Sept 1904 and Clayton Vernon-10 PITKIN born 25 Dec 1905)
    1493. Percy L.   born 24 May 1886

989. ALBION J-8 DAY, brother of above, was born 30 Jan 1848 at Cooper, Maine. He married Martha
DAVIS on 5 July 1873. She was the daughter of James DAVIS and Lucinda CATES.

Children of Albion J-8 DAY and Martha DAVIS:
    Surname DAY   (children born Wesley, Maine)
    1494. Elgie   born 8 Dec 1875; married Alice HUFFMAN 25 Ddec 1899 Colfax, WA
            (2 ch: Mona-10 DAY born 21 Sep 1900 WA; Vernon-10 DAY born 31 July 1902 WA)
    1495. Earle   born 8 Dec 1879

990. FRANK O-8 DAY, brother of above, was born 8 May 1854 at Wesley, Maine. He married Jessie
DURLING on 24 July 1874. She was the daughter of James DURLING and Rebecca CLARK, and was
born ___. Frank O-8 DAY died 2 Mar 1909 at Bangor, Maine.

Children of Frank O-8 DAY and Jessie DURLING:
    Surname DAY   (children born Wesley, Maine)
    1496. Roscoe J.   born 17 June 1876; died 8 Apr 1879 Wesley, ME
  + 1497. MINNIE   born 21 Mar 1878; married Burton GROSS 20 Jan 1897 E. Thorndike, ME
    1498. Julia   born 23 Nov 1886; married W. N. HARMON 30 Apr 1905 Portland, ME

994. MARTHA-8 FOSTER   see HENRY GILBERT-8 DAY # 985

996. GEORGE HARRIS-8 FOSTER, son of Elisha Barton-7 FOSTER (Elias-6; Woodin-5; Benjamin-4;3;
Isaac-2; Reginald-1) and Mary Elizabeth NOYES, was born ca 1845 Machias, Maine. He married Sarah
PENNELL ca 18__. She was the daughter of ____ PENNELL, and was born ca 18__; died ___. George H-
8 FOSTER was a ship's captain and/or owner.

Children of George-8 FOSTER and Sarah PENNELL:
    Surname FOSTER
  + 1499. CORRIS born ca 18__; marr Llewellyn McGOULDRICK   1500. Gertrude Pennell born ca 18__

997. LUCY BARTON-8 FOSTER, sister of above, was born 31 Mar 1847 at Machias, Maine. She married
Joseph S-5 CRANDON on 25 Jan 1868 at Columbia Falls, ME. He was the son of Joseph-4 CRANDON
and Alice B. FRANKLAND Small, and was born ca 1843; died after 1882. Lucy-8 FOSTER died 26 Jan
1882 at Machias, Maine.

Children of Lucy-8 FOSTER and Joseph CRANDON:
    Surname CRANDON
    1501. George   born ca 1871; died 18 May 1921 Fairfield
    1502. Lyman Brown   born ca 1873
    1503. Ella P.   born ca 1875; married George GARDNER 23 Oct 1901 (1 ch: Mary-10 GARDNER)
    1504. Mary N.   born 17 Aug 1877; died 20 Dec 1901; unmarried

1002. HERBERT-8 FOSTER, son of A. Loring-7 FOSTER (Elias-6; Woodin-5; Benjamin-4;3; Isaac-2;
Reginald-1) and Lydia WILSON, was born ca 18__. He married Elizabeth ELLIOT ca 18__.

Children of Herbert-8 FOSTER and Elizabeth ELLIOT:
   Surname FOSTER
   1505. David W.   born ca 18__; d y   1507. Abraham born ca 18__
   1506. Lydia   born ca 18__; res. Liverpool, ENG 1508. Sarah   born ca 18__; d y

1006. LAURA-8 FOSTER, daughter of Charles-7 FOSTER (James-6; Woodin-5; Benjamin-4;3; Isaac-2; Reginald-1) and Lavinia-5 CHASE, was born ca 18__. She married George Ruggles CRANDON 30 May 1858. He was the son of _____ CRANDON, and was born ca 18__; died _____.

Children of Laura-8 FOSTER and George R. CRANDON:
   Surname CRANDON   (all children born at Jonesboro, Maine)
   1509. Henry D.   born ca 1859; d y
   1510. Sophia S.   born ca 1864; married Clayton LEEK
   1511. Charles F.   born 31 Dec 1865; married Ulva Mabell-3 FEENEY 18 Apr 1888
                     (she dau/o Julia C-8 DRISKO (# 1168 Drisko section) and John W. FEENEY)

1007. J. KELLAR-8 FOSTER, brother of above, was born ca 18__. He married Augusta WHITTEMORE ca 18__. She was the daughter of _____ WHITTEMORE, and was born ca 18__; died ___. (he possibly married second to Julia CHALONER , and had 2 more children: Annie and Marie)
                  Reference: History of Machias, by George W. DRISKO, page 422.

Children of J. Kellar-8 FOSTER and Augusta WHITTEMORE:
   Surname FOSTER
+ 1512. LUCY H.   born ca 1869; married Herbert Lincoln FENNO 1 Oct 1890
                  (he son/o Jesse FENNO and Mary SPEAR, he born 12 Dec 1864 Canton, MA)
   1513. Emma   born ca 18__

1008. FREDERIC AUGUSTUS-8 FOSTER, brother of above, was born ca 18__. He married first to Abbie WESTON ca 18__. She was the daughter of _____ WESTON, and was born ca 18__; died ___. He married second to Lizzie/Elizabeth LORING ca 18__. She was the daughter of _____ LORING, and was born ca 18__.

Children of Frederic-8 FOSTER and Abbie WESTON:
   Surname FOSTER
   1514. Mabel   born ca 18__; married Herbert T. LANE   1515. Paul   born ca 18__

1009. J. LORING-8 CHASE, son of Louisa-7 FOSTER (James-6; Woodin-5; Benjamin-4;3; Isaac-2; Reginald-1) and Simeon CHASE, was born ca 18__. He married Amanda ENNIS ca 18__.

Children of J. Loring-8 CHASE and Amanda ENNIS:
   Surname CHASE
+ 1516. ELIZABETH   born ca 18__; married Charles GRAY
   1517. Frederic   born ca 18__; married Carrie RYAN (Child: Bessie-10 CHASE)
   1518. James (twin) born ca 18__; married Agnes JASPER (Ch: Jasper and Charles-10 CHASE)
   1519. Jennie (twin) born ca 18__   1520. Charles   born ca 18__

1010. OLIVE-8 CHASE, sister of above, was born ca 18__. She married James O. POPE ca 18__. He was the son of Colonel William POPE of Charleston, SC and Peggy Dawes BILLINGS of Boston, MA, and was born ca 18__; died _____.

Children of Olive-8 CHASE and James O. POPE:
   Surname POPE
   1521. John A.   born ca 18__   1523. Helen born ca 18__; dy
+ 1522. WARREN F. born ca 18__ ; married Kittie STUART   1524. Macy S. born ca 18__

1011. HELEN-8 CHASE, sister of above, was born ca 1841, probably at Machias, Maine. She married Thomas M. SANBORN ca 18__. He was the son of Cyrus SANBORN and Susan GARDNER, and was born 31 Dec 1838 at East Machias, ME; died ___ (still living 1897).

Children of Helen-8 CHASE and Thomas SANBORN:
   Surname SANBORN   (all children born at East Machias, Washington County, Maine)
   1525. Emily F.   born ca 1869
   1526. Lucy F.   born ca 1870
   1527. Arthur   born ca 1873; married Julia M-10 WISWELL (# 1657)
                        (she dau/o Frank H-9 WISWELL (# 1287) and Antoinette CHALONER)
   1528. Susan   born ca 18__

1012. LUCY-8 KELLAR, daughter of Lucy Ann-7 FOSTER (James-6; Woodin-5; Benjamin-4;3; Isaac-2; Reginald-1) and Josiah P. KELLAR, was born ca 1831. She married first to Captain Ambrose BROWN of Brooklyn, NY. He was the son of Jesse BROWN and Deborah WALLACE, and was born ca 18__; died ____ (about 6 months after their marriage, from a fever, at Havana, Cuba). Lucy-8 KELLAR married second to Daniel F. GARDNER ++ on 8 Oct 1881. He was the son of Thomas GARDNER and Sarah BERRY, and was born 25 Jan 1825; died ___ (still living 1895). Lucy-8 KELLAR died 19 Nov 1895.

Child of Lucy-8 KELLAR and Captain Ambrose BROWN:
   Surname BROWN
   1529. Susan   born ca 18__; married Captain J. Bartlett STROUT/STUART
          Children: Ruth-10 and Paul-10 STROUT/STUART
             Note: There were 2 other children who died in infancy
             Reference: The GARDNER Family of Machias and Vicinity; published 18__
       ++ Daniel F. GARDNER was married first to Sarah S. LINCOLN, daughter of William LINCOLN and Leah LEIGHTON.
             Sarah was born 20 Dec 1826; died 7 Dec 1878. They had 7 children.

1017. CHARLES-8 DWELLEY, son of Frances U-8 FOSTER (James-6; Woodin-5; Benjamin-4;3; Isaac-2; Reginald-1) and James DWELLEY, was born ca 18__. He married __?__. Charles-8 DWELLEY was a school teacher, a farmer, a joiner, and a painter. The History of Machias by DRISKO (page 374) states " an all 'round, ever busy man."

Children of Charles-8 DWELLEY and __?__:
   Surname DWELLEY
   1530. Raymond   born ca 18__   1531. Esther   born ca 18__   1532. Evelyn   born ca 18__

1018. MARGARET-8 HEINE see JOHN-7 FOSTER # 685

The Ninth American Generation

1128. ASA T-9 GAMAGE   see Nancy Thurston –8 FOSTER (# 780)

1143. ALEXANDER-9 GAMAGE, son of William-8 GAMAGE (Joshua, Jr-7; Elinor-6 FOSTER; Nathan-5; Caleb-4; 3; Abraham-2;Reginald-1) and Abigail THOMPSON, was born ca 1840 at Bristol, Maine. He married Mary BURNHAM on 30 June 1861 at Bristol. She was the daughter of Thomas BURNHAM and Emily H. BENNETT, and was born ca 1846 at Bristol..

Children of Alexander-9 GAMAGE and Mary BURNHAM:
    Surname GAMAGE
    1533. Charles Wilson   born 14 Apr 1866 Southport, Lincoln, ME
                                died 30 Mar 1947 Skowhegan, Somerset, Maine
    1534. Ellsworth   born ca 1868 Southport, ME   1535. Nora   born ca 1870 Maine

1168. ELIZABETH-9 NORTON, daughter of Mary-8 FOSTER (Francis-7; Nathan-6; 5; Caleb-4; 3; Abraham-2; Reginald-1) and Joseph P. NORTON, was born 17 May 1832. She married first to Elisha SNOW ca 18__. She married second to Henry METCALF ca 18__. He was the son of _?_ METCALF.

Child of Elizabeth-9 NORTON and Elisha SNOW:
    Surname SNOW
    1536. LaForest   born ca 1859; married Kate QUINN (she born ca 1859; died ____)
Child of Elizabeth-9 NORTON and Henry METCALF:
    Surname METCALF
    1537. Elizabeth   born ca 18__; 1m. _?_ CHEEVER; 2m. William NEEDHAM (no issue)

1169. SARAH F-9 NORTON, sister of above, was born 5 Apr 1834. She married Edgar MAKER ca 18__. He was the son of ___ MAKER, and was born ca 18__; died ____.

Children of Sarah-9 NORTON and Edgar MAKER:
    Surname MAKER
    1538. Horace   born ca 18__; died ___ unmarried
    1539. Eugenia   born ca 18__; married Samuel STEWART (2 sons)
    1540. Mary   born ca 18__; died ____ unmarried

1174. HORACE FOSTER-9 NORTON, brother of above, was born 19 March 1843. He married Asenath ELWELL on 18 Apr 1868. She was the daughter of ____ ELWELL, and was born 9 Apr 1848; died 1 Jan 1925. Horace-9 NORTON died 29 Nov 1911.

Children of Horace-9 NORTON and Asenath ELWELL:
    Surname NORTON
    1541. Arthur Herbert   born 19 Apr 1870; married Emma Lydia HACKER 3 Aug 1899   (EOL)
    1542. Mary Belle   born 19 Dec 1871; died 8 Apr 1934
    1543. Clara Minerva   born 26 May 1873; married Nelson PATENAUDE; died 1940
    1544. Ralph Horace   born 10 June 1875; married Alice Iola HADLOCK 19 Jan 1904
                               ch: a dau who d y; and Horace Eugene-11 NORTON born 19 Jan 1909
    1545. Hannah Grace   born 15 July 1877; died ___; unmarried
    1546. Fred A.   born 9 Dec 1879; died ____; unmarried
    1547. Susan   born 31 Mar 1882; married Edward POPE
  + 1548. WILLIAM JOHN born 8 Apr 1883; married Effie COMSTOCK
    1549. Ruth Valla   born 22 Apr 1892; died ____; unmarried

1175. RUBY ANN/ANNIE RUBY-9 NORTON, sister of above, was born 9 July 1845. She married the Reverend Greenfield Harrison BOWIE ca 18__. He was born ca 1843; died ____. Ruby Ann-9 NORTON died 25 Apr 1920.

Children of Ruby Ann-9 NORTON and Rev Greenfield BOWIE:

Surname BOWIE	(children born Phippsburg, Sagadahoc, Maine)		
1550. Frank	born ca 1867	1554. Kate	born ca 18__
+1551. EMMA NORTON born 18 Jan 1869		1555. Horace Elkanah	born 22 Oct 1874
married Charles Edward LILLEY 3 June 1896		1556. son	born ca 18__
1552. Harry	born ca 18__	1557. son	born ca 18__
1553. dau	born ca 18__		

1180. SUSAN A-9 FOSTER, daughter of Horace-8 FOSTER (Francis-7; Nathan-6; 5; Caleb-4; 3; Abraham-2; Reginald-1) and Nancy LIBBY, was born 30 Nov 1849 at Machiasport, Maine. She married Judah RICE on 18 Jan 1868. He was the son of Benjamin RICE and Jane LARRABEE, and was born 18 Jan 1843, Machiasport, ME; died 30 March 1922 at Northfield, ME. Susan-9 FOSTER died there 27 Nov 1912.

Children of Susan-9 FOSTER and Judah RICE:

Surname RICE	Reference: FOSTER/RICE Bruce E. LIBBY, Augusta, Maine		
1558. Edwin A.	born 24 Oct 1868	1559. Clara	born 20 June 1870
1560. William W.	born 11 Oct 1871 Machiasport, ME; died 21 Mar 1892 Centerville, ME		
1561. Merton A.	born 22 Apr 1873 Machiasport		
1562. Annie B.	born 10 Jan 1875; married Wellington E.CALER/KALER 28 Aug 1892		
1563. Ernest O.	born 30 Jan 1880		
+ 1564. ELMER H.	born 2 Apr 1882; married Frances C. ARCHER		
	(she born 7 Sep 1887 Wesley, ME; died 29 Mar 1972 Bangor, ME)		
1565. Clyde Garvey	born 21 Nov 1883 New Portland, ME; died 30 Apr 1962 Northfield, Maine		
	married Etta Mary BURNS 22 Sep 1922 (she born 24 Jul 1885; died 25 Apr 1958 Bangor, ME)		
1566. Virgil W.	born 10 Sep 1885; married Vesta Beulah DILL 19 Mar 1914; died 9 Apr 1965		
1567. Thurman C.	born 7 Mar 1887; married Mabel H. LUBERHATT		
	(she born 18 Nov 1895 Wesley, ME; died 7 June 1922 Marshfield, ME)		
1568. Benjamin Harrison born 9 Feb 1893; died 18 Aug 1893 Centerville, Maine			
1569. Grover Cleveland born 9 Feb 1893; died 25 Mar 1893 Centerville, Maine			

1183. ANNIE M-9 FOSTER, sister of above, was born 27 Sept 1855 at Machiasport, Washington County, Maine. She married James Alvin FLYNN on 3 June 1875. He was the son of Hiram Marston FLYNN and Phoebe TUPPER, and was born 27 Feb 1852; died 12 July 1938.

Children of Annie-9 FOSTER and James FLYNN:

Surname FLYNN	
1570. Idella	born ca 1876; d y
1571. Bessie Grace	born 10 Oct 1877; married William Corthell DINSMORE
	(he born ca 1879 Machiasport, Maine)
1572. Carl	born 3 Mar 1880; marr. Carrie MUNRO (of New Haven, CT) on 12 May 1905
1573. Alta	born 10 Nov 1882; married Frank TRAFTON 12 Dec 1905
1574. Howard A.	born 13 May 1885; married Cora-10 FOSTER (# 1580)
	(she dau/o Eben-9 FOSTER (# 1202) and Laura HUNTLEY)
	(he a member of SAR; his # 46544; New York # 4849)
1575. Hammond	born 11 Nov 1887; married Lucy GUPTILL 23 Jan 1915; died Feb 1970 ME.
1576. Fred	born 4 June 1894; married Maria SMALL 10 May 1917
	(they were both lost aboard the Schooner *DEAN E BROWN* Sept 1917 in the Gulf of Mexico)
1577. Florence	born 10 Nov 1898; died 9 Mar 1997 Rockland, Maine
	married John G. SNOW (of Rockland, ME) 10 Nov 1919

1202. EBEN-9 FOSTER, son of James-8 FOSTER (Nathan-7; 6; 5; Caleb-4; 3; Abraham-2; Reginald-1) and Mary Ann-7 LIBBY, was born 27 Apr 1857 at Machiasport, Maine. He married Laura HUNTLEY on 30 Dec 1882 at Cutler, Maine. She was the daughter of ____ HUNTLEY of Cutler, Maine, and was born 20 Apr 1861; died 1 Apr 1915 at Boston, MA. Eben-9 FOSTER died ca 1952.

Children of Eben-9 FOSTER and Laura HUNTLEY:
    Surname FOSTER

1578. Blanche	born 3 Mar 1883;; died 24 Sept 1918
	married Lt. Roscoe G. SANBORN 7 Jan 1909 Machiasport, Maine
1579. Edwin H.	born 9 Nov 1885; married Florence HEFFRON
	(he was lost in the sinking of the *USS SIXEOLA* on 28 Feb 1919)
1580. Cora	born 23 Sept 1887; married Howard-9 FLYNN (# 1574) on 7 Nov 1907
	(he son of Annie-9 FOSTER and James A. FLYNN)

1210. SARAH JOSEPHINE-9 GARDNER, daughter of Margaret-8 FOSTER (Nathan-7; 6; 5; Caleb-4; 3; Abraham-2; Reginald-1) and George GARDNER, was born ca 1846/47 at Machiasport, Maine. She married Sewell C. TRAFTON ca 18__. He was the son of Joseph TRAFTON and Temperance ACKLEY, and was born ca 18__; died ____. Sewell TRAFTON was a seaman before moving to Syracuse, NY where he worked as a fireman on the New York Central Railroad. They resided 28 Slocum Ave., Syracuse, NY.

Children of Sarah Josephine-9 GARDNER and Sewell TRAFTON:
    Surname TRAFTON

+ 1581. DELIA E.	born Nov 1864, Maine; married Herbert John NORTH
	(he born 2 Apr 1860 London, ENG; died ____, NY)

Note: Herbert NORTH, the son of John NORTH and Mary Susannah SPENCER, emigrated to America in 1864.
He was a naturalized citizen, and worked in Syracuse, NY as a Patternmaker.

1582. Nettie M.	born ca 1869/70 Maine
1583. Freddie B.	born Aug 1879 Syracuse, Onondaga County, NY

Sarah Josephine-9 GARDNER

1211. MARIETTA/HENRIETTA-9 GARDNER, called " Etta ", sister of above, was born ca 1849/50 at Machiasport, Maine. She married George W-4 LOOMIS ca 1867. He was the son of Eli-3 LOOMIS (Thomas-2; Timothy-1) and Mary COUSINS, and was born ca 1848 at Hudson, Columbia County, NY. They resided Syracuse, NY., where he worked for the New York Central Railroad as an Engineer.

Child of Etta-9 GARDNER and George W. LOOMIS:
    Surname LOOMIS
    1584. Charles Walter   born 1875 poss at Hudson, Columbia County, NY

1212. GEORGE AUGUSTUS-9 DRISKO see Drisko section # 1164

1215. NATHAN FOSTER-9 HOLWAY, son of Sarah G-8 FOSTER (Nathan-7; 6; 5; Caleb-4; 3; Abraham-2; Reginald-1) and William-4 HOLWAY, was born ca 1838, probably at East Kennebec, Maine . He married Harriet A. MOORE 1 Jan 1862. She was the daughter of _____ MOORE, and was born ca 18__.

Children of Nathan Foster-9 HOLWAY and Harriet MOORE:
    Surname HOLWAY

+ 1585. GEORGE M.	born 17 May 1863 Machias, ME; married Fannie SPINNEY/SPRINGER 28 July 1884 Cape Elizabeth, ME		
1586. Albert	born ca 1864/65		
1587. Lendall C.	born 28 Sept 1866	1589. Edith M.	born 28 Jan 1872
1588. Keller F.	born 2 Feb 1869	1590. Nathan	born ca 187_

1216. EMILY J-9 HOLWAY, sister of above, was born ca 1839/40. She married J. Hamilton SCHOPPEE ca 18__. He was the son of _____ SCHOPPEE, and was born ca 18__; died ____.

Children of Emily-9 HOLWAY and J. Hamilton SCHOPPEE:
    Surname SCHOPPEE

1591. Abbie	born ca 18__; married Charles BICKFORD (Ch: Katherine-11 BICKFORD)
1592. Elizabeth	born ca 18__; married Fred MITCHELL (Ch: Margaret-11 MITCHELL)
1593. Kate	born ca 18__

1218. MARY E-9 HOLWAY, sister of above, was born ca 1842. She married Charles A. HILL ++ ca 18__. He was the son of Hezekiah HILL and Elizabeth ELSEMORE, and was born ca 18__; died ____.

Children of Mary E-9 HOLWAY and Charles A. HILL:
    Surname HILL

1594. Sarah	born ca 18__; married Fred COLCORD (Ch: Elmer-11 COLCORD)		
1595. Martha	born ca 18__; married Charles BULLOCK		
1596. William H.	born ca 18__; married Cora BEVERLY		
1597. Blanche	born ca 18__	1598. F. Herbert	born ca 18__

++ Information about Charles A. HILL

JOSEPH- HILL, was probably son of Joseph HILL and Abigail LIBBY,and was born 15 Sept 1743 Scarborough, ME. He was one of five brothers who went to Machias, from Scarborough, ca 1763.64. He settled at Gardner's Lake, which later became the Town of Whiting. He married Sarah WISWELL, and for a few years they lived in New Brunswick where their son Enoch- HILL was born 23 Nov 1775. They returned to Maine and Enoch- HILL married Hepzibeth/Elizabeth GARDNER and had 16 children, including Hezekiah- HILL, who was born ca ____; and married Elizabeth ELSMORE. They were the parents of Loring; CHARLES; Benjamin and Elizabeth HILL.

1220. ELLA-9 HOLWAY, sister of above, was born ca 1847. She married Lowell CASWELL ca 18__. He was the son of ___ CASWELL, and was born ca 18__; died ___.

Children of Ella-9 HOLWAY and Lowell CASWELL:
    Surname CASWELL

1599. Mina	born ca 18__	1601. George	born ca 18__
1600. Edna	born ca 18__	1602. Katherine	born ca 18__

1221. SARAH HELEN-9 HOLWAY, sister of above, was born ca 1848/49. She married Charles H. SCHOPPEE ca 18__. He was the son of _____ SCHOPPEE, and was born ca 18__; died ____.

Children of Sarah H-9 HOLWAY and Charles SCHOPPEE:
    Surname SCHOPPEE

1603. John H.	born ca 18__; married Rena STODDARD (Ch: Paul and Hollis-11 SCHOPPEE)		
1604. Emily	born ca 18__	1606. Eugene	born ca 18__
+ 1605. BESSIE	born ca 18__; married A. J. COLE		

Children of Sarah H-9 HOLWAY, continued:
    Surname SCHOPPEE

1607. Lewis	born ca 18__	1610. Fred	born 29 Jan 1885; died Dec 1969
1608. James	born ca 18__	1611. Millard	born 24 May 1886; died Mar 1963
1609. Ella	born ca 18__	1612. Nathan	born ca 18__

1222. CAROLINE-9 HOLWAY " Caddie ", sister of above, was born ca 1850. She married Olin TUPPER ca 18__. He was the son of _____ TUPPER, and was born ca 18__; died _____.

Children of Caroline-9 HOLWAY and Olin TUPPER:
    Surname TUPPER:

1613. Helen	born ca 18__	1614. Ethel	born ca 18__	1615. Hazel	born ca 18__

1223. WILLIAM B-9 HOLWAY, brother of above, was born ca 1853. He married Isabel BRADEEN ca 18__. She was the daughter of _____ BRADEEN , and was born ca 18__; died _____.

Children of William-9 HOLWAY and Isabel BRADEEN:
    Surname HOLWAY

1616. Adelaide	born ca 18__	1617. Eva	born ca 18__	1618. Alice	born ca 18__

1226. FRANK H-9 HOLWAY, brother of above, was born ca 18__ (after 1860). He married Minerva BRYANT ca 18__. She was the daughter of _____ BRYANT, and was born ca 18__; died _____.

Children of Frank-9 HOLWAY and Minerva BRYANT:
    Surname HOLWAY

1619. Ethel born 18__	1620. Claude born 18_	1621. Mildred born 18__	1622. Frank born 18__

1227. LEON A-9 LIBBY, son of Hannah-8 FOSTER (Nathan-7; 6; 5; Caleb-4; 3; Abraham-2; Reginald-1) and Henry Allen-7 LIBBY, was born 10 June 1853 at Machiasport, Maine. He married Lucy E-7 LIBBY on 6 Aug 1874. She was the daughter of Deacon Mariner F-6 LIBBY and Mary Cary NASON.

Children of Leon-9 LIBBY and Lucy-7 LIBBY:
    Surname LIBBY

1623. Leon Leroy	born 20 Mar 1877	1624. Henry Henderson born 20 Dec 1879

1239. WILLIAM H-9 BATES, son of Maria-8 CHALONER (Louise-7 FOSTER; Jacob-6; Col. Benjamin-5; Benjamin-4; 3; Isaac-2; Reginald-1) and Winslow BATES, Esq., and was born ca 18__. He married ?.

Children of William-9 BATES and __?__:
    Surname BATES

1625. Janet born ca 18__	1626. Virgil born ca 18__	1627. Randolph born ca 18__

1240. JOSEPH C-9 BATES, brother of above, was born ca 18__. He married Harriet Augusta PEARSON of Boston, MA ca 18__. She was the daughter of _____ PEARSON, and was born ca 18__; died _____.

Children of Joseph-9 BATES and Harriet PEARSON:
    Surname BATES

1628. George	born ca 18__	1630. Edith	born ca 18__
1629. Herbert	born ca 18__	1631. Theodore	born ca 18__
	married Eda TIBBETTS of Lincoln, NEB		

1243. JOHN F-9 TALBOT, son of William Henry-8 TALBOT (Mary-7 FOSTER; John-6; Benjamin-5; 4; 3; Isaac-2; Reginald-1) and Martha POOR, was born ca 18__. He married Georgie E. FISHER of Foxboro, MA on _____. She was the daughter of _____ FISHER, and was born ca 18__; died _____.

Children of John-9 TALBOT and Georgie FISHER:
   Surname TALBOT
    1632. Frederic W. born ca 18__   1634. Florence born ca 18__   1636. Richard   born ca 18__
    1633. Edward   born ca 18__; d y   1635. Agnes   born ca 18_

1245. GEORGE A-9 TALBOT, brother of above, was born ca 18__. He married Ida GRAHAM ca 18__.
Children of George-9 TALBOT and Ida GRAHAM:
   Surname TALBOT
    1637. William A.   born ca 18__   1639. Ralph P.   born ca 18__
    1638. Emma   born ca 18__   1640. Mary   born ca 18__; res Kansas City, MO

1247. MARTHA-9 TALBOT, sister of above, was born ca 18__. She married Charles CUSHMAN.
Children of Martha-9 TALBOT and Charles CUSHMAN:
   Surname CUSHMAN
    1641. Barbara   born ca 18__   1643. Elizabeth born ca 18__
    1642. Martha   born ca 18__   resided South Andover, MA

1249. MARY H-9 TALBOT, daughter of John Coffin-8 TALBOT, Jr. (Mary-7 FOSTER; John-6;
Benjamin-5; 4; 3; Isaac-2; Reginald-1) and Clara WASS, was born ca 18__ at Lubec, Maine. She married
Prentiss M. WOODMAN, Jr. of Minneapolis, MN ca 18__. He was the son of Prentiss M. WOODMAN
and Elizabeth __?__, and was born ___; baptized 29 Oct 1846 at New Gloucester, Cumberland, Maine.
Children of Mary H-9 TALBOT and Prentiss WOODMAN, Jr.:
   Surname WOODMAN   1644. Prentiss   born ca 18__; d y   1645. Joseph C.   born ca 18__

1258. THOMAS L-9 TALBOT, son of George FOSTER-8 TALBOT (Mary-7 FOSTER; John-6;
Benjamin-5; 4 ;3; Isaac-2; Reginald-1) and   Elizabeth LINCOLN, was born ca 18__. He married Alice B.
SPRING ca 18__. She was the daughter of ____ SPRING, and was born ca 18__; died ____.
Children of Thomas-9 TALBOT and Alice SPRING:
   Surname TALBOT   1646. Edith L.   born ca 18__   1647. Samuel S.   born ca 18__

1263. FREDERIC FROTHINGHAM-9 TALBOT, brother of above, was born ca 18__; baptized 25 Mar
1864 at Portland, Cumberland County, Maine. He married Mary FRANK ca 18__. She was the daughter
of ____ FRANK, and was born ca 18__; died ____.
Children of Frederic-9 TALBOT and Mary FRANK:
   Surname TALBOT   1648. George F. born ca 18__   1649. Melvin F.   born ca 18__

1265. LUCINDA M-9 STUART, daughter of Susan-8 AVERY (Betsey-7 FOSTER; Levi-6; Benjamin-5;
4; 3; Isaac-2; Reginald-1) and James STUART , was born ca 18__ at Machiasport, ME. She married
Harlan P. SMITH ca 18__.
Children of Lucinda-9 STUART and Harlan SMITH:
   Surname SMITH
    1650. Susan   born ca 18__   1651. Frank   born ca 18__
               married George RICE   1652. Lillian/Lizzie born ca 18__

1272. EDWINA-9 AVERY, daughter of L. Trescott-8 AVERY (Betsey-7 FOSTER; Levi-6; Benjamin-5;
4; 3; Isaac-2; Reginald-1) and Sarah HOYT, was born ca 18__. She married George W. POPE of East
Machias, Maine ca 18___. He was the son of Colonel WIlliam POPE and Peggy Dawes BILLINGS, and
was born ca 1832; died 9 Dec 1875. Edwina-9 AVERY died ____. (still living 1903).

Children of Edwina-9 AVERY and George W. POPE:
   Surname POPE
    1653. Grace B   born ca 18__; married Capt. Benno von HEINECCINA
              (he was in the Prussian Army- they resided at Berlin, Germany (no issue)
+ 1654. EDITH   born ca 18__; marr Wallace BUELL   1655. Georgia born ca 18__; res Brookline, MA

1287. FRANK H-9 WISWELL, son of Lydia Drusilla-8 FOSTER (Benjamin-7; Deacon Samuel-6; Benjamin-5; 4; 3; Isaac-2; Reginald-1) and John WISWELL, was born ca 1846 at East Machias, Maine. He married Antoinette CHALONER ca 18__ . She was the daughter of Benjamin Gooch CHALONER and Sarah GOOCH, and was born ca 1845; Machias; died ____ .

Children of Frank-9 WISWELL and Antoinette CHALONER:
  Surname WISWELL
  1656. Rev. Thomas C.   born ca 18__; married Hessie/Bessie DOYLE (1 ch: died in infancy)
  1657. Julia M.   born ca 18__; married Arthur SANBORN(E) (# 1527)
                         (he son of Thomas M. SANBORNE and Helen CHASE)
  1658. Hovey M.   born ca 18__; 1m. Nettie STEVES 10 Dec 1900 East Machias, ME
                         1 ch : Sarah C. WISWELL ; marr. Henry C. FESSENDEN 3 July 1926 Machias
                         2m. Inez R. McLAIN 31 May 1934 (she of South Portland, ME)

1291. BENJAMIN FOSTER-9 KILBY, son of Julia E-8 FOSTER (Benjamin-7; Samuel-6; Benjamin-5; 4; 3; Isaac-2; Reginald-1) and Charles H. KILBY, was born 1 March 1852 at Dennysville, Maine. He married Lucy CORTHELL ca 18__ . She was the daughter of ____ CORTHELL, and was born ca 18__ .

Children of Benjamin-9 KILBY and Lucy CORTHELL:
  Surname KILBY
  1659. Edith L.   born ca 18__; married Charles C. RUMERY 17 June 1907 Eastport, ME
  1660. Marcia M.   born ca 18__; married Frank C. JEWETT 4 Apr 1905 Eastport, ME
  1661. Mary   born ca 18__; d y

1292. CHARLES HENRY-9 KILBY, brother of above, was born 3 July 1854 at Dennysville, Maine. He married Eliza COX ca 18__ . She was the daughter of ____ COX, and was born ca 18__; died ____ .

Children of Charles Henry-9 KILBY and Eliza COX:
  Surname KILBY
  1662. Julia   born ca 18__   1663. Gertrude   born ca 18__
  1664. Angus M.   born ca 18__; married Gertrude M. COX of Perry, ME 26 Nov 1902
  1665. Alice W.   born 12 June 1880; died June 1968
                      married Dana Estes EDWARDS 26 July 1904 So. Portland, ME
                      (he son/o Theodore Brown EDWARDS and Lovinia Angie BANGS
                      (born 10 July 1883 Gorham, ME; died July 1967)
  1666. Richard F.   born ca 18__; married Ella F. PETTINGILL 25 Sept 1906 So. Portland, ME
  1667. Frank C.   born ca 18__; married Cora M. ALLEN 9 May 1908 So. Portland, ME
                      (she born 3 Sept 1889; died July 1973 South Portland, ME)
  1668. Ruth   born ca 18__; married A. I. DYER 23 Feb 1907 So. Portland, ME
  1669. Alden   born ca 18__

1293. EMILY U-9 KILBY, sister of above, was born 30 Oct 1856 at Dennysville, Maine. She married Henry Howard KILBY 7 June 1884. He was the son of Benjamin KILBY and his 1st wife Eliza RICE, and was born 4 Feb 1855 at Dennysville, ME; died ____ .

Children of Emily-9 KILBY and Henry KILBY:
  Surname KILBY
  1670. Horace   born 10 Mar 1885; died Mar 1966
  1671. Esther T. born 18__; married William WATSON 25 Aug 1926 Dennysville, Maine
  1672. Hope   born ca 18__

1296. MARIA-9 HOBART, daughter of Drusilla-8 FOSTER (Benjamin-7; Samuel-6; Benjamin-5; 4; 3; Isaac-2; Reginald-1) and Charles HOBART, was born ca 18__ . She married Oscar CHALONER ca 18__ . He was the son of ____ CHALONER, and was born ca 18__; died ____ .

Children of Maria-9 HOBART and Oscar CHALONER:
    Surname CHALONER
    1673. Ruth   born ca 18__   + 1676. SIDNEY   born ca 18__
    1674. Amy   born ca 18__   married Ada MORONG
    1675. Earl   born ca 18__

1300. CLARA-9 INGRAHAM, daughter of Rebecca-8 FOSTER (Alfred-7; Samuel-6; Benjamin-5; 4; 3; Isaac-2; Reginald-1) and George INGRAHAM, was born ca 18__. She married __?__ BELL ca 18__.

Children of Clara-9 INGRAHAM and __?__ BELL:
    Surname BELL
    1677. Aubrey   born ca 18__; d y   1679. Edna   born ca 18__
    1678. Albert   born ca 18__   1680. Rae   born ca 18__

1303. DEBORAH R-9 FOSTER, daughter of Solomon M-8 FOSTER (John Woodin-7; Wooden-6; 5; Benjamin-4; 3; Isaac-2; Reginald-1) and Elizabeth WILDER, was born 21 Feb 1832 at Dennysville, ME. She married Albert Robinson LINCOLN on 11 Feb 1857 . He was the son of William LINCOLN (Otis) and Elizabeth THOMPSON, and was born 3 Oct 1831 Dennysville, Washington Co., ME; died 18 Oct 1899 at Dennysville, Deborah-8 FOSTER died 3 Mar 1901.

Children of Deborah-8 FOSTER and Albert R. LINCOLN:
    Surname LINCOLN   (all children born at Dennysville, Maine)
    1681. Elizabeth Maria born 11 Nov 1857
    1682. William   born ca 1858
    1683. Albert E.   born 15 Oct 1859; married Ellen M. JONES; died 1 Mar 1920
        Ch: Albert R. LINCOLN born 13 Nov 1899; marr Marcia Ricker ANDERSON; died 29 Aug 1984
    1684. Harry F.   born 30 Aug 1867; died 24 Sept 1931 OR
    1685. Olive E.   born 5 Oct 1875

1309.   ALMIRA/ELMIRA-9 FOSTER, daughter of Elias-8 FOSTER (John Woodin-7; 6; Woodin-5; Benjamin-4; 3; Isaac-2; Reginald-1) and Hannah HANSON, was born ca 1825, possibly at Bocala, New Brunswick. She married ____ HANSON ca 18__.

Child of Almira/Elmira-9 FOSTER and __?__ HANSON:
    Surname HANSON
    1686. Alma   born ca 18__ at St. David, New Brunswick; married __?__ POLK
        Child: Eva V-11 POLK born ca ____; married ____ AMIDON
                Reference: Eva V. AMIDON, 636 Salisbury Street, Holden MA 01520

1311. SAMUEL ALONZO-9 HOWE, son of Gilbert D-8 HOWE, was born 23 Feb 1833 at East Machias, Maine. He married Harriet Melissa Thompson SIMPSON on 6 Jan 1851. She was the daughter of Andrew SIMPSON and Clarissa Hanlow NOYES, and was born 31 Mar 1832 at East Machias; died 7 Apr 1910 at Shamokawa, Wahkiakum County, Washington. Samuel A-9 HOWE died 27 Dec 1907 at Astoria, Oregon.

Children of Samuel-9 HOWE and Harriet SIMPSON:
    Surname HOWE
    1687. Viola E.   born 11 Apr 1851 East Machias, ME; died 8 Feb 1924 Hailey, Blaine Co., ID
                           1m. David WEST 22 Feb 1868, OR (div); 2m. George SHIRLEY Apr 1889
    1688. Etta Mae "Ettie" born 23 June 1866 Clatsop Co., OR; marr John C. ELEASON (born 1862 OR)
    1689. Orin   born 29 Nov 1873 Clatsop County, Oregon

1346. CHARLOTTE-9 PATTANGALL, daughter of Laura-8 HARRIS (Drusilla-7 FOSTER; Moses-6; Woodin-5; Benjamin-4; 3; Isaac-2; Reginald-1) and N. Page PATTANGALL, was born ca 18__. She married George L. WHITTEN ca 18__. He was the son of ____ WHITTEN, and was born ca 18__.

Children of Charlotte-9 PATTANGALL and George WHITTEN:
  Surname WHITTEN
  1690. Nathan   born ca 18__   1691. Mae   born ca 18__   1692. George   born ca 18__

1357. BENJAMIN F-9 HARRIS, JR. , son of Benjamin-8 HARRIS (Cynthia-7 FOSTER; Moses-6; Woodin-5; Benjamin-4; 3; Isaac-2; Reginald-1) and Elizabeth-4 HANSCOM, was born ca 18__. He married first to Nettie HAMMOND ca 18__. He married second to Jennie FIELD ca 18__.

Children of Benjamin-9 HARRIS, Jr. and Nettie HAMMOND:
  Surname HARRIS
  1693. Samuel   born ca 18__   1695. William born ca 18__   1697. Josie   born ca 18__
  1694. Elvira   born ca 18__   1696. Loring   born ca 18__   1698. Elizabeth born ca 18__

  1699. Benjamin F. born 17 Mar 1872; died Oct 1967 Orrs Island, Maine
                     married Meta Kennier WILLSON of NY, NY on 1 Oct 1903
                     (she born ca 1874 Ireland; died 25 Oct 1958 Portland, ME)

1358. ELIZABETH-9 HARRIS, sister of above, was born ca 18__. She married Fred TAYLOR ca 18__.
Children of Elizabeth-9 HARRIS and Fred TAYLOR:
  Surname TAYLOR
  1700. Leland   born 3 Dec 1910, ME; died 13 Dec 1992 Oxford, Maine
  1701. Edith   born ca 18__   1702. Harris   born ca 18__

1386. MARILLA F-9 STRONG, daughter of Deborah-8 FOSTER (James-7; Paul-6; Woodin-5; Benjamin-4;3; Isaac-2; Reginald-1) and David E. STRONG, was born ca 1849 at Alma, Albert, New Brunswick, Canada. She married Stephen Stiles HOAR on 2 Feb 1885 at Alma, NB. He was the son of George Mills HOAR and Isabel STILES, and was born 27 Oct 1848 Hopewell Hills, NB; died 15 July 1927 at Shell Lake, Washburn, WI. Marilla F-9 STRONG died 6 Nov 1890 at Shell Lake, WI.

Children of Marilla-9 STRONG and Stephen HOAR:
  Surname HOAR
  1703. Harry Herbert   born 16 Oct 1885 Alma, Albert, NB; died 4 Aug 1959 Pine City, MN
  1704. David Eaton   born 13 Sep 1886 Shell Lake, WI; died 20 Jan 1979 Little Falls, MN

1439. JENNIE-9 GETCHELL, daughter of Delia-9 CARY (Eliza-7 FOSTER; Paul-6; Woodin-5; Benjamin-4; 3; Isaac-2; Reginald-1) and Stephen J. GETCHELL, was born ca 18__. She married Harvey LEITH

Children of Jennie-9 GETCHELL and Harvey LEITH:
  Surname LEITH
  1705. Fred   born ca 18__   1706. Delia   born ca 18__   1707. Mary   born ca 18__

1444. EDWIN FOSTER-9 CARY, son of Martin Luther-8 CARY (Eliza W-7 FOSTER; Moses-6; Woodin-5; Benjamin-4; 3; Isaac-2; Reginald-1) and Mary Ann WATTLES, was born 13 Apr 1869 at Providence, Rhode Island. He married Clara Louise PERRY on 14 Sept 1898 at Reheboth, MA. She was the daughter of Charles PERRY and Anna Powell PIERCE, and was born 18 July 1874, MA. Edwin Foster-9 CARY died 12 June 1942.

Children of Edwin Foster-9 CARY and Clara PERRY:
  Surname CARY
  1708. Hope Shepardson born ca 1902 Providence, Rhode Island
  1709. Eleanor Foster   born 24 July 1904 Providence, RI; died 17 May 1979 E. Providence, RI
                          married Robert Spencer PRESTON 11 Aug 1928 Seekonk, MA (he born ca 1900 Providence)

1460. LAURA-9 GRAY, daughter of Julia-8 DAY (Mary-7 FOSTER; Elias-6; Woodin-5; Benjamin-4;3;

Isaac-2; Reginald-1) and Sheldon GRAY, was born 15 May 1830 at Wesley, Washington County, Maine. She married first to James Randolph BROTHERTON on 5 Dec 1870. She married 2nd to Richard OLNEY.

Children of Laura-9 GRAY and James BROTHERTON:
Surname BROTHERTON
1710. Irene   born 7 Mar 1872; married James ZANDER
1711. Harry   born 10 June 1873; died 18 Dec 1887

1462. HERBERT L-9 DAY, son of Elias-8 DAY (Mary-7 FOSTER, Elias-6; Woodin-5; Benjamin-4; 3; Isaac-2; Reginald-1) and Joan STANCHFIELD, was born 22 Apr 1855 at Wesley, Maine. He married Rebecca E. McRAE on 3 Aug 1878. She was the daughter of Asa T. McRAE and Margaret MUNSON, and was born ___.   Herbert-9 DAY manufactured bedsprings and mattresses at Bangor, Maine.

Children of Herbert L-9 DAY and Rebecca McRAE:
Surname DAY
1712. Nellie   born 22 Nov 1879; married Horace WELCH 27 Mar 1901
1713. Cora C.   born 9 Nov 1882
1714. Arthur L.   born 17 June 1885; married Grace BLAKE 25 June 1907; died Apr 1971 FL.
1715. Clarence L.   born 14 Apr 1892; died Dec 1970   1716. Hazel E.   born 20 Aug 1899

1463. HIRAM F. DAY, brother of above, was born 17 Mar 1858. He married first to Ida M. ARCHER on 23 Dec 1879. She was the daughter of Samuel ARCHER and Harriet WILLIAMS, and was born ___; died 9 Apr 1884 (after giving birth to her only child). He married second to Mary J. McRAE on 31 Dec 1885. She was the daughter of Asa T. McRAE and Margaret MUNSON. Hiram-9 DAY was a Baptist minister, and died 18 Dec 1901.

Child of Hiram F. DAY and Ida M. ARCHER:
Surname DAY   1717. Ida M. born 6 Apr 1884 ; a trained nurse; resided at Augusta, ME

1466. SHELDON G-9 DAY, brother of above, was born 22 Apr 1866 at Wesley, Maine. He married Ida/Ada M. FOSTER on 8 Nov 1899. She was the daughter of Nathan O. FOSTER and Sarah J. WHALEN. He was a farmer at Wesley, Maine.

Children of Sheldon-9 DAY and Ida M. FOSTER:
Surname DAY   (first child born Machiasport. ME; 2nd born Wesley, Maine)
1718. Winifred M.   born 18 Sept 1900   1719. Kenneth Foster   born 31 Oct 1901

1467. MANLEY E-9 DAY, brother of above, was born 17 July 1868 at Wesley, Maine. He married Abbie M. WEBBER of Houlton, ME on 20 Mar 1890. Manley-9, a farmer, died 14 Feb 1901 at Bangor, ME.

Children of Manley-9 DAY and Abbie WEBBER:
Surname DAY   (all children born at Wesley, Maine)
1720. Pearl Florence born 5 June 1891   1723. Ruth Ann   born 6 June 1896
1721. Karl Webber   born 20 Feb 1893; died Dec 1971   1724. Paul Hiram born 17 June 1898
1722. Merrit Doris   born 6 May 1894

1472. JULIA ADELIA-9 DAY, daughter of Lewis-8 DAY (Mary-7 FOSTER; Elias-6; Woodin-5; Benjamin-4;3; Isaac-2; Reginald-1) and Mary Melancy ELSEMORE, was born 9 Feb 1863 at Wesley, Maine. She married Fred RICH on 1 Nov 1879 at Chico, CA.

Children of Julia A-9 DAY and Fred RICH:
Surname RICH
1725. Walter   born 20 Dec 1881 Springfield, OR; died 3 May 1896
1726. Pearl A.   born 18 Sept 1885 Butte Meadows, CA

Children of Julia A-9 DAY, continued:
    Surname RICH
    1727. Harold   born 3 Mar 1888 Chico, CA   1728. Rex   born 3 May 1896 Springfield, OR

1474. FANNIE B-9 DAY, sister of above, was born 28 Nov 1867 at Wesley, Maine. She married Fred LAKE on 29 Nov 1888 at San Francisco, CA.
Children of Fannie-9 DAY and Fred LAKE:
    Surname LAKE

1729. Elsemore	born 27 Sept 1889	1732. Alice	born 28 Aug 1895
1730. Allen F.	born 4 June 1893	1733. Constance	born 10 Mar 1897
1731. Wesley	born 4 Aug 1894; d y	1734. Bernice B.	born July 1901

1477. LUCY E-9 DAY, daughter of John Willard-8 DAY (Mary-7 FOSTER; Elias-6; Woodin-5; Benjamin-4; 3; Isaac-2; Reginald-1) and Josephine GUPTILL, was born 18 Aug 1866. She married Charles DURLING of Crawford, ME. on 1 Oct 1883. She died 31 Jan 1894.

Children of Lucy E-9 DAY and Charles DURLING:
    Surname DURLING

1735. J. Willard	born 5 Dec 1885; married Elsie DAY 30 Sept 1905 Wesley, ME
	(she dau/o Josiah DAY and Maria BIRD)
1736. Walter	born 6 Jan 1888; died Sept 1966

1737. Flora	born 7 Mar 1890	1738. Hattie	born 18 Oct 1893

1478. ALTHEA/ELTHEA M-9 DAY, sister of above, was born 25 Apr 1867 at Wesley, Maine. She married Tholmena BROOKS of Steuben, ME on 28 June 1885.
Children of Althea-9 DAY and Tholmena BROOKS;
    Surname BROOKS

1739. Josephine	born 19 Feb 1886	1741. Stella M.	born 1 July 1893
	died 15 Dec 1892	1742. Lester H.	born 30 Aug 1897
1740. Samuel	born 8 June 1889	1743. Marjorie E.	born 8 July 1900

1479. CORRIN J-9 DAY, brother of above, was born 19 Feb 1869 at Wesley, Maine. He was the twin brother of Orrin (below). He married Carrie GUPTILL on 27 June 1891 at Wesley. She was the daughter of Alexander GUPTILL and Mehitable HOLMES.

Children of Corrin-9 Day and Carrie GUPTILL:
    Surname DAY   (all children born at Wesley, ME)
    1744. Harold   born 7 May 1892; died Oct 1978
    1745. Arnold   born 28 Jan 1895; died Apr 1969
    1746. Norris E.   born 5 Sept 1896; died June 1982 Bangor, ME
                              marr Florence I. MADDOCKS 25 June 1921 Bangor, ME
    1747. Alton   born 7 Oct 1899
    1748. Christine L.   born 3 Dec 1900; married Lowell R. HAYWARD 19 Oct 1919 Wesley, ME
    1749. Marcia J.   born 29 Sept 1904; married Harry P. HAYWARD 12 Jan 1920 Wesley, ME
    1750. Gertrude Gratto   born 30 Jan 1908; died 25 Aug 1999 Calais, Maine
                              married Rupert K. DAY 4 July 1928 Wesley, ME.
                              (he born 30 Mar 1903; died 8 May 1991 Calais, Maine)

1481. HORACE A-9 DAY, brother of above, was born 10 Oct 1873 at Wesley, ME. He married Lynnie M. HANSCOM of Crawford, ME on 22 Aug 1904. She was the daughter of Ellsworth HANSCOM and Angelina GRAY, and was born ___.
Children of Horace-9 DAY and Lynnie HANSCOM:
    Surname DAY   1751. Almon Wesley   born 23 Nov 1905; died 12 Jan 1906
    1752. Horace Hanscom born 16 Jan 1907; died 16 Jan 1907   1753. Phyllis Eileen born 8 June 1908

1488. LULU-9 DAY, daughter of Jacob Lincoln-8 DAY (Mary-7 FOSTER; Elias-6; Woodin-5; Benjamin-4; 3; Isaac-2; Reginald-1) and Lizzie HOLLINSWORTH, was born 10 Apr 1871 at Wesley, Maine. She married Lincoln BRIDGHAM on 11 Dec 1895.

Children of Lulu-9 DAY and Lincoln BRIDGHAM:

Surname BRIDGHAM

1754. Vera Geraldine	born 13 Aug 1898	1756. Laurel Justin	born 22 Jan 1904
1755. Harold Allison	born 23 Dec 1901	1757. Carl Edward	born 28 Oct 1906
			died 2 May 1998 Carmel, ME

1497. MINNIE-9 DAY, daughter of Frank O-8 DAY (Mary-7 FOSTER; Elias-6; Woodin-5; Benjamin-4; 3 ; Isaac-2; Reginald-1) and Jessie DURLING, was born 21 Mar 1878 at Wesley, Maine. She married Burton GROSS of East Thorndike, ME on 20 Jan 1897.

Children of Minnie-9 DAY and Burton GROSS:

Surname GROSS

1758. Jennie R.	born 1 Apr 1899	1761. Frank Wellington born 18 July 1906
1759. James Rufus	born 9 June 1901	died 26 Jan 1992 Sonoma, CA
1760. Rolland Day	born 4 Aug 1904	1762. Alice Marguerite born 29 Apr 1908
	married Olive GILBERT 27 Oct 1924	died 19 Mar 1909

1499. CORRIS-9 FOSTER, daughter of George-8 FOSTER (Elisha B-7; Elias-6; Woodin-5; Benjamin-4; 3; Isaac-2; Reginald-1) and Sarah PENNELL, was born ca 18__. She marr Llewellyn McGOULDRICK. .

Children of Corris-9 FOSTER and Llewellyn McGOULDRICK:

Surname McGOULDRICK

1763. Philip (twin) born ca 18__   1764. Paul (twin) born ca 18__   1765. Harris   born ca 18__

1512. LUCY-9 FOSTER, daughter of J. Kellar-8 FOSTER (Charles-7; James-6; Woodin-5; Benjamin-4; 3; Isaac-2; Reginald-1) and Augusta WHITTEMORE, was born ca 1869. She married Herbert Lincoln FENNO 1 Oct 1890. He was the son of Jesse FENNO and Mary SPEAR, and was born 12 Dec 1864 at Canton, MA.

Children of Lucy-9 FOSTER and Herbert FENNO:

Surname FENNO

1766. Mary   born ca 18__   1767. Jesse   born ca 18__   1768. Emma   born ca 18__

1516. ELIZABETH-9 CHASE, daughter of Loring-8 CHASE (Louisa-7 FOSTER; James-6; Woodin-5; Benjamin-4; 3; Isaac-2; Reginald-1) and Amanda ENNIS, was born ca 18__. She married Charles GRAY.

Children of Elizabeth-9 CHASE and Charles GRAY:

Surname GRAY

1769. Lucy	born ca 18__		
1770. Fred A.	born ca 18__; married Rebecca J. McKENZIE 29 Apr 1903 Westbrook, ME		
1771. Jennie	born ca 18__	1773. Jasper	born ca 18__
1772. James	born ca 18__; married Agnes _?_	1774. Charles	born ca 18__

1522. WARREN F-9 POPE, son of Olive-8 CHASE (Louisa-7 FOSTER; James-6; Woodin-5; Benjamin-4; 3; Isaac-2; Reginald-1) and James O. POPE, was born ca 18__. He married Kittie STUART ca 18__.

Children of Warren-9 POPE and Kittie STUART:

Surname POPE

1775. Morrill	born 2 July 1891; died Aug 1967 Long Beach, WA		
1776. Helen	born ca 18__		
1777. Winona	born ca 18__; died young	1779. Ralph	born poss 23 Feb 1899
1778. James	born ca 18__		died May 1977 Sanford. ME

The Tenth American Generation

1548. WILLIAM JOHN-10 NORTON, son of Horace-9 NORTON (Mary-8 FOSTER; Francis-7; Nathan-6;5; Caleb-4;3; Abraham-2; Reginald-1) and Asenath ELWELL, was born 8 Apr 1883.   He married Effie COMSTOCK ca 19__. She was the daughter of ____ COMSTOCK, and was born ca 1891; died ca 1979.

Children of William John-10 NORTON and Effie COMSTOCK:
    Surname NORTON
    1780. John Comstock   born 15 Oct 1916, Maine; married June __?__; died 6 Jan 1996, NJ
                    Children : surname NORTON
                        12.i.   Mary Sue   born ca ____
                        12.ii. James H.   born ca ____
                        12.iii. William   born ca ____
                        12.iv. Florence   born ca ____

1551. EMMA NORTON-10 BOWIE, daughter of Ruby Ann-9 NORTON (Mary-8 FOSTER; Francis-7; Nathan-6; 5; Caleb-4; 3; Abraham-2; Reginald-1) and Rev Greenfield BOWIE, was born 18 Jan 1869 at Phippsburg, Maine. She married Charles Edward LILLEY on 3 June 1896 at Smyrna, Aroostock, Maine. He was the son of Samuel LILLEY and Hannah CRANE, and was born 1 Aug 1856; died 14 Jan 1932 at Northborough, Worcester, MA. Emma Norton-10 BOWIE died 3 May 1952 at Northborough, MA.

Children of Emma Norton-10 BOWIE and Charles LILLEY:
    Surname LILLEY
    1781. Frank Samuel   born 13 Aug 1897 Patten, Penobscot, ME; died July 1981 Fallbrook, CA
                    married Iva Etta FELTON 12 Aug 1931 Northborough, MA
                    (she dau/o William Jacob FELTON and Florence Emma WILLIAMS)
                    (she born 2 Nov 1912, Worcester, MA; died 21 Sept 1977 Oceanside, CA)
                    Children: (5) 4 un-named (surname LILLEY)
                    12.i. Marjorie Iva   born 25 May 1936 Marlborough, MA; died 17 Dec 1975
    1782. Ruby Etta   born 19 Jan 1899 Smyrna, Aroostock, Maine
                    married Lindsey Luther JONES 27 Aug 1919 (divorced)
                    (he born ca 1895 Smyrna, Maine)
                    died Oct 1971 Robesonia, Berks Co., PA
    1783. Caroline Emma   born 9 Mar 1900 Smyrna; married Ernest Albert WILLIAMS 7 Oct 1922
                    (he born 15 June 1897 Smyrna , ME; died Oct 1979 Fairfield, ME)
                    died Apr 1978 Northboro, Worcester, MA
    1784. Edward Wellington born 20 June 1903 Smyrna, ME; died 20 Sep 1908
    1785. Florence Hannah   born 15 Mar 1907 Canaan, Somerset, ME; died 25 June 1910

1564.   ELMER H-10 RICE, son of Susan-9 FOSTER (Horace-8; Francis-7; Nathan-6; 5; Caleb-4; 3; Abraham-2; Reginald-1) and Judah RICE, was born 2 Apr 1882 , probably at Machiasport, Maine. He married Frances C. ARCHER ca 19__. She was the daughter of ____ ARCHER, and was born 7 Sept 1887 at Wesley, Maine; died 29 Mar 1972 at Bangor, Maine. Elmer-10 RICE died ____.

Children of Elmer-10 RICE and Frances ARCHER:
    Surname RICE:
    1786. Lucy M.   born 10 Mar 1906; died 7 Oct 1993 East Corinth, ME
                    married Percy J. PRAY 5 Apr 1924 Bradford, ME
                    (he born 30 Oct 1897; died Jan 1984 East Corinth, ME
    1787. Isabelle L.   born ca ____; married Earl L. MORRISON 5 July 1927 Bradford, Maine
                    (he born 15 Feb 1905; died Oct 1969 Bradford, ME)

1581. DELIA E-10 TRAFTON, daughter of Sarah Josephine-9 GARDNER (Margaret-8 FOSTER; Nathan-7; 6; 5; Caleb-4; 3; Abraham-2; Reginald-1) and Sewell TRAFTON, was born ca 1846/47 at

Machiasport, Maine. She married Herbert John NORTH ca 18__. He was the son of John NORTH and Mary SPENCER, and was born 2 Apr 1860 in London, England; died ___, NY.

Children of Delia-10 TRAFTON and Herbert NORTH:
    Surname NORTH
    1788. Josephine   born Aug 1886, NY   1789. Herbert   born July 1890, NY

1585. GEORGE M-10 HOLWAY, son of Nathan Foster-9 HOLWAY (Sarah G-8 FOSTER; Nathan-7; 6; 5; Caleb-4; 3; Abraham-2; Reginald-1) and Harriet MOORE, was born 17 May 1863 at Machias, Washington County, Maine. He married Fannie SPINNEY/SPRINGER 28 July 1884 at Cape Elizabeth, Maine.

Children of George M-10 HOLWAY and Fannie SPRINGER/SPINNEY:
    Surname HOLWAY
    1790. A. Carlton   born ca ____
    1791. Ralph O.   born ca ____
    1792. Marion B.   born ca ____; married Patrick E. JOYCE 6 Oct 1913
                             (he born 12 Jan 1892; died June 1968 Portland, ME)
    1793. Ruth B.   born ca ____; married Alfred A. TRAFTON 4 Dec 1909 Machiasport, ME

1605. BESSIE-10 SCHOPPEE, daughter of Sarah Helen-9 HOLWAY (Sarah G-8 FOSTER; Nathan-7; 6; 5; Caleb-4; 3; Abraham-2; Reginald-1) and Charles H. SCHOPPEE, was born ca 18__. She married A. J. COLE ca ____. He was the son of ____ COLE, and was born ca ____; died ____.

Children of Bessie-10 SCHOPPEE and A. J. COLE:
    Surname COLE
    1794. Emily   born ca ____   1798. Eugene   born ca ____
    1795. Ida   born ca ____   1799. Carol   born ca ____
    1796. Laura   born ca ____   1800. Neal   born ca ____
    1797. Christina   born ca ____

1654. EDITH-10 POPE, daughter of Edwina-9 AVERY (L. Trescott-8 AVERY; Betsey-7 FOSTER; Levi-6; Benjamin-5; 4; 3; Isaac-2; Reginald-1) and George POPE, was born ca 18__. She married Wallace BUELL ca ____. He was the son of ____ BUELL, and was born ca ____; died ____.

Children of Edith-10 POPE and Wallace BUELL:
    Surname BUELL
    1801. George P.   born ca ____
    1802. Trescott A.   born 23 Jan 1900; died Mar 1979 Suffern, NY
    1803. Wallace, Jr.   born ca ____

1676. SIDNEY-10 CHALONER, son of Maria-9 HOBART (Drusilla-8 FOSTER; Benjamin-7; Samuel-6; Benjamin-5; 4; 3; Isaac-2; Reginald-1) and Oscar CHALONER, was born ca ____. He married Ada MORONG ca 1892 . She was the daughter of ____ MORONG, and was born ca ____; died ____.

Children of Sidney-10 CHALONER and Ada MORONG:
    Surname CHALONER
    1804. Clara   born ca ____   1809. Drusilla   born ca ____
    1805. Benjamin   born ca ____   1810. Alice   born ca ____
    1806. Ralph   born ca ____   1811. Edmund   born ca ____
    1807. Richard   born ca ____   1812. Ada   born ca ____
    1808. Chester   born ca ____

MISCELLANEOUS and UNPLACED FOSTER INFORMATION

US Federal Census 1850	Milbridge, Maine		US Federal Census 1860		Milbridge, ME
FOSTER, Lewis	36	Sea Captain	FOSTER, Lewis	45	Sea Captain
, Mary	30	wife	, Almira/Mary	40	wife
, George W.	11		, George W.	20	day laborer
, Albion W.	9		, Albion	18	
, Lucy H	7		, Helen	16	
, Eugene	5		, Eugene	13	
, Augustus	2		, Augustua	11	
			, Edgar	10	
FOSTER, James	26	Sea Captain	, Alice	6	
, Elizabeth	25	wife	, Affa (?) F	2	
, Georgianna	3				
, Arletta	1				
FOSTER, Wm.Godfrey	30	Sea Captain	FOSTER, Wm Godfrey	40	Sea Captain
, Catherine	28		, Kate	38	wife
(nee CAMPBELL)			, John H	19	store clerk
, John	9		, Lizzie	18	school teacher
(married Laura LEIGHTON)			, Margaret	16	
, Elizabeth H.	8		, Warren	14	
, Margaret J	6		, Frank	5	
, Warren	4		, Wm. G.	2	
(married Phebe Parker LEIGHTON)					
, Edgar D.	10/12	(born Sept 1849)			
FOSTER, Eli	55	Sea Captain			
, Sarah	37				
, Mary L.	3				
, Bartlett W.	2 born 1848				

FOSTER,Captain Ira born ca 1791 Eastport, ME; married Eliza-6 LINCOLN. She daughter of Jacob-5
      V   LINCOLN and Sarah CLARK (Joseph CLARK and Mehitable _?_).
dau (5) Mary Richardson FOSTER,   born 19 Jan 1823
            V   married Henry Bond WAIDE (he born 4 Jul 1821)
     Child: Kate Aubra WAIDE born ____ married Frederick O. TALBOT
          V
            Children: Edward E.; Mary W; Fred O; Clara S; Kate D; E. Jerome
Other children of Captain Ira FOSTER: (1) George born ca 1817 Eastport; (2) Lincoln born ca 1819;
(3) Jacob born ca 1821; (4) Sarah born ca 1823 (poss twin of Mary, (5) above) (6) Elizabeth Maria
born 17 Aug 1827; died 11 Aug 1902 at Malden, MA

FOSTER, Abigail married Thomas-8 HANSCOM 28 Oct 1810 He was the son of John-7 HANSCOM
        (Thomas-6-5-4-3-2; John-1) and was born 11 Dec 1788; died 1834.
     2 children: William Cutter HANSCOM born 1815 ; and Simon Parker HANSCOM
FOSTER, Abigail (1790-1830) 2nd wife of Isaac HANSON of Jackson, NH (Ref 2nd Boat May 1989)
FOSTER, Charles of Guysboro, NS , was lost from the Schooner FLORENCE REED (Nov 1868)
FOSTER, Charles R marr Jane ALBEE 10 Oct 1865 (both of East Machias, ME)
FOSTER, Daniel , 2nd settler of Hiram, ME; was born 7 Jan 1726 at Andover, MA; died 1782.
     Married Anne INGALLS of Andover, went to Hiram, ME ca 1774. No children.
FOSTER, Diantha H. of North Yarmouth, ME marr John CORLISS of Woolwich, ME on 10 Mar 1832
FOSTER, Esther married John McFARLAND 16 Sept 1784 Bristol, ME
FOSTER, George Malcolm   born 1 June 1868 Winthrop, Kennebec, ME
     He son/o Charles Oliver FOSTER and Angelia PARLIN
FOSTER, Lewis R marr Mary ALBEE 15 June 1869 (Both of Whitneyville, ME)

FOSTER, Lucia married Fred HILL 10 Sept 1859 at Machias, Maine
FOSTER, Mary L (of Machiasport,ME) marr Wm H. ALBEE 7 Apr 1866 (he of Whitneyville , ME)
FOSTER, Miriam married Daniel McFARLAND 9 Nov 1783

FOSTER, Peregrin Dwight s/o Frederick Augustus FOSTER and Sarah ARNOLD was born 18 Feb 1819 at
Lancaster, OH (Note: he poss desc of # 246 Peregrine-6 FOSTER and/or # 164 Peregrin-5 FOSTER)
FOSTER, Uriah possibly married Elizabeth S. WARE 27 May 1846 at Kennebec, Maine

Maine Natives in Kitsap County, Washington 1860-1880 – taken from the Territorial Census
                 Port Gamble, WA (13 June 1870)
                         FOSTER, Phineas   born ME 1832 (38 yr)   sawmill
                                , Nellie   born ME 1840 (30)   wife
                                , Annie   born ME 1861 (9)   daughter

107th Psalm
"They that go down to the sea in ships,
That do business in great waters;
These see the works of the Lord
And his wonders in the deep."

MACHIAS, MAINE REGISTERS AND ENROLLMENTS CAPTAINS LIST
FOSTER CAPTAINS

Captain	Vessel	Enrollment Date and Number	
FOSTER, FRANCIS	Schooner *LOUISA* of Jonesport	28 July 1862	# 1143
(# 1171)	Owner: Horace FOSTER		
FOSTER, JAMES M.	Schooner *WILLIAM PENN*	2 July 1840	# 1954
(# 763)	(built 1833 Warren, Maine) (78'l. x 23'w x 8' d.)		
	Schooner *MAYFLOWER* of Machias	26 June 1846	# 1309
	Brig *BONAPARTE* of Machias	1852	# 220
	Schooner *MECHANIC* of Machiasport	17 Sept 1858	# 1312
	(he was the Captain and part owner (1/8) of this vessel)		
FOSTER, JOHN WM.	Schooner *GENERAL JACKSON* of Mchsprt	1831	# 696
(# 760)	(also part owner of this vessel)		
	Schooner *CHAMPION* of East Machias	1833	# 286
	(built 1827 Warren, ME; 81' 1 x 23' w x 8' d)		
	Schooner *PRESIDENT* of Machias	1840	# 1553
FOSTER, NATHAN	Schooner *RANGER* of Boston	1812-14	# 1578
(# 457)	Schooner *GENERAL GATES* of Mchsprt	1816	# 695
	Schooner *FAVORITE* of Ellsworth	1818	# 605
	Schooner *CAROLINE and NANCY* of Mchias	1818	# 262
	Schooner *CONSTELLATION* of East Machias	1824	# 351
	Schooner *PLEIADES* of Machiasport	Sept/Oct 1825/26	# 1542

Note: This vessel was registered to Nathan FOSTER, JR. His father was also Nathan – and he may have been called JR .at times.

	Brig *GEORGE WASHINGTON* of East Machias	1826	# 1711
	Schooner *HUNTER* of Salem, MA (# 856 Enrolled 1834 --)		
FOSTER, NATHAN, JR	Schooner *GENERAL JACKSON* of Machiasport	1832	# 696
(# 760)	(built 1827 Thomaston, ME)		
	(part owners were Nathan FOSTER; Nathan, Jr; John W; and William H. FOSTER)		
	Schooner *MARY SPEAR* of East Machias	Jul/Nov 1834	# 1271
	(built 1815 Rockland, Maine)		
	Brig *MARTHA ANN* of Boston	1837	# 1235
	(Owners included the Heirs of Nathan M. FOSTER)		
	Schooner *HENRY CLAY* of Machiasport	1840	# 826
	(built 1830 at the Thomaston ME shipyard of Edward O'BRIEN)		
	(77' 1 x 22'w x 7' d)		
	Schooner *HANNAH* of Machias	1841	# 778
	Schooner *HENRY CLAY* of Machiasport	1842	# 826
	(this vessel built 1830 Thomaston, ME by Edward O'BRIEN and William HOLWAY)		
	Schooner *HANNAH* of Machias	1843	# 778
	Schooner *JACOB LONGFELLOW* of Machias	1849	# 932
	Brig *NORTH AMERICA* of Machias	1852	# 1425
	Brig *BONAPARTE* of Machias	1853	# 220
	Schooner *DOLPHIN* of East Machias	7 July 1854	# 419
		17 May 1856	
	Schooner *B A TUFTS* of Machiasport	1856	# 1860
	(built 1846 at Machiasport by James STUART)		
FOSTER, PAUL	Schooner *MARTHA* of East Machias	8 Dec 1838	# 1233
CROCKER (# 765)	Schooner *CAROLINE* of Harrington	Sept 1844	# 254
FOSTER, WILLIAM H.	Schooner *GENERAL JACKSON* of Machiasport	1832	# 696
(# 762)	(also part owner of this vessel)		
	Schooner *BOSTON* of East Machias	1835	# 225
	Schooner *FREDERICK REED* of Machias	19 May 1841	# 664
	Schooner *GEORGE EVANS* of East Machias	1 Sept 1845	# 703

FOSTER CAPTAINS, CONTINUED

Captain	Vessel	Enrollment Date and Number

FOSTER, WILLIAM H.   Schooner *GEORGE EVANS* of East Machias   9 Apr 1846   # 703
    (# 762)   Schooner *WILLIAM POPE* of East Machias   4 Dec 1846   # 1955
                       also enrolled 7 June 1848; and 5 May 1851
                 Schooner *CRUSOE* of East Machias   10 June 1856   # 365
                 Schooner *ALCORA* of East Machias   21 Mar 1864   # 70
                                          23 Aug 1865
                 Schooner *RENO* of East Machias   # 1599
         (Enrolled; 6 June 1866; 26 July 1868; 3 Aug 1869; 5 Sept 1870; 10 Jul 1871;
     7 Oct 1871; 23 July 1872; 30 Sept 1872; 9 Dec 1875; 9 Mar 1876 and 24 Mar 1877)
FOSTER, ZEBEDEE M.   Schooner *ELIZA HUPPER* of East Machias   # 490
    (# 766)

Note: William HOLWAY who built the *HENRY CLAY* of Thomaston, ME, also built the
                Brig *MARGARETTA* in 1842.

CAPTAINS RELATED TO THE FOSTER LINE

AMES, ISAAC   Sloop *THREE SALLYS* (# 12) Enrolled Machias 26 Sept 1806
                 (Owners: Stephen TALBOT; Timothy WESTON, Machias ; Daniel WESTON;
         Francis FOSTER, Cushing, ME; Arunah WESTON, Bristol, ME)
BROWN, AMBROSE   (husband of # 1012)
BROWN, DAVID   Bark _____ (# 249)
  (husb/o # 646)   (built at E. Machias by Charles FOSTER and Josiah KELLAR)

HOLWAY, JOHN, Jr.   Schooner *HENRY CLAY* of Machiasport   1832 (Master/part owner)
                  Schooner *WILLIAM AND JOHN* of Machias   1833
                  (this vessel built 1883 at Warren, ME by Edward O'BRIEN)

LeBALLISTER, CHAS.   _____

LONGFELLOW, STEPHEN (master and part owner of the following vessels)
                  Schooner *OLD HUNDRED* of Machias (built 1828 East Machias) 1832
                  Schooner *ELIZA ANN* of Machias   (built 1819 Warren, ME)   1835
                  Schooner *OREGON* of Machias (built 1833 Brewer, ME)   1837
                  Bark *VIRGINIA* of Machias (built 1852 Machias)   1852

RONEY, JOHN   (he of Thomaston, Maine)
                  Schooner *WILLOW* of Thomaston (# 243) built 1844 Thomaston
                  Master 1844-47
                  Brig *DENMARK* of Thomaston (# 769) built 1848 Thomaston
                  Master and part owner   1848
                  Schooner *LUCY WATTS* of Warren (built 1847 Warren, ME # 3063)
                  Master 1852

WESTON, TIMOTHY   Sloop *THREE SALLYS* of Bristol, ME
                 (# 1 Enrolled 1 Apr 1805 Machias)
                 (built 1796) Owners: Francis FOSTER, Daniel WESTON of Cushing, ME;
                          and Arunah WESTON of Bristol

DEATH, John	375		DRESSER, Nathaniel	382
, John , I	371		, Nehemiah Charles	389
, John, II	371		, Prudence	381
, John, III	367, 371, 375		, Rebeckah	382
, Lydia	372, 376		, Richard	372, 376
, Mary	371, 375		, Sally	382
, Oliver	371		, Samuel	373
, Ruth	372, 375		, Sarah	381, 382, 389
, Samuel	372		, Sarah Foster	389
, Thomas	371		, Selena / Silena	389
, Waitsill	375		, Simeon	382
DELAP, Sarah	408		, Stephen	382, 389
DENNISON, Charles	433		, Susanna	389
, Ezra	411		, Thomas	382, 389
, Frank P.	433		, Thomas Newman	389
, Gilbert	411		, William F.	389
, Parker	411		, William Otis	389
DeWOLFE, Caroline	395		, Zilpha	389
DICKINSON, Mercy	372, 377		DRISKO, Capt. George W.	406, 428, 429
DILL, Vesta Beulah	446		, Capt. John	428
DILLOWAY, Mary	394, 407		, George Augustus	429, 447
DINSMORE, William Corthell	446		, Julia C.	443
DORMAN, Hannah	371		, Laura	429
, Jabez	399		, Margaret Foster G.	429
, Lucy	386, 399		DUNNELL, Sarah	372, 377, 382
, Mary	371, 375		DUNSTER, Rose	412
, Thomas	367, 371		DURLING, Charles	441, 455
DOURING, Hannah	365, 369		, Flora	455
DOWNING, Abigail	387		, Hattie	455
, Hannah	365, 369		, J. Willard	455
DOYLE, Bessie / Hessie	451		, Jessie	416, 442
, Eunice	414		, Walter	455
DRESSER, Abigail	376, 381, 389		DUSTIN, Betsey	403, 423
, Asa	376, 381		, Florinda	423
, Benjamin	376, 381, 382		, Freeman	423
, Betsey	389		, George W.	403, 423
, Chloe	382, 389		, Hannah	403, 423
, David	381		, Harriet	423
, Elbridge Gerry	389		, John	423
, Eliza C.	389		, Jonathan	403, 423
, Elizabeth	382, 389		, Lemuel	423
, Emelia	389		, Lydia	403, 423
, Enoch	382, 389		, Mary	403, 423
, Eunice	382		, Mary Jane	423
, Hannah	381		, Moses	387, 403, 423
, Harriet	389		, Nathaniel	403
, Isaac	381		, Polly	403
, Jacob	376		, Robie	423
, Jane	382		, Sally	403, 423
, Job Abbott	389		, Samuel	423
, John	372, 376, 377, 381, 382, 389		, Sewell	423
, John Foster	389		, Sukey	423
, Jonathan	377, 382, 389		, Timothy Wilder	423
, Jonathan Foster	389		, Walter	423
, Joseph	381, 389		, Warren Sargent	423
, Leonard P.	389		, William Sargent	423
, Levi	382		DWELLEY, Arthur	436
, Louisa	389		, Bessie	436
, Lydia	382		, Charles	418, 444
, Mahaliah	389		, Esther	444
, Mary	369, 373, 377, 382		, Evelyn	444
, Mary / Polly	389		, James	399, 418
, Mary Jane	389		, Mary E.	436
, Mehitable	382		, Raymond	444
, Mercy	377, 382		, Sylvanus	413, 436
, Molly	382		DWIGHT, Brig Gen. Joseph	376, 381
, Nancy	389		, Dorothy	376, 381
, Nathan	372, 377		DYER, A. I.	451

BIBLIOGRAPHY

ALDEN Genealogy
ALDRED Family Bible (Judith MATHEWS, desc)
A Maritime History of Bath, ME by Wm. A BAKER 1973
A Maritime History of Maine by W. H. ROWE 1948
Ancestors Tables of Judith Ann WHITE
Ancestors and Some of the Desc of Joseph DRISKO
   (compiled by Clarence H. DRISKO 29 p. transcript)
Ancestry of Abel LUNT (INGERSOLL) pp 63-67
Annals of Warren, Maine p. 531
Bagley, Joyce Lillian DRISKO, Robbinsdale, MN
BANGS (History and Gen of the BANGS Family) pp 9 & 16
Barnstable (MA) Town records Volume 1: p 21
Berwick, Maine VR
Boston Transcript # 2675 17 Jul 1912
Bowdoinham (ME) Deaths p 407
BOYNTON Genealogy (History of the Boynton Family)
Bristol, Maine VR
BRITTON, Ann H (Glen Mills, PA) (KNOX/RICKER)
Burke, Carol Richmond, Maine

CARVER (The Rev Eleazer CARVER Genealogy)
Cemetery Records from:
        Clark's Hill Cemetery, St. George, ME
        East Machias (ME) Cemetery
        Laurel Grove Cemetery (Woolwich, ME)
        Machiasport (ME) Cemetery
        Maple Grove Cemetery (Belfast, ME)
        Muscongus Cemetery (ME)
        Oak Grove Cemetery (Bath, ME)
        Patridge Cemetery (Woolwich, ME)
        Riverside Cemetery (Woolwich, ME)
        Ward Cemetery (Bath, ME)
        Witch Spring Cemetery (W. Bath, ME)
Centennial Celebration of Machias, Maine p 158
CHUTE Family in America, Wm CHUTE 1894
COBB (History of the COBB Family Part 1) Phillip L. COBB
COFFIN Family Newsletter (David COFFIN)

DAR Vol 14, 16, 25, 31, 118, 268
DECKER, Helene, Oxford, Maine
Descendants of Edmund WESTON
Diary of Simeon PERKINS, Toronto: Champlain Soc 1948-49
Dictionary of New Hampshire by SAVAGE Vol 2:562
Downeast Ancestry Vol 8, 1984-85; pp 66-67
           Vol 4, # 1; pp 14-15
           Vol 12 # 1
Dover, NH VR 1693-1838
DRISKO Clarence H, Columbia Falls, ME (Dec'd)
DRISKO, John Bucknam , Easton, PA
DRISKO, Shapleigh, Columbia Falls, ME
Duxbury, MA VR

Earliest Records of Machias , ME 1767-1827
        By Beulah JACKMAN, Concord, NH
Early Families of Gouldsborough, ME
Early Families of Limerick, ME
Early Marriages of Machias 1767-1827 JOHNSON
Early Marriage of Strafford County , NH
Early Pleasant River Families by LAMSON & TIBBETTS
Early Records of Cushing, ME
Early Settlers of Brunswick, Maine
Early Settlers of Rowley, MA p 20
Early Settlers of Standish, ME by Albert SEARS p 59
EASTMAN, Rich Topsham, ME

Ebenezer POLE Manuscripts of Rockport (MA)
        by John MARSHALL 1888
Ecclesiastical History of New England FELT
EMERY (Genealogy of John and Anthony EMERY) 1890
Essex Co. (MA) Gen and Hist Record page 59
Essex (MA) Deed lib 13:206
Essex Genealogist Feb 1988 (the GOWING Family)
        Aug 1988, p 143

FALLA, John , Tenants Harbor, ME
Falmouth Friends Records (Maine Hist Soc)
Families of Old Salisbury and Amesbury 1897
Family Records of Berwick, ME (typescript)
FINCK (Major Andrew FINCK 1751-1820) 1906
        First Baptist Church, St. George, ME
First Congregational Church Records, Scarboro, ME
Foltz, Gertrude North Haven, ME (KILTON)
FOSTER, Frank, Jr. Machiasport, ME
FOSTER Genealogy by Frederick Clifton PIERCE 1899
Fraser, Marian FOSTER, Bahia, Brazil
FREEMAN Family in Nova Scotia

GARDNER Family of Machias, ME C.L. ANDREWS, Esq
GARDNER (Thomas GARDNER, Planter and Some of his Desc)
GATES (Stephen GATES of Hingham, MA)
Gen & Family History of the State of NY Ezra STEARNS
Gen Dict of ME & NH NOYES p 208; 483; 643
Gen Boston and Eastern MA p 1299
Gen & Family History of the State of ME LITTLE 1909
Groton Marriages (VR 1850) p 48

HALL, Marvin Scarsdale, NY
HAMMAT Papers
Hayward, Nancy Wilmington, MA
HEARD/HURD Genealogy 1610-1988 p 9 & 34
History of Belfast, ME p 726-728
History of Cape Elizabeth, ME Wm JORDAN 1965
History of Durham, NH (2 vol) by STACKPOLE & THOMPSON
History of Gloucester by BABSON
History of Gorham, ME by McKELLAN p. 69 & 419
History of Old Broad Bay and Waldoboro by Jasper STAHL
        Vol 2 Appendices (p 536) CROCKER
History of Machias by George W. DRISKO 1897
History of Martha's Vineyard
History of Portland, ME by SOUTHGATE 1853
History of Rowley by Thomas GAGE 1840 p 167-178
History of Scarborough, ME
History of the County of Annapolis. NS; p 192-195
HULL Family Genelaogy page 252

INGERSOLL (Desc of Richard INGERSOLL, Salem, MA) p 2, 3

JORDAN Memorial, pub 1882 by Tristam F. JORDAN
JORDAN, Roland G. Auburn, ME

KILTON (Notes on the KILTON Family, Jonesboro, ME)

LAMSON, Darryl Cherry Hill, NJ
Lebanon, ME VR
Lebanon, ME Genealogies 1750-1892 CHAMBERLAIN
LEIGHTON Genealogy
LIBBY, Bruce Augusta, ME
LIBBY (The LIBBY Family in America) by Chas. LIBBY 1882
Lighthouses of the Maine Coast Brattleboro 1935 by STERLING
Lynn, MA VR Vol 2: 110; 166

Machias Union Newspaper 29 Dec 1865 (DRISKO)
                       14 June 1881 (CROCKER)
Machiasport Hist Soc. (Gates House) (CROCKER)
Magnalia Christi Americana p 591
Maine Census Records 1790-1880
Maine Families in 1790 Vol 1 Maine Gen Society
Maine Hist & Gen Recorder Vol 1: 78, 81
        Vol 3; 1401; Vol 9; 81
Maine Historical Magazine Vol 8 1893
Maine Maritime Museum   Bath , Maine
Maine Place Names by CHADBOURNE
Maine Province and Court Records
Maine Wills 1610-1760 by SARGENT
Marblehead (MA) VR Vol 1 p 339 (MARTIN)
Maritime Museum of the Atlantic, Halifax, Nova Scotia
MA Soldiers, Sailors of the War of the Revolution
            pp 126-127 (CROCKER)
MA Archives Vol 95: 407
MA Historical Society Vol 1: 144
MA/ME Direct Tax Census of 1798 Vol 1: 39-75
            Addison, Machias and Twsp # 23
Mayflower Descendants Vol 1: 3: 16
McCUTCHEON/CUTCHEON Family Records
     Compiled by Florence McCUTCHEON McKee 1931
MESERVE (The First 4 Generations of Portsmouth, NH)
            Edited by Michael DENIS (Typescript)
Meservey, Mrs Ralph   Klamath Fall, OR
Milton, Strafford County, NH 1850 Census

Narragaugus Valley by J A MILLIKEN
National Ocean Service Map # 13326
New England Historical Register 1925 Vol XXIX
            Vol XIV: 155;124; VOL XVII: 30
New England Marriages Prior to 1700 by Clarence TORREY
New Englanders in Nova Scotia 1759-62 by Fred CROWELL
New Hampshire Census   1732 and 1776
New London Day (NH)   Sunday 8/4/88 Nostalgia D/2
            Article of DRISCO House of Strawbery Banke
NH Genealogical Record (1905-06) Vol 3: 3
NORWOOD Genealogy

Old Families of Salisbury and Amesbury p 173
Old Kittery and Her Families 1903 STACKPOLE p 764-66
Old Norfolk County Court Records p 610
Old Times in No. Yarmouth (ME) by CORLISS

PABODIE Genealogy (PEABODY)
PARKER (Robert PARKER of Barnstable, MA)
PARLIN (Desc of Nicholas PARLIN of Cambridge, MA) 1913
Penobscot Maritime Museum , Searsport, ME (MAYHEW)
PLUMER Genealogy by Sidney PERLEY
PLUMMER, Wayne L, Moorhead, MN
Probate Records of Lincoln County, ME

Records of the Lower St. Georges and Cushing, ME 1605-1897
            Cushing Historical Society
Records of Shipping of Yarmouth, Nova Scotia
Records of the Town of Machias, Maine
RICHARDS Genealogy (The Family of Emery RICHARDS
            of Round Pond, Maine)
RICKER (A Genealogy of the RICKER Family)
            by Percy Leroy RICKER 1919

Saco Valley Settlements pp 121; 128
Salem VR Births pp 146-149
Salisbury MA VR p 74
SANBORN (The American SANBORNS)
SAWYER (The Early SAWYER Families of New England)

Scarboro Church Records
SCHOPPEE, Marion   Machias, ME
SCOTT Genealogy
Ships Registers & Enrollments of Machias 1780-1930
SIMMONS Family Genealogy (Desc of Elizabeth SIMMONS)
SMALL Genealogy (Genealogy of Edward SMALL)
            CHANDLER Family pp 1079-1082
                       Vol 3: 1398; 1401; 1726
SMITH (The John SMITH'S of Berwick, ME) by Dotty KEYES
Soldiers, Sailors & Patriots of the Rev War by FISHER p 23
Steuben (ME) Town Record Book # 1: 57
Storey, Betty ANDREWS Hales Corners, WI
Suffolk Surnames (DRISKO) p 19

Tall Ships of Annisquam
The Book of Names by MacWETHY (FINCK)
The Coast of Maine by Louise Dickinson Rich 1962; 1965
The Forerunners – The Tragic Story of 156 Downeast Americans
            by Reed M. HOLMES 1981
The Trial of Mrs. Elizabeth Howe, the Witchcraft Delusion p 27
THORNDIKE Genealogy (MARTIN)
Town Records of Gloucester, Portland and No. Yarmouth
TIBBETTS, Dr. Leonard F.   South Yarmouth, MA

Vessels of Downeast by Joyce KINNEY
Vital Records of Dover, NH
            Births & Marriages 1639-1838 pp 30-31
Vital Records of Marshfield, MA to 1850 (Plymouth Co)
Vital Records of Old Bristol and Nobleboro
            ME Historical Society   1947

Wakefield VR   1850 NEHGS 1912 ; p 34
WENTWORTH Genealogy
WHITNEY Genealogy
Will, Edna STERLING Cape Elizabeth, ME
Windships of Warren, Maine
Woburn (MA) Records 1640-1873 pub 1890 p 227
WOODS, Kendall   Gorham, Maine

Yankee Magazine Sept 1964 Article entitled
            " Picture Behind a Picture " by Lowell A NORRIS